Advertising Management

ITS ROLE IN MARKETING

The PennWell Marketing and Management Series

Louis E. Boone,
Consulting Editor

Advertising
Management

Its Role
In Marketing

William Sachs

PennWell Books
PennWell Publishing Company
Tulsa, Oklahoma

Copyright © 1983 by
The PennWell Publishing Company
1421 South Sheridan Road/P.O. Box 1260
Tulsa, Oklahoma 74101

Library of Congress Catalog Card Number: 83-42926
International Standard Book Number: 0-87814-240-1
Printed in the United States of America

1 2 3 4 5   87 86 85 84 83

To Inge

Preface

As evident by its title, the book is written from a managerial point of view. Its main concern is the management of the advertising function.

But whose decisions shall be uppermost? The advertising function actually involves a number of different entities, with differing views and objectives. Managers exist in all these organizations, and at different levels of authority.

The perspective of this book is that of the advertiser. To advertising agencies, this firm is known as "the client." While most of the planning, creation, and placement of advertisements are done by outside advertising agencies, responsibility for managing the advertising process ultimately falls upon executives at the client organization. It is the offerings of this firm that provides advertising's reason for being. It is the name of this firm that appears as the signature in all commercial messages. It is the budget of this firm which initiates the chain of various advertising activities. As the old saying goes, he who pays the piper calls the tune. Whether presto or largo, fortissimo or pianissimo, the tunes which reverberate in the halls of the advertising industry are those ordered and paid for by client organizations. Accordingly, the book views planning, implementation, and control of advertising from the standpoint of firms whose products are being advertised.

Decisions of advertising managers at client organizations are, in the main, eminently pragmatic. As a former practitioner of advertising, I firmly believe in a practical, real world approach to the subject. Yet that approach would be a feeble and insufficient attempt at understanding the advertising process without examining the theoretical underpinnings of its decisions. The book thus attempts to combine the pragmatic with the analytical, and to present illustrations and examples of the resulting inquiries.

Because advertising employs many different skills—those of the product manager, copywriter, art director, researcher, television producer, to name only a few—it amalgamates values and ideas of different professions and intellectual traditions. Attempts to relate these diverse elements are carried only so far as they are relevant to the management of advertising. A conscious effort is made not to get bogged down in the narrow methodologies of marketing research or of social psychology. The emphasis thus lies on business aspects, which form the underlying reasons for advertising being undertaken in the first place. Since the advertiser firm provides the focal point of the book, its orientation can be said to be microeconomic.

The book is divided into seven parts. This division is meant to follow along lines which logically delineate the various phases of the advertising process. Thus:

Section 1 sets the framework for advertising management. It presents advertising as an economic activity, and from a microeconomic point of view, as part of a firm's marketing mix. The communication aspect in fact becomes a means for achieving economic goals.

Section 2 analyzes advertiser-agency relationships from the standpoint of channel management. In effect, these relationships represent a special case of a marketer using facilitating agencies in a channel of distribution. This section thus emphasizes such subjects as compensation for advertising services and control of the advertising function, including audits.

Sections 3 and 4 take up the planning process. They deal with formulation of the advertising plan and its three primary elements—the budget, the creative programs, the media plan.

Section 5 examines placements of commercial messages in national media, by far the most important type of advertising being carried on. The book takes the view that advertising in national media is not a homogeneous process. For example, consumer advertising is not the same as industrial advertising. It faces different problems, and therefore requires different solutions. Similarly, corporate advertising run in national media is unique in many ways and warrants separate analysis. Accordingly, this section analyzes programs designed for different media, and having different goals and target markets.

Section 6 focuses on sales-specific advertising, which is quite different from the general-type advertising handled in Section 5. The main forms of the sales-oriented type of advertising are retailing and direct marketing.

Section 7 examines the regulatory environment in which advertising must work. Here, the firm must deal with government laws and regulations, organizations for self-regulations, and outside pressure groups.

Many people have contributed to the writing of this book. Foremost are my colleagues in the marketing department of St. John's University, Joseph Chasin and Lawrence Deckinger, who have reviewed parts of the manuscript and offered valuable insights. Louis E. Boone of the University of South Alabama has read the original manuscript and his suggestions resulted in a number of improvements.

My thanks to two graduate assistants, Steven Chasin and Katherine T. Driscoll. The first helped in checking facts and running down sources of information. The second prepared the Instructor's Manual which forms a valuable supplement to the text. I am also indebted to Elizabeth McCall, who helped immeasurably with numerous clerical chores to get the manuscript ready for publication. And my most enduring thanks is to my wife, Inge, who checked footnotes, read proofs, and carried out many other tasks to bring the book to fruition. To her I dedicate this book.

WILLIAM S. SACHS

St. John's University
Jamaica, New York

Contents

PART FOUR

CHAPTER 8

CHAPTER 9

CHAPTER 10

CHAPTER 11

PART
ONE

DIMENSIONS OF
ADVERTISING:

ECONOMIC and COMMUNICATIVE

Advertising as an Economic Activity

Advertising is everywhere. It is always around us in our society. When extended to its full size, it accounted for about $61 billion of society's expenditures in 1981. It is like the proverbial elephant examined by blind men: it can be described in many different ways.

Diversity is its hallmark. Its participants are of many kinds. Their presentations are many sided in content, form, motif, and are addressed to audiences as varied as the subject matter. Despite differences in aims, tasks, and starting points, most advertising activities proceed along routes which converge in the sphere of economics.

This chapter probes into the different aspects of advertising, classifies the variegated patterns, and traces the convergence to common ends which practitioners seek. Specifically, the chapter examines:
* **Types of participants in the advertising process**
* **Types of tasks**
* **Subject matter which they present**
* **Audiences for which their messages are intended**
* **Common purposes which tie together diverse elements into a cohesive whole**

WHAT IS ADVERTISING?

Advertising is so pervasive in our culture, so ubiquitous in our society that it has quietly coalesced with the main body of our environment. Advertising is virtually taken for granted as the normal way of things, like the routine of eating breakfast, going to work at a certain time, or sending children off to school. A person customarily encounters hundreds of advertisements in the course of a normal day. The pages of our daily newspapers carry notices, interlaced between news reports, that proclaim the excitement of a current movie thriller, the fantastic bargains of a closeout sale, specials on meat, fish and poultry just put on the counters of the local supermarket. Millions of radios, between spasms of news and music, implore their listeners to visit someone's used car lot for impossible-to-refuse deals, to spray their underarms with Brand X for alluring fragrance, to brush their teeth with Brand Y toothpaste for irresistible charm and sex appeal. TV programs about swaggering private detectives and self-sacrificing doctors are only entertainment devices to gain attention for the more lucrative business of hawking wares more varied than those of the most fabulous oriental bazaars.

Advertising is used for different purposes, and consequently, takes on various meanings. One widely-accepted view defines advertising as paid communication in media, wherein the messages transmitted are identified with their sponsors.[1]

Insofar as this definition readily sets advertising apart from communication, which has similar forms and purposes, it is commendable. It distinguishes advertising from other forms of sales promotion, such as exhibitions, displays, contests, premium offers, and the like. These activities are sponsored by individual organizations, but can be carried out without the use of media. Many of them enjoy advertising support. Trade shows and exhibits are widely popularized by paid messages in media. Printed ads often carry cents-off coupons, which can be disengaged from the main body of copy and redeemed at the store. But media are not absolute necessities; they can be dispensed with. Discount offers can be made by mail or "in-pack," with off-shelf displays, or through other point-of-purchase devices.

This definition also distinguishes advertising from publicity. Though the latter avails itself of media, it is actually part of the editorial format. The very appearance of a publicity item, its form and content, arises from decisions of a medium's editorial staff. The medium, not the dispatcher of the press release or public announcement, determines what is said, when, and how. Publicity is thus communication with no fee attached, regardless of benefits to the recipient of favorable news stories or editorial comments.

Some authors object to this definition of advertising because it is too restrictive, and point out that some advertisements are not paid for. Each year, for example, the Advertising Council as a public service function places free advertisements worth hundreds of millions of dollars in various media. Many firms in the advertising industry generously donate their materials and labor. One group of authors have thus defined advertising as "controlled, identifiable" communication in mass media.[2] But, overall, the quantities of advertising contributions to worthy causes are relatively small and inconsequential. This modicum of altruism hardly alters the nature of advertising. One might also argue about the control which an advertiser can realistically hope to exercise. The degree of control relates only to the creation and scheduling of messages, not to their effects.

Besides, a definition of advertising should not be taken as a detailed, exact description of a process. It is, to fall back on analogy, somewhat like a pegboard. The area within its perimeter is filled with pins of wood or metal, arranged to accommodate the things which are to be hung. But the board itself gives no clue as to the items displayed. In similar fashion, the definition of advertising tells nothing about what is communicated, who originates the messages, or for what reasons such efforts are expended in the first place. Any definition is only a beginning to understanding. A richer and fuller meaning of advertising requires an inspection, so to speak, not merely of the bare pegboard, but of the objects which grace its pins.

WHAT IS ADVERTISED?

While individuals can engage in advertising—and many do in the classified sections of newspapers—the vast preponderance is performed by organizations. From this standpoint, advertising can be viewed as organized behavior; it has become institutionalized. The process itself involves individuals or groups who carry out different functions. But functional units and decision units within an organization are not necessarily identical.

The subjects of advertisements can be grouped into two parts: product and nonproduct. Even though they are related in part, this classification is used in order to clarify our message for purposes of analysis and exposition.

Product Advertising

Products encompass both goods and services, and have come to dominate the advertising scene. They probably account for more than 90 percent of all advertising, though there is no precise figure that measures their volume. *Product advertising* is used by both buyer and seller. Buyer advertising occurs when firms are seeking productive inputs, such as labor, commodities, or capital. Advertising by the armed services is an example of buyer advertising, for this branch of government is seeking personnel, and is competing with private business for services, if labor can be regarded as such.

The bulk of product advertising is done by sellers, not buyers. This is in keeping with the traditional concepts of marketing, which have emphasized product flows from producer to consumer or user. In the acts of exchange which characterize our market economy, it is customary for sellers, in competition with other sellers, to establish their channels of distribution and promote their wares. The exchange mechanism can be likened to a propose-dispose system; the seller proposes, the buyer disposes. While a product's disposition in the final analysis is governed by the decisions of buyers, its proposal rests on the decisions of sellers. Advertising is one way among several for proposing a product to would-be buyers in a market.

Nonproduct Advertising

Nonproduct advertising is all advertising that does not directly feature products either by sellers or buyers. Such advertising is often defined as "institutional." In recent years, the terms "corporate advertising" and "corporate image advertising" have been used for institutional advertising. The main reason for the change was because the word "institutional" evoked connotations of coldness, aloofness, or unconcern—images which were contrary to those which the advertising was trying to create. An institution is normally thought of as something established by law or custom, and not affected by the pressing needs of the marketplace. Imagine an institution working hard to effect "better living through chemistry" or "to make weekends."

The change in name was thus one of semantics rather than of content. Nevertheless, the word "corporate" in the new terminology suggests advertising conducted by business firms. Most of such advertising does indeed come from the private business sector. But some of it also derives from governmental agencies and nonprofit organizations. Not only do they market goods and services, but they also attempt to build favorable images of themselves, and may look to advertising as a felicitous way of doing the job. For example, it is essentially the public's perception of them that enables charities and universities to meet fund-raising goals and enlist armies of volunteers.

Although the nonproduct category accounts for a relatively small proportion of total advertising, its subject matter is highly diverse. Nonproduct messages can be divided into two major types.

The first, for lack of a better term, might be called organizational advertising. The messages focus on the organization which transmits them. They deal with such themes as quality of an organization's outputs, its philosophy, its performance, its employee policies, and its social and economic contributions. The goals of this type of advertising are primarily economic, though they are long term and discursive.

The second kind of nonproduct message involves ideas which are usually social or political in nature. Such messages in mass media have often been referred to as idea advertising. The focus falls not on the organization or its products, but on societal issues. Exemplifying idea advertising are campaigns such as those to reduce pollution, save energy, plan parenthood, or change current tax policies. Figure 1–1 contains an example of idea advertising prepared by the Advertising Council, a voluntary industry group.

The exact dividing line between products, organizations, and ideas are not always clear. Political advertising, for example, is usually thought of as being in the idea category. But alternative ways of looking at it are possible. Because it promotes the interests of organizations, in this case political parties, it might be viewed as organizational. Product advertising is a possibility too, since candidates are products of political parties. Political office seekers could be regarded as offering the public certain services, though such an interpretation appears a bit far-fetched.

"Thou shalt not take the name of the Lord thy God in vain."

"Remember the Sabbath day, to keep it holy."

"Honor thy Father and thy Mother."

"Thou shalt not bear false witness."

Love thy family. Worship together.

A Public Service of This Magazine & The Advertising Council

Fig. 1—1 *Ad Council. Sample of an Idea Advertisement.* Courtesy The Advertising Council.

THE CLASSIFICATION SYSTEM

The division of advertising into product and nonproduct messages, as presented in the previous section, can be regarded as the beginning of a classification system. Components which make up each group display certain similarities. It is possible, of course, to carry the divisions further, making for finer and finer breakdowns. For example, nonproduct advertising might be classified by type of organization, such as private sector business, government, or nonprofit organization. Business firms might further be categorized by product line or size. Other divisions are also feasible, limited only by the imagination of the analyst and the practicality of the subdivisions.

In like manner, product advertising can be coded in a number of ways. It can be conceptualized in accordance with the simple, three-way gradation of Melvin Copeland, which divides all consumer goods into convenience, shopping and specialty categories.[3] Or it can be conceived in terms of the more elaborate Standard Industrial Classification (SIC), used by the government for national accounting. Products can also be grouped into smaller, more homogeneous units—as most firms do—the data sets of which are composed of competitive offerings. These groupings are useful insofar as they involve different types of decisions, as well as different methods of data collection and modes of operation.

DEFINING THE MARKET

Another approach to classification is by defining the market. To advertise something is to communicate to someone, for products and markets are inseparable. One cannot exist without the other. Product categories are thus modified by market designations, or vice versa. No matter which assumes primacy in the scheme of things, products or markets, the two go together.

Organizations define their markets in a bewildering variety of ways, depending upon their objectives and resources. Few firms have identical goals because their capacities for effecting a result are not the same. Given the demand for soft drinks, Dr. Pepper can hardly be expected to compete head-on with Coke and Pepsi for the mass, general market. Insurance companies sell protection, but not necessarily against all the hazards besetting humanity. Their policies specialize in covering such items as homes, autos, or health. Their operations emphasize one type of adversity over another, offering financial recompense for fire damage, accident loss, burglaries, medical and hospital expenses, or for the final human misfortune, death. The differences in capabilities and expectations lead to a variety of market definitions. Nevertheless, the diversity in perceptions of what constitutes a relevant opportunity—which is a firm's definition of a market—can be pressed into the service of classifying advertising. Two fundamental elements are geography and user types.

Geography

This is a traditional basis for describing markets and maintaining records of orders, shipments, and revenues. When advertising expenditure data are kept by geographic segments they can easily be matched with sales and can therefore be used to set future budgets and evaluate past advertising performance.

Many firms with heavy television schedules formulate their operating plans using "areas of dominant influence" (ADIs). Made popular by Arbitron, a television rating service, an ADI consists of counties which contribute significantly to the viewing of "home market stations." The A.C. Nielsen Company offers an equivalent measure called "designated market areas" (DMAs), which do not always agree with Arbitron statistics as to cut off points for counties with relevant viewing levels. Companies using ADIs or DMAs for planning and monitoring can, with little or no difficulty, allocate print audiences, circulations, and costs along the same geographical lines as those of television. Such data manipulation enables firms to match their markets with print and broadcast schedules, and compare revenue and advertising expenditures for the same areas.

The factor that determines, or rather limits, the size of the area in which advertising should take place is a company's distribution network. The logic of circumstance restricts promotional effort to areas in which products are made available. Advertising an item in an area where people cannot obtain it yields no sales. It may also be harmful to a brand's future, for later expansion plans may have to shake off negative feelings previously formed, in addition to overcoming the customary hardships of product introduction. By the same token, the greater the relative intensity of a product's distribution, the higher the probability that advertising would appear in the sales territory.

Advertising is occasionally suggested as a means of getting retailers to stock an item. When customers come in and ask for a brand, the reasoning goes, stores become more anxious to order it. Attempting to "force" distribution through advertising, however, is an expensive and inefficient strategy. Its chances of success are not good. Seldom can the power of advertising, as though by magical incantation, cause goods to appear on retail shelves. A heavy media schedule may indeed heighten dealer acceptance, since it increases the likelihood of better sales and faster turnover farther down the trading channel. But advertising is seldom the prime determinant in middlemen transactions. The distribution mechanism must be in place before, not after, advertising begins, for the media campaign plays a supportive, not a leading, role in channel management. Like a shadow, advertising follows product availability; rarely does it lead distribution.

The limitations imposed by physical distribution present firms with different sets of advertising options. The most restrictive adhere to products with less-than-national distribution. Their advertising must of necessity be confined to media with local coverage. Regional brands represent an aggregation of localities which form a regional market. Consequently, these products are advertised by combining local media to fit a regional configuration of distribution channels.

Nationally distributed brands enjoy a wider range of alternatives. They can be advertised nationally, locally, or both simultaneously. National programs are often supplemented by local advertising, such as network television being supplemented by station buys in particular markets. Maxwell House coffee, for example, runs commercials on network lineups as well as on spot tv. Similarly, ads in national magazines can be combined with insertions in regional editions. Giant retailers, food chains and franchisers with outlets spread across the length and breath of America split up their advertising budgets in various proportions, covering national, regional, or local boundaries, such as efforts in specific metropolitan areas, individual counties, or even parts thereof.[4] Refer to Figure 1–2 for an example of a retail advertisement for national media.

If the market-oriented approach is pursued with inexorable logic, advertising can be thought of as being national, regional, or local, from the standpoint of the area covered by the message. It might be argued that all advertising is essentially local in nature, for both national and regional schedules are actually the sum of local ones. Surely, network time charges can be allocated to different stations or markets in a lineup. Space costs for a national advertisement can also be assigned to smaller areas in accordance with the distribution of magazine copies. But there is still a vast gap between advertising coast-to-coast in one swoop and advertising in a series of local markets. These dissimilarities involve the media environment, timing, and weight of the commercial message, all considered important by practitioners in running an advertising campaign.

But in the advertising industry, as in Mr. Carroll's Wonderland, words do not always mean what they seem to mean. Terms "national" and "local" refer to the business of the advertiser and not to the geographic coverage of the message. For example, a manufacturer of a branded product is called a national advertiser, and the firm's advertising is called "national" no matter where or how far the message reaches, even if the ad appears only in a small town newspaper. If General Foods were to run a test market in Peoria, its advertising would still be classified as national, ostensibly because it has the potential of becoming nationwide in scope. Thus, many brands with limited distribution, advertising locally or regionally, are deemed "national," such as Coors and Schaefer beers. On the other hand, advertising by local retailers are tabbed "local." As such, the distinction of the industry classification system is really between general and retail advertising, and not between that of national and less-than-national message coverage. A more logical system would be the one in Table 1–1.

Fig. 1—2 *J. C. Penney. Sample Retail Advertisement Placed in National Media.*
Courtesy J. C. Penney Co.

TABLE 1–1 *Hypothetical Geographic Classification of Advertising*

Type of Advertiser	Coverage of Advertising Message		
	National	Regional	Local
General			
(Subgroups if desirable)			
Retail			
(Subgroups if desirable)			

The general advertiser in fact employs a record-keeping format similar to that shown in Table 1–1. Message coverage is made to conform to the firm's particular sales territories or markets, while the types of advertisers are restricted to vendors of competitive products. If applied to the entire industry, this classification scheme would have to standardize coverage areas and types of businesses. To some extent, standardization of geographical areas and product groups is already being done even with the specious definitions.

The anomalies arising from the current form of industry data gathering, as in most conventional practices, are a consequence of historical development. The main impetus to industry statistics of time and space utilization came from media, which required information about their sources of revenue. Newspapers were in the forefront, since they are the oldest media accepting advertising. These data enabled them to define their markets by the type of reader they had, which helped them plan their sales programs and set different rates for "national" and "local" advertisers. The classification system is thus market-oriented from the standpoint of media suppliers, but not from the perspective of the advertisers. The advertisers can easily keep tabs on their competitors' spending, for they are often few in number, and so do not require a comprehensive information system. In the absence of strong pressure for change, or rationalization, the presentation of media expenditures has continued in its current form, with hard-to-understand explanations of why national advertising is not really nationwide.

According to industry statistics compiled by Robert J. Coen, of McCann-Erickson, Inc., the ratio of national to local advertising over the past five years has remained fairly constant at 55% to 45%. These expenditures, observing industry definitions, are shown in Table 1–2.

If the figures in Table 1–2 were recalculated on the basis of geographical media coverage instead of type of advertiser, the local and national percentages would be reversed. Breaking down the totals into their component parts and estimating expenditures according to the geographic area covered by a message, projections for 1980 are reckoned at approximately 55 percent for local advertising and 45 percent for nationally-transmitted

TABLE 1–2 *Estimated U.S. Expenditures for National and Local Advertising*

Year	Expenditures National (Millions of Dollars)	Local (Millions of Dollars)	Percent Distribution National	Local
1976	18,555	15,135	55.1	44.9
1977	20,850	17,070	55.0	45.0
1978	24,025	19,925	54.7	45.3
1979	27,085	22,495	54.6	45.4
1980	30,315	24,285	55.5	44.5
1981	34,280	27,040	55.9	44.1

Source: Robert J. Coen, of McCann-Erickson, prepared for *Advertising Age.*

messages. The comparable figures for 1981 are 56 percent and 44 percent respectively. This calculation strongly indicates that general advertisers pay a great deal more attention to local markets than might be inferred from industry-ordered figures.

Type of Users

Another approach to classification, which can also be combined with the geographical one, is to break down markets into product user categories. The resulting classes of users are commonly referred to as *targets*, a nomenclature borrowed from the military establishment meaning something at which to shoot. In the commercial lexicon, however, the word target means a group—individuals, organizations, or both—to which advertising is to be directed. Designations of these marketing targets are as varied as those of geographic markets. But again, there are common methods which can be used to direct advertising to specific user types.

One broadly-based method of classification separates the target audience into either consumer or industrial divisions. The first relates to individuals or households, depending upon a product's use patterns and buying influences. Products designed for personal use are generally targeted to individuals, although many purchasing decisions may be made jointly by husband and wife. Higher-priced durable goods, for example, tend to fall into the shared decision category.

In other instances, characteristics of households are as important as those of individuals, even though one person may be responsible for the shopping. Manufacturers of linens, detergents, cleansers, and numerous other sundries find it helpful to describe their markets in terms of both households and individuals. And irrespective of importance assigned to various buyer groups, consumers are the end users of all products. The largest share of U.S. advertising expenditures is funneled into consumer markets.

In contrast, business firms buy goods and services for the purpose of producing other goods and services. It does not matter whether these purchases are raw materials, semi-finished goods and components, capital equipment, supplies, or business services. They are regarded as productive inputs, and their demand is therefore said to be derived from that of the consumer sector, or end user in the case of government and quasi-public services.

The smaller volume of expenditures devoted to industrial advertising misrepresents its broad scope and diversity. There are three major targets for industrial advertisers: entire industries, certain professions or occupations, and trade groups.

Messages may be directed to specialized industries, such as steel, electrical equipment, dairy, and so forth. This type of advertising is often referred to as *vertical advertising*, and may be specifically tailored to certain individuals within a firm. These individuals make up what is known as buying centers. In general, more people get involved in the buying decision when the cost is significant.

In contrast, *horizontal advertising* is aimed at certain professions or occupations which cut across industry lines. Computer manufacturers, for example, may target programmers and systems analysts, regardless of the industry in which they are employed. Accountants, lawyers, real estate department personnel, and engineers are other illustrations of marketing targets that overlap industry groupings.

The third kind, *trade advertising*, promotes a company's products to wholesalers and retailers. Its purpose is to enlist the support and cooperation of businesses which participate in the transactional processes of distribution channels.

THE MARKETING MIX CONCEPT

It should now be evident that advertising is an integral part of the marketing function. This function, popularized by McCarthy as the four P's— product, price, physical distribution, promotion, is commonly known as the *marketing mix*. Advertising is usually considered a part of promotion, making it in this context a subsystem within a subsystem, so to speak. Under certain circumstances, however, advertising assumes the dominant form of the promotional mix, that unique combination of revenue-generating devices a firm chooses to employ in pursuing marketing goals.

Neil Borden originated the marketing mix concept—mixing the functions in various proportions. Many writers have likened this mix to a cake bake in which each cook combines ingredients in somewhat different proportions.[5] In keeping with the cooking metaphor, the exact makeup of the marketing batter will depend upon the particular cake that is being prepared and the preferences of the cook.

Following in the footsteps of Borden, the dominant view tends to regard the marketing mix as a selection of productive inputs which is particular to time, place and circumstance. That choice, write Dunn and Barban, "depends on the situation as well as on how you define a particular factor."[6] The dynamic nature of business, maintains another author, renders the blend of marketing inputs unique to an individual company, for "each new situation is sufficiently different so that it requires a new method."[7] Other authors, agreeing with this assessment, extend its logical corollary that "a variation [in the marketing mix] will likely produce different results."[8]

It is almost a truism that no two companies will ever confront an identical set of marketing circumstances. Both goals and tasks vary from firm to firm, and budget allocations follow divergent, twisting routes. Even the same company can never quite duplicate a marketing plan from year to year. The passage of time, like rolling ocean waves, brings on a perpetual surge of change to which an organization must adjust.

This aspect of contingency, situational as it were, raises a number of interesting, perplexing questions. If the advertising function is company-specific, or brand-specific, how valid are generalizations about it? Surely, there can be no guarantee that a testimonial for a household cleanser will achieve a result similar to one for a microwave oven, if the same amount of advertising was budgeted for its marketing. And if advertising's importance in the marketing mix is time-related, then any particular product may find past performance of little value as a guide to future planning. How can learning take place? Of what value is experience? Advertising relationships in growth situations, for example, cannot be expected to continue into future periods of comparative stability and subdued market expansion. Consequently, authors have cautioned against generalizations on grounds that they are as tenuous as morning mist evaporating under warm rays of the sun.[9]

The billions of dollars spent annually on advertising imply that generalizations are being made regarding the effect of advertising. Else money is being spent foolishly. Without synthesis there can be no understanding of how advertising works, and of how to use it to accomplish organizational tasks. Yet most advertising executives seem to have definite ideas as to what to expect from their budget, though performance does not always accord exactly with expectations and goals. Nor can performance always be measured precisely, as with other weights and measures. The fact is that advertising operates in an environment, as does most business activity, that is tinged with uncertainties and attended by factors which a firm cannot control. But the functions are, nonetheless, subject to underlying forces and constraints which, common to many situations or sets of circumstances, permit deductions concerning principles of operations and norms of behavior.

Despite its multiformity, advertising can be considered an economic activity. Assuredly, the great preponderance of advertising is carried on for the attainment of economic goals. But not all economic goals are met by advertising. Then, on the most elementary level the question arises: "Under what circumstances might advertising be used, and where or when is its utilization unthinkable?"

On a negative note, advertising cannot exist in an environment which resembles that postulated by the theory of "pure competition." This economic model visualizes large numbers of firms producing homogeneous products, with none able to exercise any influence over the market. In this imaginary world, not only advertising, but almost all other marketing mix elements are reduced to irrelevancy.

If competitive products are identical, no particular vendor can look to product policy for an advantage. Nor can pricing be a factor, since that policy is determined for the firm by an invisible hand. Even physical distribution functions are relegated to routine logistics of delivery. In this abstract world of sameness it makes little sense for a seller to advertise more than the bare minimum, such as listing an address, phone number, and product availability.

Certain commodity markets resemble the model of pure competition, where there is actually no competition at all. But the remainder of our economy has firms—from small gas stations to large combines—vying with each other to differentiate their goods and services and to form customer attachments. This struggle for a differential advantage takes place by firms working changes in their four P inputs.

Some authors have assigned such competition to profit organizations only.[10] But this is somewhat doubtful. The fact that an organization is tax exempt does not mean it is less interested in the bottom line of its financial statement. Off Track Betting (OTB), a New York sponsored agency, has set up an extensive network of betting centers and advertises heavily. The National Geographic Society derives a substantial amount of "nonprofits" from magazine subscriptions, totaling some 8.4 million, and from book, map and record sales. Colleges and universities compete with each other, though not in identical market segments, by offering a variety of educational programs. Of late, competition has been increasingly conducted by direct mail advertising. Institutions of higher learning have about $1 billion more current income than current expenditures in the aggregate, which also includes outlays for plant expansion. Whenever there are substitutable but non-standardized products, rivalries flare up using differentiating techniques.

Nonprofit organizations may also engage in interproduct competition. This takes place when a trade association promotes a whole product category which has similar uses to another product class. Asphalt producers through their association compete with concrete manufacturers as suppliers of road paving materials. Or gas may contest oil as a source of energy. Figure 1–3 contains an example of an advertisement for an entire industry.

Any attempt to make a good or a service more desirable is an attempt at product differentiation. Efforts at influencing or changing buyer preferences therefore encompass this broad outlook, applicable to profit and nonprofit organizations alike.

Often linked with the model of pure competition, and a requisite for its operation, is the theory of *consumer sovereignty*. This notion was developed by classical economists to explain demand. They saw consumers as entirely rational, all-knowing buyers, unswervingly pursuing their self-interests. They, like firms, went about maximizing their benefits—in this case not profits, but utility. This theory implies that demand is independent of supply. In an affluent, highly diversified economy, it would follow that demand would be heterogeneous—an inconsistency with the assumption of identical products contained in the competitive model. If demand is independent and heterogeneous, how can producers satisfy it with standardized products?

The two incongruous notions, consumer sovereignty and differentiated supply, were brought together by the marketing concept. This philosophy, which in the 1950s and 1960s became the focal point of marketing theory, regards buyers as having specific wants, needs, and desires, the amalgam of which forms market demand. Since supply must follow demand, the theory regards the prime function of the business firm as the fulfillment of that demand, which more often than not is differentiated, or nonstandardized.

Yet a market in which consumer sovereignty rules supreme is one in which advertising is largely unnecessary. As clearly set forth by Peter Drucker, a firm which adheres to the marketing concept would consider persuasive advertising and promotion a waste of resources. Such a firm would see that "the aim of marketing is to make selling superflous. The aim of marketing is to know and understand the customer so well that the product or service fits him and sells itself. . . . All that should be needed is to make the product or service available, i.e., logistics rather than salesmanship, and statistical distribution rather than promotion."[11] In short, a firm operating under the marketing concept philosophy would differ little from one operating passively in the benumbed environment of the hypothesized pure competition.

ADVERTISING TASKS

As part of the promotional mix, advertising works with two other variables—personal selling and sales promotion. All elements of this mix are both complementary and substitutable for each other. They must work together. But to some degree they are also replacements for each other. For

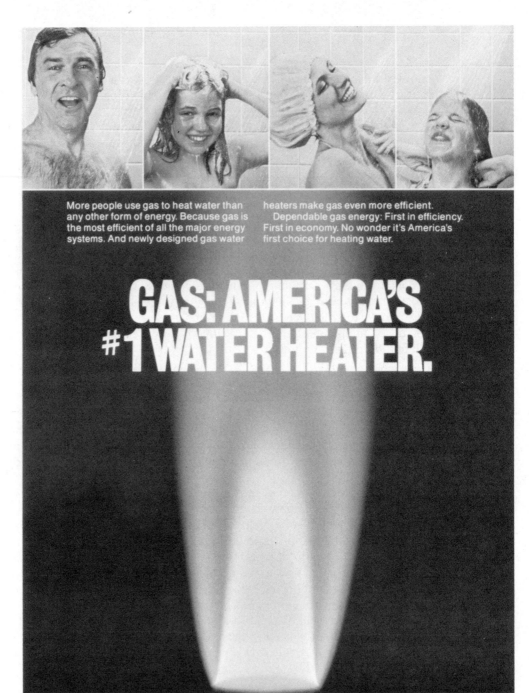

Fig. 1—3 *Gas Assoc. Sample Advertisement for an Entire Industry.* Courtesy of American Gas Association.

example, if costs of sales calls go up in relation to advertising costs, it is conceivable that more advertising will be employed in lieu of salepeople's visits. The rapid rise in recent years of sales promotion expenditures, which now exceed advertising outlays, may be a case of substitution in an inflation-ravaged economy. Firms can exercise considerable latitude in their choices of promotional means, and the selections often reflect the tasks which these factors are called upon to perform.

From a promotional perspective, tasks can be assigned to product or nonproduct advertising. In the first category, advertising tasks can be visualized as a continuum. At one end, advertising does the entire selling job; at the other end it is responsible for only an infinitesimal part of the sales effort. For illustrative purposes, product advertising might be sliced into three parts, though the points of demarcation are not exact:

1. Where advertising tasks are *subsidiary* in sales transactions.
2. Where advertising tasks are *dominant* in sales transactions.
3. Where advertising tasks *consummate the entire* sales transaction.

Nonproduct advertising can likewise be separated into different parts: where the ultimate objective is a transaction and where the objective contemplates a nontransactional end. This method of classifying advertising tasks is diagrammed in Figure 1–4.

Product Advertising Tasks

These tasks make up the preponderance of all advertising, better than 90 percent. The major portion of this 90 percent-plus total is devoted to jobs in which advertising is cast in a supporting role to personal selling. Sidney Bernstein, columnist for *Advertising Age*, a trade magazine, has appropri-

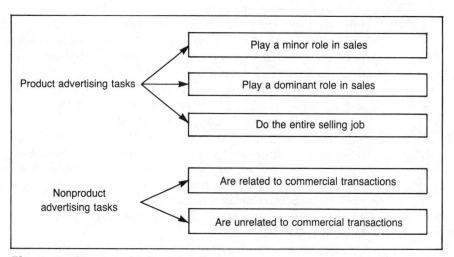

Fig. 1–4 *Diagram of Advertising Tasks.*

ately described this sort of advertising as a "salesman's helper."[12] It is found primarily at the retail level. Advertising here builds store traffic. It brings in customers who want to see, touch, feel, and compare the merchandise before they buy. Advertising draws customers to assortments of goods, and prospects to sales personnel behind the counters.

The "salesman's helper" concept can also be extended to general advertising at the national level. Here, however, advertising takes on tasks beyond those of traffic builder. While it draws prospective customers to showrooms, to auto dealers, for example, it aims at creating positive consumer impressions. As such, it makes the salesperson's job easier because the would-be buyer is favorably inclined to the product in the first place. The salesperson has less resistance to overcome.

The same principles follow in service industries, such as airlines and insurance. Though agents and sales personnel actually close the sale, advertising predisposes sales prospects. It provides a more conducive atmosphere for completing a transaction. Advertising also generates leads, informs the public about particular services, such as special tours and features, and carries sales promotion messages.

Industrial advertising serves principally as an assistant to a company's sales force. The extent of such assistance varies considerably from industry to industry and firm to firm, going from an absolute minimum to lead generation and preference creation.

When the salesperson has disappeared, advertising takes on the burden of persuasion. Considering all goods and services, a comparatively small number of products falls into the group that employs advertising to act as representative and spokesperson to the public. These products have big ad budgets, and it is here that advertising techniques have been developed to the highest level of sophistication. To fill the sales void left by a self-service distribution system, here advertising must "presell." It must be capable of affecting buyers' perceptions of brands and shaping buyers' preferences. In the jargon of economics, advertising strives to make a firm's demand curve more inelastic.

Efforts at influencing consumer choice are not unique to advertising. Indeed, these endeavors lie at the heart of competition and form the core of marketing. Every local shopkeeper, gasoline station, or professional service tries to hold and build customer attachments. In the industrial field, this is done in numerous ways: cumulative discounts, open-purchase contracts, missionary selling, technical support, to name a few. Service contracts with consumers do the same thing—they keep customers coming back. Goods catering to low-priced, self-service markets have no such options, and must turn to advertising as the foundation upon which to build brand loyalty.

Sometimes advertising is expected to complete the entire selling job, as in direct selling. Buyers can respond to ads directly by placing mail or phone orders. Such advertising constitutes a small piece of the total.

Nonproduct Advertising Tasks

Such advertising, called corporate or institutional, is concerned mainly with image building. The ultimate objective of most of these activities is to increase sales of goods and services. This type of advertising has the same goal as product advertising—commercial transactions. But it goes about the job in a different manner, indirect and long-term.

A small portion of nonproduct advertising has no commercial or transactional goals in sight. These messages concern themselves primarily with public issues of a social and political nature. See Figure 1–5 as an example of an advertisement which contains no transactional goal.

ADVERTISING AS ENTREPRENEURSHIP

As just outlined, the tasks advertising is called upon to perform are highly diverse as well as highly demanding. They require people with many skills and many talents, for they cut across almost all organized activity in our society. Advertising uses research data in the performance of its tasks, but it is not research. Advertising uses art forms in putting messages together, but it is not art. Pleading for "well-argued risk" before the 1980 annual meeting of the American Association of Advertising Agencies, Norman Berry, executive creative director of Ogilvy & Mather, accented a persistent theme as to where advertising tasks belong. "It's a selling business," Berry declared, "not an art or science."[13]

From an economic point of view—which certainly takes in all but a small portion of paid-for media messages—there is some justification for regarding advertising as selling. Business accountants list advertising under selling expenses. Advertising, though, is more than just selling. It unveils an aspect of business often not appreciated, and easily overlooked. It is essentially entrepreneurship, explained by the economist Israel Kurzner. According to Kurzner, entrepreneurship is a search for exploiting existing opportunities. Its requirement is not substantive knowledge of market data, but an "alertness" to possibilities for gaining a differential advantage.[14] These entrepreneurial tasks of advertising, unlike those of product development, work in the sphere of human psychology. They are concerned with mental states—perceptions, attitudes, preferences, decisions to buy—all intangible attributes that impel consumer behavior. But these insubstantialities, to paraphrase the Shakespearean magician, Prospero, are the stuff dreams are made on, and the fleeting impressions, like the little lives of the men and women who create them, are rounded by a sleep.

Advertising does the bidding of many different organizations, with different perspectives and different goals. Yet chameleon-like, advertising adapts to changing environments. But a chameleon is a chameleon, regardless of the color of its skin. And advertising is advertising, regardless of goals, as long as it does its job through paid, mass media.

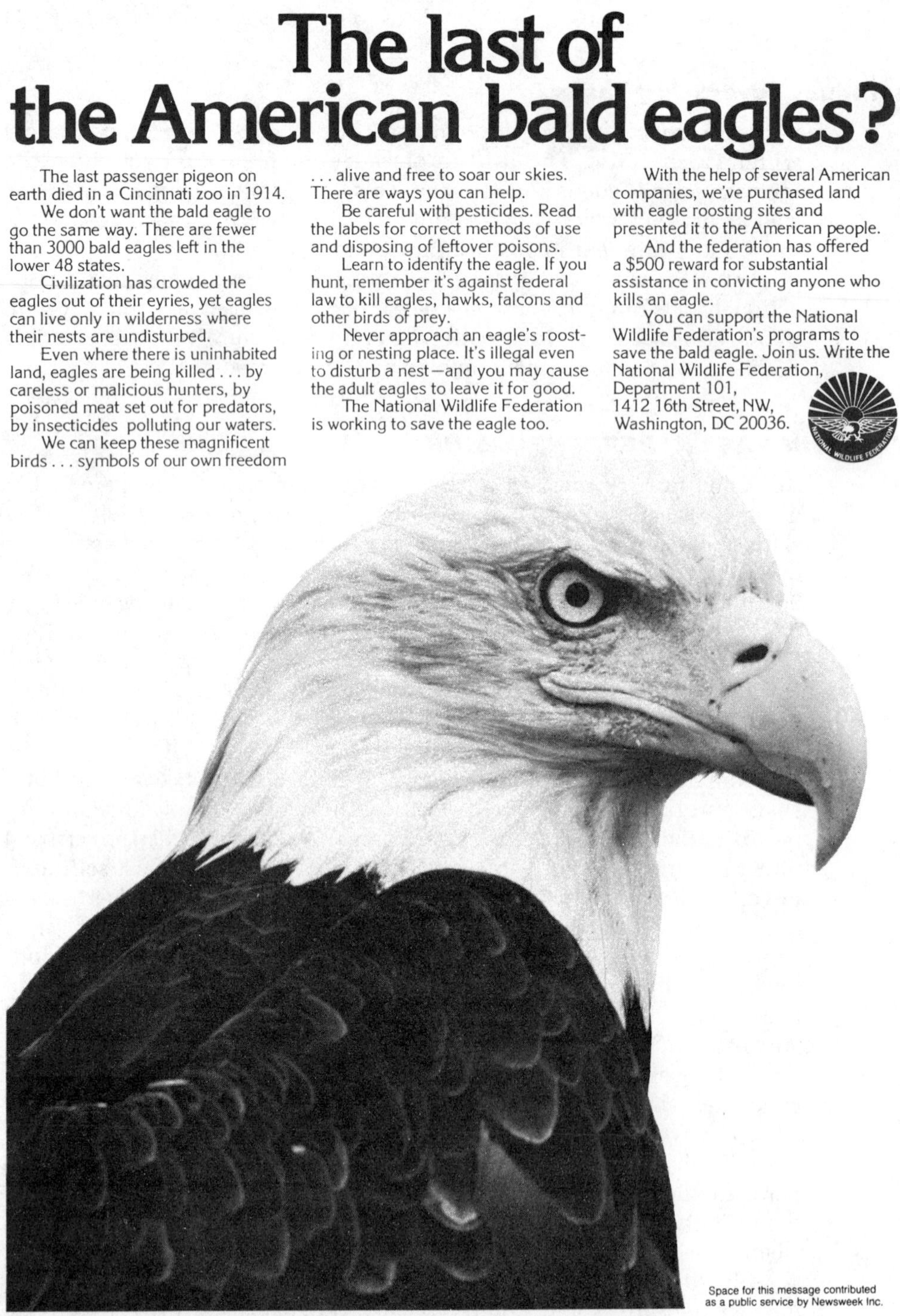
The last of
the American bald eagles?
The last passenger pigeon on earth died in a Cincinnati zoo in 1914.
We don't want the bald eagle to go the same way. There are fewer than 3000 bald eagles left in the lower 48 states.
Civilization has crowded the eagles out of their eyries, yet eagles can live only in wilderness where their nests are undisturbed.
Even where there is uninhabited land, eagles are being killed . . . by careless or malicious hunters, by poisoned meat set out for predators, by insecticides polluting our waters.
We can keep these magnificent birds . . . symbols of our own freedom . . . alive and free to soar our skies. There are ways you can help.
Be careful with pesticides. Read the labels for correct methods of use and disposing of leftover poisons.
Learn to identify the eagle. If you hunt, remember it's against federal law to kill eagles, hawks, falcons and other birds of prey.
Never approach an eagle's roosting or nesting place. It's illegal even to disturb a nest—and you may cause the adult eagles to leave it for good.
The National Wildlife Federation is working to save the eagle too.
With the help of several American companies, we've purchased land with eagle roosting sites and presented it to the American people.
And the federation has offered a $500 reward for substantial assistance in convicting anyone who kills an eagle.
You can support the National Wildlife Federation's programs to save the bald eagle. Join us. Write the National Wildlife Federation, Department 101, 1412 16th Street, NW, Washington, DC 20036.
NATIONAL WILDLIFE FEDERATION
Space for this message contributed as a public service by Newsweek Inc.

Fig. 1–5 *National Wildlife Federation. Sample Advertisement Which Contains No Transactional Goal.* Courtesy of National Wildlife Federation.

SUMMARY

Advertising is paid for media messages of either products, institutions or ideas. These messages are directed to particular markets, which can be classified according to geography and type of user or customer.

In a practical sense, the geographic region of advertising is restricted to the area of distribution. Consequently, nationally-distributed brands have a greater range of media alternatives than those with less than nationwide coverage. User types are market designations, which vary markedly from company to company. Markets can be categorized by types of individuals or households with respect to consumer products, and by types of organizations, professions or occupations with respect to industrial products.

Advertising is part of the marketing mix, made up of product policy, pricing, physical distribution operations, and promotional decisions. Actually, it is a part of promotion. This mix can be employed most profitably when markets feature substitutable but nonstandardized products. However, the optimal combination of factors making up the mix is difficult, if not impossible, to come by despite a plethora of computer models.

Advertising is both a complement and a substitute for other promotional mix variables. The amounts of each variable that are employed in marketing depend upon their costs, tasks, and expected returns. But above all, the most important tasks of advertising are essentially entrepreneurial.

Questions for Chapter 1

1. Why would a company advertise rather than use publicity to announce a new plant opening to surrounding communities?

2. Set up a schematic for classifying organizations from an advertising standpoint.

3. Because advertising does not conform to the theory of pure competition, it represents anticompetitive behavior. Discuss this statement.

4. Does advertising support or contradict the marketing concept?

5. Is advertising more important to companies in which R&D is less innovative?

6. What problems might nonprofit organizations encounter in advertising social issues?

Footnotes for Chapter 1

[1]For example, see American Marketing Association, "Report of the Definitions Committee," *Journal of Marketing* (October 1948), p. 202.

[2]John S. Wright et.al., *Advertising*, 4th edition, (New York: McGraw-Hill, 1977) p. 9.

[3]Melvin T. Copeland, "Relation of Consumers' Buying Habits to Marketing Methods," *Harvard Business Review* (April 1923), pp. 282–289.

[4]See Jack Engel, *Advertising: The Process and Practice* (New York: McGraw-Hill, 1980), p. 33.

[5]Neil H. Borden, "The Concept of the Marketing Mix," *Journal of Advertising Research* (June 1964), p. 3.

[6]S. Watson Dunn and Arnold M. Barban, *Advertising: Its Role in Modern Marketing*, 4th ed. (Hinsdale, Ill: Dryden Press, 1978), pp. 200–201.

[7]Maurice I. Mandel, *Advertising*, 3rd ed. (Englewood Cliffs, N.J.: Prentice-Hall, 1980), p. 167.

[8]Wright et. al., *Advertising*, p. 79.

[9]For example, see C. H. Sandage and V. Fryburger, *Advertising Theory and Practice*, 9th ed. (Homewood, Ill: Richard D. Irwin, 1975), p. 8.

[10]William M. Weilbacher, *Advertising* (New York: Macmillan, 1979), p. 10.

[11]Peter F. Drucker, *Management: Tasks, Responsibilities, Practices* (New York: Harper & Row, 1974), pp. 64–65.

[12]S. R. Bernstein, "What is Advertising?" *Advertising Age* (April 30, 1980), p. 32.

[13]"Creatives Bemoan Current State of Advertising," *Advertising Age* (May 26, 1980), p. 10.

[14]Israel Kurzner, *Competition and Entrepreneurship* (Chicago: University of Chicago Press, 1973), pp. 35–42, 66–68.

2 *Advertising and the Marketing Mix*

Advertising is a means, not an end; a method, not a result. Since it is one of several possible means for achieving marketing objectives, it presents management with the problem of resource allocation. Advertising is enmeshed with other revenue-generating devices in an intricate pattern of infinite possibilities. Since variances from company-established goals of all these marketing inputs are difficult, if not impossible, to calculate, the marketing mix problem is rendered all the more poignant. Yet resources must be allocated among the different elements of the marketing mix in spite of uncertainty and doubt.

Conceptually, the problem can be approached from two start-off points, theoretical and empirical. These are not mutually exclusive, and both can yield valuable inferences about relationships between advertising and other marketing mix variables.

The primary goals of this chapter are:
- **To explore potentials of both theoretical and empirical methods for marketing mix allocations**
- **To explore factors associated with varying degrees of advertising intensities**

THE MARKETING MIX PROBLEM

To place advertising within the marketing mix, or within a subgroup called the promotional mix, implies it is a device in the distribution of goods and services. But this by itself is not very helpful to marketers. It tells nothing about how advertising should be combined with other elements of that mix. To remain in keeping with the cooking metaphor, the marketer is told that he must prepare a cake, but there are no specific recipes for how to whip up the concoction.

Trial and error yields valuable experience. In actuality, even a cursory view reveals that products vary enormously in the extent to which they are advertised. Some products are not advertised at all, while others rely heavily on messages in mass media. Towering dissimilarities spring up among different product groups, and even among firms within the same industry. Why should advertising be embraced in one set of circumstances and ignored in another? Do varying conditions cause differentials in advertising efficiency? If so, what are they?

The pattern of inconstancy has evoked a search for explanations from both academic and business communities. Both groups have for many years sought reasons why advertising intensity rises and falls, and why effectiveness waxes and wanes. The exploration has proceeded in both theoretical and empirical directions. This endeavor at understanding, it is hoped, will move firms to make better allocations of resources.

There exists a vast body of economic literature dealing with resource allocation as it relates to advertising. Most of it treats the subject as macroeconomics; analyses aim to assess how advertising affects the welfare of society. From the standpoint of society, a misallocation of resources does not necessarily have an adverse effect on an individual firm. There are two situations where possible losses accrue to the firm because of advertising misallocations. First, a company may advertise excessively. This happens when the excess does not expand demand. Put in economic terms, the demand curve is not shifted further to the right. Second, a misallocation can occur when advertising is underutilized. In this situation, the firm foregoes opportunities. This decision prevents production and certain distribution functions from achieving potential economies by keeping operations too small.

But what is excessive and what is too little? And what is the base by which these relative values are gauged? These are the primary questions with respect to the marketing mix.

THEORETICAL APPROACHES

One approach toward solving the marketing mix problem has been theoretical, following marginal concepts of economics. On this basis, the best allocation is one in which incremental expenditures for each element of the marketing mix yield the same incremental returns. This principle is illustrated graphically in Figure 2–1.

The illustration in Figure 2–1 supposes that advertising and personal selling are the major variables in a promotional budget at a certain level. In accordance with the marginal productivity theory of distribution, returns to productive inputs completely exhaust their total value. The problem then boils down to selecting the best combination of factors within a range of alternatives.

Accordingly, points on the constant budget line, $ByBx$, represent all possible combinations of advertising-selling expenditures. Bx represents a situation in which the entire promotional budget is spent on personal selling. At By the entire budget would go to advertising. The line connecting By and Bx embodies all possible mixes of advertising and personal selling, with total expenditures being a constant sum. Q_1 and Q_2 are constant net revenue curves. All points on a particular curve will yield an identical net revenue, but by a different blend of advertising and personal selling. For the given budget, $ByBx$, only one point produces an optimum. This is at E, where the iso-revenue curve Q_2 is tangent to the budget line $ByBx$. In this particular problem, almost equal amounts should be allo-

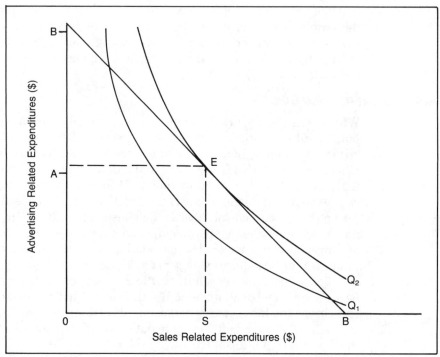

Fig. 2—1 *Advertising-Personal Selling Mix.*

cated to advertising and personal selling—OA dollars to the former and OS dollars to the latter.

This simplistic but basic model can easily be extended to encompass other budget levels and more elements of the marketing mix.[1] The mathematical proofs were worked out by Robert Dorfman and Peter Steiner in 1954.[2] They postulated a situation wherein a firm has almost complete market power, with a demand curve dependent upon two factors. In these circumstances, the marginal value of a promotional mix is equal to the elasticity of demand for the product with respect to each productive input or element of the mix. Elasticity refers to the relative change in sales or output effected by a relative change in input. The Dorfman-Steiner conclusions rest on the assumption that the independent variables have continuous and differential functions. In Figure 2–1, for example, sales were regarded as a function of two variables, advertising and personal selling.

The theorem carries the implication that management has at its disposal the means of maximizing revenue whenever advertising can exert an effect on the demand of the product. It suggests that a manager bent on getting the most out of an operation should set the advertising budget so that the net revenue which results from the last dollar expended equals the product's elasticity of demand. Advertising effectiveness must therefore be presumed at some point to display decreasing returns, or else expanding budgets and commensurate revenues could be maintained indefinitely.

MAXIMIZATION MODELS

With the increasing use of computers, marginal theories have been incorporated into advertising maximization models. These, however, have been criticized on many counts. The most serious charges assert that the theories are not operative in real flesh and blood situations. Advertising elasticity of demand is largely unknown. With certain exceptions, revenue cannot be traced unambiguously to advertisements. Competitive behavior cannot be accounted for. The models also treat advertising as homogeneous, without assessment of media and copy differences. To seek points of tangencies in a set of abstract relationships, the values of which are unknown, critics allege, represents a sterile academic exercise.[3]

The model builders admit to the creation of norms which may be beyond the realm of attainment. But they insist that models improve practices by seeing more clearly certain implications, relationships, and even anomalies.[4] A model offers a systematic way of looking at things and how their parts are put together.

Although the efficiency of maximization models have not been resolved, a number of companies have nevertheless pressed ahead with computer programs for profit maximizing solutions. Since revenue effects of marketing mix variables are often not known, managers are asked to insert values based on their best judgment.[5] The rationale for this procedure is that under any circumstance, a decision must be made. It is therefore better to use experience, which is a form of accumulated knowledge, than to make a blind guess. But even this assumption has been questioned. Several researchers investigating popular models in which advertising was a major variable found that poorer decisions were just as likely as good ones when managers' judgments were used as data.[6]

The spreading use of these computer models does not, however, constitute *per se* evidence that firms are indeed maximizing advertising functions. There have been very few studies of the computer's impact on advertising efficiency and effectiveness, and the work that has been done turned up inconclusive results. If man is as adaptive as sociologists claim, there is no reason for thinking of these computer-begotten decisions as other than extensions of human intuition, no matter that the subjective thought processes go by such scientifically-sounding names as Bayesian decision models, probability decision techniques, or decision trees. By substituting judgmental for factual data, the electronic machines might have enhanced middle management's power over "discretionary" corporate funds, and its proclivity to overspend on marketing programs in the process.[7]

The greatest obstacle to the rational approach stems from the absence of relevant empirical data. Despite a massive literature on advertising, there still remain wide gaps in knowledge about how advertising works, or does not work, in a market setting. After a thorough and critical review of the published material, Richard Schmalensee concluded that the veritable throng of studies, which would reach dizzying heights if stacked on one another, provides little evidence with which to generalize about the effects of advertising.[8] He was even unable to find any reliable relationships between changes in advertising and corresponding changes in sales of cigarettes, though that industry claims to have more complete and extensive data than any other.[9]

THE PIMS STUDY

Another line of inquiry into the marketing mix is that of empiricism. Unlike the theoretical approach, the empirical one assumes no optimum. It accepts the fact that advertising practitioners do not know all they wish to know, and that often their only guide is trial and error. But if pursued systematically, learning and modifying behavior along the route, firms move toward a more satisfactory position. They may never attain the sought-after optimum. But if one is willing to settle for more modest goals, valuable inferences can be drawn from existing information sources.

An important body of empirical data is that of *PIMS*, an acronym for "Profit Impact Marketing Strategies." This project, initially begun by Marketing Science Institute and now being carried on by Strategic Planning Institute, has accumulated records from a large number of businesses. A recent study of 227 consumer businesses from this data base sheds considerable light on advertising-price-product quality relationships.[10] This particular investigation covered a seven-year period, from 1971 to 1977.

The participating companies were asked to compare their budgets, as a percent of sales, with those of their closest competitors. The questionnaire contained a five-point scale for ranking spending levels. Respondents were also asked to rate their factory prices as a percentage above or below those of their competitors.

According to the pattern traced out in the PIMS study, heavier advertising goes together with higher prices. Low-budget advertisers price their products, on the average, from 2 percent to 3 percent below the market. In contrast, businesses with above-average ad budgets command prices of some 4 percent to 7 percent higher than the going market rate.

The study offered two alternative explanations, both standard ones, which bring to mind the renowned chicken-and-egg argument. First is the claim that retailers and consumers will pay more for popular, better-known brands. This interpretation accords with the generally accepted view that sees advertising as a technique for influencing the demand curve, shifting it to the right. More advertising thus becomes a means for getting higher prices, without at the same time reducing total dollar sales.[11] Here, greater advertising intensity begets higher prices.

Second is the assertion that firms are more inclined towards advertising when higher prices widen the spread in gross margins. Here causation runs the other way, from pricing decisions to advertising decisions. In this interpretation, a firm sets its price first, depending upon its assessment of market factors, and then adjusts its advertising level accordingly. Here, price policy begets advertising policy.

The PIMS study relates to producer prices, not those at the retail level. Prices to consumers need not parallel exactly those to middlemen.[12]

Regardless of prime cause, there seems to be a tendency for relative price and relative advertising to move in the same direction.[13] This positive relationship reflects the main choices of price-advertising options available to a business. It can compete on the basis of price, and reduce ad expenditures. Or it can heavy up on advertising, thereby hoping to obtain better net profits through higher prices. Other strategies are also practiced, such as one calling for low prices and heavier-than-usual advertising. But PIMS researchers give this option less chance of being successful.

Marketers of highly-advertised, national brands often claim that their higher prices come about because of superior quality, and not because of advertising. To assess this argument the PIMS survey elicited management judgment as to product quality, both for their own brands and competitive ones. Having managers rate products on quality introduces some bias because any ensuing exaggeration will not be uniform. Some qualitative differences will be perceived by virtually everyone in the same way, while others will engender a variety of opinions.[14] Included in the first type are products subject to what Lawrence Abbott calls, "vertical quality differences." For example, a Cadillac is regarded as qualitatively superior to a Chevette. These differences usually involve cost differentials. The second kind, termed "horizontal," arises largely from subjective tastes and preferences, and normally entails no significant variations in production costs.[15] Despite the inherent difficulties in dealing with the subject of quality, PIMS results are highly revealing.

The study indicates that prices embody a surcharge for quality. But advertising joins the qualitative factor in giving prices an upward nudge. Businesses which outadvertise their competitors and turn out better-made products get the highest prices, 6.5 percent above market. Without the benefit of advertising, prices for superior products command no premium. They approach the market average. On the other hand, products of relatively inferior quality obtain better-than-average prices when they are supported by heavier-than-average advertising. Usually, these low quality products were found to sell some three percent above market.

The conclusions of Farris and Reibstein, who supervised this study, have far-reaching implications. Given products of equal quality, heavier-advertised brands will sell for more than lesser-known brands. And regardless of any promotionally-induced economies in production or distribution, a price differential will remain between advertised and unadvertised brands.

One implication, and probably most important for corporate management, concerns the bottom line. Since revenue is calculated as price times quantity sold, price becomes a direct factor in the profit equation. Insofar as advertising affects prices, it can tip, albeit indirectly, the revenue-cost scale.

A number of studies, including PIMS, have consistently found a significant association between advertising intensity and profit.[16] Can a company, then, raise its earnings by spending liberally on advertising? The answer is emphatically no. There is a multitude of reasons why it can't.

As has been repeated over and over, advertising does not work alone. In most instances, it is not even the dominant factor in a marketing program but functions in a supportive role. When advertising does assume primacy, its effects remain contingent upon the operation of the other marketing elements. Either way, its influence on profits is indirect. To assess this influence, therefore, presents great difficulties. This is why econometric studies have found relationships between advertising and profits, as well as with prices, modest at best and usually weak.

In addition, the sales response which advertising evokes is uneven and unstable. There are two main reasons for such results: the advertising itself and the nature of products and markets.

First, some campaigns leave an indelible impression on sales, while others come and go with hardly a trace that they were ever run at all. Both advertisers and advertising agencies pay the highest tribute to creativity, a gift that defies measurement and prediction. Practitioners just don't know why some ads work and others do not. Second, some products and markets more so than others present advertising with a favorable climate or setting within which to operate. The efficiency of advertising will then vary.

CONSUMER VS. INDUSTRIAL MARKETS

The previous section dealt with "relative" advertising. It compared advertising in firms marketing competitive products. But there are also striking dissimilarities among industries. On an absolute level, some industries expend vast sums on advertising, while others spend relatively little.

All products and markets can be divided into consumer or industrial. The consumer segment, on the average, exhibits an advertising-to-sales ratio from three to four times larger than that of the industrial sector.[17] In absolute terms, the bulk of advertising funds are used to promote consumer products. This is evident from the expenditure records of the leading 100 national advertisers, as shown in Table 2–1.

Among the 100 leading national advertisers in 1981, only a handful had major product lines which were not sold directly to the general public. The same held true in past years, going back as long as records are available. A closer look at the exceptions, such as Mobil, DuPont, Eastman Kodak, and Union Carbide, reveals that they are all highly diversified companies, and that the largest portions of their advertising budgets were earmarked not for their industrial goods but for their smaller consumer lines.

For example, of Mobil's $293.1 million spent on advertising, $60.4 million was in measured media, listed by *Advertising Age* as newspapers, magazines, televison, radio, outdoor. Of the $60.4 million total, $20.8 went for Montgomery Ward, a Mobil subsidiary. Another $7.1 million supported its motor oil, while $12.2 million was spent promoting its Hefty line of products, ranging from paper plates to plastic bags. Another $4.2 million was budgeted to advertise gasoline, Mobil's primary consumer product.

The chemical companies in the top 100 advertisers similarly spent the bulk of their advertising budgets on consumer products. Of $65.0 million expended by Eastman Kodak in measured media, practically the entire amount was used to promote cameras, film and photographic paper. Union Carbide registered $56.2 million for measured media. Some $49.6 million of that total went into three consumer product lines—Eveready batteries, Glad plastic bags, Prestone anti-freeze.

Expenditures on a brand rather than a company basis tells the same story. The fifty largest brand advertisers in 1980, which also includes retail establishments, are shown in Table 2–2. These figures are reported by *Marketing and Media Decisions,* and are on a slightly different basis than those of *Advertising Age.* Spending levels from year to year, over the past four, illustrate the high degree of consistency in advertising budgets.

RATIO OF ADVERTISING TO SALES

A refinement of absolute expenditure levels is to calculate advertising as a percentage of sales. This ratio eliminates the effects of scale, and constitutes a more accurate reflection of the importance companies attach to advertising as part of their marketing efforts. This measure, despite numerous detractors, continues as a highly popular guideline for managers in setting budgets.

The advertising sales ratio serves as a rough indicator of advertising efficiency to an industry. A low ratio suggests that advertising is not deemed important in the marketing mix. Conversely, a high ratio identi-

TABLE 2–1 Advertising Expenditures of 100 Leading National Advertisers

(Total ad dollars in millions: 1981)

Rank	Company	Advertising	Rank	Company	Advertising
1	Procter & Gamble	$671.8	27	Unilever U.S.	188.9
2	Sears, Roebuck & Co.	544.1	28	Anheuser-Busch Cos.	187.2
3	General Foods Corp.	456.8	29	Heublein Inc.	187.0
4	Philip Morris Inc.	433.0	30	Dart & Kraft	177.0
5	General Motors Corp.	401.0	31	Esmark Inc.	175.0
6	K mart Corp.	349.6	32	Gillette Co.	171.9
7	Nabisco Brands	341.0	33	Beatrice Foods Co.	170.0
8	R. J. Reynolds Industries	321.3	34	Consolidated Foods Corp.	166.4
9	American Telephone & Telegraph Co.	297.0	35	General Electric Co.	164.7
10	Mobil Corp.	293.1	36	H. J. Heinz Co.	160.2
11	Ford Motor Co.	286.7	37	Warner Communications	159.0
12	Warner-Lambert Co.	270.4	38	International Telephone & Telegraph Co.	153.0
13	Colgate-Palmolive Co.	260.0	39	Norton Simon Inc.	149.9
14	PepsiCo Inc.	260.0	40	Richardson-Vicks	149.0
15	McDonald's Corp.	230.2	41	Seagram Co. Ltd.	145.0
16	American Home Products Corp.	209.0	42	Loews Corp.	141.4
17	RCA Corp.	208.8	43	Time Inc.	141.1
18	J. C. Penney Co.	208.6	44	American Cyanamid Co.	138.0
19	General Mills Corp.	207.3	45	Chesebrough-Pond's	136.2
20	Bristol-Myers Co.	200.0	46	CBS Inc.	134.0
21	B.A.T. Industries PLC	199.3	47	Pillsbury Co.	131.0
22	Coca-Cola Co.	197.9	48	Schering-Plough Corp.	119.8
23	Johnson & Johnson	195.0	49	Mattel Inc.	110.6
24	Chrysler Corp.	193.0	50	Revlon Inc.	106.6
25	Ralston Purina Co.	193.0			
26	U.S. Government	189.0			*(continued)*

TABLE 2–1 Advertising Expenditures of 100 Leading National Advertisers

(Total ad dollars in millions: 1981)

Rank	Company	Advertising	Rank	Company	Advertising
51	Toyota Motor Sales	106.2	77	Beecham Group Ltd.	69.1
52	Gulf & Western Industries	106.1	78	American Honda Motor Co.	68.3
53	E. I. du Pont de Nemours & Co.	105.0	79	S. C. Johnson & Son	66.6
54	Kellogg Co.	102.1	80	MCA Inc.	63.6
55	Eastman Kodak Co.	101.0	81	Wm. Wrigley Jr. Co.	63.5
56	Quaker Oats Co.	95.6	82	Kimberly-Clark Corp.	62.4
57	Trans World Corp.	95.2	83	Pfizer Inc.	59.0
58	Union Carbide Corp.	90.0	84	Exxon Corp.	58.1
59	Sterling Drug Co.	89.7	85	Jos. Schlitz Brewing Co.	56.8
60	SmithKline Corp.	89.3	86	Hershey Foods Corp.	56.5
61	Nestle Enterprises	88.0	87	Eastern Air Lines	54.1
62	Nissan Motor Corp., U.S.A.	87.9	88	Polaroid Corp.	51.8
63	CPC International	87.0	89	American Airlines	51.5
64	Xerox Corp.	84.2	90	Columbia Pictures Industries	47.5
65	North American Philips Corp.	83.9	91	Delta Air Lines	44.5
66	American Brands	82.2	92	Borden Inc.	44.0
67	Volkswagen of America	81.0	93	Liggett Group	43.5
68	Clorox Co.	80.8	94	Morton Norwich Products	42.5
69	Mars Inc.	78.4	95	Hiram Walker Resources Ltd.	42.3
70	Brown-Forman Distillers Co.	78.0	96	Noxell Corp.	41.1
71	American Express Co.	76.0	97	Jeffrey Martin Inc.	41.0
72	Greyhound Corp.	75.6	98	International Business Machines Corp.	40.7
73	Miles Laboratories	72.1	99	American Broadcasting Cos.	40.0
74	Campbell Soup Co.	70.8	100	Canon U.S.A.	36.5
75	UAL Inc.	70.6			
76	American Motors Corp.	70.0			

Source: Reprinted with permission from September 9, 1982 issue of *Advertising Age.* Copyright 1982 by Crain Communications Inc.

TABLE 2–2 *Top Fifty Brand Advertisers in 1980*

Brand Name (and Parent Company)	Classification	1977	1978	1979	1980
1. Sears (Sears Roebuck)	Retail	$430,048,000	$501,450,000	$405,835,000	$442,160,000
2. K-Mart (K-Mart)	Retail	218,002,000	231,245,000	244,365,000	304,050,000
3. Penney's (J. C. Penney)	Retail	185,164,000	245,623,000	250,979,000	259,170,000
4. Ford (Ford Motor)	Cars, trucks	106,266,000	163,184,000	175,264,000	197,763,000
5. Wards (Mobil Corp.)	Retail	132,268,000	149,794,000	159,821,000	166,600,000
6. Woolco (F. W. Woolworth)	Retail	111,505,000	113,416,000	131,886,000	151,000,000
7. Chevrolet (General Motors)	Cars	131,231,000	150,924,000	161,123,000	138,741,000
8. AT&T/Bell (AT&T)	Communications	69,365,000	68,359,000	93,050,000	136,515,000
9. McDonald's (McDonald's Corp.)	Restaurants	98,016,000	118,016,000	142,569,000	130,862,000
10. Toyota (Toyota Motors)	Cars, trucks	48,459,000	70,110,000	67,203,000	91,707,000
11. Kellogg's (Kellogg Co.)	Cereals	61,716,000	67,293,000	79,528,000	85,428,000
12. Purina (Ralston Purina)	Pet foods, feeds, pest control	56,188,000	62,394,000	76,890,000	78,824,000
13. Kraft (Kraft, Inc.)	Cooking, dairy, prepared foods	61,524,000	72,192,000	74,470,000	77,785,000
14. Miller (Philip Morris)	Beer	32,317,000	50,444,000	59,237,000	76,234,000
15. GE (General Electric)	Appliances, radio, tv	54,768,000	52,944,000	62,701,000	71,896,000
16. Salem (R. J. Reynolds)	Cigarettes	33,294,000	36,620,000	48,193,000	66,831,000
17. Datsun (Nissan Motors)	Cars, trucks	54,101,000	61,818,000	65,477,000	65,711,000
18. Vantage (R. J. Reynolds)	Cigarettes	34,089,000	30,269,000	46,176,000	59,689,000
19. Chrysler (Chrysler)	Cars	58,952,000	55,952,000	47,170,000	57,035,000
20. Kent (Loews)	Cigarettes	32,261,000	42,184,000	55,205,000	56,063,000
21. Merit (Philip Morris)	Cigarettes	41,961,000	43,806,000	51,777,000	55,640,000
22. Pepsi-Cola (PepsiCo)	Soft drinks	43,700,000	45,819,000	57,186,000	55,001,000
23. Kodak (Eastman Kodak)	Cameras, film	52,758,000	53,325,000	60,090,000	54,400,000
24. Budweiser (Anheuser-Busch)	Beer	27,116,000	28,719,000	36,518,000	49,032,000
25. Marlboro (Philip Morris)	Cigarettes	38,700,000	43,180,000	45,388,000	48,678,000
26. Winston (R. J. Reynolds)	Cigarettes	44,826,000	38,573,000	59,230,000	48,344,000
27. Clairol (Bristol-Myers)	Hair products, toiletries	49,921,000	53,338,000	59,737,000	47,487,000
28. United (UAL)	Passenger travel	26,233,000	40,467,000	37,008,000	47,377,000

(continued)

TABLE 2–2 Top Fifty Brands Advertisers in 1980

Brand Name (and Parent Company)	Classification	1977	1978	1979	1980
29. Volkswagen (Volkswagenwerk)	Passenger cars	32,641,000	33,395,000	30,915,000	46,063,000
30. Now (R. J. Reynolds)	Cigarettes	14,540,000	9,313,000	10,057,000	45,578,000
31. Mercury (Ford Motor)	Passenger cars	28,092,000	34,446,000	30,870,000	45,534,000
32. Maxwell House (General Foods)	Coffee	16,039,000	34,011,000	51,011,000	45,090,000
33. Burger King (Pillsbury)	Restaurants	27,233,000	36,607,000	45,109,000	45,075,000
34. Coca-Cola (Coca-Cola)	Soft drinks	29,424,000	40,956,000	46,364,000	44,988,000
35. Anacin (Amer. Home Product)	Medicines	33,981,000	34,290,000	39,671,000	43,513,000
36. Dodge (Chrysler)	Passenger cars	64,836,000	75,396,000	62,640,000	43,124,000
37. Seagram's (Seagram)	Liquors	18,582,000	41,627,000	43,151,000	42,366,000
38. American (American Airlines)	Passenger travel	25,109,000	25,267,000	29,132,000	41,958,000
39. Oldsmobile (General Motors)	Passenger cars	29,520,000	33,904,000	29,195,000	41,673,000
40. GMC (General Motors Corp.)	Cars	34,765,000	54,550,000	52,575,000	41,125,000
41. DuPont (E. I. DuPont)	Paints, fabrics, auto access.	13,269,000	19,423,000	34,166,000	40,609,000
42. Johnson's (Johnson & Johnson)	Hair care, baby products	26,151,000	35,180,000	35,734,000	40,298,000
43. Eastern (Eastern Air Lines)	Passenger travel	25,541,000	22,326,000	29,216,000	40,182,000
44. Buick (General Motors)	Passenger cars	33,596,000	45,618,000	36,114,000	39,931,000
45. American Express (Amer. Ex.)	Financial, travel	22,089,000	36,999,000	33,811,000	37,723,000
46. Polaroid (Polaroid)	Cameras, film	26,068,000	40,955,000	38,241,000	37,334,000
47. ABC (American Broadcasting)	Tv, radio stations	19,976,000	26,890,000	31,572,000	36,972,000
48. Pontiac (General Motors)	Passenger cars	35,596,000	39,565,000	37,686,000	36,664,000
49. Columbia (Columbia Pictures)	Motion pictures	12,525,000	14,249,000	24,073,000	36,317,000
50. Wrigley (Wm. Wrigley, Jr.)	Gum	29,114,000	40,415,000	43,516,000	35,617,000

Source: *Marketing & Media Decisions* (July 1981), pp. 66–68.

fies those products and markets which generally impose an advertising requirement on all firms competing for a piece of the industry sales pie.

Besides publishing advertising expenditure figures for the 100 largest national advertisers, *Advertising Age* shows sales and advertising sales ratios for each firm. The next table summarizes these data for various industries. It shows weighted ratios for 1979–1981 for major product groups. Although the firms within each industry are not necessarily the same in all years, the averages remain fairly constant.

The figures in Table 2–3 are less than complete. The percentages shown in the table are biased on the downward side for several reasons.

First, most companies which make up a product category operate in several business fields. Yet a firm is listed in the product cateogry which accounts for the most important part of its revenue. For example, Procter and Gamble, the largest national advertiser, is classified under "soap, cleansers." But the firm is highly diversified, marketing foods, toiletries, and paper products, each with different advertising-sales ratios. The company has recently developed a profitable and growing business in hospital and medical laboratory supplies, where advertising is relatively light compared with consumer products. Philip Morris, classified under "tobacco," is a major manufacturer of beer. R. J. Reynolds similarly derives a substantial part of its revenues from non-tobacco sources, mainly food and beverages. These anomalies in classification cause some distortion in a product group's average, generally downward.

TABLE 2–3 *Advertising-Sales Ratios for Leading National Advertisers by Major Product Group*

Product Group	Number of Companies			Advertising as a Percent of sales, Average*		
	1979	1980	1981	1979	1980	1981
Airlines	5	5	5	1.4%	1.3%	1.5%
Appliances	3	2	3	1.1	1.0	1.2
Automotive	9	9	8	0.6	0.7	0.8
Communic., Entertainment	6	6	6	3.3	3.9	3.9
Drugs	8	8	6	8.2	5.2	5.4
Food	20	21	19	3.2	3.1	3.4
Soap, cleansers	5	5	5	5.4	5.7	5.6
Tobacco	5	5	5	3.1	3.0	3.1
Toiletries, cosmetics	7	9	11	5.9	5.9	5.6
Wine, beer, liquor	5	5	6	6.6	6.4	5.0

*Weighted
Source: Calculations based on statistics in *Advertising Age* (September 11, 1980), p. 8; (September 10, 1981), p. 8; and (September 9, 1982), p. 8.

Second, advertising outlays refer to spending in the United States only. Therefore, foreign sales must be excluded from the totals, so that revenues and expenditures come from the same domestic sources. Unfortunately, this is not always done by suppliers of public information. When a firm's total sales are used in the calculations, the result will depress the advertising-sales ratio. The greater the proportion of overseas business, the larger the understatement of advertising intensity. Accordingly, 10K reports were examined so that advertising outlays could be matched more properly with sales.

Not all firms file 10K reports with the Securities and Exchange Commission, nor necessarily break out domestic sales from totals. Table 2–4

TABLE 2–4 *Advertising Sales Ratios for Selected Leading National Advertisers*

Company	Advertising Age Ratio			U.S. only Ratio		
	1979	1980	1981	1979	1980	1981
Appliances						
General Electric	0.6	0.6	0.6	0.8	0.8	0.9
RCA Corp.	2.1	2.1	2.6	2.5	2.5	2.9
Automobiles						
General Motors	0.5	0.5	.06	0.6	0.7	0.7
Ford Motor Co.	0.5	0.8	0.7	0.9	1.5	1.1
Chrysler Corp.	1.0	1.6	1.8	1.1	1.8	1.9
Drugs						
Pfizer Corp.	3.7*	1.6	1.8	3.7	3.7	4.2
Sterling Drug	11.2*	5.7	5.0	11.2	9.4	9.1
Schering-Plough	5.4	5.7	6.6	10.1	11.4	13.0
Smithkline Corp.	8.0	4.6	4.5	15.0	8.5	8.7
Richardson-Merrell	11.4	11.1	13.7	24.9	33.8	29.6
Soap, cleansers						
Procter & Gamble	5.7***	5.7***	5.6***	9.1***	8.5***	8.4***
Colgate-Palmolive	2.7	9.4	4.9	6.9	11.3	12.0
Tobacco						
Philip Morris	3.5	3.7	4.0	4.7	5.0	5.8
R. J. Reynolds	2.9	2.9	2.7	4.4	4.4	4.1
Toiletries						
Amer. Home Prods.	5.6	4.8	5.1	8.7	7.5	7.6
Bristol-Myers	7.7	6.2	5.7	11.1	8.9	8.1
Warner-Lambert	6.8	6.8	8.0	12.2	12.5	14.6
Chesebrough-Ponds	9.1	9.3	8.9	12.7	12.7	12.6
Gillette Co.	6.4	6.5	7.4	16.1**	16.5**	17.1**

*Ratio based on U.S. sales.
**Sales are based on U.S. and Canada.
***Sales are for the fiscal year ending June.
Source: *Advertising Age* ratios are as reported in issues of September 11, 1980; September 10, 1981; and September 9, 1982.
Note: Richardson-Merrell in 1981 divested itself of the Merrell ethical drug division, and its name was changed to Richardson-Vicks.

compares *Advertising Age* ratios with U.S. only ratios for a selected number of advertisers to indicate the extent of the reporting bias.

Despite their imperfections, the advertising-sales ratios in Tables 2–3 and 2–4 are indicative of broad trends. The highest advertising intensities are to be found in consumer products which are nondurable, low-priced, purchased with some degree of regularity, sell in self-service outlets, and have open or intensive distribution.

The FTC has been publishing line-of-business reports since 1975, compiled from actual company records. This first report listed 217 product categories where advertising sales ratios stood at 0.1 percent or higher. Of this total, only sixteen lines of business had advertising-sales ratios of five percent or better. In just seven product lines did this ratio exceed 10 percent. Though the exact ratios were different—higher than those based on total company sales—the characteristics of the products were strikingly similar to those inferred from statistics of advertising expenditures reported by *Advertising Age*. The FTC figures are more sensitive to marketing factors. The seven product lines with the highest media advertising expenses, expressed as a percentage of their sales, were as follows:

Industry Category	Ratio of Media Expenses to Sales (Percent)
Drugs, proprietary	20.1
Perfumes, cosmetics, toiletries	13.8
Cutlery	12.8
Chewing gum	12.3
Distilled liquor	11.9
Periodicals	11.2
Cereal breakfast foods	10.2

Adapted from Advertising Age (October 19, 1981), p. 42.

PRODUCTS AND MARKETS

As is abundantly evident from advertising-sales ratios, the intensity of advertising is related to products and markets. A summary of product-market characteristics associated with high and low advertising intensities is presented in Table 2–5.

The characteristics shown in Table 2–5 are interrelated to a high degree.[18] They are listed separately for purposes of exposition. In reality, however, they come bundled, with the combinations of elements varying among different product categories.

Product Type

By definition, durable goods last longer than nondurables. Consequently, they are purchased infrequently and their markets are more constricted. There are many nondurables which are also bought infrequently, such as

TABLE 2–5 *Product-Market Characteristics and Relative Advertising Intensity*

Product-Market Characteristic	High Advertising Intensity	Low Advertising Intensity
Product type	Convenience Nondurable	Shopping, specialty Durable
Price	Low	High
Purchase frequency	High	Low
Nature of distribution and retail selling	Self-service Open and/or intensive	Personal selling Limited and/or exclusive

window cleaners and shoe polish. But that is beside the point. Thin markets afford less scope for efficient advertising. In marketing briefs to incontinent adults, Procter & Gamble, the largest advertiser, went to direct response marketing because of low retail demand.[19] Advertising-sales ratios for drug, soap, and toiletry manufacturers are many times those of appliance and automobile makers. In some instances, drug marketers have advertising intensities from fifteen to twenty-eight times greater than the average for the appliance or automotive category. The Gillette Company's advertising, expressed as a percentage of sales, is 25 times greater than that of General Motors (See Table 2–3 and 2–4.)

Price

If product is given, the price level can expand or contract a market. The amount of such change depends upon the elasticity of demand. If a market is given, higher-priced products may find advertising more "affordable," especially when trading margins are higher. In a study of 103 businesses manufacturing consumer products sponsored by Marketing Science Institute, trading margins had the highest positive correlation with promotion-sales ratios among nineteen independent variables.[20] Higher prices thus allow auto makers to have bigger ad budgets than hardware producers, though both types of manufacturers make durable goods.

One reason why high prices result in low advertising intensities is that they bring about greater deliberation on the part of consumers. When the price tag is a large percentage of total income, consumers seek more information. That is not to say that purchases will be completely rational. But advertising must compete with evaluations of independent agencies, advice from friends and acquaintances, and personal experience based on observation. Comparison shopping and bargaining become an important factor in sales, and greater emphasis is placed on personal selling. Advertising becomes a device for bringing prospects to showrooms, and the salesperson takes over from there. In other instances, advertising is used as an aid to permit salespeople to be sent to prospects, as in high-priced services. The insurance business is one in which salespeople go to prospective customers.

Advertising assumes a more important role in marketing low-priced items. Consumers do not usually engage in an extensive search, and advertising becomes their vital information source. Whether the advertising is given full credence or not is another story. The fact remains that consumer's knowledge about these products is often derived from advertising, regardless of the way in which information is presented or the method by which it is processed.

Low-priced items are also more amenable to flow production techniques. The output is more standardized. There is less customization, less fragmentation, less variation. General Motors, for example, produces some 250 different models of automobiles in a given year. In contrast, the largest producer of household supplies will put out a half dozen or so different brands of detergents. Reduction of product variation exerts pressure to sell the standardized items. Stakes are high in such mass production industries. Because a strong demand reduces risks, marketing effectiveness is essential. Advertising therefore becomes, to borrow a phrase from John Kenneth Galbraith, a "technological imperative."[21]

Purchase Frequency

When items are bought infrequently, a large percentage of potential customers are out of the market at any given time. Conversely, products bought at relatively close intervals expand the size of the market in a particular period.

For example, sales of new cars average about 11.5 million units a year. This is equivalent to less than 15 percent of all U.S. households. Since buyers rarely purchase more than one car a year, any given period of time must have substantially less than 15 percent of the household population in the market. Prospective buyers for, say, a three-month period amount to only 3.5 percent of the household count, on the average. The opposite is true for high turnover items, since virtually their entire potential market is poised for action at any point in time. Cigarettes exemplify this proposition; smokers buy cigarettes almost every day of the year. Even bulk purchases, cartons, do not last very long.

A high purchase frequency stimulates advertising intensity in many ways. It affords marketers more opportunities to influence consumer choice. It makes advertising more productive, for it offers a larger percentage of active customers per dollar of advertising expenditure. Even when purchases are of a routine nature, advertising can be effective. It can act as a reminder by keeping the brand name before shoppers. As such, it can reinforce the patterns of loyal users.

Distribution

Both the nature of distribution and forms of retail selling are related to market size. Narrow markets, for example, make intensive, open distribution impractical. There is simply not enough sales volume to justify the same item being widely stocked by competitive retail outlets. In turn, the limited or exclusive distribution system enhances the marketing role of the retailer, as compared with that of the manufacturer.

On the other hand, a constant flow of would-be customers, such as in self-service retail outlets, permits manufacturers to pursue open and intensive distribution. In such stores there are no salespeople to push a particular brand. A preference must be created beforehand if buyers are to choose one brand over another. Advertising in this case must presell by building consumer preferences.

High advertising intensities are further nurtured because manufacturers have to act as channel captains. They must create their own customers. They can't expect help from retailers, who often compete with them through private labels. Brand name manufacturers in the packaged goods field regard retailers somewhat like common carriers. They carry goods for many firms. But unlike common carriers, the retail outlets practice discrimination. They make shelf space available only if the manufacturer can assure them an adequate revenue per linear foot. High turnover merchandise is avidly sought, and retailers are willing to stock such goods at low margins. Space is at a premium, for retailers are offered more items than they can carry. To induce retailers to provide adequate shelf facings, the manufacturer can only fall back on demand-generating promotion.

Sales volume under such conditions is more than a mark of success. The pressures of open distribution have transformed it into an absolute necessity for the right to compete. It is no accident or irrationality that firms often emphasize sales growth even at the expense of present earnings. Otherwise, their chances for profits are greatly diminished. Paradoxically, these modern, market-oriented firms admirably demonstrate Says Law, a concept long outmoded, which says that production creates its own demand.

COMPANY SPECIFIC FACTORS

The product-market characteristics dealt with in the previous section apply to all firms in an industry. However, individual companies have some latitude in their choice of characteristics. Given markets, they can alter their product offerings somewhat. Given products, they can vary the relevant marketing options. For example, Avon produces cosmetics which fall in the same product category as those of Revlon. But Avon's distribution system is substantially different, and its reliance upon advertising is minimal. But once corporate strategy sets certain product-market characteristics, it also determines, to a large extent, the relationship of advertising to the marketing mix.

Other influences on advertising intensity are company specific. The most important of these are a company's competitive position and the stage of a brand's life cycle. Both of these factors are not completely independent of each other. A brand life cycle must be distinguished from a product life cycle. The first refers to the life cycle of a specific company's product. The latter refers to the life cycle of the entire product category.

New products normally disclose high advertising-sales ratios. During the early stages of a brand's life cycle, sales are obviously low. Advertising, though, starts out at a relatively high level, particularly when it must carry the burden of creating new product awareness among prospective customers. Consequently, the advertising-sales ratio has larger values built into its numerator compared with those in its denominator.

New products can be either of the following:

1. They can represent something new to the market.
2. They can represent something new to the company, but not to the market.

In the first instance, the company's offering appears in the introductory stage of the product's life cycle. The brand may perform functions similar to those of older products, which implies interproduct competition. In the majority of cases, the new brand vies for the customers of older, established brands, but in another product category. And the type of advertising is often indistinguishable from any other kind. For instance, when digital watches first caught on in the early 1970s they stressed the same utilitarian themes as those of Timex's mechanical watches. They were durable, reliable, and moderately priced.

But a product new to the market may perform completely new functions or call for new usage patterns. The more an innovation departs from established patterns of behavior, the more effort is required to familiarize consumers with its key features or benefits. For example, some two years after a publicity-filled market rollout, the Magnavox advertising strategy still sought to educate people about its videodisc. "The awareness level for videodiscs," claimed a company spokesperson, "on a scale of 0 to 100, now has to be somewhere between 0 and 1."[22]

Products with new usage patterns may have an advertising intensity of similar magnitude to other new products, but the type of advertising required is different. The messages must stimulate primary demand to sell the particular brand. The first advertising for hand calculators had to explain how they worked and what they were capable of doing. The early advertisements for personal computers had a similar job—to familiarize consumers with the product's potential uses and benefits. The advertising for Electra's Freedom Phone cordless telephone aimed essentially at creating a primary demand, with an offer of gaining more product information by calling an 800 number. This advertisement, shown in Figure 2–2, received in excess of 22,000 consumer inquiries.

The vast majority of new offerings, however, are not new to the market. Primary advertising can serve little purpose, especially in mature markets. The new entry must embrace a selective advertising stance, emphasizing the particular brand, not the product category. Here, the only way to gain customers is to win them from competitors.

In fact, rivals are often brands of the same company. When General Foods launched Maxwell House freeze-dried coffee in 1981, it already had two other brands in the same field. Procter & Gamble in 1982 introduced a new version of Pampers despite the fact that its regular Pampers and Luvs had garnered a combined 70 percent share of the $1 billion-plus disposable diaper market.

Sometimes, primary and selective factors operate simultaneously. One such situation is when the market is experiencing growth. Wang, for example, expected the total market for microcomputers to expand when IBM in 1981 got into the business. Another situation is when a mature market has been underpromoted, and a new entrant with heavy promotional outlays can increase total industry sales.

But the more usual situation is for a new brand to encounter several large, well-entrenched brands dominating the market. This tendency towards concentration has been characterized as "the rule of three or four." A market seems to stabilize when it has about three significant competitors, with market shares distributed roughly in a 4:2:1 ratio.[23] Under such conditions, new entrants find it necessary to allocate higher promotional expenditures than those of the competitors in order to break established buying patterns.

In any event—in a new market or an old one, a product life cycle in the growth stage or in a mature one—as the brand gains sales, its advertising intensity decreases. This must be so or the business will fail. And if the brand should happen to carve out the lion's share of the market, it will probably enjoy a lower advertising-sales ratio than that of its smaller competitors. One possible explanation is that market leaders adopt maintenance strategies, translating their marketing success into strong cash flows. In such cases, relatively less advertising is essential to maintain high brand shares.[24]

Whether new products or old, advertising-sales ratios vary enormously by products, markets, and companies. Firms that operate in an advertising-conducive environment, implying high advertising intensity, subordinate marketing mix variables to promotion. Market-oriented activity rather than product development serves as the fulcrum for swings in consumer preferences. Convenience products especially, a mainstay of advertising, typifies this tendency. For one thing, they offer few alternatives at differentiation through technical design or physical features. Product

THIS DEVICE MAKES
ORDINARY TELEPHONES OBSOLETE.

Actual size.
(1" x 5⅛" x 2¾")

The Freedom Phone® Cordless Telephone Model FF-3500 has more features than any ordinary telephone. But one ordinary feature is missing.

There's no cord to tie you down. The compact handset measures 1" x 5⅛" x 2¾" and weighs just 7 ounces. So it's really easy to take or make calls anywhere within its operational range. That's upstairs, downstairs, in the front yard, backyard, at the neighbors, up the street, or down the block.

Instead of going to the phone to talk, you take the phone with you.

Buying a Freedom Phone Cordless Telephone is an intelligent move if you prefer the convenient over the conventional. But there's more to it than meets the eye or ear.

Designed and built exclusively for the Electra Company, makers of Bearcat® Scanners, the Freedom Phone 3500 provides crisp and clear cordless calls. An audible tone and pulsing light confirm dialing. The touch of a button automatically redials the last number entered.

The Freedom Phone Cordless Telephone is as easy to install as it is to use. Its attractive and compact base station plugs into your existing phone line and electrical outlet.

If the idea of using a Freedom Phone Cordless Telephone has a nice ring to it, get up, walk to your obsolete telephone, and call 800-428-4315 (800-382-1076 in Indiana). You'll learn more about the Model FF-3500 and get the name of the nearest Freedom Phone Dealer.

THE FREEDOM PHONE® CORDLESS TELEPHONE.

Electra Electra Company
Division of Masco Corp. of Indiana • 300 East County Line Road • Cumberland, Indiana 46229 • International Business Office • Suite 102, 1828 Swift • North Kansas City, Missouri 64116
© 1981 Masco Corp. of Indiana

Fig. 2—2 *Electra Telephone. Sample Advertisement of a New Product—The Cordless Telephone.* Courtesy Electra Company.

innovations are easily imitated. How different can one brand of toilet paper be from another? Or one aspirin tablet from the next? Blind tests have consistently shown that consumers cannot tell which brand is which by sampling them. Yet they emphatically claim to drink Brand X because they like its taste, to smoke Brand Y cigarette because they enjoy its flavor, to use Brand Z toothpaste because they obtain whiter teeth. For brands with small, imperceptible physical differences from those of competitive items, advertising emerges as the dominant form of product differentiation, and as the main thrust for achieving a competitive advantage.[25] The same principle holds for products where their attributes are not readily apparent. It is not the item, but the perception of the item, which assumes market importance. The competitive struggle in the marketplace or at the retail level is then joined with that for a share of the consumer mind.

SUMMARY

Because of large variations in marketing inputs even within the same industries, the marketing mix has been a subject of intensive investigation. The exploration as to when advertising intensity is justifiable, and at what level, has proceeded both theoretically and empirically. The theoretical route has followed marginal concepts of economics. The empirical approach has studied advertising-sales ratios.

Marginal theories, which aim at finding an optimal combination of marketing inputs, have been incorporated into computer models. Unfortunately, the information needed is not complete, especially that information which relates to sales response functions. Managers are often asked to arrive at values based on their best judgment. Although these opinions often represent hard experience, the effectiveness of these decisions have been widely questioned.

A major body of empirical knowledge has been built up by PIMS. A study using the PIMS data base has yielded valuable inferences about relationships among advertising, pricing, and product quality.

The study of advertising-sales ratios has also revealed important insights into marketing mix relationships. Factors associated with advertising intensities, high and low, are product-market characteristics and company-specific variables. Prominent among the former are product type, price, purchase frequency, and nature of distribution. Outstanding among the latter is the product life cycle.

Although advertising is a means, this chapter has explored factors associated with economic ends. It now remains to focus on the other part of the means-end chain—communication.

Questions for Chapter 2

1. Why do companies fail to use media mix maximization models, despite increased computer usage and greater detail of reporting?

2. Does advertising raise prices of consumer products?

3. Would a firm benefit by lowering product quality and increasing its advertising budget?

4. Why do you think that many studies have found an association, though a weak one, between advertising intensity and profits?

5. In your opinion, what are the main reasons why consumer durable goods have generally lower advertising-to-sales ratios than nondurables?

6. What are some of the problems in analyses of advertising-sales ratios?

7. In what ways is advertising related to distribution?

8. How would advertising for a product new to the market differ from one new to the company but not to the market?

Footnotes for Chapter 2

[1] Philip Kotler, *Marketing Management*, 4th ed. (Englewood Cliffs, N.J.: Prentice-Hall, 1980), pp. 264–265.

[2] Robert Dorfman and Peter O. Steiner, "Optimal Advertising and Optimal Quality," *American Economic Review* (December 1954), pp. 826–836.

[3] See Julian L. Simon, *Issues in Economics of Advertising* (Urbana, Ill.: University of Illinois Press, 1970), p. 25.

[4] Paul W. Farris and Mark S. Albion, *Determinants of Variations in the Advertising-to-Sales Ratio: A Comparison of Industry and Firm Studies* (Cambridge, Mass.: Marketing Science Institute, 1980), pp. 1–2. For an application of the Dorfman-Steiner thesis, see Lester G. Telser, "How Much Does It Pay to Advertise?" *American Economic Review* (May 1961), pp. 194–205.

[5] Kotler, *Marketing Management*, p. 261.

[6] Dipankar Chakravarti et. al., "Judgment Based Marketing Decision Models: Problems and Possible Solutions," *Journal of Marketing* (Fall 1981), pp. 13–23. For a rejoinder, see John D. C. Little and Leonard M. Lodish, "Commentary on 'Judgment Based Marketing Decision Models,'" *Journal of Marketing* (Fall 1981), pp. 24–29.

[7] See Oliver E. Williamson, *The Economics of Discretionary Behavior: Managerial Objectives in a Theory of the Firm* (Englewood Cliffs, N.J.: Prentice-Hall, 1964), pp. 34–60; R. Marris and D. C. Mueller, "The Corporation, Competition and the Invisible Hand," *Journal of Economic Literature* (March 1980), pp. 33, 38–40.

[8] Richard Schmalensee, *The Economics of Advertising* (Amsterdam: North-Holland, 1972), pp. 9–12, 36, 107–124, 242–243.

[9] Schmalensee, *The Economics of Advertising*, pp. 125–215.

[10]P. W. Farris and D. J. Reibstein, "How Prices, Ad Expenditures, and Profits are Linked," *Harvard Business Review* (November/December 1979), pp. 173–184.

[11]For the argument that this leads to generally lower prices, see Phillip Nelson, "Advertising as Information," *Journal of Political Economy* (July/August 1974), pp. 729–754.

[12]See Robert L. Steiner, "A Dual Stage Approach to the Effects of Brand Advertising on Competition and Price," Marketing Science Institute, *Report No. 78-105* (July 1978), pp. 127–150.

[13]See William S. Comanor and Thomas A. Wilson, "The Effect of Advertising on Competition: A Survey," *Journal of Economic Literature* (June 1979), pp. 454–458.

[14]This runs counter to the assumption of the PIMS study, which postulates relative uniformity in the degree of exaggeration. Farris and Reibstein, "How Prices, Ad Expenditures, and Profits are Linked," pp. 177–178.

[15]Lawrence Abbott, *Quality and Competition* (Westport, Conn.: Greenwood Press, 1973), pp. 125–130.

[16]See William S. Comanor and Thomas A. Wilson, "Advertising, Market Structure and Performance," *Review of Economic Statistics* (November 1967), pp. 423–440; Richard A. Miller, "Market Structure and Industrial Performance: Relation of Profit Rate to Concentration, Advertising Intensity, and Diversity," *Journal of Industrial Economics* (April 1969), pp. 104–118; Federal Trade Commission, *Economic Report on the Influence . . . of Food Manufacturing Companies* (Washington, D.C., 1969).

[17]Miller, "Market Structure and Industrial Performance," pp. 112–113.

[18]See Robert Buzzell and Paul W. Farris, "Marketing Costs in Consumer Goods Industries," Marketing Science Institute, Working Paper, Report No. 76-111, p. 10.

[19]Jennifer Alter, "P&G, K-C Going Direct," *Advertising Age* (November 30, 1981), pp. 1, 79.

[20]Buzzell and Farris, "Marketing Costs," p. 9.

[21]See John K. Galbraith, *The Industrial State* (Boston: Houghton Mifflin Company, 1967), pp. 11–21; Joan Woodward, *Industrial Organization: Theory and Practice* (London: Oxford University Press, 1965).

[22]Jacques Neher, "Disc Shootout," *Advertising Age* (December 22, 1980), p. 1.

[23]Robert D. Buzzell, "Are There 'Natural' Market Structures," *Journal of Marketing* (Winter 1981), pp. 42–51; R. D. Nelson and S. G. Winter, "The Schumpeterian Tradeoff Revisited," *American Economic Review* (March 1982), pp. 124–129.

[24]Buzzell and Farris, "Marketing Costs," pp. 19–20.

[25]See Michael E. Porter, *Interbrand Choice, Strategy, and Bilateral Market Power* (Cambridge, Mass.: Harvard University Press, 1976), pp. 20–27.

3 Advertising as Communication

Regardless of objectives, advertising is a form of social intercourse. The act of doing is the art of communicating. It is thus understandable that advertisers should exhibit a keen interest in communication theories. Understanding is the conduit to improvement and performance excellence.

Yet the intellectual abstractions—most of them nurtured by social psychology—do not form a coherent, consistent body of knowledge which is universally accepted. The main concepts applied to advertising may reflect diverse academic traditions, uphold conflicting views, and when blended with advertising practices, support differing philosophies of communicating with media audiences.

The aim of this chapter is as follows:

- **To evaluate various theories which underlie advertising communication**
- **To evaluate their applicability to solving advertising problems**

THE ACT OF COMMUNICATION

Although the results of advertising are largely economic, they are accomplished basically by communication. Communication is implied in the very definition of advertising—paid for messages in mass media. As such, the advertising process can be viewed as an act of communication.

In order for communication to take place, regardless of content, at least three structural forms must exist: a sender, a medium, and a destination. Two processes link these structures: transmission and reception.[1]

Five elements, three structural and two procedural, make up the generalized communication model shown in Figure 3–1. The diagram represents a simplified abstraction of a model proposed by Claude E. Shannon more than thirty years ago, and which has since become the cornerstone of communication theory.[2]

The main components of this system can be described as follows:

1. *Source*—that which produces the message. Sources are usually

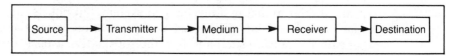

Fig. 3–1 *Generalized Communication Model.*

human beings, though they can also be machines. Sources in advertising are most often organizations, or combinations of organizations, such as companies and their advertising agencies.

2. Transmitter—that which encodes the message by converting it into a signal. The classical model regards the encoder as the first terminal receiving the message from the source and tailoring it to fit the channel that will carry it.[3] Since advertising uses various channels, it employs different transmitters.

3. Medium—the carrying device for relaying the signal from transmitter to receiver. Magazines, newspapers, radio and televison are the major carriers of advertising messages.

4. Receiver—that which reconstructs or decodes the message from the signal. Technically, it is a terminal at the receiving end of the channel.

5. Destination—the person or thing that is designated as the final recipient of the message.

The Shannon model proved extremely valuable to the communications engineer. It was applied to mechanical systems, and concerned itself primarily with the faithful transmission of messages in transit. To what extent does a picture transported by electrical current maintain its original clarity? A voice its tone and distinction? Engineering measurements are thus preoccupied with fidelity or rather the loss of information in the transmission process.

Does this mechanical model, however, apply to human communication, of which advertising is a part? To a certain degree, parallels exist. From an engineering standpoint, the purpose of a sender is to have a message accurately decoded by a receiver and forwarded intact to a destination. So it is with advertising. The firms which pay for sending out commercial messages want them seen or heard by media audiences (destinations) as they are initially transmitted. As in mechanical systems, advertising messages may encounter interference or "noise" that would destroy or warp the information transmitted. Like their engineering counterparts, advertisers regard feedback as necessary to well-run operations. The responsibility for measurements fall to their marketing research departments. And like engineers, advertisers believe that if communication can be measured—although the measurements differ from those of engineering—it should be possible to pinpoint and correct trouble spots.

But here the parallel ends. If the analogy is stretched too far, it becomes pseudo-science. Only the framework of advertising communication appears similar to that of a mechanical system, but not its inner workings. The analysis of advertising as communication must therefore probe beneath the outside shell and into the substantive aspects of the process itself.

ADVERTISING AS MASS COMMUNICATION

Although advertising information flows through channels linked by transmitting and receiving mechanisms, its communication is a more complicated process. In fact, the focus is not the purely technical aspects. For example, a television commercial is conveyed by an electric signal which is decoded by a television receiver and picture tube. But communicators of advertising messages see decoding as extending beyond the mere reception of electronic impulses by a television set.

Advertising involves human communication. Individuals make up the audiences of mass media. They must perceive and understand the words and images coming over the airwaves into their living rooms, and unless they decode a message properly, communication does not take place. From this point of view, a secondary and more important set of decoding facilities comes into play—that of human beings. The electronic communication system thus serves as an intermediary, a linkage, between organizational sources and the eyes, ears and brains of human receptors, which can no longer be disassociated from destinations. Indeed, a receiver and a destination is the same thing. Commercial messages in a human communication context are essentially stimuli to sensory organs, primarily those of sight and sound. Advertisers employ the skills of the journalist, of the graphic artist, of the audio-visual producer, in order to appeal to these human senses.

But human decoders do more than just mirror the sounds and images which are transmitted to them. They do not reproduce messages word for word; they attach meanings or no meaning to the communication. Messages can indeed be translated into action, but most frequently there is no action.

Though advertisers and their agencies spend millions of dollars on research, measurement of the information flow lacks the fine details available to the communications engineer. There is no way of getting into people's minds and observing with methodical accuracy which messages reach the brain, how they are decoded, and where the information is stored. Feedback is indirect, inferential, and of low quality. Firms often assess their communication efforts by ill-defined, error-prone surveys, which ask people about their exposure to various media and about advertisements they recognize and remember. Companies also may use sales-related statistics as proxies for communication results. However, advertising is not a science. Also, it cannot be assumed that what is valid for the physical universe applies to human relationships.

The most outstanding feature of advertising, when viewed as communication, is its use of mass media. By providing the context for commercial messages, the format in which they make their appearance, media exerts a pervasive influence over advertising operations.

For one thing, mass media lend themselves to the production of large quantities of identical messages which can be transmitted simultaneously. A commercial or a printed advertisement goes into millions of homes in exactly or almost exactly the same form, and with the same content. Because message output is high relative to advertising input, communicators derive certain efficiencies from mass media.

The same media also thrust advertising into a one-way communication mold. Commercial messages move in one direction, from organizations to a dispersed and often diverse public. There is no back flow. Audiences do not talk back to commercials; they don't ask questions, dispute claims, or relate problems they may have had with their products. Because feedback is limited or delayed, senders seldom know how much contact, if any, their messages made with their intended destinations.

Critics of advertising have denounced this one-way information flow as evidence of socially-unacceptable behavior. Marketing, the argument goes, should enable consumers to influence the decisions of producers in accordance with the ideals of the marketing concept. Marketing should permit a dialogue between participants in transactions, between creators and users of want-satisfying products. Instead, advertising stands as a monologue, forbidding any meaningful exchange of information between buyer and seller. Advertising itself is perverted from a true communication course into a control system, the purpose of which is to manage human behavior and to compel it along predetermined lines.[4] And marketing research, though frail and limping, is enlisted to supply producers, never consumers, with an assessment of costs and benefits.[5]

Two-way communication is referred to as interactive. Here the role of sender and receiver is reversible. A prerequisite for a user-producer dialogue, however, is the ready availability of suitable media. As of now, only personal selling, done face-to-face, offers marketing a reciprocal communication system. But for many products, especially those which rely on advertising, personal selling is highly inefficient. Some vendors of home computers have drawn scenarios of interactive marketing in their promotional literature: consumers tapping large data banks; querying their machines and inputting information directly, such as opinions, suggestions, orders for goods and services, and instructions to banks for deposits and payments. Perhaps the society of some hypothetical tomorrow will unravel the secrets of fulfilling routine needs and wants and desires by a beneficent technology. But mankind has not yet reached the threshold of this brave new world.

Another effect of mass media is that they dilute the control the advertiser seeks to establish. Control implies a power of regulating or dominating specific actions, and it is evidenced by a correspondence between desired results and actual outcomes. To achieve particular effects through advertising, communicators transmit persuasive messages. These are distinguished from other types of communication by the intent of the source and the explicit objective of the message itself.[6] Recipients of such messages are asked to do something, either to act or to think in a certain way. But mass media are indiscriminant as to the information they carry or the advertising clients they strive to accommodate. Each medium accepts competing advertisements. The claims of one is thus offset by the counterclaims of another, but with no parity among the contestants for consumer patronage. As each advertisement shouts the virtues of its own offering, a great deal of the shouting gets drowned out in the collective roar.

Even more important, the media context is somewhat incompatible with the persuasive messages emitted by advertisers. The editorial content of mass media remains heavily weighted with entertainment or information, though it is difficult to draw a hard and fast line between the two. Both news and entertainment do not overtly tell their audiences how to use whatever data is conveyed. These media messages do have various effects, but not necessarily on economic behavior. It can be said with certainty that most people watch television, listen to radio, read magazines or newspapers to relax, to be entertained, or to obtain knowledge, but not to evaluate articles of commerce. Many people no doubt do notice, and even absorb, the content of an advertisement which they happen to come across. But it is uncertain that a majority of an audience will do so, much less give credence to a persuasive message that is out of character with the editorial format of a medium. Advertising people themselves often refer to television and magazines as "involuntary" media, ostensibly because they are voluntarily chosen by the public not for the commercial messages they carry, but for entertainment or informational reasons. As noted by Dick Wasserman, creative director of Foote, Cone & Belding, "most customers have to be charmed or 'seduced' into listening to a commercial."[7]

Unlike the receivers in mechanical systems, those of mass media are largely independent of transmitters. The amount of advertising messages picked up by human receivers are distressingly small compared with the number sent out. A typical adult is said to be subjected to hundreds of commercial messages each day. Yet how many are attended to or register in the mind? How many are retained for any length of time? Relatively few.

Lastly, the world of mass media can be described as an "open system." Its communications are not directed with exacting precision to specific destinations, as by a phone call, a letter, or a personal contact. Americans spend more of their leisure time watching television than doing anything else. Yet audiences are highly fragmented, and broadcasters cannot determine who will see a program and who will not. Print circulation may initially go out to specific destinations. But subscribers may not read the issue, and many magazines find the major part of their readers made up of nonsubscribers.

In this respect, advertisements take on the characteristics of their carriers. They are generalized messages, addressed "to whom it may concern." They reach out, as it were, in unrestricted fashion to find receivers. Yet the coupling is a chance encounter. Media behavior patterns are irregular, and exposure to advertising is more so. Consequently, only a probability attaches to any person of being exposed to an advertising message. All messages do not have an equal chance of being seen or retained in the mind, and for advertising as a whole, this probability is exceedingly low.

SELECTIVE MESSAGE RECEPTION

The generalized, open nature of mass media, and the dependent advertising, ultimately lead to a communication system separated into two interrelated parts. That at the front end of the communication chain is highly organized. Activities are conducted by professional communicators, who create and transmit advertising messages. At the other end are groups who make up the destinations, the target markets of the advertisers. These recipients are individuals whose actions are somewhat disorganized, haphazard and autonomous.

Senders of advertising messages can only influence, not control, the end part of the communication process. They are able to do so in two ways, by message encoding and by media selection. The more appealing the advertisement, the greater its probability of being "received." The better media selection can be matched with marketing targets, the larger the number of potential receivers becomes, all other things being equal.

The characteristic which dominates the reception of mass-produced messages, however, is selective behavior. In ways not completely understood, the human brain selectively chooses particular stimuli from a countless number. It labels this stimuli, stores the abstractions, and makes use of some in future behavior and in building new experiences.

Audience statistics, running into millions of viewers and readers, reflect large numbers of individual decisions. People choose the media they wish to see and hear, sometimes unconsciously and without deliberation. In a similar vein, they select the advertisements they will absorb. The process doesn't end with consciously-directed exposure to a commercial message. Humans perceive selectively, and can easily twist the intended meaning of a message to conform to their inherent biases and predispositions. Retention of information, too, is selective. People store in their memories the important and the relevant, and disregard or forget the inconsequential and the trivial. But what might be seen as trifling by one individual or group may be considered as significant by another person or group of prospective customers.

The selective reception of an advertising message makes for a progressive deterioration of communication effectiveness. This process can be likened to a giant funnel that tapers to ever narrower dimensions as it goes from one end to the other. The broadest part can be likened to a medium's audience, which represents the number of potential advertising message recipients. This figure sets the upper limit of advertising communication. Any particular advertisement cannot have an audience that is larger than that of the medium in which it is placed.

Out of this total media audience, only some fraction will register a memory trace or a mental impression of the commercial message. The mental images formed may be at either the cognitive or affective levels. The first refers to a phase of knowledge or comprehension which takes place. The second involves a change of attitude towards the product or idea advertised. The desired end result of advertising is usually some form of action which the message seeks to bring about. At this behavioral level an even smaller proportion of the audience will respond.

From the perspective of the advertiser, communication can be thought of as a series of probabilities beginning with media audience and ending with response evidenced by behavior. Between this initial phase and the concluding phase are mental impressions of various types and intensities, created from a person's contact with the advertising. The communication of an advertising message might then be expressed as

$$Ca = [P]M \times [P]I \times [P]R$$

where

Ca = communication effect of an advertising message

$[P]M$ = probability of a person in the target market being exposed to a media vehicle

$[P]I$ = probability of a mental impression occurring from exposure to an advertisement

$[P]R$ = probability of behavioral response caused by the advertising impression

Advertising research expends most of its efforts on the first two terms of the foregoing equation. Deriving probabilities for media exposure boils down to audience measurements and analyses. Investigations of mental impressions left by particular advertisements go under the description of copy research. But attempts to link impressions (I) with either media audience (M) or behavior (R) have encountered formidable problems.

The communication equation implies that behavior resulting from an advertising message is arrived at through a given sequence. However, there is no agreement about the kind of impressions that makes audiences act upon advertising propositions. This subject has been the object of endless debate among the research fraternity, and a consensus seems as far away as ever.

It might be held that I is not needed at all if R is the ultimate goal of the message. For example, a sales objective would call for R being defined as so many units or dollars of sales. The size of media audiences (M) is mainly a function of advertising expenditures, assuming media is bought efficiently. If a relationship can be established between M and R, then the spending level—which is controlled by the advertiser—becomes the determinant of sales. Buying so much audience will also buy so much sales. Every budget level will have a definite audience configuration and its own predictable response. The communication formula is thus simplified to

$$Ca = [P]\ M \times [P]\ R$$

with the latter term being in effect a function of M. This, advocates of direct measurements of response argue, is really all that is necessary for effective operations.

The conventional wisdom within the advertising industry, however, has never accepted this judgment. Detractors call it the "black box" approach. It records the inputs and outputs of a system, but provides no explanation of why things happen. It surrenders no inferences about causal factors. The absence of such "intervening variables," it is felt, offers little hope of improving communication efforts.

Besides, attempts at measuring effects beyond purely communicative ones have up to now been barren of practical results. Endeavors to relate sales to either M or I have proved elusive. In most instances, sales response cannot be traced directly to particular messages in specific media. Some forms of behavior can, such as making inquiries, participating in contests, visiting showrooms, taking advantage of premium offers. But these actions, by and large, are not those elicited by general advertising.

On the other hand, researchers' preoccupations with I have resulted in many inferences. But without firmly-established relationships between I and R, theory has remained in the realm of speculation.

ADVERTISING COMMUNICATION: MASS OR MINIM?

The fact that reception of commercial messages is selective alters to some extent the concept of advertising as mass communication. It remains mass communication in the sense that it uses media with wide circulations. It stays mass in the sense that it transmits messages to large population segments, often heterogeneous and far-reaching. But selectivity invites modifications to creep into the mass concept.

This postulate can be illustrated by observing industry convention, which subscribes to the idea of using M and I as measures of communication effectiveness. According to this view, there are three prime elements: target markets, audiences, and impressions. If it is assumed that

$$Ca = [P]\ M \times [P]\ I$$

educated guesses can be made by following the logic of this equation.

To begin with, suppose a company designated adult males as its relevant market. To reach this group, the firm runs advertising on network television, during prime time, when viewing is at its height. This schedule is the most expensive, but will ostensibly yield maximum audiences. Yet an average telecast during the fall season, according to industry sources, reaches about 11 percent of all men in the United States.[8] The probability of an individual in the marketing target being exposed to a media vehicle used by the company is thus .11. This seemingly low percentage still amounts to more than eight million males.

The next step is to estimate how many of this 11 percent acquire some meaningful impression from the commercial. These estimates vary depending upon the research method used to measure impressions. They can be defined in several ways: awareness, brand recognition, and message recall after a period of time. The most popular technique is the day-after recall; a commercial is run one day and people are interviewed on the next day. They are given a brand-product cue, and asked what they remember about the commercial on the program they supposedly watched. The resulting recall figure—if they play back anything at all that was in that commercial they are credited with a recall—represents a cognitive measure. On this basis, some 20 percent of a show's male audience will remember some element of the typical commercial. Consequently, the probability of a single message leaving a memory trace of a one day duration on the target group comes to .02 (.11 × .20 = .02).

Yet this paltry 2 percent figure may be overly optimistic. Relatively few products would define all adult males as logical prospects. Even if this were so, the entire potential would not be in the market at all times. Such frequently purchased products as beer would perhaps count 30 percent of the men as being prospective customers at any given time. Under such conditions, our hypothetical commercial would still make an impression on two percent of prospects, but that target group would comprise only six-tenths of one percent of males aged 18 years or older (.02 × .30 = .006). Products bought less frequently, such as automobiles, appliances, or airline travel, must contend with much smaller cognitive effects, in relation to the American population.

If cognitive effects of an advertising message are of such low proportions, behavioral response must be smaller yet. The calculations are admittedly rough. But any upward adjustment for error would not alter the conclusions significantly. Then how accurate are the portrayals of mass communicators as giants who bestride modern society like a colossus? They well may be, but not for wares hawked over the airwaves or print media.

There are many actions which indicate response to the appearance of an advertisement—mail orders, telephone calls, and store visits are examples. These situations have piled evidence upon evidence to support the proposition of low response levels emanating from individual messages. Orders received through the mail, expressed as a fraction of a medium's audience, normally amount to well below one percent. Large metropolitan dailies claim millions of readers. Yet many retailers would be satisfied if their ads were to pull only several hundred customers into their stores. Indeed, retail ads seem to score their greatest success in prompting store traffic among those who are already on the verge of buying.[9] A special, a new line of merchandise, a holiday sale, seems to trigger action which was previously intended but not made definite as to a particular time and place.

Response to general advertising messages cannot be as easily assessed as results to ads which solicit immediate and direct action. But there is no reason to assume that what cannot be measured does not exist. Nor can general advertising be assumed to work differently. Its "soft," nonprice, indirect approach may produce an even weaker response than the hard-hitting direct mail and retail ads.

Instead of mass communication, the advertising process might be better described as mass transmission. Messages are transmitted *en masse*. But reception may be another matter. The effects may be minim, not mass, depending upon market definitions and response measurements.

This reality is roundly acknowledged by the advertising industry, at least implicitly. It has also led to three fundamental principles for the conduct of general advertising: the theory of a threshold, the idea of a campaign, and the concept of joint effects.

Theory of a Threshold

The communication effect of a single message, as previously demonstrated, has about the same impact as that of a stone tossed into an ocean. The object is immediately swallowed up by the sea and the irrepressible waves roll on as before. Even several advertisements may do little. Therefore, it is necessary to establish some minimum message transmission.

Advocates of the so-called threshold theory maintain that an advertising rate which falls below the minim produces imperceptible results and is hardly worth the effort. The exact bottom point, however, has seldom been specified. The outspoken David Ogilvy, head of a prominent Madison Avenue agency, was one of the few advertising executives to publicly volunteer an opinion on the subject. Ogilvy stated in 1963 that unless a budget amounted to at least $2 million, continuous, national advertising should be foregone.[10] This figure like any other, is admittedly conjectural. It represents an intuitive judgment, but by a man with an intimate knowledge of the advertising business. If that estimate were taken as a benchmark and adjusted for inflation, the absolute minimum number of messages in today's economy would require an expenditure of better than $6 million.

The Campaign Idea

Since isolated, *ad hoc* messages are seen as ineffectual, they are usually combined so that a greater effect might be obtained. The overall effect of retail advertising essentially involves the same thing—the aggregation of outcomes brought about by individual message units. Each advertisement brings back modest returns, but when added together can grow into imposing sums. The campaign idea suggests that general advertising works in similar fashion, though the results of individual messages cannot be scrutinized as carefully as in the retail trades.

A campaign calls for single messages to be strung together in some coherent manner—spaced at definite intervals and interconnected by a common theme or repeated a certain number of times. The combination of messages into a pattern forms the core of planning the advertising campaign.

The logic of the advertising campaign rests upon the twin postulates of accumulation and repetition. Because one commercial message leaves its impression on a small proportion of a market, subsequent transmissions will encounter new prospects who had previously been unfamiliar with the information being disseminated. Consequently, repetition of the same message accumulates impressions among the target market. At the same time, previous impressions are reinforced. One commercial impression is thought to be too weak to accomplish a communication task meaningfully.[11]

Theory of Joint Effects

No matter how far above the minimum expenditure level, campaigns used exclusively are not considered capable of continually gaining sales. Even the most avid believer in the power of advertising cannot deny the necessity of other marketing inputs, such as product quality, price, availability, and service. Procter and Gamble, the largest national advertiser, has always insisted on the primacy of product quality. This merely echoes a common-sense view that promotion pays when there is something worthwhile to promote. In short, messages in mass media are most effective when working in unison with other elements of the marketing mix.

But the marketing mix differs considerably from company to company, even for those producing similar products. These differences induce substantial variations in how messages are put together in a campaign. What is an optimal number of messages for one company may not be for another. Thus, there is no best way of planning a campaign, and trial and error continues to play a major role.

MESSAGE TRANSMISSION

When a firm advertises, it transmits a commercial message in mass media. It usually researches its markets in advance, analyzes available media, but supervises only the encoding process. The other parts of the communication system, encompassing media and reception functions, are outside the domain of management. The advertiser might just as well regard them as something given, for they comprise its environment.

A company may influence certain aspects of a particular media, such as business policies, but it cannot affect its basic nature of communication. To use a medium effectively, the advertiser must accommodate itself to the medium's relevant characteristics.[12] Likewise, a marketer cannot force consumers to pay attention to advertising messages. The firm can only create messages to which consumers will want to pay attention.

If information is not getting through, or if results seem disappointing, the advertiser can only change its *modus operandi*. The firm may switch media vehicles, create a new pool of advertisements, or reposition its brand. It may also change its marketing mix, such as modifying its product, altering its prices, or starting a series of new promotions. But unlike the communication engineer, it cannot adjust the basic functions of media and receptors. It cannot alter the way in which the human mind works. The only avenue open for more effective advertising is through improved message transmission.

The word communication derives from the Latin *communis*, meaning common. To communicate with someone is to form a "commoness," a bond of shared experience with respect to a message. If one person speaks in Chinese but the other understands only Russian, there can be no verbal communication between the two. The words of the speaker would be taken as gibberish by the listener. In contrast, the greater the degree of commoness, the higher the probability of communication taking place.

Advertising communicates through signs or symbols, the most important of which is language. But advertisements are also made up of nonverbal codes to support the oral or written message. The nonverbal alternatives are limited by the type of media selected to convey the message. For example, a televison commercial might employ background music, sound effects, gestures, or illustrative material to heighten its effect. Copy tests have consistently shown that audiences recall more nonverbal than verbal elements of advertisements in both television and print media. This realization may have come about partly due to the nature of research methods. People may find it easier when being surveyed to describe nonverbal symbols than to articulate verbal codes. Partly, the high nonverbal feedback is occasioned by the coding itself. Commercials usually contain a paucity of information expressed by words.[13] Similarly, printed ads in consumer magazines devote more space to illustrative material than to textual. Consequently, there are relatively few verbal symbols that can be recalled. Nevertheless, nonverbal elements form a significant part of the typical advertising message.

Psychologists describe an idea conveyed by signs or symbols as "signified," and the thing to which it refers as a "signifier." In these terms, advertisers use signifieds to evoke sets of images, attitudes, and feelings about signifiers, which are usually products. But for the message to have its intended effect, or communicate its intended meaning, the audience must perceive the signs in a particular way. Response depends not solely upon the actions of those transmitting messages, but upon the behavior of those receiving information. It is they who translate them faithfully or misinterpret them, convert them into something of meaning, or disregard them as something of inconsequence. People who receive messages are the real creators of meaning.[14]

It is precisely because meaning arises from an individual that communication through mass media poses questions which seem to have no answers. Advertisers are virtually unanimous in the opinion that public announcements should be in a easily understood language. All advertising texts suggest the use of signs that are familiar, so that they can be related to experiences of the audience. Since mass media appeals to a varied audience, the question arises as to what experiences are relevant.

Human experience is both homologous and singular. Members of the same culture have many experiences in common, and so attach the same meaning to certain symbols. All Americans know a red traffic light means stop. Meaning assigned to symbols by virtue of cultural affinity is referred to as denotive. But our society also contains many groups whose experience differs from each other. A "bagel" is something known to Americans in larger metropolitan areas, but residents in North Dakota may have trouble with the word. Other symbols have meanings that vary from person to person. The word "abortion" denotes the expulsion of a fetus before it is viable. But for those with deep religious convictions, the word may mean something more. "Pro Life" supporters go so far as to call it murder. Others see abortion as a liberating instrument, freeing a woman from the unhappy consequences of an unwanted pregnancy. When symbols bear meanings that are attitudinal, emotional, or personal, they are said to be connotative. Mass communication would suggest the use of symbols with denotive meanings. But as mass media do not necessarily offer audiences that see symbols alike, a portion of the advertising content is distorted, misconstrued, wasted.

Advertising has an enormous interest in symbols because message transmission is its business. Which symbols are the most potent? And in what circumstances?

Human message reception draws nourishment from at least two sources. The first affects the senses, and is physical in nature. The sense organs, absorbing light and sound waves, transmit neural impulses to the brain. There, the sensations are converted to perceptions of sight and hearing. The second source is cognitive, and relates to such factors as beliefs, attitudes, and habits. In order to communicate meaning with some degree of cogency, an advertisement must satisfy both sensory and cognitive faculties.

SENSORY FACTORS

Sensory factors deal with relationships between physical stimuli and human sensation. The pioneering studies were done in Germany by E.H. Weber in the nineteenth century, and the basic generalization still bears his name. Weber postulated that attention depends not only upon the stimulus, but upon the context in which it is perceived. For example, a drip from a faucet, lost in the noises all about the house in daytime, can become a sharp irritating sound in the dead of night that interferes with sleep. The headbeam of an automobile has little effect in twilight, but can be blinding on a dark road.

According to Weber's law, any noticeable change in the intensity of a stimulus is proportional to the existing intensity level. This principle can be expressed mathematically as

$$K = \frac{\Delta I}{I}$$

where

K = constant value
ΔI = minimum change in intensity that would be noticed
I = existing level of intensity

Weber's formulation is represented graphically in Figure 3–2.

In Weber's equation, the term K is a ratio which yields a value that is constant over a certain portion of the range. Any value of ΔI on the line of average relationship will be constant when expressed as a proportion of I. This generalization holds near and about the midpoint of the range, but breaks down at the extremes. For example, if I in the above diagram was

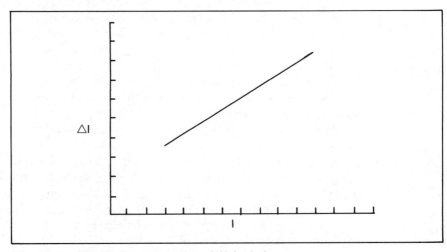

Fig. 3–2 Graphic Representation of Weber's Law.

the noise level, it is conceivable that at the extremes the ratio of change needed to obtain a perceivable difference would be vastly altered from the ratio needed at lower noise levels. In effect, ΔI is the variable that is manipulated to obtain the desired result—the perception of a difference. Once K is determined, then ΔI is expressed as a percentage of I, which actually is a rearrangement of terms to $\Delta I = KI$.

Psychologists have found many applications of Weber's law to advertising.[15] For example, how large must an illustration be for a consumer to perceive some product feature as being unique or different? How colorful must an ad be so that it stands out from other ads or pictures in a magazine? Sometimes, advertisers try to create advertisements that resemble the editorial features of magazines in order to get better readership. In these instances, the question of ΔI might be reversed. How much change in format can be made before readers immediately notice the difference between advertising and editorial?

The same principle is implicit in media as well as copy decisions. Advertisers have long held a preference for having printed advertisements interspersed with editorial matter, and most publishers have willingly complied. Advertisers also object to television commercials being bunched together, and disparagingly call this practice "clutter." But with stations' available advertising time limited, broadcasters have resisted demands to lower the number of commercials run back-to-back.

Somewhat related to Weber's law, but more in line with the later Gestalt theories, is the concept of "perceptual isolation."[16] Here, there is no attempt to alter relative intensity. Rather, attention is directed to something by differentiating it from its surrounding field. This is done by presenting the object so that it differs from the context in which it is contained. The upside-down Crown Royal ad in Figure 3–3 is so unexpected that it looks as though there was an error in printing. How many readers, whose curiosity is piqued, would actually turn the page around to see what it says?

Perceptual isolation achieved through more complicated forms is sometimes referred to as "psychical distance." The complexity or consistency of the advertisement undergoes change, either in total or in part. For example, an animated commercial may be a pleasant change of pace, and easier to notice, in a setting of messages which feature real people and things. Other applications in the same vein include unique verbal or text elements, out of the ordinary visual perspectives, different forms of words or images.

Illustrative of perceptual isolation are the advertisements in Figures 3–4 and 3–5. The Tree Top apple juice advertisement shown in Figure 3–4 accomplishes psychical distance by juxtaposing discordant elements. It shows a gigantic bottle towering over the New York skyline. The Hertz television commercial shown in Figure 3–5 which has O. J. Simpson, a

Fig. 3—3 *Crown Regal. Upside-down Crown Royal Advertisement.* Courtesy of Seagram Distillers Co.

Fig. 3—4 *Tree Top Apple Juice. Psychical Distance with Discordant Elements. Courtesy of Tree Top, Inc.*

Fig. 3–5 *Hertz. Perceptual Isolation with a Startling Visual. Courtesy of the Hertz Corporation.*

former football player, floating in air, is startling enough to gain attention.

Recently, television advertising has begun exploiting perception by a new mode which Hooper White has dubbed product graphics.[17] These techniques, developed initially in Great Britain and in Europe, focus upon the product through imaginative, beautifully-produced graphics. Illustrative of this approach are the commercials for the Lynx automobile, directed by Howard Guard of England. One of them, called "Genesis Fuel Economy," is shown in Figure 3–6. The commercial sets its stage at the dawn of creation, with a gigantic white ball standing amid freshly-formed volcanic rock. The only living thing is a lynx. After examining the car and its main features, the lynx leaps up and sits on its haunches atop the white ball, which becomes the world, with its skies and seas and continents. The entire scene gives the impression of a breathtaking landscape painting.

Through its investigations of perceptual organization—how the senses arrange and relay impulses—Gestalt psychology has contributed greatly to various aspects of copy practices. Of particular significance to layout and design is the figure-ground principle. Gestaltists found that people see geometric patterns, called figures, against a surrounding environment, called a ground. Though figure and ground may complement each other, they are perceived separately, not at the same time. This implies that the focal point of an advertisement be harmonious with its background, but still remain clearly distinguishable.

Figure 3–7 illustrates the figure-ground principle. The advertisement displays a bottle of Beefeater gin by a highly conventional technique in design. By showing a light bottle against a dark background, attention is focused on the product. The package, in this instance a bottle of Beefeater gin, is highlighted by the contrasting elements of the figure and the ground.

At times, advertising designs attempt to give objects and backgrounds near equal emphasis. This treatment in effect reverses the roles of figures

YOUNG & RUBICAM INTERNATIONAL, INC.

CLIENT: LINCOLN-MERCURY DIV. OF FORD MOTOR COMPANY
PRODUCT: 1981 LYNX
TITLE: "GENESIS FUEL ECONOMY" (49 STATE DIVISION)

LENGTH: 60 SECONDS
COMM. NO. FMLX 0357
DATE: 10/20/80

1. (MUSIC UNDER)
2. ANNCR: (VO) Something is about to happen to the American automobile.
3. Introducing the totally new Lynx from Lincoln-Mercury.
4. (MUSIC)

5. Lynx.
6. Its hemispherical head engine,
7. advanced transmission
8. and aerodynamic shape

9. have combined to produce exceptional fuel efficiency.
10. Lynx.
11. Not just front-wheel-drive. But four-wheel independent suspension for smoothness.
12. Lynx.

13. Not just advanced computer technology.
14. But a special inner world that's a pleasure to be in.
15. Starting today,
16. the world belongs

17. to an American car.
18. Starting today,
19. the world belongs to Lynx.
20. (MUSIC OUT)

Fig. 3—6 *Lynx. Illustration of New Product Graphics.* Courtesy of Lincoln-Mercury Division, Ford Motor Company.

Fig. 3—7 *Beefeater. Advertisement Illustrating the Figure-Ground Principle.*
Courtesy of Kobrand Corporation.

and grounds. It is sometimes used to call attention to details without detracting from the major brand recognition elements. A reversal would occur, for example, if the bottle or glasses of the Beefeater gin ad were to become the background for figures which, like mythical genii, were submerged in the liquid-filled vessels.

The advertisement in Figure 3–8 for Chloé perfume makes use of the figure-ground reversal to support the idea of a woman entering a fragrance. The focus becomes the woman, who is submerged in the bottle. The container is actually relegated to a background element.

Another concept of Gestalt psychology, though less structured and operationally feasible, is that of closure. If parts of a configuration are missing, the human mind strives to fill in the gaps, even by distorting the original stimulus. A famous quotation, like a well-known nursery rhyme, will be completed in the mind if started and broken off before its end. In like manner, reminder advertising may contain cues which stimulate past associations, and produce a perceptually-complete entity without being explicit.

Advertisers often make shortened or simplified versions of a commercial from the same shooting. This practice not only reduces costs, but reinforces previous learning. Audiences are supposed to imagine what has been left out, assuming the material is familiar. Shortened commercials which are to maintain an original meaning involve editing. Although judgment is essential, the incomplete rendition does not stray too far afield. Closure tenets in a broader sense become more subjective and more difficult to implement.

The omission of relevant data introduces an element of ambiguity or vagueness. The same is done whenever implicitness is substituted for explicitness. For example, some commercials show sleek felines and cat-like women in velvety gowns turning into automobiles. Do these connotative symbols make viewers associate particular models with the vicarious excitement of a romantic hunt? Or do a series of unspoken images in certain jean commercials evoke sensations of erotic pleasures and make people want to jump into the advertised pair of pants? At times, suggestive words and pictures may have their intended effects. But at other times they do not, for ambiguity poses a danger of irrelevancy. An extreme example may be that of a beautiful model dominating an advertisement for earthmoving machinery, and the most memorable impression is that of a female torso and not of an excavated landscape. The meaningful issue is not whether to use closure principles, but at what point does ambiguity lapse into something meaningless? Unfortunately, there are precious few guidelines.

Despite applications of psychology to sensory perception, the role of the "scientific method" can easily be overstated. Generalizations have remained general, indeterminate, and virtually impossible to put into

Fig. 3—8 *Chloe perfume. Illustration of Figure-Ground Reversal.* Courtesy of Elizabeth Arden.

Disappears rather quickly, doesn't it.

Fig. 3—9 *Chivas-Regal. Example of Advertisement Using Closure Concept.*
Courtesy of Seagram Distillers Co.

practice in a systematic manner. For example, perceptual isolation implies that attention is enhanced when competition wanes. Yet there is a strong tendency for individual media to carry advertisements for the same or similar product groups. Women's magazines are heavy with food advertising. Various brands of golf balls are advertised during a golf tournament on television. Afternoon soap operas carry a repetoire of tiring commercials, appearing one after another, for competing brands of detergents, cleansers and pain killers. The main reason is because competitors sell to the same markets, and therefore seek to promote their wares to the same audiences.

The ways of influencing perception through sensory effects, whether intensifying the stimulus or achieving isolation, are innumerable. An endless variety of word forms and visual configurations are possible, constrained only by the mind of the designer. But psychology so far has utterly failed to assess the comparative value of the alternatives. It can be this way or that way or some other way. When all roads lead to Rome, and are equally good, it doesn't matter which one a traveler takes.

COGNITIVE FACTORS

Perception involves not merely the senses, but cognitive factors—motives, interests, and past experiences. One school of psychology regards people as inherently conservative, clinging to the old familiar ways. These views go under the psychological umbrella of "consistency theories," of which there are numerous versions.[18]

According to these theories, people do not feel comfortable with views that conflict with their own. They do not embrace novelty, they shun it. They do indeed perceive selectively, and strongly favor information which supports their opinions, confirms their biases, and justifies their behavior. Messages which have an old, familiar ring have higher probabilities of being perceived. If true, advertisers face interesting dilemmas when their proposals are at odds with existing opinion. As put by Charlotte Beers, chief operating officer of Tatham-Laird & Kudner Advertising, in Chicago, in these situations "we reached for a bridge between what we wanted to say and what we thought the prospect wanted to hear."[19]

Following the logic of consistency theories, advertisements for well-known brands have an edge over those for new, unheard-of products. All other things being equal, people will notice ads for popular brands more readily. This thesis implies that new products or low share brands must spend more on advertising than market leaders to gain the same level of attention.

Consistency theories supply the rationale for advertising campaigns noted for their uniformity in message content. Running a series of different advertisements is seen as a vacillating, ill-defined campaign, leaving audiences with dissipated and confused impressions. Rather, consistency theory urges a concatenation of messages which are highly similar, even identical.

This dogma was forcefully presented by Rosser Reeves while top executive officer at Ted Bates Advertising Agency.[20] His first prescription for effective advertising was to keep the message simple and bland, with one idea dominating all others. That central theme he called the "unique selling proposition." His second pronouncement was to repeat that message over and over, so that people would become as familiar with it as they are with letters of the alphabet, with everyday routines, or with fairy tales learned as children and reread as adults to their children.

An extreme form of consistency theory is that of conditioned response. This notion has always been intuitively appealing to the advertising industry. Marketers are consistently striving to routinize transactions, to make them almost automatic so that acts can be carried out with little or no deliberation. If learning derives from associations of response to stimuli, then why cannot advertising messages bring about learned behavior of a desired type?

This concept visualizes repeated stimuli—in this instance commercial messages—as capable of evoking purchase behavior in roughly the same fashion as Ivan P. Pavlov, in his famous psychological experiments, got dogs to salivate whenever he rang a bell. In the 1930s, J. Walter Thompson even hired the psychologist John B. Watson, who tried unsuccessfully to apply behavioristic principles to the agency's advertising efforts. The mechanistic theories of behaviorism gradually gave way to the concept of instrumental learning, as initially set forth by N. W. Miller and J. Dollard.[21] This theory supposes a drive-cue-response-reward sequence. Given a particular inclination, a cue—here an advertisement—is seen as able to induce a response, usually a purchase. The reward hopefully comes from product usage, which in turn reinforces the association of cue with response.

An opposing school of thought asserts that the power of persuasion resides not in the familiar, but in the novel. How would one react to seeing an elephant walking down the street? Startled, to say the least, if the street were Madison Avenue, despite its reputation for showmanship. But probably indifferent if the site were somewhere in India.

Communication which diverges from the norm, this group of psychologists points out, is more prone to attract attention, like our make-believe pachyderm on a busy thoroughfare. This view has come to be known as the complexity theory. It sees people as suffering from *ennui*, and welcoming the novel, the unusual, the unexpected. Even arguments contrary to one's point of view, the theory claims, are apt to be more persuasive than old assertions which have become shopworn through repetition.[22] This penchant for change, welling irresistibly within the human breast, is seen as the force that tears people from their traditional ways of thinking about things and doing things. In this view, a new product would have a decided advantage over an older, established product under similar circumstances. It is the underlying explanation for new brands being able to carve out large market shares and for modified products boosting sagging sales.

In line with this theory, Ogilvy once asserted that the word "new" was one of the most powerful that can be inserted in a headline. His recommendations for writing potent copy included the following terms: new, announcing, introducing, just arrived, improvement, amazing. All these words connote some element of novelty. The reason why these cliches work, according to Ogilvy, is "because the consumer is always on the lookout for new products, or new ways to use an old product or new improvements in an old product."[23]

A campaign with many different messages is costlier than one which transmits the same message over and over. It entails expanded creative efforts, higher production expenses, and more complicated logistics. But its proponents argue that perceptual effects become more pronounced throughout the campaign.[24]

Though the complexity and consistency theories are basically at odds with one another, reality embraces both at the same time and in the same individual. A strong preference for steak may not change easily, and supports consistency. But neither would this predilection make a person want a steak dinner every day, thus upholding the argument for variety.

In practice, there are many possibilities and compromises between sameness and variety in an advertising campaign. But psychology cannot tell when to use what. In the absence of any clear directive, intuitive decisions of practitioners must act as the guiding force.

HIERARCHY OF EFFECTS

Since advertisements are persuasive messages, advertisers have an understandable interest in consumer behavior. They are interested in how people come to choose the brands they do.

These decision-making processes are conceived of as being composed of a series of mental phases through which an individual must pass on the way to action. There are several versions of such progressions, but they all belong to a class of theories which has become known as the hierarchy of effects.

One of the first such models came from sales management in the 1920s. It was called AIDA, an acronym for attention, interest, desire, action.[25] It proposed that the ideal sales presentation was one which brought prospects from an initial state of awareness to one of interest, and next to that of desiring the product. Once desire was achieved, the sale could be closed expeditiously.

In the 1930s some psychologists suggested there were natural courses which people took when making decisions. Alan H. Monroe called these steps the "motivational sequence." He listed five of them: attention, need, satisfaction, visualization, and action. The first gains a prospect's attention. Next, the prospect must be given convincing reasons why he needs whatever is being sold. If successful, the argument should arouse his interest. The third step demonstrates how the suggested solution would satisfy the proposed needs. Visualization then shows the advantages of that particular solution over others. Finally, the presentation would recommend specific actions for achieving the desired results.[26]

In 1955, a committee of rural sociologists postulated an adoption process for innovations which consisted of five ascending steps: awareness, interest, evaluation, trial, and adoption. This prototype was popularized by Everett M. Rogers, and became diffused in marketing.[27] Carried increasingly by models of consumer behavior, the theory gained wide acceptance in advertising circles. A popular rendition was the six-phased conception of Lavidge and Steiner, which stipulated a chain of awareness, knowledge, liking, preference, conviction, and purchase.[28]

Regardless of the particular version one accepts, the hierarchy of effects theory draws a picture of the consumer as an information seeker. It assumes purchase decisions involve deliberative acts, and many proponents of the theory have equated product choices with problem-solving decisions. The theory also presupposes that decision processes take place in a given order—from cognitive to affective impressions—which, in turn, influence behavior, the final step in the hierarchy. Each event is a contingent one, depending upon the fulfillment of preceding conditions.

A number of advertising companies and agencies have sought to put this theory into practice. One application has been the incorporation of the hierarchy of effects theory into computer models for new product planning.[29] Most of these constructs assume certain relationships between awareness, product trial, and continued usage. Of greater significance to advertising has been the approach which regards the supposed hierarchy as a set of marketing segments.[30] For example, some prospects will be "unaware" of the offer and not even stand on the bottom step of the hierarchy. Some people will have "knowledge" of the brand. Among the "knowledgeable" will be those with favorable attitudes, or those with unfavorable ones. The idea is to classify all people within a market according to their position on the hierarchy so that they can be led up the steps to its apex, the point of taking action.

Applications of the hierarchy of effects theory have been in existence for almost two decades, but a verdict on their effectiveness has still not come in. Up to now they have produced no evidence of outstanding results. Companies which use them have been no more successful than those which do not. The reasons are both operational and conceptual.

It is easy enough to say that advertising should move prospects up the hierarchy. But to which positions should the advertising be directed? To address people on each step means running several campaigns simultaneously, a highly impractical undertaking. Some authorities have fallen back on the paradigm of concentrating on the level which contains a large number of prospects in relation to the next higher level. The logic is that advertising so directed would move the largest numbers up the ladder to purchasing. But this proposal really begs the question. It assumes that all prospects are of equal importance irrespective of their position in the hierarchy. Conceivably, the movement of a person into the purchase category can be much more important than the transition of another individual from awareness to knowledge. But how should such weights be assigned?

The concept further supposes that advertisers know what appeals are appropriate for each step of the hierarchy. For example, consider for a moment the Lavidge-Steiner model. What sort of copy would move people from liking to preference? Or from preference to conviction? The presumption of such knowledge being readily available is either grossly audacious or incredibly naive.

The validity of the hierarchy of effects has also come under attack from several quarters. One assault was mounted by dissonance theorists, who hold that when cognitions are inconsistent with behavior, people seek evidence to support what they are doing. Since people rationalize their actions rather than act rationally, a change in attitude need not precede a change in behavior. Leon Festinger, a pioneer in the development of dissonance theory, examined secondary sources for evidence that attitude changes cause behavioral changes. Surprisingly, his search in the psychological literature turned up only three studies which were relevant to the issue, and they all indicated a negative relationship.[31]

Another volley of criticism came from a school of thought which regards advertising communication as an inherently "low involvement" activity. Its leading spokesperson is Herbert Krugman, manager of public opinion research at General Electric. Krugman argues that for many products, particularly the low-priced, high-turnover items that enjoy large advertising budgets, purchasing takes place without any significant change in attitudes.[32] This line of reasoning goes as follows: An attitude is basically a deep-seated emotion. But the persuasive messages about products represent so much trivia to consumers. Does a shopper really form an attitude about a roll of toilet paper, notwithstanding the tongue-in-cheek antics of the affable Mr. Whipple in the Charmin commercials? Would smokers really "fight than switch" if their favorite brand were not available at a tobacco counter? It is exaggerated nonsense to think so! In Krugman's view, purchases of convenience goods are not the result of rational, deliberative acts. Recent research with brain wave frequencies shows that television viewing is not only characterized by low levels of mental activity, but that the parts of the brain affected have little or nothing to do with reasoning or logical thinking.[33] Rather, advertising is observed and learned as meaningless material, quickly forgotten, and then learned a little more with subsequent exposure. It is the perceptual factor, not attitude change, that brings forth a response, with the purchase situation acting as the catalyst.

The controversy about the hierarchy of effects, often debated in obtuse, esoteric language, is not academic bickering over some fine points of psychological theory. The issue is real enough and gets down to the very root of advertising planning.

If the hierarchical concept is a valid one, agencies which use it as a framework for planning their communications are obviously on the right track. So are those members of the marketing research fraternity who talk about predicting behavior from attitudinal measurements and segmenting markets by analyzing the components of an attitude.[34] Their ability to do so, however, may be another matter. On the other hand, the acceptance of dissonance theory would lead an advertiser to direct its messages to current customers and create ads to help them rationalize their decisions. Methods for garnering new buyers would emphasize those other than advertising, such as sales promotion, merchandising, pricing, or personal selling. A belief in "low involvement" theory would call for yet a different approach. Communication would have to appeal to cognitive, not affective, elements. It would have to enhance such intangibles as gaining attention, brand awareness, product image, in a word: perception. A reticence to subscribe wholeheartedly to any theory might lead to eclecticism, whereby the advertiser grasps at all these approaches, shifting from one to the other depending upon the situation.

It is difficult to see how they can all be right. Yet each group can dig up cases to prove its approach brought success. Perhaps there is more than a touch of irony in the oft quoted remark of Wanemaker that half his advertising worked but that he didn't know which half.

SUMMARY

Although the objectives of advertising are economic, its means are those of communication. Mass media provides the context in which advertising takes place, and as such wields an important influence over the process. Communication is one-way rather than interactive. The media dilute advertising effects by carrying competitive messages, appealing to people who have little interest in commercial messages, and communicating to self-selective audiences.

The open nature of mass communication leads to selective perception of advertising. Consequently, advertisers control message transmission but not message reception. That resides within the individuals. The small effects of single advertisements has led to three widely-accepted principles: the theory of a threshold, the idea of a campaign, and the concept of joint effects.

Because consumers perceive messages selectively, advertisements attempt to use signs and symbols that are familiar and relevant. Both denotive and connotative characteristics are thus brought into play.

Symbols have both sensory and cognitive effects. The first involves physical stimuli. One useful generalization is Weber's law. Another is the concept of perceptual isolation. Yet both theories are not specific enough to employ operationally, except in a general kind of way.

There is less agreement about cognitive factors, and theory follows two diverse paths. One encompasses a set of postulates called consistency theories. The other route is known as complexity theory.

The conventional wisdom sees the consumer decision-making process as one described by a series of mental steps beginning with attention or awareness and ending with action. This theory is called the hierarchy of effects. But the view has also been challenged by dissonance theory and low involvement concepts of learning.

In advertising, the core of communication theory is concerned with application. In order to do something, participants are required, which in business, means organization. The next two chapters discuss the business structures set up for advertising purposes.

Questions for Chapter 3

1. A network tv rating measures the average minute to which a television set is tuned to a program. From the standpoint of the generalized communications model, is this rating an appropriate measure of advertising message reception?

2. Why is feedback of advertising communication much less effective than that of mechanical communication systems?

3. Because advertising is one-way communication, certain authors have likened it to a "control system." Comment on this view.

4. Since the goal of advertising is to cause some form of behavior, only this end result need be measured in order to advertise effectively. Do you agree?

5. Given equal audience size and copy goodness, why would an advertisement for a detergent have an effect different from that for a washing machine?

6. The advertising campaign bases its rationale on the idea that communication effects of a message is low. Discuss.

7. What are the major methods of designing advertisements to appeal to the senses?

8. How would an advertiser subscribing to consistency theory run advertising different from one upholding a complexity theory?

9. What assumptions are made when accepting a hierarchy of effects theory?

10. Outline an advertising approach for razor blades using a theory of hierarchy of effects. Of cognitive dissonance. Of low involvement.

11. Are advertisements whose purpose is persuasion appropiate for low involvement products?

Footnotes for Chapter 3

[1]See Wilbur Schramm, "How Communication Works," *Dimensions of Communication*, ed. Lee Richardson (Englewood Cliffs N.J.: Prentice-Hall, 1969), pp. 3–4.

[2]Claude E. Shannon, "The Mathematical Theory of Communication," *Bell System Technical Journal* (July and October 1948).

[3]Ernest R. Kretzmer, "Communication Terminal," *Scientific American* (September 1972), p. 131.

[4]See William G. Nickels, *Marketing Communication and Promotion*, 2nd ed. (Columbus, Ohio: Grid, Inc., 1980), pp. 9–15, 82–85; B. Stidsen and T. F. Schutte, "Marketing as a Communication System: The Marketing Concept Revisited," *Journal of Marketing* (October 1972), pp. 22–27.

[5]Bent Stidsen, "Some Thoughts on the Advertising Process," *Journal of Marketing* (January 1970), p. 49.

[6]Nickels, *Marketing Communication and Promotion*, p. 15.

[7]Dick Wasserman, "Do Clients Hate Agencies?" *Advertising Age* (March 30, 1981), p. 50.

[8]W. R. Simmons, *Selective Markets and the Media for Reaching Them* (New York: Simmons Media Studies, 1978).

[9]Leo Bogart, *Strategy in Advertising* (New York: Harcourt, Brace & World, Inc., 1967), p. 297.

[10]David Ogilvy, *Confessions of an Advertising Man* (New York: Atheneum, 1963), p. 88.

[11]Michael J. Naples, *Effective Frequency: The Relationship Between Frequency and Advertising Effectiveness* (New York: Association of National Advertisers, Inc., 1979), pp. 21–25, 40, 61, 63.

[12]See Marshall McLuhan, *Understanding Media: The Extensions of Man* (New York: McGraw-Hill, 1965).

[13]A. Resnik and B. L. Stern, "An Analysis of the Information Content in Television Advertising," *Journal of Marketing* (January 1977), pp. 50–53.

[14]Judith Williamson, *Decoding Advertisements* (London: Marion Boyars, 1978), pp. 40–41.

[15]See Stuart H. Britt, "How Weber's Law Can Be Applied To Marketing," *Business Horizons* (February 1975), pp. 21–29; Edmund W. J. Faison, *Advertising: A Behavioral Approach For Managers* (New York: John Wiley, 1980), pp. 97–98.

[16]Kenneth A. Longman, *Advertising* (New York: Harcourt Brace Jovanovich, 1971), pp. 270–276.

[17]Hooper White, "A New Wave Has Landed," *Advertising Age* (November 2, 1981), pp. 55–56.

[18]David A. Aaker and John G. Myers, *Advertising Management* (Englewood Cliffs, N.J.: Prentice-Hall, 1975), pp. 314–331.

[19]"Effective Messages Are Interesting, Dramatic, and Relevant to Audience," *Marketing News* (April 17, 1981), p. 8.

[20]Rosser Reeves, *Reality in Advertising* (New York: Knopf, 1961).

[21]Faison, *Advertising*, pp. 145–146.

[22]D. O. Sears and J. L. Freedman, "Effects of Expected Familiarity with Arguments upon Opinion Change and Selective Exposure," *Journal of Personality and Social Psychology* (February 1965), pp. 420–426; M. Venkatesan, "Cognitive Consistency and Novelty Seeking," S. Ward and T. S. Robertson, eds., *Consumer Behavior: Theoretical Sources* (Englewood Cliffs, N.J.: Prentice-Hall, 1973), pp. 354–384; R. W. Hughes et. al., "Variety Drive in Consumer Behavior," V. Bellur, ed., *Development in Marketing Science*, Vol. 3 (Marquette, Mi: Academy of Marketing Science, 1980), pp. 22–27.

[23]Ogilvy, *Confessions*, p. 105. Also see Edmund W. J. Faison "A Neglected Variety Drive: A Useful Concept for Consumer Behavior," *Journal of Consumer Research* (June 1977), pp. 172–175.

[24]Robert C. Gras and Wallace H. Wallace, "Satiation Effects of TV Commercials," *Journal of Advertising Research* (September 1969), pp. 3–8.

[25]Aaker and Myers, *Advertising Management*, p. 103

[26]See A. H. Monroe and D. Ehminger, *Principles of Speech*, 5th ed. (Chicago: Scott Foresman and Company, 1964), pp. 221–223.

[27]W. S. Sachs and G. Benson, *Product Planning and Management* (Tulsa, Okla.: PennWell Publishing Co., 1981), pp. 346–347.

[28]R. J. Lavidge and G. A. Steiner, "A Model for Predictive Measurements of Advertising Effectiveness," *Journal of Marketing* (October 1961), pp. 65–67.

[29]Sachs and Benson, *Product Planning*, pp. 273–278.

[30]See Aaker and Myers, *Advertising Management*, pp. 105, 118–227.

[31]Leon Festinger, "Behavioral Support for Opinion Change," L. Richardson, ed., *Dimensions of Communications* (New York: Appleton-Century-Crofts, 1969), pp. 105–116.

[32]Herbert Krugman, "The Impact of Television Advertising: Learning Without Involvement," *Public Opinion Quarterly* (Fall 1965), pp. 349–356.

[33]"New Studies of Brain Functioning" *Marketing News* (March 25, 1977), pp. 1, 7.

[34]Harry E. Heller, "A New Theory of Attitude Change: Or How Advertising Works to Change People's Attitudes," *Marketing Review* (April/May 1977), pp. 15–17.

ORGANIZATIONAL STRUCTURE OF ADVERTISING

4 Organizing for Advertising

Scholars of industrial organization, such as Alfred E. Chandler and Richard E. Caves, have amply documented the fact that structure is a response to strategy. That is, an organizational structure is a unique arrangement whereby, given a long-term plan of action, a firm seeks to use its productive inputs in the most efficient manner.

The organization of the advertising industry manifests no significant departure from this generalization. But, as advertising is one of several marketing inputs, its organizational structure must accommodate itself to the ascendant strategies of marketing.

From this perspective, the chapter analyzes the structure of firms involved with advertising. To be more precise, it focuses on:

- **Differences in structure relating to different types of advertising**
- **Options in centralizing or decentralizing advertising functions**
- **Internal developments among marketers to which advertising tasks must adjust**
- **Ways in which advertising agencies organize to carry out the assignments of their clients**

ORGANIZATION OF THE ADVERTISING INDUSTRY

The advertising industry is divided into three main parts—advertisers, advertising agencies, and media. In a delightful little book written more than two decades ago, Martin Mayer, well-known author on advertising matters, quotes an officer of a research company describing a meeting of the Advertising Research Foundation, the members of which are drawn from all three industrial segments:[1]

> The media people come first, usually about ten minutes early. Then about the time the meeting is supposed to start, the agency people show up and start kicking the media people around. The advertisers come about fifteen minutes late and for the rest of the meeting they kick the agency people around. Then everybody goes out for a drink.

Mayer astutely notes that this nimble-witted vignette is a microcosm of the real world, with advertisers ordering, agencies suggesting, and media requesting. Today, it still superficially represents the commercial relationships of clients, agents and suppliers. The advertisers produce the branded goods or services and pay to have them advertised. The advertising agencies work under contract as the agent of the advertiser, on whose behalf they prepare and place advertisements and commercials. Media are suppliers of space and time, offering their publications and broadcasts to carry the commercial messages.

Not all advertisers make use of agencies. Of total U.S. advertising expenditures, perhaps half are funnelled through agencies. The remaining half are made by clients directly.

Firms most prone to go the do-it-yourself route are industrial marketers and retailers. Compared with consumer products, industrial goods and services are promoted heavily by methods which fall outside the domain of agency expertise, such as direct mail, trade shows, company brochures and literature, publicity-type releases. Since these tasks can be done just as well by an internal staff, and at lower cost, there is little reason to employ an outside agent.

Similarly, retail establishments have few incentives to place advertising through agencies. Media alternatives are relatively few, and seldom require the elaborate analysis of experts. Local media usually allow no commissions to advertising agencies, preferring to carry out many production jobs on their own. Television stations have studios for hire. They make available production facilities, staffed by people who shoot and edit their programs. Newspapers, the major medium of retailers, do layouts and set type according to customer specifications. These services are included in the space rates. Featuring sales, specials, price, and having a one-day life, these merchandising advertisements are evidently simple in design and ordinary in production quality. These characteristics are sufficient for their marketing requirements.

Larger retailers use to advantage the more specialized talents of outside ad agencies. These are usually employed for partial services, such as special campaigns in national media, radio and television production and placement, and package design. In general, the larger the store, the greater the variety of jobs and specialized functions it takes on even while using outside help. Figures 4–1 and 4–2 illustrate organization charts for medium and large-sized stores.

Most general advertisers turn in varying degrees to agencies for advertising services. But ultimate responsibility must rest with the advertiser. They are the organizations whose messages are transmitted. They pay the media charges for carrying the messages, and as the old saying goes, he who pays the piper calls the tune. And invariably, it is the client organization which in large measure determines how people both inside and outside the firm will work together.

Since an organization is a means for getting things accomplished, structure normally follows strategy.[2] Once management decides what it wants to do, structures are set up to carry out the decisions.

There are numerous ways in which firms can organize themselves for the advertising function, about as multitudinous as the endless possibili-

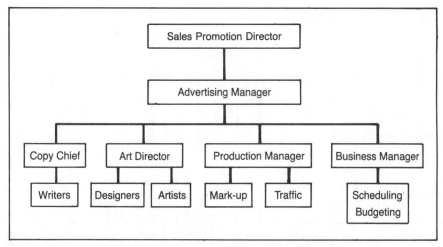

Fig. 4–1 *Advertising Organization in Medium-sized Store.*

Source: Judy Y. Ocko and M. L. Rosenblum, How To Be A Retail Advertising Pro *(New York, National Retail Merchants Association, 1977), p. 288. Published with permission of National Retail Merchants Association.*

ties for strategy. One line of inquiry into the subject is to examine the extent to which the advertising function is centralized.

Firms with narrow product lines, typically small companies, have few options. If advertising is deemed important, a top official might take charge. It is more common, however, for advertising to be in a functional department, such as marketing or sales.

Large companies usually operate in many different businesses, selling very dissimilar products in highly diverse markets. As early as the beginning of the 1970s less than 2 percent of the Fortune 500, the biggest manufacturing firms in terms of sales, were single business companies.[3] These complex, diversified organizations enjoy more varied choices. From the standpoint of centralization, a multidivisional firm has three broad alternatives. It can:

1. Centralize advertising at the corporate level
2. Set advertising responsibility at the divisional level
3. Decentralize to operational units below the divisional level

These three basic alternatives are not mutually exclusive. They can coexist in different combinations, with tasks parceled out between them in varying amounts. Each arrangement may also display variations in the chain of command or place of control. Though few companies will have identical structures, the basic types will distinctly show through the organizational maze.

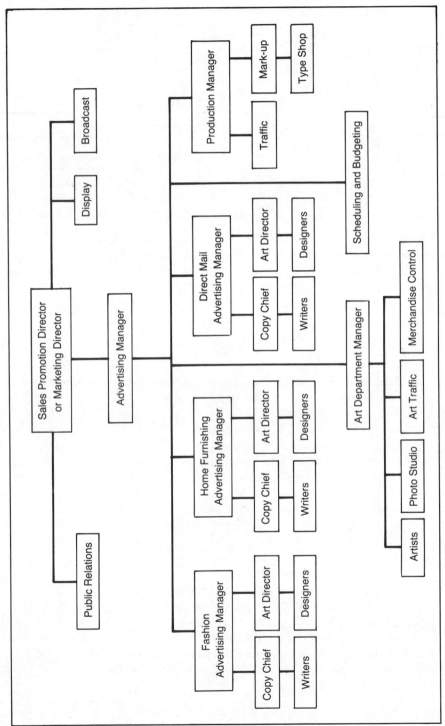

Fig. 4–2 *Advertising Organization in a Large Store.*

Source: Ocko and Rosenblum, How To Be A Retail Advertising Pro (New York: National Retail Merchants Association, 1977), p. 289. Published with permission of NRMA.

CENTRALIZATION AT THE CORPORATE LEVEL

Placing sole responsibility for advertising at the corporate level represents extreme centralization. This central unit is put in charge of getting advertising done for the entire company. Figure 4–3 depicts this form of organization for a company with several divisions.

This arrangement appeals to a multidivisional company under a wide range of circumstances. The structure is brought out in bold relief by industrial marketers to whom advertising is comparatively unimportant. If the various divisions advertise sparingly, it does not pay for them to hire personnel who specialize in advertising. But by sharing the overhead of a centralized department, they are better able to obtain quality services and lower costs than if each division did its own promotion.

Eminently illustrating this cost-sharing approach of divisions is the organization of Beckman Instruments. The firm's eight divisions market more than 5,000 products in about 30 markets, and advertise in a large number of business publications. The total budget for trade book advertising is relatively small, making up about a fourth of a not-too-large promotional allocation. To take advantage of pooled resources, ads are placed in business magazines by a single agency. Direction comes from internal managers, who are assigned to divisions by the corporate manager of marketing communications. All other promotional work is done internally, with outside services used where appropriate. According to company spokespersons, substantial economies are realized in art and production by concentrating purchasing authority at one place within the corporation.[4] Figure 4–4 shows how Beckman Instruments organizes for marketing communication.

Another set of circumstances favoring a corporate thrust is when divisions serve related markets and partake of similar promotional activity. A division is usually a profit center built around a family of affinitive products and markets. When divisions lean in a horizontal direction, the product families tend to move into surroundings which resemble each other. In

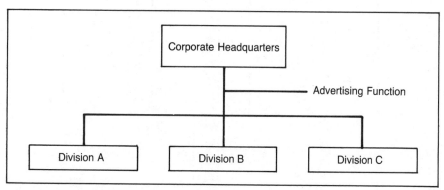

Fig. 4–3 *Advertising at the Corporate Level.*

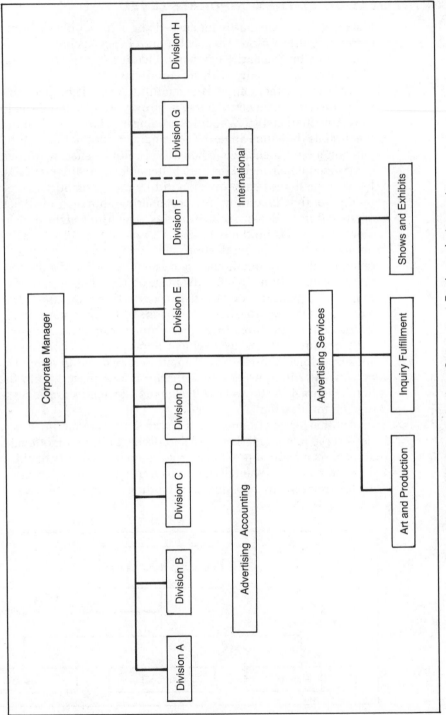

Fig. 4—4   *Communications Structure at Beckman Instruments.*

these instances, efficiency can be increased by centralizing the common elements of their operations. The effects produced by such unions are said to be synergistic.

Service-type industries seem especially suited to benefit from synergistic fusion of efforts. The Fidelity Group, for example, admirably demonstrates this principle. This financial giant markets a diverse assortment of services, such as money market funds, investments in corporate and government securities, or stock brokerage. Yet advertising and promotion for all these services are of the same type and appear in the same financial publications. This financial institution, like its industrial counterparts, stands to gain from centralized purchasing of artwork, production, and creative talent, and from discounts through corporate planning of media schedules. Opportunities, indeed, abound for cross-selling, such as piggybacking diverse services in the same advertisements. Likewise, many banks and insurance companies can do promotion more economically through a single unit than by fragmented efforts. Figure 4–5 shows a basic organizational chart for marketing in a bank.

A third kind of situation that moves promotional activity to the corporate offices comes with a decision to do corporate advertising. The way in which a company projects itself, the face it shows to the public, is clearly the responsibility of the chief executive officer.[5] It cannot be left to subordinates. Nor can the job of shaping public attitudes be delegated to marketing people whose main concern is selling products. Consequently, the task of advertising a corporation most often falls within the domain of public relations. These departments, reporting directly to top management, play a key role in corporate advertising decisions. They are the leading source of ideas concerned with corporate image. Besides originating the concepts for corporate communications, public relation depart-

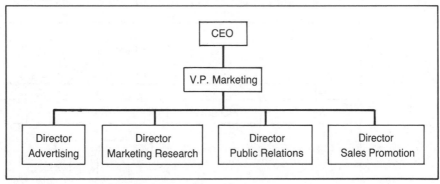

Fig. 4–5 *Organization of Bank Marketing.*

Source: Derived from R. A. Sandgren and J. M. Murtha, Sales Promotion for Banks *(Chicago: Bank Marketing Association, 1976), p. 11.*

ments have an extremely high involvement in the formulation of the ensuing advertising programs.[6]

DECENTRALIZATION OF ADVERTISING

When divisions operate in dissimilar and varied markets, as in conglomerate organizations, an advertising department at the corporate level becomes unwieldy. To assemble the personnel needed who are familiar with diverse businesses is a costly undertaking. At the same time, corporate functions more and more overlap divisional ones, and redundancy grows. The advantages of a decentralized approach are particularly obvious when divisions are large, with advertising volume capable of supporting a competent, self-sufficient staff.

At the divisional level, advertising will normally be lodged within a functional department, depending upon the unit's importance. Most often, this will be the marketing department. A firm with this form of organization is diagrammed in Figure 4–6.

Compared with the centralized approach, divisional effort would bring the advertising function closer to the markets in which a firm operates. Those who work on advertising would be more conversant with marketing problems, more attuned to the exigencies of the marketplace, and more able to respond quickly to changes in the business scene. Lines of communication are shorter, and company efforts tend to be more cohesive. Lastly, advertising people are under the same authority as other personnel doing the job of marketing.

Advertising is further decentralized in firms which have adopted the product management system. This form of organization is prevalent among packaged goods manufacturers having many products which contribute materially to earnings, despite the 20–80 principle: some 20 percent of the brands usually account for about 80 percent of total company sales. But most large packaged goods firms have no brand or product line which is so dominant as to reduce all others to insignificance.

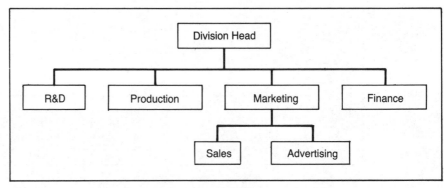

Fig. 4–6 *Advertising at the Divisional Level.*

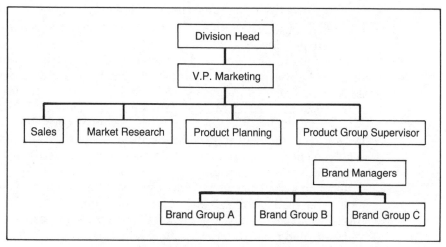

Fig. 4–7 *Product Management System in Packaged Goods.*

The product management system dates back to more than half a century. It is said to have originated at Procter & Gamble, when Neil H. McElroy in 1927 was given responsibility for marketing Camay soap. But the system was not widely adopted until the 1950s, as consumer demand enticed all types of marketers to increase the number of available products by leaps and bounds. The proliferation of goods and services severely taxed the resources of most marketing departments, organized along functional lines. To ease the burden of the marketing head and his traditionally small staff, a layer of management was superimposed upon the functional units. All departments, except advertising, remained intact. Managers were added, often for each brand, to plan, coordinate and monitor marketing endeavors.

Product management can take many forms. A rather common one for consumer goods divisions is depicted in Figure 4–7.

As shown in Figure 4–7, the typical packaged goods company will have no advertising department. With the advent of brand managers, advertising departments were dismantled for several reasons. First, firms ere able to reduce costs by getting rid of overlapping functions between advertising departments and brand manager groups. Second, the consensus was that brand managers would better coordinate and control their marketing responsibilities if they were given advertising functions. This shift in jobs from the advertising department to the brand manager was made possible, in the opinion of many, because the advertising agency possesses the necessary specialists to make the system work.[7] In essence, the advertising agency assumes a role which is almost tantamount to that of a company advertising department.

Some firms maintain a corporate advertising department along with a product management system. The main function of this department, however, is to provide services used in common by all divisions, such as those of media planning. The coordination of media purchases is usually done in consultation with the advertising agency involved. Some corporate departments also act in advisory and administrative capacities. The advertising head at General Motors, for example, reviews advertisements for several divisions.[8] For the most part, however, corporate headquarters lacks direct authority in product decisions, and refrains from any active involvement in planning and implementation of advertising for either its divisions or product groups.

Though widely used throughout industry, the product mangement system never realized the dreams of its early proponents. The idea of the product manager as a "little president," running his or her own business and being held accountable for profits, turned out as unsubstantial as the reveries which brought it into being. Disappointments frequently turn into strong negatives. Product management has even been accused of fostering poor financial results by encouraging wasteful and misguided marketing plans.[9]

As far as advertising is concerned, criticism of product management comes from two directions. Advertising agencies complain about manager inexperience. Most product managers are young, generalists rather than specialists, and unfamiliar with the fine points of creative endeavors. Product managers, it is charged, seek to compensate for their insecurity in judgment with exuberant cautiousness. They spend too much time on trivialities, and blow inconsequential issues out of proportion. Unable to judge creative work, they take refuge in copy testing as the final arbiter of goodness. But more often than not, the tests yield uncertain results and the numbers become the subject of endless debate. Instead of furthering the creative process, critics affirm, brand managers impede and discourage it.[10]

Another source of disenchantment with product management has been internal, within the companies themselves. Product managers seldom stay with a brand more than a few years. They regard brand assignments as stairways to better things and loftier positions. The high personnel turnover works against smooth, continuous marketing operations for individual product lines and brands.

The product management system has also been characterized as management without authority. In the past, when the number of products were comparatively few, product managers may have been a step or so removed from senior executives. But as product lines expanded, the gap grew. More and more product managers were added, while a short span of control necessitated new groups of supervisors intervening between product managers and higher echelon executives. Today, a large company may have the once-regarded "little presidents" two to four levels beneath an office with decision-making powers and enough authority to put a stamp of approval on plans to be carried out.

The response to these shortcomings has been varied. A few companies have actually done away with their brand managers, reverting to the traditional form of functionalism.[11] But the overwhelming majority of firms which have adopted the product management system regard such measures as overly harsh. Top executives generally acknowledge the system's flaws, and advocate revisions to make it work better.[12] One form seems to be a trend away from extreme decentralization towards rationalization.[13]

The most common revisions have stripped the brand manager of all major decisions, leaving him or her with the unimportant, routine tasks. Companies will obviously differ over what constitutes a major and minor decision. Nevertheless, there has been a marked tendency for job descriptions to have the brand manager responsible for gathering and analyzing information for purposes of product planning, budget control, and performance monitoring. When advertising decisions are deemed important, such as those dealing with brand strategy, they are pushed up the corporate ladder, mainly to the divisional level. But managers are still charged with implementation. Divisions seem to be opposed to relinquishing authority to corporate headquarters. Some companies have established divisional staffs to provide creative counsel, hoping thereby to rekindle a lost art. The shifts in responsibilities have resulted in greater fragmentation of the advertising function within the corporate structure. The chart in Figure 4–8 illustrates graphically the loci of decision making within corporations having a product management system.

ADVERTISING AGENCIES: INDUSTRIAL STRUCTURE

Although advertising agencies sell services to advertisers (referred to by agencies as clients), they are thought of as operating from the demand side of the industry. As representatives or agents, they come into the market to buy various services. The main expenditures are for media time and space, but agencies also buy typesetting, printing, art, film production, and a host of related services.

There are some 7,000 or so companies which call themselves advertising agencies. The agency field is still one where a talented individual can hang up a shingle, go into business for him or herself, and do fairly well in competition with larger, well-established firms. But the significant numbers composing the industry are much lower than those indicated by the self-defined totals.

According to the annual compilation prepared by *Advertising Age,* billings and gross income of only 791 companies were listed in 1980. Another 98 firms were excluded because they gave incomplete information. Of those reporting, just 366 registered gross income from U.S. sources of more than $1 million in the 1980 fiscal year.[14] Agency gross income rep-

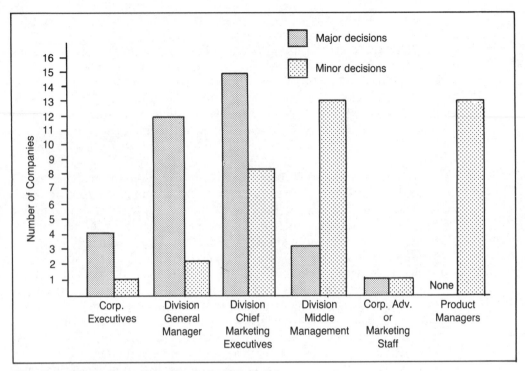

Fig. 4—8 *Where Advertising Decisions Are Made.*

Source: V. P. Buell, Changing Role of the Product Manager in Consumer Goods Companies, *Journal of Marketing* (July 1975), p. 8. Reprinted by permission of the American Marketing Association.

resents revenue from operations, made up of commissions, service charges and fees. The more than 6,000 companies not included in the *Advertising Age* survey are small shops, individually owned and managed, whose gross incomes are presumably too meager to bother about when reporting industrial revenue patterns. A statistical summary of agency revenue, as reported by *Advertising Age,* is given in Table 4–1.

The agency structure clearly shows concentration tendencies, though they are far less than those of American industry in general. As shown in Table 4–1, the top 40 firms make up 5 percent of all agencies reporting, but they account for 66 percent of the total gross income. At the other extreme, the bottom 54 percent of the companies garner but 5 percent of the total gross income reported in *Advertising Age.* Using the more traditional measures of industrial concentration, four, eight, and twenty-five firm ratios are as follows:

4-firm ratio : 17% share of gross income
8-firm ratio : 30% share of gross income
25-firm ratio : 58% share of gross income

TABLE 4–1 *U.S. Advertising Agency Revenue in 1980*

Income Class	Agencies Reporting		Gross Income	
	Number	Percent	Amount ($000,000)	Percent
Over $15 million	40	5	2215	66
$5 million to $15 million	54	7	405	12
$1 million to $5 million	272	34	549	17
Under $1 million	425	54	178	5
Total	791	100	3347	100

Source: Derived from *Advertising Age* (March 18, 1981).
Note: The above computation assumes that agencies reporting less than $5 million in gross income derived their entire revenue from domestic sources.

A more detailed description can be found in Table 4–2. This shows the billings, gross income and number of employees for the leading twenty-five advertising agencies in terms of U.S. business volume.

As expected, billings bear a close relationship to gross income. Revenue for the top twenty-five agencies comes to 14.8 percent of billings, on the average. This ratio has a remarkable uniformity, varying little from agency to agency. The standard deviation of the distribution is 1.5 percent or about 15 percent of the average. Regardless of how agencies are paid for their efforts, their revenues will come close to 15 percent of the business volume they handle for their clients.

ADVERTISING AGENCY FUNCTIONS

Advertising agencies have traditionally been linked with two basic functions: creating ads and placing them in media. The creation of advertising calls upon the talents of writers, artists, musical composers, and the like. Once the advertisements are composed, the skills of typographers, engravers, printers, and film producers are brought into play to transform the arrangements of words, sounds and pictures into a reproducible mode.

The creative function is the heart of the advertising agency, pumping life-giving fluids to all of its other parts. Creativity is the only unique service an agency has to offer. It is innovative, arising from the imagination. It is particular to a specific individual, and except for that person, would not have happened in the same way. It cannot be anticipated by someone other than the creator. It cannot be duplicated. Though good ideas may be imitated, imitation can occur only after the original idea has been conceived.

The placement of ads involves a multi-stage procedure. It begins with media planning, the art of devising a schedule for achieving predeter-

TABLE 4–2 *Top Twenty-Five U.S. Advertising Agencies in 1980 by Billings, Gross Income, and Employees*

Agency	Billings $000,000	Gross Income ($000,000)	Employees
Young & Rubicam	1333.7	200.0	3,804
J. Walter Thompson	918.9	137.8	2.474
Ogilvy & Mather	837.1	125.5	2,160
Foote, Cone & Belding	749.3	109.1	2,330
Leo Burnett	734.6	108.2	1,481
Ted Bates	720.3	108.0	1,884
BBDO Intl	806.4	105.8	2,049
Doyle, Dane, Bernbach	671.0	98.1	1,800
Grey Advertising	524.9	78.7	1,522
Benton & Bowles	492.0	73.8	1,447
Dancer Fitzgerald Sample	505.0	70.3	1,179
N W Ayer ABH Intl	443.7	68.1	1,346
D'Arcy-MacManus & Masius	449.3	67.4	1,446
McCann-Erickson	431.0	64.6	1,277
Wells, Rich, Greene	411.5	61.7	904
William Esty Co	390.0	58.5	616
Bozell & Jacobs	383.6	57.5	1,269
Marschalk Campbell-Ewald	372.4	55.8	983
Compton Advertising	352.0	51.4	1,035
Needham, Harper & Steers	341.6	51.2	980
Marsteller Inc	298.0	44.7	980
Kenyon & Eckhardt	279.1	40.9	741
SSC&B	254.4	38.1	575
KM&G Intl	219.2	32.9	777
Cunningham & Walsh	240.8	31.3	604

Source: Reprinted with permission from March 18, 1981 issue of *Advertising Age,* Copyright 1981 by Crain Communications, Inc.

mined advertising goals. The media selection process entails not merely a detailed analysis of markets, circulations, audiences and costs, but negotiations for space and time purchases. Media buyers have an obligation to get the best possible terms for their clients. Upon completion of media contracts, the agency sees to it that the appropriate materials are forwarded to publishers and broadcasters in accordance with production schedules.

Advertising agencies that go beyond the twin functions of creating and placing advertisements refer to themselves as "full service." The additional services usually cover marketing research, campaign planning, merchandising and sales promotion. Other agency offerings may encompass direct mail, point-of-purchase, public relations, and even specialties such as product testing, generating new product ideas, package design, exhibits and trade shows. To offer clients a veritable myriad of services, or ones which span the full range of marketing, an agency must have a large enough volume of business to support the overhead of specialized departments. For this reason, the full service concept is found primarily among the larger firms within the industry. A client utilizing a truly full service agency should theoretically be able to obtain virtually all the promotional work it requires.

Agencies rely chiefly on people for carrying out their appointed tasks. Their fixed costs are low. Their principal assets are investments in people, and their operating costs are heavily weighted by payrolls. Executives at advertising agencies generally concur with the view that advertising is a people business.

The twenty-five largest U.S. agencies in 1980 averaged one employee per $369,200 of billings, as calculated from the statistics in Table 4–2. Revenue per employee came to $54,645. With the onrush of inflation, these figures keep going up each year. The elite twenty-five in 1979, which included the same companies as in 1980, recorded an average per employee of $338,000 for billings and $49,720 for revenue. The top twenty-five agencies in 1981, which were the same group except one, experienced a rise to $409,686 in billings per employee and $60,401 in revenue.

The relationship between employees and gross income or revenue, expressed as a line of regression, is shown in Figure 4–9.

The line of average relationship in Figure 4–9 is virtually at a 45° angle. This indicates that in 1980 the number of employees were strictly proportional to revenue for the top group of agencies.

But there seems to be large variations from year to year. The same analysis of 1979 data portrays smaller firms among the largest twenty-five having less employees in relation to both revenue and billings. This pattern is evident in Figure 4–10.

The dotted line in Figure 4–10 expresses a situation which would prevail if the number of employees were in proportion to revenue. The solid line depicts the actual situation, as it existed in 1979. The two lines tend to converge as operations get larger, indicating a higher employee-revenue ratio for bigger agencies. However, in 1981 the solid line sloped in a contrary direction, suggesting a reversal in employee-revenue relationships between agencies of various sizes.

Why the difference between 1979 and 1980? The year 1980 was marked by recession and financial stringency, which prompted agencies to trim fat, primarily in payrolls. The previous year was one of rising billings after adjustment for inflation. Buoyed by higher expectations, some agencies added staff in order to prepare for that eventuality. However, no apparent pattern is related to agency size.

This explanation is also supported by the value of the coefficients. In 1980, R^2 stood at .90, indicating high uniformity among agencies. In 1979, the corresponding value was .56, expressing a moderate relationship and

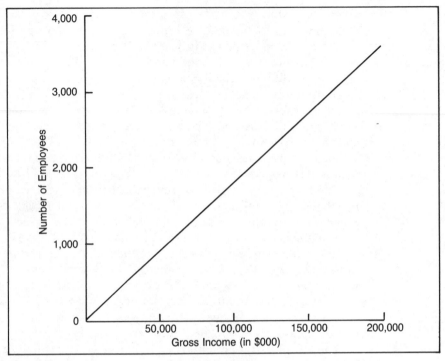

Fig. 4–9 *Employee-Revenue Relationship (25 Largest U.S. Advertising Agencies in 1980).*

Source: Adapted with permission from material in the March 18, 1981 issue of Advertising Age. *Copyright 1981 by Crain Communication, Inc.*

greater variability. The standard error of the estimate in 1979 was some 50 percent of the value of the dependent mean, as compared with 40 percent in 1980. This suggests that advertisers should exercise diligence in evaluating agency operations if contracts specify certain internally-performed functions included in agency remuneration.

ADVERTISING AGENCY ORGANIZATION

The organization of advertising agencies, like that of all other business firms, is related to their functions. It is a device for doing work. Company size and the nature of accounts weigh heavily in the structural arrangement an agency adopts. But individual style cannot be disregarded. People must feel comfortable with an organization. They must be able to work together in the chosen system.

There are two broad types of structures for large and medium-sized agencies. The most common one is that based on functional departments, illustrated in Figure 4–11.

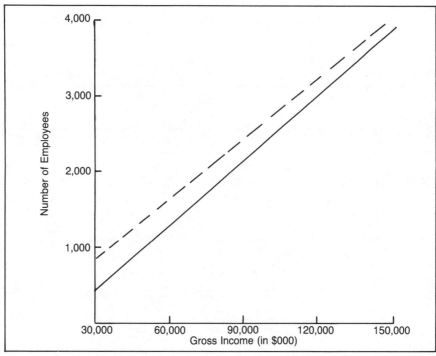

Fig. 4–10 *Employee-Revenue Relationship (25 Largest U.S. Advertising Agencies in 1979).*

Source: Adapted with permission from material in the March 19, 1981 issue of Advertising Age. *Copyright by Crain Communication, Inc.*

As Figure 4–11 indicates, the advertising functions are compartmentalized. Writers and artists in the creative departments will be assigned to different accounts. Media specialists will similarly apportion their time by drawing up media plans, negotiating contracts, and placing ads in print media and on the air. An account in need of marketing research, sales promotion, or merchandising plans would take its request to the appropriate department.

The job of coordinating the various activities falls to the account executive, who is responsible for handling a product's advertising. This manager usually has a marketing background and familiarity, if not expertise, with the client's line of business. The makeup of an account depends largely upon the size of the budget. Accounts doing high volume business will be headed by the more experienced executives, assisted by adequate staffs. Low budget brands may necessitate a single-person account group, sharing a secretary from the typing pool.

The account executive is the nucleus around which all activity revolves. He or she manages the advertising effort from the agency side.

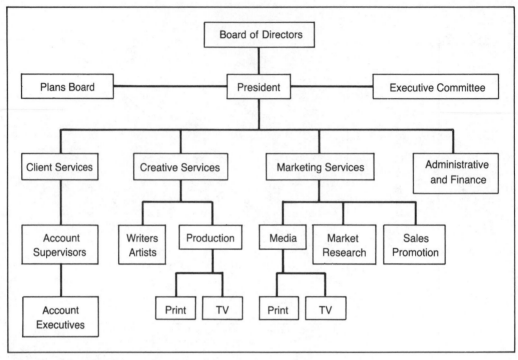

Fig. 4—11 *Advertising Agency Organized into Functional Departments.*

Besides being a coordinator, this executive is charged with planning strategy and evaluating results as the work progresses. The account executive is also the liason between agency and client. All communication regarding the product being advertised passes over his desk. He or she presents to the client organization all agency proposals for approval. He or she receives all client requests and complaints. He or she, more than anyone else in the agency, identifies him or herself with the success or failure of an advertising campaign. His or her business future is bound up with that of the brand whose advertising he or she manages for the agency.

Many advertising agencies boast of plans review boards. These committees are made up of top executives from separate departments. Their chief function is to review the advertising plans of individual campaigns. This system supposedly instills a more uniform quality into services rendered to different clients. All accounts benefit from the experience of senior management. But review boards have also been accused of hampering creative effort—perhaps implicitly rather than overtly—by discouraging new approaches. Lower level executives display little enthusiasm for parading before their bosses recommendations which are unconventional, untried, and unsure. Committees can criticize but cannot create; they frequently complain.[15]

Another type of structure, adopted in recent years by several large ad agencies, is the Group Plan. This arrangement is akin to a matrix form. Figure 4–12 illustrates the manner in which a group is organized.

In the matrix organization, specialists are organized into teams. The work unit may be one large account or group of accounts. Each account is headed by an account executive, and utilizes the services of specialized teams, such as creative personnel, production people, media planners, and so forth. The rationale for the team approach is that advertising is carried on more cohesively, without individuals working at cross-purposes. This form of organization, however, is a complicated one and requires greater managerial effort. Agency size is also a factor. Particular accounts operated by teams must be sufficiently large to warrant the group approach.

SPECIALIZED SERVICES

The advertising landscape is spotted by firms selling ancilliary services, such as typography, printing, photography, or film production. Such companies have had a long and notable history. They have been partly responsible for advertising agencies being concentrated at certain locations—in and around Madison Avenue in New York or Michigan Avenue in Chicago. These patterns of cohesion provide the narrow specialists with markets large enough to support their activities. At the same time, advertising agencies can purchase the necessary specialities at a reasonable cost, for they would certainly pay more if they had to buy at a distance what are essentially customized services.

The last two decades have witnessed the upsurge of specialization of another sort. These new entrants do not complement the work of full service agencies. Instead, they offer their services as substitutes. Their services compete directly with the traditional agency functions.

One such specialist is the boutique shop, which focuses on creative work as art and copy. The firm takes its name from the retail trades, where a boutique suggests a store selling stylized products of high quality. These small, specialized agencies justify themselves on the premise that the differential advantage to be gained from advertising arises from creative effort. All other functions, the reasoning goes, are logistical, cut and dry, virtually routine, and can be done equally well by anyone. To use an analogy, a boutique is to advertising what a designer is to manufacturing. It is the design that differentiates a product from competitive ones, not the production line. By eliminating the technical and clerical chores, boutiques contend there are no distractions from the really important work, and creative output is superior. Boutiques also operate with low overheads, and thus lay claim to delivery of quality service at low costs.

Another specialist is the media buying service, which first emerged in spot television. These companies work in various ways. Some act as

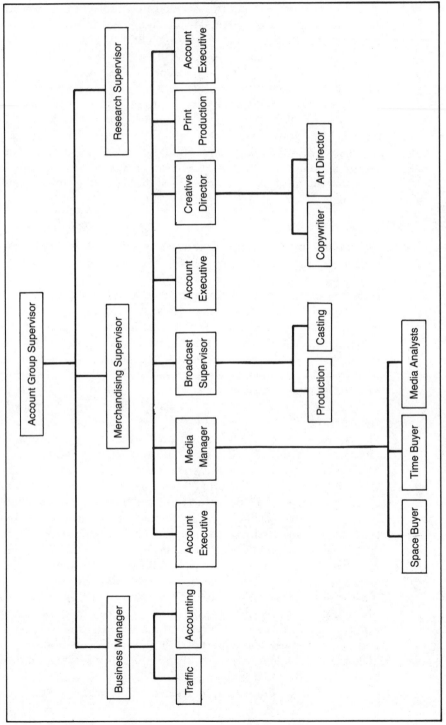

Fig. 4-12 *Organization of an Advertising Agency Group.*

agents or contractors. They negotiate schedules with stations and charge clients a fee for their services. Fees may be fixed or predetermined. They may also be based on a percentage of savings effected, similar to the system used by transportation auditing firms. A number of media buying services are actually media middlemen, purchasing station time at wholesale and reselling at discount rates. Their revenue, like that of any other reseller, comes from the spread between prices at which they buy and prices at which they sell. Because they buy in large blocks, they can often undersell the conventional advertising agency. Their client lists include many small agencies, which regard the discounters as a means of equalizing any agency size differential in the placement of advertising.

The rise of specialization has been accompanied by what might be called "scrambled advertising services." This trend has blurred traditional organizational functions. As in retailing, firms have taken on diverse products, no matter how dissimilar from their regular lines, if they think the addition will generate greater business volume. Thus, some media buying services have added research departments and acquired sophisticated computer models in order to do media planning and analysis. Marketing research companies vie for assignments to formulate strategy, pretest copy, draw up advertising plans, and evaluate campaigns. Full service agencies are content to contract for specific tasks on a project basis, competing with the specialized, limited service shops. This hybridization, resulting in a hodgepodge of services, has widened the range of alternatives for all firms in the industry—advertisers, agencies and media—in ways of conducting business affairs.

IN-HOUSE OPERATIONS

The overwhelming proportion of advertisers make use of independent advertising agencies. But there has been a marked tendency in recent times for advertisers to do more and more work by themselves and assign less and less to the outside agencies. There are varying degrees with which in-house work can be carried on. This can range from doing the entire job to doing very little.

At one extreme is the full-fledged house agency such as that of American Home Products. This organization is set up in much the same way as its outside counterparts, fully-staffed with advertising specialists and account executives assigned to specific brands. This type of house agency for all intents and purposes is a full-service agency, but owned and operated by an advertiser. These agencies may also handle accounts of other companies and compete for business with the independents. At the other extreme, the in-house operation may be confined to an advertising department taking over some peripheral function.

The impetus for in-house work in both industrial and consumer advertising stems for the same cause—a desire to reduce costs. Companies with house agencies think they can do as good a job as outsiders more economically.[16] Most firms which have instituted in-house operations, however, have adopted hybrid forms. They have opted for a modular approach, doing some portion of the work themselves and giving out the rest. The number of modules, or tasks, can be expanded, reduced, or combined in any arrangement that a situation warrants.

In the industrial field, it is common for magazines to have small circulations and low space costs. The standard commissions are sometimes so low as to be hardly enough to cover an agency's time and effort. Also common are skimpy budgets earmarked for commissionable media. In all these instances, advertising agencies may with a good deal of justice ask for remuneration over and above the normal commission. Yet the industrial marketer, especially if the company makes heavy use of non-media promotion, might be paying top dollar for ad agency services which cannot be employed to full advantage.

One solution for such problems of mismatched resources is the modular method.[17] In actuality, a company usually handles by itself certain advertising and promotional functions. For example, the advertising agency is often by-passed for such material as sales literature, direct mail, trade exhibits and audio-visual displays. These jobs are done either internally or contracted for with specialized collateral shops. If media alternatives are narrow, or if media vehicles are relatively stable from year to year, the advertising agency is not really necessary to handle the function. If the task happens to be complicated, a media buying service might be considered as a possible alternative. Of all advertising functions, creative ones will invariably fall outside the capabilities of the industrial firm. But even here, boutiques and conventional agencies will contract for work on a project basis. The advertiser thus has a wider choice of creative talent. But the firm using a variety of suppliers must assume the responsibility of management and all that it implies. The advertising agency under these conditions serves as a supplier, not an agent, of the advertiser.

Firms marketing consumer goods have similarly turned to the modular solution in larger numbers. Those with big budgets in particular already possess stout proficiencies in advertising. By accepting sole responsibility for functions within areas of competence a firm can substantially reduce duplication of effort between it and its advertising agency. Of equal if not greater importance, in-house operations enhance the degree of control that an advertiser can exercise over marketing efforts.

A major area into which large advertisers have entered and taken over traditional agency functions is that of media. Exemplifying this trend, Lever Brothers in 1976 established an in-house media group.[18] This organization handles about 85 percent of total billings, mainly in network tv. It does both media planning and buying. Only spot tv, which is more complicated than network, is left to J. Walter Thompson, one of the company's advertising agencies.

But in-house media operations vary markedly from company to company. Bristol Myers, for example, does all of its own media buying, covering both broadcast and print. But media planning is split, some being done internally and some by agencies. The firm also boasts of a tv production department, which bids competitively on jobs. This department runs in the same way as those of ad agencies, contracting for work on the outside and acting in a supervisory capacity. By having its own facilities competing directly with agencies, the company obtains a better assessment of production costs and job specifications.

With large companies having their own marketing research departments, they are not as dependent upon agencies for gathering market information. Many firms routinely do copy testing and evaluate campaigns. Most large companies carry on marketing research for purposes of advertising planning and formulating strategy.

The once traditional functions which separated agencies from clients have become less distinct. But not all. The on-rushing takeover of advertising functions has halted, at least temporarily, at the creative end. Even the advertising giants have, in the main, not crossed the creative boundary, beyond which lies the last stronghold of the advertising agency.

SUMMARY

The advertising industry serves those firms marketing products, with advertising agencies placing commercial messages on their behalf and media supplying the space and time. The most extensive use of advertising agencies are made by general advertisers of consumer products.

Multidivisional firms, which describe most of the large manufacturing and service corporations, can set responsibility for advertising at the corporate, divisional, or operational level. The first two alternatives call for advertising to be carried out by a functional department. The last option represents complete decentralization, with advertising usually under the direction of product managers. Large, complex organizations will often have some melding of the functional department with product management.

There are slightly more than 7,000 advertising agencies in the United States. Tendencies towards concentration are patently evident, with the 37 largest firms accounting for almost two-thirds of total agency revenue. An agency's revenue is close to 15 percent of total billings, regardless of differences in methods of compensation for services. The larger agencies tend to have more employees in relation to both revenue and billings. The reason is because the large firms will do relatively more work internally, while the smaller companies will buy proportionately more on the outside.

Advertising agencies are organized in two ways. The conventional one is along functional department lines. Some larger agencies have recently adopted the group plan, where advertising specialists work as a team on one, or on a group, of accounts.

A recent trend is the emergence of specialized firms, such as boutiques and media buying services. This trend has been accompanied by scrambled advertising services, where individual services offer a diverse selection of related services. Advertisers have been taking on more advertising tasks formerly left to agencies. These trends have resulted in a fragmentation of advertising functions and a blurring of once traditional lines of business.

Questions for Chapter 4

1. Why would a local retailer not use an advertising agency?

2. In what circumstances would a firm benefit by centralizing advertising functions at the corporate level?

3. What have been the main criticisms of brand management coming from advertising agencies? Do you think they are justified?

4. Does a corporate advertising department waste resources if brand managers work directly with outside advertising agencies?

5. List the major responsibilities of the advertiser and advertising agency.

6. What values might an advertiser derive from studying billings-income-employee relationships?

7. What are the advantages and disadvantages to a company in contracting with an advertising agency for full service?

8. What are the drawbacks to performing all advertising functions in-house?

Footnotes for Chapter 4

[1] Martin Mayer, *Madison Avenue, U.S.A.* (New York: Pocket Books, 1959), p. 15.

[2] Alfred E. Chandler, *Strategy and Structure* (Cambridge, Mass.: MIT Press, 1962), p. 14.

[3] M. S. Salter and W. A. Weinhold, "Diversification Via Acquisition: Creating Value," *Harvard Business Review* (July/August 1978), p. 166.

[4] Robert Crittenden, "Beckman Instruments Finds Blending of In-House, Outside Services Works Best," *Industrial Marketing* (February 1976), pp. 56–65.

[5] Harry L. Darling, "How Companies are Using Corporate Advertising," *Public Relations Journal* (November 1975), pp. 26–29.

[6] "How PR Executives Shape Corporate Advertising," *Public Relations Journal* (November 1976), pp. 32–33; "Public Relations Role in Corporate Advertising," *Public Relations Journal* (November 1977), pp. 34–35.

[7]See Victor P. Buell, "The Changing Role of the Product Manager in Consumer Goods Companies," *Journal of Marketing* (July 1975), p. 5; R. M. Gray and J. B. Wilkinson, "Advertising in the Corporate Structure," R. Barton, ed., *Handbook of Advertising Management* (New York: McGraw-Hill, 1970), p. 3.

[8]"Marketing and Advertising at GM," *Industrial Marketing* (March 1979), pp. 68–74.

[9]See Terry Haller, "An Organizational Structure To Help You In The '80s," *Advertising Age* (August 25, 1980), pp. 45–46.

[10]See Robert S. Marker, "Advertising Management in Transition," *Industrial Marketing* (June 1979), pp. 64–66.

[11]"The Brand Manager: No Longer King," *Business Week* (June 9, 1973), pp. 58–66.

[12]Buell, "Changing Role of the Product Manager," p. 6.

[13]Nancy Giges, "Brand Manager Competition Waning?" *Advertising Age* (April 28, 1980), pp. 88–90.

[14]Also see U.S. Dept. of Commerce, *1977 Census of Service Industries SC 77-S-1*, pp. 1–13, 1–99.

[15]Edward Buxton, *Creative People at Work* (New York: Executive Communications, Inc., 1975), pp. 51–57.

[16]See Roger Patterson, "In-House Agency has Faster Reaction Time," *Industrial Marketing* (August 1979), p. 76; Charles L. Leighton, "In-house Agencies Can Produce Creative 'On Target' Programs More Economically," *Industrial Marketing* (February 1976), pp. 66–67.

[17]See Gary Lewis, "In-house vs Full Service Agency: Why Not Consider a Consortium," *Industrial Marketing* (June 1979), pp. 68–74; M. E. Ziegenhagen, "Survey: Advertisers Continue Trend From Full-Service Agencies," *Advertising Age* (December 26, 1977), pp. 32–33.

[18]Robert E. McGhee, "Lever Exec Tells His Media Cost-cutting Methods," *Advertising Age* (September 26, 1977), p. 76.

The Advertiser-Agency Relationship

The advertising budgets of many consumer goods producers well exceed net after-tax profits. Yet these vast sums are often entrusted to agents who haven't the slightest connections to the banking or financial industries. These outside companies not only disburse advertising funds, but do much of the planning as to what these expenditures will buy.

This chapter examines the key aspects of client-agency relationships from the standpoint of the advertiser. Specifically, it seeks to answer such important questions as:

- **What advantages are to be gained by employing an advertising agency?**
- **What criteria are used in the selection of an advertising agency?**
- **What methods are available for compensating agencies for their work?**
- **How can an advertiser evaluate and control the performance of an advertising agency?**

ADVERTISING AGENCIES AS CHANNEL MEMBERS

As advertising is part of the marketing mix, so are organizations which perform advertising functions as part of a larger whole. Such firms are subsumed in a marketing system referred to as distribution channels. All goods and services in our economy flow from producer to consumer through these organized conduits.

Channels of distribution consist of two types of organizations, middlemen and facilitating agencies. Firms dealing in advertising are of the latter kind. Like common carriers, advertising agencies do not partake directly in transactional processes. But their functions are allied in varying degrees with transactions of all kinds. Advertising tries to stimulate sales, and in some instances, to brace up buyer-seller relationships after the fact.

It is for this reason that marketers must give thoughtful consideration to their choice of an advertising agency, provided they cannot do the whole job themselves. That choice will ultimately affect their channel relationships in some way.

Companies regard the channel members with whom they deal—their suppliers, their distributors, their agents—as long-term participants in their distribution system. It takes time, effort, and money to build up an efficient network. It is a long range undertaking. Advertising agencies are looked upon in the same way as other channel members, as valuable economic entities which are not to be turned over like inventory. Though agency switches make headlines in the trade press, the monetary value of these changes amount to a small fraction of total advertising volume. Perhaps this is why account shifts make headlines; they are out of the ordinary. In 1981, some six percent of advertising billings moved from one agency to another.[1]

Advertising agency relationships are marked by stability, firmness, conservatism and not by changeability, unsteadiness, erraticism. This is not to say that discord and friction do not exist. They emphatically do. But most differences are settled amicably or tolerated patiently without breaks in ongoing associations. Ruptures are undesirable on many counts. They hinder smooth marketing operations. They put undue strains on company personnel. They may, depending upon the relative importance of advertising, prove quite costly. If at all possible, discontinuity is something to be avoided. One essential for reaching this wished-for end is to select the right advertising agency in the first place.

NATURE OF THE ADVERTISER-AGENCY RELATIONSHIP

What is the right agency for achieving a sound business relationship? The question defies an exact answer. It is contingent at best. It depends mainly upon two factors: marketing requirements and the internal capabilities of the firm. Because these are highly variable, the right agency for one firm is not necessarily the right one for another.

When advertising is comparatively unimportant, agency functions tend to be confined to those of communication. Illustrative of this pattern are products destined for the industrial market. Firms plying this line of business stress personal selling. A reliance on their own sales force enables companies to exercise greater control over their distribution channels. A client possessing these primary marketing skills is not apt to demand them from agencies. Instead, the services most wanted are those pertaining to communication.[2]

Advertising agencies are not likely to offer expertise in fields outside their main sphere of competence. Working with small advertising budgets, the purely industrial agency cannot afford the luxury of increasing overhead by hiring specialists drawn from diverse marketing areas. In fact, the talented, aggressive agencies have tried to transform themselves from industry-oriented shops into general advertising practitioners. Twenty-five years ago the two best known industrial agencies were the Basford Company and Fuller, Smith & Ross. Today, both firms are part of Creamer, Lois, FSR, whose public relations department has been trying hard to impart an image of creative consumer advertising. Other agencies with strong capabilities in industrial advertising—Marsteller, Rumrill-Hoyt, Griswold-Eshleman, and Ketchum McLeod—have not given up their traditional source of revenue. But they have concentrated their new business efforts on soliciting accounts for consumer products, because these offer the greatest opportunities for agency growth and profits.[3]

Some consumer goods manufacturers and service companies find their situations much like those of industrial marketers. Advertising is of little significance. This is particularly true for products that are complex, technical, or custom-made. Insurance, for example, is closely related to underwriting. Ground transportation companies see their critical variables as routes, schedules, and rates. Many financial organizations, like their industrial counterparts, focus on personal selling and customer service.

Companies do not usually try to cultivate marketing skills on the outside. These are regarded as a last resort, to be used only when dictated by necessity. Companies make every effort to develop them internally. When nonadvertising factors dominate a business, there is even less reason to demand such expertise from agencies. Consequently, agency activities in these industries are tightly constricted, limited mainly to creative and media assignments. Agency functions tend to be simple and direct; responsibilities cover advertising only. Agencies do not get involved in other facets of marketing.

In the past decade, advertising agencies have also been moving in the direction of piecemeal services. Specialized firms such as boutique shops and media buying services emphasize this trend. But today, even full-service agencies are willing to offer their talents on a project basis. Depending upon its needs, a firm can buy such individual services from agencies as direct mail assignments, point-of-purchase, audiovisual and film, product and package design, sales promotion, exhibits, trade shows, and public relations. Agency functions sold on a project basis transform the client-agency relationship into one which resembles the arms-length behavior of a customer with respect to suppliers. A goodly portion of industrial advertising gives this sort of appearance.

Large advertising budgets typical of many consumer goods industries tend to move the agency towards the mainstream of marketing. When advertising is the dominant factor in the marketing mix, the agency automatically plays a central role in marketing operations. Here, advertising is marketing for all intents and purposes, and agencies become active participants in company planning.

Under certain circumstances, an agency is drawn into a similar position even when products exhibit low advertising intensities. One such occasion is when advertising expenditures are small as compared with sales volume but bulk large in total. This happens in such industries as food, consumer durables, and airline travel. The big three auto manufacturers, with an advertising-to-sales ratio of about one percent, collectively, spent almost $881 million on advertising in 1981. General Electric has approximately the same advertising-sales percentage but a total advertising bill that exceeds $164 million. Though amounting to less than two percent out of every sales dollar, the advertising tab for the five leading airlines that year ran to some $288 million.[4]

The sheer size of these expenditures gives eloquent testimony to the importance of advertising—important enough to be taken under active consideration and carefully scrutinized in market planning. As in industries with high intensities, advertising must be integrated with other elements of marketing, with any contemplated price change or sales promotion or product development project. The advertising agency thus figures prominently in the marketing plans of the client, no matter whether advertising is provided *à la carte* or across a full spectrum of services.

Advertising is perhaps the only activity in which an outside company is invited to take part regularly in operational decisions. These resolves can run into millions of dollars. With stakes that high, it behooves companies to choose their marketing assistants in the same way they select other long-term assets—on the basis of expected returns.

CRITERIA FOR SELECTING AN AGENCY

The idea of expected returns from agency effort is one that is bandied about by agencies themselves. Marion Harper, in the early 1960s, then head of McCann-Erickson, popularized the concept "advertising accountability." He proposed that advertising agencies show demonstrable outcomes flowing from their efforts. This same proposition has taken many different forms. It has been alluded to in numerous public relations pieces and new business presentations. Yet the notion is an elusive one, for the returns of advertising are difficult to measure.

Nevertheless, expectations are cogent influences in agency selection. Exact, measurable results may not be an accurate description of anticipated benefits. But companies seeking advertising agencies have well-defined standards by which to make a choice. Criteria which swing the greatest weight in the selection process cover four general areas: creative potential, size of the agency, experience with the product, and accounts currently being handled.

Agency Creativeness

Of all criteria, creativity is far and away the most important. It is avidly sought for in an agency because it is thought to make the greatest impact on advertising results, notwithstanding measurement obstacles. Creativity is precious at all times, but never more than when competitive products are highly similar. In these instances, product development by itself gives no single producer a competitive edge. If so, why would Tide be preferred by many more homemakers than Dash or Dreft or Fab? Why would Comet cleanser be the overwhelming choice of consumers over Ajax or Bon Ami? When all other things are equal, or nearly so, firms pin their hopes for a differential advantage on the persuasive power of advertising messages.

Creativity, like a passing thought, represents an intangible quality. How is it possible to judge whether an agency can provide creativity? Virtually all agencies can on demand muster up a contingent of success stories and display a portfolio of advertisements that received industry awards. The agency per se, however, is not the relevant element to be evaluated for creativity. Rather, it is the people who will be assigned to work on the account. It is their originality that counts, not that of the organization as a whole. It is they who will be producing the commercial messages for the brand. Yet there is no sure way of assessing the creative potential of individuals. The best method seems to be evaluation of past performance. Though final judgment may be deferred, the truest indicator of creative talent is the record of what an individual has previously created. Output is past deeds, not fair words.

There is also merit in the oft-cited recommendation for clients to insist that key individuals proposed for an account actively participate in the agency presentation.[5] This exposition, mockingly called "a dog and pony show" in advertising circles, usually comes at the last stages of the selection process. The few agencies which pass a client's preliminary screening are invited to give presentations.

These new business solicitations occasionally contain finished copy and artwork for the account. A format of this sort is known in the industry as a "speculative presentation." In some instances they come at the request of the prospective client. In others, they emerge from urging of agency executives who think that a more complete and polished presentation would give them the nod over their competitors. Either way, whether its source is the client or agency, the practice is highly controversial. Most firms in the industry frown upon it, and many advertising agencies have explicit policies against it, although the ethical-sounding enunciations may be violated with impunity when profits can be made by departing from the course of virtue. The greatest objection to speculative presentations is that agency resources are siphoned off from present clients and used to chase new accounts. Although some advertisers reimburse the agency for out-of-pocket costs, the remittance does not overcome all negatives. It is also doubtful that an agency working under severe constraints of time and money can turn out advertising that is typical of the job it would do under more normal conditions.

The conventional wisdom in advertising defines creativity in a restricted sense. Creative personnel are seen as those with training in the liberal and fine arts, and found exclusively in agency departments concerned with the composition of the advertising message, such as copy and art. Employees in account handling, marketing research and media departments are widely regarded as numbers people, necessary for the performance of administrative and management tasks. It's as though this part of an agency exists solely to provide support functions for copywriters, artists and broadcasting specialists so that they can generate creative output, called copy.

This view is eminently correct insofar as the copy, art, and audiovisual departments produce the actual advertisements. Since ads are arrangements of elements in new ways, the process of making up these commercial messages is a creative art. But creativeness is not precluded from other areas of agency operations.

If advertising is considered an economic activity, creativity takes on a broader meaning. It can be thought of as innovativeness as defined by Joseph Schumpeter, the first economist to highlight this quality as a driving force in the development of the Western world.[6] To Schumpeter, economic innovation meant any combination of productive inputs in new ways for the purpose of gaining a competitive advantage.

From an economic standpoint, any entrepreneurial function can be innovative. An account executive who proposes a new way of doing things can be as creative as a copywriter who composes a new headline. A new media format may call into being a novel concept for promotion. Even statistically-oriented marketing researchers, who talk in a strange, incomprehensible language, have the potential to think creatively. The psychologists who brought motivation research to marketing, people like Ernest Dichter, Burleigh B. Gardener and Hans Zeissel, admirably illustrate innovative qualities. They engaged in an art which many of their critics likened to black magic. But they turned out numerous new product concepts and advertising ideas during their illustrious careers. Thus, it can be demonstrated that if creativity is an important criterion for selection of an agency, it applies to all key personnel on an account.

Agency Size

Agency size must be fitted to the level of advertising expenditures. The association between the two stems from the agency's responsibility to provide clients with personnel and experience to a sufficient degree. This requirement drives advertisers of varying sizes to seek agencies at their own levels. Products that enjoy big budgets will gravitate towards large agencies; low budget brands will move towards smaller shops.

The matter of size is basically a matter of economics. The industry norm puts agency profit margins at about 20 percent of gross income before taxes. This figure is often used as a benchmark in cost-based fee arrangements.[7] Since overhead is factored into the bottom line estimate, allocated costs loom large in calculations of profitability. The larger the account, the broader the base over which to spread fixed costs. These overhead charges run high in large agencies, and so make small accounts unprofitable, unless somehow direct costs can be trimmed. But these reductions often lead to cutting corners, like putting in less time on an account than warranted, using less qualified personnel, or producing advertisements of inferior production quality. This behavior is undesirable for both agency and client. On the other hand, small agencies lack the necessary personnel for handling accounts which go beyond their normal scale of operations.

The nature of an account is also a factor in choosing an agency of appropriate size. Servicing requirements are not necessarily equal even though expenditure levels are the same. Some clients demand agencies with branch offices. This may occur when a company is engaged in cooperative advertising and its agency must work with groups of local distributors. A branch office requirement is actually a special case of a situation where clients place varying emphasis on individual markets.

For a given budget, highly uneven workloads appear when advertising weight varies from market to market. A spot television plan, for example, demands more extensive analyses and negotiating effort than a network buy. A magazine schedule made up of regional editions is similarly more complicated than one using national editions only. The larger agencies, with fuller staffs and branch offices, are better equipped to handle geographically-fractionated media schedules and sales promotion programs. To offset this size disadvantage, smaller agencies have organized themselves into networks. These are loose associations of noncompeting agencies located in many different parts of the nation. Affiliated members counsel and advise one another and, being familiar with local media and distribution outlets, can conceivably act as branch offices in carrying out assignments for distant associates.

A third consideration when choosing an agency of sufficient size is the quality of service. In small agencies, the principals are apt to give clients their personal attention. Many of these agency heads have built reputations while in the employ of large agencies and are apt to possess a high degree of expertise, usually along creative lines. The drawback of the small agency is that it cannot offer the range of services available at the larger shops.

The question of size also has a relative aspect. A client is thought to receive better service when the account represents a good-sized chunk of total agency billings. A client may thus have to consider a trade-off between the range of service and quality of service.

Product Experience

A number of agencies tend to specialize in particular kinds of products. Certain agencies are staffed to handle industrial accounts. Others are geared to service financial organizations, retail establishments, direct response marketers, and the like. Such specialization is, to a large extent, related to agency size. The larger the firm, the higher the probability that it would shun specialization. Larger agencies usually enjoy a client roster in diverse fields.

Nevertheless, even large agencies often become identified with particular categories of products and markets. This comes about in the normal course of business. For instance, an agency with a food account may be running a test kitchen in which dieticians conduct experiments with different food forms and menus. The agency may also have working arrangements with photographers and designers who are adept at creating appealing settings for advertised products. Thus, an agency with one food account in the house will have developed a capability which can be applied to a variety of food products. The same principles hold true for other lines. Agencies heavy in packaged goods and in the use of television would have evolved a style and expertise which could be used to advantage for similar lines. In any event, there is a certain amount of synergism that carries over from one account to another operating in analogous markets with similar products.

A corresponding philosophy of advertising seems to carry over as well. An agency which features a hard sell for one packaged good, for example, is prone to use the same approach for other similar items. This affords a prospective client an opportunity to judge an agency on the basis of performance with products resembling the client's.

Current Accounts

The accounts currently handled by an agency are not independent of its size or product experience. However, after allowing for these associated variables, the criterion of accounts turns out to be a negative factor. It is generally acknowledged that, with certain exceptions, an agency should not handle or solicit competitive accounts. This rule rests on the obvious premise that an agent, subservient to a principal, cannot serve two antagonistic masters at the same time. Lists of current accounts thus indicate to a future client which agencies to stay away from.

The question as to what constitutes a competitive account, however, is an open one. Agencies prefer the narrowest of definitions, that of substitutable items in the same product category. Advertisers espouse a broader interpretation, that of the company as the competitive unit. For example, Young & Rubicam handles Cheer detergent for Procter & Gamble and Betty Crocker cake mix for General Foods. Clearly, these two products are not competitive. But Procter and Gamble also competes against General Foods with its Duncan Hines line of cake mixes and with its Folger's coffee. Is Young & Rubicam therefore housing competitive accounts?

Present trends lend more and more credence to the narrow definition. Companies over the last two decades have moved steadily in the direction of product proliferation and greater diversity. A giant firm such as Procter & Gamble operates in such diverse fields as soaps, detergents, household supplies, cosmetics and shampoos, foods, skin and health care, beverages, and paper. In each of these product categories the company might produce multiple brands, some of which amount to better than half a dozen. In line with a policy of keeping competing brands in different advertising houses, the company would be hard pressed to find a major agency having no account that contests with P & G in some area. When the relentless fractionization of advertising is added to the diversification trend, a company basis for defining competitive accounts is rendered hopelessly impractical, if not intractably chaotic.

Yet gray areas exist, and differing interpretations come to the fore from time to time. Red Barn in 1976 reportedly pulled out of J. Walter Thompson because of the agency's interest in Pizza Hut.[8] Both chains are in fast foods but do not offer identical specialties. The same agency in 1979 lost a $25 million account when it apparently flouted Gillette's no-compete-anywhere policy by accepting a Shick assignment in Brazil.[9]

If an account conflict is anticipated, the company should spell out the details and come to an understanding with the agency at the very beginning. However, change is incessant and there can be no guarantee that controversy will be muted forever. Agencies are independent firms with interests which may diverge from those of their clients, and both cooperation and conflict will continue to characterize management in this sector of the distribution channel.

Exacerbating the problem has been the recent spate of agency mergers. These unions have sought to minimize account conflicts by a judicious choice of partners. But competitive accounts have not been eliminated entirely. One solution has been the holding company, pioneered in the agency business by McCann-Erickson. Each agency in the family operates as completely independent, giving and expecting nothing from the others. Only certain financial functions and administrative tasks are controlled by the parent company. This form of organization has been ostensibly successful in preserving revenue by halting the flight of clients which perceive an agency conflict of interest. But the holding company form of organization also foregoes economies that might be achieved by reducing overlapping functions of the operating units.

MULTIPLE AGENCY MANAGEMENT

Many companies employ more than one agency. This practice comes about from the dictates of circumstances and the predilections of clients.

One reason is the attempt to make the most out of agency specialization. A company branching off into unrelated businesses may employ agencies which have developed fine skills in these respective fields. A firm catering to both consumer and industrial markets can find it advantageous to appoint one agency to handle its consumer products and another to advertise its industrial lines. Or assignments can be divided on the basis of job types, such as product versus corporate advertising. There are an endless number of ways in which to exploit the specialized talents of advertising agencies.

Another reason for working with more than one agency is multiple brand marketing. In some product lines, such as packaged goods, marketers offer brands which compete with each other. The outstanding example is Procter & Gamble, which puts out more than a half dozen brands of detergent, each vying with the other for a share of the consumer dollar. The company sustains an internal environment that is highly competitive among its brand groups, even to the extent of each making superiority claims to the general public. From here it is only a small step to insist that no single agency carry more than one brand in any product category. Because P & G is a marketing leader, this one brand-one agency philosophy has been widely emulated. A number of multiple brand marketers, however, prefer to consolidate operations in one agency so as to get rid of redundancy.

A third reason for a multiple agency set up is the desire to avoid what some executives call agency inbreeding. They argue that several agencies offer broader experience and wider scope for creative talent than a single agency. They also think that interagency competition is highly beneficial, spurring agencies on to greater effort.

AGENCY COMPENSATION

There are two basic ways of compensating an agency. The first is the billings-based method, known in the industry as the commission system. The second is the cost-based method, popularly referred to as the fee system. Both methods have numerous variations, and can be combined with each other in different arrangements to produce hybrid-like forms.

The exact method of compensation is the outcome of negotiations between advertiser and agency. All sides agree that agencies should receive fair pay for their work. But there can be different versions of what is fair and different opinions about the means of assuring fairness. At any rate, negotiations are greatly influenced by the specific nature of an account—its size, its risks, and its requirements.

Commission System

The commission system is the oldest and traditional method of agency compensation. It has its roots deep in the past, going back to the nineteenth century space brokers. These agents sold space for publications and were paid a commission on business they brought to their employer.

Despite the transformation of the space broker from a media representative to an agent of the advertiser, the commission system has persisted over the years. Basically, it works with extreme simplicity. An agency retains a percentage, usually 15 percent, of the value of all advertising it places in media. This is accomplished by billing the client for the gross

TABLE 5–1 *Agency Payables and Receivables under a Commission System*

Agency Bills Client

Magazine space	$50,000
Art and production	10,000
Charges for art and production @ 17.65%	1,765
Total bill to client	$61,765

Agency Pays Vendors

Magazine space costs	$50,000
Less: 15% discount on space cost	7,500
Agency total space cost	42,500
Art and production cost	10,000
Total agency payments	52,500
Agency gross income (receivables minus payables)	$ 9,265

media expenditure and taking a 15 percent discount when paying for the space or time which has been contracted. Supplies and services bought on the outside are charged for accordingly. The agency adds a markup to the client's bill, customarily 17.65 percent. This markup derives from the idea that a 15 percent commission should be based on the sales price received by a broker—the price to the reseller plus the selling margin. Thus, a $17.65 markup on an out-of-pocket expense of $100 is equivalent to a 15 percent commission on an item selling for $117.65 ($17.65/$117.65 = .15).

To illustrate how the commission system works, suppose an agency buys magazine space for a client worth $50,000. Its out-of-pocket expenditures for art, type and film negatives run to $5,000. The relevant financial calculations can be seen in Table 5–1.

Agency revenue derived from the transactions shown in Table 5–1, labeled gross income, amounts to $9,265. This is the difference between what an agency takes in and pays out for placing and producing the advertisement. In the industry's accounting procedures, gross income comprises commissions, service charges and fees. Any discount for prompt payment, usually given by media at terms of 2/10 net 30 days, accrue to the advertiser. The reason for rebating cash discounts is because agencies do not finance clients out of their own funds. They send out their bills in advance of due dates for accounts payable to media and other vendors, and pay after they receive the money from their clients. Otherwise, agency working capital would be quickly exhausted.

Over the years, the commission system has been vigorously berated by advertisers even while it was being used. The first sturdy blow to its rationale was struck by an Association of National Advertisers-sponsored study, conducted by Frey and Davis in 1958. The main criticisms leveled against the commission system, well-founded now as then, were as follows:

1. Commissions are not necessarily related to the cost of a service.
2. Commissions give agencies incentives to increase costs.
3. If all other things are constant, an agency has a vested interest in media plans which are easiest to administer.
4. Although the agency is by contract an agent of the advertiser, payments for the service are made by media.

These conclusions raise a number of urgent issues. First, it becomes patently obvious that one client may be paying more than the service is worth while another may be underpaying. The 15 percent commission package also hides unnecessary payments by all clients, encouraging them to order services because they seemingly come free. Consequently, the system spawns a waste of resources.

Second, the commission system has built-in biases for escalating costs. The fixed percentage of media and out-of-pocket charges makes higher costs yield higher gross incomes. Agencies are then provided incentives for recommending bigger budgets and benefiting from price increases by suppliers.

Third, the system tenders premiums to agencies operating with efficient media plans but not necessarily with effective ones. Given a budget of fixed size, an agency can increase its profits if its media schedule is attended by low internal administrative costs. Network television, for example, requires less effort than spot television in practically all phases of operations—planning, execution, and monitoring. The commission system thus tempts agencies into recommending programs with comparatively low administrative charges regardless of their effectiveness. Nor is this cost reduction passed on to clients.

Fourth, the commission system reflects a form of payment born in an age that is no more. It made sense when agencies acted as space brokers for publications and were paid a commission by their principals. But for media today to pay agencies for services rendered to a third party is an anachronism, a practice hopelessly out of tune with a changed world. The logic once offered as an intellectual defense of the system no longer rings true.

Variations of the Commission Method

The incidence of the traditional agency compensation method has experienced a continual decline. The Association of National Advertisers (ANA), in 1976, estimated that about two-thirds of its members paid agencies in accordance with some billings-based method. The percentage had fallen from 78 percent in 1974, when another ANA study was reported.[10]

The survey also noted considerable flexibility within the 15 percent commission framework. The most frequent deviations from the standard commission system were of four kinds: fixed percentages, variable commissions, profit-based rates, minimum-maximum rates.[11]

Changes in Fixed Percentages This method raises or lowers the negotiated commission from the normal 15 percent whenever that level is considered to be inequitable. Increases are likely to occur when budgets are small and advertisements are spread among many low-priced media vehicles. A situation of this sort is common to industrial marketing firms which operate in many different business lines. Larger commissions, which in effect add up to supplemental payments, allow agencies to realize "normal" profits from their endeavors in unfavorable environments.

Contrariwise, commissions are apt to be decreased when the standard 15 percent rate showers agencies with windfall profits. This can happen with large television budgets which schedule the same commercial to be run over and over on a network lineup. In such instances, the agency will rebate to the client a portion of its customary 15 percent commission received from media.

Variable Commission Rates Advertising often involves conditions in which agency profits soar rather quickly after the budget reaches a certain level. This occurs when incremental costs are low compared with incremental advertising expenditures. Agencies operating in such fortunate circumstances are recipients of abnormally high profits by virtue not of their own efforts but of their clients' budget allocations. Agency effort here is largely irrelevant with respect to profits. To redress the balance, some contracts call for variable commission rates. That is, the contracting parties agree on a commission schedule with a sliding rate scale for successive levels of advertising expenditures. An example of such a schedule might be as follows:

Media Budget	*Commission Rate*
First $8,000,000	15%
Next $1,000,000	14%
Next $1,000,000	13%
.	.
.	.
.	.

Profit-based Rates This method attempts to adjust commissions to profits agencies would normally earn under a traditional setup. The standard system literally defines an agency's gross income as 15 percent of capitalized sales. Using the sales figure as a base, after-tax profits tend to average out at about two percent. This figure merely expresses profit as a percentage of billings. Allowing for a certain amount of variation, the norm might then be established as an interval going from 1½ percent to 2½ percent of capitalized sales. Should profit fall below the 1½ percent mark, the advertiser would make up the deficit. Conversely, any excess above 2½ percent would be returned to the client on a before-tax basis. An illustration of how profit-based rates work is as follows:

Suppose an account provides an agency with $1,000,000 in commissions paid out by media. This sum is equivalent to $6,666,666 of capitalized sales ($1,000,000/.15 = $6,666,666). An after-tax profit of between 1½ percent and 2½ percent would set normal margins at between $100,000 and $166,667. Clients, however, prefer to calculate profit margins on a pretax basis because agencies can influence the bottom line in many ways after meeting tax obligations. At any rate, if agency profits were to fall between the 1½ percent and 2½ percent, adjusted for tax considerations, neither rebates nor supplementary payments would take place. A bottom line below the prescribed minimum would bring forth additional funding to lift agency earnings up to the minimum level. Any excess profits, calculated on a pretax basis, would be restored to the client.

Minimum-Maximum Rates This sort of compensation plan places upper and lower limits on allowable commissions. In contrast to profit-based methods, there are no guarantees of profit margins. Rather, the contracts seek to build desirable management practices by combining cost and commission philosophies.

One version of this form of agency compensation is that of Richardson-Vicks, Inc. The pharmaceutical firm pays its agency an amount that equals cost plus a 20 percent markup if agency compensation turns out to be less than 15 percent of billings. For example, an account of $5,000,000 in billings would yield the agency a gross income of $750,000 were it to operate under the traditional 15 percent commission system ($5,000,000 × .15 = $750,000). This amount by conventional standards should be sufficient to defray all costs and expenses, including normal profit. This figure then constitutes an upper limit. But when actual costs are lower than "standard" costs, a downward adjustment is made from the 15 percent standard. For example, suppose that agency costs amounted to $600,000. In that event, the firm would pay the agency an additional $120,000 ($600,000 × .20 = $120,000). This would bring total agency compensation up to $720,000 ($600,000 + $120,000 = $720,000). The difference between the standard, in this case $750,000, and $720,000 is regarded as a savings. This amount is then divided equally between agency and client, so that both firms benefit from cost reduction.

Cost-based System

Cost-based methods for remunerating agencies are of comparatively recent vintage. Since fee arrangements are related to work done, the price of a service is tied more closely to its costs. This relationship between costs and factor prices is seen as bringing greater efficiency to advertising management.

The attempt to force prices into line with costs has also been responsible for important changes in advertiser-agency relationships. In this system, client companies, which are the ultimate sources of advertising funds, assume more direct control in the application of their resources. The fee method literally mandates that advertisers insinuate themselves into what was previously the domain of agency decision-making, and give direction to the advertising process. The price of an agency's service depends upon the work that the client requests. The advertiser thus regulates its payments to agencies by parceling out the work. The advertising firm is, more than before, thrust into internal agency matters—such as specific personnel to be used, work schedules to be set, and cost accounting procedures used to keep track of costs. Advertising companies no longer have agency services at their beck and call as under the 15 percent umbrella. Advertisers now are obliged to analyze their needs and to negotiate prices for having the required services carried out. These tasks necessitate a thorough understanding of an agency's cost structure and diligent cost-accounting procedures.

Methods for compensating agencies on the basis of costs display a number of varieties. But all these different plans can readily be grouped into three basic categories: fixed fee contracts, cost plus agreements, and incentive programs.[12]

Fixed Fee Contracts As the name implies, with a fixed fee arrangement agency and client agree on work to be done, stipulating in advance prices to be charged. This method is usually employed for specific projects. Because all terms are agreed upon in advance, both negotiating parties must make work estimates. The agency must be sure of the job specifications so that there will be no surprises later and that the fee will cover all costs and allow for a fair profit. The client must place some value on the project so that the price paid the agency can be compared with expected benefits. The advertising firm has the option of getting competitive bids on the work in order to assess going market prices. Decisions, however, cannot avoid the encroachment of subjective elements, for advertising services are not uniform or standardized. They possess qualitative characteristics which are extremely difficult to evaluate.

Fixed fees work best when jobs are simple and clear-cut, so that few misunderstandings crop up. Other circumstances which favor fixed fees are those in which the contracting parties have had a prior working relationship which was carried off in a satisfactory manner.

Cost Plus Agreements An agreement of this sort is far and away the most popular cost-based method. It discloses an incredible number of variations. Regardless of the exact form, fees are essentially constructed by calculating the direct costs expended on an account, adding an allocation for overhead, and factoring into the sum a markup for profits. The fee formula in essence thus becomes direct costs plus overhead plus profits. A summary of an agency fee proposal to a hypothetical prospect is illustrated in Table 5–2.

The items over which clients can exercise a high degree of control are those expended directly on the account—salaries, fringe benefits, unemployment insurance, travel and entertainment, communication, and shipping charges. These direct costs comprise the bulk of agency expenses. It therefore becomes incumbent upon clients to take an active part in directing and managing these monetary flows.

Agency direct labor costs can be arrived at in several ways. One possibility is the "agency team" method. The first step here is to postulate the time requirements for the group or team working on the account. The next step is to estimate salaries and related payments. Because calculations of individual hourly rates are cumbersome, most agencies use standard costs, which are later adjusted to actual employee remuneration. Table 5–3 illustrates how direct costs can be estimated.

TABLE 5–2 *Fee Proposal to Company X*

Type of cost	*Amount*
Estimated Direct Costs:	
Salaries and fringe benefits	$200,000
Direct facility utilization	40,000
Out-of-pocket expenditures	24,000
Total direct costs	$264,000
Allocated company overhead	160,000
Total costs	$424,000
Profit @ 25%	106,000
Total annual fee	$530,000
Monthly fee	$ 44,167

TABLE 5–3 *Direct Labor Cost Estimates*

Job function	*Estimated hours spent on account*	*Hourly rate*	*Annual labor cost*
Management supervisor	450	$65.00	$29,250
Account executive	900	35.00	31,500
Research supervisor	230	20.00	4,600
Creative personnel	650	45.00	29,250
Art supervisor	320	30.00	9,600
Media planning	420	20.00	8,400
Production coordinator	540	15.00	8,100
Traffic	200	8.00	1,600
Accounting	300	12.00	3,600
Total	4,010		$125,900

Another application of direct costing is the so called "composite man" method. This technique begins by estimating the direct labor requirements for an account. For example, the schedule might specify an account executive and one copywriter working full time, a media buyer spending half of his or her available time on the account, a research person putting in a quarter of his total time, etc. The sum yields a total figure of employees working on the account throughout the year. The agency would then rely on its historical cost record to estimate a cost per person and update this figure by anticipated rises in salaries and related expenses for the current year. These estimates are usually reconciled with actual costs by standard cost accounting methods. The adjustment normally considers the cost per person as a fixed amount. This system benefits agencies which are successful in keeping salaries in line with projections.

The management of work schedules to a surprising degree affects production costs, another area in which important savings can be achieved. According to Arthur Bellaire, who heads his own consulting firm, the greatest enemy of cost control in television is the rush into production.[13] It may take an agency several weeks, or even months, to work up a final storyboard. With little time left in which to produce the commercial, pressure is put on people involved in its production. Outside studios are asked to make bids while lacking full details or specifications. Under such circumstances, they are most likely to pad their bids for possible oversights and unforeseen emergencies. Or the production houses may not be given adequate time to develop the best logistics for effecting the ideas of the creative team. These tactics include such matters as sets to be used, selection of sites, etc. Each combination of logistical elements carries its own price tag. Better forward planning in the utilization of agency personnel would go a long way to rectifying such deficiencies.

Tight schedules also raise costs for print production as well. It is common for agencies to send copy to composition houses with orders for overnight delivery of type proofs or galleys. Night work usually bears a hefty premium. Worse yet, alterations are made after type has been set, and even after mechanicals are made up. These last minute changes incur disproportionately higher costs. Only an inspection of itemized bills would reveal the amount of overpayments attributable to poor management in production.

Incentive Programs Unlike cost-based methods, incentive systems tie agency compensation to sales results. These methods are used sparingly because of the difficulty in isolating advertising's contribution from that of other marketing variables. It may be appropriate for direct response marketing or certain advertising-intensive situations, but hardly for most national brands.[14]

Incentive plans resemble the quota systems of salesperson's compensation, and like them, come in different shapes and sizes. Illustrative of the general category is Romrill-Hoyt's "profit on performance" compensation plan.[15] It works as follows:

Given an advertising budget, the client and agency jointly set a sales goal. If that objective is reached, the agency is awarded its full profit, calculated as 20 percent of costs on a before tax basis. Revenue over and above the established sales quota produces extra income for the agency. But the additional revenue cannot exceed 100 percent of the profit norm. The Romrill-Hoyt plan contains a floor as well as a ceiling on profits from an account. Smaller than expected sales call for agency profits to be decreased accordingly, but they cannot be negative. Net costs define the lower limit.

AGENCY EVALUATION

The advertiser approval function is still regarded as a necessary means of controlling advertising operations. But it is no longer accepted as sufficient. Monitoring, by almost universal acclaim, has become a close companion of good business practice. How else can management know if its policies are being adhered to? Or if its programs on paper followed in fact? Or if its objectives are being met expeditiously? The desire to control an operation rather than being controlled by it necessitates getting feedback on what is being done and on the consequence of those actions. Only then can organizations take measures to bring actual performance into line with their expectations, and real outcomes with desired goals.

Monitoring of advertising includes work performed by agencies. Many such assessments are done informally. But the trend has been emphatically in the direction of formal, systematic evaluations, especially when advertising involves substantial sums of money. Like other bureaucratic procedures, once begun, the evaluations become institutionalized. They are repeated in a fixed pattern, undergoing alterations from time to time, but accepted as standard operating procedure. The motivating force is control. There are basically two types of agency assessments, a financial audit and a qualitative one, both of which can be carried out together.

The Financial Audit

The financial audit concerns itself with how an advertising agency operates as a business. Assessments that are financial in nature take place periodically, with intervals varying from company to company. Most agencies can expect auditors from client companies to visit them at least once a year. These audits usually include verification of costs and expenses, the number of hours various personnel worked on accounts, and analysis of payments to media and outside suppliers.

The popularity of financial audits spring from the proposition that agencies are clothed with fiduciary responsibilities. They consummate numerous transactions on behalf of others. They enter into contracts which are legally binding to their clients. These actions, in legal parlance, are proper when they fall within the scope of authority granted by the principal. The financial audit is the chief means of ascertaining whether an agency is discharging adequately its obligations of stewardship.

Fiduciary mismanagement carried out with intent to defraud is rare among agencies. According to Price Waterhouse & Co., the greatest problem is a complicated billing and payment system which lets errors slip in easily—bills going to clients for costs never incurred, and payments going to media and production houses for services never rendered.[16] Taking care of bills, both incoming and outgoing, should be more or less routine. But if poor monitoring exists, the system gets bogged down in error-prone procedures. Consequently, financial audits often serve to improve agency accounting practices and to put agency functions on a sound business basis. Spokespersons for Price Waterhouse recommend the following four basic principles to reduce irregularities:[17]

1. The client company must make sure that it approves in advance every expenditure incurred on its behalf by the agency.
2. Every agreement or approval of an action should be put in writing. The documentation should also be readily accessible.
3. Possibilities of cost overruns should be cleared ahead of time. This will reduce misunderstandings later.
4. Procedures must be carefully monitored to make sure that all parties involved adhere to the terms of a contract.

Yet shoddy, if not shady, practices are occasionally discovered even in the most reputable agencies. Ford, the car manufacturer, audited its agency, J. Walter Thompson, in 1978, and uncovered billing irregularities which reportedly ran into the high six figures. The agency's New York art subsidiary was said to have billed the agency at retail rates, and Thompson embellished the bill with another 17.65 percent, in effect taking a double markup. Outrageously high entertainment expenses were also reported as a point of contention. Agency charges for wining and dining Ford executives purportedly ran far higher than allowable maximums set by the auto manufacturer. An Eastman Kodak audit of the same agency was said to have turned up a number of other irregularities.[18]

A financial audit which embraces production activities is much more than a perfunctory examination of receivables and payables.[19] All related services are analyzed in relation to established standards and explicit goals. For example, practically every company seeks to achieve a given level of productive quality at minimum cost. Records would then reveal if an agency had obtained competitive bids, compared them item for item, and negotiated contracts which were cost effective. Reasons for budget overruns and possible violation of client instructions are other matters into which auditors delve.

The timing of agency payments to media and other suppliers is another prime area of concern. Two separate issues are involved: the proper use of clients' money and liability for agency debts.

Client payments form a relatively high proportion of the cash flowing through agency bank accounts. Without adequate safeguards, pressures build up in times of financial stringency. Remittances earmarked for specific purposes can easily come to be regarded as "floats." Money received from promptly paying clients might be diverted to financing agency operations, or even to meeting debts of slower paying clients.

Rumors of agency finagling always rise along with high interest rates. In early 1979 it was estimated that some 30 percent of agencies had broadcast bills outstanding for more than 60 days. Amounts ranged from small sums to thousands of dollars. Charges abounded that agencies were slowing down payments to media and funneling cash into commercial paper.[20]

There are actually few documented instances of agencies manipulating the float to make extra profits by investing clients' money. But, the opportunities for financial juggling are there and gains can be substantial. For example, an agency billing $350 million collects from clients about $1 million on an average day. If that agency can slow down payments for just one day, it has $1 million to invest for one year. At 15 percent interest, a heady rate that has prevailed for considerable periods of time in recent years, the agency would stand to make $150,000 extra before taxes. A deferral of payments for two days would add up to $300,000, three days $450,000, etc. The exact amount of profit would depend on the size of the float and the timing of payments. More than anything else, financial audits are preventive devices. They discourage agency personnel from yielding to the temptations which high money costs dangle, and so help preserve ethical standards.

The issue of liability concerns itself with another matter. Who is responsible for an unpaid balance? This question has been hotly debated in advertising circles for close to a decade. It came to the forefront in 1972 when Lennen & Newell, a leading agency along Madison Avenue, was plunged into bankruptcy and left behind a horde of unhappy creditors. One such claimant was CBS, which brought suit for payment against the agency's former clients on grounds that as principals they were liable for the actions of their agency. Stokely Van Camp, a food processor which had paid all its bills to the defunct agency, was sued for more than $450,000.

After years of litigation, the courts ruled in favor of the advertiser. But the question of advertiser liability is still not clear. The court supposedly upheld the "sole liability" concept, a position long supported by the American Association of Advertising Agencies and its large member firms. But the case applied to litigants in particular circumstances, and left enough gray areas to cloud the general issue of client-agency relationships.

The court said that Stokely Van Camp was not liable for the debt because Lennen & Newell was an independent contractor, not an agent. Weighing heavily in that decision were three sets of circumstances:[21]

1. There was no written contract that expressly conferred authority on the agency.
2. Stokely Van Camp did not appear to direct closely the activities of the agency.
3. CBS made no attempt to inform the client that bills were not being paid until the collapse occurred, ostensibly to keep the agency's goodwill.

It thus seems that the legal status of agent or contractor is created by the advertiser. An agent arises only when a principal confers in writing specific authority to draw up, modify, or terminate contracts. Or an agent relationship can be apparently established, in a legal sense. This is done when both parties behave as though agent authority has been bestowed and media, relying on such behavior, accept contracts from the agent in the name of the advertiser.[22] Supervision and auditing of bill-paying activity contribute to the behavior which gives rise to agent-principal relationships in fact.

Even if an advertiser tries to avoid double jeopardy, paying its agency and still being liable, it may not be able to do so. In 1975, the Institute of Broadcasting Financial Management recommended to its member stations a contract form which holds advertisers liable if they are told of an agency's delinquency.[23] Similarly, numerous publishers specify on their contracts that in the event of an agency's failure to pay, liability is assigned to the advertiser.[24] Lastly, the concept of sole liability does not extend outside of media for contracts in the name of a client.

The Qualitative Audit

The qualitative audit focuses on the procedures and programs by which a firm expects to attain certain results in the marketplace.[25] The ultimate value of this assessment lies in the firm's ability to correct relevant shortcomings in the recognition of market opportunities, the formulation of advertising messages, and the use of corporate resources. This audit covers both planning and implementation.

Many companies have formalized these efforts at agency evaluation, though there remains considerable variation in methods and styles. For example, Borden Inc. rates its agencies twice a year on the basis of 100 points.[26] The largest part of the total score, sixty percent, deals with agency performance in achieving a share of market goal. The analysis assumes that Borden can measure the sales effects of agency efforts. The remaining forty percent of the score is split 20-20 between creativity and cooperation, defined as the diligence with which an agency services an account. The twenty points assigned to creativity are split as follows:

eight points for market strategy formulation

four points for conceptual ability

two points for television creative ability

two points for print creative ability

two points for new product development

Scott Paper, another firm with a formal method of agency evaluation, reviews the work of its agencies three times a year. As part of its creative assessment, Scott rates message output, for which it uses the following criteria:[27]

Consistency in copy strategy

Conveyance of clear, simple benefits or relevant selling ideas

Ability for attention-getting inherent in the message

Integration of visual and verbal elements

Emphasis on "product is hero" without too much "theater"

Advertising believability

Communication leading to cognition of consumer choice

Most of these formal systems involve three elements: criteria for evaluation, a notion as to the relative importance of each criterion, and a score for agency performance on each criterion. A scheme of this sort can be expressed as a summated rating, which multiples the score by the weight for each criterion and adds the resulting values to derive an overall rating. A possible system of this kind is visualized in Table 5–4.

As shown in Table 5–4, a scoring system devised for illustrative purposes, each criterion is given a weight (f) in accordance with its presumed importance. The sum of all weights add up to 1.0. The ratings (X) are set on

TABLE 5–4 *Example of Summated Ratings for Agency Evaluation*

Criterion	Criteria Weight (f)	1	2	3	4	5	Total
1	.30			X			.90
2	.20		X			X	1.00
3	.10				X		.40
4	.10		X				.20
5	.08					X	.40
6	.08		X				.24
7	.05				X		.20
8	.05					X	.25
9	.02				X		.08
10	.02				X		.08
	1.00						3.75

Header spanning columns 1–5: *Rating (X)*

a scale which has five points, 1–5. Other scale values are possible. If a hypothetical agency was rated five on all criteria, its overall score would be 5.0. This is the theoretical maximum. The checks indicate how one scorer might have rated his agency on the various criteria. The summated rating of this scorer adds up to 3.75, or 75 percent of the theoretical maximum. A rating system of this nature can be expressed mathematically as

$$R = \Sigma f_i x_i$$

where

R = overall rating
f_i = weight for the ith criterion
x_i = rating value for the ith criterion

The summated rating as a model for agency evaluation has a number of weaknesses. The glaring one is that it is subjective. But then, so are all other qualitative auditing methods. If more than one person does the rating, care must be exercised that all scorers interpret rating values in the same way. This might be done by setting forth exact definitions of what each value means with respect to each criterion.

Another difficulty is ascertaining the weights for the various factors on which agencies are rated. The danger always lurks that unimportant things will be overemphasized, or that really vital elements will be bypassed. The problem of interpretation also persists. What is a good score as opposed to a bad one? When does a rating, either partial or total, warrant corrective action. These decisions can only come with experience. Although formal systems do not by themselves solve these problems, they inaugurate systematic thinking about agency operations, and about their role in the broader framework of marketing.

SUMMARY

Advertising agencies form an important part of the distribution channel. The nature of the advertiser-agency relationship therefore depends on marketing requirements and capabilities of the client firm. The advertiser will select an agency to fit those needs.

The choice of an advertising agency rests upon four main criteria: creative ability, size, experience, and accounts currently being handled. An advertiser can actually perform all advertising functions with the exception of creating the commercial messages. This does not, however, detract from the importance of the other three criteria.

Advertising agencies are compensated either by a commission or by a cost-based method. The former is the traditional way and calls for a percentage, usually 15 percent, to be paid on billings placed for the client.

Though still widespread, this method has been declining in favor of the cost-based method.

The cost-based system is essentially a fee arrangement. The fee system has virtually forced advertisers to intrude into the internal operations of advertising agencies as never before. There are three basic categories of cost-based plans: fixed fee contracts, cost plus agreements, and incentive programs.

Two kinds of monitoring are carried on for the purpose of evaluating an advertising agency. One is the financial audit, which is handled by accountants. The other is a qualitative audit, which focuses on marketing programs and assessment of their results.

Questions for Chapter 5

1. Why would an industrial advertiser have less need for a full service agency than a packaged goods manufacturer?

2. If you were the advertising director of an insurance firm, how would you go about evaluating the creative capability of agencies?

3. Do you think it proper for companies to concern themselves with new business solicitations of their advertising agencies when, admittedly, they are independent businesses?

4. Should a company with a $15 million advertising budget seek a large advertising agency?

5. What are the pros and cons of a company with multiple brands in the same product line using different advertising agencies for each brand?

6. When would a company benefit from not contracting with an advertising agency for the traditional 15 percent commission?

7. Why would a company remunerating its agency by a profit-based method prefer to calculate the rate base before taxes?

8. Does a fixed fee system overcome the main objections to the conventional 15 percent commission system?

9. What major items should a financial audit cover?

10. What are the advantages of establishing a principal-client relationship instead of a buyer-contractor association?

11. Why would qualitative audits of advertising agencies differ from advertiser to advertiser?

Footnotes for Chapter 5

[1]Nancy Millman, "Record $1.4 Billion Changed Hands in '81," *Advertising Age* (February 1, 1982), p. 3.

[2]See Booz, Allen, Hamilton, *Management and Advertising Problems* (New York: Association of National Advertisers, Inc., 1965), pp. 44–47

[3]Donald H. Miller, "Justifying Role Vexes Business Admen," *Advertising Age* (June 12, 1978), p. 38.

[4]See *Advertising Age* (September 10, 1981).

[5]Henry Obermeyer, *Successful Advertising Management* (New York: McGraw-Hill Book Co., 1969), p. 72.

[6]Joseph A. Schumpeter, *The Theory of Economic Development*, R. Opie, trans. (Cambridge, Mass.: Harvard University Press, 1961), pp. 65–85.

[7]Association of National Advertisers, *Agency Compensation* (New York: Association of National Advertisers, Inc., 1979), p. 6.

[8]Louis J. Haugh, "Burger King Now Top Prize in Current Fast-food Shop Shuffle," *Advertising Age* (July 5, 1976), p. 1.

[9]John J. O'Connor, "Gillette Pulls $25 Million from JWT," *Advertising Age* (February 5, 1979), p. 2.

[10]"More Advertisers Shift to Fees, ANA Report Says," *Advertising Age* (May 10, 1976), p. 1.

[11]Association of National Advertisers, *Agency Compensation*, pp. 14–18.

[12]See *Agency Compensation*, pp. 14–18.

[13]Arthur Bellaire, "Why Do Some Advertisers Pay More While Others Pay Less?" *Advertising Age* (November 15, 1976), p. 50.

[14]Herb Zeltner, "Sounding Board: Clients, Admen Split on Compensation." *Advertising Age* (May 18, 1981), p. 64.

[15]*Agency Compensation*, pp. 115–116.

[16]Bernice Kanner, "Client Audits of Agencies Becoming More Common," *Advertising Age* (December 3, 1979), p. 10.

[17]Kanner, p. 10; also see Robert Roth, *A Guide to Accounting Controls for Advertising Agencies* (New York: Price Waterhouse & Co. 1979).

[18]"JWT Pays a Six-figure Sum to Ford Motor Co. After Audit," *Advertising Age* (November 28, 1978), pp. 1, 98.

[19]See Robert E. Roth, "Production Audits Aid Agency, Client," *Advertising Age.* (September 1, 1980), p. 36; Price Waterhouse & Co., *A Guide to Accounting Controls for Advertising Agencies* (New York: Price Waterhouse & Co., 1980).

[20]Colby Coates, "Broadcast Slow Pay Mounts, but It's Termed Under Control," *Advertising Age* (February 19, 1979), p. 3.

[21]Bob Donath, "Judge Backs Sole Liability Concept, Rules in Favor of Stokely vs CBS," *Advertising Age* (October 10, 1977), pp. 1, 111.

[22]Donald R. Holland, Lessons to Learn: How to Avoid Lennen & Newell's Fate," *Advertising Age* (April 9, 1979), p. 54.

[23]Bob Donath, "Who Has To Pay? Sole Liability Issue Awaits Court Action," *Advertising Age* (April 4, 1977), p. 4.

[24]Roy A. Heckerback, "You can—and Should—Audit How Well Your Agency Performs as Your Agent," *Industrial Marketing* (November 1976), p. 68.

[25] See Robert L. Anderson and Thomas E. Barry, *Advertising Management: Text and Cases* (Columbus, Ohio: Charles E. Merrell, 1979), pp. 431–437.

[26] Rance Crain, "How Agencies Are Evaluated: Will Run vs Share Increase," *Advertising Age* (October 25, 1976), pp. 3, 114.

[27] Nancy Giges, "How Scott Agency Reviews Aid Stability," *Advertising Age* (December 29, 1980), p. 29.

PART THREE

FORMULATING THE OPERATIONAL PLAN

6 *The Advertising Plan*

Modern management builds its operations from formally devised blueprints. These include written details as to what is to be done, how and when to do it, and what results are to be expected.

Since advertising is part of marketing, its plans are part of a larger system. Advertising is like a gear within gears, impelling some and in turn being impelled by others. For this reason, the chapter regards the advertising plan not merely as an entity by itself, but as a document related to other marketing activities.

This chapter analyzes:

- **Role of the marketing plan in formulating an advertising plan**
- **Main elements which comprise an advertising plan**
- **Method of setting advertising goals, both behavioral and nonbehavioral**
- **Positioning concept, and how it affects relationships between advertising and other marketing activities**
- **Models of rationality and involvement which, implicitly or explicitly, remain inherent in most advertising plans**

LEVELS OF ADVERTISING PLANNING

Advertising, like most business operations, has succumbed to the necessity of planning. This is particularly evident in large, diversified corporations, characterized by decentralized management and specialization. The plans, turned out as formal documents, serve various purposes. The main advantages of an advertising plan are:

1. It permits all elements given consideration to be combined into a united, cohesive whole.
2. It makes all assumptions and reasons for key recommendations explicit. More thoughtful operational programs are the result.
3. It evaluates alternative courses of action, and reduces the likelihood of important ones being overlooked.
4. It draws up a timetable for all activities and expenditures. This helps to coordinate the work of different departments and outside agencies.
5. It serves as a means of delegating authority for each task. All groups and individuals working on a project should know what is expected of them.
6. It creates the criteria for judging the quality of ongoing assignments.

Work can thus be approved, modified, or rejected on some kind of objective basis.

Planning for advertising may take place at many different levels within a corporation. Some plans come from corporate or divisional headquarters. These usually involve corporate advertising, which cannot stray too far from the top executive suites. Other advertising operations are only partly controlled by central management, such as broadcast purchases and coordination of advertising schedules to achieve maximum discounts. In these instances, individual units must still do their own media planning. But selection of specific media vehicles may be subject to negotiation between corporate planners and functional units, and sometimes choices may be legislated.

For the most part, however, an advertising campaign is many times removed from corporate planning. Advertising mainly entails the promotion of individual products, and in a number of instances, of closely related products handled as a group. As such, it is carried out at the operating levels within a corporation. Its procedures, as well as relationships of its participants, depend upon organizational structure and management style.

Product advertising, which consumes the largest share of all advertising expenditures, derives from the marketing plan of which it is a part. It is essentially a program or a series of programs for attaining marketing goals.

When advertising plays a subordinate role in marketing, advertising plans can best be formulated after the marketing plan is in place. This procedure is quite common with industrial advertising. When advertising is an important part of the marketing mix, or is intricately meshed with other promotional factors, its planning may take place concurrently with that of marketing. For example, product advertising in large department stores relies so heavily upon merchandising programs that schedules must be drawn up in conjunction with buyers and various functional departments. Brand managers of packaged goods often work with their advertising agencies on planning at the same time they are devising their marketing plans. If the two sets of plans are mutually dependent upon each other, it is evidently more efficient to do both simultaneously. Advertisers may seek assistance in drawing up a marketing plan from outside sources, and often from their advertising agencies. Companies without large marketing departments often find themselves short on planning capabilities. Final approval, nevertheless, is lodged with the advertiser. No matter how firms go about it, the advertising plan is a creature of the marketing plan, which in turn is almost always the responsibility of the advertiser.

THE MARKETING PLAN

The marketing plan is usually a formal document which goes by different names, depending upon the preferences of the company. All marketing

TABLE 6–1 *Main Parts of the Marketing Plan*

1. Situational Analysis
   a. Sales trends for the total product category and product types (units, dollars). It should include other categories, if interproduct competition exists.
   Sales trends by region, customer characteristics, distribution channels.
   b. Competitive data for principal competitors. The analysis should delineate competitive marketing strategies, market shares, promotional effort, pricing, distribution patterns.
   c. Trade relations by types of outlet, market, distribution channel. Included should be markups, discounts, cooperative programs.
   d. Problems and opportunities. These are inferences based on the above situational analysis.
2. Marketing Objectives
   a. Sales estimates over time in both dollars and units, market share, contributions to profits and overhead.
   b. Subfunctional objectives. These may include goals of a sales force, sales promotion, pricing, middlemen, physical distribution, advertising, inventory levels, technical service.
3. Strategy and Action Programs
   This section is the heart of the marketing plan. It should include exact details of the strategy, and methods by which it is implemented in order to achieve the firm's objectives.

Source: Adapted from Clarence E. Eldridge, *The Role and Importance of the Marketing Plan* (New York: Association of National Advertisers, 1966).

plans deal with activities which are associated with sales generation. They establish the outer parameters of a product's "mission" and spell out the specific marketing strategies and functions in minute detail.

The core of the marketing plan is taken up with the elements of the marketing mix, a topic which forms the backbone of many marketing books. For this reason, the subject is considered beyond the scope of this book. But, to understand how it shapes the advertising plan, it might be desirable to capsulize its main parts. This can be seen in Table 6–1.

Naturally, different firms will concentrate on different aspects of the marketing plan. But no matter what points are stressed, the advertising plan is really a subsection of the marketing plan.

ROLE OF THE MARKETING PLAN IN ADVERTISING

The advertising plan is derived from the marketing plan. The advertising plan takes the marketing plan as input and uses it to devise a set of advertising programs. From this standpoint, marketing decisions are primary. Advertising decisions are tactical ones, concerned with how to achieve through communication in mass media the goals of marketing.

The marketing plan includes two key decisions vital to advertising—the product to be offered and the market to be served. Both product and marketing strategy are prominent in the marketing plan.

The nature of the product, which is the consequence of the firm's product policy, restricts advertising as to what can be said. Unique attributes, superior quality, and specialized features facilitate the task of presenting the product to the public. Parity products which lack these characteristics are harder put for a promotional theme. Although advertisers have wide latitude, their claims must pass the test of substantiation to avoid legal action. Product characteristics thus provide references as to what can and cannot be communicated.

The markets to be served delineate to whom the messages are to be directed. Related to market definition are seasonality, size, and dispersion or concentration of buyers. Seasonality regulates the timing of commercial messages. Changes in spending must correspond to changes in sales. Seasonality may also exert an influence on the content of messages, for certain times of the year are associated with particular buying practices. For example, Christmas is linked with gift giving. Factors of size and dispersion to a large extent determine the choice of media. It would hardly make sense, for instance, to air a commercial on a network lineup if markets are small and localized.

Closely allied with the market definition are two related concepts, market potential and market segmentation. The latter is especially significant for consumer products.

A potential does not imply actual sales. According to the American Marketing Association, it is the "maximum possible sales opportunities for all sellers of a good or service." One author defined market potential as "the limit approached by market demand as industry marketing effort goes to infinity, for a given environment."[1]

For example, a firm producing a fluoride toothpaste might regard its market as being only families with children. Another manufacturer with a similar product might add young adults to the list of potential users. A third firm might stretch its definition of possible customers to take in more mature citizens. Or all three companies might cater to the same age groups but attach different degrees of importance to each.

The concept of market potential, though somewhat inexact and decidedly elastic, carries important ramifications for advertising. The process of denoting a theoretical maximum involves a description of marketing targets against which promotional efforts are directed. If this potential is defined too narrowly, opportunities will be lost. If the definition is too broad, advertising effort will be wasted on impractical goals. Overadvertising is often caused by an overreaching definition of market potential.

The theory of market segmentation refers to division of a whole market into smaller parts or units and the concentration of all marketing activity on one or more of these segments. The firm's options are thereby expanded. They can run a wide gamut from going after the whole market, called undifferentiated marketing, to cultivating parts thereof, described as selective marketing.

Segmentation philosophy stems from the fact that markets are seldom uniform. Consequently, diverse segments contain within themselves unique patterns of behavior and thought. As explained by Wendell Smith, who first popularized the concept in the mid-50s, market segmentation is a strategy designed for a "heterogeneous market by emphasizing the precision with which a firm's products can satisfy the requirements of one or more distinguishable market segments."[2]

Lastly, a marketing plan allocates resources to promotional activities. This decision expands or contracts the scope of advertising, for tasks must accommodate themselves to the money available. This budget tells advertising how much funds it has to work with.

ELEMENTS OF THE ADVERTISING PLAN

The advertising plan, like all the other aspects of corporate planning, follows a certain generic form. It is composed of three basic elements: 1) objectives and goals, 2) an operating plan, and 3) monitoring. This format can be visualized as follows:

Objectives and goals outline what is intended to be accomplished. The former term typically implies a long-term end. A goal is an objective made specific as to performance and time period, usually over a short duration. Plans for general advertising cover about one year. However, the advertising industry uses the two terms interchangeably.

The operating plan outlines in great detail what is to be done in order to achieve the goals set forth. It includes two main parts: creative and media. The creative part explains what will be said, how it will be said, and to whom the messages will be directed. The media part specifies where and when the messages are to be transmitted to the desired marketing targets. It will contain a schedule of the media vehicles to be used during the campaign. Once finalized, the advertising plan serves as a blueprint for the various departments at both the advertiser and its advertising agency in carrying out their respective assignments.

Monitoring refers to performance evaluation. The operating plan articulates a series of intentions and expected results. But there is often discordance between the word and the deed, between the dream and the reality. For this reason operations are monitored; to see whether plans on paper are, in fact, carried out and whether actual results accord with those postulated in the operating plan.

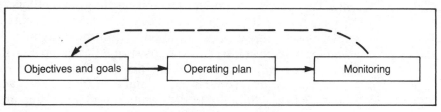

Fig. 6—1 *Generic Planning Representation.*

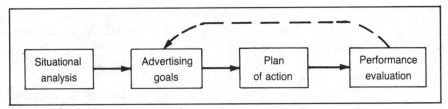

Fig. 6–2 *Elements of an Advertising Plan.*

Many advertising plans detail the type of research and measurements by which programs are to be judged, but most probably do not. However, a judgment of the program's success or failure is implied. It is inconceivable that a company would spend large sums and form no opinion as to what it received for its money, or whether it was all worth the effort.

When a plan contains no details as to how advertising is to be assessed, disagreements can arise among the interested parties. It therefore seems sensible to put into the advertising plan the proposed evaluative measurements. This would by no means eliminate all varying opinions. But the disputes would surface before the plan is put into effect, not after, and all individuals with a stake in the outcome would be committed to the resolution which ensues. Results are accepted—good, bad, or indifferent—and are used as input for next year's planning and for possible modification of current operations.

Going from the generic to the particular planning form, an advertising plan can be composed of four main sections: situational analysis, list of advertising goals, proposals for programs of action, and a research program for evaluating operations. This is depicted graphically in Figure 6–2.

SITUATIONAL ANALYSIS

The planning process begins with a situational analysis. This is the basis of goal setting and operational planning. It contains three main types of information: data pertaining to products, markets, and environments. The situational analysis is lifted directly out of the marketing plan which, if done properly, furnishes the basic facts.

The product-market data encompass the attributes and performance in use of the company's product and of its leading competitors. This analysis must confine itself not only to a single product category, but to all offerings which pose a threat of substitution. All-purpose liquids and powders, ammonia, disinfectants, and various specialties compete with each other in cleaning various surfaces around the home. The same is true for numerous other products, both consumer and industrial. For example, Wisk is actually a heavy duty liquid detergent. But its most common usage is for stains, such as dirt rings around a collar, and its closest competitors are spot removers. Arm and Hammer baking soda competes more as a deodorant than as a cooking ingredient. Economists refer to this sort of interproduct competition as cross-elasticity of demand.

The environment is an amalgam of influences which are external to the firm. These influences are beyond direct company control, and are usually regarded as something which is given. But they do undergo change with the passage of time. Of particular importance to consumer goods marketers are population trends, for people are markets. Another issue of growing concern is the role of government in product development and marketing.

Advertising planners may gather marketing intelligence relating to creative approaches, media statistics, or consumer motivations. But most information about products and markets lies imbedded in the marketing plan. One need go no further than that basic document to extract relevant product-market data.

When advertising agencies are employed to draw up an advertising plan, it is the client's responsibility to supply all product-market information which has a bearing on the assignment. People at the client company should know more about their company's products and markets than an outside agency. But practice varies widely. The large firms producing consumer goods normally supply their agencies with vast quantities of highly detailed information. In the industrial field, such fine detail is often superfluous. Advertising is used sparingly and in limited ways. Firms may thus give their agencies just enough information to enable them to come up with a satisfactory plan. Sometimes, the data in industrial fields include nothing more than a set of goals.

When completed, the situational analysis should reveal a product's strengths and weaknesses. The advertising plan must then address itself to two issues. How can the product's advantages be exploited? How can its deficiencies be overcome? The answers to these questions, in large part inferential, make up the programs for turning to good account business opportunities through advertising.

ADVERTISING GOALS

Advertising goals, which usually follow the situational analysis, make up a vital part of the advertising plan. Since advertising is part of marketing, its goals must seek to accomplish the broader objectives of the marketing plan. Advertising goals thus must be subordinate to, but compatible with, those of marketing. They have two main functions: planning and monitoring.

By setting forth the tasks which advertising is called upon to perform, goals give direction to the operating plan. They must therefore be specific and clearly spelled out or the progress will be ineffective. How can anyone draw up a plan of action without being sure of exactly what is to be accomplished?

Goals also serve as a basis for monitoring. This involves a comparison of intended outcomes with actual results. As such, goals act as standards for judging a program's success or failure. But these standards are only as good as the analyses from which they arise and the realism with which they are promulgated.

The goals contained in the advertising plan must be stated in terms which are operational and quantifiable. Unless a firm exercises control over an operation, it lacks the ability to make things happen. All desirable events cannot be decreed, for that would imply the absence of all uncertainty. But the more an operation can be brought under control, the greater the likelihood of satisfactory results. Since monitoring is essential to control, goals must be stated so that outcomes can be measured.

An advertising plan may contain three types of goals: behavioral, cognitive, or affective.

Behavioral Goals

Behavior by definition is objective and can be defined quantitatively. Behavioral items appear in virtually all advertising plans as lower-level goals. For example, media plans carry printed advertising schedules. In the course of the campaign, copies and tearsheets are examined to determine whether advertisements have been run in accordance with instructions. Broadcast schedules give estimates of viewers. Once programs are aired, ratings are checked to see if the expected audience size had been obtained.

A higher-level goal that is behavioralistic relates to sales. Whether phrased as brand leadership, market share, or dollar volume of sales, this goal is appropriate only if that outcome is the result of advertising. However, it is generally conceded that purchases caused by advertising cannot be measured accurately. Nevertheless, sales stand out as the basic reason for advertising. Therefore, the advertiser is faced with an Ibsen choice: what is most desired cannot be had, and what is readily available is not greatly valued.

The sales issue actually boils down to a trade-off between relevancy and errors of estimation. Setting goals in terms of sales makes advertising tasks highly germane to management. However, managerial decisions are often diluted by monitoring inaccuracies. As a rule, the more influence advertising has on sales, the more meaningful a sales goal becomes. The exact points of decisive influence and acceptable meaningfulness are matters of judgment. If sales goals are set, management believes they are relevant. However, advertising's effect cannot be estimated by normal monitoring. In general, the greater the influence of advertising, the more accurately its effects on sales are estimated. But the points at which research gives significant answers or leads to effective decisions cannot be determined.

Sales goals are often written into advertising plans when communication via mass media assumes a dominant position in the marketing mix, such as in packaged goods. This procedure is rationalized as follows:

Since the bulk of sales takes place in self-service outlets, the effects of store policies and personal selling are minimal. If the firm can maintain a high degree of internal control, nonadvertising activities will stabilize at a satisfactory operating level. This is particularly true with mature products, the categories of which display little change in unit sales. Consequently, all things remain fairly constant with the exception of advertising, which may alter its expenditures, its messages, or both. Therefore, changes in sales can be associated with changes in advertising programs.[3]

A purist would quickly raise objections to the presupposition that all things are equal. If advertising of a single firm changes over time, so does the advertising of all firms in an industry. Equally important, sales promotion has made leaping advances in recent years. Its expenditures today, even for packaged goods, exceed the dollar volume spent for advertising. The rise to prominence of sales promotion makes more untenable the assumption of constancy in all marketing variables except advertising.

Nevertheless, advertising campaigns are not prone to be evaluated favorably when sales are going badly. Conversely, advertising will meet with approving smiles when sales are booming. The fact that these sales cannot precisely be traced to advertising does not matter. If advertising is regarded as an important cog in the marketing machinery, falling sales raise the presumption of defective advertising and vice versa. Under these conditions, sales as a goal will continue to be put into advertising plans, regardless of flawed logic and faulty measurements.

Nonbehavioral Goals

When advertising is somewhat removed from the purchase transaction, it is assigned tasks which fall short of sales generation. Some of these tasks may be behavioral, such as visiting showrooms, requesting information, or entering contests. But in the main, nonbehavioral goals are phrased in communication terms, mental constructs such as brand awareness, product knowledge, attitude formation, and predisposition to buy. Cognitive goals and affective goals are nonbehavioral goals.

These psychological factors are referred to as "intervening variables." The desired action, usually a sale, is not the direct result of a stimulus, in this case the advertising. Rather, certain nonbehavioral responses, cognitive or affective, are seen as necessary and prior conditions for purchase behavior to occur. These psychological variables are regarded as acting in an indirect, intermediary capacity, as "intervening" between advertising and sales.

Advertising goals which specify communication goals may also include sales objectives. One does not preclude the other. Either way, the intervening variables are means to ends which are behavioral. The key decisions involve the determination of which means are most relevant in the means-end chain.

The selection of any intermediate factor as a goal assumes a causal relationship between that variable and an end result. If a campaign is earmarked to increase awareness, then that objective, however defined, is supposed to exert a significant influence over purchases. If advertising is assigned the task of changing consumer attitudes, then these states of mind are indeed taken as proxies for eventual sales.[4]

The ways in which these intervening variables relate to behavior are not well understood. Models based on psychological constructs have fared rather badly in ability to predict market behavior. The advertising profession abounds with contradictory psychological theories and competing explanations of events. Copy tests find little relation between research scores and buying behavior. Similarly, improved attitudes as evidenced by consumer surveys are not necessarily followed by increased sales. These anomalies have spurred eclecticism. Advertising works differently in different situations, it is reasoned. If this is so, effective planning must determine the appropriate tasks for particular circumstances.

THE POSITIONING PHILOSOPHY

The positioning philosophy ties together various parts of the advertising plan. Positioning came into vogue during the last decade, and its popularity has continued to grow. Hardly an advertising plan today does not make some reference to a brand's position. Yet, there are disagreements about exactly what the word means.

The concept is rather old. Originally it meant product positioning of packaged goods—a product's physical features as compared with those of the competition. Product characteristics embrace such elements as size, shape, color, texture, package, price, and so forth.

A classic example of traditional positioning is that of Dove soap, introduced to the market in 1957. Lever Brothers then decided to position its new entry as a complexion bar for dry skin rather than a soap for personal cleansing. The item was given an oval shape to connote femininity. It came to market in a box, like a cosmetic, instead of a paper wrapper. Even the name aroused visions of a beauty aid. The advertising was designed to fit the brand's product strategy with the promise that the soap "creams your skin while you wash."[5]

Positioning, as used by Lever Brothers, is essentially a marketing concept. It refers to the products against which Lever's entry was to compete and the markets in which this rivalry was to take place. The specific selling idea was a tactic which, if not an afterthought, bowed dutifully to the market niche envisioned by the brand planners.

The positioning concept was greatly expanded in the 1970s, and it took on more varied meanings. The main change involved a shift away from products to the objectives of the advertising itself. A tactic was, on many occasions, elevated into a strategy. The position moved away from tangible product characteristics to disembodied perceptions or images. The position was no longer a location defined in terms of sales or market share, but in terms of some nebulous "share of mind." The new definition of positioning came to mean the art of locating a product in the consumer psyche.[6]

On the surface, the new interpretation of positioning seems subtle and but a small extension of the main body of thought. In reality, what is seen on the surface is like the proverbial tip of the iceberg; the most important part of the icy mass lies beneath. The change in meaning of positioning has already brought about dramatic alterations in advertising practice, and its implications have far-reaching effects.

IMPLICATIONS OF POSITIONING

If customers think that Avis works harder than Hertz because it is Number Two, the exact service levels of both companies are not critical factors in the struggle for share. If customers associate Timex with durability, other watches just as durable cannot hope to gain an edge by making such claims in their advertising. Ironically, when Timex in the late 1970s switched strategy to the more stylish digital and quartz watches, it ran into trouble. The new positions were associated with the more fashionable brands of Timex's competitors.[7]

Faced with the problem of how to get its Cella brand noticed among an increasing number of imported wines, Brown-Foreman Distillers created a fictitious character, Aldo Cella, a funny little man who sweeps beautiful women off their feet with, you guessed it, Cella wine. Figure 6–3 shows a typical Aldo Cella commercial stressing this romantic motif.

On a more serious note, the Aldo commercial admirably illustrates the relationship between product and consumer perception. Although Aldo has recently become a little more subdued, the brand had built its reputation on the romantic escapades of a make-believe personality. Aldo told people in a facetious kind of way that you need not be handsome to be a great lover. The commercial was highly effective. Irrepressible Aldo sold wine. The once little-known brand increased its sales from 750,000 cases in 1977 to 2,400,000 cases in 1980.[8] Today, Cella is the second largest

"Italian Village"

CELLA BIANCO

:30 TV Commercial

MUSIC UP: OFFSTAGE WOMAN: Senor Cella, Senor Cella!
VO: This is Aldo Cella.

He is not a slave to fashion.
OFFSTAGE GIRL: Aldo, Aldo!

VO: He speaks no French.
GIRL: Ca vas Aldo?

ALDO: Si.

VO: But Aldo Cella knows what women like.

Cella Bianco,

A very special white wine.

ALDO: Chill-a-Cella!
GIRL: Aldo!

MUSIC FADES.

Fig. 6—3 *Aldo Cella Commercial. A Personality Created for a Wine.* Courtesy of Joseph Garneau Co.

wine import. Are then sidewalk cafes and whirlwind romances any more a true attribute of Cella than of any other wine? Certainly not. But then, the question may have little relevancy, at least to Brown-Foreman.

From the consumer's perspective, a product may well be a perception rather than a good or service which can be defined objectively by its inherent attributes. When advertising accentuates this separation, the perception and the physical entity drift further apart. In fact, advertising may work to keep the consumer image substantially different from the true product characteristics. The vast outpouring of line extensions and nearly identical products impel advertising in that direction. Otherwise, advertisements for these parity products would all be saying pretty much the same thing. Minimal product differences as with beer, cigarettes, detergent, gasoline, soft drinks, or banking services prompt companies to turn to communication rather than to product policy in the quest for a differential advantage.

When the focus falls on advertising, the manner in which an idea is communicated becomes as important as the idea itself. For example, when Tareyton was introduced, its only distinctive feature was a charcoal filter. Perhaps a dozen other brands could claim the same attribute, and its resultant benefit of a "smooth" taste. But Tareyton advertising communicated to the public the idea of belligerent smokers, so loyal to the brand that they would "rather fight than switch." If position means a mental perception, then what was that of Tareyton? Was it the charcoal filter, "smooth" taste, or some rowdy user who fights at the drop of a hat?

The view of a position as residing in the consumer mind blurs the traditional distinction between product strategy and tactics. It also obscures the fine divisions between marketing and advertising. Since positioning is a long-term affair, advertising is invested with traits of strategic planning. Marketing decisions on packaging, product design, pricing, and distribution must now support that basic rationale created by positioning. From this standpoint, advertising infringes on the prerogatives traditionally reserved for marketing. It also creates an additional burden on product managers to coordinate the efforts of advertising with those of other marketing functions, especially when advertising has a major role in product sales.

It is patently obvious that if a position can be created by how a brand is projected to the public, decisions by outside agencies can determine a brand's strategy. But strategic planning has always been the responsibility of a company's management. It has never been delegated explicitly to an advertising agency. For this reason, advertisers have begun to participate more actively in creative processes. Their research departments have become more involved in positioning concepts, unwilling to leave creative decisions solely in the hands of their agencies. As a consequence, conflicts often flare up between researchers and creative personnel. If creativity is not actually sacrificed, as many copywriters maintain, its freedom of action is surely circumscribed.

Another tactic that is used to establish a position is that of comparative advertising. Highly contentious, this maneuver makes no oblique allusions to the competitor as Brand X. It names the opponent. It is normally shunned by market leaders who have successfully differentiated their products.[9] Instead, it is taken up by new brands or market laggards who, by positioning themselves directly opposite the leader, insinuate themselves into a prospect's "consideration frame." It is a means whereby a relatively unknown contender lists itself with a front-runner and asks to be considered as a feasible alternative in buying decisions.

The rise of the positioning philosophy has taken place concurrently with the demise of the marketing concept.[10] Both trends are related to the same causes. The marketing concept implores corporations to study consumers' needs and wants, and promises gratifying rewards to those who satisfy them. The wants and needs remain, but open no road to riches. This is aptly stated by ad agency heads Trout and Ries: "Knowing what the customer wants isn't too helpful if a dozen others are serving his wants and needs."[11] The critical difference, which lies at the root of most advertising, relates to the competitor, not to the customer. Product advertising attempts in almost every instance to swing consumer choices away from competitive brands to the brand advertised.

IS POSITIONING SEGMENTATION?

Many authors have described positioning as segmentation. In fact, it is and it isn't. Like the cerebral processes to which it is related, the positioning philosophy is a bit vague, indefinite, surreal.

Insofar as positioning attempts to carve out a share of mind, it can be thought of as psychological segmentation. But from a marketing perspective, there are many difficulties with this interpretation.

The segmentation concept literally sees market segments as already being in existence. The marketer takes advantage of this splintering by putting together an offer which would appeal to a particular group as is. Positioning goes further. It is not passive. It can create its own "segments."

For example, there has been a veritable boom in the licensing of cartoon characters as marketing tools. Bugs Bunny, Fred Flintstone, Little Orphan Annie, and a host of fictional beings are endowing products with personalities. In some industries, such as children's sleepwear, the cartoon-created positions hold the key to success, and even survival.[12]

Just to say that customers perceive competitive products differently is almost universally true. It does not, however, segmentation make. Traditional segmentation philosophy lists five basic requirements for proper application. These are, though not necessarily in order of importance, a differential response, sufficient size, stability, quantifiability, and accessibility.[13] Positioning as segmentation fails completely on the last two counts.

How does one quantify the "Uncola" segment? Or the "Pepsi generation"? Or the "Number Two" segment in the rent-a-car market? Are people who think in these terms readily distinguishable from those who don't? If they cannot be identified unambiguously in quantitative designations, there is no way of taking advantage of their existence.

These segments must also be accessible in the sense of being reached efficiently by promotion. Then does the "Pepsi generation" have media habits which differ substantially from those of the "Uncola" segment, or from those of people who have decided to be Peppers? All soft drink brands rely heavily upon television, a medium with general audiences, to establish their positions. Messages go out to all people, young and old, rich and poor, product users and nonusers—a violation of the segmentation concept. No economies are achieved by "targeting" messages to specific segments. Perhaps positioning can be better described by an older concept of differentiation, be it through product or pricing or advertising, rather than as segmentation.

CONSUMER RATIONALITY

The choice of advertising options flows from views of buying behavior. These models may be formal or informal. Their basic assumption may be implicit or explicit. But they all involve some explanation of how consumers go about deciding what to buy and the role of communications in those decisions.

There are many different theories, and numerous variations of each, concerned with the purchasing decisions. One possible way of classifying them is on the basis of rationality. That is, they can be visualized as existing on a continuum going from highly reasoned choices to completely irrational decisions.

The reasoning end of the spectrum finds expression in the utility theories of economics. Ordinal utility, with its focus on preferences and indifference curves, has largely replaced the neoclassical notion of cardinal utility, with its diminishing marginal utils. Still, the consumer is depicted as a deliberating buyer who consistently chooses the item offering the maximum utility per dollar of expenditure. In its most extreme form, the theory erects a vision of the "economic man." In its current form, utility may include psychological satisfactions, and hence be somewhat less than wholly governed by flawless logic. Any subject involving value judgment raises questions about objectively determined standards for maximizing behavior.

The model of rational purchase behavior is best exemplified by industrial and commodity markets. Since purchases rest on certain assumptions, they are not always wise. But they are rational, value-seeking deci-

Fig. 6—4 *Beechcraft. A Rational Argument for Business Executives.* Courtesy of Beechcraft.

sions, and in the main, logical. For consumer goods, the most thoughtful purchases are those of high-priced durables, such as automobiles, major appliances, or houses. Certain financial services also fall into the same category. But considerations of price and value may also arise with respect to low-priced packaged goods, as evidenced by private labels and generics. Several large companies have veered from their traditional policy of brand advertising towards value items and generic products.[14] The recent spat of price-off coupons for convenience goods—more than 100 billion in 1981—also implies a utilitarian approach to selling.

The irrational portion of the purchase continuum thrives upon several social and psychological theories. One is the almost mechanistic stimulus-response theory of psychology. When buying becomes an automatic, routine purchase, each succeeding purchase reinforces past behavior. Many frequently purchased convenience goods are thought of as falling into this category of fixed behavior. It is but another name for brand loyalty, as evidenced by repeat purchases. Though all advertisers strive to create such routine transactions, leading brands normally have the greatest amount. Their advertising, regardless of content, serves mainly to remind buyers to continue their habit.

A second theory of irrationality has a social basis and seeks explanations in group dynamics. Opinion leadership and badges like status and prestige are regarded as important facets of consumer behavior. Illustrative of this fact is the present craze for jeans with trademarks sewn on the rump.

A third theory is steeped in psychology of the individual. It holds up to view a consumer swayed by emotional impulses and even unconscious desires. Under such conditions, ego involvement and self-actualization become powerful motives, and attitudinal factors outweigh functional ones in buying decisions. These appeals are highly prominent in liquor, cigarette, cosmetics and toiletry advertising.

From an advertising standpoint, however, the question of rational or irrational behavior is but one part of the problem. The other portion deals with consumers' reactions to advertising itself.

CONSUMER INVOLVEMENT

The traditional view of how consumers handle information derives primarily from social psychology, the principles of which have been applied to the marketplace. One result was the emergence of hierarchy of effects theories, which postulate attitudes as forerunners of action.

Attitudes may indeed be central to an understanding of human relationships regarding social issues. They cause excitement. They are subjects of arguments and demonstrations. They are focal points of political upheavals and ghastly wars. They are objects for praise and contempt.

They are profaned and sanctified. In a word, people are moved and become highly involved.

But can these theories of social involvement be transferred to commercial transactions? A shift of market share from one parity brand to another involves no earth-shaking issues. Consumer research reveals many inconsistencies, such as buying patterns unaccompanied by changes in attitudes. New explanations were obviously necessary as to why behavior deviates from the routes marked out by the conventional wisdom. The new theories which arose did away with the old mental hierarchies, at least for certain classes of products, and hypothesized a nation of consumers doing their shopping chores with little concern and low involvement with respect to issues which grip marketers.

To define "consumer involvement" is not easy. It connotes degrees of interest, concern, anxiety, and attention. Thomas Robertson has described it as a "commitment" associated with strongly held beliefs.[15] Although involvement is a relative concept, products do not command equal amounts. Following this line of logic, consumer behavior can once again be thought of as existing on a continuum—this time on an "involvement dimension" which ranges from extremely low to very high.

The involvement concept has important implications for advertising planning. An involved customer, as portrayed by hierarchy theories, comes forward as a buyer who, though perceiving messages selectively, wilfully processes information and welcomes advertising.[16] This is not to say that a prospective automobile buyer bases his decision on advertisements. He might distrust them all and turn to *Consumer Reports*. But there is some evaluation. When consumers make an effort at obtaining information, the primary goals of advertising communication are likely to be those dealing with cognition, affect, and conation.[17] The latter is an attitudinal component that is related to action tendencies, such as intention to buy.

Products standing at the ebb tide of consumer involvement inspire no evaluation of symbolic messages. Their advertising encounters passive, apathetic audiences whose most likely response is a yawn. Goals of increasing sales through attitude formation are far-fetched and unrealistic. But neither do competitors enjoy strong buyer commitments. It does not take much to induce trial and brand switching. The conveyance of minimal information may be sufficient to accomplish the purpose. Indeed, the slightest exposure to an advertisement equates to persuasion if only the barest memory trace, such as the brand's name, is enough to make a difference at the point of sale. Advertising in this situation sees its main job as creating awareness.[18] Since purchases are to a considerable extent influenced by situational factors, recollection of a name or some other image may be just enough to tip the scales in favor of the advertised brand.

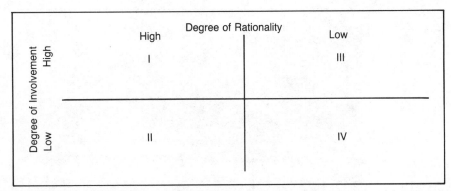

Fig. 6–5 *Rationality-Involvement Matrix.*

THE RATIONALITY-INVOLVEMENT MATRIX

Since any offering must contend with customer rationality and involvement, an advertising plan should consider both factors simultaneously. The combination of both dimensions can be represented as a quadrant, although the strength of the factors is theoretically given by the exact position on the space map. This is shown graphically in Figure 6–5.

As indicated in Figure 6–5, rational and involvement factors are complementary for products falling into quadrants I and IV. The two elements move in the same directions. Advertising for products in the high rationality-high involvement sector (I), can benefit from data related to product options and rational appeals. Refer to Figure 6–6 for an example of a rational appeal advertisement directed at involved consumers.

In contrast, advertising designed for quadrant IV tends to lack product-related data and draws attention to itself by other means. For example, advertising for 7-Up shows boxer Sugar Ray Leonard in a touching father-son scene. But what this has to do with a soft drink is entirely obscure. AT&T advertises its long-distance telephone lines with emotional scenes of children, parents, and grandparents holding back tears of joy as they are touched by someone "reaching out for them." Unlike the Sugar Ray Leonard commercials, those of AT&T are related to its service. But the attention is focused on people—their emotions and hangups—and not on the service. After all, no one can get very excited about a phone.

Products in quadrant III, though involving to consumers, require a paucity of facts for transactions to be consummated. Advertising here will stress image, with emotion-arousing and ego-directed appeals. See Figure 6–7 for an example of an emotional appeal for an emotional occasion.

Quadrant II presents conceptual difficulties. How can a buyer act rationally yet pay little attention to informational sources? Behavior of this kind occurs in the industrial sector when contracts call for purchases stretched over time. To avoid negotiations with every purchase, ordering

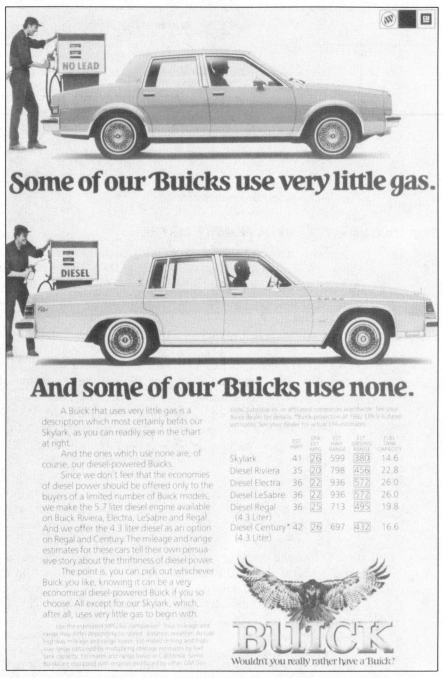

Fig. 6—6 *Buick. Example of an Advertisement Offering Rational Appeal to Involved Consumers.* Courtesy of Buick, a division of General Motors.

"For all those Saturdays you never complained."

Nothing else feels like real gold.
Nothing else makes any moment so precious.

Give her the gleaming, elegant, enduring gift she will treasure all of her life.
KARAT GOLD JEWELRY

For more information about Karat Gold Jewelry or the specific jewelry pictured here,
write to Jewelry Information, International Gold Corp. Ltd., 645 Fifth Avenue, New York, N.Y. 10022.

Fig. 6—7 *International Gold Corp. Advertisement Showing an Emotional Appeal for an Emotional Occasion. Courtesy of International Gold Corp., Ltd.*

is reduced to a routine. In the consumer field, a parallelism exists with replacement parts and services under warranties. But such products do not demand much advertising.

Rationality and involvement considerations make themselves felt not only in creative strategy. They reach deeply into the media portion of the advertising plan. The copy treatment decided upon cannot be carried out in all media with equal effectiveness. More directly, planners must assess the different levels of involvement which take place with respect to media content.

The brain wave activity level is extremely low when watching television. Laboratory tests have recorded alpha waves with frequencies of eight to twelve cycles per second, which are characteristic of wakeful but inattentive adults.[19] At this level of cerebral activity, viewers are probably incapable of absorbing anything but the simplest information handed out in small doses. Reading evidently requires more effort, and brain wave activity is at a higher level.[20] More information can thus be crammed into printed advertisements. The need here is to get readers to want to exert themselves mentally when reading an advertisement.

THE FCB PLANNING MODEL

The ideas of rationality and involvement are nearly always present in advertising plans. They may not be expressed in bold terms because they are implicit, hidden within unstated assumptions. But they are there, bending the plan in the direction of their biases.

An attempt to integrate these theories into planning was recently made by the advertising agency, Foote, Cone & Belding/Honig. This planning model was built around the twin concepts of rationality and involvement, but characterized in terms of learning, feeling, and doing.[21]

The rationality factor was translated to a thinking-feeling dimension. That is, goods and services are classified as to whether thinking or feeling dominates the purchase decision. This transformation probably makes the rationality dimension more operational. Involvement is defined as the degree of importance a product holds for the buyer. Conceivably, this can be measured, somewhat crudely, by some form of rating scale. This model, illustrated as a matrix, is shown in Figure 6–8.

The arrows in the graphic presentation of the FCB model (see Figure 6–8) indicate consumer tendencies of thinking and importance. The dotted lines which separate the quadrants denote a "soft" partition between them. This suggests possible overlaps of advertising strategies associated with each quadrant: to convey data, to be affective, to support habit or routine buying, and to promote self-satisfaction.

As described by agency spokespersons, the model serves as a guide for setting objectives and formulating the strategic and tactical elements of the advertising plan. "If done properly, the parts should fit together," claims its author.[22]

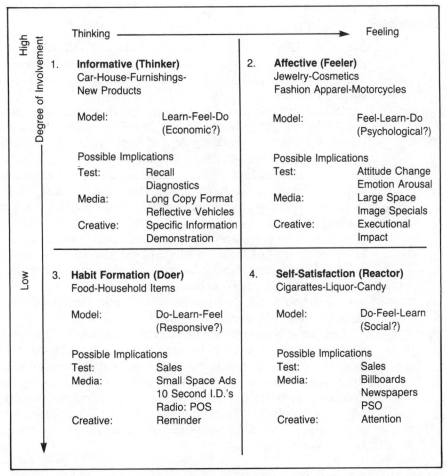

Fig. 6—8 *FCB Planning Model. Source: Richard Vaughn, "The Consumer Mind: How to Tailor Ad Strategies," Advertising Age (June 9, 1980), p. 31. Reprinted with permission from Advertising Research Foundation, Inc.*

But the model is not a mathematical one, which, if given relevant data would yield an exact solution. Numerous variations are possible, and these reside in the imagination of those who do the planning. The exact position of any product within the rationality-involvement matrix is unknown. Even were research able to determine the existing "information-emotion-action" leverage, and this is doubtful, the question of strategy is still an open one. Should advertising go along with what is or try to alter what is, including the leverage?

Undoubtedly, the model is a useful planning tool. It provides a framework for organizing thoughts. But the usefulness of the plan still rests on the creativity of its architects.

SUMMARY

The advertising plan embodies the goals, operational programs, and in many instances, the monitoring methods for a promotional campaign. Most advertising plans deal with individual products or groups of closely related products.

The advertising plan usually begins with a situational analysis, which is actually a part of the marketing plan. Two related concepts are of particular significance, market potential and market segmentation.

The decade of the 1970s witnessed the adoption of a positioning philosophy which moved its focus from tangible product characteristics to mental constructs, such as perceptions and images. This philosophy impinges on the traditional distinctions between advertising and marketing.

Advertising goals are of three main types: behavioral, cognitive, and affective. The most important behavioral goal is that of sales, which, in most circumstances, cannot be measured accurately. But the selection of nonsales goals implicitly assumes a causal relationship between the intervening variables selected and sales results. In turn, the choice of variable rests on views of buying behavior.

Consumer behavior can be based on rational or irrational considerations. Another factor is the degree of consumer involvement, which differs from one product to another. An attempt to make the concepts of rationality and involvement operational is the model formalized by Foote, Cone & Belding/Honig. But the advertising plan still depends largely on the creativity of the planner. Implementation of the plan also depends on the size of its budget. This financial aspect of planning becomes the subject of the next chapter.

Questions for Chapter 6

1. Industrial marketers often draw up the advertising plan after the marketing plan is in place. Do you think that this is a good procedure?

2. Why might a firm's advertising intensity be high when the gap between market potential and actual industry demand is large?

3. How does segmentation differ from differentiation? How would advertising strategy be affected by these differences?

4. A college decides to promote a number of courses in a continuing education program. Outline a research plan for evaluating the advertising effort.

5. A brand with a small share of the total market is not considered as competing with brand leaders. Would there be any advantage in setting formal advertising goals under such circumstances?

6. The Hoyt-Rumill agency has proposed a remuneration plan based on sales results. Would you, as an advertising director, be willing to set these goals for advertising?

7. The modern concept of positioning emphasizes "share of mind." What are the managerial implications to an advertiser owing to this approach?

8. Do basic appeals for high-priced automobiles differ from those for low-priced cars? Why or why not?

9. Would you consider Miller Lite commercials which stress "tastes good" and "less filling" to be rational appeals?

10. The FCB Planning Model implies attention-getting ads for soft drinks (low involvement-feeling quadrant). Do you agree with this recommendation?

Footnotes for Chapter 6

[1] Kotler, *Marketing Management*, p. 217.

[2] Wendell Smith, "Product Differentiation and Market Segmentation as Alternative Marketing Strategies," *Journal of Marketing* (July 1956), p. 4.

[3] Weilbacher, pp. 127–128.

[4] For example, see R. A. Roy and M. J. Nicolich, "Planner: A Market Positioning Model," *Journal of Advertising Research* (April 1980), pp. 61–66; "Brand Awareness is Best Measure of Ad Effectiveness for New Product," *Marketing News* (May 16, 1980), p. 14; "Attitude Share Of Market Predicts Better Than Behavioral Measured," *Marketing News* (May 16, 1980), p. 7.

[5] Kenneth Roman and Jane Maas, *How to Advertise* (New York: St. Martin's Press, 1976), p. 2.

[6] See Jack Trout and Al Ries, *The Positioning Era* (Chicago: Crain Communications, 1972), pp. 8–11.

[7] Jeffrey H. Birnbaum, "Falling Profit Prompts Timex to Shed Its Utilitarian Image," *The Wall Street Journal* (September 17, 1981), p. 29.

[8] *The Wall Street Journal* (January 29, 1981), p. 27.

[9] J. J. Boddewyn and K. Martin, *Comparative Advertising* (New York: International Advertising Association, 1978), p. 13.

[10] See Sachs and Benson, "Is It Time to Discard the Marketing Concept," *Business Horizons* (August 1978), pp. 68–74.

[11] Jack Trout and Al Ries, "Positioning: Ten Years Later," *Industrial Marketing* (July 1979), p. 42.

[12] Dean Rotbart, "Licensing Boom Envelopes U.S. Industry as Makers Search for a Competitive Edge," *Wall Street Journal* (June 1, 1981), p. 29.

[13] See Sachs and Benson, *Product Planning*, pp. 40–41; Kotler. pp. 205–206.

[14] For example, see Sam Harper, "L & M: Generics Rush to the Rescue," *Advertising Age* (June 1, 1981), p. 4; Larry Edward, "Also-ran Brands Periled," *Advertising Age* (May 11, 1981), pp. 3, 72.

[15]Thomas S. Robertson, "Low-Commitment Consumer Behavior," *Journal of Advertising Research* (April 1976), pp. 19–24.

[16]Raymond A. Bauer, "The Obstinate Audience," *American Psychologist* (May 19, 1964), pp. 319–328.

[17]See W. R. Swinyard and Charles H. Patti," The Communications Hierarchy Framework for Evaluating Copytesting Techniques," *Journal of Advertising* (Summer 1979), pp. 29–36; David J. Reibstein et. al., "The Direction of Causality Between Perceptions, Affect and Behavior: An Application to Travel Behavior," *Journal of Consumer Research* (March 1980), pp. 370–376.

[18]Robertson, "Low-Commitment Consumer Behavior," pp. 20–22.

[19]V. Appel et. al., "Brain Activity and Recall of TV Advertising," *Journal of Advertising Research* (August 1979), p. 10.

[20]S. Weinstein et. al., "Brain-Activity Responses to Magazine and Television Advertising," *Journal of Advertising Research* (June 1980), pp. 57–63.

[21]See Richard Vaughn, "The Consumer Mind: How to Tailor Ad Strategies," *Advertising Age* (June 9, 1980), pp. 45–46.

[22]Vaughn, "The Consumer Mind," p. 46.

7 *Budgeting for Advertising*

The bottom line, actually the difference between revenue and cost, is a powerful motivator of business. It is the central idea of cost accounting and operational control.

This process, matching monetary inflows and outflows, makes up the underlying theme of this chapter. What budgeting methods are available and used by management for the purposes of calculating advertising's bottom line? Accordingly, the chapter will deal with such topics as:

- **Marginal concepts in setting advertising expenditure levels**
- **Theoretical models assuming conditions of oligopolistic markets**
- **Guideline methods for determining advertising spending levels**
- **Budgetary adjustments to business cycle fluctuations**
- **Long-term effects of advertising and investment spending decisions**

THE ADVERTISING BUDGET

The advertising budget is derived from forward planning. This financial document becomes especially compelling when advertising makes up a significant portion of operating costs, as in certain lines of packaged goods. Manufacturers of cigarettes, cosmetics, detergent, soap, or personal care products, for example, may find their advertising expenditures outrunning their net profits after taxes. The larger advertising's share of gross profits is, the more top management insists on formal procedures for dispensing corporate funds and gets involved in the budgeting process. It is not uncommon for advertising budgets in such companies to go through several layers of management before they come to the finance committee and chief operating officer for the final stamp of approval.

The budget expresses the operating plan in financial terms. It puts hard cash figures on the proposed action, and on the expected benefits to be derived therefrom. By doing so, information about the use of corporate resources undergoes a subtle conversion. It is distilled. Verbal descriptions of numerous acts are reduced to monetary terms, to simple sets of numbers. This transformation permits upper echelon executives to concentrate on the financial consequences of action, and to forego the myriad details of the operating plan. When finally approved, the budget serves as an instrument of financial control.

The company chart of accounts, an expenditure classification system, lists all items that belong in an advertising budget. Each item is identified by a code number, which is used to record spending authorizations and payments. To facilitate monetary control, advertising budgets should be prepared in accordance with the company's chart of accounts. Expenditures should also be broken down by time periods, monthly or quarterly, depending upon company practice, so as to permit sound management of cash flow.

Two questions, both related to each other, are paramount in expenditure decisions:

1. How much should be spent on advertising?
2. How should the total be allocated?

The allocation question is primarily the concern of lower-level managers charged with the responsibility of devising an operating plan. Therefore, this question can best be handled in chapters dealing with campaign strategy and media selection. This chapter will focus on the issue of setting a total amount, though in real life situations the allocation of expenses cannot as readily be severed from the determination of an aggregate.

THE BUDGET AS AN ADJUSTMENT PROCESS

The budget, like goals, plays a dual role. It is both a planning device and a standard for evaluating performance.

The practice of measuring performance against a financial standard was first developed in production. There, cost accountants analyze past experience, determine a set of standard costs for various functions, and compare actual costs with standard ones. This form of financial evaluation is called variance analysis. The factors analyzed are those which induce costs to fluctuate, such as output volume, raw material prices, labor costs, and production efficiency.

The same techniques are highly appropriate to marketing tasks, such as those of physical distribution, which bear a close resemblence to production.[1] In those instances, the nature of the job is one of order-filling. So much is to be produced and shipped, either directly to customers or to inventory. Since these jobs are repetitive, they can be boiled down to a routine, and operation costs can be predetermined.

But advertising entails an order-getting activity. Unlike order fulfillment, output is not something that is given. The amount of sales to be produced from some predetermined amount of advertising cannot be as readily standardized as bills of materials made up by engineers. Nor can companies easily ascertain relationships among marketing mix variables, which include advertising. When sales targets are met or missed it is difficult to put a finger on the exact reason.

In fact, the sales forecasts themselves often become the standards by which results are judged. An advertising campaign with a less-than-anticipated sales figure, for example, is often viewed as unsatisfactory. But though budget reviews frequently itemize advertising costs, variances are not traced to causal factors. The ability to do so is ostensibly lacking.

Nevertheless, the procedure calls attention to instances in which performance deviates from plans. These out-of-balance situations indicate that either corrective action is needed or that the plan is unrealistic and should be changed. Monitoring thus emerges as an adjustment process by which a firm adapts to changing events, continuously receiving market intelligence and, on the basis of the up-dated information, modifying its behavior.

APPROACHES TO SETTING BUDGET LEVELS

There are two basic approaches to setting budget levels for advertising—theoretical and guideline. In turn, each of these has several variations.

The first approach is advocated by many economists, management scientists and marketing researchers. It rests squarely on the marginal concepts of economics, which seek to maximize returns of advertising inputs. This method is quantitative, and may involve mathematical modeling and experimentally-designed studies.

The guidelines approach is the more traditional one, widely practiced by advertising managers. It embraces a variety of techniques, the most popular being the percent-of-sales, unit-of-sales, competitive parity, affordable and task methods. They are essentially rule-of-thumb procedures, but espouse a high degree of pragmatism. Their underlying rationale finds justification in experience. They are attuned to the shifts and turns of the marketplace, which, sweeping up many firms in a widening vortex, contribute to the formation of particular budget norms for different product lines.[2]

Table 7–1 depicts the extent to which these methods are practiced by general advertisers, as determined by two surveys. The first was conducted in 1975 by San Augustine and Foley, advertising practitioners; the second in 1981 by Patti and Blasko, both Arizona State University professors.

The Augustine-Foley study is based on samples of 50 major consumer advertisers and 50 industrial advertisers. The Patti-Blasko study derived its information from a mail questionnaire to the 100 leading national advertisers. Since the latter is composed mainly of companies marketing consumer goods and services, its results should be roughly comparable to those of major consumer advertisers of the Augustine-Foley study. However, the figures presented by these surveys differ substantially from each other.

Nevertheless, several general conclusions can be reached. First, the percentages in both studies add up to more than 100 percent because of multiple responses. More than half the firms said they used more than one method.

Second, for all their sophistication and acclaim, theoretical methods remain speculative. The Augustine-Foley study reported only two percent

TABLE 7–1 *Methods Used to Set Advertising Budgets*

| Method | San Augustine-Foley Survey | | Patti-Blasko Survey |
	Consumer Products (Percent)	Industrial Products (Percent)	100 Leading Advertisers (Percent)
Quantitative methods models	2	—	51
Percent of sales	64	44	73
Unit of sales	14	14	22
Affordable	30	26	20
Task	6	10	63
Arbitrary	12	34	4
Others	28	12	24
Base: Companies	(50)	(50)	(54)

Source: Adapted from A. J. San Augustine and W. F. Foley, "How Large Advertisers Set Their Budgets," *Journal of Advertising Research* (October 1975), p. 12; C. H. Patti and V. Blasko, "Budgeting Practices of Big Advertisers," *Journal of Advertising Research* (December 1981), p. 25. Reprinted with permission from Advertising Research Foundation, Inc.

using quantitative models. The Patti-Blasko survey put the figure at 51 percent for use of quantitative methods. These do not necessarily mean theoretical models. Since companies in that survey used an average of 2.6 methods, the probability of a mathematical construct being a major determinant of budget level is not high. Instead, it is much more likely that computer printouts are regarded as research data to assist executive decision making—helping to form judgments as to whether familiar guidelines should in some way be modified.[3]

Third, both studies indicate that the cruder, trial-and-error guidelines hold almost universal sway in the advertising community. The most popular rule of thumb is to set the advertising budget as a percentage of sales, though its incidence is significantly higher among firms catering to consumer markets. The affordable approach also has a substantial following in both consumer and industrial fields. The so-called arbitrary method, which implies budgeting decisions uncontrolled by prescribed rules, appears particularly widespread among companies marketing industrial products. Such erratic conduct presumably occurs whenever advertising budgets are relatively small and inconsequential in affecting sales.

Theoretical Approaches

Theoretical approaches to budgeting came to the fore in the 1950s. Their immediate impetus came from operations research, which applied many of the theoretical economic concepts to marketing.

At the heart of virtually all theoretical approaches lies the well-known economic principle of marginal productivity. It enjoins management to increase expenditures as long as they are exceeded by an incremental net revenue resulting from the added spending. Each additional dollar put out, the reasoning goes, would then bring back more than a dollar of profit. Advertising is maximized when the last dollar spent yields a dollar of net revenue, defined as total sales less all costs and expenses, save those of advertising. To stop before reaching this optimal point is to forego opportunities. To spend beyond that point would produce a loss on the incremental outlay, provided the budget level has reached an area of decreasing marginal returns.

But to equate marginal revenue with marginal cost of advertising necessitates, among other things, certain assumptions about how sales will react to incremental outlays. Practitioners commonly envision what might be termed a stimulus-response function, with advertising regarded as the stimulus and sales as the response. From this point of view, sales become a function of advertising. This proposition can be expressed mathematically as $S = f(A)$, with S denoting the amount of sales and A representing the level of expenditures. Most of these disbursements are "programed" rather than "fixed," and are reflected in prices for time and talent, space, and production. But the critical element in setting the budget through marginal analysis is the exact pattern of sales response to different levels of advertising expenditures. Figure 7–1 depicts two generalizations about advertising-sales relationships.

The dominant theory sees the advertising function as best described by the logistic curve labelled S_1, actually a second degree polynomial, in Figure 7–1.[4] According to this version, very small amounts of advertising produce only meager and negligible results. Implied is the existence of a

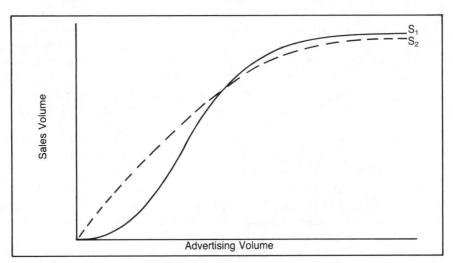

Fig. 7–1 *Hypothetical Sales Response Curves.*

threshold which must be pierced before advertising effects can be observed. As the budget is increased beyond this threshold of effectiveness, sales grow noticeably, and at an increasing rate. The jump in sales is more than proportional to the increment of advertising. But sooner or later this coveted state of affairs must cease, and this does happen as the saturation level is approached. Sales still go on rising, but at a subdued rate. Eventually they flatten out, having reached their limit, and no further additions to the promotional budget will give them a desired boost.

The other theory of sales response to advertising postulates an exponential curve, as shown by the dotted line marked S_2 in Figure 7–1. Here, there are no thresholds and no increasing marginal returns at any point.[5] Sales do increase from the beginning, but at a declining rate. This curve, too, will ultimately reach the limit of sales growth, where additional spending will be superfluous in terms of new sales.

The question as to which model portrays the real sales response curve is largely academic. The hypothetical S-curve may apply to small companies and new brands with tight budgets. When actual budgets lie at low levels of the advertising-sales configuration, a company would obviously be under-advertising, and would stand to gain revenue by upping its budget. But most firms in established industries would in all probability find themselves to the right of the point where the S-shaped curve turns concave downward. In that area, both logistical and exponential curves display similar patterns of sales response—diminishing marginal returns to scale.

Leading brands in the consumer field are more apt to suffer from overkill than from scanty advertising. This was never more forcefully evidenced than by the experience of Anheuser-Busch.[6]

Beginning in 1962, Anheuser-Busch conducted a series of marketing studies for its Budweiser brand of beer to determine how sales would respond to changes in advertising expenditures. The first test used a three-level design, decreasing the budget by 25 percent in one set of markets, having no change in another set, and adding 50 percent to the budget in a third. The results of this level-of-spending test revealed no significant interaction between changes in advertising budgets and changes in sales.

Encouraged by these early results, Budweiser expanded its market research program. The country was randomly divided into groups of markets, some designated as experimental and others as control. Each of these groups, seven in all, were assigned different budgets, ranging from a low of no advertising, or a decrease of 100 percent, to a high of 200 percent over and above current levels. The results were similar to those of the first experiments.

The research data were interpreted as Budweiser being far out on the right of the sales response curve, in an area of no return. At that point, variations in spending levels evoke virtually no change in market response. Accordingly, Anheuser-Busch began to gradually reduce its advertising commitment. From 1962 to 1968 advertising expenditures fell from $1.89 to $.80 a barrel. But sales rose from about 7.5 million to 14.5 million barrels, and market share grew from 8.1 percent to 12.9 percent. Obviously, the decline in per capita spending for advertising did not cause a growth in dollar sales and market share. Other factors were evidently at work. Nor can it be said that Budweiser achieved a maximum return, though its profits were ostensibly improved. As claimed by those who carried out the research project, the advertising budget reduction did no harm. But neither did the studies, despite care and expense, evince any clear-cut relationships between advertising and sales.

The simplest application of the marginal concept presents itself in mail order operations, where results are immediate and one time occurrences.[7] Each advertisement is keyed, so that revenue can be matched directly with costs. Under these conditions, the profit derived from an advertisement can be expressed as

$$\pi = VB - A$$

where

$\pi =$ profit from advertising
$V =$ value of a buyer—calculated as the average value of an order minus all costs, except those of advertising
$B =$ number of buyers
$A =$ advertising expenditure

The above formula states that profits of advertising equal the value of a customer multiplied by the number of buyers garnered by an advertisement, less the cost of advertising. The decision rule for optimizing is to add advertisements, or mailouts, as long as VB remains greater than A for each addition.

The same principle applies to retail businesses which feature product advertising. Following the appearance of an advertisement, sales are compared with those of a "normal" period, or with sales that would take place had there been no advertising. If the net revenue (VB) delivered by the advertisement is greater than the cost of advertising, the promotion is profitable. Retailers understand this principle well, and seek to evaluate their efforts in this manner. This is why retail advertising takes on the appearance of piecemeal decisions, planning done ad by ad. In reality, each individual message can be, and often is, evaluated on its own merits. Retailers' product ads may also generate sales for unadvertised brands by attracting more shoppers to a store. These secondary effects can only be arrived at by finding the relationship between sales of unadvertised items and the additional store traffic caused by an advertisement. This is apparently a more difficult task than tracing sales directly to an advertisement.

The problem changes radically, however, when resulting sales are not immediate and one-time events. A nursery catalogue mailed in the spring may bring unsolicited orders for fall planting. New buyers gained by an advertisement in January may continue as customers in the months ahead, especially for products which have to be replenished at periodic intervals. The higher the frequency of purchase, the greater the probability that the incremental business occasioned by an advertisement will be continued. To estimate these carryover effects, it is necessary to know the customer retention rate, or the percentage of current buyers that will continue patronage in subsequent periods. This proportion is customarily regarded as being constant from period to period or month to month. By making this assumption, firms can calculate the net revenue of an advertisement from early returns, or from those of the initial period. But the retention rate must be known in order to do this. The way to ascertain this rate is to withhold all advertising to new customers and observe their behavior. But even then, marketers can never quite be sure that the initial ad should get all the credit for return customers.

The nature of things undergoes further substantive changes as advertising veers away from retailing and direct response marketing. Unlike mail order operators, general advertisers do not possess customer lists and individual purchase records. Nor are advertising results immediate, capable of being attributed to this or that ad. Companies work on a campaign basis, emitting a series of advertising messages, with no individual ad, singly or in combination, leaving testimony by which its selling contribution can be appraised. How, then, can a firm optimize its budget when the sales response curve to advertising remains shrouded in uncertainty? Proponents of the theoretical methods offer two possible ways out of the dilemma: experimentation and regression analysis.

Market Experiments The usual type of test employed is the so-called field experiment, essentially a sales area test. The idea is to advertise at different levels in different but equivalent markets. The disparities in sales can then theoretically be attributed to variations in budgets, and the vital sales response curve can be derived.

For such experiments to be vested with external validity, the capacity to generalize results, a number of rather exacting conditions must be met. The markets selected have to be representative of those to which research findings are to be projected. They must typify that larger universe in terms of purchasing behavior, sales outlets, competitive efforts, and media patterns. Also recommended is "media isolation," so that sales measurements can be ascribed only to test areas, and no others. This self-containment aspect has two faces. First, no outside influences should impinge on sales in the experimentally-designated areas. Second, there should be no wasted circulation—media messages transmitted to areas beyond the boundaries of the test markets.

Nevertheless, market experiments have engendered heated debate and controversy in the advertising industry. One issue pertains to the magnitude of spending levels tested. Market researchers generally concede that differences in spending levels must be substantial before sales effects are discernible. Joseph Plummer, a former vice-president of Leo Burnett, a large, Chicago-based advertising agency, estimates that an increase of 50 percent in the spending level is needed to obtain a 5 percent increase in net sales, on the average.[8] The products alluded to were presumably packaged goods. Plummer also noted that Leo Burnett had conducted some fifty market experiments between 1971 and 1978, but had "fairly complete data" for twenty. Of these, only seven yielded "statistically significant and logical results."[9] Under these circumstances, it is hardly surprising that marketing departments have displayed no great enthusiasm for experimentation.

Another set of issues deals with selection and control of test markets. Critics have amassed impressive evidence which brings into question the ability to choose representative markets, to hold all things constant except advertising, and to obtain generalized results relatively free of large errors.[10] In fact, the same test market data can yield different sales estimates, depending upon the technique used to make the forecast.[11]

A third point of contention comes to focus on the problem of stability. Assuming a sales response function can be calculated from an experimental study and projected to the firm's market, its degree of permanency is still open to question. This function, like all other things, submits to the ravages of time, though the rate and direction of change remain variable.

This dynamic aspect of marketing was prominently exemplified by Anheuser-Busch, whose research efforts in the 1960s were heralded as an unparalleled triumph of scientific budgeting. Market experiments spanned the largest part of the decade, and the brewer spared no expense in seeking a solution to the problem of how much to spend on advertising. Test markets were conducted in accordance with best-prescribed procedures. The company acted on research recommendations. It reduced the budget drastically and, in a mood of magnanimity, assured its ad agency that no income would be lost from budget reductions. And for a while, the company profited as market share and net earnings rose.

But the prescription for success was short-lived. The 1970s brought more intense competition to the beer industry, and conclusions drawn from the years of research seemed no longer valid. What was once considered gross overspending was now seen as stark underspending. Advertising costs per barrel for Anheuser-Busch skyrocketed, jumping from $.52 in 1974 to $1.60 in 1977, an increase of more than 200 percent. During the same period, the per barrel expenditures of its major competitor, Miller Brewing Company, rose from $1.50 to $1.78, an increase of only 19 percent.[12]

If yesterday's results are not relevant to today's problems, of what use is experimentation? One answer to the problem of a changing world has been the adaptive model. Sales arising from advertising are regarded as a process with parameters which are ever changing in value. To account for such change, adaptive models seek to modify themselves periodically by altering the parameters of the sales response function. It is theoretically feasible to change the model itself so that it will conform with each new situation as it appears. But, as of now, this has not been done.

A pioneer in laying the theoretical foundation for adaptive models is John D. C. Little of the Massachusetts Institute of Technology. According to Little, the average sales rate at any given time can be described by the quadratic function

$$S = \alpha + \beta X - \gamma X^2$$

where

$$S = \text{sales rate}$$
$$X = \text{advertising rate}$$
$$\alpha, \beta, \gamma = \text{parameters}$$

The gross margin of a product (M), which is the incremental profit expressed as a fraction of sales (S), is conceived of as being a constant. The advertising rate that will maximize profits (X*) works out mathematically to be described by the equation

$$X^* = \frac{M\beta - 1}{2M\gamma}$$

Little assumes that β is subject to random disturbances, such as effects of competitive activity, product changes, economic fluctuations, and will therefore change over time. To account for such changes in budgeting for a future period ($t+1$), Little uses the difference of sales rates between two sets of experimental markets, one above the national average and the other below. The β coefficient in $t+1$ is a weighted average of β in the present and β in the experimental markets. The optimizing rule[13] for the new budget then becomes

$$X^*_{(t+1)} = \frac{M(t+1) - 1}{2M\gamma}$$

Although adaptive models have been in existence for more than fifteen years, they have been strictly confined to academic conclaves and professional journals. Few, if any, companies actually use them to set their advertising budgets.

Regression This approach, unlike the marketing experiment, cannot manipulate variables. It cannot enhance or pare advertising spending to desired levels and observe what happens to sales. It must accept what is, or what was, as inputs to its investigative procedures. Using the historical record for its evidence, regression analysis is retrospective. It infers possible future events from those of the past. But if offers already available, cost-free data from which to estimate a sales response curve.

The amount expended on advertising (X) is normally taken as the independent variable. The volume of sales (S) is regarded as the dependent variable, and inferred from its past relationship to X. The values of S are then estimated from values of X in the form of the equation, $S = a + bX$ if the relationship is linear, or $S = a + b(\log X)$ if curvilinear.

There are basically two ways of proceeding with regression analysis: cross-sectional or time series. The first approach calls for examining different markets for the same time period. It has been likened to snapshots taken at the identical instant, so that people and objects which make up a market stand, as it were, mute and motionless, forever frozen in time. The second approach requires a market, or group of markets, to be observed chronologically over a relevant span of time.

Regardless of method, cross-sectional or time series, the analysis is bound to encounter troublesome problems in attempting to ascertain the sales effects of advertising. To derive meaningful results from cross-sectional analysis, substantial budget differences must exist among the various sales territories or geographical regions. But most companies willfully try to smooth out such anomalies, so that markets of comparable potential receive similar amounts of advertising. A second condition for an effective solution demands no systematic influences other than those of advertising. Market size or sales potential, for example, must not be associated with observable variations in sales. The same principle applies to time series, though the variation is temporal rather than spatial. But, here again, the realities of the marketplace do not usually comply with statistical requirements for precise, unambiguous information that can be neatly fitted into mathematical equations. If the analysis is cross-sectional, there persists the questionable assumption that a given budget change in Wyoming or Montana has the same effect as in Los Angeles or New York. If the analysis takes the time series route, data must be available for relatively short periods, so as not to reflect changing tastes and habits.[14]

Lastly, regression analysis runs headlong into the enigmatic subject of causality. The designation of sales as the dependent variable in the equation implies that changes in advertising expenditures cause changes in sales. The analyst can only hope that this is so. But in practice, most companies set their budgets as a fixed percentage of sales. A high correlation between advertising and sales therefore indicates, not a likely sales result, but a strict adherence to the percent-of-sales rule in budgeting.

To explore a possible reverse flow of causation—in this case from sales to advertising—statisticians have proposed a two-way equation. All variables involved in this reciprocating relationship are expressed as both dependent and independent variables, and the entire set of equations is solved simultaneously.[15] Two or three-stage least square procedures are also feasible to handle causative effects flowing in more than one direction. Using simultaneous equations, the simple sales-advertising relationship, assuming linearity, can be expressed as follows:

$$S = a + bX$$
$$X = c + dS$$

If the b coefficient is sloped positively and values of d are negligible, it might be assumed that advertising (X) was responsible for variations in sales (S). But if a contrary result appears, the opposite might be inferred.

Simultaneous equations may yield better insights than the traditional least square estimates. But they do not resolve the question of how to estimate a sales response curve when relationships are topsy-turvy, and when sales, in effect, determine the level of advertising.

BUDGETING IN OLIGOPOLISTIC MARKETS

Most of the theoretical models ignore competitors, or possiblities that action by one company might set off a spurt of defensive spending by others. Such eruptions, errant and unpredictable, are most likely to come in oligopolistic markets where leaders use advertising as an important competitive weapon. Illustrative of a reliance on advertising to ward off marketing inroads by aggressive rivals is the cigarette industry. The success of Philip Morris' Merit, coupled with the Edsel-like failure of Real, brought a higher wave of advertising by R. J. Reynolds in a bid to maintain its faltering market dominance. "We believe in the Procter & Gamble and General Foods approach," Gerald Long, executive vice president, was quoted as saying in a telephone interview in June 1980. "You've got to spend more against the consumer than the competition."[16] Beer and analgesics seem to have been similarly affected at the time by advertising wars.

A market structure dominated by few firms is fairly typical of American industry. The four leading firms are responsible for about 40 percent of all American manufacturing, on the average. The average eight-firm concentration ratio amounts to approximately 60 percent. Service industries, such as airlines, banks, and insurance companies, all leaning upon heavy doses of advertising to support their marketing efforts, are similarly characterized by high concentration ratios. When oligopolistic industries reach a mature status, with demand close to the saturation level, marketing settles into what might be called a sum zero situation; a firm gains sales by taking customers away from competitors. Under these conditions, an aggressive maneuver by one company is apt to provoke strong counter-measures by others. It is also customary for firms to monitor each other's activity and manipulate advertising budgets in relation to market share.

Working from the Dorfman-Steiner thesis regarding the marginal value of promotion, economist Richard Schmalensee proved mathematically that the optimum point for a firm selling in an oligopolistic market is a ratio of advertising elasticity to price elasticity.[17] The relationship of this formula to advertising expenditures can then be stated as follows:

$$\eta(A)/\eta(P) = N \times C/P \times Q = \text{Advertising expenditure(\$)/Sales(\$)}$$

where

$\eta(A)$ = elasticity of demand in relation to advertising
$\eta(P)$ = elasticity of demand in relation to price
N = number of advertisements
C = cost per advertisement
Q = number of units sold
P = price per unit sold

Schmalensee argues that if demand elasticities are constant, or if the ratio between them is constant, the optimal decision for a firm is to keep a fixed advertising to sales ratio. This policy seems most appropriate when sales are relatively stable, and firms are content to undertake no forceful actions to upset the balance. In this business setting, the formula lends support to the rationale of setting advertising budgets as a fixed percentage of sales. But if this policy is carried out, as it seems to be, estimating the sales impact of advertising becomes an almost hopeless task.

Although the economic theorem defines the optimal point, it is not helpful in practical matters of budget-setting. It only states that the ratio of advertising expenditures to sales should equal the ratio of advertising elasticity to price elasticity. But it does not tell how to arrive at this ideal.

There have been several advertising models prominently featuring brand share. An early model was that of Robert Weinberg, then market research manager of IBM.[18] A key concept in keeping with competitive efforts is what Weinberg called the "advertising exchange rate," which can be described as follows:

$$\text{Exchange rate} = \frac{\text{Company advertising expenditure/Company net sales}}{\text{Residual industry advertising expenditure/Residual industry net sales}} = \frac{\text{Company advertising expenditure per \$ of sales}}{\text{Industry advertising expenditure per \$ of sales}}$$

The exchange rate's logarithm is calculated for each year and related to changes in market share. The logarithmic values comport with the concept of diminishing returns to scale. According to Weinberg, the results of the calculations should predict sales that are most likely to occur at various levels of advertising expenditures. However, the method maintains an utmost dependence on past data to develop functional relationships, and can thus reflect, as most economic models do, a reverse causation if advertising budgets are being set as a percentage of sales.

Another market share-advertising expenditure model is that of the Hendry Corporation, first developed in 1962. The company has never described its methodology publicly to enable a complete evaluation. According to the Hendry Corporation, the model requires three items of information; direct manufacturing margin (presumable sales minus variable production cost), advertising expenditure level, and share of market. It then supposedly determines the relationship between varying levels of advertising and resulting market shares and profit contributions.[19]

The information inputs, it seems, are manipulated in the context of a purchase behavior model based on brand switching derived from a consumer panel. The notion of entropy, a concept in physics which deals with internal energy in a thermodynamic system, is used to calculate a theoretical brand switching constant. This figure enables an analyst to estimate consumers' probable brand choices from share of market information.[20] The greatest value of the Hendry model is not in budgeting, but in the insights it provides about market structure when evaluating relative product positions and formulating brand strategy.

GUIDELINES—PRACTITIONERS' VIEWPOINTS

Despite the continued output of ever more refined and elegant models which appear in professional journals, the industry has remained more or less indifferent. Businesspeople's rejection of the theoretical prescriptions stems from a widely-held opinion that the models are defective.

One of the strongest objections to theoretical models is their underlying assumption that revenue caused by advertising can be separated from that engendered by other marketing mix variables. This idea, to the practitioner, is both naive and damaging. If advertising can be set apart from everything else and have its functions diagnosed, like viruses in a medical laboratory, industries relying upon promotion as the mainstay of their marketing programs would seldom witness unexpected product failures, or even excessive inventories. A firm need only calculate its sales response curve to know exactly how to proceed.

But the marketplace is not like an experimental laboratory, and uncertainty follows the practitioner at each step. The prevailing business view follows the lines laid out at the annual meeting of the Association of National Advertisers by Robert Rechholtz of the Joseph Schlitz Brewing Company. Identifying forty factors which influence sales and profits, Rechholtz listed only ten, or one-fourth of the total, as being capable of being controlled by a company.[21] How can one then assess the interrelationships of all variables, weight them properly, and predict the point at which marginal returns equal marginal costs?

The greater the effect of uncontrolled variables, the more a firm comes under the sway of market forces, reacting to them rather than mastering them. Given these external factors managers hold, guidelines lend themselves better to flexibility and fast response.

The theoreticians argue that the existence of uncontrollable influences should not deter the use of rational decision making. Few things in marketing are error free, but decisions must be made nevertheless. And a scientific approach, they claim, leads to better decisions than an intuitive one.[22]

Practitioners, however, reject this argument on many grounds. First, they regard the association of science with modeling and intuition with the nonuse of models as semantics which would be absolutely deceptive if put into an advertisement. They point out that the model builders are quite willing to accommodate managerial judgment, incorporating it into their formula with complete credence under the Bayesian dispensation. Are then these "subjective probabilities" made any less intuitive, managers may ask, because they are manipulated by a computer? The fact is that both guidelines and mathematical models may use intuitive pronouncements. These opinions may indeed have a firm basis in experience, but no more so in one method than in another.

Second, practitioners see the main question not as whether decisions will be improved, but the degree of improvement. The adoption of a theoretical system is normally an expensive proposition, especially if experimental testing is necessary, which is often the case. This incremental cost must be judged in the light of what can be gained. Costs can be estimated. But the proponents of models cannot put a figure on expected gains, either in the form of increased revenue or savings. The promised benefits are phrased in generalities. Under such circumstances, hardnosed managers can seldom justify the incremental costs. The effects of uncontrolled variables, coupled with joint influences of marketing mix factors, render sales unresponsive over a relatively wide range of advertising expenditures. This imperviousness minimizes the likelihood of changes in advertising inducing major changes in sales.

Third, the thesis of greater effectiveness through science is highly debatable. If market experiments alter spending by substantial amounts, as they must for the market to be "read," some areas are apt to receive budgets which are far from optimal, or further than they would normally be. If advertising is excessive, the overspending represents waste. If advertising is insufficient, the firm exposes itself to possible deterioration of market position. Lost customers are not easily regained. As a consequence, market experiments are not always conducive to better decisions, and they can also be accompanied by higher risks.

The rebuff to theoretical models and experimental design for setting budgets does not mean that companies have turned their backs on marketing intelligence. Most marketing plans are based on extensive research data. Spending level tests are commonplace in packaged goods industries, where markets can easily be fragmented. But they are not conducted as a means of gathering inputs for computer models which trigger spending decisions. Nor are they carried out on a scale which might jeopardize a company's standing in the market. Rather, they are used to feel out the market, to approach the theoretical optimum by changing guideline values incrementally. Operating in an environment permeated with uncertainty, firms grope as it were by trial and error towards a position of economic equilibrium.

Practitioners also assert that questions of how much to spend on advertising cannot be divorced from questions of where to spend it and on what to spend it. Media discounts, for example, may allow firms to deliver more advertising messages for the same dollars. Thus, media selection can alter "advertising weight" though total dollar spending remains constant. Moreover, the advertising presentation might have a far greater impact on sales than the size of the budget. But there is no practical way to assess quantitatively the sales value of creative inputs. Hence, attempts to measure the effects of advertising only in terms of changes in expenditures may be as unrealistic as dreams could make them.

PERCENT OF SALES

Of all guideline methods, the percent-of-sales rule enjoys the greatest popularity. It has two major variations; the percentage factor can be applied either to past sales or to future sales. In the first instance, company records are taken as data and used as a base. In the second, a sales forecast is made and the percentage is applied to this projection. When sales of a previous period are used, budgets follow, often by as much as a year, changes in sales. When forecasted sales are used, alterations in ad spending are expected to be concurrent with variations in sales. Futuristic sales are more common than past sales as a basis for budgeting, ostensibly because it is desirable to match revenue with expenses.

The so-called unit-of-sales method is a variation of the percent-of-sales technique. The difference between the two is in the method of computation. Instead of multiplying a dollar sales figure by a decimal, the unit-of-sales method allocates to advertising a certain sum of money based on the number of units sold, past or prospective. This approach is sometimes referred to as the "assessment" method. Each sale is charged with an assessment for advertising. The method is widely used by auto manufacturers and certain packaged goods companies.

The advertising budget appropriated by the unit-of-sales method is identical with that calculated by a percent-of-sales approach, if price remains constant. This proposition is illustrated as follows:

Suppose a company were to forecast sales of one million cases of product, priced at $2 a case. Also assume the firm spends about $.20 on advertising for each case sold, which comes to 10 percent per unit of revenue. Under the percent-of-sales method, projected revenue would come to $2,000,000 (1,000,000 cases × $2). The advertising budget would then be calculated as forecasted sales multiplied by 10 percent, or $2,000,000 × .10 = $200,000. The unit-of-sales method would project sales of a million units and allocate $.20 to each, arriving at the same $200,000 figure (1,000,000 × $.20 = $200,000).

One advantage claimed for the percent-of-sales method, or variations thereof, is that advertising budgets can be regarded as variable. This assumes that they are based on future sales and that forecasts are reasonably accurate. But the proportionality of advertising expenses to sales can be maintained even when past sales are used, if the industry undergoes little change from year to year. The method operates best in stable markets. Its proponents claim that stability is encouraged when leading competitors tacitly follow a fixed advertising-to-sales ratio, for firms avoid advertising spending wars to uphold profit margins.

When sales are subject to wide fluctuations, some mechanism for rapid adjustments must be resorted to. If not, the objective of keeping expenditures as a predetermined percentage of sales cannot be achieved. A sharp drop in sales because of a recession, for example, would raise the advertising-sales ratio if the original budget were strictly adhered to. For this reason, most companies have flexible or contingent budget plans. These allow quick alterations in projected spending in order to conform to changing conditions.

The percent-of-sales method has been sharply criticized for illogical thinking. Sales determine advertising rather than being seen as a determinant of advertising. At best, promotional expenditures are regarded not as sales-generating devices, but as a cost of doing business. When a brand is growing, the damage may not be great because it is getting promotional increments to spur sales. Whether the additions are just right, too much, or too little can only be conjectured—as it is with other systems. Declining brands, however, may drift into patterns of overspending, especially if business keeps coming from loyal, established customers whose buying habits would be the same without any prompting from commercial messages. The hallmark of good management is knowing when to begin harvesting an aging product.

THE TASK METHOD

The task method was formalized in 1961 by Russel H. Colley, who sought to bring a "management by objective" philosophy into advertising.[23] Colley argued, cogently and plausibly, that the budgeting process must begin with a definition of objectives. This is essential to all planning, no matter what phase of business. Only after setting forth what advertising is intended to do, Colley affirmed, can the failure or success of the activity be ascertained.

The task method builds up a budget in three main stages. First, it specifies the advertising objectives. Second, it chooses the appropriate means to use to reach these objectives. Accordingly, it draws up an operating plan, spelling out in detail what must be done to meet the designated goals. The third step is more or less routine. Each task of the operating plan is costed out. The sum of the individual costs becomes the recommended level of spending.

A central consideration is the choice of means. What tasks? Here lies the fatal flaw. The tasks visualized by Colley and the subsequent throng of disciples were nonsales goals, such as awareness, comprehension, and conviction. The management by objective system thus came to rest on the fundamental assumption that advertising works through a "hierarchy of effects." But the validity of this psychologically-based model of advertising is conjectural. There are, as of now, no known relationships between the different levels which make up the supposed hierarchy and the apex, which is represented by sales.

When intermediary, nonsales goals are comparatively straight-forward, and can be directly related to revenue, the task method presents few problems. For example, many industrial marketers aim at generating inquiries through reader service cards offered by trade publications. In these instances, the leads furnished by the advertisements can be monitored to see how many result in sales. Thus, the task of getting X inquiries can be translated into Y sales. Similarly, retail ads featuring loss leaders are designed to increase store traffic. In turn, the store traffic objective can be related to additional sales.

But a different picture comes into view when goals are far removed from sales, and the exact relationships are speculative and indistinct. Let us say, for example, that a company sets an advertising goal of increasing brand awareness by 20 percent, as measured by aided recall. Well and good! The intention is stated in specific, quantifiable terms as recommended by management consultants, and may seem as something good to do for the product. After all, a higher awareness must be a plus if cognition influences human action. But whether that end justifies the cost is another matter. Who knows? The projected 20 percent more awareness may evoke a highly-disappointing contribution to profits. To set objectives without a clear understanding of how they relate to other marketing variables, or to end results that are manifest in action, critics charge, is to designate tasks both arbitrarily and somewhat foolishly.[24]

THE AFFORDABLE METHOD

The affordable method, as the name implies, pegs spending levels to a judgment of how much can be afforded. The amount affordable is actually

TABLE 7–2 *Illustration of the Affordable Method*

Forecasted sales	$ xxx
Less: cost of sales	xxx
Gross profits	xxx
Less: sales and administrative, except advertising	xxx
Less: profits	xxx
Amount available for advertising	$ xxx

a residual, a leftover after all other obligations, including profits, are deducted from gross revenue. Table 7–2 illustrates this method.

This manner of budgeting is top-down, and sometimes called the controller's method. The rationale here is to manage the firm's profits, or contribution to profits, as the case may be. This is done by altering the firm's programed expenses, for the values of fixed and variable costs usually cannot be changed in the short run.

To affect profits by an affordable budget procedure, advertising must comprise a relatively large proportion of marketing expenses, so that any variation would make a meaningful impact on the bottom line. This form of budgeting implicitly assumes that advertising contributes little to sales in the short run; revenue will stay pretty much the same no matter how the ad budget is manipulated. The method seems most feasible when the advertising budget contains significant amounts of slack funds not regarded as absolutely necessary. That nonessential part might be considered as discretionary, and lopped off whenever the profit standard is threatened. But if sales are sensitive to the volume of advertising, the affordable budget may be something that a firm can ill afford.

A somewhat unique twist in applying the method is the approach of Schlissel and Giacalone, combining the affordable budget with the task method.[25] In this formalized scheme, profit goals act to impose an upper limit on the marketing budget. A set of tasks are then passed down to particular groups, with allowances proportionate to the presumed importance of each job. Table 7–3 illustrates this top-down, task-setting procedure.

Table 7–3 shows a hypothetical budget which contemplates two prime objectives, servicing present customers and gaining new ones. The total of $10 million is apportioned to goals in accordance with management's judgment as to the relative importance of each. For example, some $8.5 million of the $10.0 million total, or 85 percent, is to be directed to already established business relations, goal number one. The remaining $1.5 million, or 15 percent, is to go towards new prospective customers, goal number two.

Given this 85-15 split, managers are called upon to devise ways of meeting objectives. Table 7–3 lists these programs as 1a to 1d, and as all

TABLE 7–3 *Illustration of a Top-down Task Method for Budgeting*

Objectives or Tasks	(1) Task Value	(2) Personal Selling	(3) Advertising	(4) Sales Promotion	(5) Physical Distribution	(6) Other
			(All dollar figures are in millions of dollars)			
All Tasks	$10.00					
1. Sell to existing customers	8.50	$1.67	$4.51	$1.06	$ .63	$ .63
a) Increase distribution		(75%)	—	—	(25%)	
to___%	1.70	1.28	—	—	.42	—
b) Increase brand		—	(85%)	(15%)	—	(3%)
awareness to ___%	4.25	—	3.49	.64	—	.12
c) Develop new uses		(15%)	(60%)	(20%)	—	(5%)
for product	1.70	.26	1.02	.34	—	.43
d) Create more package awareness		(15%)	—	(10%)	(25%)	(50%)
at point of purchase	.85	.13	—	.08	.21	.43
2. Add new customers	1.50					
a) Build better brand		(10%)	(60%)	(25%)	—	(5%)
attitude	.75	.07	.45	.19	—	.04
•						
•						
•						
etc.						

Source: Adapted from Schlissel and Giacalone, "Budgeting the Strategic Marketing Plan." Paper presented to the Academy of Marketing Science Annual Conference, April-May 1980.

subgroups under objective number two. The respective money allocations of each are shown in column number one.

The next step is to assign funds to each functional unit in accordance with its presumed importance and program requirements. Thus, task 1a will get $1,280,000 for personal selling programs and $420,000 for physical distribution. Each functional unit, of course, will spell out both tasks and programs in greater detail. For example, the sales department may spend so much on increasing the sales staff, so much on sales training, so much on number of calls per salesperson, etc. Similarly, the advertising department, to achieve task 1b, an increase in brand awareness, would draw up a detailed media schedule, together with a creative presentation.

Figures for each line of the plan tell the extent to which a functional unit is involved in a given task. Going down a column vertically reveals a department's role in different programs. The sum of each column is the amount budgeted to a functional unit.

The procedure described by Schlissel and Giacalone does not constitute a radical departure from current practices. Though an overall amount is set by the "affordable" method, it can just as readily be designated by any other, such as the percent-of-sales or the competitive parity approach. This sum is then broken down in various ways—by functional units, tasks, markets, etc.

The greater the formality of the system, the more ends and means are made explicit. The latter, unlike that in the task method, has no open-ended, blank checks. The system introduces a certain degree of discipline into the budgeting process.

But the system does not overcome the glaring weaknesses of the basic guideline methods. It is still subject to inherent limitations of arriving at a total figure, and of determining the relative importance of specific tasks in meeting predetermined goals.

COMPETITIVE PARITY

Strictly speaking, competitive parity means that a company attempts to set its advertising budget in accordance with its share of market and competitive spending. To illustrate: A firm has a 20 percent market share, while its closest rival boasts a 40 percent share. If the competitor is spending $10 million on advertising, the parity budget becomes $5 million. This would make relative advertising proportionate to relative sales.

Faithful compliance with the parity principle implies a passive marketing role that is self-imposed. A firm copies its competitors in a follow-the-leader routine. This follower philosophy strongly suggests an optimal policy that considers share of advertising equal to share of market.

In practice, however, companies that look over their shoulders when setting budgets stray far afield from the proportionality notion. There are many reasons for this divergence. Cost structures are not the same for all firms in an industry. Nor do all firms use marketing mix variables in the same proportions. In fact, the share of advertising seems to decline with market share increases. For example, General Motors consistently spends less on advertising as a percentage of sales than does Ford. And Chrysler, with the weakest market share among the top three auto manufacturers, has the highest advertising to sales ratio. The same principle seems to hold for industrial products.[26] This suggests that management acts as though advertising were possessed of economies of scale, so that higher market shares can be maintained at smaller percentage outlays for promotion.

At any rate, firms that embrace a competitive parity strategy proceed similar to those relying on a percent-of-sales method. They do not attempt to achieve a proportionality of relative advertising to relative sales. Rather, they set their budgets as a ratio of advertising to sales which may be, and usually is, different from that of their competitor. But they will adjust this ratio to match changes in competitive ones. The strategy can thus be described as one of trying to keep the advertising budget as a constant percentage of sales in relation to changes in competitive ratios.

BUSINESS FLUCTUATIONS

Despite society's best efforts, business remains subject to alternating waves of prosperity and recession. These cyclical patterns leave unmistakable imprints on budgets. In economic parlance, advertising is a "lag series." Variations in expenditures tend to follow variations in sales. Thus, businesses are prone to increase their advertising spending in good times and cut back in hard times. Many firms assure such results almost automatically by contingency or step budgets, especially when using a percent-of-sales method. Essentially, step budgets designate different amounts of advertising for different levels of sales. When forecasts turn downward, budgets are quickly adjusted to head in the same direction.

These practices have been both attacked and defended by people in the advertising industry and in academic circles.[27] Critics maintain that depressed markets require more stimuli, not less, and have therefore urged increases in advertising during recessions. But business has almost universally resisted spending-out-of-recession solutions, and for good reason. It is highly doubtful that liberal doses of advertising can significantly push up sales which are depressed by a cyclical downturn. Consumers are not likely to go on spending sprees, no matter how much advertising is directed to them, when their incomes are threatened by shorter work weeks, layoffs, and fewer available jobs.

Probably the most cogent case for maintaining advertising levels during a recession was made by the National Broadcasting Company in 1975. Among other things, the NBC report cited studies which measured advertising and sales for five different recessions: 1949, 1954, 1958, 1961, 1970. The data encompassed from 95 to 133 different advertisers in each recession period. The findings showed that companies which did not cut their budgets pushed sales higher, as compared with firms which retrenched their media spending.[28] Similar conclusions were drawn by a McGraw-Hill study of 468 industrial companies operating in the recession of 1974–1975.[29]

This implied causality between advertising and sales in times of adversity rests on somewhat specious reasoning. Not all product categories are affected by recession in the same way, and variations among them are considerable.[30] High-priced durables, which represent discretionary consumer spending, are highly sensitive to business fluctuations. Other products are completely unaffected, such as common, everyday necessities. Here, reductions of promotional spending make little sense. If advertising is a lag series, it should be expected that reduced budgets go with lower sales and that more spending is accompanied by more sales. These relationships by no means imply that higher budgets lifted sales out of recessionary declines.

Businesses caught up in the recession may resort to greater use of specials and promotions while they reduce advertising outlays.[31] For example, automobile manufacturers offered attractive rebates in 1975 to break out of the sales doldrums. But timing is important. These price discounts came during the later phase of the recession when the low point in the business cycle had already been passed. Many marketers claimed at the time that the deep price cuts bought sales at the expense of future business. Be that as it may, there is an advantage to speeding up cash inflows. In the 1980 slump, however, the same tactics did not work. They came at the very early stages of the business slump, and were disappointing, probably because of the poor timing.

In most instances, firms have little control over drooping sales caused by general business conditions. These external forces impose serious obstacles and definite constraints on a firm's ability to influence sales. These limitations force companies to fall back on methods which are more amenable to internal control, such as the time-honored ones of cost cutting. Advertising budgets are not exempt from the process, and consequently, variations in advertising spending will tend to follow the expansions and contractions of business in general.

ADVERTISING AS AN INVESTMENT

The previous discussion perceived advertising as an operating expense, and accounting practices lend credence to this view. Budgets are drawn up for periods of no longer than a year. Plans are reviewed monthly, bimonthly, quarterly; seldom do reviews take place at longer intervals. Outlays are charged to the period in which they are incurred, which presumes the benefits accruing from advertising are being used up in the current accounting period.

Because firms treat advertising as a current expense does not necessarily mean that effects do not carry over into future periods. For example, the now classic study made by Lydia Pinkham of a vegetable compound that was popular in the 1930s suggested cumulative effects.[32] The economist Joel Dean argued that advertising belongs in the capital budget because of long-term effects.[33] Expensing these costs, some critics charge, enables corporations to write off the outlays immediately so as to obtain a higher rate of return. On the assumption that advertising effects do in fact last for several years, Harry Block held that some forty firms avoided an average of $2 million a year in income taxes by the IRS allowing them to expense promotional charges rather than to capitalize them.[34]

Industry spokespersons also talk of advertising as an investment, though their practice contradicts the theory. This is evident in such phrases as "building a brand franchise," developing "customer goodwill and loyalty." A quarterly report to stockholders by Consolidated Foods contained a special report entitled: "Investment Spending: Advertising." The report noted that the company considers "advertising as necessary investment spending for building long-term consumer franchises."[35]

In 1978, the Association of National Advertisers established a task force to study the subject of return on advertising investment.[36] The advertising-as-investment thesis professes to see long-term carryover effects resulting from advertising effort. An advertisement, it is argued, may be responsible not merely for an individual's one-time trial of a product. That customer may continue to buy for a long time, and generate a flow of revenue stretching into the future. All customers are also not in the market at all times. An advertisement may be noted, filed in the memory, and called up by the mind at a later date. When a purchase occasion arises, an advertisement in the musty past may thus wield an influence in the here and now. Lastly, it may take a series of advertising messages to move someone into a buyer category, and early ones can be just as vital to that sale as current ones.

The long-lasting effects of advertising, if true, have important managerial ramifications. The proponents of the investment thesis take the position that internal analysis should separate itself from public reporting. That is, financial analysis for long-range planning should not be constricted by the straightjacket of accounting for tax purposes and custodial reporting. As an investment, advertising must compete for funds with alternative projects on return-on-investment criteria, such as profitability, rate of return, discount cash flow.

To treat advertising as an investment requires a knowledge of how long, and in what amounts, affected sales will continue beyond the current period, conventionally accepted as one year. If effects last only a few months, or less than twelve, they are treated as a delayed response, not as a cumulative effect. The latter is usually estimated by econometric methods known as distributed lags. Sales are regarded as functions of advertising in various periods:

$$(Y_t = f(A_t, A_{t-1}, A_{t-2}...)$$

This functional relationship can then be expressed in direct fashion by the equation:

$$Y_t = a + \sum_{j=0}^{n} b_j A_{t-j} + u_t$$

where

Y_t = sales in time t
A_{t-j} = advertising in time $t-j$
u_t = independent, normally distributed error, with a mean of zero and a standard deviation of 1

The above conceptualization is seldom used, however, because of difficulties in application. One of these is in determining n, the number of lagged independent variables which are to be included in the estimating equation. The most popular method of distributed lags has become the Koyck model, named after its originator. Sales in a given period are conceived as being shaped by two factors: the ubiquitous present and the residual effects of the entire past. This relationship can be described by the equation,

$$Y_c = a + \lambda Y_{t-1} + bA_t + u_t$$

This formula, evidently more efficient, still heaps gnawing problems upon its users. Many companies may lack historical data that are suitable for the model, especially values for the decaying effects of advertising over time (λ). Its absence would suggest some sort of controlled experiment whereby all advertising is stopped in order to observe how far sales fall.

Besides the obvious limitations of estimates coming from sales area tests, a company may incur additional risks by the discontinuance of all advertising. The Koyck model is also susceptible to certain computational biases which are not inconsequential in the derivation of the lagged series.[37] But the most serious objection to the usual calculation is that all repeat purchases are attributable to advertising, and only to advertising. Endowing advertising with such powers, critics contend, is illogical, for even if it evoked initial trial, repurchase decisions are affected by many factors. Brand loyalty may require satisfaction in usage, which comes from product policy. Or it may emerge from astute pricing or favorable comparisons with other brands or convenience in brand availability. The marketing mix variables which might convert a trier into a loyal customer are numerous indeed. To capitalize advertising budgets without a similar treatment of other marketing expenditures working for long-term benefits can lead to suboptimization of resource allocations.

But the basic question has until now been skirted. Are there really cumulative effects from advertising? Darral G. Clarke examined seventy published studies in consumer goods industries dealing with the subject.[38] Some sixty of the seventy econometric studies related to low-priced, frequently purchased items. Clarke concluded that the studies yielded inconsistent results, varying radically among product categories as well as among individual brands. The duration of advertising effects ranged from a low of three months to a high of fifteen months, indicating a short-term span. When Clarke adjusted the findings to correct for computational biases, the duration range dropped to three to nine months, well within the current period. A companion study undertook an extensive examination of communication effects rather than just sales effects. This study did an exhaustive survey of behavioral science literature.[39] The authors concluded that the impressions made by advertising lasted no longer than a few months. It thus seems that the advertising investment issue may turn out as nothing more than the proverbial tempest in a teapot.

SUMMARY

The budget represents an operating plan expressed in financial terms. Upon approval, it becomes an instrument of financial control by serving as a standard against which performance is measured. But budget variances are not associated with causal factors as in conventional cost accounting. Nevertheless, the budget is an important factor in an adjustment process whereby a firm modifies its behavior in the light of unfolding events.

There are two basic approaches for setting budget levels: theoretical and guideline. The latter is the most prevalent in the advertising industry.

Theoretical methods rest on marginal concepts of economics. Their employment requires a knowledge of sales response to different levels of expenditures. The marginal theories are most appropriate to situations involving an immediate and traceable response to an advertisement, as in direct mail and retail operations.

Response to individual advertisements cannot be ascertained for general advertising. To circumvent this difficulty, proponents of theoretical budget-setting methods offer two alternatives for deriving estimates of sales response—market experiments and regression analysis. Both of these methods have major shortcomings.

Of all guideline methods, the percent-of-sales rule is the most popular. The affordable method also has a substantial following. Both of these methods tacitly regard advertising as a cost of doing business.

The task method, another guideline technique, espouses management by objective. However, its usage seems limited. The main reason is because designated tasks cannot be directly related to sales.

Budgets are also affected by cyclical fluctuations. Advertising is a lag factor, and will tend to follow change in general business patterns. Despite urging by some to deviate from a philosophy wherein promotional budgets follow demand fluctuations, it is doubtful whether advertising is capable of altering cyclical behavior in sales.

Conventional accounting treats advertising as an expense. One school of thought holds that advertising should be regarded as an investment. However, there is little empirical evidence which supports this proposition.

Questions for Chapter 7

1. Why do most cost accountants consider variance analysis as inappropriate for evaluation of advertising budgets?

2. Why would you imagine the affordable approach to budgeting as appealing to corporate controllers?

3. Do you agree or disagree with the statement that it is better to overspend than to underspend on advertising? Why?

4. What are the limitations of spending level tests to ascertain advertising budgets?

5. Under what conditions would a percent-of-sales method of budgeting be advantageous?

6. Though a management-by-objective philosophy permeates business thinking, its adoption to advertising budgets has lagged badly. Why do you think this is so?

7. Economist Joel Dean has argued that advertising belongs in the capital budget. Do you agree or disagree? What are the implications if companies were made to report financial results in the manner suggested by Dean?

8. Annual advertising expenditures rose in 1982, a recession year. How do you explain spending increases when sales were falling?

Footnotes for Chapter 7

[1] See Gayle L. Rayburn, *Financial Tools for Marketing Administration* (New York: AMACOM, 1976), pp. 101–105; A. S. Johnson, *Marketing and Financial Control* (New York: Pergamon Press, 1967), pp. 180–208; F. H. Mossman et al., *Financial Dimensions of Marketing Management* (New York: Wiley, 1978), pp. 130–135.

[2] For example, see P. W. Farris and R. D. Buzzell, "Relationships Between Changes In Industrial Advertising and Promotion Expenditures and Changes in Market Share," Marketing Science Institute, *Working Paper* (December 1976), pp. 2–3.

[3] Seymour Banks, "Trends Affecting the Implementation of Advertising and Promotion," *Journal of Marketing* (January 1973), pp. 19–28.

[4] For example, see "Computerized Model, 'Real World Data' Can Produce Better Advertising Budget Decisions," *Marketing News* (May 16, 1980), p. 10; J. K. Johansson, "Advertising and the S-Curve: A New Approach," *Journal of Marketing Research* (August 1979), pp. 346–354; A. G. Roa and P. B. Miller, "Advertising/Sales Response Functions," *Journal of Advertising Research* (April 1975), p. 8.

[5] See Julian Simon, "Are There Economies of Scale in Advertising," *Journal of Advertising Research* (June 1966), pp. 16–19; and "New Evidence for No Effect of Scale in Advertising," *Journal of Advertising Research* (March 1969), pp. 191–202.

[6] See R. L. Ackoff and J. R. Emshoff, "Advertising Research at Anheuser-Busch," *Sloan Management Review* (Winter 1975), pp. 1–13.

[7] See Julian Simon, *Management of Advertising* (Englewood Cliffs, N.J.: Prentice-Hall, 1971), pp. 14–15, 85–96; and "A Simple Model for Determining Advertising Appropriations," *Journal of Marketing Research* (August 1965), p. 285.

[8] Joseph T. Plummer, "A Researcher's Viewpoint," *Return On Advertising Investment* (New York: Association of National Advertisers, 1979), p. 24.

[9]Plummer, "A Researcher's Viewpoint," pp. 24–25.

[10]See Frank Stanton, "What is Wrong with Test Marketing," *Journal of Marketing* (April 1967), pp. 43–47; Jack Gold, "Testing Test Market Predictions," *Journal of Marketing Research* (August 1964), pp. 8–16; Nielsen Marketing Service, "To Test or Not to Test," *The Nielsen Researcher* 30, no. 4 (1971), p. 4.

[11]Edwin M. Berdy, "Testing Test Market Predictions: Comments," *Journal of Marketing Research* (May 1965), pp. 196–198; Jack Gold, "Reply," *Journal of Marketing Research* (May 1965), p. 199.

[12]*Advertising Age* (October 9, 1978), p. 122.

[13]See John D. C. Little, "A Model of Adaptive Control of Promotional Spending," *Operations Research* (November/December 1966), pp. 1075–1097, and "Adaptive Control Systems in Marketing," *How Much to Spend for Advertising*, M. A. McNiven, ed., (New York: Association of National Advertisers, Inc., 1969), pp. 111–121.

[14]See Simon, *Management of Advertising*, pp. 27–29; D. R. Corkingdale and S. H. Kennedy, *Measuring the Effect of Advertising* (Westmead, England: Saxon House, Teadfield, Ltd., 1978), p. 9; Richard E. Quant, "Estimating Advertising Effectiveness: Some Pitfalls in Econometric Methods," *Journal of Marketing Research* (May 1964), pp. 52–58.

[15]See Frank M. Bass, "A Simultaneous Equation Regression Study of Advertising and Sales of Cigarettes," *Journal of Marketing Research* (August 1969), pp. 291–300.

[16]John J. O'Connor, "Reynolds Vows It'll Beat Back PM," *Advertising Age* (June 30, 1980), pp. 1, 54.

[17]Schmalensee, pp. 22–43.

[18]Robert S. Weinberg, "Developing an Advertising Planning Procedure—An Econometric Approach," M. A. McNiven, ed., *How Much to Spend for Advertising* (New York: Association of National Advertisers, Inc., 1969) pp. 47–66; and *An Analytical Approach to Advertising Expenditure Strategy* (New York: Association of National Advertisers, 1960).

[19]B. F. Butler et al., "Quantitative Relationships Among Advertising Expenditures, Share of Market, and Profits," M. A. McNiven, ed., *How Much to Spend for Advertising* (New York: Association of National Advertisers, Inc., 1969), pp. 67–71.

[20]See Jerome Herniter, *A Comparison of the Entropy Model and the Hendry Model* (Cambridge, Mass.: Marketing Science Institute, 1973); M. U. Kalwani and D. Morrison, "A Parsimonious Description of the Hendry System," *Management Science* (January 1977), pp. 467–477.

[21]Robert A. Rechholtz, "An Advertiser's Perspective," *Return on Advertising Investment*, pp. 2–5.

[22]For example, See Julian Simon, "A Simple Model for Determining Advertising Appropriations," *Journal of Marketing Research* (August 1965), p. 288.

[23]Colley, *Defining Advertising Goals*.

[24]See S. H. Kennedy and D. R. Corkindale, *Managing the Advertising Process* (Westmead, England: Saxon House, D. C. Heath, Ltd., 1976), p. 183; Weilbacher, p. 103.

[25]M. R. Schlissel and J. A. Giacalone, "Budgeting the Strategic Marketing Plan." Paper presented to the Academy of Marketing Science Annual Conference, April-May 1980.

[26]Gary L. Lilien, "MIT Plan Helps to Budget, Allocate Promotion Dollars," *Marketing News* (February 25, 1977), p. 7.

[27]For example, see Simon, *Issues in the Economics of Advertising*, pp. 67–74; Wright et. al., p. 559; S. W. Dunn and A. M. Barban, *Advertising: Its Role in Modern Marketing* (Hinsdale, Ill.: Dryden Press, 1978), p. 74.

[28]National Broadcasting Company, *Advertising During a Recession* (New York: National Broadcasting Company, 1975).

[29]McGraw-Hill Publications, *Lap Report # 5262.*

[30]See Charles Y. Yang, "Variations in Cyclical Behavior in Advertising," *Journal of Marketing* (April 1964), pp. 25–30.

[31]See Wally Tokarz, "Recession Bothers Them But They're Trying to Cope," *Advertising Age* (August 11, 1980), pp. S1, S14.

[32]Kristain S. Palda, *The Measurement of Cumulative Advertising Effects* (Englewood Cliffs, N.J.: Prentice-Hall, 1964). For a contrary interpretation, see Schmalensee, pp. 9–13.

[33]Joel Dean, "Does Advertising Belong in the Capital Budget?" *Journal of Marketing* (October 1966), pp. 15–21.

[34]Harry Block, "Advertising and Profitability: A Reappraisal," *Journal of Political Economy* (March/April 1974), pp. 267–286.

[35]Consolidated Foods Corporation, *Third Quarter Report, 1980;* also see Nariman K. Dhalla, "Assessing the Long-term Value of Advertising," *Harvard Business Review* (January/February 1978), pp. 87–95; Charles S. Mill, "Advertising: A Business Investment," *Industrial Marketing* (March 1979), pp. 95–96.

[36]Association of National Advertisers, *Return on Advertising Investment*, p. i.

[37]See F. Bass and D. G. Clarke, "Testing Distributed Lag Models of Advertising Effects," *Journal of Marketing Research* (August 1972), pp. 298–308; M. Nerlove and K. F. Wallis, "Use of the Durbin-Watson Statistic in Inappropriate Situations," *Econometrica* (January 1966), pp. 235–238; Zvi Giliches, "A Note on Serial Correlation Bias in Estimates of Distributed Lags," *Econometrica* (January 1961), pp. 65–73.

[38]Darral G. Clarke, "Econometric Measurement of the Duration of the Advertising Effect on Sales," Darral G. Clarke, ed., *Cumulative Advertising Effects: Sources and Implications* (Cambridge, Mass.: Marketing Science Institute, 1977), pp. 31–70.

[39]A. Sawyer and S. Ward, "Carry-Over Effects in Advertising Communication Evidence and Hypotheses From Behavioral Science," Darral G. Clarke, ed., *Cumulative Advertising Effects: Sources and Implications* (Cambridge, Mass.: Marketing Science Institute, 1977), pp. 73–170.

**PART
FOUR**

CREATIVE AND MEDIA DECISIONS

8 Copy Strategy and Tactics

Creative decisions, in theory at least, follow a strategy-to-tactics sequence. The first link in this chain rests on a "positioning" concept. Entrepreneurial in nature, the position statement of an advertising plan sets forth the presumed differential advantage to be stressed for competing in the marketplace. Tactical decisions, alternatives for implementing the strategy, are then formulated.

Accordingly, this chapter explores:

- **Components of the product position strategy**
- **Various types of copy strategy which advertisers employ in the quest for a differential advantage**
- **Relationships between strategy and tactics in the creation of advertising messages**
- **Different approaches to the formulation of message content**

CREATIVE STRATEGY

Practically all operating plans have a major section devoted to copy, defined as that part of the plan related to the creation and production of advertising messages. Creative strategy is usually subsumed in that section of the plans. Sometimes it goes under the name of positioning or brand image. Many large, highly structured advertising agencies do not allow copywriters and artists to begin an assignment until the account executive has reached some agreement with the client on creative strategy.

What is creative strategy? If a dozen agency executives and a dozen advertisers were asked to define it, their answers would probably yield two dozen varying definitions. About the only concurrence attained is that the definition contains two words, "creative" and "strategy."

Something that is creative gives the impression of newness. It connotes that which is imaginative, innovative, original. Some advertising contains all these qualities, but most advertising messages are lacking in these areas. The description of strategy as creative, like many adjectives contained in headlines of advertisements, stretches the facts somewhat.

The word creative may also imply that strategy emanates from the so-called creative departments of the advertising agency, which is made up of copywriters, artists, and production people. Sometimes it does, but most of the time it does not. The primary source is usually the client organization. In any event, "copy strategy" may be a more appropriate term.

The second word of the definition, "strategy," comes from military usage. Literally, it means generalship. It is concerned with managing large movements or operations in order to get the better of an adversary and win a war. It provides general direction for implementing programs, which are tactics.

In like manner, strategy in marketing deals with warfare in the marketplace. It focuses on how a product will compete against its rivals, not only today but in a long succession of tomorrows. In this respect, it is future oriented. Insofar as advertising is one among many means of attaining long-term marketing goals, it can be argued that its decisions are essentially tactical. Advertising is mainly concerned with ways it can contribute to the master plan for winning the marketing war.

Everyone in the advertising field aspires to be a general—account, creative, and research people alike. Everyone wants to provide input for that master blueprint in the war room, which is basically a marketing stratagem that assigns roles to various operating units. When advertising plays a minor role in the scheme of things, its decisions are decidedly tactical. When advertising assumes a leading part, copy decisions have a closer association with a firm's strategy. But even here it might be maintained that the basis of strategy resides in the marketing plan and not in advertising, if a distinction is made between the two. The latter must support the former, and can consequently be thought of as a tactic.

For example, Polaroid created a new market in the photographic field. Cameras were not something new. But the Polaroid camera was different, positioning itself as a device which offered pictures in a matter of seconds. The advertising strategy was this position of instant photography. It had to convince people that they could and that they wanted to get pictures without waiting for them to be developed.[1] Advertising was thus supportive of the marketing strategy, and actually tactical.

The marketing strategy established for advertising usually deals with some basic idea by which a series of communications will build preferences for a product. A strategy is seldom altered, and many successful brands have maintained virtually the same strategy throughout their existence. Outstanding examples are such brands as Maytag appliances, Virginia Slims cigarettes, and Bounty paper towels. Table 8–1 demonstrates the relationship between strategy and tactics. The commercial messages which follow illustrate how strategy is implemented with advertising copy. (See Figures 8–1 and 8–2.)

The strategic idea conveyed by advertising must either create or support a product's position in the marketplace. This objective is expressed as the creative strategy in the advertising plan: it is actually a "position" statement. That position locates the cornerstone for building advertising messages and entire campaigns.

TABLE 8–1 *Examples of Strategy and Tactics*

Brand	Strategy	Tactics
Virginia Slims	A cigarette for the modern, independent woman.	Compares the smoking woman now with one of a past age, tongue-in-cheek, with the slogan, "You've come a long way, baby."
Maytag	Highly dependable.	Features the person who makes repairs as old and lonely, having nothing to do.
Bounty	Superior absorption qualities.	Demonstrates how Bounty absorbs spills, which makes it "the quick picker-upper."

ELEMENTS OF PRODUCT POSITION

Though not necessarily included in every statement of creative strategy, three basic elements determine the position of a product. These are: the context, the marketing target, and the point of difference.

The context describes the relevant forces a product encounters in its markets. It includes customers' perceptions and usage patterns of strengths and weaknesses, as compared with competitive offerings. These relationships, some positive and some negative, spell out both opportunities and dangers which lie ahead. The strategist must choose, usually from among many alternatives, which opportunities to exploit or which shortcomings to rectify.

The market framework embraces all viable marketing targets, the obvious destinations for advertising messages. Their selection emerges from the decision regarding which opportunities are to be pursued. Which buyer loyalties and vacillations, desires and aversions, are to be addressed? Which groups of the population offer the most alluring prospects?

But marketing targets may also be related to the point of difference stressed by the advertising. That selling point, for example, may be meaningful to some segments and not to others. Contrariwise, it may cut across various demographic and socio-economic lines, reducing the importance of these conventional market groupings. Hence, the three main elements of product position are mutually dependent.

The point of difference forms the core of advertising strategy. A product may have many differentiating possibilities. But a strategy must usually settle upon one underlying characteristic, around which all advertising communication will revolve. This basic idea need not be related to a product's physical features, as in the case of Virginia Slims. But that preemptive point of difference, once established in consumers' minds, sets the product apart from its competitors. The product becomes differentiated.

In 1910, Esther Fortner thought her vacation would be a perfect time to be open about smoking cigarettes.

Unfortunately, her vacation soon came to a close.

You've come a long way, baby.

VIRGINIA SLIMS *Lights*

In the crush-proof purse pack.

Fashions: J.G. Hook

9 mg ''tar,''0.8 mg nicotine av. per cigarette by FTC Method.

Warning: The Surgeon General Has Determined That Cigarette Smoking Is Dangerous to Your Health.

Fig. 8—1 *Virginia Slims. Implementation of Female-Oriented Strategy. Reprinted by permission of Philip Morris Incorporated.*

Bounty

"NICE CATCH" :60

CLIENT: PROCTER & GAMBLE COMM'L. NO.: PGBN 3786

Fig. 8—2 *Bounty Commercial. Implementation of Product Quality Strategy.*
Courtesy of The Procter & Gamble Company.

The point of difference has been described in many ways. Reeves called it the "unique selling proposition." Another writer defined it as the "consumer's impression of the product reduced to its essence."[2] No matter which course is taken, the point of difference concept implies an attempt at stereotyping, a condensation of information to convey one fixed, essential meaning.

The choice of this differentiating concept is entrepreneurial in nature. It represents a continual search for a competitive advantage. It determines the rationale with which the product will press its claims for market share. It marks the rallying point around which all marketing units will marshal their forces and rush forth to do battle for sales. Advertising messages must proclaim this concept's virtues over the noisy airwaves and in the crowded pages of print media.

Very similar products may adapt radically different positioning strategies. Candy, for example, is usually promoted to children. Yet M&M advertises to adults and stresses the fact that it keeps clothes from becoming messy with the slogan, "It melts in your mouth, not in your hand."

The key to product differentiation is not the inherent characteristics of the product, but the point of difference which creeps into customers' minds. A differential advantage, like beauty, lies in the eye of the beholder, in this instance, the eventual consumer. It is the buyer who makes the decision that counts. For that reason, the basic concept must be attractive and convincing to prospective customers.

A position is a long term affair, neither easily acquired nor shifted. Its establishment requires effort, time, and money. Of the thousands of different brands in the marketplace, how many are widely associated with some favorable attribute? Or, how many are even known to exist? Advertising studies have consistently turned up high levels of misidentification and unfamiliarity even for brands with large promotional budgets.[3] Nor can a position, once established, be readily altered. Avis had long ago dropped its boast of being Number Two, but has yet to erase the idea from the collective mind of customers. Seven Up is still thought of as an uncola despite the fact that it has not been promoted as such for several years. Merrill Lynch is still regarded as having a bullish stock market outlook, though it has not touted that philosophy for some time.

An established position tends to persist. A change is undertaken only when the original conditions no longer hold; when a radical alteration has occurred with respect to the marketing context, the marketing targets, or the point of difference. This is called repositioning. A modification in strategy at any other time indicates that the position was not quite right to begin with.

DIFFUSE AND SELECTIVE STRATEGIES

The adaption of a creative strategy, actually a marketing stance, depends heavily on how a firm defines its potential market. IBM sees the vast and worldwide computer market as being within its reach, and consequently promotes its corporate symbols as synonyms with computing. It puts out machines and equipment for the main body of the market, and its advertising is designed for the largest possible aggregation of potential customers. At the other extreme, Cray Research produces about a dozen super computers a year. To Cray's management, that small number of units is enough for satisfactory growth and profits.[4] Somewhere between IBM and Cray, but overlapping, lies the sales areas marked out by Control Data, which concentrates on electronic data processing for scientific fields. These different lines of approach to markets, etched in the intense heat of experience, guides what is said, and how it is said, to a corporation's numerous publics.

Firms pursuing a course of undifferentiated marketing can avail themselves of a diffuse copy strategy. This approach hitches a campaign to some vague, undefined image. For example, what is the "Pepsi generation"? Any person can ascribe to it whatever meaning he or she wishes. It is all things to all people, yet promises nothing that is specific. The advertising can feature many different versions of the main theme, or even appeal to particular segments of the population without offending others at the same time. The Pepsi generation, like an astute politician, draws its popularity by being grandly vague but constantly visible. The king of beers, the green giant, the brokerage house that is bullish on America, have built national reputations with advertising symbols which defy exact meaning and which are no more substantial than a mirage.

Companies conforming to the segmentation line would normally subscribe to a selective copy strategy. This strategy highlights a specific attribute—a product feature or a benefit, actual or implied—which would hopefully give the advertised brand a competitive advantage. The strategy chosen, however, must appeal to the segment or segments for which the advertising is intended. Close-Up and Ultra-Brite, catering to young adults, stress their teeth-whitening power so as to make a person more attractive to the opposite sex. Crest's cavity-fighting messages make their greatest impression on families with children, whose teeth are more susceptible to decay.

Market segmentation by definition disregards some groups in the marketplace. Should a firm try to reverse that policy, a selective copy strategy might hinder the effort. Marlboro cigarettes, for example, would find it difficult to sell to women after perfecting a he-man image for so many years. Yet the brand has come out with a "light" cigarette which, whether it appeals to females, is still to be seen. Camay, advertising itself as the soap for beautiful women, would have trouble doing an about-face. The change in direction takes on importance if market expansion is feasible at some future time. But the attributes touted to the old segment must appeal to the new one. Thus, Johnson & Johnson had no problem promoting its baby oils, shampoos and powders as adult products. The women's liber-

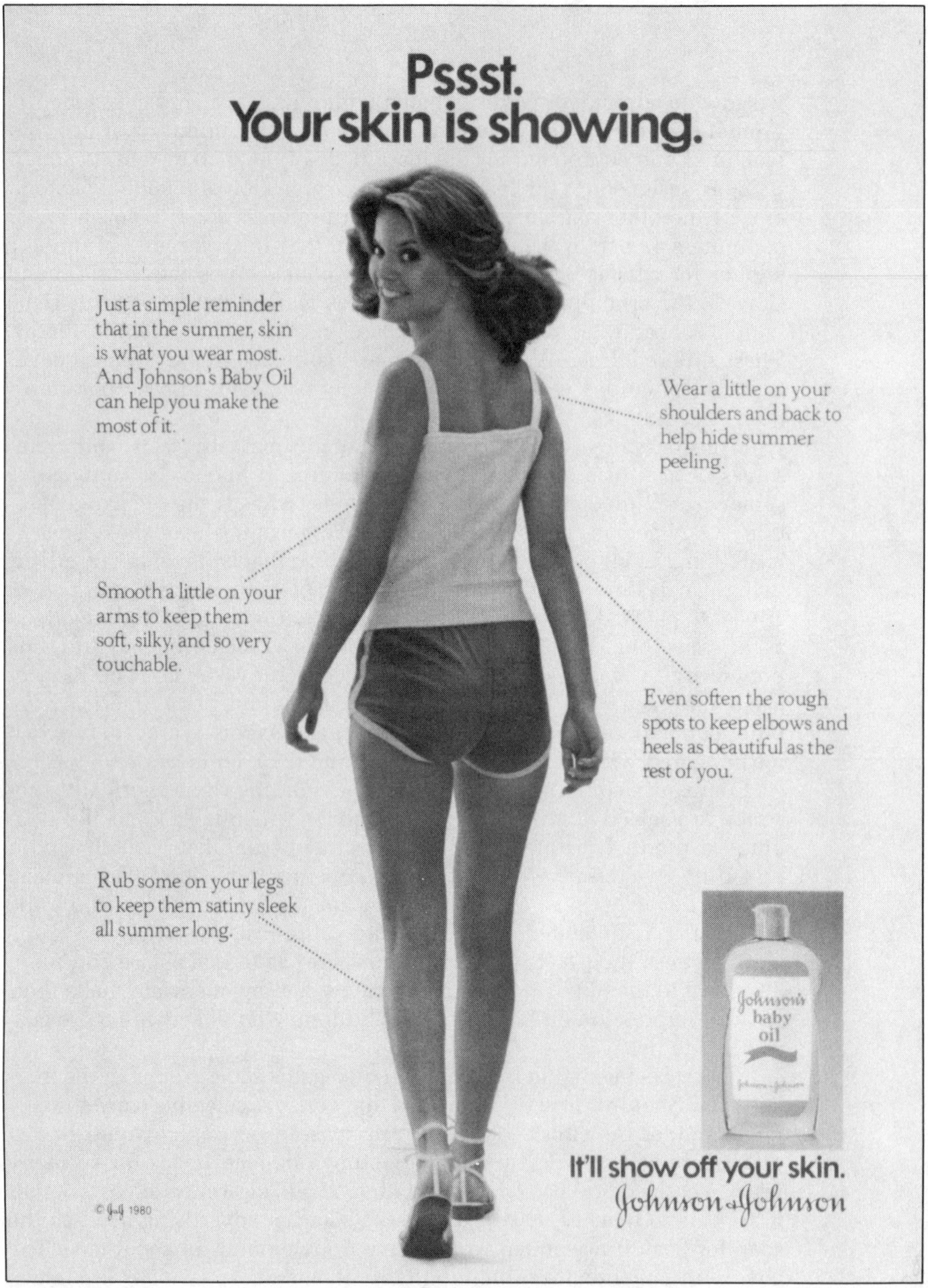

Fig. 8–3 *Johnson's Baby Oil. A Baby Product Repositioned for Adults.*
Courtesy of Johnson & Johnson.

ation movement has in no way dampened the female desire for baby-soft skin. The softness theme for adult usage is illustrated by the Johnson's Baby Oil advertisement (Figure 8–3). Gerber Products Company, though, met with stiff resistance in marketing fruits and dessert products to teen-agers under the name associated with baby food.[5]

Diffuse and selective copy strategies, however, do not always go hand in hand with the way a firm defines its market potential. A brand leader trading on a large, diverse market may easily do so with a selective copy strategy. Conversely, a firm operating in a segment of a market can adroitly employ a diffuse image strategy.

The first situation arises when a particular attribute or product feature is universally regarded as desirable. A detergent that cleans white, or "whiter than white," casts its claim into the mainstream of the market. All purchasers expect a detergent to get dirt out of clothes. A softness claim for toilet paper represents an obvious selective copy strategy. It emphasizes a specific attribute. Abrasiveness is not pleasant for skin contact, but it is widely looked upon with favor in household cleaning agents, such as those which are used on porcelain surfaces. Comet cleanser is promoted as effective in removing stains. The broad demand for such characteristics encourages brands to stake out specific claims even while catering to an undifferentiated market. In these instances, all segments want essentially the same thing, and advertising to one is tantamount to advertising to the entire market.

The second situation occurs when a product is associated with a variety of different features but the advertiser does not wish it to be identified with any particular one. Banks which offer a broad range of services frequently adopt a diffuse copy strategy though they may be catering to certain market segments. Featuring a "wide variety of loans to meet your needs," the Chemical Bank promotes itself as having its "chemistry just right." The Chase Manhattan Bank advertises the "Chase advantage," recently changed to the "Chase is on." Chase offers many advantages: special large safe deposit boxes, convenience banking, six-month savings certificates of deposit, etc. As explained by Chase's marketing vice-president," We believe our advertising and marketing programs should speak with one voice . . . through a unifying theme, look and attitude, yet permit the various businesses of the bank to communicate specifics about those products and services that are most important to each division."[6]

Higher-priced automobiles can also make successful use of a diffuse copy strategy and feature many sorts of individual traits under a catchall theme. Cougars, lynxes, and colts run across television screens in attempts to imbue certain cars with positive attributes such as freedom, sportiveness and grace.

Diffuse and selective strategies, however, are not mutually exclusive. They may be combined in various ways. One occasion for such blending is when a brand, often a leader, attempts to make inroads into markets outside its usual product category. A textbook example is that of Arm & Hammer baking soda, a cooking ingredient which attained success as a deodorant. Consequently, its promotion features a variety of selective uses to different marketing targets. The market expansion strategy of Knox unflavored gelatin runs along similar lines. Because of its high nitrogen content, the brand has promoted itself as a plant food. (See Figure 8–4.)

Bacardi rum, long a leader in its product category, exemplifies this eclectic approach of selective themes to different market segments. With about 60 percent of all rum sales, Bacardi cannot realistically expect high growth by vying for market share with other rums. By no means has the brand abandoned its rivalry with like products. Nor has it given up in attempts to encourage higher per capita usage among current customers. But the central idea of its marketing strategy is to position itself in the fast-growing family of mixes.

Thus, Bacardi has put on many faces to the diverse public. Without foresaking such traditional themes as rum and cola, its advertising has promoted Pinacoladas and rum with orange juice, a clear challenge to vodka. (See Figure 8–5.)

FORM-CONTENT RELATIONSHIPS

Some authors present advertising strategy as the determination of what will be conveyed, as opposed to how the job will be done.[7] This distinction is one between content and form. It is commonly made in disciplines as diverse as mathematics and art, because it is useful in analysis and exposition. In this line of reasoning, form follows content. The advertising strategy is developed first. The structural elements, of which there are countless varieties, represent possible tactics. They are alternative ways of expressing a strategy.

The subject of how a concept will be presented to an audience appears in the copy platform of the advertising plan. It sets forth the main theme, the anticipated mood of the messages, and the selling points to be made. An advertising campaign results when all commercial messages have a common strategy, bear a structural affinity to each other, and run in a series or some pattern over time.

Yet many astute advertising people take issue with the separation of form and content. Without denying the value of separating the two for certain purposes, they question its overall appropriateness to advertising. A foremost critic of the form-content division was William Bernbach, reputed for his creative skills and copywriting virtuosity. He argued that what is said has no significance unless it is said memorably and effectively. A Shakespearian play may contain old, hackneyed plots copied from printed material of the day. But how scenes unfold, and how ideas are expressed by the characters, have imbued Shakespeare's plays with

THIS LITTLE IVY HAD KNOX.®

THIS LITTLE IVY HAD NONE.

*3 Applications

GIVE YOUR HOUSEPLANTS KNOX® UNFLAVORED GELATINE AND WATCH THEM GROW FULLER AND GREENER.

Knox Unflavored Gelatine has no artificial ingredients. But it does have lots of nitrogen, just what houseplants commonly need to flourish.

Just mix one envelope of Knox with one cup of very hot tap water to dissolve. Then slowly add three cups of cold water to make a quart of liquid. Prepare only as much of the mixture as you plan to use at one time. Once a month, use the Knox mixture as part of your normal watering pattern and you'll see amazing results as we have shown above.

And here's another important fact to remember. To help your plants grow, they need to be periodically repotted into larger pots using a standard potting soil.

For fuller, greener plants, nourish them with Knox.

Fig. 8—4 *Knox Gelatin. An Edible Presented as a Plant Food.* Courtesy of Thomas J. Lipton, Inc.

Fig. 8—5 *Bacardi. The Many Faces of Bacardi. Courtesy of Bacardi Imports, Inc.*

immortality. In like manner, Bernbach held that it is not possible to divorce the content of an advertisement from the execution. A unique selling proposition, he once told an annual meeting of the American Association of Advertising Agencies, is virtually useless without a "unique selling talent."[8]

If content is inextricably bound with form, there is a question about who really formulates a copy strategy. Although agency personnel may be consulted, the responsibility for a position statement rests with the client. It is an integral part of the marketing plan. This focal point of marketing strategy is aped in the creative strategy section of the advertising plan. But if implementation modifies content, as it indubitably must, then copywriters, designers, and production people all have their say, though not the last word. Copy strategy in these circumstances is the outcome of a collective decision.

Shirley Polykoff, in 1981, was admitted to the American Advertising Federation's Hall of Fame. She had for many years produced truly outstanding advertisements. Some of her better-known creations were, "The closer he gets . . . the better you look," and "Only her hairdresser knows for sure." To mark the occasion of her admittance to the Hall of Fame, Ms. Polykoff let the audience witnessing the ceremonies in on a secret. She related that while working on the Clairol account at Foote, Cone and Belding, she wrote the strategy only after the commercials were finished. Her well-wishers roared with laughter.

Yet, on reflection, this apparent violation of management procedure was impeccably logical. If form interacts with content, how can advertising strategy be known until the advertisements are done? Ms. Polykoff might well have written another version of her memorable slogan: "Only the copywriter knows for sure."

This creative Gordian knot, neither compliantly unravelled nor easily severed, makes for difficulties in operational control. The way creative people present the message can divert, often inadvertently, communication from its intended strategy. Although the advertiser has the prerogative to accept or reject a piece of copy, it is difficult to judge beforehand how a message will be perceived. The more the creative presentation departs from traditional or past practice, the greater the uncertainty. Past events can no longer serve as a reliable guide for the future. There are few facts which relate to the novel and the untried.

Thus advertisers are confronted with a no win situation. They're damned if they do and they're damned if they don't. If they give free reign to creativity—which implies new ways of doing things and presenting ideas—they have no previous experience to fall back on. If they discourage new approaches, they negate the main value of the agency, the creative talent for which they pay a handsome price. This quandary has furnished the major rationale for testing ads before they are run. Though the research may often yield equivocal conclusions, it is argued, judgment alone may be even more hazardous.

ANATOMY OF PERSUASION

Regardless of the form-content relationship, practically all commercial messages are persuasive instruments. What distinguishes persuasion from information is the intent of the communication source and the objective of the message. Although the dividing line between the two types of communication is not always clear, an informative message does not try to influence the recipient. A news story may be inaccurate, but it shouldn't enjoin readers to do things, even by innuendo. Walter Cronkite, who brought subjectivity and interpretation into news reporting, never harangued people to join demonstrations, write to their congressperson, or vote for certain candidates.

A movie or a television program may stir emotions, bring tears or laughter, but as entertainment should not suggest a course of action to its viewers. Its creators are not concerned about audience loyalty, unless the show is a serial. In that case, they would want the audience to come back for more entertainment. On the other hand, a persuasive message seeks to affect the behavior and thinking of its intended audience along certain lines.

Advertisements seek to be persuasive messages. Most of them carry sales ideas bound together in an artistic format. But the art forms are not solely meant to entertain or enlighten. If they do, it is incidental to their main purpose, which is to influence people's thought processes with respect to commercial transactions. Society may insist upon certain standards or norms of conduct as a condition for message transmission. But this in no way detracts from the persuasive character of advertising.

The logician, Stephen Toulmin, reasoned that all persuasive messages, called arguments, no matter what their particular intent, can be identified by a set of common characteristics.[9] According to Toulmin's thesis, all arguments bear an identical structure which, to a greater or lesser degree, contains three components: a claim, data, and a warrant.

As related to advertising, the claim is the proposition. It is a conclusion that a sender of a message asks the recipient to accept. Since the overwhelming proportion of paid for messages in mass media represent product advertising, the claim is in most instances a sales proposition. It exhorts readers, listeners, or viewers to take some kind of action—to buy a product, visit a showroom, try a recipe, and so forth.

The data, in Toulmin's view, are made up of facts and reasons which support the claim. Any proposition which lacks data becomes an assertion, and turns the message down the path of irrationality. Advertising appeals to data are conveyed by visual or verbal symbols. But the quality of the data, in conjunction with the use of the warrant, governs the extent to which the message is rational or nonrational.

The warrant connects the data to the claim. It may be implicit, insinuated, or stated in such a way as to be inferred by the audience. In any shape or form, it is the crux of the argument; it bridges the gap between the proposition and the evidence offered to support it. Printed advertisements often insert the warrant in headlines or body copy. Television has more complex and varied formats than does print, and displays more diversity in how claims are supported by data.

Unfortunately, conventional wisdom followed the views of economist Alfred Marshall in categorizing advertising as persuasive or informative. Advertising has since been defended and upbraided on this score. Yet this dichotomy even in Marshall's day (the early 1900's) ran counter to decades of economic experience. The English common law clearly recognized the vested interest and inherent bias of sellers, and for this reason never allowed the principle of libel to be applied to commercial speech. Not until recently was advertising accorded protection in the United States under the First Amendment, having sneaked in through the back door on the heels of action taken by consumer advocates. But even then, the court let stand a number of important qualifications. Sales messages are not expected to be completely neutral in content, and from the standpoint of intent, are therefore persuasive. They are public arguments for particular articles of commerce.

RATIONAL VS NONRATIONAL MESSAGES

Once advertising is accepted as a form of persuasion, differences in type can be regarded as differences in the rationale that is given for action. One possible way to begin classification is to separate messages into those that are rational and nonrational. These two kinds of appeals, however, are not mutually exclusive in advertising, and are mingled in varying proportions within the same message.

The rationally-oriented message presents objective, factual data. The soundness of the argument can be judged by intellectually-accepted standards. In the field of advertising, such commonly-accepted criteria include relevancy, clarity, timeliness, truthfulness, and completeness. These are presumably the standards by which Alfred Marshall categorized advertising, as either being informative or combative. A long succession of his followers, including members of the Federal Trade Commission, believe that these attributes can be shaped so as to permit consumers to exercise their right to know.[10]

Conceptually, an advertising message may find it difficult if not impossible to fulfill the conditions of relevancy and completeness. Relevant evidence may fall short because of time and space limitations. Not too many facts germane to a transaction can be jammed into a thirty-second commercial. Nor can complete information be given.

In a larger sense, completeness can never be wholly satisfied, even in a system of rational messages that are essentially persuasive. Except for health and safety reasons, such as in cigarette advertisement warnings, no seller is expected to promote the deficiencies of his product. Advertisements tell why a product should be bought, not why it should not. The arguments contained therein are like those of an attorney pleading a case. The facts are carefully sifted, and what is submitted as evidence is done so to further a client's cause. Advertising can then be viewed as a case of product advocacy. Andrew Kershaw, president of a Madison Avenue agency, epigrammatically stated that his skills could tell the public "the truth, nothing but the truth, but not the whole truth."[11]

The nonrational message resorts to appeals which have little basis in logic. The argument uses questionable data, warrants, or both, as ground for its claim. Hence, the claim is intellectually indefensible.

The uses of each type of argument—both rational and nonrational— depend upon how sellers perceive buyers going about their shopping. If sellers think that buyers would be swayed only by well-grounded arguments, advertising takes on a rational demeanor. A good deal of industrial advertising follows this sort of rational prescription. Copy backs its warrants with facts, and many advertisements offer more information upon request, because purchasing is viewed as a rational, evaluative process.

In contrast, much consumer advertising proceeds along nonrational lines. The main reason is because consumers are regarded as generally uninformed, and in many instances not desirous of information. For technical, complex products, expert buyers are few and far between. When vital product features are not evident, consumers may have no way of judging performance. Surveys of the Food and Drug Administration found widespread consumer misconceptions about nutrition.[12] Search activity for many low-priced products is not feasible because costs would exceed the price of the item. Under these conditions, buying decisions are emotional, nondeliberative, or motivated by factors which do not conform to rules of logic. Nonrational advertising rests on the premise that it is inappropriate to present a rational argument to a consumer who makes decisions on a different basis.

Products which have been on the market for a long time and have gained a high degree of familiarity have little need to stuff their messages with much data. An extreme example is reminder advertising which mentions only the name or displays just the brand. A claim is presented with no supporting data—facts are superfluous. Even a warrant is lacking or is supposed to be understood. Such advertisements are gentle reminders to consider the brand should a buying occasion arise. An example is Izod LaCoste, whose ads highlight the small alligator emblem appearing on men and women's casual attire. The emblem represents the essence of casual, popular style, and unmistakably promotes a significant consumer brand awareness.

Another kind of nonrational advertising is that which attempts to promote an image with intellectually unsupportable evidence and warrants. The Coca-Cola commercial shown in Figure 8–6 is a near classic execution of a nonrational message. It features a small boy on a runway offering his drink to Mean Joe Greene, the famous Pittsburgh Steeler tackle, after an especially hard game. The warrant skillfully links this tender, sentimental scene with the proposition, "Have a Coke and a smile." That the sweating Mr. Greene would appreciate a cold drink is understandable. To anyone watching Sunday mayhem in the comfort of his or her living room, the reason given for wanting a Coke is logically unsupportable. But the commercial is great advertising.

Figure 8–6 is reproduced here from slides. Though no words accompany the visuals, the story is obvious and reaches its climax when Joe Greene empties the bottle. The sequence and composition demonstrate how the visual elements carry the message. It is highly memorable, emotionally compelling, and expertly executed. It is the only commercial that was made into a tv show.

A high proportion of nonrational advertising attempts to link the sales proposition with some motive deemed powerful enough to galvanize people into action. Motives for buying something are of various kinds. Some are practical or utilitarian. A homemaker must replenish an empty pantry. The noon hour sets off a pang of hunger and an urge to eat lunch. Or Mean Joe Greene, who had worked up a great thirst on the football field, had no compunction about emptying a kid's bottle of Coke in one gulp.

Other motives transcend the biological drives of thirst and hunger, and rise into the nebulous clouds of psychology. Such motives are learned, and apt to vary from person to person.

Although there is some tendency for advertisers to try matching the content of their messages with the presumed motives of buyers, there is no connection necessary between the two.[13] A nonrational argument can be used for utilitarian motives. For example, the previously mentioned emotional Coca-Cola commercial aims to satisfy a strictly physiological drive—to quench one's thirst. Similarly, a rational appeal can be made for products bought for nonutilitarian reasons. Most developers of prestigious recreational communities believe that buyers act on the basis of psychological motives. Yet several sellers of such second homes abide by rational, matter-of-fact arguments, send out promotions which resemble an HUD property report, and get satisfactory results. Besides, the same product can be purchased for a variety of reasons, and the same buyer may be motivated by several factors simultaneously. An automobile is a case in point. It provides personal transportation. But buyers may prefer certain

Fig. 8–6 *Coca Cola. The Irrational Appeal of Mean Joe Greene. Courtesy of Coca-Cola, USA.*

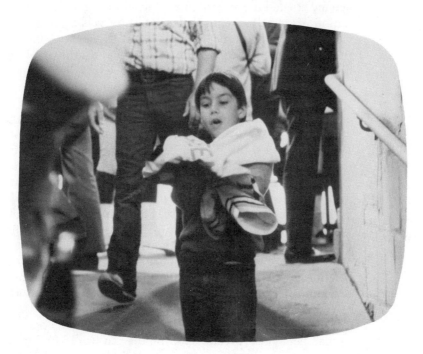

styles, colors, or interior decors. Many durable goods fall into the same category.

BUYER MOTIVATION

The subject of human motivation has numerous theories and theorists. Probably the most popular in advertising is some variation of the "hierarchy of needs" thesis proposed by Abraham Maslow almost four decades ago.[14] Maslow postulated that human needs, of which there are many, can be ranked in order of their importance. A typical person will then start with the most important. Once that need is satisfied, the drive subsides, and the person moves on the the next, and so on all the way up the hierarchy. According to Maslow, motivation proceeds through five broad layers of needs in the following direction: physiological, safety, belongingness and love, esteem and status, and self-actualization.

In an advanced consumer economy such as that of the United States, the most important needs of survival and safety have been fairly well fulfilled, though sections of some major metropolitan areas have tended to revert to veritable jungles. A high standard of living encourages hedonistic desires and egocentric modes of thought.

An appeal to self-actualization is the slogan for Clairol's Nice 'n Easy hair coloring: "It lets me be me." As related by William Bernbach, whose agency created the advertising, "the ad played up to a woman's own evaluation of herself, saying that her beauty was there all the time but that Clairol was just helping to bring it out."[15] The "me" theme is widely used with respect to personal care products and articles of fashion, the purchases of which are supposed to be guided by self-concept attitudes. These refer to how people see themselves or would like to see themselves.

Many of these products have sex appeal themes. The items are touted as agents for enhancing personal attractiveness to the opposite sex. This sort of appeal can be regarded as a special case of self-concept, provided people like to think of themselves as attracting admirers. But the sex motive can also be interpreted in accordance with Freudian theories, which also enjoy a goodly following in the avertising industry. In this view, the id and superego are locked in continual combat for mastery over an individual's action. The first is the impulsive source of human drives, while the latter represses the animal instincts and modifies them to conform with socially sanctioned conduct. The ego, which represents an individual's consciousness, may not reveal even to its owner the true motivation for any action. Noxema Medicated Shave Cream has for many years been running commercials with sexual overtones, such as "take it off" and references to feeling "skin."

The theories of Maslow and Freud are general, open-ended vistas into human behavior. Anyone entering therein would find him or herself on a journey to nowhere. The itinerary might be pleasant enough, but it never reaches a destination. Neither Maslow nor Freud was explicit as to which of the myriad of motives apply to which specific set of circumstances. They marked out a general direction, but without guideposts. Nor was either explicit as to what kind of external stimuli will trigger a specific type of action. A food, for example, can be advertised with appeals to purely biological motives of pleasing the stomach rather than the heart. Or it can exploit motives of belongingness and love, such as the cook's concern for the family or loved ones. Or it can play on motives of esteem and status, such as showing the food being prepared by the finest chefs and served in the most exclusive bistros. Or it can be presented as a food "just for your discriminating taste," an obvious ploy of self-actualization. A little imagination would extend the list of possible motives to a directory. The longer the list, the less are motivation theories operative. Which motives are strongest for what and when?

Some books draw up checklists of appeals.[16] These enumerations, however, are of dubious value. The ways of appealing to the same tastes, proclivities and motivations stretch endlessly into the imagination. Few copywriters would consult such rosters for guidance.

Although marketing research has been enlisted to supply answers to appeals and motives, its results up to now have been inconclusive. Few generalizations have emerged which, given a problem, can be used to derive a solution. Rather, research has proceeded on a piecemeal basis, undertaken for this or that situation but applicable to no other.

There are many reasons for the inability of research to demonstrate a clear-cut conclusion; some would call the conclusions dismal failures. One reason is because the underlying process of making advertisements involves creativity. The problem confronting marketing research is not simply one of search. That is, given unknown possibilities, which combination would yield the most effective means of reaching a stated objective? The fact is that the possibilities themselves are not known. A copywriter can blend elements in ways which research cannot possibly anticipate. The advertising output is not predictable, and that being so, alternatives cannot readily be tested. Though marketing research may help in part, or in spots, it gropes as blindly as the copywriter for the argument that would give a product a differential advantage.

APPROACHES TO ADVERTISING CONTENT

Decisions on positioning, type of arguments, appeals to certain motivations, do not by themselves determine the content of an advertisement. Other things enter, such as mood, tone, ways in which ideas are expressed. These "approaches" are all part of an advertisement's content, irrespective of type of argument—rational or nonrational. They are blended into a unified whole, and distinctions often rest on subtle points of emphasis. These elements are pulled apart only for purposes of analysis. But if such a dissection is necessary, the most important categories can be laid out as follows: product or nonproduct orientation, positive or negative appeal, and hard or soft sell.

Product vs Nonproduct Orientation

Actually, almost all advertising is product related. It tells prospective customers something about a good or service which is being offered for sale. The orientation of an advertisement can thus be viewed as a matter of emphasis, a matter of degree.

At one extreme is advertising which focuses entirely on attributes inherent in the product. These characteristics may encompass design, functions, shape, color, package, price, style, etc. Advertising which adheres strictly to a product-oriented message in fact contemplates a "positioning" strategy which seeks to achieve differentiation based on physical characteristics. It assumes that product attributes are the main reason for a purchase.

As advertising moves away from the extremes of product orientation, the approach in varying degrees takes on "people themes." The positioning becomes associated with consumer benefits, life styles, or other frames of reference. Product features are pushed to the background. This view supposes that consumers are not particularly enthralled with products but are interested in things which the use of a product confers. Consequently, this approach follows the long-standing advice of Elmer Wheeler, a well-known 1930's promotion executive: "Don't sell the steak, sell the sizzle." Following this line of thought, marketers of beds sell comfortable nights, manufacturers of motorcycles offer conviviality, and makers of perfume peddle dreams.

The nonproduct orientation in its extreme form produces advertising which is unrelated to a brand's physical properties. Commercials for jeans say little about the product. About the only reference to product features is a shot of the trademark sewn onto well-rounded back pockets. An outstanding example of this type of advertising is that of Chanel No. 5. Its commercial invites women to share a thirty-second fantasy (See Figure 8–7). The visuals, words, and music are blended artistically to create a sensuous mood in a woman's daydreams. Nothing is said about the product; its components, its fragrance, its price, etc. The name, "Chanel No. 5", appears at the very end, almost as an afterthought. Yet how many women associate that voluptuous scene beside the tranquil pool with a bottle of that forbidding perfume?

Many advertisements, perhaps most, fall somewhere between the two poles of product and nonproduct orientation. They combine elements of both product and people approaches. They may give one or the other greater weight, and sometimes it is difficult to determine which is primary and which is secondary.

CHANEL N°5
"SHARE THE FANTASY"

Director: RIDLEY SCOTT
Music: VANGELIS

:30 TV

(MUSIC THROUGHOUT)

WOMAN: (VO) I am made

...of blue sky

...and golden light

...and I will feel this way

...forever.

MALE: (VO) Share the Fantasy.

CHANEL N°5

Fig. 8–7 *Chanel. Example of Advertising Unrelated to Product's Physical Properties. Courtesy of Chanel, Inc.*

For example, the main benefit of Crest toothpaste, that of preventing tooth decay, is combined with ingredients in the product, primarily fluoristat. Miller Lite beer commercials, lighthearted and lightheaded, feature personalities in festive settings. But they always get into arguments about whether the brew tastes good or is less filling. Does the commercial then stress a consumer benefit or a physical product feature? The elimination of discomfort, such as headache, indigestion, or pain, can be depicted as a consumer benefit. But at the same time such claims strongly imply product performance, and it becomes a fruitless task to try separating the benefit from the product's attributes.

Indeed, benefits can be used to support a rational argument. Those trumpeted by discount brokerage houses are certainly measurable in commission savings. Benefits of various financial houses can be translated into hard, cold quantities. Benefits advertised for industrial supplies and business services can be phrased in dollar costs and unit outputs. See Figure 8–8 for an example of an advertisement presenting a rational argument.

The approach to positioning, actually numerous alternatives along a continuum, most commonly veers towards the product-oriented axis. The main reasons for the position's popularity is ease of management and less risk.

The preponderance of products are not exact duplicates of each other. The differences, though frequently minor, were supposedly considered with care when the product was in its developmental stage. If deficient in some respect, it can also be modified by research and development. Well known to their product managers and marketing personnel, these physical differences become fundamental in the formulation of positioning strategy. If the physical features of a product are of no consequence, why was so much time and money spent on designing them in the first place? Both logic and the sequence of events thus lead marketers to position their brands from a product-oriented perspective.

The product management system also favors the primacy of product attributes. All managers have the same frame of reference. They all set their strategies in the same straightforward manner. They are aided by their research staffs, who can probe markets in terms of relatively few variables. Once the basic strategy is set, managers can concentrate on tactical decisions — on how to communicate the unique selling proposition to the public.

When a brand enjoys technical superiority or a unique feature that is highly valued, advertisers would naturally want to highlight that in promotion. For advertising to take this route, the advantages of these product attributes should be patently obvious to prospective buyers.[17] There is an implicit assumption in this approach that buyers will infer the benefits from the description of how the product works. When products lack physical distinctiveness, or when buyers cannot readily perceive them, the

HOW TO PROVE TO YOUR COMPANY'S MANAGEMENT THAT OWNING AN AIRPLANE HAS BECOME AN ECONOMIC NECESSITY.

Your reasons for wanting a company airplane are easy enough to articulate:

☐ IT SAVES ENORMOUS AMOUNTS OF TIME.
☐ IT FREES YOU FROM RIGID FLIGHT SCHEDULES AND ROUTINGS.
☐ IT MAKES YOUR TOP PEOPLE MORE PRODUCTIVE.
☐ IT OFFERS YOU GREATER PRIVACY AND SECURITY ENROUTE.
☐ IT LETS YOU FLY DIRECT TO ANY AIRPORT THE AIRLINES SERVE, PLUS OVER 12,000 MORE THEY DON'T.
☐ IT ELIMINATES A LOT OF MOTEL AND TRAVEL EXPENSES, LETTING YOU SPEND FEWER NIGHTS AWAY FROM HOME.
☐ IT LETS YOU TAKE ALONG THE EXTRA PEOPLE YOU NEED AT NO EXTRA CHARGE.
☐ IT ELIMINATES ALL THAT STANDING IN LINE AT TICKET COUNTERS, SECURITY CHECKS, BOARDING GATES, AND BAGGAGE CLAIM AREAS.
☐ IT CONVEYS THE IMPRESSION THAT YOUR COMPANY IS GOING PLACES.

MEASURING THE IMPACT.

Clearly, the advantages offered by a company airplane are attractive enough on their own merits.

But, translating those advantages into hard facts and figures you can justify to a finance committee or board of directors becomes the real issue in many cases.

One way to approach this is to put a dollar value on your management's time. And then weigh the projected savings against the projected costs.

To arrive at this time/value figure, start by dividing the annual salary for each of your firm's frequent travelers by 2,000—which represents the number of hours an executive works if he puts in 50 40-hour weeks a year. Next, multiply this hourly compensation rate by an agreed-upon "productivity factor" (a commonly used figure is 2.5, which assumes that an executive generates revenues for the company equal to two and a half times his salary).

Thus, if you and another executive are paid a total of $100,000 a year, your combined hourly worth, according to this formula, is $125 ($100,000 ÷ 2,000 hours = $50/hr. × 2.5 = $125).

At that rate, a four hour layover between flights begins to look very unprofitable.

And once you've estimated the projected time savings a company airplane can help you achieve (5 hours a week is typical), you can arrive at a pretty good numerical factor for comparing the real costs of business travel to your management.

NEED HELP WITH THE NUMBERS?

Of course, if all this sounds a bit more complicated than you care to get into right now, there's only one number you really need to remember: 316-681-8219. It's Del Chitwood's phone number. And if you'll call him collect, he'll put you in touch with your area Beechcraft representative—who'll be glad to work out all the math for you and provide your company with a detailed cost analysis of how a business airplane can pay off for your company. If you'd rather write, just address your letterhead to: Beech Aircraft Corporation, Dept. 00, Wichita, Kansas 67201. We'll send you our free portfolio of Business Airplane Reports with all the factual ammunition you need to start building your case for a company airplane.

Beechcraft
50 YEARS
1932-1982

A Raytheon Company

Member General Aviation Manufacturers Association

Fig. 8—8 *Beechcraft. A Rational Argument for Airplane Ownership by a Corporation.* Courtesy of Beech Aircraft Corporation.

pure product-oriented approach gets to be modified by nonproduct appeals. The latter is thought of as easier for consumers to relate to, and is dominant in the advertising of many brands in product categories such as soft drinks, cigarettes, toiletries and cosmetics.

Positive vs Negative Appeals

Another consideration is whether the argument is to be expressed in a positive or negative way. The relative effectiveness of a do or a don't has never been proven. But there seems to be a strong preference for accentuating the positive. "Don'ts" and "nots", it is widely felt, have unfavorable connotations, and produce images of unpleasant associations.

Certain products, such as proprietary drugs, are normally associated with pain or discomfort. Though advertisers have an option, many prefer to dramatize these negative aspects to impress upon consumers the goodness of their remedies. To put it somewhat facetiously, many analgesic commercials first give the viewer a headache in order to demonstrate how the pill gets rid of it.

An extreme case of negativism is advertising that resorts to motives of fear. Insurance advertising is especially notorious for themes of impending disaster—cars getting banged up, trees falling on houses, accidents at every turn. Yet protection, not against the occurrence of calamity but against its financial consequences, is precisely why people buy insurance. They don't like to spend money on the service but feel they have to, like going to the doctor. That the fear motive has been appealed to for so long testifies to its apparent success in selling insurance, disquieting images notwithstanding.

A recent trend in life insurance advertising has been the exploitation of death itself. Whereas the issue had previously been skirted, it has lately been met head on by some advertisers. Prudential, the largest insurer, did this in a somewhat whimsical fashion. One of its commercials had two angels entering a bowling alley to call on their unsuspecting host, a healthy looking man in the prime of his life. To his remark that he thought he had more time on earth, one of the angels responds: "Doesn't everybody?" And all three, arm in arm, ascend the escalator to heaven.

Other life insurance firms have tried more serious approaches to death, having no reluctance to putting the undertaker at the doorstep. These dismal ads often portray hapless widows and orphans forced to give up their ambitious dreams because their providers failed to provide in death as in life. Whether serious or comic, death topics seem to perform well in advertising tests.[18]

There is nothing that says perfume must evoke glamorous fantasies, or that insurance must scare the consumer in order to advertise effectively. The same product can be presented in different ways. A contrasting view is that of Sun Life of Canada, whose advertising features Tracy Austin, the youthful tennis star. "To Tracy Austin," the copy reads, "security is many happy returns." And her broad, content smile which dominates the ad supports the proposition. (See Figure 8–9.)

Advertisements appealing to fear have not all had outstanding success. Antismoking campaigns, it has been pointed out, did not significantly decrease the incidence of smoking. Car safety ads seem to have had little effect in getting drivers to strap themselves into the seats of their vehicles, or in making partygoers forego drinking before taking to the road. This has lead some observers to infer that appeals to fear do not work when they try to get people to break away from ingrained habits. But then, probably no advertising will.

Hard vs Soft Sell

In many situations, there is a question of whether to use hard or soft sell. The distinction between the two is the kind of action an advertisement urges its audience to take. The hard sell calls for doing something now, immediately, in the present. The soft sell also pleads for action, but it can wait. There is no time limit set. The matter of timing is left entirely up to the consumer.

The hard sell is common in retail advertising, which tries to create a sense of urgency. Supplies are limited and go on a first come-first served basis. A sale takes place only on a certain date. An offer is good only within a particular time span. The tone of the hard sell message displays substantial variation, ranging from a noisy, high pitch to a subdued, low key. But loud or soft, the hard sell is designed for getting immediate action.

National consumer advertising is a mixed bag. In the main, it adheres to the soft sell. The primary job of advertising is to keep the brand in the consumers' minds until such time as they are ready to buy. The soft sell does not attempt to influence action at any specific time. Rather, it accomodates itself to the behavior of the audience. It is like a salesperson who never tries to close on any particular call so that regardless of what the prospect does, sends in or witholds an order, the calls continue without interruption.

National advertising contains a goodly percentage of hard sell as well. Coupons and sales promotions carried by advertisements anticipate immediate or short-term action. New products exhort their audiences to try now, as though the product will not be on the market if they didn't. And it might not. Product categories which experience low brand loyalty and considerable switching can expect advertising with high pitched shrills and more hardness in sell.

Whatever the approach, it must be attuned to the shifts and turns of the marketplace. The closer it is, the better will advertising perform its economic function.

Fig. 8—9 *SunLife. Looking at the Brighter Side of Life Insurance.* Courtesy of SunLife of Canada.

SUMMARY

Marketing objectives establish advertising strategy, which actually represents a product's position. There are three basic components of position: market context, marketing targets, and the point of difference.

A position is a long-range affair. Repositioning is undertaken when there has been a fundamental change in the components of a product's position.

There are two main strategies, diffuse and selective. The first is associated with undifferentiated marketing; the second with segmentation. But the two strategies can reverse their respective functions, regardless of the firm's strategy of market undifferentiation or market segmentation.

Copy strategy decisions emanate from the marketing departments of client companies. But if advertising content cannot be easily separated from form, agency creative people in greater or lesser degrees influence strategy decisions.

Almost all advertising is persuasive in nature. A persuasive argument can be rational or nonrational. The type of message that will be used leans heavily on patterns of consumer behavior.

Many nonrational arguments try to associate their messages with some consumer purchasing motive. Two popular theories of human motivation are those of Abraham Maslow and Sigmund Freud. But neither of them is explicit about which motives apply to which situations.

The context of an advertising message is also determined by mood, tone, and expression of ideas. Important considerations include whether to stress product features or people themes, a positive or negative appeal, and a hard or soft sell.

Content comes embodied, like thoughts contained in a book, in a message structure. The latter is discussed in Chapter 9.

Questions for Chapter 8

1. Is advertising a strategy or a tactic?

2. Why may companies with highly similar products have different positioning statements?

3. Under what circumstances would a change in the marketing context suggest repositioning?

4. How would you characterize the positioning strategies of the following brands of beer: Miller, Lowenbrau, Budweiser?

5. What problems arise for brand managers when the form of a message cannot be separated from its content?

6. Select a rational and nonrational message for two brands in the same product category. Contrast the two in terms of proposition, data, warrant.

7. An advertising agency recommends research to find the best copy appeal. Would you as an advertising manager approve the recommendation?

8. Can the Chanel No. 5 commercial, "Share a Phantasy," (illustrated in chapter) be characterized as an attempt at benefit segmentation?

9. Why is appliance advertising usually product-oriented?

Footnotes for Chapter 8

[1] William H. Bolen, *Advertising* (New York: John Wiley & Sons, 1981), p. 109.

[2] Stephen Baker, *Systematic Approach to Advertising Creativity* (New York: McGraw-Hill, 1979), p. 185.

[3] Roy Paul Nelson, *The Design of Advertising* (Dubuque, Iowa: W. C. Brown, 1977), p. 227; "From ¼ to ⅓ of What is Viewed on Television is Miscomprehended," *Marketing News* (June 27, 1980), p. 1; Fred Danzig, "Keep it Simple, 4A's Study Shows," *Advertising Age* (May 19, 1980), p. 128.

[4] Harlan S. Byrne, "Seymour Cray Shows Computer World How to Build Big Machines," *Wall Street Journal* (April 12, 1979), pp. 1, 32.

[5] Gail Bronson, "Baby Food It Is, But Gerber Wants Teen-Agers to Think of It as Dessert," *Wall Street Journal* (July 17, 1981), p. 29.

[6] J. H. Silverman, "Banking on a Single Image," *Advertising Age* (May 10, 1982), p. M-36.

[7] Weilbacher, p. 174; David W. Nylen, *Advertising*, 2nd ed. (Cincinnati: South-Western Publishing Co., 1980), p. 370.

[8] "Creatives Bemoan Current State of Advertising," *Advertising Age* (May 20, 1980), p. 10.

[9] Stephen E. Toulmin, *The Uses of Argument* (Cambridge, England: University Press, 1964), *passim*.

[10] John A. Howard and James Hulbert, *Advertising and the Public Interest* (Chicago: Crain Communications, Inc., 1973), pp. 80–87.

[11] *Advertising and the Public Interest*, p. 87.

[12] See Food and Drug Administration, *Consumer Nutrition Knowledge Survey*, Report No. 1, (FDA) 76-2058, and Report No. 2, (FDA) 76-2059.

[13] See Nylen, *Advertising*, p. 374.

[14] Abraham H. Maslow, "A Dynamic Theory of Human Motivation," *Psychological Review* (July, 1943), pp. 370–396; Abraham H. Maslow, *Motivation and Personality* (New York: Harper and Row, 1954).

[15] "Today's Ads Need More Creativity, Less Reliance on Science, Research," *Marketing News* (June 13, 1980), p. 5.

[16] For example, see C. L. Bovee and W. F. Arens, *Contemporary Advertising* (Homewood, Ill: Richard D. Irwin, 1982), p. 305.

[17] Philip W. Burton, *Advertising Copywriting* (Columbus, Ohio: Grid Publishing, 1978), p. 10.

[18] *Wall Street Journal* (January 29, 1981), p. 27.

CHAPTER 9 *Message Structure and Production*

Victor Hugo may well have been right when he wrote that no army can withstand an idea whose time has come. But victory can be hastened if the idea is presented in an effective form, interestingly, forcefully, and expertly. To mount its assaults on the consumer mind, advertising uses various art forms.

This chapter will concern itself with the structures for creating advertising messages. In particular, it will analyze:

- **Components of the advertising message in television and print**
- **Layouts both of printed advertisements and messages in broadcast media**
- **Classes of television commercials and their respective uses**
- **Integration techniques for advertising campaigns in multimedia**

ADVERTISING STRUCTURE

An advertisement embodies a persuasive argument in an integrated structure. This format, stated again, is, in reality, intertwined with the content of the message. But for purposes of analysis and exposition, it is useful to separate the two and treat them as though they were entities to themselves. The last chapter emphasized content. This one will focus its attention on structure.

Most advertisements are created by teams of specialists which, in advertising agencies, are lodged in the creative departments. A creative team must have at least one copywriter and one art director. The copywriter is the head of the team. He or she is responsible for the content, makes up the copy platform, supplies the theme, verbalizes the ideas that go into the advertisement, and writes up all the nonvisual portions of the commercial message. In many instances, the visual elements dominate the advertisement and bear the main burden of conveying the message. Nevertheless, the art director enters the scene to dramatize the ideas advanced by the copywriter.

The art director specializes in design, defined as the art of arranging the various parts of an advertisement. He or she cannot neglect content, for the structure must be compatible with the theme. The important content decisions have already been made by the copywriter. To the designer, content is something that is given. His or her main job is to arrange the elements in a pleasing, unified form. For an illustration of an advertisement unifying content and design, see Figure 9–1.

ANNOUNCING
THE SMALLEST
PRICE
IN YEARS.
A JEEP CJ
FOR JUST
$6765.*

Fig. 9—1 *Jeep. An Impression of Smallness in Price Through Use of Blank Space in Design.* Courtesy of American Motors, Inc.

At each step of the creative process the client must approve plans and executions. In organizations with functional departments, personnel who deal with advertising agencies are likely to have an intimate familiarity with creative functions. Though they may not be copywriters or artists, they are usually capable of critical evaluation.

Firms with product management systems ordinarily lack creative expertise. Managers are primarily marketing specialists with no prior experience in advertising. But they are cast in liason roles, having to work with the agency in planning and approving its copy.

The formulation of strategy presents few problems. It derives from the marketing plan, which is a prime responsibility of the product manager. The strategy may have to be filtered through several layers of management within the firm. Further, discussions may be held with the agency. But these are conducted with account executives who are also marketing specialists. At this point in time, the strategy is still an abstraction, for there is no concrete prototype.

Major difficulties are encountered when the copywriter and art director enter the scene. Now abstract concepts must be translated into actual advertisements. When the strategy statement is specific and tightly written, there is little argument about what the ad should communicate. The copywriter can devote his or her entire attention on communication of the objectives. Possible disagreements are not eliminated, but the range of differences is narrowed. When strategy is vague, broad, and all-encompassing, the copywriter must obviously set strategy while creating the ad.

The amount of freedom that should be given to copywriters is a matter of great debate. One school holds that a narrow scope usually necessitates a heavy reliance on marketing research. The strategies which emerge, the thesis goes, emphasize product attributes. It is easier to draw up a list of product characteristics and ask consumers to rate them than to measure vague, undefined, and perhaps inexpressible emotions. These research-oriented strategies, it is held, suppress creativity and produce dull, uninspired advertisements. On the other hand, opponents point out that to allow creatives free reign is to subordinate factually-based judgment to intuitively-based decisions. In turn, they feel these self-engendered impressions can easily divert marketing from the main track into frivolities and irrelevancies.

Many of the basic ideas for the advertisement come from outside the creative team—the client organization, the research department, and the account executives. Product managers can usually judge the copywriter's output, though they cannot suggest a substitute if they do not like what is proposed. They can request several different approaches or versions so that they can select from alternatives. But they normally provide no other input.

The look...the feel...
of silk from the Orient.

Now yours in a pantyhose.

Sheer Elegance*

Imagine...pantyhose that looks and feels like real silk.™ It's Sheer Elegance.
Silky, smooth, radiant! In Sheer Elegance Control Top, too.
Nothing beats a great pair of L'eggs.™

*Sheer Elegance is a registered trademark of L'eggs Products for pantyhose. ©1981 L'eggs Products

Fig. 9—2 *L'eggs. Illustration Conveying the Idea of Oriental Silkiness.* Courtesy
of L'eggs Products.

In contrast, neither product managers, researchers nor account executives have any proficiency in design. The art director thus enjoys greater latitude than the copywriter, and works with a relatively free hand, but with well marked goals. He or she translates content through art and design. This transformation is admirably demonstrated in the advertisement for L'eggs pantyhose, shown in Figure 9–2.

The proposition in the L'eggs advertisement is primarily carried by the designer's fine touch, in this case the illustration. The exotic beauty who models the pantyhose adds more than oriental charm. The everyday pantyhose becomes imbued with some mysterious, Far Eastern sensuality. The art director's expertise is especially vital in television commercials, where unspoken, unpictured, and unsung elements can communicate images, feelings and impressions.[1]

COMPONENTS OF A PRINT ADVERTISEMENT

Copywriters depend strongly upon the headline and illustration to carry a message. Regardless of its limitations, copytesting emphatically shows that visual elements make the strongest impression on consumers' minds. Recall studies show that virtually all readers who remember anything about an advertisement recall an element of the illustration. And of those who recall seeing an advertisement, an overwhelming percentage read only the headline.[2]

Headlines are normally set in larger type than other text material. They have multiple functions which are often interrelated. Though their appraisal cannot avoid subjective opinion, like for that of a painting or an essay, it should be related to what the advertisement intends to communicate.

A major purpose of a headline is to gain attention. If a reader passes over the ad completely, the opportunity to communicate with that person is lost.

Along with the "stopping power" of a headline is the reader-qualification function. A good headline tells what the ad is about so that interested readers can then give the message their attention. It frequently capsulates the main selling proposition in an interesting way.

For example, an army recruiting ad makes quite evident the benefits offered to high school students aspiring to a college education. "The army," says the headline, "has helped send more people to college than there are people in college today." (See Figure 9–3.)

Another example of a good headline can be seen in a Speed Queen advertisement. "Speed Queen. Washers built for a world where washday never ends." The headline, "Noxzema introduces the first beauty pad for oily skin," leaves little doubt as to the selling proposition or the intended audience. It leads adroitly into the body copy, another important function

Norman Griner, Director

THE ARMY HAS HELPED SEND MORE PEOPLE TO COLLEGE THAN THERE ARE PEOPLE IN COLLEGE TODAY.

A lot of people, like Norman Griner, got where they are today because the Army helped them get there. By helping finance their college education. These people are proud to have served. Proud to have succeeded.

Today, the Army introduces the new Army College Fund. A high school graduate can join it, upon qualifying,when he or she joins the Army.

For every dollar they put in, Uncle Sam puts in five. Or more. So, after just two years in the Army, they can have up to $15,200 for college. In three years, up to $20,100.

Call this toll-free number for your free copy of the Army College Fund booklet. In California, call 800-252-0011. Alaska and Hawaii, 800-423-2244.

This could be the most important book a high school student ever reads.

ARMY. BE ALL YOU CAN BE. 800-421-4422

THE ARMY COLLEGE FUND

The Veterans' Educational Assistance Program with extra Army benefits.

Fig. 9—3   *U.S. Army. An Army Ad Which Headlines its Offer.*

of a headline. Females with oily skin who are interested can read further about what the beauty pad does. (See Figure 9–4.)

Headlines seldom work alone. Their most common associate is the illustration. If a reader scans the headline and illustration, he or she should get the main idea of the message in a majority of instances. These two components should, therefore, be closely related to each other. The headline usually states the proposition. The illustration should supply the supporting data in the form of nonverbal symbols. An excellent example of how headline and illustration can work together is the advertisement for Converse shoes. Indeed, the illustration of a knee is virtually part of the headline itself, which announces, "Good news for bad knees." Each element—headline and main illustration, reinforces the primary idea of the ad.

One suggested test of headline-illustration integration is to put a hand over the logotype of a given advertisement. If it could be any number of products, the headline and illustration are doing a bad job. If the association with the advertised brand is unmistakable, the functions of the two elements have been well executed.[3]

Rudy Nardelli, president of a New York advertising agency, once took travel advertisements to task. Figure 9–6 shows four advertisements Nardelli had singled out for criticism, and his comments about each one. Judgments on what is creative and what is effective are subjective, even when peers do the judging. Do you agree with Mr. Nardelli's verdict?

Some advertisements are comprised almost wholly of a headline and an illustration. Under these conditions, the two entities must present the proposition, the data, and the warrant. When body copy is present, it shares with the illustration the task of communicating the supporting data, and ties the evidence to the proposition. Rational messages will usually contain more text than nonrational ones.

Regardless of its importance, body copy is the element least often read. People read selectively, and this holds for both editorial and advertising matter. Headlines and illustrations serve as cues for further reading. They tell readers at a glance whether the advertisement holds interest for them. Headlines and illustrations thus function as devices for enticing prospective customers into the body copy.

Reader selectivity has probably been the main reason for practitioners taking a single-minded approach. If people must be coaxed, cajoled, goaded into reading an advertisement, they will not exert much effort to understand the proposition. Unless they are actually seeking information, they will not be greatly involved with content of a message. This lack of interest, for some products more so than others, has led copywriters to advocate simplicity. Although an advertisement may contain several points, normally one will dominate. This is called the one point-one ad principle. It has gained wide acceptance throughout the advertising industry.[4]

Fig. 9—4 *Noxzema. A Headline Which Creates Attention, Qualifies Prospects, Leads into Body Copy. Courtesy of the Noxell Corporation.*

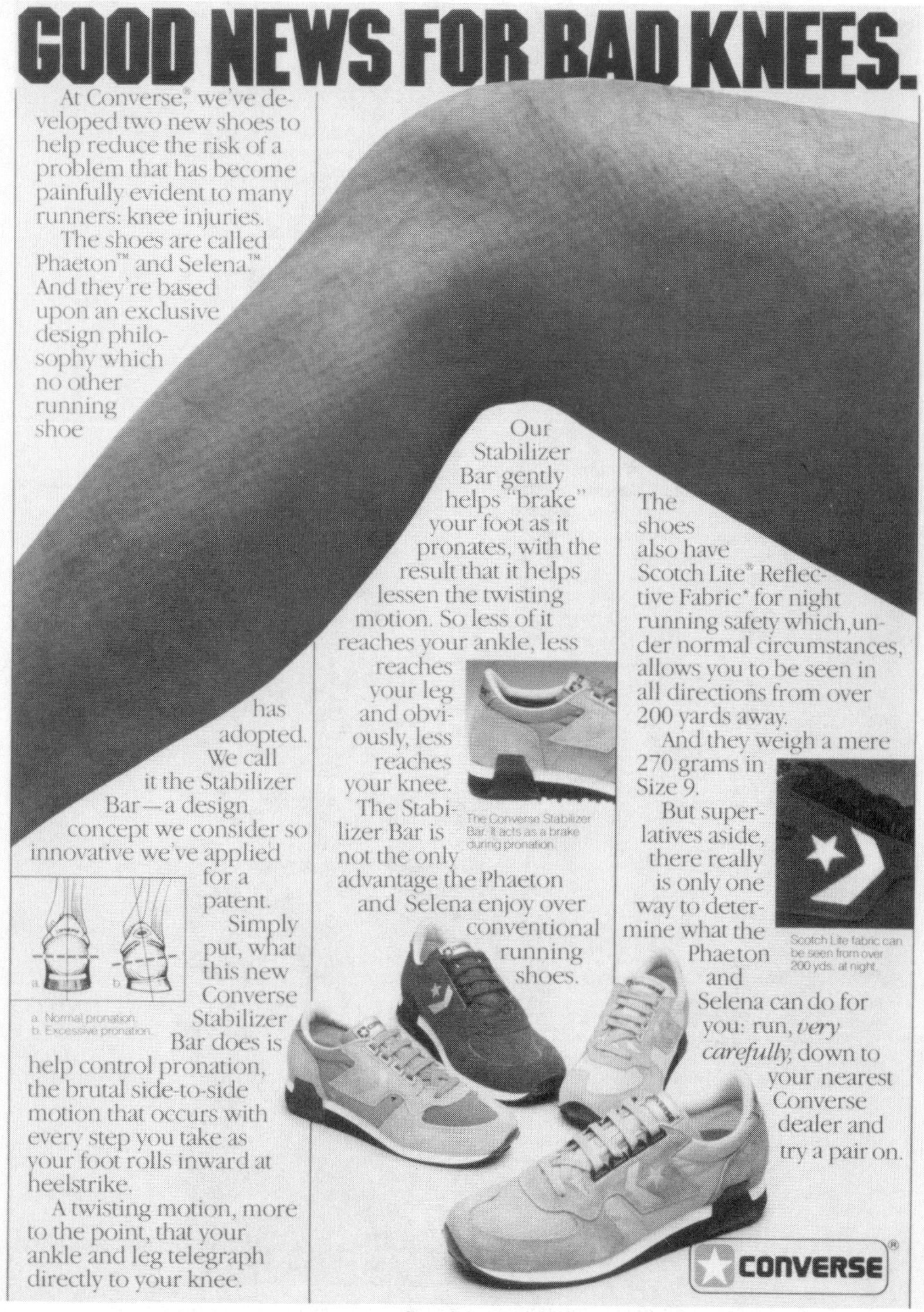

GOOD NEWS FOR BAD KNEES.

At Converse, we've developed two new shoes to help reduce the risk of a problem that has become painfully evident to many runners: knee injuries.

The shoes are called Phaeton™ and Selena™. And they're based upon an exclusive design philosophy which no other running shoe has adopted. We call it the Stabilizer Bar—a design concept we consider so innovative we've applied for a patent.

Simply put, what this new Converse Stabilizer Bar does is help control pronation, the brutal side-to-side motion that occurs with every step you take as your foot rolls inward at heelstrike.

A twisting motion, more to the point, that your ankle and leg telegraph directly to your knee.

a. Normal pronation.
b. Excessive pronation.

Our Stabilizer Bar gently helps "brake" your foot as it pronates, with the result that it helps lessen the twisting motion. So less of it reaches your ankle, less reaches your leg and obviously, less reaches your knee.

The Stabilizer Bar is not the only advantage the Phaeton and Selena enjoy over conventional running shoes.

The Converse Stabilizer Bar. It acts as a brake during pronation.

The shoes also have Scotch Lite® Reflective Fabric* for night running safety which, under normal circumstances, allows you to be seen in all directions from over 200 yards away.

And they weigh a mere 270 grams in Size 9.

But superlatives aside, there really is only one way to determine what the Phaeton and Selena can do for you: run, *very carefully*, down to your nearest Converse dealer and try a pair on.

Scotch Lite fabric can be seen from over 200 yds. at night.

★ CONVERSE®

Fig. 9–5 *Converse Shoes. Sample Headline and Illustration Integration.*
Courtesy of Converse, Inc.

"Who can relate to a bride in the water? This ad for Jamaica is foolish. It does nothing to promote a honeymoon in Jamaica."

" 'Virginia is for lovers' has served it well—but this ad does not competitively distinguish Virginia from surrounding states."

"Mexico has to be one of the most beautiful places on earth, but this ad doesn't capture that beauty. It could be Central Park."

"What's sensuous about two wet people? The ad should prove Niagra Falls is sensuous, not just say it."

Fig. 9—6 *Travel ads from* Advertising Age *article. Examples of Four Travel Advertisements. Reprinted with Permission from June 1981 issue of* Advertising Age, *Copyright (1981) by Crain Communications, Inc.*

The signature or logotype usually appears at the end of the body copy. It aims to enhance brand identification by displaying some sign or visual symbol.

In the past several years firms have begun adding four other symbols to their advertisements: ®, ™, ℠, and ©. These encircled letters may show up anywhere in the advertisement. To consumers they are meaningless, and consequently have nothing to do with making a better advertisement. Rather, their sole function is to protect the exclusive ownership of brand names, trademarks, and processes.

An ® signifies registration at the U.S. Patent Office. A ™ stands for trademark. It puts all firms on notice that an ® status application is in the works and that any unauthorized use of the name is illegal. ℠ says the product is a service but its legal position is similar to that of ™. The letter © is a copyright claim, declaring the right of sole ownership to everything in the advertisement. According to lawyers, the elimination of these seemingly obscure marks could result in a loss of exclusivity to the name.[5]

COMPONENTS OF A BROADCAST ADVERTISEMENT

Like the printed advertisement, a commercial draws its inspiration from the copy platform. But its components are those of time, running from the opening to middle to close. It makes no difference whether the commercial is on radio or television. The former must rely more on the imagination of the listener. The latter adds pictures to the voice, making everything more explicit. Since sight and sound dominate broadcasting, the spotlight will be turned on television.

The opening of the commercial performs functions which are similar to those of a headline. First, it sets out the proposition in a simple manner so that even if a viewer sees nothing more than the mere beginning he or she will have gotten the gist of the message. Second, it acts as a lure to get the audience into the main body of the message.

The audience holding power of the opening is crucial to the success of the entire commercial. From 25 percent to 40 percent of a television audience is said to leave the room during station breaks, when commercials come on.[6] The loss of viewership may often be completely unrelated to the quality of the commercial. The normal practice of stations is to transmit commercials in a series. If a particular message is the third or fourth in the sequence, by the time it gets aired a large proportion of the audience may already have gone on their break from the television set. Copywriters and producers have no control over this type of audience loss. Responsibility for obtaining a time slot with maximum audience traffic falls to the media department.

But even those who stay in the room can by no means be regarded as "captive." The mind can wander and attention can wane. Distractions can spring up. Viewing is as selective as reading, and an opening must work hard to hold the viewer.

The opening has one other function which is somewhat unique and has no counterpart in print. Broadcast has no obvious devices, such as pages and borders, which separate messages from each other. When several commercials follow in quick succession, they can easily merge into one another. Because of this bunching, or clutter as it is called, an opening must strive to keep the beginning distinct. In order to counteract this problem, many experts suggest that producers observe their creations in a group of other commercials before the final editing.

The middle portion of the commercial incorporates the heart of the argument. It supports the opening proposition through voice, sound, pictures, music, or any combination thereof. The most important element is video, which allows the television media to be exploited to its utmost advantage.

But, as in print, the advertising industry remains wedded to the one point-one commercial principle. A good commercial, it is held, focuses on a central idea and results in the registration of a single, penetrating impression. After examining more than 22,000 commercials in the television library that bears his name, Harry Wayne McMahan pointed to the "key visual" as the indicator of successful commercials. According to McMahan, "It is the distinctive, relevant scene you hope will stick in the minds of the viewers."[7] McMahan illustrates his point with a cutaway picture for Titleist which compares itself with another golf ball to show it has 30 percent more backspin. (See Figure 9–7.)

How fast or for how long must a commercial stick in one's mind to be effective? There is no answer to this question. Marketing research usually examines memorability at what may be called the conscious level. Though cues may vary, some kind of recall is elicited.

Advertising Age and SRI Research Center, Inc., in April, 1982, began monthly tracking studies to measure consumer awareness of advertising. Its first wave interviewed by telephone a national sample of 1,262 adults chosen by probability methods. As expected, the majority of advertisements remembered, 69 percent, were linked to television. But 44 percent of all consumers answered "don't know" when asked to identify which brand comes to mind from all the advertising they have seen in the previous 30 days.[8]

It might be argued that failure to play back advertising does not mean the consumer is completely unaware of the the brand. But, the fact that such a large proportion of adults could not recall the advertising of a single brand is startling. Not only do the transmitted messages suffer from severe attrition, but those that do get through to viewers' minds are quickly forgotten. An advertising impression is a highly perishable item. This is all the more reason for keeping message content down to its essentials—a single idea, expressed simply and forcefully.

Fig. 9—7 *Golf Balls. Illustration of a Key Visual.* Reprinted with permission from Advertising Age, *Copyright (1977) by Crain Communications, Inc.*

The close of the commercial often contains the warrant, the clincher, as to why a person should do something. Along with the advertiser's signature or signoff, the commercial might repeat a slogan. For example, Mazda leaves its viewers with the rhythmical message, "The more you look, the more you like." Merrill Lynch signs off with a qualifier to its name, "A Breed Apart." Clorox prewash closes with the slogan, "Cleans circles around the leading prewash."

PRINT ADVERTISEMENT LAYOUT

The design of print advertisement is often referred to as the layout. It is an arrangement of the components which make up the advertisement, as visualized by the art director.

Layouts proceed in a number of stages. Artists begin with a thumbnail sketch, a small drawing in which the elements are indistinct. These thumbnails, done rather quickly, represent possibilities which might be considered. The best ideas are chosen and progressively refined until a particular arrangement is decided upon. At that point the artist will go about preparing a comprehensive.

A comprehensive shows the exact size and position of each element in the advertisement. The layout is supposed to look as much as possible like the finished advertisement, so that it can be approved for production. Once that is done, the layout goes into production to be readied for printing.

The comprehensive is not the last stage where changes can be made, but for economic reasons, it should be. Once type is set, afterthoughts become expensive. For example, making changes in a mechanical pasted up for offset printing is a tedious process which disrupts the production flow of a composition shop. The alterations, no matter how small, necessitate a set-up charge. The phototypesetter must be readjusted, with proper fonts and settings, even if the change involves one word or one line. A pasteup person must strip out the old copy before inserting the new. Depending upon the equipment used, typists may be interrupted from straight text to prepare a special tape which incorporates the change. If the work has already been put on film, expenses mount further. Company auditors should always examine these composition procedures for indications of work which could have been avoided by thinking before doing.

At first glance, advertising layouts display elements of different shapes and sizes, and in various positions. But all these can be reduced to certain basic forms, though there is no unanimity of what is a basic design. According to Jugenheimer and White, arrangements can be classified in six types, and most advertisements will fall into one of these categories. Of these six, the first four are the most popular. The six categories are:[9]

1. Conventional headline—illustration—body copy layout
2. Poster ad
3. Editorial-dominant layout
4. Picture-caption format
5. Comic strip
6. Continuous strip

The most popular design is layout number one. It is a highly conventional arrangement in which the reader is led from headline to illustration to body copy.

This layout is exemplified by the advertisement for a Whirlpool washer, shown in Figure 9–8. The headline and illustration dominate, and given the content, readers who scan the page—as most of them do—would have no trouble in picking up the gist of the message. In these instances, a passing glance at the advertisement would be enough to keep the brand name in consumers' minds.

This advertisement has a purpose other than just reminding. Readers who are interested in a washer are welcomed, as though a red carpet ran right up to the door, into the body copy. This section goes into more detail about the machine's features and benefits.

The design of the Whirlpool advertisement achieves balance by a symmetrical arrangement of elements. If a vertical line were drawn down the middle of the advertisement, the elements on both sides would be equi-

Fig. 9—8 *Whirlpool. Example of Conventional Headline—Illustration—Body Copy Layout. Advertisement used by permission of Whirlpool Corporation.*

distant from the line and have the same weight. The optical center would be about two-thirds from the bottom of this vertical line, which is where the eye would fall naturally upon first seeing the advertisement. This would be at the middle of the control panel on top of the washer. The optical center is the fulcrum around which all elements revolve.

If the body copy of the Whirlpool ad were removed and the illustration expanded, the result would be a poster-type advertisement. This form is designated as layout number two. Its main use is for reminder advertising. Well-known brands in mature markets gravitate to this kind of design.

An example of layout number two is the advertisement for Marlboro Lights, shown in Figure 9–9. The prominent text material displays only the brand name and the Surgeon General's warning. But the picture which forms the ad is in keeping with Marlboro's image of cowboys and macho men.

An illustration-dominated advertisement can actually take on many functions when used creatively. It can create product images, not merely reinforce them, actively urge people to buy, not merely remind them of the brand when they buy.

Most of the pictures in today's advertisements are photographs rather than illustrative drawings. The preference for photography stems from the belief that photographs are more realistic and credible than interpretations of artists.

At the other extreme of the poster-type design is layout number three, where editorial material dominates. The advertisement often resembles the editorial style of the publication carrying it. Many corporate and industrial advertisements are made up in an editorial format. This design works best when the argument follows rational lines and the target audience tends to be selective and highly involved.

Layout number four, the picture-caption format, represents a compromise between the all-illustration and the all-editorial approach, as is layout number one. The difference between one and four is the way the illustrations and text are blended. Layout four contains several illustrations, each accompanied by a copy block. This design conforms with situations which call for more than one product characteristic, or more than one product, to be featured in the same message. Breaking up the advertisement into separate units, each illustrating a point, makes for quicker reading and better understanding.

The picture-caption advertisement comes in many versions. It can emphasize text or illustration. Or it can walk a thin line between the two.

Heavy weighting of text material becomes manifest in the advertisement for KitchenAid dishwashers, shown in Figure 9–10. The layout resembles the editorial design, except that the body copy is broken up by small pictures which symbolize portions of the text. The argument takes a

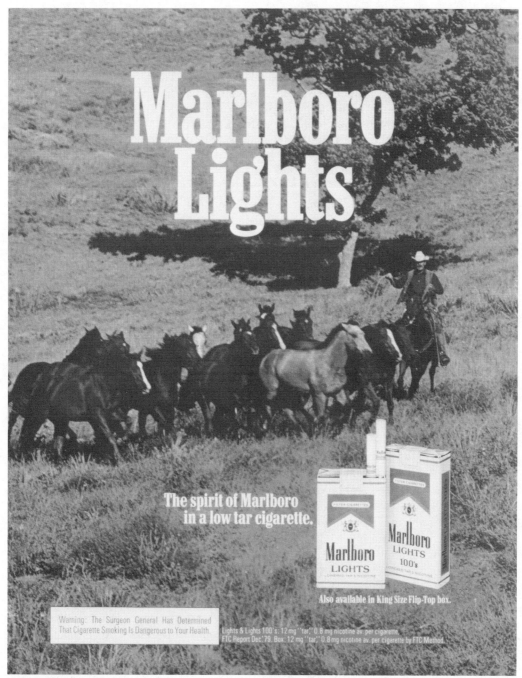

Fig. 9—9 *Marlboro Lights. Illustration of a Poster Advertisement. Courtesy of Philip Morris, Incorporated.*

rational course, offering an array of factual data for intellectual support. Another version of the picture-caption format is the advertisement for Frost & Tip hair lightener. (See Figure 9–11.) It tells how to get four different hair shades mainly by illustrations, not text. Captions are brief and words are at a minimum. Except for the short captions, the design looks like layout number six, which develops its theme using pictures only.

Layout number five, employing a comic strip technique, has no big following. Its greatest use occurs in advertising to children. Essentially, the message plays down literalness with a touch of humor.

BROADCAST ADVERTISEMENT LAYOUT

The design of a broadcast advertisement can also be thought of as a layout insofar as its elements are arranged in some order. But the components are ordered in time.

The radio commercial is quite simple, and requires no more than a script. Television commercials combine the script with pictures. In fact, the layout begins with a script and is progressively refined to include visual elements. The video portion, however, is not a simple appendage of the audio but assumes a prominent place in the scheme.

The layout of a television commercial is called a storyboard. It is a series of sketches which depict key scenes and major changes in the action flow. Beneath each drawing or frame are two sets of instructions: a verbal description of what the frame represents and any spoken words which belong to the scene. The number of frames differ from storyboard to storyboard, depending upon the contents. Sequence takes primacy, for action must flow smoothly and logically yet form a unified whole.

Like the print layout, the storyboard cannot go into production until it is approved by the advertiser. But from this point onward, the design function in television departs radically from that of print.

When a print layout is approved, it is final. The ensuing advertisement will look exactly like the mechanical, the images of which are replicated on the printing plates. In turn, these images are transformed onto paper by the medium in which the advertisement appears. The only factor involved is the fidelity of reproduction, which becomes a function of the press and paper used by the publication. Quality of reproduction also is largely dependent on the medium. For all purposes, the copywriter and designer have done their job with the completion of the mechanical or layout.

For the television commercial, the approved layout is only the beginning. The storyboard is sent out to production houses for bids. To make sure that all bids are comparable, the client should insist on a standard form in which all estimated costs are itemized. The Association of Independent Commercial Producers is one organization which publishes such costing forms.

NOW KITCHENAID USES LESS ENERGY, USES LESS TIME, USES LESS WATER.

Our new dishwashers are the most energy efficient we've ever made. They even heat their own hot water for superior cleaning every time.

Most dishwashers depend on the temperature of the hot water in your home. But that can vary quite considerably.

If you've ever had a hot shower suddenly turn cold, you know what we mean.

Now KitchenAid automatically heats its own hot water in every complete cycle. Heats it as high as a steamy 150° for superior cleaning every time.

Save energy, time and water.

Our new Low Energy Wash Cycle uses 25% less energy.* 30% less time, and 30% less water than the Normal Wash Cycle it replaces. There's even optional Heat Off Drying for additional energy savings. And you can save even more energy by setting your home water heater 20°F lower than any other dishwasher recommends.

And everything will still come out clean.

More loading convenience.

Only KitchenAid gives you a completely usable lower rack. No lost space. No cut-out portion to accommodate the wash system.

And KitchenAid also gives you true upper rack loading flexibility. Our exclusive 16-position adjustment lets you lower one side or raise the other. The dividers even fold down. So odd-shaped items fit in easily.

Quick change color front panels.

Each new KitchenAid comes with a Stainless Steel Trim Kit and two front panels installed one behind the other. The flip side of each is a different color. Almond. Harvest Wheat. White. Onyx Black. Or you can insert your own custom wood panel. Easily change your kitchen's decor.

Weigh the alternatives.

KitchenAid dishwashers are the heaviest you can buy. Because we build them sturdy and strong. We use a rigid steel frame to give all the parts solid support. Others use just a base plate with a few struts for support.

We use a solid steel tank with two coats of porcelain and a tough overglaze. No one else does. Some even use a tank or inner door made of plastic.

Most others settle for a motor with only one-third horsepower or less. We use a hefty one-half horsepower motor.

A stronger motor strains less. So it's a lot less likely to wear out.

Triple Protection Warranties.

We're so confident of the quality that goes into a KitchenAid we give a 10 Year Limited Warranty on the porcelain tank and inner door. A 5 Year Limited Warranty on the motor. And a One Year Full Warranty on the complete dishwasher. Check what the others offer.

Don't settle for less.

Certainly there are dishwashers that cost less than KitchenAid. Because they give you less than KitchenAid. Compare for yourself. We think you'll find the difference in dishwashers is a lot bigger than the difference in price. For additional information, write KitchenAid Division, Troy, Ohio 45374.

KITCHENAID. DON'T SETTLE FOR LESS.

Fig. 9–10 *KitchenAid. Illustration of Text Weighted Picture—Caption Format.*
Courtesy of KitchenAid (a registered trademark of Hobart Corporation).

Four ways to turn on the lights in your hair.

Turn on soft lights...by using only the dots on the front section of the Frost & Tip "Designer" Cap.

Bright lights...use the dots on the front and top sections.

Brighter lights...use the dots on the front, top and first three rows in the back section.

Outtasight lights!...use *all* the dots.

With Clairol Frost & Tip.

It's easy. With Frost & Tip. Because only Frost & Tip has the special "Designer" Cap with clearly marked "how-to" dots.

Just slip on the cap. Pick your "look." And pull out just the strands you need to get it.

And Frost & Tip conditions your hair to make it soft, silky, even more manageable.

So turn on the lights. And turn 'em on.

Fig. 9–11 *Frost & Tip Hair Lightener. Example of Illustration Weighted Picture—Caption Format. Courtesy of Clairol, Inc.*

The production house hired takes the storyboard as a guide. But a producer can render the storyboard in many different ways. Because of the different renditions which are possible, a client should always keep on top of preproduction sessions. The advertiser should also have a representative on the scene when the commercial is being shot, for decisions made on these occasions can have a strong bearing on costs.

Expenses for producing a commercial can range from as low as $10,000 to as high as $100,000 and up. Exotic settings, faraway locations, elaborate musical numbers, or difficult stunts, can send costs skyrocketing.

Should a company approve or reject creative proposals which seem lavish or frivolous? The answer is twofold.

First, the basic structure as represented by the storyboard is crucial. If the design visualizes scenes which resemble those of a De Mille extravaganza, payrolls for stage hands will be costly. If the plan contemplates helicopters dropping automobiles on mountain tops, authentic shots will be costly. On the other hand, storyboards which call for close-ups of the product from almost start to finish will be relatively cheap because there are no actors. A number of these "product-as-hero" commercials show up each year among the "100 best" in the McMahan library.[10]

Second, execution moves to the forefront only after the structure is decided. Here, too, there can be wide variations in costs. If a producer shoots a skiing scene in the Alps, he will pile up expenses for travel, lodging, eating, and drinking. The choice of film or videotape involves different production techniques, and consequently alters the cost structure.

No matter how the question of production cost is phrased, the answer rests on judgment. Does the additional cost yield more than proportionate benefits? Put this way, the question must take up both production and media transmission costs. It must be answered from the standpoint of total costs.

If a commercial is run nationwide, and repeated a number of times, any incremental outlay amounts to a small proportion of the total. The addition is spread over a larger base. This is why networks generally carry better quality commercials than local stations. Relative costs of production run lower, and even if returns from the enhanced quality cannot be precisely measured, advertisers with national schedules can afford to spend more.

The total cost approach also gives rise to a number of possible trade offs. For example, better quality can be offset against a schedule with more frequency per message. That is, telecast the commercial at the same intervals but over a longer time span. Or the commercial portfolio can be constructed with fewer different messages. Reducing the number of commercials in the pool has the effect of running the same message more times, but without lengthening the time period.

Any decision to increase repetition of messages must consider content, which seems to be an important variable. A commercial that contains humor, for example, is often thought to lose appeal quickly with repetition. It is also possible to reduce repeated showings if more versions of the same commercial can be produced through editing. At any time, more film is shot than actually used. With a little planning, producers can create somewhat different versions with only minor increments in expenses.

CLASSIFICATION OF TELEVISION COMMERCIALS

Classification forms the core of any professional discipline, be it art, law, or advertising. Unless names of things are widely accepted by a profession, meaningful communication is hardly possible. Unless things are well defined and grouped in some systematic way, techniques cannot be evaluated, perpetuated, or improved upon.

There have been a number of attempts to classify commercials, but no unanimity has resulted. Book and Cary identify as many as thirteen separate types.[11] But they are not mutually exclusive. Systems with the smallest number of classes list six.[12] The taxonomical scheme adopted here is that of Ray P. Nelson, which settles on seven classes.[13] The Nelson plan seems to have the highest proportion of agreement with other classificatons, and therefore represents a consensus to a greater degree than others. Categories, rated by dominant characteristics, are as follows:

1. Story
2. Slice-of-life
3. Testimonial
4. Announcer commercial
5. Demonstration
6. Song and dance
7. Special effects

The Story

This type of commercial, as the name implies, contains a plot. Normally, the story begins by posing a problem. It ends with a successful conclusion by showing how the advertised product solved the problem, and the once distraught person lived happily ever after.

Slice-of-Life

This type, too, is a story. But whereas the conventional story does not try to hide its fictitious character, the slice-of-life commercial gives the impression of being nonfiction. For example, it may feature two women talking over a fence about what they use to clean their sinks.

To be effective, the slice-of-life approach shows common, everyday people with whom viewers can identify. Agency casting departments or freelance casting directors look for actors who are ordinary looking, or they may even pick nonactors to do the commercial.[14] But the stress is on reality. This is vital. If the commercial fails to impart that sort of atmosphere, it will usually fail to accomplish the advertising objective.

Figure 9–12, a commercial for Bold detergent, exemplifies a skillful implementation of the slice-of-life technique. The characters are so like people viewers know, that even Moose Mountain takes on a certain reality.

The main character who delivers the product pitch is vital to the effectiveness of the slice-of-life commercial. Such "authority figures" as Mr. Whipple, Cora, Madge the manicurist, have been around for years. But the average life expectancy of such characters is a year or two.[15] The Whipples and Coras and Madges are the exceptions, not the rule, and their longevity only attests to the difficulty of success.

Testimonial

This is a very old technique which predates television. Usually, a well-known personality stands up, relates from personal experience why the product is good, and recommends it to viewers. According to the Federal Trade Commission, if a celebrity is used, he or she must have actually used the product. Mohammed Ali must be a regular Brut user in order to tell his audience that the product makes him smell sweet. Bruce Jenner, the former decathlon champion, must have eaten Wheaties as a kid to be able to urge other children to have it for breakfast. Another type of testimonial is done by unknown actors, such as commercials which try to simulate shoppers caught by a candid camera. Both kinds of testimonials, by celebrities or ordinary people, give authenticity to the message.

The choice of celebrity depends upon the target audience and the kind of impression intended. Perrier water, advertising to better educated, higher income individuals, would hardly use the same spokesperson as used for a beer commercial appealing to blue collar workers. The agency usually searches and recommends the personality, and the client must be actively involved in the decision.

Care must be exercised if the person considered does testimonials for another product. At times, these figures become so identified with a particular item that other recommendations go unheeded. Or worse, audiences may relate them to another product. Research studies constantly turn up people being associated with products long after they had stopped their testimonials.

Another concern is the interplay between the character and the product. A study conducted by Advertising Age and SRI Research, Inc. found the greatest confusion was linked to a Polaroid commercial. Respondents mentioned "the James Garner" commercials but were unable to name the brand Mr. Garner touts.[16] Apparently, the actor was so dominant, or his performance so overpowering, as to detract attention from the product.

GREY ADVERTISING INC.

CLIENT: PROCTER & GAMBLE CO.
PRODUCT: BOLD-3
TITLE: "HIKING"   LENGTH: 60 SECONDS

DATE: 5/18/81
CODE NO.: PGBO 4816

1. HUSBAND: We climbed Moose Mountain!

2. ANN: On your elbows?

3. RUTH: Think that's easy? ANN: Well washing that sweatshirt won't be. It needs a good old-fashioned cleaning.

4. RUTH: No problem. I've got what it takes. ANN: Oh, c'mon...you don't do anything old-fashioned. RUTH: You're right.

5. But I know how to get an old-fashioned clean...plus softness with Bold-3.

6. ANN: An old-fashioned clean

7. from a detergent with a new-fangled fabric softener? RUTH: Absolutely.

8. ANN: Bold-3'll clean this sweatshirt? RUTH: Plus leave it snuggly soft.

9. ANN: If I see it and feel it,

10. I'll climb Moose Mountain.

11. ANNCR: (VO) We took the softening and static control

12. of a full-strength fabric softener...

13. and concentrated it into a powder. Then we combined it with...

14. Bold-3's powerful powdered detergent.

15. ANN: Now everything looks like you didn't leave home. That is a good old-fashioned clean.

16. RUTH: Of course...and feel it. ANN: Soft enough to sleep in.

17. RUTH: Even our hiking socks slide apart... ANN: No static cling.

18. I see it. And feel it.

19. RUTH: So... BOTH: Start climbing.

20. ANNCR: (VO) Bold-3 for an old-fashioned clean plus a new-fangled fabric softener.

Fig. 9—12 *Bold Detergent. A Slice-of-Life Commercial.* Courtesy of The Procter & Gamble Company.

The Announcer Commercial

This type of commercial has several versions. One is the staff announcer, who looks right into the camera and speaks to the audience. If the announcer is well known, the commercial takes on aspects of a testimonial. This format has a long history, having been used in the very early days of television.

Another version of an announcer commercial does not show the announcer, but records his voice accompanying the video elements. One advantage of the announcer commercial is its comparatively low production cost. This advantage also applies to the testimonial.

Demonstration

A demonstration may show how a product is made, how it functions, or how it compares with competitive offerings. The demonstration is one of the most popular forms of television commercials, because of the suitability of the medium. At least one-third of all advertising on television employs this technique.

Song and Dance

This structural form tries to capture the mood and flavor of a musical show. It is used mainly when the objective of advertising is to remind. One of the most successful song and dance commercials is that for Dr. Pepper, featuring Mickey Rooney. (Refer to Figure 9–13.) The entire argument — proposition, data, warrant—is part of the song and dance.

Special Effects

This type of commercial employs unusual shots and other visual devices in order to attract attention. Trucks being driven separately and then coming together, or O. J. Simpson floating through an airport, are examples of special effects. Some of these commercials depend upon technical wizardry, creating an illusion. The O. J. Simpson commercial shown in Figure 9–14 was produced in this way. Its effectiveness stems not merely from the startling special effects, but from the integration of the unusual visuals with the proposition of Hertz putting customers in drivers' seats faster than anyone else.

PRESENTATION METHODS

There are basically three ways in which commercials can be presented: live, film, or videotape.

The live commercial had its heyday when television was young, In fact, it was the only way commercials could be presented. Nowadays, it is rare, having been replaced by film or videotape.

Fig. 9—13 *Dr. Pepper. Illustration of Song and Dance Commercial.* Courtesy of
Dr. Pepper Company

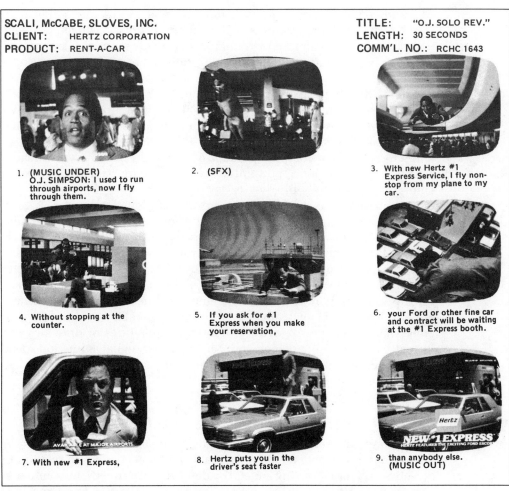

SCALI, McCABE, SLOVES, INC.
CLIENT: HERTZ CORPORATION
PRODUCT: RENT-A-CAR

TITLE: "O.J. SOLO REV."
LENGTH: 30 SECONDS
COMM'L. NO.: RCHC 1643

1. (MUSIC UNDER)
O.J. SIMPSON: I used to run through airports, now I fly through them.

2. (SFX)

3. With new Hertz #1 Express Service, I fly non-stop from my plane to my car.

4. Without stopping at the counter.

5. If you ask for #1 Express when you make your reservation,

6. your Ford or other fine car and contract will be waiting at the #1 Express booth.

7. With new #1 Express,

8. Hertz puts you in the driver's seat faster

9. than anybody else.
(MUSIC OUT)

Fig. 9–14 *O. J. Simpson. Illustration of Special Effects Commercial. Courtesy of The Hertz Corporation.*

Film is more expensive than videotape, but it is also more versatile. It has an advantage for on-location shots and animation. It offers cheaper copies than videotape. This becomes a factor to consider if the media schedule contemplates running the commercial in a large number of spot markets. Film also has a higher reuse rate than videotape. After about a hundred showings of a videotape, magnetic dropout begins to deteriorate the quality.

The videotape's biggest advantage lies in its possibilities for reducing shooting time. A film must be sent to a lab for development before editing can take place. This necessitates keeping the cast and production crews on call until the final copy. Studios normally rent by the day, along with crews, even if a change requires but one hour. In contrast, videotape needs no processing and can be edited immediately. This permits a commercial to be finished the same day as editing. Reshots can be taken at one sitting if the instant replay reveals any mistakes.

About five percent of television commercials involve animation.[17] What are its advantages over live action? First, it can produce visual exaggeration which live action cannot. Second, it presents a way of getting inside an object and demonstrating how it functions. This technique also helps to simplify a complex product by demonstrating it symbolically. Third, it offers humor opportunities which are impossible in real life.[18] Humor is used widely in advertising to children.

But animation is a relatively expensive and lengthy process. A fully animated commercial of 30 seconds duration, at 24 frames per second, requires 720 drawings. To do these drawings by conventional methods and get them onto film normally takes from ten to fourteen weeks. Lead time can be cut to as low as ten days by recently developed computer programs, known as digital animation. An artist draws the key frames directly into the computer. Color, brightness, line intensity, and texture, are also fed into the machine. Given these basic data, the computer generates the "in-between" artwork. Enormous quantities of drawings can virtually be ground out on demand. Not only does digital animation speed up completion time, but it enables the artist to make more changes and to exercise better control over production.[19]

MEDIA INTEGRATION

Many companies run advertising campaigns in more than one medium. A major reason is to obtain a more favorable audience pattern in relation to objectives set for marketing targets. By definition, an advertising campaign conveys the same selling proposition, regardless of media. Every message in the series is thought of as having a certain similarity to each other, either visually or verbally. Since different media lend themselves to different copy treatments, accomplishing an effective array of look-alike messages can be a problem.

Integration is easier when two media have characteristics in common. For example, a sound track of a television commercial can often be adapted to radio with minimal change. Because radio acts as the junior partner in this media combination, it functions as a booster for television. The audio-only commercials are said to make the audio-visual commercials more memorable when scripts are similar.

The print-television mix discloses more varied ways of integrating messages in the two media.[20] The advertisements reproduced in Figures 9–15, 9–16, and 9–17 exemplify different methods of media matching.

Fig. 9–15 *Aqua-Fresh. Reinforcing the Television Commercial in Print Media.*
Courtesy of Beecham Inc.

The advertisement for Aqua-fresh in Figure 9–15 involves little more than reproducing the storyboard in print. The advertisement simply displays the key visuals, with the audio portion of the commercial printed under each frame. The function of the printed message appears to be one of reinforcing the impression conveyed by the commercial.

The Anacin advertisement in Figure 9–16, featuring Eleanor Newcomb, arthritis sufferer, contains the same key elements found in the Anacin commercial. But they are rearranged to fit print media. The headline and picture are closely related, as in other print advertisements. The advantage of Anacin—handled as comparative advertising in television—appears at the bottom of the advertisement and supports the body copy.

The Dove advertisement in Figure 9–17 illustrates yet another method of using different media. It makes the same selling point as the commercial—Dove contains a moisturizer which creams the skin and leaves it smooth and soft. Except for this main theme, there is no relationship between the advertisement and commercial. The advertisement is a testimonial, but tailored to fit print media.

SUMMARY

The creative team is headed by a copywriter, whose ideas are dramatized by an art director. The structure of a print advertisement has four main components: headline, illustration, body copy, and signature. The first two are the most important.

The major components of a broadcast commercial are those of time. The message has an opening, a middle, and a close. The most important element of a television commercial is video, which permits utilization of the full potential of the medium.

Most print advertisements fall into one of six layouts: conventional headline-picture-body copy sequence, poster layout, editorial advertisement, picture-poster format, continuous picture format, and comic strip. The major television structures are: story, slice-of-life, testimonial, announcer, demonstration, song and dance, and special effects.

When a print layout is approved, it should be final. The finished advertisement will look like the mechanical. When a storyboard is approved, it can still be rendered in different ways by the producer. Television production offers various trade offs in costing decisions.

Multimedia users face the problem of integrating the individual messages of a campaign. There are numerous ways in which this can be done. Messages in one medium can be used to reinforce those in another. Or the same selling points can be made, with no relation whatsoever between advertisements in different media.

Eleanor Newcomb, arthritis sufferer

"Before I took Anacin for my Arthritis pain, I could hardly open the jar."

After Anacin® pain reliever went to work, Mrs. Newcomb opened the jar easily.

Anacin has more pain reliever. Two tablets of regular strength aspirin or non-aspirin products contain only 650 milligrams of pain reliever. But Anacin contains more. 800 milligrams. And Anacin is a special combination of medical ingredients. Mrs. Newcomb got hours of relief from her minor arthritis pain. Shouldn't you be using Anacin for your arthritis?
Tablets or capsules. Use only as directed.

Get the Anacin difference.

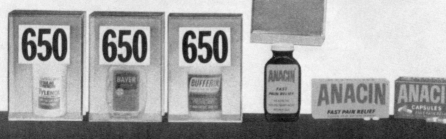

Fig. 9—16 *Anacin. Print Version of a Television Theme.* Courtesy of Whitehall Laboratories.

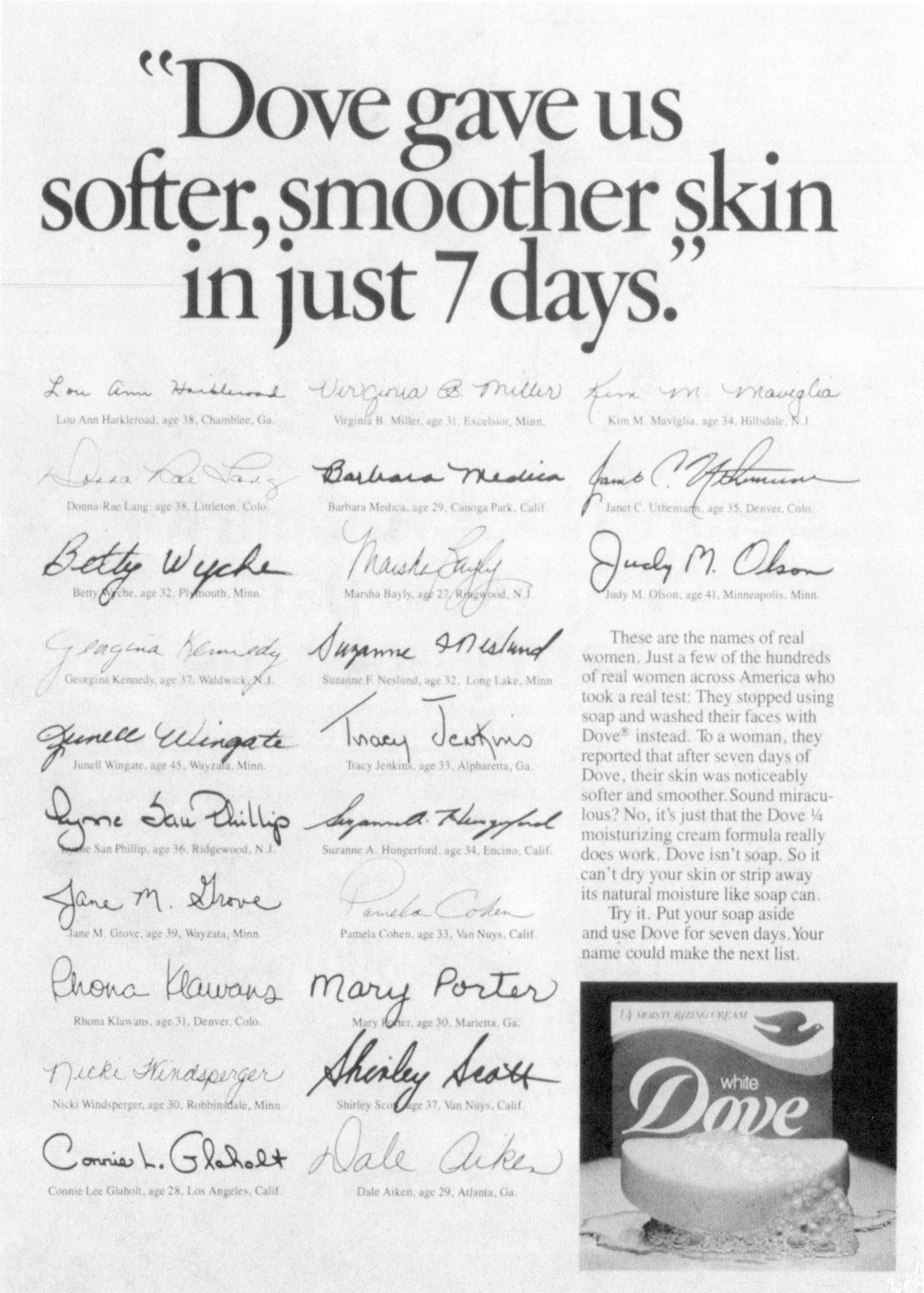

Fig. 9–17 Dove. Print Advertisement with No Relationship Except Main Theme to Television Commercial. *Courtesy of Lever Bros.*

Questions for Chapter 9

1. Should creative personnel be involved in strategy formulation?

2. Why would an art director be less constrained than a copywriter?

3. What are the main functions of headlines?

4. Under what circumstances might advertisements display long copy?

5. What is the rationale for having each commercial stress a single proposition?

6. What are the various uses of printed ads in which the illustration dominates?

7. Demand for commercials from national advertisers are more inelastic than the demand of local advertisers? Why?

8. Why would a slice-of-life commercial have a higher probability of being used for a detergent than for an automobile?

9. What are some major problems in integrating television and print messages in a campaign?

Footnotes for Chapter 9

[1]Julius Harburger, "Commercial's Vibes May Say Opposite of What's Intended," *Advertising Age* (February 12, 1979), pp. 57–58.

[2]"Ads Should Focus on Products, not Themselves, say 2 from O&M," *Marketing News* (August 12, 1977), p. 7.

[3]Janice Chlopowicz, "Popularity Isn't Success," *Advertising Age* (December 29, 1980), p. S–4.

[4]Nelson, pp. 44–45.

[5]Richard C. Douglas, "Ad Symbols Warn, Protect, Muddle," *Advertising Age* (March 30, 1981), p. 50.

[6]Book and Cary, p. 93.

[7]Harry W. McMahan, "How to Make Them Better: Seven Deadly Sins in Writing Television Commercials," *Advertising Age* (November 28, 1977), p. 44.

[8]Joseph M. Winski, "Coke is It in First Ad Age Poll," *Advertising Age* (May 17, 1982), p. 1.

[9]Donald W. Jugenheimer and Gorden E. White, *Basic Advertising* (Columbus, Ohio: Grid Publishing, 1980), pp. 140–141.

[10]Harry W. McMahan, "Selling on a Trimmer Budget," *Advertising Age* (June 2, 1980), p. 46.

[11]Book and Cary, p. 14.

[12]I. M. Hefzallah and W. P. Maloney, "Are There Only Six Kinds of TV Commercials?" *Journal of Advertising Research* (August 1979), pp. 57–62; Robert Hilliard, *Writing for TV and Radio*, 3rd ed. (New York: Hastings House, 1976).

[13]Nelson, pp. 228–232.

[14]Hooper White, "Ins and Outs of Commercial Casting—Is an Actor More Real Than a Real Person? *Advertising Age* (April 10, 1978), pp. 50–52.

[15]Lawrence Ingrassia, "As Mr. Whipple Shows, Ad Stars Can Bring Long-Term Sales Gains," *Wall Street Journal* (February 12, 1981), p. 27.

[16]Joseph M. Winski, p. 76.

[17]Nelson, p. 236.

[18]Hooper White, "How to Liven TV Spots: Animate," *Advertising Age* (March 9, 1981), p. 50.

[19]Dylan Landis, "Creative Input, Creative Output," *Advertising Age* (December 29, 1980), p. S–7.

[20]William D. Tyler, "Marriage of Print, TV: Today's Misunderstood Media Mix," *Advertising Age* (May 23, 1977), pp. 50, 54.

Advertising Research: The Message

As marketing outgrew its local status, it became more institutionalized. Marketing managers, divorced from line operations, lost personal contact with customers. The gap grew further as management layers were piled upon management layers within a corporation. Specialization brought into being marketing research departments, charged with the responsibility of supplying decision makers with relevant information.

This chapter turns the spotlight on the role of marketing research as a means of creating advertising messages and in the monitoring of results. The first area, concerned with the creation of advertising messages, covers four main fields:
- **Concept testing**
- **Motivation research**
- **Focus groups**
- **Attitudinal research**

The second aspect of marketing research usage, concerned with monitoring, takes up major copy testing methods. These include:
- **Market Behavioristic methods**
- **Physiological methods**
- **Affective measurements**
- **Cognitive measurements**

ROLE OF ADVERTISING RESEARCH

Advertising research is to advertising what marketing research is to marketing. Both research activities supply information to their respective fields. Since advertising is part of marketing, advertising research is part of marketing research.

The reason research is necessary for advertising is the same as for marketing. Roundabout production of our modern economy removes the producer several times from the consumer in channels of distribution. The expansion of the market, first nationally and then internationally, separates management further from the classes of customers it attempts to woo.

There is no personal contact between seller and buyer, at least for nationally distributed brands. There is no direct feedback of customer satisfaction, frustration, experience, or desires. There are no first hand observations of consumer buying behavior. Such knowledge can only come from indirect, impersonal sources. Advertising research acts as the eyes and ears of the advertising industry in keeping abreast of what goes on in the marketplace.

The research function plays a dual role, one in planning and the other in evaluation. Both are interwoven with each other, like a design embroidered in fine cloth. Market intelligence is used in planning. These plans are evaluated in the light of experience. In so doing, the analysis turns back on itself and becomes input for future planning. The research process thus moves in a cycle, as depicted in Figure 10–1.

The planning part of the cycle concerns itself with the creation of messages. Basic is the product position which, from an advertising standpoint, means reaching the right people with the most effective message. But what is right, and what makes a message effective?

THE DEED VS. THE THOUGHT

For advertising research, questions of rightness and effectiveness translate into information which pertains to the marketplace. Yet advertising is seldom called upon to provide intellectual support for either the marketing plan or the strategy included therein. But the advertising executive must be familiar with the marketing information upon which the strategy rests.

Both marketing and advertising are industries which deal with people. The single most important source of information about people is the Bureau of the Census. The agency conducts population censuses every ten years, primarily for purposes of apportioning Congressional seats in the lower house. But a census is much more than a simple head count. It includes a wealth of demographic and socio-economic data, such as sex, age, household composition, occupation, income, education, and so forth. These data can be broken down further by different geographical units such as census regions, states, metropolitan areas, counties, census tracts,

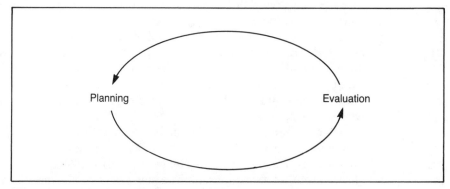

Fig. 10–1 *The Planning-Evaluation Cycle.*

and zip codes. The bureau periodically updates population statistics, though not in the same detail as the census counts, and does special studies of demographic and social trends. Companies can also acquire summary tapes from the government and do analyses on their own computers.

Marketing plans usually combine population statistics with sales data. Sources of purchase information differ radically from industry to industry. Packaged goods get sales figures from store audits, supplemented by warehouse retrievals. Automobile registration is gathered by R. L. Polk and stored in its data bank. Numerous trade associations and private companies supply market statistics. An important source used in advertising planning is the annual *Survey of Buying Power*, which provides estimates of population, income and retail sales for states, cities, metropolitan areas and counties.

Information can be generated in various ways, depending upon the objectives of the marketer. Cigarette, gasoline and liquor sales are estimated from government taxes. Other sales figures come from company reports accumulated by trade associations. *Information Sources*, a membership directory of the Information Industry Association (IIA), contained data on 159 companies supplying business information. Still other statistics come from sample surveys of businesses, retail outlets, or consumers directly. An IIA survey, for example, published results of a survey of more than a thousand U.S.-based companies in the field of information. Marketing services was the largest segment of the business.

The largest proportion of corporate expenditures for marketing research goes towards behavioristic measurements. These are derived by observation. The nation's top twenty-eight research companies in 1981 boasted total revenue of $974 million. The largest three, A. C. Nielsen, IMS International, and SAMI had $599 million in combined sales, or 60 percent of the twenty-eight firm total.[1] All three leaders offer syndicated research based on observational methods and large data banks. A. C. Nielsen concentrates on audits of grocery and drug outlets. IMS International, serving the pharmaceutical industry, does in its field what Nielsen carries out in packaged goods. It measures sales of ethical drugs in retail stores, hospitals, laboratories, and nursing homes. More than half the Nielsen and IMS gross revenues, however, come from foreign sources. SAMI, an acronym for Selling-Areas Marketing, Inc., produces warehouse movement statistics for thousands of individual brands. Its entire revenue of $72.6 million in 1981 was generated domestically.

Behavior which cannot be as readily observed as product flows must often be measured by consumer surveys. The studies ask individuals to report their conduct either to an interviewer or in a self-administered questionnaire. As compared with observational methods, surveys with individuals have larger errors owing to faulty reporting and nonresponse.

Though the magnitude of these nonsampling errors cannot be measured, they are thought to greatly exceed sampling errors.[2]

Management's interest in consumers focuses on behavior. The objective of marketing effort is to create sales which are profitable. Consequently, behavioristic aspects are monitored and fed back.

One school of thought holds that an understanding of behavior alone is all that is necessary to operate efficiently. In accordance with this thesis, an analysis of products and markets serves as the basis for brand strategy. The process is one of problem solving, using both deductive and inductive reasoning. Implied in this approach is the supposition that the best predictor of future action is past behavior.

Somewhat along the same line of thought is the view of Victor Wademan, president of his own advertising agency. Wademan argues that product positioning should be based on corporate economics, which he defines as a handful of factors that have a decisive effect on profit and long-term competitiveness.[3] This view may be commendable for situations where advertising has a low profit leverage. It makes for a more realistic perspective of advertising in the total corporate structure. But then, it really doesn't much matter what tasks are assigned to advertising because its function is basically unimportant in the strategy. When potential profits caused by changes in advertising are greater than profits coming from proportionate changes in other areas, the argument takes on a different complexion. Now it is necessary to know the relationship between changes in advertising components and changes in profits, which Wademan admits is "very imprecise" and may not be measurable at all.[4]

On the whole, the advertising industry is willing to settle for behavioristic criteria for determining market parameters. Sales and market share are basic in practically every market analysis. So are such objective measurements as population demographics and socio-economic variables. But, most practitioners maintain they are not the entire story.

Causal elements that induce behavior, this view holds, are to be found in human psychology, and not in demographics or social status or sales statistics. Sales are an effect, not a cause. Ries and Trout's excellent book on positioning has as its subtitle, "The Battle for Your Mind." Positioning, explain the authors, "is not what you do to a product. Positioning is what you do to the mind of the prospect."[5] This definition sums up the prevailing philosophy. It also implicitly assumes that whatever is done to the mind will result in the desired behavior. In short, advertising creates sales by first doing something to the mind.

But doing what? Here there is no agreement. And even those who do agree on some psychological trait do not agree on how to measure it. Consequently, advertising research has gone off in many directions at once. Wave after wave of advertising prophets rise up with a revealed truth about a psychological process which will make advertising research a true science, only to be dashed on the rocks of experience. Predictive values are extremely low. Results are often described as "inconclusive," a euphemism for no definitive or firm conclusion after money had been spent on the project. Yet the quest for explanations rolls on as inexorably as the ocean tides. Psychologically-oriented research which has had the greatest impact on advertising practices has concerned itself mainly with the creation of messages. Though not mutually exclusive, the most important research methods undertaken for the purpose of creating advertising messages can be summarized as follows: concept testing, motivation research, focus group interviews, and attitude measurements.

RESEARCH METHODS

Concept Testing

Concept tests apply mainly to new products, including product modifications and line extensions. Testing which occurs at the early phases of new product development, as in screening, attempts to select alternative ideas for research and development.[6] This kind of marketing research has little relevance to advertising.

Concept tests done at later stages of new product development have positioning as their aim. Specifically, their purposes are:

1. To indicate target audiences or marketing segments for ensuing test marketing.
2. To develop advertising appeals to differentiate the new brand from competitive ones.

Concept tests are carried out with prospective customers in a variety of ways. Concepts may be presented as short descriptions of several sentences or as advertisements. Either way, questionnaires can cover a broad range of possibilities, such as likes and dislikes, preferences, attitudes, and intentions to buy. Questions can be structured or unstructured, open- or closed-ended, or yes or no or multiple choice answers. The interviewing forms often resort to rankings or scaling techniques.

The limitations of concept testing are many. The form of the material has a significant effect on test results. There is an ambiguity as to whether people's answers reflect a response to the concept or to the creative quality of the material. Finished advertisements would usually end up with higher ratings than mock ups or semi-finished art.[7] Answers to intention-to-buy questions, which are part of most concept tests, can hardly be taken at face value.[8] What people say they will do in response to conjectural questions is not predictive of what they will do in real life situations.

Because concept testing lacks external validity—the ability to generalize results—the majority of such studies do not select respondents by probability sampling. Most firms have no intention of projecting results to a given universe. Under such conditions, the tests may yield nothing more than what researchers call hypotheses, or in plain English, hunches. On the optimistic side, the tests yield comparative measures of alternative positions. But there always remains the haunting possibility that even the winner is the best of an all-bad lot.

This is what might have happened to Reynolds Tobacco when, in June 1977, it went full speed ahead after concept testing to introduce Real, a cigarette composed of natural ingredients. The brand was supported with a $40 million budget for its first six months, and advertisements trumpeted Reynolds' strategy in bold headlines "Nothing artificial added." But sales were disappointing. Almost a year later the brand was repositioned, with headlines now reading, "Real's got strong taste. More like a high tar." The brand staggered for two more years, eking out less than half a percentage point share of market, and finally went off the market. On the other hand, there is always the possibility of poor implementation of correct strategy. In any case, the real reason for failure is conjectural.

Motivation Research

Motivation research was a major attempt to make advertising strategy seek its rationale in the underlying reasons why people buy the brands they do. Its leading exponent was Austrian-born Ernest Dichter, who brought the theories and practices of clinical psychology into marketing during the 1950s.

The philosophy rests on the premise that the real reason for action is to be found below the level of consciousness. While people express one thing, they feel another. While they profess to be emancipated, they hold value judgments formed many years ago. While they offer rational arguments for their actions, they are moved by deep-seated emotions that they are probably unaware of. To get at these inner feelings, motivation researchers offered depth interviews and projective techniques with which to probe the consumer psyche.

The depth interview comes from psychoanalysis, which encourages the patient to pour out his or her fears, hopes, and dreams on the doctor's couch. Marketing research dispensed with the couch, but tried to preserve the rambling discourses. The verbatim comments from these interviews were often typed up and given to copywriters in the hope that consumer outpourings would spark ideas for advertisements. The same probing techniques can be applied to groups. For example, Dr. Dichter conducts "therapy" sessions with small groups, perhaps a half dozen or so, of consumers.[9]

Projective techniques use more structured interviewing forms, but are designed to hide the real intent of the investigation. These include a battery of different approaches, such as word association, sentence completion, balloon filling, story telling, Rorschach tests. Common to all these methods is the assumption that when a person fills in some vague, incomplete part of a stimulus he is really projecting his inner self and revealing his true personality.

Can such clinical techniques, when applied to ships, shoes, and sealing wax, wring from the mind the secrets that lie buried deep in the id? Most unlikely.[10] Yet motivation research helped shift marketing emphasis to the intangible qualities of the mind, even though a scientific body of knowledge never materialized.

When motivation research was at its peak in the soaring 1950s, its major users were advertising agencies. It gave more credence to intuitive processes by clothing them with a mantle of science. Account executives were better able to sell an advertising program if they were able to tell clients that a basic idea or a particular execution was indicated by a study using the latest psychological techniques. Yet even in those days motivation research was looked upon with suspicion, if not downright skepticism. One reason was that its methods ran counter to the research tradition which stressed mathematical results and replication.

The influence of motivation research in the business community has ebbed considerably since the 1950s. The voice of Sigmund Freud and his disciples has become fainter, but not muted. Motivation research still holds a certain fascination for those having to deal with the collective mind of a populace. And many of its techniques, though shorn of their psychoanalytical trappings, have crept into other research activities, especially focus groups.

Focus Groups

Probably the most widely used technique of advertising agencies, the focus group, is in reality an extension of the depth interview. It is a "therapy" session going under another name, since motivation research has fallen out of favor. Its advantages over the old depth interview are speedy results, ease of application, and cost reduction.[11] The traditional depth interview required one interviewer for each respondent. The focus group necessitates one interviewer, called a moderator, for eight to twelve respondents, the average size of a session. All depth interviews are conducted at the same time and at the same place, reducing interview and travel time.[12]

Focus group interviews suppose that people engaged in similar activities or who have similar problems, are more willing to talk about them when put in the same room. Research practitioners therefore recommend that group session participants have similar social and demographic characteristics, especially age and sex.[13] Mixed groups of men and women, or adults and teenagers, have not been productive.

While there are variations in how sessions are conducted, almost everyone agrees that the role of the moderator is central. He or she must maintain control of the discussion, keeping it on a fixed course and preventing it from straying too far off track. Yet, the atmosphere must be easygoing and relaxed, so that people feel uninhibited and speak freely. Many of the methods for running these rap sessions were worked out years ago, as far back as the 1930s, when agencies held brainstorming meetings to arouse creative ideas regarding promotions, copy treatment, slogans, and names for new products. For example, adherence to what is known as "deferral of judgment," which discourages all negative comments, traces back to the brainstorming practices of a past decade.

The discussions are usually tape recorded for later analysis. Interested parties can observe sessions through a one-way mirror, and sometimes they even participate. Kelly, Nason, an advertising agency, conducts group sessions in people's homes, with copywriters and art directors attending and taking part in the proceedings.[14]

Focus groups are applied to a wide range of advertising and business problems.[15] These applications fall into three broad groups: search, evaluation, and idea generation.

1. *Search problems.* These deal with "why" questions, seeking reasons for certain aspects of human behavior. The issues are essentially the same as those of motivation research.
2. *Evaluation problems.* These issues pertain to assessment of alternatives, such as comparison of different possible strategies or advertising executions.
3. *Idea generation problems.* These refer to methods of generating ideas, either for advertising strategy, themes, or particular advertisements. The objectives here run parallel to those of brainstorming, except that the research is done with actual consumers rather than employees.

The first two categories of focus group usage are the most controversial. Critics regard them as both invalid and unreliable. Conclusions, they say, are highly subjective. Session recordings gush out words which can have as many interpretations as interpreters. Participants are mainly women who are articulate, outgoing, and blessed with free time. They can hardly be taken as representative of consumers. Nor can results be generalized beyond this untypical half dozen. To use a handful of women as a basis for decisions which may run into millions of dollars, detractors charge, is the height of folly.[16] Although focus group users may conduct several sessions, sample size remains small and samples do not improve their unrepresentative qualities.

Focus groups are more defensible when used as an idea-generating device. But even here there are problems. Harold Bay, Chairman of D'Arcy, MacManus & Masius, wrote: "We do a lot of focus group pretesting and if you take every comment literally, you're in trouble."[17] That may be the biggest understatement of the year. Acceptance or rejection of any comment can neither be defended nor condemned. There is no way to inspect comments and separate what is true from what is false, what is right from what is wrong. The decision, like that of any metaphysical proposition, is an act of faith.

The important thing in using focus groups to come up with ideas is not the market research but the people who make use of it. Tom Dillon, former head of BBDO, once related how in his early days of advertising he acquired knowledge about consumers. "I used to go to gas stations and ask people questions and then go back and write."[18] Focus group interviews are not much different from this unscientific process. But, instead of the copywriter spending his time interviewing customers, it is cheaper to get a handful of people to come to a central location and talk about a product. The copywriter may hear the conversation when the tape is played back.

If the focus group serves as a device to stimulate the imagination of the copywriter, well and good. If it sparks the fires of imagination, it doesn't matter whether the group is representative or not. But the copywriter must have freedom to either use or not use the information obtained from the session.

By the same token, a brand manager must exercise the same prerogatives in approving or rejecting ideas. The focus group is not a valid basis for strategy. The fact that a technique stimulates ideas does not say or intimate that the ideas are right. The focus group is helpful in creative implementation rather than formulation of strategy. If so, the session should be channeled in the direction of a predetermined strategy and researchers should not look to that narrow respondent pond for alternative positions.

Attitudinal Research

The advertising industry sustains a deep and abiding faith in attitudes as the way to sales. Some industry gurus claim predictive powers for attitudinal measures, though they have yet to demonstrate these assertions.[19] Hierarchy of effects theories, widely accepted as true despite their failure to become operational, see attitude change as a precursor of behaviorial strengths, such as the degree of loyalty or probability of repeat purchase attached to a brand. The act of carving out a position in the consumer mind, the very core of advertising strategy, carries no meaning without reference to the images registered in the brain.

Few would argue about the key role of attitudes in consumer decisions. But heated arguments spring up as to how attitudes are formed, how they work, and how they can be measured, if they can be measured at all. The reason is because attitudes, though a force in the marketplace, can neither be seen nor felt. They represent a state of mind, and elude precise definition.

TABLE 10–1 *Example of a Multiattribute Model*

(Column 1) Attribute	*(Column 2)* Importance Weight	*(Column 3)* Delivery Brand A	*(Column 4)* Evaluation Ratings Brand B
1	6	4	6
2	3	5	5
3	2	6	4
Overall Attitude Rating		51	59

One theory which has gained wide currency is that of an "evoked set" of products, often referred to as the "consideration frame."[20] The theory holds that confronted with a purchase situation, a person will narrow his or her alternatives down to several items. These favored brands comprise the set from which the final choice is made. Comparative advertising is essentially an attempt to push a brand into a buyer's "consideration frame." The advertising for the North Star personal computer, which touts its advantages over IBM and Apple, the giants of the industry, well exemplifies this technique. (See Figure 10–2.)

Social psychologist Martin Fishbein extended this notion into a more elaborate theory. In Fishbein's view, the evoked set of any individual is determined by the importance attached to certain attributes, such as benefits sought. The person then goes about evaluating how well particular brands in the set deliver the desired attributes. A person's predisposition, according to Fishbein, can then be expressed mathematically as a weighted sum of attribute values by the following formula:

$$A_j = \sum_{i=1}^{n} V_i B_{ij}$$

where

j = Product
i = Product attributes or characteristics
A_j = Overall attitude toward the jth product
V_i = Value or importance attached to the ith attribute
B_{ij} = Belief as to whether the jth product delivers the ith attribute.

The above formula represents what is called a linear compensatory model. The concept is simple and easily understood. The hypothetical example in Table 10–1 illustrates how it works.

Suppose a person thinks that three attributes are important, and weights them as 6,3,2 respectively. Suppose further the individual considers two brands, A and B, and evaluates their delivery potential as shown in columns 3 and 4 in Table 10–1. Which brand is he or she prone

North Star's Advantage over IBM and Apple is easy to see.

The North Star ADVANTAGE desktop computer has higher precision graphics, better software, and greater disk capacity than the IBM Personal Computer or the Apple III. Plus, nationwide on-site service and free business graphics software. See it for yourself. Then check the price. You'll see how easy it is to own the North Star ADVANTAGE.

FOLLOW THE STAR
NorthStar™
14440 Catalina Street, San Leandro, California 94577

(dealer name/address here)

North Star's Advantage over IBM and Apple is easy to see.

The North Star ADVANTAGE desktop computer has higher precision graphics, better software, and greater disk capacity than the IBM Personal Computer or the Apple III. Plus, nationwide on-site service and free business graphics software. See it for yourself. Then check the price. You'll see how easy it is to own the North Star ADVANTAGE.

FOLLOW THE STAR
NorthStar™
14440 Catalina Street, San Leandro, California 94577

(dealer name/address here)

FOLLOW THE STAR
NorthStar™
North Star Computers, Inc. 14440 Catalina Street
San Leandro, CA 94577, USA

2935

Fig. 10–2 *North Star. Applying the Theory of an Evoked Set by Comparative Advertising. With permission from North Star.*

to choose? The overall attitude value for Brand A is calculated as: $(6 \times 4) + (3 \times 5) + (2 \times 6) = 51$. The comparable sum for Brand B is: $(6 \times 6) + (3 \times 5) + (2 \times 4) = 59$.

This concept, which surveys can implement with relative ease, has enjoyed wide popularity. Attitude research usually contains questions about product attributes in the form of rating scales. Though tabulating procedures may not follow Fishbein's formula exactly, the underlying rationale is present. Whatever the version, these surveys make implicit assumptions that product attributes are the main reason for a purchase, consumers can rate them, and the aggregate ratings are meaningful.

The Fishbein model raises many issues in advertising strategy. A position can be achieved in one of three ways: changing people's opinion about what is important; changing people's perceptions about benefits a product delivers; or changing people's ideas about both attribute importance and benefits delivered. Which way to go is indeed a difficult question and not answerable by a survey.

The model suggests that a position in the mind is an ever-shifting thing. It can become undesirable even while consumer perceptions of a brand remain basically unaltered. This can come about if consumers change their opinions about what is important, as in articles of style and fashion. But this can happen with almost any product. Foods once thought healthy suddenly are shunned because of their cholesterol content, their sweeteners, or country in which they were produced. Once luxury features on automobiles were avidly sought; now the cry is for economy. These considerations give rise to a host of questions.

What is an effective approach to strategy when there is a threat that consumers may change the importance criterion of a product set? If a brand has an attribute advantage which might decline in importance, should it still exploit that advantage? Or should the opportunity be traded for another position which has greater stability? Such questions, too, have no firm answers.

While the Fishbein model exudes an intuitive appeal, it has encountered criticisms from many quarters. It has been accused of using variable scales for measuring attitudes.[21] This is like using rulers which mark off inches in different lengths. For the model to work properly, attribute evaluation must be consistent with overall attitude scores. But tests of this kind have turned up weak correlations between the two, indicating a fractured model.[22]

Since the model places no limits upon the number of beliefs or values which make up an attitude, the equation can contain an immense number of terms. More important, these psychological variables must come from people, and it is highly dubious whether they can catalog with mathematical precision every belief and value stored in their minds.

Some critics have taken Fishbein to task for assuming that consumers add attribute values, as implied in the model's equation.[23] But there are more serious shortcomings, not only with Fishbein's, but with other multiattitude measurements. Whether they are predilections, preferences, degrees of liking, or attitudes, they are measured by scaling devices. People responding to surveys are asked to rank or rate different things, presuming they are able to assign numerical quantities to their emotions. The component values are often handled as cardinal numbers, manipulated mathematically, and combined into a single figure which purportedly measures an attitude. Although proponents of these methods insist ordinal scale values represent a conservative approach, many have questioned the meaningfulness of such a number.

This leads to the last, all-important question of validity. How can one tell whether any figure represents what it is supposed to measure? Of all possible approaches, attitude researchers fall back on "face validity" evidence. The method they use is assumed to be so self-evident that no reasonable person would choose to quarrel with it.[24] In short, if a researcher were asked how one knows whether his or her study accurately reflects an attitude, he or she would whip out a questionnaire and assert that a particular question measures a particular attitude. Not only are such self-evident truths unconvincing, but there is little agreement among researchers as to what questions should be used.

At the American Marketing Association's 1979 Conference of Attitude Research, Rudolph W. Struse III recounted a strange experience that happened at Oscar Mayer. It seems the company acquired two attitude research studies covering the same product category with "precisely the same objectives" made by two research houses. But the results were "markedly disparate." Struse called the experience "disturbing."[25] But it was not surprising. Different questions, regardless of objectives, yield different results. Sometimes even identical interviews conducted by different research houses produce contrary conclusions. This anomaly is referred to as "organizational bias."

In recent years, a technique known as perceptual mapping has emerged to deal with scaling data. It falls into a class of statistical methods known as multidimensional scaling (MDS). MDS is a computer-based method which transforms attitudinal data into a set of points in multidimensional space. Figure 10–3 depicts on a two-dimensional map how consumers perceive different models of pickup trucks.

According to the authors who generated the map in Figure 10–3, individuals utilize two dimensions with which to evaluate pickup trucks, durability and stylishness. The data were developed from preference rankings and judgments about which models were most similar. The distances between them denote psychological proximity. The closer the distances,

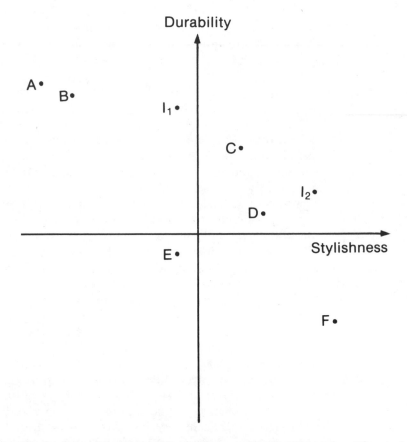

Fig. 10—3 *Space Map from a Sachs/Benson title. Multidimensional Space for Pickup Trucks. Sachs and Benson,* Product Planning and Management *(Tulsa, OK.: PennWell Books, 1981), pp. 198–199.*

the greater the degree of competition between brands, it is assumed. The ideal points, labeled *I*, are derived from preference rankings. They presumably indicate combinations of attributes which are highly valued by groups of consumers. When ideal and perception points are plotted on the same map, it is referred to as a joint space configuration.

If ideal points are viewed as market segments—groups of consumers with similar tastes and preferences—gap analysis can be used to establish positions. This approach calls for seeking out areas near ideal points which contain no existing brands. A strategy made to fit this void, it is reasoned, will appeal strongly to the segment located in close psychological proximity. However, the limitations of information gathering for multiattitude models also apply to multidimensional scaling.

RESEARCH AND ADVERTISING STRATEGY

The role of research in the formulation of advertising strategy is an ambiguous one. In part, the equivocacy arises because marketing research is multifaceted. Most studies are descriptive, such as census data, sales information, and many surveys of attitudes and preferences towards products. When strategies are based on descriptive information, they involve not merely inference but an awareness of what is possible and feasible. The decision makers, usually one or more individuals in the marketing department or in product management, translate the descriptive statistics into opportunities and courses of action. In this situation, marketing research takes on more or less a neutral, data collecting function.

For example, Roy Nelson adapts this interpretation in explaining how to go about writing an advertisement. His first step is to overindulge oneself with facts. Only after analyzing all the data, says Nelson, does a copywriter "decide which of several advantages a product offers should get the principal play in the ad."[26]

Nelson's strategy, subscribed to by most copywriters and agency management, is the time-honored method of how creative people used to work, perhaps more than a decade ago. They still do work in this manner on small accounts and with clients that lack advertising know-how. In this view, advertising strategy emerges when research data are properly sifted and combined with judgment. But to large, sophisticated marketers this procedure raises a rather sticky question. Whose judgment is considered?

Nelson apparently sees no conflict between the copywriter's choice of what to emphasize and the marketer's choice of brand strategy. The copywriter's opinions are precisely what many big advertisers want to avoid— having copywriters select the selling proposition. They almost uniformly regard that choice as an infringement on their responsibility to determine a brand's position, which means determining the points of difference to be highlighted in promotion. Marketing managers thus have a narrow view of creativity as being a device for implementing decisions about what points to emphasize. That copywriters often find themselves in the midst of strategy discussions stems from the difficulty, if not impossibility, of separating advertising strategy from tactics.

Though descriptive data form the bulk of marketing studies, leading researchers stress problem solving as the core of their discipline. Viewed from this perspective, research ceases to be a neutral, fact gathering endeavor. Accepting the tenets of decision theory, research presumes it has the capacity to choose the best strategy, the best theme, and even the best manner of presenting it. For example, concept tests are designed to evaluate ideas as a basis for strategy. The one with the highest numerical value is obviously the logical candidate. Attitude research, often using forms of experimental design, aims at determining the strongest appeal, the most important buying motives, or the most salient variables in consumer behavior. Perceptual mapping is undertaken to discover a brand's position options and their palpable efficiencies.

In these problem-solving projects, the decision is explicit in research results. Because decision oriented research provides marketing managers with more systematic ways of making choices, it has enjoyed increasing usage. Its outcomes though, have been mixed and controversial.

The problem-solving approach to research has undoubtedly reduced intuitive decisions. Conclusions drawn from concept tests, attitude studies and perception maps frequently worm their way into positioning statements, even as "mandatories" to specifically be put in the copy.[27] The net effect has been a constriction of the copywriter's influence on advertising strategy.

Many advertising people, especially creatives, are wary of research recommendations which guide strategy. The annual conference of the American Association of Advertising Agencies in 1980 saw a panel blaming uninspired advertising on research. Norman Berry, creative director of Ogilvy & Mather, highlighted the basic theme, "We can't duck behind research that's gone wrong."[28] The annual meeting of the Association of National Advertisers that year was told to "beware of the process barriers such as rigid application of research."[29]

The objections to research as a mediator of advertising strategy, in the main, rest on two counts: prediction and explanation. These two items are crucial to the assessment of any theory or practice in the social sciences.

Market researchers have had considerable success at predictions which have a bearing on strategy. Forecasts of sales, product usage rates, and population trends have been extremely useful in defining markets and segments thereof. But when research departs from the objective, behavioristic measurements, predictions encounter trouble.

There is no secret as to why this happens, even putting aside the vital issue of measuring by surveys such things as attitudes, predilections and other states of mind. The goodness of any prediction depends upon the variability of the data. The less variable, the better the forecast. Behavioristic measurements are direct. For example, Nielsen estimates of sales come from measurements of sales. But surveys of psychological characteristics are several times removed from what marketers really want to predict—sales. Opinion surveys were even unable to forecast accurately how people would vote for president in an election that ended in a victory of landslide proportions.[30]

As a consequence, marketing research has performed unevenly in strategy decisions. It has been instrumental in defining target markets. It has been hopelessly inept at predicting results of particular advertising messages. It has been unable to say with any assurance what to advertise or how to do it.

Marketing research as a tool to explain consumer behavior has also been an issue of pros and cons. There are many social science theories which, unable to accurately predict, are nonetheless valued. Econometric models, for example, have had a poor record of forecasting economic performance. Yet they are highly valued because they provide explanations of economic behavior. In like manner, marketing theory and research studies are a source for insights on how advertising works. But managers must exercise prudence in their choice of research, for data may be useless or misleading in particular circumstances.

ENTREPRENEURSHIP AND STRATEGY

Advertising agency leaders have raised somewhat unique objections to the use of research in setting advertising strategy. Actually, their objections are variations of the prediction-explanation themes, but they bear a strong relation to the broader question of entrepreneurship.

With respect to prediction, William Bernbach argued that research provides only a picture of what is or what was. No matter how helpful it is in providing insights to the marketplace, research lies in the past and cannot by itself be used to influence the future. Success here, holds Bernbach, "depends on something new and fresh and exciting which has never been seen before."[31]

The second argument is that research focuses on incorrect variables, and hence, recommends incorrect strategies. Marketing surveys, mainly from pragmatic considerations, tend to emphasize product attributes. It is easier to draw up a list of product features and ask questions about them than to measure ill-defined psychological processes. But agency people, especially those from the creative departments, claim the things that sell are feelings, images, reputation, or just plain force of habit. Allen G. Rosenshine, BBDO's president, once told an industry gathering that the loss of emotion in advertising signified "a victory of research over judgment" in the creative process.

A commonly-held agency view is that reluctance to embrace creativity, meaning strategy decisions of copywriters, is in effect an attempt to avoid risk.[32] Insofar as an innovative program connotes something new and unknown, it is accompanied by risk.

But the question is not whether to take a risk or not, it is the degree of risk to be taken. What many agencies fail to recognize is that risk must be weighed on a success-and-failure scale. Nor do the consequences of the two different outcomes have the same importance. A marketing success to a large company shows up as an increment in sales and profits, depending upon size of the company and volume of the sales gain. But a failure may signal the demise of an important business sector. In such circumstances, the consequences of an action are not distributed equally about the mean of all possible outcomes, and a risky strategy appears not only rash but foolhardy.

Agencies also fail to appreciate the demands that are necessary to keep large organizations operating smoothly. To use intuition in setting brand strategy is anathema. Without any evidence that decisions would be better, the practice would encourage brand managers to fly off in all directions. It would violate the very essence of control, which lies in the fidelity of a system and not in actions of gifted individuals. Research may indeed yield uncreative, and even less effective strategies. But all groups in the company do things the same way are impelled by the same rationale, and move with a unity of purpose.

Brand managers come and go. Waves of trainees settle into new jobs. Still, operations continue as before, despite human frailties and inconsistencies. If the fires of creativity are dampened in the process, a firm has many ways of compensating for the loss, such as increasing the number of messages, doing more sales promotion, enhancing product quality, etc. The alternatives for manipulating the marketing mix are numerous and may well prove a small price to pay for organizational effectiveness.

Minnetonka, Inc. in April 1980 introduced a new liquid soap which in less than a year captured seven percent of a $1 billion U.S. soap market. Wallace A. Marx, vice president of the firm's Softsoap Division, credited intuition, often defined as judgment, rather than formal research for the success. "Our success," Marx told an American Marketing Association conference, "wasn't the result of . . . formal research. It was the result of old methods and marketing fundamentals."[33]

On August 11, 1981, Procter & Gamble disclosed plans to enter the liquid soap market.[34] Without doubt, this marketing giant will display a different management style. It will predictably go through the entire gamut of research and testing. It will first study all aspects of market-product features, distribution, purchasing data, sales, consumer profiles, marketing segments, prices, etc. If the company should then decide to go ahead, the agreed strategy will be the same irrespective of who receives appointment as brand manager.

More importantly, every relevant part of the company will move with a monolithic purpose, as though controlled by some master brain. The sales department will cover retail outlets like a blanket. Research and development will design a product of relatively high quality. Marketing effort will be supported with ample funds for merchandising, sales promotion and advertising. The critical instruments of the product introduction will depend not upon a superior strategy but upon a superior organization and superior resources. And success, if it should come, will not be because the research guessed right but because marketing was done right.

In a way, the difference between Minnetonka and Procter and Gamble symbolizes two diverse managerial approaches. The first reflects that of "creatives" who draw inspiration from conventional entrepreneurial values in which the individual is paramount. The second approach is more in keeping with the bureaucratic values of the modern, giant corporation. Advertising agencies, basically small firms, still think in the business terms of a bygone era.

COPY TESTS

The term copy test refers to research dealing with individual messages. Usually these tests relate to execution; strategy should have been taken care of before work began on actual advertisements.

The main reason for copy tests is to reduce risks. The greater the advertising effort, the stronger the reason for copy testing. An advertising campaign can run into millions of dollars. It is only natural that before embarking on a expensive program a company should look for some assurance that their messages will be adequate. In general, companies with large advertising budgets are more prone to dictate evaluative policies. It is estimated that corporations spend more than $25 million annually on copy tests.[35]

The research on advertisements can be carried out as either pretests or posttests. The latter is the most common type, presumably because it tests the message exactly as it appears to the consuming public. Pretests often involve semi-finished or rough versions, and leave nagging questions about how people would have reacted had they been tested on the real thing. Some pretests use practically finished advertisements but save money by not testing in actual media. These forms again raise questions about what might have been were the research conducted with actual audiences.

But a posttest, one might object, means that production money must be spent. To test under normal circumstances necessitates placing the advertisement in media, and piles up more expenses. Isn't this like locking up the barn after all the animals have taken off? Yes. But production costs and a one-time showing may be a small fraction of total campaign costs. Under such conditions, the posttest is a small price to pay for insurance. If the message does not meet standards, it can be held back and replaced by another version of the agreed strategy.

Whether in print or broadcast, there are four basic methods for testing copy: market behavior, affective, cognitive, physiological. Each of these methods have numerous variations, and can be combined with one another. The four categories, together with their main variations, are outlined in Table 10–2.

The choice of method boils down to a trade-off between relevancy and errors of estimation. As one moves from left to right in Table 10–2, the farther one goes from sales. This presumes acceptance of a hierarchy-of-effects theory, the sequence of which runs from awareness, to attitude, to action. Each step away from sales make the copy test less meaningful. But the measurement becomes increasingly more accurate. An attitude, for

TABLE 10–2 *Major Copy Testing Methods*

Market Behavior Methods	*Affective Methods*	*Cognitive Methods*	*Physiological Methods*
Sales	Persuasion	Comprehension	Eye movement
Inquiries	Liking	Recognition	Eye pupil change
Coupon response	Believability	Recall	Galvanometer
Store visits			Pulse rate
			Brain waves

example, cannot be confirmed or refuted objectively. Eye movement can be measured by instrumentation; however, its relationship to advertising effectiveness is obscure. The exact points for acceptance of relevancy and survey validity are matters of judgement, and one of the reasons why firms differ in their choice of copy testing methods.

Market Behavior

When the objective of the advertisement is direct action, such as mail order or coupon response, then research will employ overt market behavior as a means of testing. The split-run, offered by many publications, lends itself to assessments of alternative executions. This method permits different advertisements to be printed in the same location of the same issue of a publication circulating in a given area. An estimation of response can be met by testing the insertion in only a portion of a publication's circulation. Broadcast media can be tested in a similar fashion. Split cable television provides a useful device for evaluating success of a commercial. It allows advertisers to run offers in one or more test markets so that data can be obtained for making projections to larger areas.

Most advertisers would prefer to test their copy in terms of sales. It is widely conceded, though, that purchases resulting from general advertising cannot be accurately measured.

Physiological Methods

These techniques are placed in Table 10–2 on the extreme right of sales, indicating an indirect relationship. Physiological measurements require equipment and technical skill, and go by the name of laboratory techniques. They have evoked a great deal of interest within the advertising industry, but are not used very much. The greatest drawback in their use is that advertisers fear that what happens to people in a laboratory does not necessarily apply to everyday living.

Affective and Cognitive Methods

General advertising, which contemplates neither immediate nor directly traceable action to its messages, embraces psychological measurements.

These are affective and cognitive measurements. The most popular of these measurements are recognition and aided recall. Both techniques furnish respondents with clues to help them remember past experiences. In this sense, they are both memory tests. But the degree of assistance given in the form of a clue is what distinguishes one method from another. Recognition shows the entire advertisement and asks people if they remember it and its various elements. Aided recall gives people less obvious clues, usually a brand or company name, to see if they can associate the clues with the actual advertisement.

Recognition The recognition method for testing copy, used primarily for print advertisements, has become virtually synonymous with the name of Daniel Starch. While on the faculty of Harvard University, Starch experimented with recognition to study how people read advertisements. He wrote about his findings in *Principles of Advertising*, published in 1923. It was not until 1932 that Starch left the quiet, ivy-covered halls at Cambridge to syndicate copy tests, the first of its kind to be done. The scholarly entrepreneur began by measuring recognition of advertisements in thirteen magazines. The service, which expanded by leaps and bounds, is now called Daniel Starch & Staff, and is part of Starch Inra Hooper. It prepares reports on more than 75,000 advertisements a year, covering more than a thousand different issues in at least 140 different publications. Over the years, the Starch Readership Report acquired competitors, especially in the business publication field.

Regardless of the research company, recognition studies follow very similar procedures. Surveys are based on judgment samples, which range in size from one hundred to two hundred readers per issue. Those who say they had read the magazine are taken through the issue, page by page, and asked which advertisements they recognize. Affirmative answers then elicit more queries about component parts of the advertisement, such as illustrations, headlines, signature and copy blocks.

The key statistic in the Starch report is the "noted" score. A reader is given credit for "noting" an advertisement if he said he remembered having seen it in the issue studied. Starch adds these "notings" and reports the aggregate as a percentage of readers interviewed.

Recognition ratings have been criticized for accepting people's claims as absolute truths. Erroneous reporting exists, and there is substantial evidence to support this fact. Reports can be incorrect in that ads that were seen are not claimed as having been "noted" and vice versa. There can be both inflation and deflation in ad reading figures. Such errors have raised doubts about the use of recognition as an accurate memory test. Skeptics say these statistics reflect a concoction of many things in addition to memorability—participant interest during the interview, guesses, respondent biases, and interviewer deficiencies.[36]

When print was the major national media, advertisements lived and died according to their noted scores. Today, variations bring less consternation and lower-than-average test scores are tolerated to a greater degree. But a large downward swing from an ad norm points a sure finger to a problem, regardless of the debates over precision or validity.

Aided Recall Aided recall methods were first used in advertising by two men, George Gallup and Claude Robinson, who in 1947 incorporated as Gallup & Robinson (G&R). The new firm first did pretesting through the use of a "dummy" publication (a magazine with no circulation), and two years later expanded its service to actual issues in several magazines.

Today, Magazine Impact Research Service, the descendant of G&R, studies advertisements in about eleven magazines with 150 readers of each sex. It uses judgment samples drawn from about ten Standard Metropolitan Statistical Areas.

The interview begins by giving respondents a brand name and product as a clue. The resulting claims of having read an advertisement are not taken as gospel truth. Rather, for each claim, people are asked a series of open-ended questions such as:[37]

1. What did the ad look like? Describe the ad as you remember it.
2. What did the ad say?
3. In your own words, what did you learn about the product/service?
4. What went through your mind when you looked at this ad?
5. The advertiser tried to increase your interest in buying the product/service. Did he increase your interest or not?

G&R grades answers to these questions by comparing them with the content of the advertisement. The firm calls its basic score Proved Name Registration (PNR), defined as the percent of readers who recall something in the ad, adjusted for space cost. It also reports verbatim comments and "idea registration profiles," which copywriters use to see if their intended points were those actually communicated.

The researcher places test issues in readers' homes, and interviews by telephone the next day. This magazine placement procedure, instituted in the mid 1960s, departed from the earlier method of interviewing actual readers. This change permitted tip-ins, inserts in magazine test copies, so that advertisements could be studied before being placed in media.

The most important application of aided recall, however, made its appearance in television. Since all viewing must be done at the same time, it is a relatively easy matter to control the interval between exposure and interview, a key variable in any memory test. Since research can be carried out under normal viewing conditions, more meaningfulness is given to the test results.

G&R's Total Prime Time Service, one of several offered by the researcher, conducts telephone interviews in the Philadelphia SMSA on twenty different days throughout the television season. The company draws random samples from telephone directories and interviews partic-

TABLE 10–3 *Illustration of G&R Content Analysis*

Commercial	DUNCAN HINES CAKE MIXES
Date	Wednesday, May 3, 1978
Position	Program commercial within Star Trek
Time/Length	7:03 P.M./30 seconds

	Idea Registration (Base: PCR), Women			
		#		%
Base		66		100
One or more copy points		66		100
Taste/appetite appeal		57		86
Tastes good	57		86	
Even without frosting	53		80	
Looked good/made me hungry	8		12	
Moist		55		83
Quality/better/best		30		45
Refer to type		9		14
Deluxe II	9		14	
Refer to flavor		9		14
Chocolate	9		14	
Enjoyable/pleasurable		7		11
Favorable buying attitude				
(Among nonusers)		14/28		50
Average copy points per respondent				2.9

30" Food Qualitative Norms	*Women*
One or more copy points	>90%
Lead idea	68
Favorable buying attitude	39
Average copy points/respondent	2.3

Source: Gallup and Robinson, *Television Impact Report.*

ipants on the previous day's commercials. An average rated show normally yields about 150 men or women per commercial, depending upon the objectives of the advertiser. The television interview uses practically the same questions as for print and follows similar procedures in coding and tabulating responses. Proved Commercial Registration, a statistic similar to PNR, expresses the overall score as a percentage of program viewers for half-hour segments. Reports to clients also include a content analysis, as illustrated in Table 10–3.

The firm that has become most closely associated with day-after recall, however, is Burke Marketing Research, a Cincinnati-based firm which got its big start testing commercials for its neighbor, Procter and Gamble. Burke carries out custom-tailored surveys in cities throughout the country. Its sample consists of about 200 program viewers screened out by telephone calls, which in turn produces a commercial audience of about 150. This figure represents viewers who were in the room when the test commercial went on the air, determined by a tedious sequence of questions. The commercial audience becomes the base for what Burke calls related recall, the percentage of people who played back some element in the commercial. Like G&R, Burke produces verbatim comments from which clients can do content analysis.

The commercial audience concept supposedly eliminates variations in scores owing to fluctuations in viewing. This, its proponents claim, puts all commercials on an equal footing, so that they can be evaluated on their own merits.

Actually, the commercial audience accomplishes little or nothing. First, derivation of the sample base is not error free. People usually watch several programs during an evening. Can they really tell, a day later, exactly when they left the room to go to the bathroom, get a cup of coffee, make themselves a snack, or do some other act? The errors in such reporting are of an indeterminate magnitude. Second, the associated variance between related recall scores geared to commercial audience and those readjusted to program audience is quite high. This suggests that scores based on program audiences would be about 20 percent lower, but produce the same relative rankings as related recall figures based on a commercial audience. But a program audience base would lower survey costs by discarding the unnecessary intellectual baggage.

Despite its widespread popularity, or perhaps because of it, aided recall has hatched endless controversies. One such debate rages over program effects. A study of on-air recall conducted by J. Walter Thompson indicates that program environment affects overall message scores. In a report on the survey, Sonia Yuspeh, research director of J. Walter Thompson, cited the example of a commercial which garnered a 41 percent recall score on one show but a 53 percent rating on another.[38] If recall measures the media effects as well as those of the message, critics maintain, then it ceases to be a test of copy.

Although Burke vehemently denies this flaw in what for many years has been the industry's standard, the weight of evidence leans heavily toward the media-message comingling thesis. Recall measurements in both print and television are highly sensitive to such factors as age, education, income, and occupation.[39] Younger, better-educated people from a higher income grouping tend to perform better on recall tests, perhaps because they have superior faculties and/or larger vocabularies in which to articulate their thoughts. Insofar as different program audiences seldom have an identical demographic mix, recall scores will be as much shaped by the medium as by the message.

Interviewing variations, such as time of telephone call and interviewer ability, also lead to variations in recall results. These factors may be responsible, though no one can ever be sure, for inter-city differences. Harry Wayne McMahan, a harsh judge of copy tests, once cited a Burke five-city test that gave the same commercial a score of 32 in San Diego and a zero in Dallas. The zero, having a relative weight of about one-fifth, brought the overall average two points below the passing grade and Purina killed the commercial.[40] The McMahan example may be an extreme locality difference, but it is not an isolated one. If so, the choice of cities and changes in circumstances account for variations in recall scores.

Persuasion Another approach to testing copy leaps from cognitive measures to affective or conative ones. The logic rests on the premise that an advertisement must do more than simply be remembered. It must, according to this school, motivate consumers, influence their purchase dispositions or attitudes towards the brand. Since these mental states are closer to the actual purchase than cognition, assuming a hierarchy of effects, attitude change or persuasion becomes a more desirable evaluative method than attention or recall of selling points.

In the foreground of the attitude-persuasion school is the firm McCollum/Spielman. The firm uses recall, too, but the emphasis is mainly on its persuasion score in judging a commercial.

McCollum/Spielman's standard test takes place in a theater with a sample of 300 or more adults. Participants are divided into groups of about twenty-five with a TV monitor for the closed-circuit system. At the conclusion of a half-hour program, the audience is asked about its reaction to the program. That is actually a decoy. The main business on hand begins right after.

First, recall is solicited about products advertised; their brand names, and information conveyed about them on the commercials. Next, the audience is treated to a second program in which four test commercials appear separated by program material. People's brand preferences obtained before the show began are compared with their selections for a "market basket award" (door prizes) at the end of the program. The gain or loss in preference is considered a measure of the persuasive power of the advertisement. This method is used for packaged goods. McCollum/Spielman employs a variety of other techniques to ascertain attitude shift for non-packaged goods.

Another firm noted for its theater-based research is ASI Market Research, Inc., which tests feature films and television programs as well as commercials. The firm uses a program analyzer, called an "instant response profile" device, and conducts focus group interviews with attendees after the showing. It uses the ruse of door prizes to compare peoples choices before and after viewing commercials.

The theater technique provides diagnositc data and savings in media expenditures. But the reluctance of many advertisers to adopt a persuasion score stems from the artificially-created conditions of viewing. Research must go this "laboratory" route because measuring an attitude change from a single commercial in a realistic setting is almost impossible. Even if one were to devise a stratagem for getting consumers' preferences before and after seeing a commercial, the change would probably be so small as to be meaningless. By the same token, there is no guarantee that brand choices which are altered in a theater would change similarly in the real world.

THE COPY TESTING CONTROVERSY

As is with strategy setting research, there has been much disenchantment with copy testing. Creative complaints center on relevancy, no matter whether they are measurements of recall, attitudes, brain waves, or whatever. Measurements, critics say, have never demonstrated any relationship between their numbers and eventual sales. Critics have pointed out a number of occasions wherein commercials which tested poorly seemingly increased sales when put on the air. The Pepsi "spirit" commercials in the early 1980s, judged by the advertiser as highly successful, would not have run had copy tests prevailed.[41]

The issue of accuracy in testing has not been neglected. Feeling or mood commercials, a Foote, Cone & Belding study indicated, fare rather poorly on recall tests, not because they do not register in people's consciousness but because they cannot be verbalized easily.[42]

In turn, copywriters and art directors are led to adjust their outputs to satisfy the measurements by which they are judged. They quickly learn the tricks and gimmicks of getting a high score on a particular testing technique. Outrageous but to the point is the prescription of David J. Scott, creative director of Ogilvy & Mather, for getting a high recall score. "I just put a gorilla in a jock strap when I want a good Burke."[43] To achieve good ratings on standardized tests, firms make use of common techniques, though not necessarily by displaying a gorilla. This practice, critics say, makes advertising lean toward a certain sameness.

The many deficiencies of copy testing, and the strong objections to it, put management in a quandary. If creative output is stifled rather than improved, research denies management the benefits it seeks. Large advertisers do their own market planning, marketing research, budgeting for advertising and promotion, and media buying. They usually possess the expertise to perform all advertising functions save one—that of creating the advertising messages. To avail themselves of that capability, the core of the advertising process, they are willing to loosen control over their operations and entrust the job to an outside organization. Then why should they destroy that which costs them dearly?

Assuming the evaluative method chosen is one a firm deems best, the only other option is to have none. Under these circumstances, all alternatives appear equally dismal. Since brand managers are essentially marketing personnel, not advertising experts, they are unskilled in judging copy quality. To rely solely on the agency is to accept a judgment rendered by an interested party. As so aptly put by John P. Andrews of General Foods, a firm that has established a minimum recall score for commercials, "few advertisers can afford to invest millions of media dollars and risk important consumer franchises on copy which has only the author's stamp of approval to attest to its effectiveness."[44]

Meanwhile, the stubborn intangibles and troublesome uncertainties keep coming neatly packaged in a statistical report. And the debates rage on.

CONFLICT RESOLUTION

Actually, the research goals of advertisers and agencies are the same. Both strive to make advertising more effective. But the means of going about it are different.

Creativity is the heart and soul of the advertising agency, its only differentiating characteristic. It is thus natural that agencies should stress the creative element above all else, surround it with a mystique, and oppose procedures which compromise its most important function.

Advertisers, too, desire creativity, but not when it threatens to alter marketing strategies or upset internal control. The product management system diffuses advertising decision making among lower level managers with little advertising expertise. Copy testing thus serves an administrative function as a liaison between brand managers and agency personnel.

In virtually every situation a creative-research conflict is resolved on the basis of legitimacy. The client's right to approve all plans pertaining to the creation, production, and placement of messages is standard in advertiser-agency contracts. But operating decisions are often modified by persuasive arguments which invoke the power of expertise.

One alternative of the expert is the research solution, which is a problem in itself. Different copy testing methods yield different results, which imply different decisions. In fact, recall and attitude change have most frequently come up with negative or inverse relationships.[45] A rather optimistic view is that of Leckenby and Wedding, who argue that a lack of correlation shows that copy tests measure two different things. Their solution is then to do testing on more than one dimension.[46] This implicitly assumes that all methods are valid. But it is difficult to rationalize why an ad which is highly memorable should affect attitudes negatively, and vice versa.

If one method or set of techniques can demonstrate an indisputable superiority over all others, an unqualified acceptance becomes likely. For example, the 1981 Advertising Research Foundation Conference on copy testing validation was an attempt in this direction. Another was the agreement of twenty-one leading agencies in January 1982 on copy testing principles.[47]

Unfortunately, the likelihood of research expertise resolving this issue is remote. Market researchers can only support their methods with face validity, the weakest form of substantiation. The Advertising Research Foundation (ARF) itself, after calling on major advertisers of the nation, was unable to uncover a single case which confirmed beyond doubt the validity of a copy testing technique.[48]

Advertising agencies often suggest "up front" research instead of the traditional copy tests.[49] Supposedly, emphasis would be put on creating better communication before all money for production is spent. Most advertisers would have no objection to such a system if it met the following conditions:

1. The developmental research does not presume to set or modify brand strategy.
2. The "up front" testing does not become a substitute for evaluative research of finished advertisements.
3. If developmental research is contemplated as a substitute for evaluative research, the former must be able to predict evaluative results with a high degree of accuracy.

The main question is, do restraints on creativity make for poorer performance? The answer is difficult, if not impossible to ascertain. If the past is any indication, truly great advertising today is no more infrequent than it was say twenty years ago, when copy testing was less prevalent in decision making. It is sheer daydreaming to uphold advertising of the past as more effective because creative personnel were given greater latitude.

Given a product category, small accounts do no better than large ones, which impose greater restrictions on a copywriter's freedom of action. One might object to this argument on the grounds that the top creative talent usually work on big-budget accounts. Yet despite all griping and backbiting, creatives themselves seem to prefer working on accounts most likely to be well funded and successful.

SUMMARY

Advertising research is the information arm of advertising. Its function is two-fold: it is used in planning and in evaluation.

Marketing plans usually combine population statistics with sales data. The Bureau of the Census is the most important source for the former. Purchase information will differ from one industry to another.

Most advertising practitioners, however, advocate going beyond the purely behavioristic data to psychological measurements. Those which have had the greatest impact upon the creation of advertising messages are concept testing, motivation research, focus groups, and attitude measurements.

Concept tests are used widely for positioning new products. Motivation research, which came from abnormal psychology, enjoyed its greatest popularity in the 1950s and early 1960s. Focus groups are widely used today, though they are highly controversial. Attitude measurements are varied. One that has gained wide currency is the multiattribute model, particularly that of Fishbein. Another, of more recent vintage, is perceptual mapping, a computer-based method which plots attitudinal data in multidimensional space.

Evaluation of advertising messages is referred to as copy testing. There are three basic methods, each with numerous variations, for testing copy: physiological, market behavior, psychological. The latter is most common, and its most popular variations are recognition, recall, and attitude change.

Despite almost universal use of research, criticism of its accuracy and relevancy abounds. Nevertheless, its use is dictated by organizational needs, even at the expense of creativity.

Questions for Chapter 10

1. Why should a firm exploit secondary sources before undertaking primary research?

2. How would you explain the fact that the major part of corporate research expenditures goes toward sales measurements?

3. Are concept tests of value for older products?

4. What are the advantages and pitfalls of focus groups?

5. How might an advertising campaign based on the Fishbein model differ from one based on motivation research?

6. An advertising agency research department looks for empty gaps on a perception map to guide copy strategy. Would you approve the resulting proposal if you were an advertising manager?

7. What are the main weaknesses of Starch ratings?

8. What are the main difficulties in testing advertisements running in actual magazines by aided recall?

9. Why would an advertiser oppose "up front" research as a substitute for a post test of a tv commercial?

10. Why are persuasion measurements used less than day-after recall, despite the fact that persuasion is considered a more meaningful variable?

11. What are the main criticisms of on-air tests?

Footnotes for Chapter 10

[1]Jack Honomichl, "Nation's 28 Top Market Research Companies See Revenues Jump 13.8% in 1981," *Advertising Age* (May 24, 1982), pp. M7, M10, M12.

[2]Henry Assael and John Keon, "Nonsampling vs. Sampling Errors in Survey Research," *Journal of Marketing* (Spring 1982), pp. 114–123.

[3]Victor Wademan, *Risk-free Advertising* (New York: John Wiley & Sons, 1977), pp. 1–37.

[4]Wademan, pp. 1, 4.

[5]Al Ries and Jack Trout, *Positioning: The Battle for Your Mind* (New York: McGraw-Hill, 1981), p. 3.

[6]Sachs and Benson, *Product Planning*, pp. 242–243.

[7]See Edward M. Tauber, "What is Measured by Concept Testing," *Journal of Advertising Research* (December 1972), pp. 36–37; Russel I. Haley and Ronald Gatty, "Trouble With Concept Testing," *Journal of Advertising Research* (June 1968), pp. 23–35.

[8]Gareth W. Jones, "New Product Development," *The Conference Board Record* (September 1976), p. 27.

[9]Leonard Russ, "Dean of the Motivation Researchers," *New York Times* (September 18, 1977), Sec. 22, p. 8.

[10]See Danny N. Bellinger and Barnett A. Greenberg, *Marketing Research* (Homewood, Ill: Richard D. Irwin, Inc., 1978), pp. 189–192; Bertram Schoner and Kenneth P. Uhl, *Marketing Research*, 2nd ed. (New York: John Wiley, 1975), pp. 258–259, 283–285; William A. Yoell, "The Fallacy of Projective Techniques," *Journal of Advertising*, vol. 3 (1974), pp. 33–35.

[11]Jennifer Stewart, "Focus Groups: A Dangerous Case of Malpractice," *Marketing Review* (December/January 1981), pp. 32–33.

[12]K. L. McGown, *Marketing Research* (Cambridge, Mass.: Winthrop Publishers, 1979), pp. 309–310.

[13]Myril Axelrod, "Ten Essentials for Good Qualitative Research," *Marketing News* (March 14, 1975), p. 10.

[14]Baker, pp. 82–83.

[15]Roger E. Bengston, "Despite Controversy, Focus Groups Are Used to Examine a Wide Range of Marketing Questions," *Marketing News* (September 19, 1980), p. 25.

[16]See Henry Schachte, "Today's (Bad) Corporate Advertising Credo Is: Don't Stick Your Neck Out," *Advertising Age* (August 15, 1977), p. 49.

[17]Harold Bay, "Creativity In Driver's Seat," *Advertising Age* (June 22, 1981), p. S-41.

[18]Christy Marshall, "Dillon: Now They Think Ads Can Do It All," *Advertising Age* (November 3, 1980), p. 3.

[19]For example, see Harry E. Heller, " 'Attitude Share of Market' Predicts Better Than Behavioral Measures," *Marketing News* (May 16, 1980), p. 7; Jon N. Zoler,

"Consumer Attitude Research Will Be Mandatory In 80s," *Marketing News* (September 19, 1980), pp. 22–23; "Ads Can Change Attitudes, Hike Sales; Effects Are Measurable," *Marketing News* (February 13, 1976), p. 5.

[20]Martin Fishbein, "A Behavior Theory Approach to the Relations Between Beliefs About an Object and the Attitude Toward the Object," M. Fishbein, ed., *Readings in Attitude Theory and Measurement* (New York: Wiley, 1967), pp. 394–396.

[21]See Schoner and Uhl, *Marketing Research*, p. 280.

[22]William L. Wilkie and Edgar A. Pessemier, "Issues in Marketing's Use of Multi-Attribute Attitude Models," *Journal of Marketing Research* (November 1973), pp. 428–441.

[23]C. Michael Troutman and James Shanteau, "Do Consumers Evaluate Products by Adding or Averaging Attribute Information?" *Journal of Consumer Research* (September 1976), pp. 101–106.

[24]David A. Aaker and George S. Day, *Marketing Research: Private and Public Sector Decisions* (New York: Wiley, 1980), pp. 192–193.

[25]"A Tale of Two Studies—Disturbing: Struse," *Marketing News* (May 18, 1979), p. 7.

[26]Nelson, p. 44.

[27]See Al Hampel, "It's Never Been Done Before... And Other Obstacles To Creativity," *Marketing Review* (December/January 1978), p. 18; "A Creative Sampler," *Advertising Age* (June 22, 1981), pp. 49–50.

[28]"Creatives Bemoan Current State of Advertising," p. 10.

[29]"Innovation Means Risk-taking, ANA Hears," *Advertising Age* (October 6, 1980), p. 10.

[30]For example, see James M. Perey, "Those Public Opinion Polls," *The Wall Street Journal* (September 11, 1980), p. 26; Jack J. Honomichl, "The Marketing of a Candidate," *Advertising Age* (December 15, 1980), pp. 3, 65–68.

[31]"Today's Ads Need More Creativity," p. 5; Carolyn Pfaff, "Bernbach Comments Ruffle Researchers," *Advertising Age* (April 13, 1981), p. 98.

[32]For example, see "Don't Overmanage Advertising Ideas," *Marketing News* (May 2, 1980), p. 10; Merle Kingman, "A Profile of The Bad Client," *Advertising Age* (May 11, 1981), pp. 49–52; Ron Burkhardt, "A Creative Mind: Will It Return in 1980s?" *Advertising Age* (March 31, 1980), p. 45.

[33]"Minnetonka Credits 'Thinking' Not Research, For Success of Softsoap," *Marketing News* (December 26, 1980), p. 1.

[34]Dean Rotbart, "P&G Profit Rose A Surprising 19% In Its 4th Period," *The Wall Street Journal* (August 11, 1981), p. 4.

[35]Swinyard and Patti, p. 29.

[36]Darrell B. Lucas and Steuart H. Britt, *Measuring Advertising Effectiveness* (New York: McGraw-Hill, 1963), pp. 50–58.

[37]Gallup & Robinson, Inc., *Advertising and Marketing Research*, p. 22.

[38]"On-air Testing Misses Differences: Yuspeh," *Marketing News* (April 6, 1979), p.

4; Sonia Yuspeh, "A Recall Debate," *Advertising Age* (July 13, 1981), pp. 47–48.

[39] Advertising Research Service, *Factors Affecting Measurements of Related Recall* (Evansville, Ind.: Research Systems Corp., 1979); Advertising Research Foundation, *PARM Bulletin No. 2* (September 19, 1956).

[40] Harry W. McMahan, "What's Wrong with TV Commercial Research and Can It Be Improved," *Advertising Age* (August 16, 1976), p. 44.

[41] Jack J. Honomichl, "TV Copy Testing Flap: What To Do About It," *Advertising Age* (January 19, 1981), p. 59.

[42] "FCB says Masked-Recognition Test Yields Truer Remembering Measures Than Day-After Recall Test," *Marketing News* (June 12, 1981), pp. 1–2; "Advertising Agency Creatives Attack Copy Research Because They Don't Understand Testing Goals," *Marketing News* (August 7, 1981), p. 11.

[43] J. J. Honomichl, "Creative Thoughts on Copy Testing," *Advertising Age* (October 26, 1981), pp. 5–26.

[44] "ARF Hears Andrews' Defense of Copy Testing," *Advertising Age* (March 24, 1980), p. 6.

[45] L. E. Ostlund, *et. al.*, "Inertia in Copy Research," *Journal of Advertising Research* (February 1980), pp. 17–24.

[46] J. D. Leckenby and N. Wedding, *Advertising Management* (Columbus, Ohio: Grid, 1982), pp. 402–404.

[47] "21 Ad Agencies Endorse Copy Testing Principles," *Marketing News* (February 19, 1982), pp. 1, 9.

[48] Edward M. Tauber, "Six Questionable Assumptions in Ad Research," *Marketing News* (September 19, 1980), p. 9.

[49] "Copy Research: State of the Art—1. The Agency View," *Marketing Review* (January/February 1978), p. 21; Roman and Maas, pp. 104–105; Shirley Young, "Copy Testing: For What? For Whom?," Advertising Research Foundation, *Annual Conference, October 1977,* (New York: Advertising Research Foundation, 1977).

11 The Media Plan

Media are the essential links between transmitting agencies and target audiences, between sources of communication and respective market destinations. The media plan, which spells out the intended schedules of advertisements, has two prime concerns: cost of time and space units and value received for the expenditures.

This theme of cost-benefit analysis is central to the chapter. The particulars involve:

- **Media mix decisions, or allocating expenditures among various media types**
- **Individual vehicle decisions, or allocating expenditures to various advertising carriers within each media type**
- **Geographic media selection, or allocating expenditures among sales territories**
- **Determination of message spacing during the advertising campaign**
- **Theories of advertising wearout and decisions of campaign length**

ELEMENTS OF A MEDIA PLAN

The media plan consists of all activities related to the use of time and space in mass media. These activities can be carried out by either: the advertiser, a media buying service, or an advertising agency. Or, a firm can split the media planning functions among the three in a variety of ways.

A company typically spends about 90 percent of its total advertising budget for media, which joins the message with appropriate markets. The objective of a media plan is essentially to formulate a course of action which gets the message to the intended markets in the best possible manner.

The process of selecting the most desirous carriers is often referred to as media strategy. But sometimes "strategy" takes on a narrower meaning, as when it is thought of as reasoning which leads to the choice. The implementation of the plan, such as negotiating media contracts, is commonly defined as tactics.[1] But the advertising strategy, including that of specifying target audiences, has already been delineated in the positioning section of the advertising plan. As such, media decisions are primarily tactical, not strategic.

Be that as it may, media planning can be broken down into four major phases: media selection, negotiation, logistics, and evaluation. These four broad categories are displayed graphically in the sequence of their occurrence in Figure 11–1.

Media selection entails not merely the choice of advertising carriers but the timing of message placement, both equally important elements. An advertising campaign represents an arrangement of messages emitted by particular media at points in time. Electronic media pose few problems with timing, for the transmission of messages is virtually coincidental with their reception. Print media have more complex timing patterns, as reading occurs over longer periods of time. Reading is also highly varied. Some people even read the same message in the same issue more than once. These time effects bring complications into media planning.

The schedule drawn up is actually a contingent one; both space and time must be contracted. Print media, which can accommodate ads of a number of different sizes in specific issues, can usually accommodate an advertiser's plan except for preferred positions which may already be taken or for positions in close proximity to specific articles, when buying ROP (run of press). Electronic media, especially television, have a fixed number of slots in which commercials can be aired. Here, the advertiser finds specific carriers unavailable at certain times. Even after it has been contracted, the schedule may alter due to unforeseen events and preemptions. Television contracts are, therefore, "best effort" agreements.

The implementation of a media plan requires logistical support, such as the cooperation of an agency traffic department. Other related tasks are billing and making payment. These logistical tasks are of a routine nature and left to functional departments.

There are two parts to the evaluation process. First, the firm must assure itself that media did what they had contracted to do—transmit the message in accordance with buyer instructions. Publications send their customers checking copies and enclose tear sheets with their bills. Broadcasters mail affidavits of performance with their invoices for spots which had been run. Broadcast Advertisers Reports (BAR) are available to advertisers compiled from extensive monitoring of radio and television with audio tape.

Second, the advertiser must ascertain whether the expected audience was reached. Print audiences cannot differ from those in the media plan

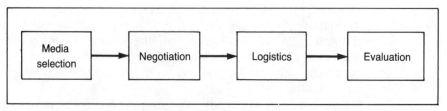

Fig. 11–1 *Elements of Media Planning.*

because surveys are done once a year, and there are no reports for individual issues. Audience statistics used in analysis are presumed to apply to issues in which advertisements run. When a publication's circulation changes materially, advertisers can adjust audience estimates accordingly. The publisher also has to meet some minimum circulation guarantee. Failure to do so incurs penalties in the form of rebates. For television, ratings serve as evaluative tools with which to gauge media performance.

Media plans can proceed from the top down or from the bottom up. The former is most common, as media planners work from fixed budgets, allocating a fixed amount of money to various media. When the task method rules the budget process, media planning is open ended, as it were. The amount of media expenditures is regarded as variable. However, even here there are constraints and certain limits which cannot realistically be exceeded.

Either way, top down or bottom up, media planning matches advertising carriers with product markets. Media considerations fall into two broad categories. First, how much should be spent for different media, such as television, magazines, newspapers, or radio? This question relates to making intermedia choices, or determining what is called the "media mix." Second, how much should be allocated to particular carriers within each type of media, such as individual broadcasts, day parts, magazine issues? This allocation of funds represents intramedia choices.

Market considerations also divide into two broad classes of decisions. First, markets can be viewed as geographic units or sales territories. From this standpoint, media planning concerns itself with apportioning media expenditures geographically. Second, markets can be thought of as buying units, groups, individuals, or households. This perspective saddles media selection with the responsibility of reaching target audiences effectively and efficiently. The end result of planning is a media schedule, which might be depicted graphically as in Figure 11–2.

THE MEDIA MIX

Conceptually, a firm can spend its entire advertising budget in one medium or spread its expenditures among many. Practically, firms employ a mix, except those with severely limited budgets or markets.

Of the 100 leading national advertisers in 1980, the median number of measured media used per firm stood at six. Fifty out of the hundred employed six out of seven alternative media. Measured media consisted of the following seven classifications: newspapers, magazines, spot television, network television, spot radio, network radio, and outdoor. Only seventeen companies confined their communication to five or less media types, and two used less than five.

Industry groupings experienced great diversity in individual choices, as evidenced by relative amounts earmarked for various media types. This

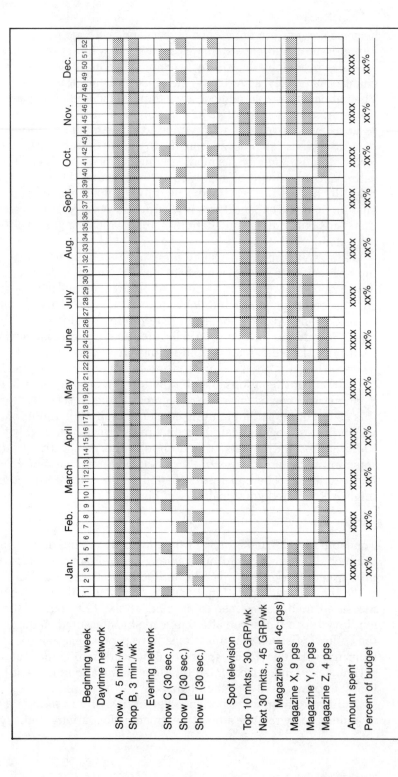

Fig. 11–2 Sample Media Schedule.

TABLE 11–1 *Relative Airline Expenditures by Media in 1980*

| | Relative Expenditures | | | | |
Media Type	American	Delta	Eastern	Trans World	United
Newspapers	42%	58%	50%	33%	33%
Magazines	10	2	11	6	7
Spot tv	26	13	16	22	25
Network tv	2	—	5	27	17
Spot radio	19	23	13	12	17
Network radio	—	—	—	—	—
Outdoor	1	4	5	—	1
Total	100%	100%	100%	100%	100%
Amount in Measured Media ($000,000)	(42.1)	(35.2)	(40.3)	(52.8)	(49.3)

Source: Adapted from *Advertising Age* (September 10, 1981).
Note: Percentages based on *Advertising Age* estimates of expenditures by media.

held true for companies producing highly similar products or services. For example, Table 11–1 shows how airlines allocated their advertising expenditures among the different classes of measured media.

Why should Delta spend nothing in network television, American Airlines only two percent, while United puts 17 percent of its budget there? Why should Delta and Eastern weight their schedules so heavily with newspapers, while Trans World and United maintain a greater balance in their media distributions? (See Table 11–1.) There are many reasons for these differences, such as variations in airline routes, product mix, sales operations, and just plain differences in individual evaluations and preferences.

But media schedules of entire corporations, it can be argued, differ from those of single brands or products. True.

Airline statistics do not pertain to passenger travel only; they include advertising for hotels. Yet the basic principles hold. Large budget brands will invariably embrace a media mix. Products with small budgets or narrow markets will adopt a more restricted outlook towards media diversification. Table 11–2 shows the relative media expenditures for the six most heavily advertised brands of cigarettes in 1980. Supplements are broken out separately as a media type.

As shown in Table 11–2, all brands use a media mix of at least three different media types, despite the confinement of cigarette advertising solely to print. Salem, Vantage and Winston are all marketed by J. R. Reynolds. Yet the variation in media usage between Winston and the other two company brands is the largest of the six. Merit and Marlboro are both put out by Philip Morris, but follow highly diverse routes as well.

TABLE 11–2 *Cigarette Advertising by Media in 1980*

| Media Type | Relative Expenditures | | | | | |
	Salem	Vantage	Kent	Merit	Marlboro	Winston
Newspapers	45%	46%	47%	52%	36%	24%
Magazines	34	38	28	25	39	49
Supplements	7	12	10	10	5	—
Outdoor	14	4	15	13	20	27
Total	100%	100%	100%	100%	100%	100%
Amount in Measured Media ($000,000)	(66.8)	(59.7)	(56.1)	(55.6)	(48.7)	(48.3)

Source: Adapted from *Marketing & Media Decisions* (July 1981), pp. 84–88.

There are several advantages of a media mix. To some extent, each medium excels over others in specific functions. A mix will, therefore, have more versatility, and do more things better than a single medium. A broadcaster planning a promotion with redeemable coupons must use print media. On the other hand, an advertiser who wants to demonstrate his product would undoubtedly consider television for that purpose. The greater the number of specialized tasks media is called upon to do, the higher the probability of a mixed schedule.

Even though the message remains the same, the audience receives different impressions when different media is used. A movie which follows an author's script faithfully cannot produce the identical thoughts as the book. A radio commercial can use the same sound track as the television message, but it cannot be as explicit. It must leave more to the imagination, and what the listener fills in with the mind cannot correspond exactly to the images derived from a television screen. Different media call forth different mental processes. A media mix, depending upon the copy treatment, can in varying degrees communicate a more reenforcing and integrated set of images. A widely-held opinion regards advertising in various channels as more conducive to learning because communication takes place in different psychological contexts.[2]

A media mix also offers more desirable audience patterns. All media tend to have a hard core of adherents, which results in lopsided media exposure. Some people read magazines with great frequency. Others watch television constantly. Some carry their radio sets with them wherever they go. The net result is that one group of individuals has very high exposure to certain media, while another portion has little or none. Advertising campaigns in the same medium thus convey messages to the same, highly-exposed group over and over, while failing to cover another sector adequately. It happens that those who are heavy television viewers are light magazine readers, and vice versa. By employing a mix, advertisers usually increase their coverage of a market and achieve a more favorable distribution of audience exposures.

Creative decisions determine the choice of media more frequently than is realized. The creative strategy and copy platform often precede the media plan. If the basic idea is visualized in a certain way, the copy writer virtually decrees the choice of media. A creative decision to use a rational argument and lengthy copy relegates advertisements to print. A resolution to place ads in colors would tilt the media choice to magazines. A determination to present the product in a slice-of-life situation shifts the advertising to television. The media planner, therefore, must select the medium appropriate to the message.

Brands embracing the media mix philosophy are faced with the problem of allocating resources to each medium. This, to them, is a vital decision.

Unfortunately, there are no hard and fast rules. Some decisions are fairly cut and dry, leaving little room for individual judgment. Others are discretionary, especially when the same advertising functions are perceived as done equally well by different media. Although most brands will exhibit one dominant medium within the mix, the concentration and dispersion of media expenditures are highly varied, even for brands in the same product category.

GEOGRAPHIC ALLOCATION

All markets can be viewed as geographically-distributed sales entities. There are basically three ways to allocate media expenditures in accordance with geography. These choices are: using national media; putting together a media package on an individual market basis; or using a combination of national and individual markets.

National media, the audiences of which generally follow population, offer the greatest ease of scheduling. This option yields economies of scale, provided an adequate budget is justifiable. Costs run high for national media, but the cost per person reached usually decreases as audience size gets larger. Brands which pursue this course of media selection are mass-produced, widely distributed, and usually vie for market share on a national basis.

A second possibility is a market-by-market approach. This alternative is desirable when a firm seeks to adjust media weight to particular markets. There are many reasons for these types of plans. They can arise from territorial fluctuations in sales or distribution, or because national media sometimes yield audience patterns which fail to meet marketing objectives, such as a national magazine which may have low readership in certain parts of the country. The same may apply to viewership of a show on a network lineup. In all these situations, a market-by-market media buy can rectify perceived imbalances.

TABLE 11–3 *Illustration of BDI and MDI Calculations*

SMSA	Column 1 Percent of U.S. Households	Column 2 Percent of Brand Sales	Column 3 Percent of Sales in Product Category	Column 4 Column 2 Column 1 BDI	Column 5 Column 3 Column 1 MDI
Detroit	1.90	1.80	2.00	95	105
Miami	0.79	1.00	0.80	127	101
Minneapolis	0.97	1.20	0.90	124	93
San Francisco	1.62	1.40	1.70	86	105

A third alternative combines national media with those covering individual markets. No matter how widespread brand sales or distribution, some unevenness among markets normally exists. A layer of national advertising assures almost all markets of enjoying an amount of advertising which the advertiser deems adequate, whereas individual market buys take advantage of local or regional opportunities.

Regardless of whether firms apply the market-by-market philosophy to all expenditures or to only a portion thereof, they have numerous methods at their disposal for making market adjustments. One technique is to apportion media dollars in accordance with sales. The firm simply cuts up the budget for each market in proportion to its sales. Under this system, the percentage of a total budget going to a particular market can be expressed as: market sales/total company sales.

Most advertisers find this rather basic method unsatisfactory, for it disregards questions of market size and opportunities. More popular techniques, especially with packaged goods marketers, entail the construction of brand development and market development indexes, designated as BDI and MDI respectively. Both indices are based on relevant buying units, usually individuals or households. Taking households as a base, index computations are illustrated in Table 11–3.

The indexes in Table 11–3 represent ratios of relative sales to relative households. A higher BDI number means that brand sales are proportionately greater than households, and indicates a better-than-average performance. The MDI shows for each geographic market the potential for an entire product category. But these analyses do not tell how advertising should be allocated by market.[3]

For example, Miami and Minneapolis have high BDIs, but these excellent results were achieved in smaller markets. Should these better performing markets get proportionately more advertising, or should the extra money be shifted to bring sales levels up in Detroit and San Francisco?

Indexes by themselves don't give this information. The decision is a matter of managerial judgment which, in turn, may be modified by actual results.

However, the indicators provide a framework for experimentation. Extra advertising can be added in some high and some low BDI markets. Or heavier expenditures can be made in several low MDI markets, on the assumption that they are low because they have been underpromoted. Or a reverse course can be taken, if the figures are interpreted as indicative of a better potential. The market-by-market approach offers a trial-and-error method for experimenting, for seeking to capitalize on opportunities and improve performance. This search for a differential advantage is the heart of marketing, sending life-giving energy to all its parts. When advertising weighs heavily in marketing decisions, individual market allocations provide a ready means for trying new alternatives.

CHOICE OF VEHICLES

If advertisers could choose the ideal basis for media selection, barring a direct sales measure, the overwhelming choice would be exposure to advertisements. Advertisers look upon media as vehicles for carrying commercial messages to consumers. Given this function, they conceive of a medium's prime responsibility as being the exposure of their messages to an audience in a favorable communication environment. How a medium does this is of little concern to the advertiser, as long as its policies do not detract from the message's impact.

Measurements for comparing advertising exposure in specific media are not available. Some agencies use Burke's commercial audience results to make rough estimates of television's potential for communicating messages. But these exposure statistics are not generated regularly for television shows, and programs cannot be compared with each other. In the absence of exposure ratings for both print and broadcast, advertisers must fall back on the next level of relevancy—audience. Television has its viewers, radio its listeners, print its readers. Though a second or third choice in order of importance, audience stands high and casts a long shadow over the media selection process.

Most firms have adopted three major criteria with which to evaluate media audiences: efficiency, market value, audience patterns of vehicle combinations. Efficiency relates audience to cost. Market value places a worth on audience based on sales potential. Vehicle combinations are required for any campaign, and produce varying audience patterns or configurations.

COST EFFICIENCY

The underlying logic of media selection is not simply to reach prospects or target groups. The idea is to reach them efficiently, or at a relatively low unit cost.

One commonly used measure of efficiency is the cost-per-thousand calculation, referred to as CPM. It shows the cost of a thousand members of each audience, figured as cost × 1,000/audience. When advertising carriers are compared on this yardstick, all other things being equal, those with the lowest CPMs are judged the most efficient. (Table 11–4 shows CPM calculations for a number of selected magazines.)

Table 11–4 illustrates the generalization that, given a media vehicle or set of vehicles, efficiency declines as a target market becomes more selective. A male audience, for example, must have a higher CPM than total audience because the denominator gets smaller. But the cost of a given space unit remains the same, keeping the numerator constant.

The audience-cost relationship implies that more selective markets must accept more waste in mass media. The amount of waste is that portion of a medium's audience who are not prospects for the product advertised, or not designated as targets in the marketing plan. A food ad aimed exclusively at women can regard all male readers or viewers as audience waste.

An alternative to buying large chunks of waste is to resort to specialized media—vehicles which cater to highly selective groups. But this approach may sacrifice coverage of the marketing target. Hence, specialized media may be efficient, but not effective. On the other hand, vehicles with large, general audiences may reach a high proportion of a target group, but also contain many nonprospects.

Every product has somewhat different efficiency norms. Even within a product category each brand has its own unique marketing goals and designated targets. This helps to explain gaping divergencies in media usage by competitive brands. Competitive expenditure and cost comparisons in

TABLE 11–4 *Cost-per-thousand Audience for Selected Magazines (Average Issue Audience)*

Magazine	Page Rate 4-color	Total Readers (000)	Total 4C CPM	Men Readers (000)	Men 4C CPM	Women Readers (000)	Women 4C CPM
Better Homes & Gardens	$68,195	37,132	$1.84	10,420	$6.54	26,712	$2.55
National Geographic	87,685	31,009	2.83	16,728	5.24	14,281	6.14
Newsweek	57,780	21,924	2.64	12,671	4.56	9,253	6.24
Reader's Digest	89,600	59,848	1.50	26,374	3.40	33,474	2.68
Sports Illustrated	49,465	16,100	3.07	12,133	4.08	3,967	12.47
Time	76,960	24,541	3.14	13,934	5.52	10,607	7.26
TV Guide	76,160	49,957	1.52	22,777	3.34	27,180	2.80

Source: Based on Mediamark Research Inc. (Fall 1981). All rights reserved. Rates are taken from Publishers' Rate Cards, August 1981.

these instances may not be too meaningful, except for products which have almost universal appeal.

Another method for evaluating media efficiency is the cost-per-percentage gross audience. To illustrate: suppose the cost of a space unit is $50,000. Suppose further that an issue garners 20 million women readers out of a total of some 80 million in the nation. The audience of that issue can be said to equal 25% of the target market. Expressing this percentage as a whole number, a one point "coverage" or gross audience would then cost $50,000/25= $2,000. The lower this figure, the more efficient the advertising carrier.

This form of cost analysis is primarily used in spot television and is particularly popular with media buying services. Spot buyers refer to it as cost per rating point. When alternative schedules rather than individual episodes are evaluated by the cost per rating point, overlapping or duplicated audiences are implicitly disregarded. Buying is said to be conducted on a gross weight or tonnage basis.

Conventional efficiency methods—cost-per-thousand audience or cost-per-percent gross audience—do not apply to intermedia comparisons. The audiences of different media do not have precisely the same meanings. The units of time or space have no equivalencies, and there is no accepted basis for assigning values to these units. Is a 30 second commercial equivalent to a black and white page in a magazine or a four-color page? Lastly, intermedia comparisons on a cost basis make the far-fetched assumption that the impact of media is alike, regardless of message content.

THE MARKET VALUE OF AN AUDIENCE

How much is a reader or viewer worth to an advertiser? Are some worth more than others? A company that buys television on the basis of ratings assumes that all viewers are equally good prospects. A division of the population into prospects and nonprospects accepts a definition of target groups as an all-or-nothing proposition. One group merits 100 percent, with all of its members being given equal value, while another group gets a zero for having no value whatsoever to a marketer.

Many large ticket items with limited appeal may have individual purchase probabilities of zero or one. But often there are gradations in the probabilities of product purchase among various segments of the population. Teenagers have the highest consumption rate for soft drinks. But senior citizens enjoy the beverage too, even though their tendency to consume diminishes with age.

There are two main techniques by which marketers place a value on the medium's audience. One is demographic matching. The marketing plan usually contains an analysis as to kind of people who make up the best prospects for a product. The media planner then seeks out publications and broadcasts which best deliver audiences having the same characteristics. A second method ascertains directly the product usage or probability of purchase which relates to a medium.

Demographic matching is the most widespread method of assigning values to audiences. In effect, it weights audience by demographic factors which are presumed to be associated with buying. This method tacitly supposes that audiences with certain demographics have the same purchase probabilities as their counterparts in the general population. It assumes, for example, that women with babies who watch Program A have the same likelihood of buying diapers as similar mothers who are nonviewers.

This supposition, however, does not always hold. The U.S. Census of Travel shows occupation of household head as the most important single characteristic associated with travel to northern Europe. Homes headed by professionals, managers, or administrators account for about two-thirds of all person trips to Europe.[4] Do readers of *National Geographic* magazine classified as professional or managerial by occupation have the same probability of taking a transoceanic flight as their counterparts in the population? Their's may be much greater, since reading National Geographic indicates an interest in far away places. Or would a reader of *House and Gardens* have the same probability as any other home owner of buying flowering bulbs just because he or she owns a residence? Not at all!

Demographic matching is most applicable when editorial interests have no relation to the products advertised. When the two factors are correlated, probabilities of population segments cannot be transferred to audiences.

The assignment of purchase probabilities to audience is at least once removed from the original source of data. Demographic matching thus contains a built-in process which feeds on estimating accuracy, for the audience characteristics serve as proxies for product usage.[5]

Direct estimates of purchase probabilities shortcut the intermediate steps. But to do so, media and product data must come from the same research source.

At present, product usage information is available only for consumer magazine audiences. These advertising vehicles, in the main, appeal to selective markets. Their specialized nature also gives rise to collinearity between editorial and product purchase variables, which makes demographic matching difficult for many products. On the other hand, the absence of product usage for television audiences does not signify a gross omission. Rather, it reflects a lack of demand for such information. Television audiences are largely undifferentiated, so that product profiles become superfluous. Program evaluations based upon the current system of ratings and broad demographic breakdowns, such as age and sex, would differ little from those based on product usage.

Still, the use of direct estimates presents many snags and frustrations. The main purpose of any audience study is readership estimates, not gathering details about product usage. The products are survey add-ons, and like most appendages, have low utility functions. The resulting product statistics are often vastly inferior to those of other sources in terms of accuracy and detail. An analyst may thus favor demographic matching, loss of efficiency and allover direct estimates which are inherently warped.

LIFE STYLE

Life style as a buying influence has been studied by sociologists and marketers for at least three decades. Though intriguing, it has remained an elusive subject. Its force is felt, like a thought crossing the mind, but it lacks definition.

Many life style measures have been applied to media audiences in the past—social class concepts, IQ scores, ratings of "venturesomeness." They evoked interest, but little else.

Psychographics came on the scene during the 1960s, though its roots go back much farther. The research stressed psychological traits of consumers. For example, one study of toothpaste classified consumers into sensories, sociables, worriers, and independents. Each segment was presented as seeking a different benefit from a toothpaste.[6] Other researchers came up with a host of other classifications for products—squares, swingers, traditionalists, liberated, outgoing, introverts, and so forth. But it was virtually impossible to identify these groups or to estimate their size from conventional population statistics. The research also seemed to lack a common method for classifying consumers according to psychological traits, so that results could not be duplicated. Nor was it ever demonstrated that these disputed labels were predictive of buying behavior, notwithstanding researchers' claims to the contrary.

In the 1970s, *Time Magazine* introduced "zip marketing," which related neighborhood and income level to product purchase. The concept proved useful in defining market parameters for many products, especially consumer durables. It was also capable of being expanded to include other socio-economic variables.[7] But the technique of clustering zip code areas into income quintiles still upheld a model wherein a $30,000-a-year college professor had the same tastes and consumption habits as a $30,000-a-year truck driver.

The amalgamation of zip codes and socio-economic data was greatly extended in 1980 by a Claritas Corporation model named PRIZM. The name is an acronym for Potential Rating Index by Zip Marketing. Claritas analyzed some 35,600 zip codes on more than 1,000 Census demographic measures, and on the basis of multivariate analysis assigned all zips to one of forty groups called zip-market clusters. These segments were so designed as to produce maximum similarity for persons within a cluster and utmost dissimilarity among people in different clusters. Each cluster was also given a somewhat colorful but descriptive name, such as Blue Blood Estates, Bunker's Neighbors, Tobacco Roads. PRIZM then went further and combined its clusters with data from magazine audiences and product usage.[8]

Figures 11–3 and 11–4 illustrate a PRIZM analysis. The first histogram shows an index of camera ownership for each of the forty "ZQ" clusters. The second chart is an overlay of National Geographic readership, displayed as dark bars. The lighter shaded bars denote ownership of 35mm cameras.

Figure 11–4 indicates a strong relationship between National Geographic's reader profile and camera ownership. The coefficient was actually calculated at slightly better than .9. Some products, of course, would have smaller coefficients. The closer the fit, the more suitable a publication is assumed to be as an advertising carrier. Or audiences can actually be weighted by "ZQ" cluster product indexes to estimate potential. However, this method cannot escape the assumption of equivalency between readers and nonreaders in terms of product purchases.

The PRIZM approach is actually a matching process, but more sophisticated than the traditional one of demographics. However, relationships between product usage, audience and "ZQ" clusters must be known. Only experience will determine whether this life style method of weighting audiences will make headway in the advertising industry.

AUDIENCE PATTERNS OF VEHICLE COMBINATIONS

Since firms advertise over time, audience patterns result from combinations of advertising carriers. Media planning deals with three basic concepts related to these configurations: gross audience, reach, frequency.

Gross audience is often called media weight because it is akin to piling up tonnage. It is calculated by simply adding up the audiences of all vehicles used. It can be expressed as an absolute number or as a percentage of the target market. For example, if an advertiser placed messages in four television programs with an average rating of 17, the gross audience would be 68 ($17 \times 4 = 68$). This figure in television is known as gross rating points (GRP).

Spot television plans are frequently phrased in GRP criteria, usually on a weekly basis. But any other time period is feasible. A gross audience represents the number of program viewings, or the number of issue readings when applied to print. But it does not tell how many prospects were reached or the frequency with which it was accomplished. The same people can be members of many different audiences.

Reach and frequency concepts involve overlapping constructs of media exposure. To illustrate how they work, assume an advertiser will run

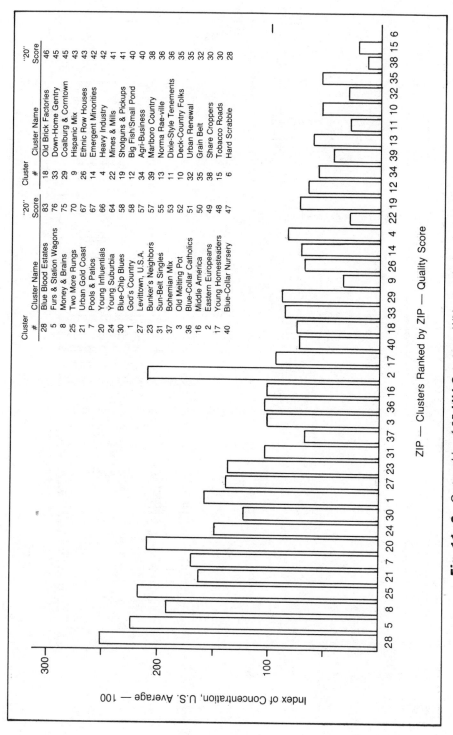

Cluster #	Cluster Name	"20" Score		Cluster #	Cluster Name	"20" Score
28	Blue Blood Estates	83		18	Old Brick Factories	46
5	Furs & Station Wagons	76		33	Down-Home Gentry	45
8	Money & Brains	75		29	Coalburg & Corntown	45
25	Two More Rungs	70		9	Hispanic Mix	43
21	Urban Gold Coast	67		26	Ethnic Row Houses	43
7	Pools & Patios	67		14	Emergent Minorities	42
20	Young Influentials	66		4	Heavy Industry	42
24	Young Suburbia	64		22	Mines & Mills	41
30	Blue-Chip Blues	58		19	Shotguns & Pickups	41
1	God's Country	58		12	Big Fish/Small Pond	40
27	Levittown, U.S.A.	57		34	Agri-Business	40
23	Bunker's Neighbors	57		39	Marlboro Country	38
31	Sun-Belt Singles	55		13	Norma Rae-ville	36
37	Bohemian Mix	53		11	Dixie-Style Tenements	36
3	Old Melting Pot	52		10	Deck-Country Folks	35
36	Blue-Collar Catholics	51		32	Urban Renewal	35
16	Middle America	50		35	Grain Belt	32
2	Eastern Europeans	49		38	Share Croppers	30
17	Young Homesteaders	48		15	Tobacco Roads	30
40	Blue-Collar Nursery	47		6	Hard Scrabble	28

ZIP — Clusters Ranked by ZIP — Quality Score

Index of Concentration, U.S. Average — 100

Fig. 11—3 *Ownership of 35 MM Cameras. With permission from National Geographic Magazine.*

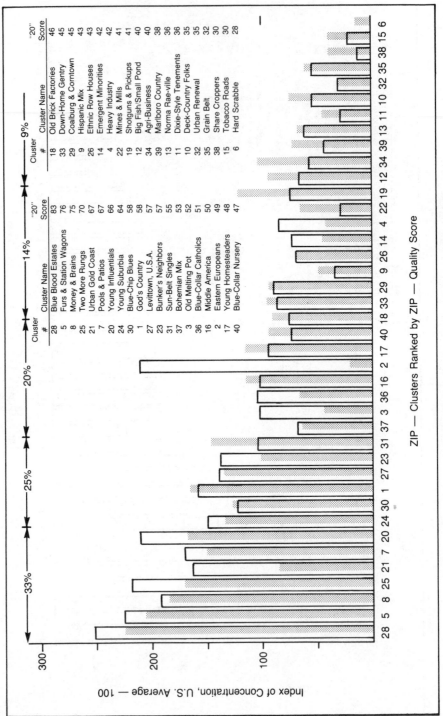

Fig. 11–4 Illustration of a PRIZM Chart—National Geographic Audience Owning 35 MM Camera. With permission from National Geographic Magazine.

TABLE 11–5 *Example of Cumulative Audience*

Program	Rating	Reach	Unduplicated Audience
1	15	15	15
2	19	28	13
3	16	37	9
4	18	43	6
GRP	68		

commercials on four different shows spread over one month. It could actually be four magazines, or two and two. The specific advertising carriers are irrelevant. No matter how the content varies, the form remains the same.

Now suppose these four programs obtained ratings of 15, 19, 16, and 18 respectively. The average is 17, which is typical for a network program in prime time. This rating means that 17 percent of all homes with tv sets have some contact with a program, on the average. But how many different homes were reached by the combination of four? This is the definition of reach, also called net cumulative audience.

The smallest number is 19 percent. If this were the case, the entire audiences of shows one, three and four would have had to be tuned in on program two, which came up with a rating of 19. The largest possible number is 68 percent which is the gross audience. This could only happen if no single home tuned in to more than one program of the four. A more likely outcome is the audience pattern depicted in Table 11–5.

According to Table 11–5, the audience builds up from 15 percent of tv households to 43 percent. But the increase occurs at a diminishing rate. With each additional program, a smaller proportion of the target market is unduplicated by programs aired previously.

The four programs reached 43 percent of all homes about 1.6 times on the average. This is calculated by the formula: Average frequency = Gross audience/Net cumulative audience. Thus, 68/43=1.6.

This model makes it impossible to maximize reach and frequency simultaneously at a fixed level of advertising weight. Given GRP, any increase in reach lowers average frequency. An increase in frequency, on the other hand, decreases reach. When a budget is determined, only certain amounts of reach and frequency are possible. These amounts are variable, and can be altered within prescribed limits. But the exact choice of a reach-frequency mix depends largely upon judgment.

The pattern of audience buildup depicted in Table 11–5 is for exposition purposes only. It may never occur in reality, especially for brands advertised continuously. This model assumes that a four-week period stands by itself, isolated from everything that has gone before and will follow.

Suppose four programs during the next four weeks achieve similar ratings and an identical cumulative audience. Suppose further a like pattern is obtained in the next four weeks. Does the cumulation stop at the end of every four weeks and begin all over again on the fifth? Every week the cumulative audience will add some new people and drop out some viewers from the previous four-week period. Cumulation would look more like a moving average rather than the traditional cumulation curve. Figure 11–5 illustrates this proposition graphically, showing the difference between a moving average concept of cumulation and the conventional step-wise audience model.

According to Figure 11–5, GRPs remain at 68 during both four-week periods. The conventional method of computation, represented by bars or steps, shows reach in both periods rising to 43 percent of the target market. The moving average method, represented by the dotted line, pictures the cumulative audience as fluctuating about 43, with an average frequency of close to 1.6 each week.

It is readily apparent that reach calculations hinge greatly on the length of the relevant period. If the time interval were extended to eight weeks

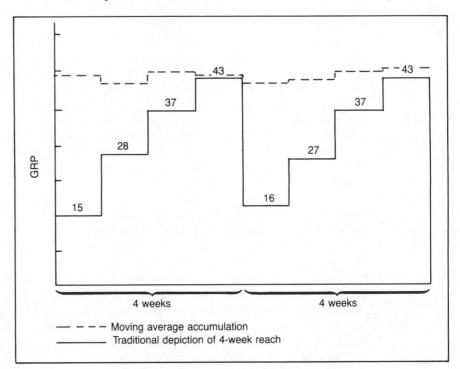

Fig. 11–5 *Illustration of Two Cumulative Audience Concepts.*

instead of four, cumulative audience would likely go to about 55 percent of all homes, assuming one telecast a week. If the time period stretched beyond eight weeks, given the same pattern of telecasts, reach would build to higher levels.

Cumulative audience is thus governed not merely by the number and types of media vehicles, but by the choice of a relevant time period. Since the increase in audience accumulation proceeds at a diminishing rate, there comes a point at which more programs add negligible amounts of viewers. This saturation point is thought to be at about 70 percent.[9]

Consequently, variations in the expenditures of large budget brands result mainly in variations in frequency. Reach is maintained by a schedule which is more or less continuous. It is hardly a coincidence that the effect of frequency is the information desired most by media users.[10] Contrariwise, small budget brands aim at maximizing reach. They would rather penetrate the target market as deeply as possible; frequency under any circumstances would be paltry.

An average frequency, like any other measure of a central tendency, describes a point of a distribution around which media exposures tend to cluster. But this statistic can be misleading under a wide range of circumstances: the distribution is platykurtic, with a wide variance; the distribution is skewed, with a small proportion of the audience doing a preponderance of viewing; the distribution is bimodal, with large percentages at high and low ends and a small one near the middle. A good media plan therefore considers not merely the average but the distribution of frequency.

Take a hypothetical situation in which eight shows are telecast over a period of time. Suppose the average rating of these episodes is 17, with a reach of 55 percent. Under these conditions, the average frequency would come to 2.5 (17×8) /55=2.5). This schedule offers nine possible outcomes ($n + 1 = 9$). In other words, any member of the marketing target can be grouped in nine possible categories of viewing, ranging from zero to eight. A distribution of media exposures resulting from this schedule might look like that depicted in Figure 11–6.

According to Figure 11–6, some 45 percent of the marketing target was never reached by the schedule. Among those reached at least once, the median viewing home was exposed three times to a program carrying the commercial.

If all viewers have an equal value, the ideal schedule is one in which each viewing home is exposed to three out of eight episodes. In that event, the effective distribution might be defined as being from two to four times. This range is shown as the area between two dotted lines.

But the ideal almost never happens. Some homes tune in to one program only, which might be deemed insufficient. Others are exposed from five to eight times, which might be considered excessive.

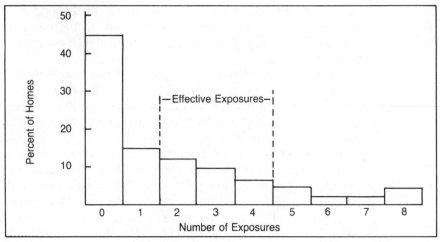

Fig. 11–6 *Distribution of Media Frequency.*

The frequency distribution issue raises two prime questions. First, what is the value of an exposure? Second, what is the relevant period for which exposures should be measured?

Figure 11–6 shows a substantial number of homes reached either insufficiently or excessively, given the definition of "effective." Are then all "noneffective" exposures entirely worthless? If worth something, how much less is their value as compared with "effective exposures?"

In fact, the term exposure in a media context is highly ambiguous. Reach and frequency in a media plan refers to exposures to advertising carriers, not to the advertisements themselves. But all viewers of a television show do not necessarily see a commercial. Nor do all readers of a magazine see every advertisement. Media audiences do not properly reflect opportunities to see or hear the advertising message.

When dealing with questions of "exposure," conventional media measurements should be adjusted downward. But there are no reliable data with which to do so. Some advertisers and agencies use Burke's "commercial audience" concept to adjust their television figures. However, such statistics are not available on a regular basis for a large number of programs. Other media users employ Starch "noted" scores to project advertising exposures for publications, which is a gross abuse of statistics. In the absence of accurate figures, estimates remain subjective and highly varied. With little agreement on how to calculate exposure opportunities, the question of the value of an exposure produces an even less definite answer.

Only a few laboratory experiments ever dealt with the number of exposures needed for effective advertising. Based on research with eye cameras, Herbert Krugman contends that no more than three exposures are needed.[11] Robert Grass, using CONPAAD equipment, reasoned that the optimal number of exposures lies somewhere between two and four.[12] Both these opinions are largely speculative with preciously few facts to support them. A study by Colin McDonald of the British Market Research Bureau, Ltd., in 1966, carried out with diaries kept by housewives, concluded that purchases were related to "opportunities to see" advertising.[13] But not all marketing factors were taken into account, and McDonald recognized his work as only a pilot study.

The question of an optimal frequency, like that of reach, relates to the time period in which exposures occur. If the time span lengthens, all other things remaining equal, frequency rises. The reverse is true when the duration contracts; less people are apt to have experienced a frequency level which is considered adequate. Therefore, the question of frequency cannot be disentangled from one of relevant time period.

The dominant view holds that the relevant duration is that of the product purchase cycle.[14] This theory has merit for products with short cycles. It counsels advertising to build enough frequency for influencing prospects on their next purchase. But the concept falters when purchases are few and far between. Two exposures may be right for a detergent. But what would two exposures mean for an automobile bought once every five years? Or for a refrigerator, which has a life expectancy of better than ten years? Though the reach-frequency mix applies to durables, the relevant time must be drastically modified as compared with that of fast turnover items.

REACH AND FREQUENCY OF MESSAGES

Reach and frequency in media planning relates only to media audiences. But an audience of any carrier represents to the advertiser merely a potential—the maximum number of people capable of receiving a commercial message. Even advertising exposure measurements signify a potential, though one that lies closer to the advertiser's objective than media audience. Nevertheless, the bottom line is how well the potential was realized from a communications standpoint.

Then why not calculate reach and frequency of the messages themselves? This would avoid the present compartmentalized approach which fails to integrate media and copy elements. The present system at best makes only peripheral use of copy quality in media planning. The direct message approach would overtly consider copy effects in reach-frequency calculations.

Little or nothing has been done on this score despite the almost universal endorsement of the proposition that copy and media effects are bound together in the communication network. Partly, the lethargy stems from lack of agreement on measurements. Partly, it persists because of institutionalized practices, which are difficult to change.

The last piece of research to grapple with the problem of how to calculate the reach of commercial messages was a pioneering study in 1964 by the defunct *Look* magazine.[15] Though the conclusions of the study are outdated, and the scope even then was restricted, the methodology still remains applicable to the electronically-dominant environment of today.

The *Look* study addressed itself to questions of how advertising impressions take shape and arrange themselves over the course of a campaign. For example, if an advertisement leaves a memorable impression on X number of readers, how many different consumer minds will be reached by Y issues? And with what frequency?

Look conducted a series of interviews with overlapping samples of 800 of its readers each month for about a half year. A total of 4,695 telephone interviews were completed with a sample that represented all metropolitan areas in the United States. Recall of advertisements were elicited by the same techniques as those employed today in evaluating television commercials. Each reader was interviewed twice, one month apart. The interval between the last reading and the interview was kept constant at roughly twenty-four hours, making results comparable with those of television copy testing.

After adjusting the data for "survey conditioning," the two observations were projected mathematically by use of a beta function. This method is quite similar to that used currently in estimating the reach and frequency of any number of media vehicles from pairs of observations. The following chart, Figure 11–7, shows how advertising impressions—defined as memorable playback of some element in the message—cumulated over thirteen issues for three different levels of recall.

Figure 11–7 illustrates certain principles which are as valid now as then, though the exact values undoubtedly differ. A basic theorem states that advertising messages which get higher initial recall register memorable impressions with more different readers as the campaign progresses. It is interesting to note that it took eight below-average ads, defined as those scoring 17 percent recall, to attain the same cumulative level as four above-average ads, defined as those scoring 29 percent recall. Also noteworthy is the observation that a campaign which starts out with a feeble impact never does catch up. Lastly, there emerges a strong implication that fair approximations of relative communication effectiveness for a campaign can be gotten from copy tests of single advertising messages, provided samples are reliable and representative of target audiences.

If the *Look* findings can be upheld, it would put a definite dollar value on creativity. Good ads deliver the same reach and frequency as bad ones,

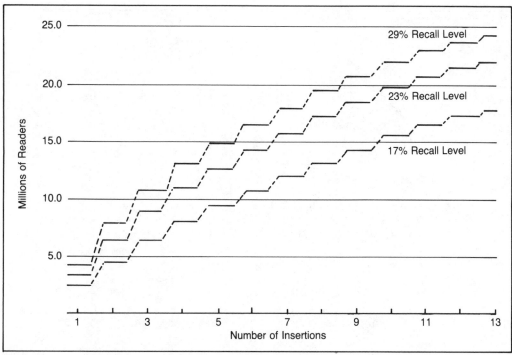

Fig. 11–7 *Cumulation of Advertising Impressions.* Look *Magazine, "Reach and* Frequency," *Communication Report No. 4 (1964), p. 11.*

but with smaller budgets. This conjecture can only become fact when the exact values are verified.

MESSAGE SPACING

Every media plan ends up with a schedule, a designation of when advertising messages will be run. These messages can be spaced regularly over time or transmitted in bursts. Between these two basic patterns a large number of variations are possible.

Conventional wisdom expresses a strong preference for a continuous schedule. Information on spacing effects, however, is sparse, and the theoretical justification for a continuous schedule rests mainly on an old study reported by Hubert Zielske in 1959.[16]

This study compared two direct mail schedules, one of thirteen consecutive weeks and the other of thirteen mailings conducted at four-week intervals. The criterion used to judge each schedule was advertising recall. Figure 11–8 illustrates graphically the main results of the study.

The study indicated that weekly mailings achieved greater awareness, but were rapidly forgotten once the mailings stopped. Monthly advertise-

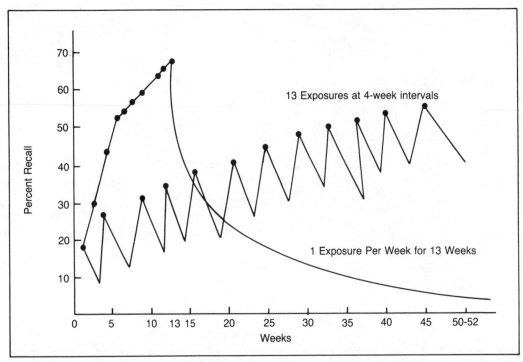

Fig. 11–8 *Recall with Different Spacings. Hubert Zielske, "The Remembering and Forgetting of Advertising,"* Journal of Marketing *(January 1959), pp. 239–243; 468.*

ments built recall continuously throughout the campaign, and it took longer to forget the advertisements when mailings ceased. The total amount of "recall weeks," calculated as the number of weeks multiplied by the appropriate recall rate, was greater for the monthly schedule.[17] These data were widely interpreted as supporting continuous spacing rather than advertising in "waves."

But there are grounds for questioning this interpretation. The recall level at any point in time depends upon two memory functions, learning and forgetting. Learning which has decayed is called forgetting. For recall to increase, more people must learn than forget. But rates of learning and forgetting change over the course of a campaign. Nor can an even pattern of advertising produce at all times an exact balance between memory gain and recall loss. Under such circumstances, a variable media pattern may be more conducive to a sustained level of high recall.[18]

Practicalities also impinge on the media schedule. For any product a range of conditions may exist which dictate a "wave strategy," often called "flighting." A seasonal sales curve would accord with an intermittent advertising schedule. A budget deemed inadequate for advertising on a

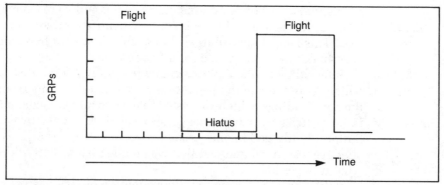

Fig. 11—9 *Illustration of Flighting.*

continuous basis might adopt flighting as a feasible alternative. Figure 11—9 depicts a "wave" schedule.

The peak advertising periods, called flights, are separated by low advertising periods, referred to as hiatuses. When sales fluctuate seasonally, peak periods normally precede the heavy selling season. In other instances, the schedule seeks to build a strong impact during the advertising flights and to begin again before the effect deteriorates too much.

LENGTH OF A CAMPAIGN

Since advertisers run series of repetitive messages, a vital question becomes: How long should a campaign be? This question is related to one of optimal frequency. If the optimum were known, then advertisements should logically change when that point has been reached.

But the optimum is not known. There are no reach-frequency estimations for messages. The question of campaign length is instead thought of as a replacement problem. Advertisements are perceived as wearing out, like light bulbs, and the issue boils down to one of when they should be replaced.

Research on advertising wearout has been confined solely to television. It has evaluated commercials according to three basic measures: attention, memorability, attitudes.

Attention measurements have been wholly laboratory tests. One set of experiments, conducted by Grass and Wallace, found attention waning after the second exposure of the same commercial.[19] The biggest objection to these tests is that they are done under artificial conditions and may not necessarily reflect behavior with real audiences.

A few studies used recall to evaluate wearout.[20] In 1971, Benton & Bowles published results of retesting eighty-one commercials from two to thirteen months apart using a day-after recall method. Only negligible declines were recorded in recall scores during the first three months, but substantial ones appeared nine months later and were from 33 percent to 50 percent. The study, however, did not control for frequency of transmission. This lack of control in effect equates time with frequency, and supposes a constant decay rate for all commercials.

Interestingly, the Benton & Bowles study found that commercials which scored low at the beginning wore out faster. This result paralleled the *Look* findings, which suggested that a poor advertisement never makes it, no matter how many times it is repeated. As argued by Greenberg and Suttoni, "only good commercials wear out. If wearout means a loss in effectiveness, a commercial that was ineffective to start with cannot lose what it never had."[21]

Attitudes do not seem to follow attention or recall. Grass and Wallace, testing corporate image commercials, disclosed a pattern of declining recall scores and steady attitude ratings.[22] This accords with many psychological studies which, while linking attitudes with cognition, have failed to find consistent and unequivocal results.[23] The subject becomes even more muddled by psychologists who contend that wearout reflects not merely "passive forgetting" but "active information processing." This view asserts that wearout occurs in spite of advertising repetition because of people's internal thought processes.[24]

The sum of all studies, theories, and speculations leave many unresolved issues pertaining to wearout. A major issue is the establishment of some correlation between evaluative measurements and behavior. If none exists, then why bother with attention or recall or attitude change? To do so in effect uses these variables as a surrogate for sales. And if information processing theories are correct, the key variables of media planning become external ones.

SUMMARY

The bulk of advertising expenditures is spent in media. The objective of a media plan is to reach prospective customers effectively and efficiently.

Media planning entails four functions: media selection, negotiation, logistics, and evaluation. Most media plans go from the top down, since planners work from fixed sum budgets. There are two basic decisions in every media plan: (1) how to allocate the budget among different media types, and (2) how to allocate expenditures among particular carriers within each media type.

The first decision involves a media mix. Practically all large budget brands use a multimedia plan.

Regardless of mix, expenditures must be allocated geographically. There are basically three ways by which this is done; national media only, a market-by-market approach, a combination of a national and individual market schedule.

Audience is the most important single factor in media selection. There are three main criteria on which audiences are evaluated: cost efficiency, market value, patterns formed by vehicle combinations.

The most popular method of evaluating audience on cost efficiency is the so-called cost-per-thousand method. Judging the market value of audiences is commonly done by demographic matching. Direct product usage and life style are other alternatives. Audience patterns formed by media combinations encompass concepts of gross audience, reach, and frequency.

Reach-frequency concepts raise the question of how much an exposure is worth. But exposure to what? Industry statistics refer to exposures to the medium rather than to the message.

The media plan must also deal with message spacing and campaign length. Messages can be spaced at regular intervals or in "waves." The advertising campaign, it is thought, should run as long as messages remain effective and do not wear out. But there is no agreement on how long it takes advertisements to wear out or how to measure wearout effects.

Questions for Chapter 11

1. What are the advantages and disadvantages of an advertiser drawing up its own media plan rather than using an advertising agency?

2. How is the media plan monitored? What problems must be overcome for proper evaluation?

3. What benefits can a firm obtain from a media mix as compared to a single medium?

4. What assumptions are made when copy decisions come before media decisions?

5. What advantages would occur from combining national media with a market-by-market approach?

6. What assumptions are made when making intramedia comparisons on a cost-per-thousand basis? Intermedia comparisons?

7. A home computer manufacturer plans on using spot television, with gross rating points as the criterion for media selection. Comment on the choice.

8. A state tourist agency selects magazines by matching audience demographics with demographics of visitors. Discuss this methodology for media selection.

9. As a measurement of lifestyle, how does PRIZM differ from one which groups people in accordance with beliefs, attitudes and values?

10. An agency recommends a tv schedule with a four-week cume of 60% and an average frequency of 2.4. What other things would you consider if you were the advertising manager receiving this recommendation?

11. Under what conditions might "flighting" be a viable schedule for television?

Footnotes for Chapter 11

[1]Donald W. Jugenheimer and Peter B. Turk, *Advertising Media* (Columbus, Ohio: Grid Publishing, 1980), pp. 7, 11; Herbert Zeltner, "How to Write and Recognize A Good Media Plan," *Advertising Age* (September 26, 1977), p. 59.

[2]Arnold M. Barban et al., *Essentials of Media Planning* (Chicago: Crain Books, 1976), p. 74.

[3]See Jack Z. Sissors and Reynold E. Petray, *Advertising Media Planning* (Chicago: Crain Books, 1976), pp. 29–33.

[4]Derived from tape of U.S. Dept. of Commerce, *Census of Travel, 1977.*

[5]Henry Assael and Hugh Cannon, "Do Demographics Help in Media Selection?" *Journal of Advertising Research* (December 1979), pp. 7–11.

[6]Thomas P. Hustad and Edgar A. Pessemeier, "The Development and Application of Psychographic Life Style and Associated Activities and Attitude Measures," *Life Style and Psychographics*, William D. Wells, ed. (New York: American Marketing Association, 1979), p. 50.

[7]Sachs and Benson, pp. 44–48.

[8]"New in Media," *Marketing & Media Decisions* (November 1980), pp. 32–33; Claritas Corporation, "PRIZM," (1980).

[9]Sissors and Petray, *Advertising Media Planning*, p. 161.

[10]Don E. Schultz, "Media Research Users Want," *Journal of Advertising Research* (December 1979), pp. 13–17.

[11]Herbert E. Krugman, "Why Three Exposures May Be Enough," *Journal of Advertising Research* (December 1972), pp. 11–14.

[12]Robert C. Grass, "Satiation Effects of Advertising," Advertising Research Foundation, *14th Annual Conference Proceedings* (1968).

[13]Colin McDonald, "What is the Short-Term Effect of Advertising?" Marketing Science Institute, *Special Report No. 71-142* (February 1971).

[14]Naples, pp. 63–64; Don Evanson, "Estimating a Product's Optimum Media Investment Based on Effective Frequency," *Marketing Review* (January/February 1981), p. 15.

[15]Look Magazine, "Reach and Frequency," *Communication Report No. 4* (1964).

[16]Hubert Zielske, "The Remembering and Forgetting of Advertising," *Journal of Marketing* (January 1959), pp. 239–243.

[17]Julian Simon, "What do Zielske's Data Really Mean?" *Journal of Marketing Research* (August 1979), p. 418; also see Hubert A. Zielske and Walter A. Henry, "Remembering and Forgetting Television Ads," *Journal of Advertising Research* (April 1980), pp. 7–13.

[18]William Katz, "A Sliding Schedule of Advertising Weight," *Journal of Advertising Research* (August 1980), pp. 39–44.

[19]Robert C. Grass and Wallace H. Wallace, "Satiation Effects of TV Commercials," *Journal of Advertising Research* (September 1969), pp. 3–8.

[20]Valentine Appel, "The Reliability and Decay of Advertising Measurements," Speech to the National Industrial Conference Board, October 28, 1966; and "On Advertising Wearout," *Journal of Advertising Research* (February 1971), pp. 11–13.

[21]Allan Greenberg and Charles Suttoni, "Television Commercial Wearout," *Journal of Advertising Research* (October 1973), pp. 47–54.

[22]Grass and Wallace, "Satiation Effects" p. 6; also see M. L. Raymond and A. G. Sawyer, "Repetition in Media Models: A Laboratory Technique," *Journal of Marketing Research* (February 1971), pp. 26–27.

[23]See Sawyer and Ward, pp. 94–108.

[24]Bobley J. Calder and Brian Sternthanl, "Television Commercial Wearout: An Information Processing View," *Journal of Marketing Research* (May 1980), pp. 173–186.

**PART
FIVE**

GENERAL ADVERTISING
IN NATIONAL MEDIA

12 *Television Advertising*

Since television is capable of reaching into almost every home in America, it has emerged as the dominant medium of national advertisers. Firms producing consumer goods for mass markets have become particularly dependent upon television to convey their messages to the consuming public.

But the electronic media are not homogeneous as carriers of advertising. In addition, the emergence of new communication forms, though still in their infancy, alludes to greater diversity in the years ahead.

This chapter, dealing primarily with consumer product advertising on television, highlights:

- **Uses of television by various types of marketers**
- **Rate structures and audience patterns in network and spot television**
- **Buying practices by users of both network and spot television**
- **Advertiser problems with commercial "clutter" on television airwaves**
- **Technical developments in communications and emerging new uses of electronic media**

THE SCOPE OF TELEVISION

Of the nation's more than 81 million households, some 90 percent possess a television set, and more than half own two or more. Americans spend more time in front of a television set than in any other activity save working and sleeping. According to the Television Bureau of Advertising, the average American household ran its television sets more than six-and-a-half hours per day in 1981. Women did the most viewing, averaging four hours and forty-seven minutes daily from October to May, which is the height of the television season. Adult males had an average of slightly better than four hours a day.

Because television engages large numbers of people, it commands the largest share of national advertising expenditures. Table 12–1 shows the percentages going into the various media.

The preeminence of television as the vehicle of mass marketers is underscored by its 37 percent share of national advertising. The amount of dollars spent on television advertising is more than two-and-and-half times that expended on magazines, the second largest recipient of accounts payable for general advertising. The miscellaneous category, though a fourth of the total, is composed of a hodgepodge of different media types.

TABLE 12–1 *Percentage of Advertising Expenditures by Media in 1981*

	Percent of Expenditures	
	National Advertising (Percent)	Total Advertising (Percent)
Television	37	24
Magazines	14	7
Newspapers	11	33
Business Papers	7	4
Radio	4	8
Outdoor	2	1
Farm Publications	—	—
Miscellaneous 25	23	
Total	100	100

Source: From data for *Advertising Age* prepared by Robert J. Coen of McCann-Erickson.
Note: The above estimates exclude direct mail because it is not apportioned between national and local.

The second column in Table 12–1 added some $27 billion of retail advertising to national advertising, and repercentaged media receipts based on total advertising. This way of looking at advertising activity indicates the strong local influences on newspapers and radio, the proportions of which move up smartly. But even then, television still garners almost one-fourth of all advertising expenditures in media.

The transmission of sight and sound is accomplished by sending video by an AM signal and audio by an FM signal. Some 757 commercial television stations beam these signals across the nation. The biggest segment of this total, 519, are "very high frequency" (VHF), the signals of which can be picked up by channels two to thirteen. Another group of commercial television stations, 238 in number, operate through the newer "ultra high frequency" (UHF), which has a more limited signal range.[1]

General advertisers, however, classify television as either network or spot. A network is comprised of a station lineup which transmits a program simultaneously to the entire nation, or at least to areas in certain time zones. Each of the three major networks has roughly 200 or more stations on its national hookup. Spot advertising is defined as a media schedule put together on a market-by-market basis, having been negotiated directly with individual stations or their representatives.

NETWORK ADVERTISING

Network television more than any other medium can lay claim to having truly mass dimensions with respect to its audiences. According to the A. C. Nielsen Company, a typical program on prime time reaches approximately 14 million households.[2] The average American adult watches prime time, a period in which networks dominate the scene, eight-and-a-half hours a week, with about twenty percent at double the national viewing average.[3] Because networks deliver these huge audiences, they have taken the lion's share of national advertising. For the past several years, about 60 percent of national advertising flowing into television have accrued to the networks. National advertisers in 1981 spent roughly $5.6 billion for advertising on coast-to-coast hookups.[4]

One of the many advantages which networks offer advertisers is that it is only necessary to deal with one representative instead of with many individual stations. But a large advertising budget is required to avail oneself of this opportunity. The basic price of running a commercial on a network is the sum of all station costs, modified by market factors. An advertiser has an option of not taking all stations in a lineup. But the reduction in costs is less than proportionate to the elimination of stations. For all intents and purposes, advertising on network television is an all-or-nothing proposition. Consequently, the medium attracts the largest advertisers, or the big budget brands.

Large advertisers dominate most media in terms of spending. But their inordinate share of media expenditures is especially marked in network television, which in 1981 was used by an average of about 565 firms. Yet the one hundred leading national advertisers, or 18 percent of the total television users, account for 76 percent of all national advertising.[5] And among the top 100, 25 network users are credited with 60 percent of the total expenditures in the medium.[6] The one hundred largest national advertisers in 1982 accounted for 77 percent of all network time. These firms all produce goods and services which are mass marketed. In no other medium is advertising so heavily concentrated.

Table 12–2 lists the twenty-five largest advertisers on network television in 1981, together with the amount each spent in the medium.

Network Rate Structure

The most important determinant of network rates is audience: its size and characteristics. A mass audience by its nature cannot be highly selective, though viewers are not exactly proportionate to their numbers in the population. Older, less educated and lower income segments of the population do more television viewing than the average. But this bias does not detract much from the generalized characteristics of viewing. With certain exceptions, such as sporting events and children's shows on weekends, the networks deliver large, undifferentiated audiences.

Analyses of audience characteristics are concerned with broad, all-inclusive groupings, such as male-female, adults under 50, and over 50 years of age. The products advertised on the networks are primarily those which lend themselves to a mass, generalized approach to marketing. The more selective the target, the greater the waste. Advertising plans are often

TABLE 12–2 *Top Network Television Advertisers in 1981*

Rank	Company	Network TV Expenditure ($000,000)
1	Procter & Gamble	392.8
2	General Foods	238.1
3	General Motors	146.9
4	American Home Products	131.4
5	Ford Motor Company	113.9
6	Bristol Myers	109.9
7	Philip Morris	99.5
8	Johnson & Johnson	97.8
9	Lever Brothers	95.0
10	Sears, Roebuck	86.8
11	General Mills	86.3
12	Warner-Lambert	76.8
13	Gillette	76.4
14	Anheuser-Busch	73.5
15	A.T. & T.	68.9
16	PepsiCo	68.7
17	Richardson-Vicks	67.6
18	Kellogg	67.2
19	Ralston Purina	66.7
20	Coca Cola	61.0
21	Pillsbury	59.1
22	Sterling Drug	55.4
23	Chrysler	54.9
24	Beecham Group	54.8
25	McDonalds	54.1

Source: Television Bureau of Advertising, *Report 82-28* (1982), p. 10.

self-contradictory when they devote much time and effort to delineating market segments and recommend their main advertising thrust in network television, which seeks audiences from every segment of the population.

Audience measurements come in the form of ratings. These statistics, based on a panel of homes hooked up with audimeters, are reported for each telecast by the A. C. Nielsen Company. The audimeter is an electronic device attached to a television set, and it makes a minute-by-minute recording of the channels to which the set is tuned. A program rating is the percentage of panel homes tuned to a program. These proportions are commonly projected to all U.S. homes in order to calculate media values as coverage and cost-per-thousand audience. Audience characteristics are derived from another Nielsen panel which keeps diaries, the data of which are forced into reconciliation with audimeter home-tuning information.

TABLE 12–3 *TV Viewing Patterns by Daypart and Month*

Month	Mon-Fri 11:00 am-4:30 pm		Mon-Fri 4:30 pm-7:30 pm		Mon-Sun 8:00 pm-11:00 pm		Mon-Fri 11:30 pm-1:00 am	
	Percent	Index	Percent	Index	Percent	Index	Percent	Index
July	26	96	36	82	49	83	45	96
Aug.	27	100	37	84	51	86	44	94
Sept.	25	93	40	91	59	100	46	98
Oct.	25	93	44	100	61	103	47	100
Nov.	27	100	48	109	62	105	48	102
Dec.	25	93	49	111	62	105	49	104
Jan.	30	111	52	118	65	110	49	104
Feb.	30	111	51	116	66	112	50	106
Mar.	28	104	49	111	64	108	48	102
Apr.	27	100	45	102	61	103	46	98
May	24	89	40	91	56	95	47	100
June	25	93	38	86	52	88	47	100
Year Average	27	100	44	100	59	100	47	100

Source: Grey Advertising, Inc., *Pocket Media Modules 1981*, pp. 10–11.
Note: Average monthly estimates cover July 1979 to June 1980. The July 1980 to June 1981 figures show a highly similar pattern.

Ratings vary with time of day and time of year. Table 12–3 shows television usage for selected day parts for different months throughout the year, beginning with July 1979, and ending with June 1980. The same patterns hold for other years, which allows conclusions to be generalized.

In every month, audience builds up throughout the day and reaches its peak in prime time, from 8pm to 11pm, eastern standard time. Since the three major networks—ABC, CBS, and NBC—account for almost 90 percent of all prime time viewing, their ratings will also reach their zenith from eight to eleven in the evening. The three network share of Monday to Friday daytime audience is estimated at about 75 percent of all homes using television.[7] This would yield an average network rating for daytime shows of about 6.7, about 40 percent of the prime time average.

Within any daypart, individual programs will fluctuate in accordance with a show's ability to attract "homes using television" (HUT). The higher the share of HUT, the higher a program's rating, and the higher the price it can command.

As evident from Table 12–3, audience levels display strong seasonal variations, with the high point coming in the winter months and the low point in the summer. The largest swings take place in early fringe and prime time, which are most affected by changes in daylight and in the amount of outdoor activity. When people are at home, a large proportion turn on their television sets as though by rote, perhaps because they have nothing better to do with their time. Viewing is more a function of competing activities than it is of program content.[8] The best shows in summer will not cause people to rush home, or go indoors, in order to watch them. And the good programs in winter do not increase total viewers; they simply get a larger share of the already existing audience who flick on their sets to be entertained.

Advertising rates invariably follow viewing patterns. Estimated network rates for different dayparts and times of year are presented in Table 12–4. The standard unit for which prices are shown is the 30-second commercial, which makes up about 85 percent of all commercial messages appearing on television.

Advertising schedules expectedly bear the highest price tags in prime time and the lowest in daytime, paralleling the flow of audience. The standard 30-second commercial costs about $65,000 in prime time for an average network show in 1981. Network list prices in 1982, which are asking prices, ranged from $70,000 to $175,000. Actual prices are much lower than network listings. Average prices for 1982 were about $75,000. Running a commercial on prime time costs about seven times as much as commercials run during the day. Fringe time costs are somewhere in between the two extremes, depending upon particular program ratings. Yearly average costs for 1982 were estimated as $11,300 for daytime, $9,000 for early morning, $13,800 for late night, and $10,400 for weekend children's programs.[9]

The table of advertising rates indicates that costs rise disproportionately higher than ratings. This is reflected in the fact that CPMs on a household basis are positively related to audience. The higher the ratings, the higher the CPMs, but not at the same percentage increase.

But network ratings, it can be argued, are based on household tuning data. Prime time, for example, having more viewers per household, would incur the biggest drop in CPM when calculated on the basis of viewers, not households. Were the CPM figures recalculated in this manner, their positive relationship with the number of viewers would still remain. The premium for a high rating would not be as pronounced. But the marketer still must pay a surcharge for broad coverage.

Costs throughout the year move up and down with the undulating audience tides. Prices are highest in the fall season and lowest in July and August. But demand and supply influences also make themselves felt. Network prices decline in the post-Christmas season despite the peak in viewing levels. Spring brings higher costs along with rising temperatures as more marketers seek commercial time for their promotions and sales pushes.

TABLE 12–4 Network Advertising Rates by Daypart and Season

Daypart	Jan.-Mar. '81 Cost/30 $(M)	HH CPM $	Apr.-June '81 Cost/30 $(M)	HH CPM $	July-Aug. '81 Cost/30 $(M)	HH CPM $	Sept.-Dec. '81 Cost/30 $(M)	HH CPM $	Year Average Cost/30 $(M)	HH CPM $
1. Daytime (Mon.-Fri.)	8.2	1.50	10.2	2.05	9.1	1.80	9.5	1.90	9.3	1.82
2. Prime time (Sun.-Sat.)	58.6	3.90	68.4	5.20	48.6	4.70	75.0	5.10	64.9	4.80
3. Fringe time										
CBS Morning News	2.5	1.07	3.0	1.33	2.0	1.22	3.5	1.80	2.9	1.40
Today Show	6.6	1.60	8.8	2.26	5.9	1.85	9.0	2.41	7.8	2.08
Good Morning America	8.9	2.05	9.5	2.19	6.9	2.45	10.9	3.10	9.4	2.50
News	25.1	2.20	34.1	3.45	23.2	2.95	32.2	3.00	29.4	2.95
Tonight Show	26.0	4.58	33.0	6.24	29.0	5.33	32.0	5.88	30.3	5.56
ABC/CBS Late Night										
Tomorrow	12.0	3.15	15.9	4.45	14.1	3.95	18.8	4.75	15.6	4.14
4. Weekend Children's Programs	5.8	1.25	8.6	2.25	6.0	1.85	11.3	2.70	8.4	2.08

Source: Grey Advertising, Inc., *Pocket Media Modules 1981*, p. 15.

Network Buying Practices

Most network time is purchased on a participating or scatter basis. A format of this kind is often referred to as "the magazine concept." As in magazines, commercial messages of many different advertisers share the identical editorial environment. The same telecast, like a magazine issue, might carry advertisements of directly competitive products. Advertisers are no longer associated with particular shows. The end result for the buyer is a schedule of commercial announcements on many different programs, and for the big television spenders, on all three major networks.

The larger the number of different programs in a schedule, the less the likelihood that an advertiser will fall short of audience expectancies or media objectives. The bad and good programs should average out, and wider selections have higher probabilities of overall ratings settling near the average of all ratings. There is a safety factor in numbers. This is the main reason why networks are willing to give CPM guarantees, particularly to their best customers. If the CPM exceeds the guarantee by a certain amount, the network makes up for the shortfall by running extra announcements.

Company sponsorship of prime time shows, popular in the 1950s and 1960s, has completely passed from the scene. The unbroken spiral of production costs, with its attendant risks, has left the show business to the networks and independent producers. Even the largest companies find it imprudent to tie up millions of dollars in an activity that is peripheral to their main lines of business. Program sponsorship today for network prime time is confined mainly to specials.

Although networks issue rate cards, the printed price lists are widely disregarded. Rather, they are talking points. They are references from which negotiations begin.

Contract discussions for the fall season commence in early spring, when major advertisers are allowed to preview pilot episodes of network offerings. Firms which get into the bidding at this early stage are said to be practicing "upfront buying." They take action at the earliest possible moment in time, and are therefore pursuing a speculative approach to transactions. The task can be accomplished in one of two ways, participation in selected programs, or purchase of a predetermined scatter plan.

The participation buy calls for negotiating with each network for spots on individual programs. Costs per audience unit normally run higher because the best programs are in the greatest demand by buyers. This sort of competitive bidding, which resembles that of open commodity markets, tends to nudge prices upward in the preseason rush for the better shows, which are limited in number.

Advertisers taking the up-front buying route must also make forecasts of program ratings six months hence, so as to maximize delivered audiences per dollar expended. Over the years, many models for predicting ratings have been developed, some of which have been made public.[10] Most of these models and predictive systems are regarded as proprietary information, and guarded as trade secrets. Several models have emphasized program content, supposing that program type and quality form the critical predictive elements. But most systems have used some kind of regression or time series analysis, which makes the implicit assumption that the best predictor of future behavior is past behavior.

This author has made successful predictions by employing the concept of a sum zero game. If homes using television (HUT) varies by time of year, regardless of program quality, then the networks divide among themselves a fixed number of viewers which can be accurately forecast in advance. When a program gains share, one or both of its competitors must lose. Hence, game theory can serve as a useful concept to assist negotiations of program participation contracts.

Nevertheless, advertisers making commitments long in advance should always push for rating guarantees. These guarantees have become all the more compelling in recent years because of networks' more frequent resort to "flexible scheduling," popularly known as stunting. In almost every week of the tv season there appears a new mini-series, a blockbuster movie, a big sports event, or a highly-promoted special. In their intense struggle for audience, networks constantly discard their lower-rated shows and alter their line-ups. In the process, regularly-scheduled shows get preempted, and when they reappear they do so in a radically altered environment. Or they may be rescheduled on a different day. Even if assigned their old slots, they may encounter a different lead-in and a completely new bunch of competitive programs. The churning and twisting of network schedules render forecasts less certain and buying more risky. The guaranteed rating shifts risks backward onto sellers. It acts as an inducement to buy in advance risk-free.

The scatter plan entails the sale of a fixed number of announcements on a set of programs. The package usually contains many different programs, with only a few spots on any particular show during the course of the advertising campaign. Because it has less control over advertisement placement, the firm buying a scatter plan usually insists on a guaranteed ratings level. The advantage of the scatter plan is its wide market coverage, or audience reach.[11] However, the participation buy can achieve the same result as the scatter plan when companies rotate their various brands among the numerous programs in which they participate.

In contrast to up-front buying is the so-called opportunistic buy. Here the buyer follows a policy of transactional postponement, waiting until the last possible moment to make network purchases.

Firms with large television budgets alter their media purchase allocations between speculation and postponement. The most preferable alternative depends upon the firm's assessment of the market. If demand is strong, up-front buying will prevail. A waiting game may shut out the firm completely, at least for the most desirable programs. But if the advertiser visualizes a bearish market, it pays to postpone purchases until the networks break price. The amount of time available for sale is fixed and cannot be stored and held for the future. An unsold minute is revenue lost forever. The closer these unsold availabilities come to actual air time, the more precipitously their prices drop. A buyer's market allows an advertiser practicing postponement to pick up bargains and come away with more audience for every dollar outlay.

SPOT TELEVISION

Spot television means advertising in local markets. All nonnetwork advertising is spot, and advertisers must negotiate for local time with individual stations or their representatives.

There are slightly more than 200 spot markets in the United States. To avoid overlapping market boundaries, Arbitron, a leading supplier of station audience statistics, developed the ADI concept, an acronym for "area of dominant influence." According to the ADI definition, each market consists of all counties in which home stations receive the major share of viewing. This system makes all markets mutually exclusive entities.

The distribution of advertising revenue bears a strong affinity to market size. The top five markets average seven television stations per market and contain about 23 percent of all U.S. television homes. Smaller markets have less stations. An advertiser running spots in the top 50 spot markets has the potential of reaching two-thirds of all households in the nation. The largest 100 markets command some 85 percent of all advertising expenditures earmarked for spot television.

There are three main classes of advertisers using spot television: the purely local advertiser, the company with no network schedule, and the marketer running commercials on network television.

The local advertiser usually sells goods or services at retail. About 48 percent of all nonnetwork revenue comes from local advertisers. When television accommodates local advertising, it usually does so in conjunction with other local media, such as newspapers and radio. Nor is television in most instances the dominant element in the media mix.

There are various types of companies which use spot as their only television advertising. Many have limited or spotty distribution, which makes advertising in nationwide media vehicles inefficient or impractical. Other firms may find networks too expensive, and so stretch their advertising appropriations by cultivating the most promising individual markets. Many such marketers may also try augmenting their national print campaigns with television advertising in selected markets, especially at times of special promotions or events.

Spot television for these multi-media advertisers are a substitutable form of promotion. When spot prices rise and market demand for television availabilities runs strong, advertisers can shift a portion of their budgets into print or radio. If market demand falters and stations run "distressed merchandise" sales, funds tend to flow out of other media to the attractive offers.

The third type of firm is the dual user of network and spot television. Typically, this category encompasses the largest advertisers who seek to supplement their schedules on national hookups with more intense coverage in selected markets. The most important markets for national advertisers are usually the largest, and it is common for selection to begin with the major areas and go down the list until the budget is exhausted. Table 12–5 shows the top twenty-five spot advertisers, and the relative importance of spot as compared with network television.

TABLE 12–5 *Top Spot Television Advertisers in 1980*

Rank	Company	Spot Tv Expenditures ($000,000)	Spot Tv as a Percent of Total Tv
1	Procter & Gamble	125.2	26
2	General Foods	76.9	28
3	McDonalds	66.6	55
4	General Mills	61.1	45
5	PepsiCo	55.6	38
6	A.T. & T.	48.3	46
7	Coca Cola	44.1	43
8	Lever Brothers	34.8	32
9	American Home Products	33.4	21
10	Mobil	30.8	78
11	Dart & Kraft	30.4	39
12	Toyota	30.4	57
13	Pillsbury	30.2	36
14	A. H. Robins	28.9	100
15	Ford	28.1	18
16	Time	27.5	78
17	Mars	27.3	43
18	I. T. & T.	26.9	60
19	Nesfood	22.8	39
20	Revlon	21.7	46
21	Philip Morris	21.6	18
22	Anheuser-Busch	21.5	25
23	Coigate Palmolive	21.4	35
24	Warner Lambert	21.3	25
25	Consolidated Foods	20.0	32

Source: Television Bureau of Advertising, *Report 82-28*, pp. 10–12.
Note: Spot expenditures were adjusted to approximate the level of FCC dollars in the 75 markets.
Investments classified as "retail/local" are included in the spot estimates.

Advertising on "national spot" is not a perfect substitute for advertising on networks. But some purchasing takes place at the margin, causing resources to shift between network and spot television with changes in relative prices. Since affiliated and network-owned stations carry more than four-fifths of all spot advertising, events in network time sales affect those in spot markets. Both local and spot-only advertisers cannot escape the pervasive influences of network television. For example, a shift of funds from networks increases competition between local and national spot advertisers over availabilities.

Spot Television Rate Structure

Pricing practices in spot television presents many more variations than those of network television. This makes for media selection and schedule negotiation a more complicated affair. Every market within the set of possible alternatives must be investigated, examined, and analyzed. The job can be long and tedious, depending upon the number of markets being considered. Although station representatives handle national spot business, buyers have to conduct dealings with several agents.

Television stations have their own pricing policies and discount structures. Most stations, however, offer dollar volume discounts which are cumulative. A firm which exceeds the volume of advertising contracted for will be charged the lower rate. On the other hand, a failure to meet discount levels results in the customer being short-rated. But the larger volume has no relation to any lower cost of rendering the service. The lower rates for big customers are in effect patronage discounts—they are given to maintain customer attachments and to solicit more business. Advertisers should keep track of expenditures so as to take maximum advantage of discount levels.

Stations carry commercials both within programs and between programs, called adjacencies. Network affiliates are precluded from selling time on network-originated shows, except in the event of an unsold slot. They therefore schedule spot commercials at station breaks when transmitting network programing. Since affiliates devote about two-thirds of their broadcast day to network feeds, the bulk of their advertising sales cover adjacencies.

Spot participations are confined to nonnetwork programing, the main fare of which consists of syndicated series, motion picture packages, and locally-originated programs. Commercial television stations, including independents, spend more than $500 million each year for syndicated programs and movie features. These shows bring into the stations about $2 billion in gross revenue. The commercial stations in the top twenty-five markets, numbering 158, account for 64 percent of all expenditures for syndicated programing.[12]

As in network, prices for spot television are largely determined by program ratings. Audience measurements for local markets are made by

Arbitron and A. C. Nielsen. Both companies do sample surveys, asking consumers to keep diaries for one week and to record viewing in their households for each quarter hour.

Most markets are rated on the basis of these diaries. But the largest markets have their audiences measured by electronic meters attached to television sets in sampled homes, and the numbers keep expanding. Arbitron, for example, plans to monitor from twelve to fourteen markets in 1985 by a combination of meter and diary. The meters indicate household tuning levels for both individual stations and total television usage. The diaries yield data on viewing and demographics, which are then made to conform with metered data.

Station rates vary with time of day, which in turn corresponds with audience levels. The dayparts are often classified by letters, such as A,B,C,D, going from the highest to the lowest viewing period. Prime time, which has the biggest audience, is the most expensive. Fringe time is less costly. Day and late night programs have the lowest ratings and are therefore the least expensive.

Another determinant of station rates is firmness of the commitment. Preemptible positions carry huge discounts, sometimes by as much as 50 percent. The dollars-off amounts are graded by the time of prior notice that must be given for preemption. Periods run from two weeks to one week to none at all. The shorter the notice, the less the cost.

The majority of national spot advertisers regard preemptible spots as risky. A buyer that wants assurance of a specific advertising weight is forced into fixed positions. These are guaranteed, but carry the highest prices. A strong demand for station time causes fixed position buying to rise sharply. The pre-Christmas season is usually one in which stations may find it difficult to provide alternative spots for those which are preempted. Consequently, advertisers must weigh the advantages of definite schedules against the higher costs for such guarantees.

In periods of weak advertising activity, guaranteed positions are of small advantage, except for the most highly-rated shows. Low demand for television time encourages companies to veer to purchasing availabilities subject to preemption. This situation permits companies with free funds to overbid on preemptibles, especially in prime time. This higher bid "bumps" the first purchaser, but preemptibles still provide a more efficient buy than what would have been obtained under the fixed position contract. An unsuccessful bidder would still be able to find an adequate substitute in a slack period, though perhaps it would mean giving up some efficiency.

Stations also offer a wide variety of package deals which have proved popular with media users. Several stations in busy markets have replaced individual spot selections by rotation plans, in effect treating television like a public utility wherein users share time. But many stations offer these schedules even when they are not mandatory. Rotation packages require each advertiser to rotate commercials among a given set of availabilities, with no substitutions. This practice extends equitable treatment to all customers of a television station.

There are two types of rotation plans, horizontal and vertical. The former refers to rotating a commercial on the same program, but on different days each week. The horizontal rotations are common in stripped programs, such as soap operas, afternoon movies, and game shows. Vertical rotations transmit commercials on different programs, but within the same time block. Both of these plans expand media reach for an advertising schedule and at the same time even out the availabilities of the station.

Bartering for Time

Another form of spot buying is barter syndication, in which the station trades time for programing. This type of transaction received great impetus from the prime time access rule adopted by the Federal Communication Commission in 1971.[13] The networks were required to reduce programing in prime time for the purpose of encouraging local stations to develop new programing formats. This never happened. Instead of greater program diversification and more varied art forms, the result was a downgrading in quality. Stations avidly sought low cost-high profit programs to fill the empty time, and were willing to accept programs developed by advertisers in return for commercial time, usually from a half to two-thirds of the available positions. Advertisers able to provide acceptable programs gain good time periods in markets important to them, and at per-market costs which are less than those of full sponsorship on a network lineup.

There are other bartering practices which are not quite as straightforward. One of them is the tie-in arrangement pushed by large advertising agencies. This system works as follows: An agency buys a program and then syndicates it to stations. The program is not paid for in cash but in future air time. The accounts payable is entered into a "time bank," usually a computer, from which the agency sells availabilities to its clients.

The agency offerings undoubtedly appeal to many stations which prefer to pay for their programs with inventory rather than hard cash. By foregoing monetary payment, agencies acquire commercial time for less than the going rate. In turn, they pass on part of the discount to their clients. In theory at least, all parties to the transaction find some advantages.

But many in the industry have roundly denounced tie-ins as unethical. They point out that full-time syndicators pick up the best shows, leaving the dregs for the agencies. Since 60 percent of national spot placements are controlled by 15 firms, a large agency has substantial market power. Nor are such firms, critics say, averse to rewarding stations which accept their programs and to witholding business from stations which do not.[14]

A more serious charge is that a time bank has no value unless it has customers. Consequently, agencies have a vested interest in unloading time on clients regardless of whether the spots meet marketing objectives. Agencies naturally deny these allegations. But they contain enough substance to make advertisers wary of barter practices, and to evaluate spot schedules in relation to built-in agency biases.

COMMERCIAL CLUTTER

A problem that haunts most advertising managers is the present tendency of stations to run clusters of commercials, known in the industry as "clutter." The bunching of commercials along with a growing amount of other nonprogram material is thought to diminish viewer attention and reduce the effectiveness of all advertising. In a recent survey of industry leaders, more than 70 percent characterized clutter as an "extremely bad" problem and likely to get worse.[15]

Many advertising and agency executives point to television promotions as the principal villain in the clutter drama. There is no denying that network and station promotions add to the already long strings of persuasive messages. But there are more basic forces at work.

A basic factor which has led to clutter is general inflation. By itself, price increases are neither beneficial nor harmful. But those of television time and talent have risen faster than the general price level. From 1975 to 1981 advertising costs in network television has jumped approximately 85 percent and in spot about 70 percent.[16] Costs per unit of time must consider growth in the number of households. Broadcasters have been delivering larger audiences. But even when audience size is taken into account, the cost of time units has exceeded the underlying rate of inflation. From 1976 to 1982 inclusive cost-per-thousand audience for evening network television experienced an annual increase of 14 percent, on the average. Comparable figures for daytime network and spot television were 13 percent and 9 percent respectively.[17]

As television prices spiraled, advertisers sought to keep their costs in line by reducing the length of their commercials. For most brands, larger budgets are the result of more revenue, not higher media costs. Packaged goods in particular, the mainstay of television advertising, find their growth tied to population trends. To contend with inexorable price advances for productive inputs, firms changed their advertising practices to stretch their advertising dollars. The standard 60-second commercial of the early 1960s became a 30-second message by the end of the decade. This in effect doubled the number of commercials in a given time span. Double, triple, and quadruple spotting became common as stations filled up their availabilities. Some advertisers have been considering 15-second and 20-second spots in place of the current 30's. It is possible by electronic means to speed up the voice pitch and accelerate the video. These time compressions, according to advocates of this technique, have little or no effect on viewers.[18] But such measures would only worsen the clutter situation.

Time standards for television stations are promulgated by the Code Authority of the National Association of Broadcasters. Not all stations, however, subscribe to the Authority's standards. According to the television code, billboards, promotional announcements, and credits of more than a certain length are combined with commercials as nonprogram material. The code was suspended in March 1982, pending an appeal of a federal court ruling that it violates antitrust law. Networks, however, have announced that they will not alter their standards. The limits which the code had set are as follows:[19]

Daypart	*Minutes per hour*
Network prime time	9.5–10.0
Nonnetwork prime time	14.0
Nonprime time	16.0
Weekend children's programs	9.5
Weekday children's programs	12.0

The amount of nonprogram material presented over the air waves continuously as a cluster also depends on the number of interruptions, defined as the "occurrence of nonprogram material within the main body of the program." The television code sets a limit of four per hour during prime time and children's weekend programs and eight in all other time segments. News, weather, sports and special events are exempt from interruption standards.

If stations were to abide by these maximums, nonprime time would have more interruptions. Prime time would have longer clusters of nonprogram material, but occurring less often. Consequently, the most expensive messages are highly vulnerable to dilution of advertising performance.

Exacerbating the cost push, and indirectly the clutter problem, is the intense competition within the broadcast industry. Network costs for original programing hit the $1 billion mark by the middle of the 1970s.[20] Today, they are well above this heady figure.

The struggle for market share by heavy outlays on programing leads to what economists call the "prisoner's dilemma." To get a bigger share of the business, a firm spends large sums on product development, in this case, on programing. Any excess profits from higher market share, attained by getting higher ratings, are dissipated by increased spending. The large expenses for producing new programs encourage, in fact mandate, huge budgets for publicity and promotion.

High ratings just don't happen. To attract audiences necessitates astute marketing. Each network spends better than $25 million a year to tout its program offerings. ABC, in 1977, spent $1 million to promote "Roots." NBC, in 1981, spent hundreds of thousands to sell the public on "Shogun," a lavishly produced film which cost the network approximately $21 million.[21] In turn, the promotion imperative increases the number of media announcements and adds to the existing commercial clutter.

THE NEW TELEVISION

Two major technical innovations, satellite broadcasting and computer technology, promise to change the shape of modern mass communication as we know it. Satellites eliminate distance as a cost factor in transmission of messages. Miniaturization in computers has expanded by many times the capacity to process, store and retrieve information. Hardware is already being produced enabling new forms of communications to come about, which some have dubbed "the new television."[22]

The most immediate effects of this new form of communication can be seen in cable television (CATV). Cable is actually an old system that was initially developed to provide reception in areas unable to pick up station signals. Later, CATV made its way into cities experiencing interference with television transmission. About 22 percent of television homes in 1981 were linked by approximately 4,300 operating systems, most of them small community affairs built since the mid-1960s.[23] But there are already several giants among the plethora of small companies, such as Teleprompter, American TV and Communications, Telecommunications, Inc., Warner Amex Cable, Cox Broadcasting, and Times Mirror Company. Each of these organizations, as of October 1980, served more than half a million subscribers. Teleprompter, the largest, had 1,300,000 participating households and Times Mirror, the smallest of the leaders, claimed 545,000 subscribers.[24]

The trend toward bigness in the cable industry has not been merely a matter of adding systems to a network or of increasing the number of subscribers. Satellite transmission has expanded channel capacity, and transformed CATV from a carrier of traditional telecasting into a viable alternative of the conventional forms. The Warner Qube system, for example, offers a thirty channel capacity, first run movies and sporting events, and the possibility of two-way communication using the television set.

One response to the enlargement of television channels has been the rise of cable networks which transmit diverse fares of many independent suppliers to nationally-linked audiences. Another has been the growth of super stations, such as WTBS-Atlanta and WGN-Chicago, which now have a means of appealing to audiences far beyond the contiguous area of their own signal.

But unlike conventional television networks, those of cable appeal to specialized audiences in much the same manner as magazines. WTBS anticipates a 24-hour news program with national distribution via cable. ABC Video Enterprises, a joint venture with Warner Amex, in 1981 launched ARTS on Satcom I, which features dance, opera, symphony, drama, jazz, painting, and poetry. The same year CBS cable began a network of pop culture, presumably to entice teenage and young adult audiences. Advertisers often get involved in programming for these new communication outlets, as in the early days of television. A USA "Sports Probe" was developed in conjunction with Backer and Spielvogel and Miller Brewing. Nearly all 160 advertisers on Modern Satellite Network entered the system with their own films and tapes.[25]

Another development is tele-text, originally created by the British Broadcasting System. Text material is digitally coded, carried over the air by telephone or cable, and decoded by a television set translator. News briefs, sports results, weather forecasts, and paid advertisements can appear as lines of moving type across a television screen.

Many publishers are currently experimenting with these systems, and some with interactive processes. Dow Jones & Company has long been supplying news-retrieval services to business customers by electronic devices. Knight-Ridder has developed viewdata, which permits viewers to keyboard requests for news, ads, consumer information such as movies and airline schedules. Gannett Company, the largest newspaper chain, New York Times Company and Times Mirror Company are all involved with cable-tv systems for possible integration with their news services.[26]

Pay television was given a great boost by satellite transmission, and has been expanding its market steadily. Although it carries no advertising, it competes with conventional television for viewing time. Households wired for pay cable-tv do substantially less viewing of network shows in prime time than the population in general.[27] Moreover, program options on the new pay-tv network have increased because more services or programs can be offered at the same time. For example, a cable system can carry offerings of two or more pay services simultaneously.[28]

Another development expected to alter contemporary viewing patterns is that of videocassette recorders (VCRs) and that of the newer videodiscs. So far, the principal use of VCRs has been to shift the time of viewing in accordance with individual predilections.[29]

The newer technologies to date have wrought only minor changes in the overall viewing behavior of the population. Network television has lost audience. But most of the loss has occurred in daytime, and is associated with the growing numbers of women who have joined the labor force. The move has taken them out of the home and into the office. The network share of prime time audience has eroded from a high of 92 percent to about 89 percent.[30] But this difference is not large enough to attribute to factors other than survey variations, let alone technical innovation.

The new technologies are still in their infancies, and their diffusion, like those of most major innovations, can be expected to proceed slowly. Cable television in 1981 was estimated as having 17 million subscribers. Future predictions are hazardous, but according to projections of Leibowitz, Donaldson, Lufkin and Jenrette, cable penetration should rise from the current 22 percent to 50 percent of households by 1990, with pay cable moving to about 40 percent.[31] The incidence of VCRs and videodiscs are expected to reach 30 percent of all U.S. households by the beginning of the next decade.

If these estimates of future trends prove anywhere near correct, then old and new technologies will exist side by side for many years. The face of the future cannot be known, though it is almost a certainty that modifications will take place. With the proliferation of channels offered by satellites, it seems reasonable to expect greater audience fragmentation. The alacrity of the events, however, must await their actual unfolding.

Advertising and the New Television

Although at least 20 cable networks are currently offering commercial time, some with CPMs comparable to those of conventional television, advertisers have been cautious. There has been no rush into cable. The reluctance to commit large sums to a relatively untried and untested medium is understandable. Advertising expenditures on cable tv in 1982 ran at a rate of about $120 million per annum. This estimated sum is only one per cent of total media spending in television, and about half of the one percent total was accounted for by station WTBS.

Adoption of cable tv, even on a limited basis, has been confined primarily to the large tv advertisers who have enough funds to try new forms without diverting money from their regular media schedules. In the main, the uses of cable have proceeded along three lines: targeting against narrowly-defined audiences; augmenting coverage by communicating with hard-to-reach market segments; and experimenting with different commercial approaches.

Despite glowing prognostications, cable tv today is essentially narrowcasting, specialized programing such as all news, sports, or cultural fare. The typical prime-time show on network tv, according to A. C. Nielsen, is tuned to by about 14 million households. A popular cable program, in contrast, reaches no more than 400,000 homes. Cable networks accepting advertising, as of March 1982 can be seen in Table 12–6.

Under present conditions, advertisers best able to take advantage of cable tv are those whose product strategies fit cable's specialized marketing targets. Maximum values accrue when program audiences match profiles of specialized targets which are not readily accessible with the more

TABLE 12–6 *Cable Networks Accepting Advertising as of March 1982*

Program source	# of house-holds (000)	% of U.S. households	Format
Black Entertainment TV	8,803	10.8	Black
Cable Health Network (3)	4,000	4.9	Health
Cable News Network (CNN)	11,072	13.6	News
Cable News Network II	1,500	1.8	News
CBS Cable*	3,400	4.2	Cultural
Continental Broadcast Network	14,700	18.0	Various
ESPN	14,138	17.3	Sports
Hearst/ABC—Arts	6,300	7.7	Cultural
Hearst/ABC—Daytime	5,000	6.1	Women
Music Television (MTV)	3,000	3.7	Music
Modern Satellite Network	4,100	5.0	Consumer/ women's information
National Spanish TV Network (1)	2,773	3.4	Spanish
Satellite News Channel I (2)	NA	NA	News
Satellite News Channel II (3)	NA	NA	News
Satellite Program Network (SPN)	3,806	4.7	Various
TeleFrance	7,500	9.2	French
USA Network	10,000	12.3	Various
Weather Channel (2)	3,000	3.7	Weather
WGN (Chicago)	11,000	13.5	Various
WOR (New York) (4)	13,900	17.1	Various
WTBS (Atlanta)	20,375	25.0	Various

Source: Geers Gross Advertising Inc., New York.
Note: NA=not available. (1) Spanish U.S. households only; (2) Launch date: Spring '82; (3) Launch date: Fall '82; (4) not sold independently of local market.
* Service discontinued.

diversified television audience. Audience gains over cable are incremental in such cases.

By the same token, commercial forms may require a certain amount of experimentation. Conventional television rarely has programing that is related to the advertising message, and when it does, it becomes a highly expensive medium. Cable has the potential of delivering program content that is compatible with the commercial message. The new technologies thus offer advertisers opportunities to develop forms that will forge stronger bonds between creative and media through customization.

SUMMARY

Because it has the largest audience, television has the greatest share of national advertising expenditures. About 61 percent of national advertising which goes into television accrues to the major networks, and is made up of the largest advertisers.

Television advertising rates are determined mainly by ratings, which are measurements of audience. Since ratings fluctuate by day part, rates follow a parallel course. However, prime time commands a premium and rates are proportionately higher than audience increase. Rates are subject to seasonal fluctuations.

Most network schedules are bought on a participation or scatter plan basis. Advertisers can practice speculation or postponement in their negotiations. To lower risks, advertisers push for guaranteed ratings, especially when the volume is large.

Spot markets are used by both national and local advertisers. The rate structure in spot television is more complicated than in network television, but as with network television, ratings are the major factor in the price structure.

A serious problem for all television advertisers is "clutter." A growing demand for television time, along with constantly rising costs, has aggravated the problem.

Satellite broadcasting and computer technology give indications of greater fragmentation of television audiences. But changes will probably come slowly, and up until now, they have had only minor impact on viewing patterns. For this reason, advertiser adoption has been slow and usage will require a certain degree of experimentation with new commercial forms.

Questions for Chapter 12

1. If you were the manager of a brand of beer, would you be willing to pay a higher price to advertise on NFL football games? Why or why not?

2. Why would a company like Procter & Gamble sponsor its own soap operas on network television?

3. Why would a Nielsen network rating be less meaningful to an appliance maker than to a soft drink manufacturer?

4. Would a brand with a strong seasonal upswing from October to Christmas be able to buy evening network time more efficiently than a brand with no seasonal variation?

5. What factors must a firm consider in "up front" tv buying?

6. How can spot tv complement a network schedule?

7. Fixed position buying was said to be especially heavy for the 1982 fall season. Why do you suppose this was so?

8. Why do many spot buyers look with disfavor upon preemptible positions and package deals?

9. What would an advertiser's objections be to a "time bank" established by its advertising agency?

10. Since cable tv appeals to small, specialized audiences, a mass marketer has no particular interest in this media form. Comment on this statement.

Footnotes for Chapter 12

[1] Television Bureau of Advertising, Inc., "Trends in Television," (April 1981), p. 7.

[2] Based on Grey Advertising, Inc., *Pocket Media Modules 1982*.

[3] *Marketing and Media Decisions* (October 1980), p. 84.

[4] From correspondence to W. S. Sachs from Robert J. Coen of McCann-Erickson.

[5] Calculations based on *Advertising Age* (September 10, 1981), p. 98.

[6] *Advertising Age* (September 10, 1981), p. 58.

[7] John Hunt, "Primetime and Daytime Viewing Trends Since 1972," *Media Message* (New York: Ogilvy & Mather, 1980), p. 2.

[8] Dennis Gensch and Paul Shaman, "Models of Competitive Television Ratings," *Journal of Marketing Research* (August 1980), p. 309.

[9] *Advertising Age* (September 21, 1981), p. 104; Grey Advertising, Inc., *Pocket Media Modules 1982*, p. 15.

[10] E.g., see D. H. Gensch and B. Ranganathan, "Evaluation of Television Program Content for the Purpose of Promotional Segmentation," *Journal of Marketing Research* (November 1974), pp. 390–398; R. E. Frank et. al., "Television Program Types," *Journal of Marketing Research* (May 1971), pp. 204–211; Farley and Bownan, "TV Viewing: Application of a Formal Choice Model," *Applied Economics* (October 1972), pp. 245–259.

[11] Jugenheimer and Turk, *Advertising in the Broadcast Media*, p. 168; and Elizabeth J. Heighton and Don R. Cunningham, *Advertising in the Broadcast Media* (Belmont, Calif.: Wadsworth Publishing Company, 1976), p. 206.

[12] Jack Honomichl, "High Costs, High Profits," *Advertising Age* (March 16, 1981), p. S–19.

[13] See Heighton and Cunningham, *Advertising in the Broadcast Media*, p. 222.

[14] Andrew Feinberg, "In the Shadows of Madison Avenue," *New York Times* (February 28, 1982), pp. F1, F7.

[15] Herbert Zeltner, "Members of the Sounding Board Zero in on Advertising Clutter." *Advertising Age* (January 8, 1979), pp. S–10—S–11.

[16] See Bill Abrams, "Firms Fret Over Rising Costs of TV Spots; Some Raise Budgets and Shun Prime Time," *Wall Street Journal* (April 4, 1980), p. 30.

[17] See Joyce G. Romley, "The Track Record," *Marketing and Media Decisions* (August 1981), pp. 123–126; "Media Cost will rise 9.3% in '82," pp. 59–61, 122.

[18] James MacLachlan and Michael H. Siegal, "Reducing the Costs of TV Commercials by Use of Time Compressions." *Journal of Marketing Research* (February 1980), pp. 52–57.

[19] National Association of Broadcasters, *The Television Code*, July 1981.

[20] Ellen Graham, "A Spending Spree by Television Networks Touches Off Worries Over Future Profits," *Wall Street Journal* (October 4, 1977), p. 48.

[21] John Cooney, "How NBC Promotes $21 Million Mini-Series: Interviews, Press Kits, Study Aids, Trips, Parties," *Wall Street Journal* (September 11, 1980), p. 48.

[22] See James W. Carey, "Changing Communications Technology and the Nature of Audience," *Journal of Advertising*, vol. 9, no. 2 (1980), pp. 3–9, 43.

[23] Television Bureau of Advertising, *TV Basics 24*, p. 8.

[24] Tony Schwartz, "Corporations Look to Cable TV," *New York Times* (October 18, 1980), p. 31.

[25] Maurine Christopher, "ABC Debuts CATV Net," *Advertising Age* (April 6, 1981), p. 2 and "Burgeoning Role for Cable Sponsors," *Advertising Age,* (March 2, 1981), pp. 2, 76.

[26] Daniel Machalaba, "More Publishers Beam Electronic Newspapers To Home Video Sets," *Wall Street Journal* (January 2, 1981), pp. 1, 4.

[27] John Hunt, "Primetime and Daytime Viewing Trends Since 1972."

[28] See Morton B. Elliot, "Showtime: We're No. 2 and So We 'Try Harder,'" *Advertising Age* (February 9, 1981), p. 56.

[29] Don Agostino and Jayne Zenaty, *Home VCR Owner's Use of Television and Public Television: Viewing, Recording & Playback.* Report prepared for Corporation For Public Broadcasting, March 15, 1980.

[30] "Networks Losing Share of National Advertising Dollars to Cable, Spot TV," *Marketing News* (October 31, 1980), p. 1.

[31] James P. Forkan, "Research Spotlight Swings to Cable TV," *Advertising Age* (March 9, 1981), p. 56.

Consumer Advertising in Print Media

With the exception of television, consumer magazines carry more national advertising than any other medium. Although magazines compete with television in several important respects, they are not viable alternatives in others. Magazines are also both substitutable and complementary with respect to other print media, especially in instances of advertising for cigarettes and hard liquor.

This chapter devotes most of its attention to consumer magazines as advertising vehicles. Specifically, it covers the following subjects:

- **Types of advertising which best lend themselves to consumer magazines**
- **Considerations in the choice of vehicles**
- **Advertising rates and estimations of value received**
- **Application of reach-frequency concepts in print schedules**

The chapter ends with a discussion of outdoor advertising. Actually, outdoor media carry less national advertising than newspapers. The ratio of retail-to-national advertising in newspapers runs at about ten to one, but about one to ten in outdoor.

MAGAZINES AS ADVERTISING MEDIA

Magazines rank next to television, but to a lesser extent, as a national advertising medium for consumer products. About 9.3 percent of all advertising in the United States finds its way into magazines having national distribution. Several major magazines, such as the *New Yorker*, *Sunset*, *Southern Living*, and *New York Times Magazine*, circulate within narrow geographical boundaries. But most magazines circulate nationally, though spotty in many instances. The giant share of magazine advertising expenditures, about 90 percent, is spent on full run editions.[1]

Magazines are not uniform, homogeneous entities. They come in many shapes and sizes, from pocket-sized editions such as *Reader's Digest*, to the oversized issues of *Variety*. Some have slick, glossy pages, with excellent reproductions, while others resemble a slightly upgraded version of newsprint. Some are colorful and abundantly illustrated with drawings and photographs, while others come in black and white, leaning heavily toward text. Magazines are published with varying frequency, from as often as daily to once a year. The overwhelming proportion of the leading magazines, however, appear weekly or monthly. Some magazines are indeed individualistic productions, bearing the imprint of their editors just as paintings carry the signature of their creators. But to advertisers, magazines are looked upon as markets held together by an editorial concept.

A leading source of media information is the Standard Rate and Data Service (SRDS). This service, owned by Macmillan, Inc., publishes a dozen separate volumes which contain a myriad of detail for all major media. For each magazine, the SRDS report supplies advertising rates, circulation statistics, editorial analysis, and production requirements such as closing dates and technical specifications of material to be submitted for printing.

The consumer group comprises the major part of the magazine industry. Leading magazines far outdistance any trade or farm journal in terms of either circulation or revenue. The consumer segment accounts for approximately two-thirds of all advertising revenue flowing into magazines.

Consumer magazines had more than $3.5 billion of advertising in 1981 and carried about 5.8 percent of the total U.S. advertising dollars.[2] As of September 27, 1981, Standard Rate and Data listed approximately 1,900 consumer magazines. But advertising revenue has a highly skewed distribution. More than half, about 53 percent, accrue to thirteen publications, each having recorded $90 million or more of advertising revenue in 1980.[3] The top twenty magazines handle a full two-thirds of total consumer magazine advertising. Table 13–1 shows the twenty leading consumer magazines and their advertising revenue in 1980.

The most frequently advertised product categories in consumer magazines, in order of importance are: smoking materials, alcoholic beverages, and automobiles and automotive-related products. These three classes of goods account for roughly 25 percent of all advertising carried by consumer magazines.[4] Of the five leading 1981 consumer magazine advertisers, four manufactured tobacco and liquor—R. J. Reynolds Industries, Philip Morris, Inc., Seagram Co. Ltd., and B.A.T. Industries. The lone exception, in fourth place, was General Motors. Its rival, Ford Motor Company, ranked seventh. The leading twenty-five magazine advertisers included four other liquor and tobacco manufacturers: American Brands, Loews Corporation, Hiram Walker, and Liggett. The top twenty-five magazine advertisers in 1980 are shown in Table 13–2.

SELECTING CONSUMER MAGAZINES FOR ADVERTISING

Some magazines cater to the tastes of mass, undifferentiated audiences. *TV Guide* and *Reader's Digest*, both with circulations of more than eighteen million copies for an average issue, go into more than a fifth of all U.S. households. Sunday supplements like *Parade* and *Sunday* similarly distribute more than nineteen million copies each week, on an average. These mass-circulated magazines, though, are the exceptions.

TABLE 13–1 *Leading Consumer Magazines Ranked by 1980 Advertising Revenue*

Magazine	Advertising Revenue (In Millions of Dollars)
TV Guide	239.5
Time	223.4
Newsweek	176.3
Parade	136.5
Sports Illustrated	128.7
People Weekly	106.5
Reader's Digest	100.0
Woman's Day	96.6
Better Homes & Gardens	96.1
Family Weekly	91.7
Family Circle	90.4
Good Housekeeping	90.2
U.S. News & World Report	73.1
Playboy	71.5
McCall's	64.0
New York Times Magazine	56.0
Fortune	55.6
Cosmopolitan	55.4

Source: *Publishers Information Bureau/Leading National Advertisers* (December 1980).

As a rule, magazines are selective media. The day of the general, mass circulation magazine as a leading carrier of advertising messages is long gone. *Look, Saturday Evening Post,* and *Crowell-Collier* are half-forgotten memories of journalistic ventures which once vied for the minds of the broad American public. They fell from grace because advertisers shifted their patronage to television in order to reach the massive consumer body of middle America. The publications that survived the onslaught of television, and even prospered, were those which succeeded in achieving selectivity.

Two kinds of selectivity are germane to advertising, and often both types are blended in varying degrees in the same publication. One engenders a specialized editorial approach. The other refers to audience characteristics which depart significantly from the average in the population.

The editorial approach supposedly brings together readers having a particular intellectual bent or interest. For example, readers of travel magazines are obviously interested in far away places and tourist attractions; outdoor publications are presumably perused by people who fish, hunters, and lovers of the great outdoors; and garden books are apparently taken up by amateur gardeners, plant growers, and botany devotees. The extent of reader interest is mainly a function of editorial policy. The more

TABLE 13–2 *Top Twenty-five Consumer Magazine Advertisers*

Rank	Advertiser	Expenditures	
		1980	1979
1	R. J. Reynolds Industries	$118,530,200	$114,869,300
2	Philip Morris Inc	79,326,700	64,650,800
3	Seagram Co. Ltd	70,624,500	84,877,100
4	General Motors Corp	55,478,600	67,551,000
5	Loews Corp	38,210,100	35,745,100
6	Procter & Gamble...............	37,162,300	40,640,400
7	Ford Motor Co..................	35,918,500	31,042,100
8	Time Inc	35,611,300	27,243,100
9	American Telephone & Telegraph .	34,521,100	25,287,200
10	American Brands	34,233,900	31,399,300
11	General Foods Corp	34,170,100	41,241,000
12	B.A.T. Industries	32,823,900	36,081,400
13	Sears, Roebuck & Co	32,057,700	13,819,600
14	CBS..........................	29,833,200	28,532,900
15	Dart & Kraft Inc.................	27,538,200	21,428,100
16	RCA Corp	24,176,800	21,773,200
17	Volkswagen	21,708,600	13,275,300
18	Du Pont	21,701,600	16,615,300
19	Bristol-Myers Co	18,386,700	19,849,200
20	Johnson & Johnson	18,359,700	15,901,500
21	American Broadcasting Co........	18,030,400	16,174,900
22	Hiram Walker-Consumers Home Ltd	17,572,400	16,806,600
23	U.S. Government	17,571,000	18,788,300
24	Norton Simon Inc	17,278,100	14,737,600
25	Heublein Inc	16,460,200	14,861,600

Source: *PIB/LNA* (December 1980).

specialized the direction, the more homogeneous the interest. Less intense specialization attracts readers with more varied interests.

Selectivity based on interest creates a favorable advertising climate for many products. An advertisement featuring a food recipe would be prone to get higher readership in a magazine emphasizing the culinary arts than in a news weekly. Readers seeking ideas for home decorating will be more receptive than others to advertisements for carpeting and home furnishings. Photography magazines have audiences with keen interests in cameras, film, and photographic equipment advertisements.

To take advantage of a journalistic climate, the product advertised must be related to the editorial content. The greater the editorial specialization of the vehicle, the more compatible the magazine environment becomes for advertisements of related products. But the more specialized a magazine becomes, the more its circulation and audience diminish in size. A narrowly targeted editorial policy offers high reader interest for advertisements in the field of specialization, but at the expense of market coverage.

Advertisers usually fit the media to the commercial message. That is, the advertisements are made up first and then media is selected to accommodate the existing copy and audience objectives. In many instances, media selection is completely unrelated to the editorial environment. Advertising design may sometimes be altered so as to be more in keeping with a publication's context. Copy concessions to media, however, are relatively minor, and at most involve tactical decisions.

Deviations from the general rule of fitting media to copy are rare. One such exception is the "endangered species" campaign of Canon camera in *National Geographic Magazine*. Here, an entire advertising campaign was built around the interests of a publication's readers.

The advertisements of the Canon campaign showed different forms of wildlife photographed in their natural habitats throughout the world. Each advertisement, reproduced in four color in the same superb photography for which the magazine is noted, displayed an eloquent testimonial to the performance of the camera. An advertisement featuring the Indian rhinocerous from this campaign series is illustrated in Figure 13–1.

The other kind of selectivity refers to reader characteristics, as opposed to content qualities. It signifies external reader attributes, such as demographics, as compared with subjective properties, such as reader interest. That is not to say the two are disassociated. Editorial content exerts an influence on the type of reader drawn to a publication. The news weeklies and *National Geographic* have similar upper scale profiles, despite dissimilar editorial content. *Sports Illustrated* is listed by Standard Rate & Data Service, Inc. as a news weekly, although its news is confined to sports events. This anomalous classification apparently came about because of the request of the sports publication which offers advertisers markets similar to those of news weeklies. In short, magazines with varied editorial policies compete directly with each other for advertising because reader profiles may be alike, and therefore substitutable.

Any advertising decision must consider both editorial and audience factors. The first suggests a degree of synergism between the editorial environment and the products advertised. The second factor, concerning the size and characteristics of an audience, indicates the market potential which a publication offers to the advertiser. The editorial-audience mix can be visualized, simply but crudely, as a two-by-two matrix, which is illustrated in Figure 13–2.

The ideal media choice, as shown in Figure 13–2, is that of cell 1, in which vehicles provide a product with audience and editorial compatibility. Many food products, cosmetics and toiletries can avail themselves of this best possible option. When target markets are defined as women, mag-

Photographed by Andrew Laurie. *Great Indian Rhinoceros: Genus: Rhinoceros Species: unicornis*
Adult size: Average 168cm tall at the shoulder. Adult weight: Average 2-1/2 tons
Habitat: Grasslands, swamps and forests in Nepal and northern India
Surviving number: Estimated 1,000—1,500

Wildlife as Canon sees it:
A photographic heritage for all generations.

In ancient Roman times, the Indian rhinoceros was a popular sight in circuses to which it had been introduced by Pompey. After the fall of the empire, it disappeared from Europe, later leading to the opinion that it had never existed, and not until 1513, when an Indian potentate sent one to the king of Portugal, did it return.

Today, this unaggressive herbivore could disappear again, and this time there would be no way to bring it back. And while photography can record it for posterity, more importantly it can help save it and the rest of wildlife.

A convenient and dependable research tool, photography can help gather the information wildlife conservationists need. And as a means of communication, it is at once accurate and expressive, opening people's eyes to the great beauty of nature. Looking at a photograph of the Indian rhinoceros, for instance, with that unique horn

and that armor-like hide, one cannot but marvel at and gain a better understanding of nature.

And understanding is perhaps the single most important factor in saving the Indian rhinoceros and all of wildlife.

New F-1

New FD300mm f/2.8L

Canon
Images for all time

Fig. 13—1 *Rhinocerous from the Canon Endangered Species Campaign.*
Courtesy of Canon, Inc. Photographer: Andrew Laurie.

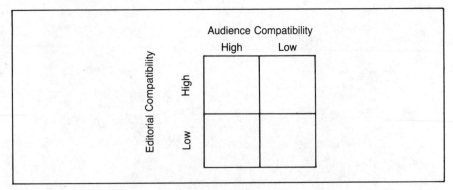

Fig. 13-2 *Editorial-Audience Options.*

azines edited for females receive large portions of advertising. Of total advertising expenditures in women's books, some 41 percent comes from foods and toiletries. The latter category also comprises about 39 percent of advertising in fashion-service publications.[5] Not only do products related to editorial compatibility reap advantages, but they benefit from audience cost efficiencies in terms of marketing targets.

The editorial-marketing relationship is a concept that is widely accepted by media planners. But it is nonetheless a supposition. There is no hard evidence which demonstrates that advertisements related to editorial content are more effective than if unrelated—given the same market potential.

In the absence of empirical data, many media planners act as though an unproven or undemonstrated event does not exist. How can they give weight to something about which they have no information? Consequently, their decisions are made strictly on the basis of available data. As described in the industry, media selection "goes by the numbers." In this case, magazine audiences are matched with markets. When a marketer's target coincides with audience selectivity, the vehicle will usually be efficient. For example, if homemakers are defined as prime targets, women's magazines become attractive because they yield low cost-per-thousand homemakers. The editorial content, though considered advantageous, has little to do with the media decision. The editorial environment is rationalized as being reflected by the audience statistics. This form of argument, though not precisely accurate, contains enough truth to be made operationally viable.

Most products advertised in magazines end up in cell 2 of Figure 13-2; they are not related to editorial content. The two leading product categories, tobacco and liquor, have few journalistic proponents to sing their praises. Both product categories must therefore select media vehicles solely on the basis of external criteria, namely audience characteristics. Editorially, content is neutral.

About one-half of all tobacco advertising in magazines finds its way into weeklies. But all types of magazines get tobacco business. The tobacco companies have no hesitation in placing advertisements in women's publications, since adult females are considered good prospects. According to Publisher's Information Bureau, advertising for smoking materials in women's magazines during 1980 amounted to $59.8 million. This compares with $148 million in weeklies, but $39.9 million in general monthlies.[6] In contrast, females are apparently not regarded as prospective customers for liquor. So books with predominantly female audiences receive negligible business, while the monthlies in 1980 garnered $75.5 million for alcoholic beverage advertising.[7]

Automobile manufacturers are similarly positioned with respect to magazines. There are several publications devoted to cars. But they are highly specialized, and their circulations are too small to provide adequate market coverage. Large magazines sometimes run articles on automobiles, especially new models. But the auto manufacturers cannot rely on special editions for advertising continuity. For the most part, the automobile companies choose print vehicles on the basis of reader characteristics, and not on editorial qualities.

The high editorial compatibility but low audience compatibility segment is relatively unimportant in terms of advertising revenue. This segment contains many small, specialized magazines which cannot provide market coverage, such as the car magazines. They may be efficient, but not effective.

Cell 4 in Figure 13–2, where magazines are low in both editorial and audience compatibility, is not a feasible option. Publications here are neither efficient nor effective, and should be avoided.

ADVERTISING RATES

Consumer magazines list advertising rates on separate rate cards. Prices are usually quoted for space units. The one-page advertisement is the most common, and is considered the standard unit. Most magazines offer fractional pages, which bear lower rates, and multiple pages, which obviously carry higher price tags. The standard one-page advertisement is confined to the area within a white border, which parallels the edge of the page.

A bleed advertisement obliterates the border, allowing the copy to go to the outer limits of the page. Since bleed is essentially an extension of the standard page, it is often priced at a premium. But pricing practices are not uniform. A number of large magazines quote four-color bleed at the same rate as a regular four-color page. *Redbook* magazine prices the four-color bleed lower than the standard page rate. Publications which have no surcharge are either incurring no additional cost for the process, or are tacking on extras as part of their standard prices, much like auto manufacturers including numerous options as standard equipment. Most publications, though, do charge higher prices for bleed, with premiums running from ten to fifteen percent above normal page rates.

Despite the long-standing availability of bleed, the subject is still a matter for debate. Most executives subscribe to the notion that bleed increases reader attention and creates more memorable impressions. However, they are not convinced that the gain in communication is equal to the increment in cost, or most advertisements would be bleed. When a cost differential exists, bleed is used on special occasions, depending upon creative factors.

The basic advertisement can be thought of as black and white, with surcharges added for color. The amount of the premium increases with the number of colors. Color is especially important for products which benefit from being presented in their natural tones, products such as fashion goods, cosmetics, automobiles, and food. Many prominent consumer magazines carry more color advertisements than black and white. The amount of color in a magazine hinges upon the type of advertisements it carries.

The degree of cost increase for color varies from magazine to magazine. The premium for four-color over black and white advertisements in magazines with circulations of one million or more ranges from as low as ten percent to as high as sixty percent. The large variation in rates makes color specification an important factor in media selection. A magazine may yield a relatively low cost-per-thousand estimate for a color advertisement but not for black and white. Another publication may produce the opposite result. As can be seen, the choice of a consumer magazine schedule must concern itself with the color requirements of advertisements in the campaign.

The reason for higher color costs stems from longer running time of printing presses. It is reasonable to expect large circulation magazines to have proportionately lower incremental color costs than smaller publications, since the set-up costs for color printing can be spread over a longer production run. Table 13–3 compares black and white with four-color rates for select magazines in three different categories and at different circulation levels: circulation of 4.3 million or more; circulation of 2.0 to 4.3 million; circulation of less than two million.

Table 13–3 shows the leading competitors in three different categories—women's magazines, news weeklies, and science and mechanics monthlies. Each category has different circulation levels, the highest in the women's group of magazines and the lowest in the science and mechanics publications.

The women's magazines indicate a tendency for four-color costs to rise proportionately less than the increase in circulation. This is consistent with expectations of economies of scale being reflected in prices. But the news weeklies display no such pattern. The color surcharge is the same

TABLE 13–3 *Black and White and Four-Color Page Rates*

Category	Circulation Rate Base (000)	Black & White (Dollars)	4-Color (Dollars)	Relative Increase (Percent)
Women's Magazines				
Family Circle	8400	45,275	54,600	21
Good Housekeeping	5000	42,030	52,745	25
Ladies' Home Journal	5500	40,800	50,200	23
McCall's	6200	45,860	56,400	23
Redbook	4300	33,195	37,365	32
Woman's Day	7600	52,040	62,320	20
News Weeklies				
Newsweek	2950	37,040	57,780	56
Sports Illustrated	2250	31,710	49,465	56
Time	4250	49,335	76,960	56
U.S. News & World Report	2000	24,310	38,365	58
Science and Mechanics Magazines				
Mechanix Illustrated	1600	16,420	23,285	42
Popular Mechanics	1600	17,400	24,695	42
Popular Science	1800	17,190	24,380	42

Source: Standard Rate & Data Service, Inc., *Consumer Magazine and Farm Publication Rates and Data* (Skokie, Ill.: SRDS, 1982).
Note: Circulation rate bases and page costs are as of October 1, 1981.

regardless of circulation size. For the group as a whole, the 56 percent color premium is larger than for the science magazines, which have smaller circulations. This suggests that production cost differentials are not the pivotal factors in pricing.

Magazine discount and circulation policies point in the same direction. Magazines usually offer discounts for ads placed by the same advertiser for volume and frequency. These discounts are in effect cumulative ones, for they have only minimum impact on publishing costs. They give each incremental page a price reduction after a certain point, not only for the most recent ad being placed but for all preceding advertisements during the contract year. Since costs for producing a current advertisement are completely unrelated to publishing costs of past editions, the discounts are devices to maintain "patronage." They are competitive tools to gain advertiser loyalty.

Multimagazine publishers may also offer combination rates which are lower than quotes for the magazines used individually. The Times Mirror Corporation permits advertisers to buy different combinations of *Popular Science, Outdoor Life, Ski, Golf,* and *The Sporting News.* Together with the standard discounts, advertisers running one-third page units or larger can attain a price cut of up to thirty-five percent from the one-time rate.

When combination rates involve magazines with unlike editorial direction, they are most advantageous to advertisers seeking audience compatibility in a magazine schedule. Multiproduct advertisers also benefit from combination rates.

CIRCULATION

Consumer magazines, which are largely paid circulation publications offer advertisers circulation guarantees. Most magazines guarantee a circulation rate base, which pertains to an average issue rather than to individual issues. An average that dips below the guarantee sets off a rebate to the advertiser. Circulation above the guarantee is regarded as a bonus delivered by the publication.

The use of circulation as a pledge for contract performance dates back to the establishment of the Audits Bureau of Circulation (ABC) in 1914. The agency still audits circulation, and its work enables both publishers and advertisers to base decisions on hard, verified data.

In general, the larger the magazine's circulation, the higher its advertising rates. But this circulation-space rate relationship holds in only a general sort of way, for it is modified by both supply and demand factors.

On the supply side, the size of a page, the number of pages, paper quality and color reproduction all go into changing cost-volume ratios. Computations of space unit costs for advertising, however, cannot be disassociated with a firm's accounting system and, oddly enough, with circulation policy.

Circulation Policy

Large publishers, with few exceptions, market their magazines as loss leaders. They sell copies to the public at prices below the cost of production, hoping to make up the deficit from advertising. Since per unit costs are largely independent of revenue for any given volume, cut-rate prices to consumers raise costs of advertisements. In recent years the trend has been away from the once disastrous "circulation wars" and towards less discounting to consumers from the "full price."[8] But even the "full price," which theoretically should cover all costs plus normal profits, may well fall short of this goal. The wider the range of price options to consumers, the more flexibility a publisher has in setting prices for advertising space.

Accounting System

The true cost also depends upon the accounting concepts in use. If the cost of a magazine is conceived of as being produced and distributed as so many copies without advertising, then commercial messages can be regarded as incremental. The cost of advertising can then be calculated as the cost of the additional pages. But if absorption costing is used, all indirect and overhead costs are allocated to both advertisements and editorial matter. The allocation would then enhance advertising costs, as compared with direct costing. However, the method of accounting as well as the selling price of a magazine are decision variables for the advertiser. Those decisions are subsumed in the space rates which an advertiser can accept, reject, or try to modify by negotiation.

AUDIENCE

Circulation audits brought business-like procedures to advertising. Buyers and sellers were able to negotiate on common, factual grounds. But, by the 1960s, interest shifted from circulation to audience. Actual number of readers, not number of copies sold, is the main criterion today for evaluating media efficiency and selecting magazine schedules. The change of emphasis introduced new considerations to decision making. This can be demonstrated in Table 13–4, which shows cost-per-thousand calculations for leading women's magazines and news weeklies on two different bases, circulation and audience.

As indicated in Table 13–4, magazine selection based upon circulation would yield a different decision from one based on audience. *Good Housekeeping* has the highest cost-per-thousand circulation in the women's group, but the lowest in terms of audience. Based upon circulation, it is the least efficient, but based upon audience, it is the most efficient. *Woman's Day* with a favorable showing in circulation, does not fare well in

TABLE 13–4 *Cost-per-thousand Calculated by Circulation and by Total Audience*

| Magazine | Cost Per Thousand | |
	Circulation (Dollars)	Total Audience (Dollars)
Family Circle	5.39	2.44
Good Housekeeping	8.41	2.27
Ladies' Home Journal	7.42	2.76
McCall's	7.40	2.81
Redbook	7.72	3.33
Woman's Day	6.85	3.25
Newsweek	12.56	2.40
Sports Illustrated	14.09	2.44
Time	11.61	2.38
U.S. News & World Report	12.16	2.45

Note: Costs are based on a black and white page rate, as of October 1, 1981, from Standard Rate & Data Service, *Consumer Magazine and Farm Publication Rates and Data* (Skokie, Ill.: SRDS, 1982). Circulation figures represent rate base guarantees. Audience figures are based on a 1981 study by Simmons Market Research Bureau, Inc.

audience figures. And it is the audience ratings, derived from sample surveys with consumers, which have become the prime determinants in magazine rate structures.

Since magazines vary in the number of readers per copy shown by surveys, the relationship between circulation and audience becomes tenuous. For the six women's publications in Table 13–4, there is no relationship whatsoever between the two. The correlation coefficient was calculated at .05. The four news weeklies had only a weak coefficient of .25.

The adoption of audience criteria in media selection has impelled advertisers to avoid using the hard, tangible circulation data and give priority to soft, intangible evidence, since readers are supposedly more relevant than the number of copies in circulation. In this sense, advertisers have traded off accuracy of information for greater meaningfulness of data.

For the publisher, the trade off has introduced greater uncertainty in operations. If circulation is not related to audience, it restricts publisher options to bring about desirable readership through circulation or editorial policies. In turn, the audience an advertiser pays for may have more defective parts.

Possible defects may arise because readership is related to circulation policy. Subscriptions require the largest amount of out-of-pocket expenditures. But they enhance publisher control over distribution and production, and minimize fluctuations in the number of sold copies per issue. Since copies go directly into the subscriber's home, the environment is most conducive to thorough reading of the magazine, and by extension, to exposure of audience to advertisements.

But subscriptions also yield less readers per copy than other circulation forms. Copies don't leave the home, and guests don't visit to read a magazine. The same people also keep reading issue after issue. As a producer of a product, the publisher benefits from repeat usage. As a seller of advertising the publisher incurs a penalty because repeat usage tends to depress audience cumulation.

If advertisers or their agencies view all readers as equal, regardless of how they acquired their copies or where they did their reading, they create incentives for publishers to debase their audiences. Why should they incur extra costs to obtain subscriber loyalty when high reader turnover brings in more advertising?

Pressure for low cost-per-thousand audience from media buyers have moved many circulation departments to adopt policies for building "pass-along" audiences, such as getting copies into business establishments such as doctors' offices, airlines, bus stations, etc. A reader is a reader, even if pages are scanned for a minute or so. In fact, *Girl Talk*, a woman's magazine, was started with the idea of distributing the publication free to beauty parlors so that it would garner a large number of readers per copy and, as a low cost producer, gain a reputation as a desirous advertising vehicle.

Since costs are less than proportionate to audience size, a high reader-per-copy figure gives a publisher an advantage in competing for advertising business. Though the dominant tendency is not to qualify audiences by some qualitative measure of reading, media selection practices are not uniform. There are a number of advertisers and agencies which discount passalong readership by factors ranging from .3 to .5, on grounds that such readers are less valuable to advertisers than primary readers. The latter is defined as a person living in a household wherein a member acquired the magazine either by subscription or single copy purchase. Probably more buyers would discount passalong readers if their relative value were ascertained. But facts are rather sparse, and any discounting must be done largely on judgment.

SELECTIVITY IN EXTERNAL AUDIENCE CHARACTERISTICS

For many reasons, most firms seek selective audiences in magazines. The largest general advertisers, such as those marketing automobiles, food, dentrifice, drugs, health care products, and household supplies, attain broad, across-the-board reach with television. These companies use magazines as a supplementary medium to bolster the advertising impact on particular consumer segments. Besides transmitting the usual campaign messages, they employ magazines in ways in which broadcast does not lend itself, as in merchandising and sales promotion.

Another group of advertisers serve narrow, segmented markets, and rely on magazines to match their unique requirements. These firms have relatively small budgets, and are predominantly in fields such as financial services, appliances, apparel, and home furnishings. Reach to select target markets is the most important objective to these companies, since budgets do not normally permit heavy frequency.

A third major group looks to magazines as the dominant medium for mass-marketed goods to general audiences. The cigarette makers and some liquor manufacturers fit into this mold. These advertisers put magazine schedules together with the aim of obtaining broad reach along with adequate frequency.

All groups of magazines have less-than-full-run options, some of which are demographic and some geographic. Standard Rate and Data Service lists 181 publications with fractional editions of either type.[9] *Time* magazine, for example, offers a number of demographic editions: one going to subscribers who are professional or managerial by occupation, excluding doctors; an edition shipped to high income zip code areas; and a top management edition, mailed to corporate officers. *Newsweek* offers an executive edition having demographics similar to that of *Forbes* and *Fortune*. Advertising to these select targets via specialized editions bears per copy rates which are generally higher than those for full runs. Also, demographic editions are spread throughout the country so the advertiser's distribution system must be national in order to avoid waste.

Geographic editions can be used to advantage by both nationwide and regional marketers. *Time* magazine, exemplifying a service offered by many large magazines, offers editions for the top fifty ADIs, which collectively cover about two-thirds of all households in the nation. These breakouts enable advertisers to combine print with television in a market-by-market approach to media planning. *Time* also offers fifty state and eleven regional editions to enhance marketing flexibility. Most large magazines will, on demand, create custom-ordered test market editions, used mainly to assess new product plans and advertising spending levels.

AUDIENCE MEASUREMENTS

Several research firms market syndicated magazine audience data. The largest of these is Simmons Market Research Bureau (SMRB); the next most commonly-used service is Mediamark Research, Inc. (MRI). Both research houses obtain audience information from sample surveys with consumers, using national probability designs. SMRB interviews 15,000 adults twice over a year's time, and tabulates readership responses from both interviews. MRI conducts interviews with about 20,000 adults in different households during the same span of time.

Although methods of measuring audiences differ, both services allegedly report for each magazine surveyed the number of readers for an average issue during the survey year. SMRB reports its figures annually, MRI every six months by using a moving average. In 1981, SMRB reported audience statistics for 124 publications. The comparable number for MRI was 140, the increment accounted for by smaller magazines which came into the latter's survey.

Because magazines have selective readership, and used that way by most advertisers, both services qualify audiences in an enormous number of ways. Their reports contain product usage information, numerous demographic characteristics, different kinds of media habits which include other than those relating to magazines, psychological measurements, and indexes of social class. Product purchase and usage information come from self-administered booklets which are left with respondents after the first interview by SMRB and picked up on the second call. MRI, which makes only one interview, requests respondents to return all material left behind via the mails, and offers them gifts for doing so. Television viewing is obtained from tv diaries placed with a subsample of respondents. Other forms of media behavior, including newspaper reading, family and household characteristics, and personal data, are derived from regular in-home interviews. Interviews also provide information regarding reading days (how long an average issue is read) and page openings (percent of pages opened by an average issue audience).

Basic magazine readership information can be combined or cross-tabulated with other items in a vast array of collected data. The possible number of combinations and permutations is so large that it boggles the imagination. This massive quantity of data, stored on computer tapes and easily retrievable, permits media planners to obtain information in almost any conceivable form desired.

This information explosion has created more problems than it has solved. Media surveys, like other population studies, face the twin issues of reliability and validity. The first pertains to sampling error, and is primarily a function of sample size. The second refers to accuracy of measurement and generalizations of results.

The selective nature of magazines encourages media planners to analyze numerous population segments and to relate them to specific media vehicles. As a practical matter, analysts use point estimates in handling large quantities of data. But analyses dealing with segments, either of markets or media audiences, require that survey data be disaggregated. In turn, each breakdown reduces the effective sample base and increases the relative error. Thus, the more specific or qualified the audience, the less reliability the audience statistics contain.

An even greater concern is nonsampling error, which cannot be computed but is believed to be many times larger than sampling error. As surveys strive to gather more and more data in a single swoop, their quality deteriorates. The exact point at which input becomes useless information is conjectural. But there is little doubt that the greater the nonsampling error, the larger the conversion of probability into uncertainty. The validity issue is a serious one, and has been widely debated throughout the industry.[10]

REACH-FREQUENCY ESTIMATIONS

Since SMRB measures magazine readership for only two issues of a publication, reach and frequency for a schedule of more than two vehicles must be estimated mathematically. The most popular form has been the beta-binomial model, first presented by G. P. Hyett in 1958. The beta function describes an individual's probability of reading for a set of alternatives and applies to both SMRB and MRI data. The estimating procedure can be described as follows:

Certain data are given, such as the average issue audience, designated as C_1. This is actually a weighted sum of all persons reading one or two issues out of the two measured, or $\frac{1}{2}R_1^2 + R_2^2$. If extended beyond two to N

issues, the formula can be expressed as $C_1 = 1/N\ R_1^N + 2/N\ R_{\frac{N}{2}} + \ldots$ R_N^N.

The same audience data provides two other vital facts: population (P) and the two-issue cumulative audience or reach (C_2). The latter refers to the number of different people reading at least one issue out of two. Given these data, SMRB computes the reach of N issues by the formula:

$$C_N = C_{N-1} + \frac{b + N - 2}{K + N - 1}(C_{N-1} - C_{N-2}),$$

where,

$$k = \frac{C_2 - C_1}{2C_1 - C_2 - \frac{(C_1)^2}{P}}$$

and,

$$b = K\left(1 - \frac{C_1}{P}\right).$$

This formula, in effect, says that the reach of any set equals the reach of N − 1 issues plus a proportion of the difference in the cumulative audiences of the two previous issues. For example, suppose one wanted to calculate the reach of three (C_3) or four (C_4) issues, given that of one and two. The procedure would be:

$$C_3 = C_2 + \frac{b + 1}{K + 2}(C_2 - C_1).$$

$$C_4 = C_3 + \frac{b + 2}{K + 3}(C_3 - C_2).$$

The frequency of reading exactly t out of N issues (R_t^N) is calculated by the equation:

$$R = \frac{a + t - 1}{b + N - t} \cdot \frac{N - t + 1}{t} \cdot R_{t-1}^N.$$

where,

$$a = K - b.$$

Projections of SMRB reach and frequency are based on two successive issues. If an advertiser uses issues with different spacings, computational efficiency decreases. According to the beta-binomial model, the entire frequency distribution is determined by the increment in the cumulative audience of successive issues. But issues spaced apart may not yield the same cumulative rates as two publications following each other. Similarly, SMRB measurements may bring about biases insofar as monthly pairs of magazines are consecutive, but weeklies are not. The expansion of the formula to a media mix with several vehicles will also encounter a decrease in computational efficiency. Reach-frequency computations should thus be used as rough approximations when developing media plans.

APPLICATION OF REACH-FREQUENCY CONCEPTS

The following section illustrates an application of the beta-binomial model in reach-frequency analysis. The advertiser in this instance was a firm marketing financial services.

The first step called for the advertising agency to draw up a list of publications deemed suitable as advertising vehicles, given criteria for defining advertising targets. This screening procedure reduces the number of alternatives to a manageable quantity.

The key market variables were income and sex. Top income groups within the population were seen as having higher probabilities of being customers than lower income households. Within each income category, males were deemed of greater value than females from the standpoint of a purchasing decision. The advertising agency thus weighted readers accordingly in devising its "consideration frame" for selection of advertising carriers.

The next step involved the choice of a schedule based on a planner's best judgment. This selection served only as a starting point, and might be called a "first feasible solution." Given a budget of about $1.5 million, the agency came up with the following schedule:

Magazines	Number of Insertions
Business Week	9
Newsweek	7
Time	7
Sports Illustrated	7
Total	30

This solution, designated as Schedule 1, yielded an audience pattern which can be summarized in terms of reach and frequency. The data was derived from a computer run based on a beta-binomial program.

The entire schedule will produce 330 million gross reader impressions over a year's time, the course of the schedule. This number is the sum of adult "issue readings," weighted by sex and income factors. The comparable net reach will be 62.3 million. This represents a coverage of 63.5 percent if the population were similarly stratified and weighted in accordance with the marketing factors set by the advertiser. This cumulative audience, on the average, will be reached 5.3 times. Ths distribution of exposure frequency is illustrated graphically in Figure 13–3.

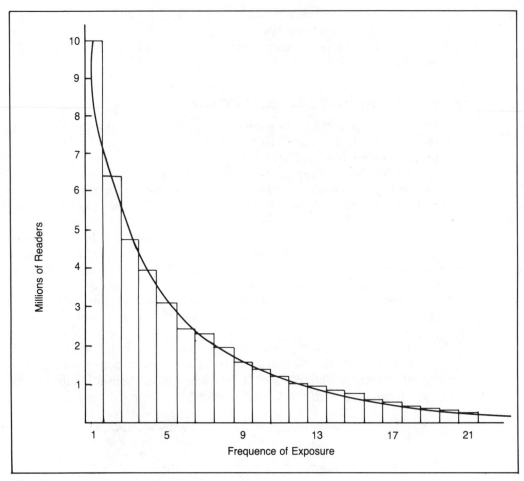

Fig. 13—3 *Distribution of Reader Frequencies.*

The last phase, and the heart of the analysis, was to improve the beginning schedule by evaluating alternatives. This was done in a logical sequence by a method of successive approximations.

For example, a significant improvement, though not necessarily the best, shows up when a general magazine is substituted for several issues in the schedule. Insertions in news weeklies were reduced to six and in Business Week to seven. The savings were then funneled into three insertions in a general magazine. The audience patterns of this new mix, denoted as Schedule 2, are compared with those of Schedule 1. Statistics of exposure frequency are presented as grouped data for ease of analysis (see Table 13–5).

As can be seen in Table 13–5, weighted gross impressions and average frequency are only slightly affected by the change in schedule. At the same time, the new combination of magazine issues picks up some 4.0 million additional readers weighted by purchase probabilities. Schedule 2 also has a more desirable distribution of reader exposures. Some 27.5 million are estimated as reading from three to eight issues, as compared with 25.2 million in Schedule 1. Both the expansion of net reach and the shift of exposures from heavy to median levels come from the same causes. The audience of the general magazine has less reader duplication with the rest of the schedule than the eliminated issues.

It might be reasoned that the subsitition of any different magazine to a schedule would yield fewer duplicated readers than issues of the same magazine. Can this process then be continued almost endlessly to increase reach and even out frequency? Decidedly not. Since it is logical to begin building a media schedule with the most efficient vehicles, improvements in readership patterns are offset by rising costs after a certain point. This tendency is exacerbated by reductions in discounts owing to the diminution of advertising volume per magazine.

The foregoing reach-frequency analysis was probably more elaborate than that undertaken by the typical media planner. Yet it did not constitute a radical departure from current modes of thinking. It may therefore be worthwhile to examine the underlying assumptions which were made, even though they were alluded to in previous sections of the book and entail repetition. The major ones, though not in order of importance, can be listed as follows:

1. A magazine is regarded as a neutral carrier of advertising.

   The analysis gave no weight to editorial format. A reader of *Sports Illustrated*, depending upon income and sex, was regarded

TABLE 13–5 *Comparison of Two Schedules*

	Weighted Number of Readers (000)	
Frequency of Magazine Exposure	*Schedule 1*	*Schedule 2*
1–2 times	24,000	26,000
3–4 times	12,100	13,000
5–6 times	7,700	8,600
7–8 times	5,400	6,000
9 or more times	13,100	12,400
Net reach	62,300	66,300
Percent coverage by media combination	63.4	67.5
Weighted gross magazine impressions	330,000	336,000
Average frequency	5.3	5.1

as interested in financial services as a reader of *Business Week*. There is also no body of information to judge comparative interests.

2. An ad has the same effect, regardless of vehicle.

This is related to point 1. The analysis assumes that, given a reader of equal value, an advertisement will be just as effective no matter what magazine carries it. The format and design of the carrier are disregarded.

3. The relevant time period is one year.

The analysis assumes that a media exposure lasts for at least a year. This is implicit in the definition of net reach, which includes one-time readers of the schedule.

In fact, reach-frequency computations were performed for quarter-year periods. But whether three months or twelve months, the media planner is presumed to know the relevant duration of an impression.

4. Weighted impressions are operationally meaningful.

The analyst is regarded as having the capacity to evaluate unerringly weighted impression statistics. For example, this analysis gave the male in the highest income group a weight of 1.0 and reduced all other cell values accordingly. It is just as logical to begin with the lowest value as one and weight upwards. Or weights can range up or down from some measure of central tendency. Depending how it is done, reach-frequency figures would alter radically. There is some question as to whether a media planner can readily translate sophisticated abstractions into actual operations.

5. Media impressions parallel copy impressions.

The computations are for issue exposures, not ad exposures. To completely disregard the latter tacitly supposes a certain correlation between the two. If an exposure is taken to mean a cognitive act related to the message, different copy treatments may yield vastly different configurations of "impressions."

It is conceptually possible to take copy effects into account. But current copy research, print more so than broadcast, is ill-suited for tying message impressions to media audiences.

6. The space unit is considered optimal.

Size and color of advertisements are taken as given, apparently in the belief that these units are right. If size and color are altered, and the budget is fixed, the number of insertions in a schedule can increase or decrease. In turn, this would change the number of gross media impressions, as well as reach and frequency estimates.

Considering these bold assumptions, a large degree of uncertainty obviously dogs the steps of media decisions.

OUTDOOR ADVERTISING

Another print medium used for consumer advertising is outdoor, which encompasses messages of standard dimensions in outside locations. Accounting for about $650 million in billings in 1981, the outdoor medium is a decidedly minor one. The annual amounts spent in the medium represents only one percent of total advertising volume, and this same rate has held for many years.[11]

The industry is widely dispersed, with more than 700 companies selling locations in U.S. markets.[12] Despite this localized characteristic, about two-thirds of all outdoor advertising comes from national advertisers. The individual outdoor advertisement plants, actually local business offices, perform many of the copy functions for retail customers. National advertisers, as is their practice with other media forms, rely upon their ad agencies for creative outputs.

In practically all instances, outdoor advertising is used in combination with other media. It seldom dominates the media mix. Rather, it is assigned a subordinate role.

Outdoor advertising functions primarily as reminder advertising. It must convey its message in a split second, for it creates consumer exposure literally on the run. Motorists do not have the time to leisurely read the commercial signs which happen along their travel routes. They cannot divert a great deal of attention from the road to a sign while driving at high speed. They must grasp the essence of the message at a glance.

For this reason, outdoor advertisements display large colorful illustrations with few words. This sort of copy treatment lends itself best to well-known brands. Their names, logotypes, and package designs are already familiar, and consumers can recognize them almost immediately. The copywriter here calls upon past experience to facilitate product identification. Not all outdoor panels are on roadways. Some are in the middle of cities and mainly encounter foot traffic. But the same principles hold. Few pedestrians will stop and gawk at a poster, no matter how attractive the subject matter.

Types of Outdoor Advertising

Although the Outdoor Advertising Association of America establishes standards for advertising carriers, they are nevertheless diverse in shape and size. A number of different forms exist. These can usually be divided into three major types, which in order of importance are posters, painted posters, and spectaculars. Costs per unit run in a reverse sequence, with the specialties priced at the top and the common units selling for the lowest prices.

Posters These are often referred to as billboards. They are standardized panels made to accommodate posters of certain sizes. The most popular is the 24-sheet poster, which got its name from the way it used to be produced. At one time it actually took two dozen sheets, fitted together and pasted up, to make a whole advertisement. The larger printing presses of today have reduced the number of sections by some 50 percent, but the name has stuck. A 24-sheet poster now merely means an outdoor advertisement of a given size, namely, one measuring 8 feet 8 inches high and 19 feet 6 inches long.

The old 24-sheet standbys are gradually being substituted by 30-sheet posters, which offer 25 percent more space for advertising. Panels of both sizes may be illuminated, especially in locations of heavy night traffic. The lighting of road signs may often conflict with energy conservation public policy.

Sellers of poster panels ordinarily offer outdoor availabilities for thirty day periods. The offer comes in the form of gross rating points (GRPs) delivered by a set of panels. For example, a package of 100 GRPs says that a plant operator will provide enough panels to yield daily consumer exposures equal to the population of the market. A 50-GRP package in the same area will produce half as many exposure opportunities. The size of the market determines the exact cost for each GRP alternative.

The Traffic Audit Bureau (TAB) is the accepted authority for GRP figures. It estimates traffic flows at each location. The exposures are derived from TAB ratings, a system whereby basic traffic counts are modified by factor weightings. The relevant locational factors are length of approach, speed of vehicles on the road, angle of driver perception, and competition from other panels.

Advertising plans which include outdoor advertising customarily cite estimates for cost-per-thousand exposures. These statistics have meaning only when comparing locations for a given type of outdoor advertising. They cannot be used to compare different media, because an exposure to one is not necessarily the same thing as an exposure to another. The nature of the impressions are not the same. Indeed, the same may be true with respect to an impression made by a 24-sheet poster and one by a spectacular.

Painted bulletins These are normally larger than posters, and designed specially for the advertiser. The messages are painted at particular outdoor plants, and because they are more durable, they have a longer life than posters. They also cost more, and contracts usually run for a year. The longer time period helps to amortize the higher cost of production. Each location is selected on its own, with no regard to GRPs resulting from a package. The advertiser can thus offset the higher cost by choosing an above average location.

Advertisers with several painted bulletins in a city may opt for a rotary plan. This permits a firm to rotate its advertisements among locations at periodic intervals, provided the messages are varied. Rotation is a device to combat campaign erosion, which is presumed to set in after repeated exposure. If familiarity does not actually breed contempt, it begets apathy and inattention. Replacing the old, shopworn images with new ones is supposed to revitalize flagging consumer interest.

Spectaculars They are few in number and occur in high traffic locations. They are almost always illuminated, hoping to take full advantage of the high density in either vehicles or people. A well-known example of a spectacular is the computerized panel towering some six stories above Times Square. It runs sequences of animated commercials over and over. The same advertisements are displayed every few minutes. Costs for getting onto this program are relatively high, amounting to several thousand dollars a week.

SUMMARY

There are two types of magazines, consumer and business. Consumer magazines make up the major part of the industry in terms of either circulation or revenue. More than half of all advertising revenue is accounted for by the top twenty magazines in the field.

The outstanding characteristic of consumer magazines is selectivity, which occurs in editorial content, audience specialization, or both. Editorial selectivity creates a favorable advertising climate for related products. Audience selectivity refers to external audience characteristics. Similar demographics can result from magazines with dissimilar but competing editorial material. Audience compatibility is the primary criterion for magazine selection in advertising; editorial compatibility is secondary and is considered only if audience requirements are fulfilled.

The one-page advertisement is the standard space unit. Surcharges are imposed for bleed, color, multiple pages and preferred positions. Magazines offer discounts for volume and frequency.

Consumer magazines are mainly paid circulation publications, and offer circulation guarantees to advertisers. But the chief criterion for advertising is audience. Audience data are gathered by sample surveys, which present serious problems in both reliability and validity.

Advertisers use consumer magazines in various ways. Those with large television schedules view magazines as supplemental to broadcasting operations. Small-budget brands aim primarily at reaching select marketing targets. When magazines are the dominant medium, as for such products as tobacco and liquor, schedules are put together to achieve reach and frequency.

Outdoor advertising is usually given a subordinate function in the media mix. It is used primarily as reminder advertising. There are three basic types of outdoor advertising: posters, painted bulletins, and spectaculars, in order of importance. Unit costs run in an inverse sequence.

For print media, as in television, the audience concept plays a key role in the selection of advertising carriers. The next chapter investigates the derivation of audience estimates.

Questions for Chapter 13

1. What characteristics would you attribute to the leading consumer magazine advertisers shown in Table 12–2?

2. What conditions might lead an advertiser to select *Newsweek* rather than *Cosmopolitan* for an advertisement for perfume?

3. If you were the advertising manager of an airline, how would you list the *pros* and *cons* of advertising flights to Mexico in *National Geographic Magazine?*

4. Why would circulation of a magazine, in general, not be as meaningful as audience? When might circulation be more meaningful?

5. In what ways can a schedule in *Time* complement one in Dallas, on network tv?

6. Why do magazine users require many more breakouts or cross-tabulations of audience data than television users?

7. Would an advertiser benefit from a reach-frequency analysis which combined both magazines and television?

8. Why would outdoor media have little likelihood of dominating a firm's media mix?

9. What advantages accrue from the use of magazines? Outdoor?

Footnotes for Chapter 13

[1] Estimated from *Publishers Information Bureau/Leading National Advertisers* (December, 1980).

[2] From correspondence of Robert J. Coen of McCann-Erickson to W. S. Sachs.

[3] Estimated from *PIB/LNA* (December, 1980).

[4] Estimated from *PIB/LNA* (December, 1980).

[5] Estimated from *PIB/LNA* (December, 1980).

[6] Estimated from *PIB/LNA* (December, 1980).

[7] Estimated from *PIB/LNA* (December, 1980).

[8] See "Turnabout," *Advertising Age* (August 24, 1981), p. 1.

[9] Standard Rate & Data Service, Inc., *Consumer Magazine and Farm Publication Rates and Data* (Skokie, Ill.: SRDS, 1982).

[10] For examples, see "Magazine Research Maze: What's the Way Out?" *Marketing & Media Decisions* (December 1979), pp. 59–63, 112–124; William S. Sachs, "Mag-

azine Research in Crisis," *Marketing Review* (May/June 1976), p. 13; "Who's Got the Answer?" *Media Decisions* (May 1978), pp. 72–75.

[11] See note 2 above.

[12] Wright, et al., *Advertising*, p. 209.

Advertising Research: The Medium

Since audience has become the major criterion by which advertisers evaluate media, it is also the central theme of media research. This chapter examines how research firms go about estimating television program and consumer magazine audiences. It is in these media that audience measurements make the greatest impact on time and space buying.

The chapter is divided into broadcast and print audience research. Each part considers such issues as:

- **Strengths and weaknesses of research methods for measuring audiences**
- **Misallocations of marketing resources owing to biases in survey methods**
- **Possible solutions to problems of resource misallocations**
- **Computer models for selection of media schedules**

AUDIENCE MEASUREMENTS

Media research deals with a vital link in the mass communications chain—the destination of advertising messages. Unless a person is exposed to the medium, he or she will not be exposed to the advertisement it carries. Media research, therefore, studies the size and characteristics of audiences.

The notion of audience was carried over into mass media from the theater. There, it meant an assembly of spectators who came to watch a performance and where business managers could check audience size by box office receipts. They tried to match revenue with their costs, just as any other seller of a good or service. Audience levels, indicated by number of tickets sold, represented the demand for their product.

Counting the house in mass media is not the same as counting tickets at the box office, with the possible exception of pay television. For one thing, media measurement concerns itself not with something tangible, such as tickets sold or seats filled, but with intangible mental activities, such as listening, viewing, and reading.

Broadcasters have no other way of assessing the demand for their offerings, for there is no real counterpart to a theater. The same radio and television sets carry alternative programs. This would be like having all plays run at the same theater at the same time, an egregious absurdity. Although publishers do count tangible things like circulation, these copy counts provide revenue figures. They tell advertisers little as to how many people are potential recipients of their commercial messages.

Different skills are required to partake of different media activities. For example, to listen is not the same as to read or to view. A box office count does not have to take into account how theatergoers pay attention to a play, but mass media measurements do.

This brings into view a set of questions pertaining to audience definitions. How much of a program must a person hear in order to be counted a "listener?" Does "viewing" imply seeing the whole show, some part of it, or just having the set on regardless of whether attention is being paid to the program? Reading is similarly differentiated. A person may read a magazine intensively or just glance at a few pages. But what should be counted here to demonstrate listenership, viewership, or readership?

Because exposure to media calls for different mental processes, and different kinds of evidence for such occurrences, audience definitions for broadcast and print are not exactly comparable. In fact, definitions may even remain incongruous with respect to the same medium. For example, a Nielsen rating for a network show has a meaning completely different from a Nielsen estimate of viewers for that same program on individual stations. Yet, both supposedly measure program popularity.

Lastly, the method used in measuring audience to a large degree determines the audience definition. Current audience measurements are undertaken primarily by syndicated services, and there are various options available for gathering data. These research houses, like any other business firm, fit their operations to their resources and capabilities. Thus A. C. Nielsen, which has had limited experience in managing large field staffs doing personal interview surveys, has focused on mechanical measurements and mail-collected questionnaires. W. R. Simmons, with a long history in print readership studies, has structured its survey along the traditional lines of the editorial interest method for measuring magazine audiences. The various methods which research firms use become institutionalized over time, and form a hard core of vested interests. Once entrenched, their proponents seek to perpetuate them even when their inadequacy or irrelevancy becomes painfully obvious.

NETWORK TV AUDIENCE MEASUREMENTS

The performance of programs on network television is gauged by the Nielsen Television Index (NTI). The so-called ratings which emanate from this service enjoy common acceptance by all segments of the advertising industry—advertisers, agencies, and networks. These statistics are the foundation of contract negotiations, which include prices and seller guarantees of performance. These ratings make up the accounting system of the television industry, spelling out what it is that buyers get for their money. And because network revenue comes mainly from advertising, the NTI ratings determine the life and death of tv programs.

Nielsen ratings derive from a fixed panel of about 1,200 homes selected to represent all households in the United States. The effective sample size at any time is probably closer to 1,100 because the full sample complement is not in operation. Television sets in each sample household are connected with audimeters, which record minute-by-minute the channels to which the sets are tuned. These audimeters are wired directly to a Nielsen central office computer by telephone lines.

A rating is the percentage of all homes tuned to a program during the average minute it was on the air. It measures home tuning, not people viewing. A set may be on with no one watching. Or it may have different numbers of viewers. Although people are not actually counted, the industry is willing to accept a measurement of household tuning as an estimate of audience size.

The ostensible reason why the industry prefers the audimeter over other known methods is its appearance of being impersonal and precise. It expresses overt behavior mathematically without becoming sullied by human beings. Researchers and academicians are of various opinions as to whether this is really so. But there can be no doubt that the audimeter reigns supreme as the ultimate arbiter of program popularity on network lineups.

Audience characteristics, such as age and sex, are derived from a diary-keeping Nielsen panel of some 2,400 households. The participants in this panel agree to enter all household viewing for each quarter hour. The panel is additionally wired with a recordimeter, which measures the gross amount of time a set was in use in much the same way as a speedometer shows the total mileage a car traveled. This device merely acts as a reminder to diary keepers to log in all viewing of their household members. It plays no part in actual computations of television viewing.

The proportions obtained from the audience composition panel are made to fit audimeter household levels so that estimates can be projected to U.S. totals. From a technical standpoint, this ratio-estimating procedure is highly questionable. But the resulting estimates are of no great consequence to advertisers since relatively few network programs are purchased for their selective quality.

The Nielsen audimeter offers several advantages: it records behavior mechanically as it occurs, unaffected by human memory lapses and motivation, and it offers the possibility of studying change over time in detailed ways, such as with turnover tables in longitudinal analysis.[1] This approach is more appropriate for networks than for advertisers. Broadcasters might use the analytical insights to relate changes in ratings to shifts in programs. But advertisers have no control over programing variables; they can only select shows after schedules have been put in place.

Since Nielsen gets viewing information from the same people week after week, changes in program ratings are more readily identifiable than they would be from independent samples. This can be a plus in analyzing program "wearout." But panels also violate probability theory based on repeat sampling, which regards observations coming from an infinite number of probable universes. One isolated rating has a range of error, but its exact position in relation to the "true" value of the universe is unknown. If random samples of tv viewing were taken each week, ratings could be expected to fluctuate up and down from the mean of the population. But not so with a panel. Since observations come from the same people, the error is fixed. It does not change direction. A person who watches a football game one Sunday has a greater liklihood than one who didn't of turning a game on the following Sunday. Behavior is patterned. This is why sampling error obtained initially from a panel tends to persist and become exaggerated with the passage of time.

Once, when network programs ran for some minimal period, the ability to detect trends may have offset the shortcomings caused by the absence of sampling error. But today, when networks change their offerings almost every week, it is difficult to rationalize any advantage of a fixed panel over independent samples.

Despite their mechanistic basis, and supposed greater reporting accuracy, Nielsen ratings raise the same nagging questions as other panels. People who participate evince a commitment not found in others, and hence may be different from individuals who do not cooperate in surveys. This difference may be reinforced by inducements given for joining a panel. The act of belonging to such a group conditions participants' behavior in many subtle ways. Just knowing that the shows they tune to influences what appears on the nation's living room screens sets panelists apart from the population in general.

Panels also suffer from attrition. People quit, move away, die, and have to be replaced. Mobility alone in the United States averages about twenty percent per annum, and is not uniform throughout the country. Large metropolitan areas on the West coast have a mobility rate roughly double that of the Northeast. All these potential changes and differences have led many research authorities to label unrepresentativeness as the major disadvantage of panels.[2] With high turnover, and no way of duplicating dropouts by replacements, panels have difficulties in keeping representative qualities.

In 1965, Alfred Politz Research conducted a national survey in which interviewers knocked on doors and observed whether a tv set was on or off. This type of survey is considered by many to be the most accurate alternative for measuring television tuning and viewing. Between 6:30 PM and 10:00 PM the Politz survey found forty-one percent of homes with sets in use, compared with fifty-five percent reported by Nielsen during the same period.

There have been numerous occasions when metered ratings of two services differed substantially in the same markets. One such market was Los Angeles in 1981. The electronically-measured ratings of Nielsen and

Arbitron showed differences of nine points in given quarter hours.[3] If this percentage were applied nationally, the magnitude of the disparity would amount to more than seven million homes! In some months the viewing levels of the two services moved in opposite directions. Naturally, the outbursts of indignation, coming mainly from stations, were directed at the service reporting the lower numbers. Who, if anyone, was right can never really be answered with any degree of certainty. But it does demonstrate that error dogs the steps of mechanical measures as long as they deal with people.

Yet ratings have had widespread acceptance, in large part because a high level of accuracy is not required. The typical network schedule consists of participations, with commercials spread out over many programs on different days and time periods. The end result of this scatter buying is an overall audience that approximates the average of all programs. It is similar to dollar averaging on the stock market, called indexing. Together with rating guarantees, risks are shifted backwards from advertisers to networks and television producers. If survey errors are randomly distributed—and this is likely because television does not yield selective audiences—an advertiser can approach optimality by using ratings to negotiate prices. An overestimate of one program will be offset by an underestimate of another. The proposition boils down to one of getting the average rating at minimum cost.

The redeeming quality of compensating errors, however, may encourage more frequent program changes insofar as ratings contain large degrees of uncertainty. It does not take much to drive a network show off the air. If a few rating points are enough, and often they are, television is the only industry in America where a differential of twenty odd homes in a survey can swing million dollar investment decisions. Higher advertising costs probably ensue, but the amount turns on the bargaining power of respective buyers and sellers. Money may also be shifted between network and spot television, depending upon relative prices, ratings, and the cross-elasticities of the two alternatives. The flimsy basis for investment decisions stems from the use of a small sample. This, in turn, is brought about by audimeter technology, which is expensive to install and maintain. In many ways, the entire research methodology totters on the absurd in an age when it is possible to monitor signals from distant planets.

SPOT TELEVISION AUDIENCE MEASUREMENTS

Ratings for spot markets, applicable to both national and local advertisers, are reported by two syndicated services, Arbitron and the Nielsen Station Index. Since their methods closely resemble each other, a description of one is sufficient to understand how local ratings work.

Arbitron, probably the leading audience measurement service for spot television, surveys more than two hundred individual markets. The frequency of these surveys vary in accordance with market size. The larger the market, the more frequently it is rated. Most markets, beginning with the smallest, are rated four times a year: February, May, July and November. These months coincide with Arbitron's "sweeps," so called because surveys cover all television markets. Arbitron's 1982 schedule called for surveying 178 out of 211 markets four times a year. Six markets were to be rated seven times; sixteen, six times; and eleven, five times.

The heart of the system is the diary, in which panelists record for a full week all home viewing for quarter-hour periods. Arbitron strives for a minimum of 200 diaries a week obtained from different households. Since ratings are reported for a period of four weeks, an ADI's effective sample size consists of 800 or so households.

Samples are drawn systematically from telephone lists supplied by Metromail. The selected households first receive a letter informing them that they were picked as a sample representing the population. Arbitron then follows up the letter with a phone call soliciting cooperation. The diaries go out to the panelists and, upon completion, back to the research house through the mail. Tabulating procedures call for weighting diary data by up to five variables for households and four for individuals in order to bring the sample into proper balance with the universe studied.[4]

Arbitron reports television viewing for both households and individuals. According to Arbitron, a program rating is defined as the percent of households or persons viewing particular stations for five minutes or more during an average quarter-hour period.

Arbitron's description of its methodology contains a section called "limitations," which details in a straightforward manner the shortcomings of its diary system. Government prodding was partly responsible for this reform. Still, Arbitron's forthright way of discussing research limitations is rare for marketing research firms servicing the advertising industry.

The major potential biases encompass both reliability and validity considerations. Reliability can be calculated, since Arbitron employs probability methods in drawing its samples. It can also be controlled, for it is essentially a function of sample size. The validity problem is far more difficult to solve, because errors are incalculable and probability gives way to uncertainty.

One obstacle to validity is nonresponse. Perhaps as many as half the initially-designated respondents refuse to cooperate by keeping diaries. If their viewing habits depart from those of diary keepers, survey results would not mirror the population in general. In addition, not all homes have telephones or listed numbers, and so have no chance of being included in the sample. Disparate viewing patterns between population segments would similarly affect representation.

Other impediments to validity deal with errors in how respondents fill out their forms. Diary entries may not have been made when viewing actually took place. When done later, the response is subject to memory failure, hearsay, and mistaken estimates of time spent watching television. In addition, the measuring instruments undoubtedly affect the behavior of what is measured. The mere acquiescence to keep a diary induces abnormal viewing patterns on the part of diary keepers.[5]

Although both Arbitron and Nielsen rely on diaries, ratings can be highly dissimilar for the same programs in the same markets. Comparing a large number of program ratings in individual markets, correlation analysis done by this author found a coefficient of determination (r^2) of less than .5. Virtually identical techniques displayed an associated variance of not quite fifty percent. Since fluctuations in one set of ratings diverge considerably from those of the other, users of different services would arrive at different decisions even if the choice criteria were identical.

MARKET RESOURCE MISALLOCATIONS

As in network television, advertisers in spot markets end up with scatter-based schedules. Rating guarantees given by stations further mitigate risks undertaken by advertisers.

The averaging principles in spot markets do not work as well as with network programs. Poor choices of program alternatives may occur in two situations: schedules selected within markets, and expenditure allocations between markets.

The first situation is brought about by station promotional activity during sweep periods, and is referred to as "hypoing." Some of these actions may affect the way diary keepers record their viewing, without any changes occurring in their watching habits. Arbitron considers such activities as "diary distortion," and threatens stations engaged in them with deletion of their audience estimates from published reports.[6]

The more pervasive and serious form of hypoing, however, results from station attempts to increase viewing during the sweep period. Stations dress up their program offerings when diaries go out. Networks aid and abet their affiliates by saving their best specials for times when the nationwide surveys are in progress. Such popular miniseries as "Roots," "The Godfather," "Shogun," and "Marco Polo," backed by large promotional budgets, were aired during rating sweeps. Other tactics include running high-rated regular shows as longer-than-usual episodes or showing the most successful films on normal movie nights.

The hypoing problem applies primarily to infrequently-rated markets. In the absence of any other information, buyers take the audience levels of a measurement month as indicative of ratings during non-rated periods. Even when hypoing is suspected, there is no possible way of adjusting ratings to normal situations. The Advertising Research Foundation issued a series of share analyses which, with monotonous regularity, came to one central conclusion: The four-week sweeps are "atypical," and "inadequate" for media selection and program evaluation.[7]

The solution to hypoing is clearly to rate markets more frequently. The Association of National Advertisers has proposed that sweep coverage be extended from four to eight weeks, at a time when sweeps were conducted during February, May, and November. This plan would in effect have been equivalent to rating all markets at least six times a year. But the proposal to increase survey frequency has met with a cool reception from television stations, which are the main supporters of rating services and would have to foot the additional costs. As long as advertisers take the position that media should pay for audience research, they cannot realistically expect that surveys will be tailored to buyer needs. As the old adage goes, he who pays the piper calls the tune.

Arbitron, in 1982, added July as a sweep month, increasing its nation-wide surveys from three to four times a year. But July is a month when viewing levels are near bottom and programs of station affiliates are mainly reruns, atypical of normal scheduling. The value of this addition for media selection remains problematical.

Misallocation of expenditures among markets stems from several factors which, in one way or another, are related to variation. Unlike network television, which is seen as broadcasting to a single, undifferentiated universe, spot television is made up of more than two hundred different entities. Its ratings are considered as evidence of tv viewing in particular, self-contained markets. But survey biases, especially non-sampling ones, are not randomly distributed among the markets measured. Consequently, the course of events will not treat all markets with an even hand; some markets will be favored as compared with others.

One source of relative error resides in the basic estimates of market size, to which ratings are projected. Both Arbitron and Nielsen base their household counts on updated estimates supplied by Market Statistics, Inc. (MSI). The benchmark for these updates is the decennial Census of Population and Housing. With the passage of time, estimates become less accurate. For example, the first counts of the 1980 Census indicated that many Sunbelt markets had received understated household estimates from MSI. This revelation resulted in a spat of station lawsuits to force the rating services to revise their base figures before the final census counts were out.[8] The revised figures showed tv household gains which were thirteen percent higher than MSI projections. It is estimated that millions of advertising dollars were diverted from television stations in these underrated markets. If so, resources were misallocated.

A second source of bias comes from nonresponse and interviewing errors which are market related. Samples in areas with high proportions of listed telephone numbers will be more representative of the population than samples from areas with low percentages. ADIs with comparatively small minority populations will yield more accurate diary entries than ADIs with large minority populations. But these distortions cannot be as readily determined as those of market size, and the misdirected advertising resources under these circumstances remain shrouded in uncertainty.

MAGAZINE AUDIENCE MEASUREMENTS

The advertising industry has relied upon two methods for measuring magazine audience: through-the-book and recent reading. Research companies have adapted numerous versions of these two methodologies over the years in carrying out their studies. The through-the-book technique, also known as the interest method, is the conventional approach by virtue of longevity. It dates back to the late 1930s, when *Life Magazine* introduced it to promote the idea that readers are many times as numerous as circulation. The recent reading method made its way into audience research during the 1960s, and has persisted as a viable alternative to the older methodology.

Simmons Market Research Bureau (SMRB), after a brief flirtation with recent reading, has settled down in getting its audience figures via through-the-book. Mediamark Research, Inc. (MRI) has committed itself to recent reading. Its management was once part of Target Group Index (TGI) which, for several years, used recent reading to grind out its audience statistics. When the firm merged with Simmons in 1978, TGI executives formed their own service to compete with SMRB, using the method which was their stock in trade before the merger.

The through-the-book technique takes qualified respondents through a stripped-down issue, page by page, and then asks whether they had seen any part of that issue previously. The qualifying question asks people whether they had looked into a magazine during the last six months. This is merely a screening device to avoid going through each book studied with each respondent.

SMRB interviews at different times for different publishing schedules; about five weeks after publication for weeklies and ten weeks for monthlies. The reason for this is to give magazines an opportunity to accumulate their maximum audiences. Each respondent on the survey is interviewed two times, one month apart. Reading claims are averaged for all issues measured, and reported once a year. The readership figure for a magazine represents its audience of an average issue.

MRI has respondents sort logo cards as a way of identifying magazines read in a given period. This span of time corresponds with the most recent publication interval—seven days for a weekly and thirty days for a monthly. The claimed readership is presumed to be equivalent to that of the average issue audience for any publication. In practice, this assumption is not quite correct, but MRI maintains that empirical data indicates a tendency of "very slightly to understate audience levels."[9]

Actually, the objective of both methods is to estimate readers of average issues. Through-the-book does this by asking about reading of particular issues; it is issue specific. Recent reading approaches the task on a time basis. It does not show respondents materials relating to particular issues. It can thus be characterized as time specific.

RESEARCH DISCORD

Despite having the same goal, the two methods for measuring readership have produced highly disparate results, both in absolute levels and survey-to-survey changes. The statistical disputes are often aired in the trade press, and sometimes wind up in the courts. The incredible has become the expected. Hardly anyone raised an eyebrow when an article in *Advertising Age* announced the issuance of the Simmons 1981 report with the somewhat facetious headline: "Simmons Out and Surprise! Challenges Fly."[10]

In 1977, the Simmons study showed 70 percent of the magazines surveyed as having audience declines from the previous year. Covering roughly the same period, competitor TGI recorded higher readership scores for 87 percent of a wider list.[11] Forty-eight of the same magazines were measured by both services within the two-year span. Of this total, 34 scored audience declines in Simmons but readership gains in TGI. Two magazines showed a reverse pattern. In only 12 out of the 48 cases, or 25 percent of the time, did the two research firms agree on the direction of change, let alone magnitude.[12]

The SMRB 1980 report listed 44 of the large magazines as being measured by the through-the-book method, and the remaining publications by the recent reading method. The result was that recent reading revealed jumps of some 90 percent over through-the-book estimates of the previous year.[13]

In general, recent reading yields higher audience figures than through-the-book. But the variation is not uniform. The largest differences occur for monthlies and the smallest for weeklies. The differential for supplements actually goes the other way. The following table compares the two services for publications credited with 12 million or more readers in the Simmons 1981 study. The table expresses the comparison by a ratio; MRI audience statistics are calculated as a percentage of SMRB results.

The prestigious Advertising Research Foundation (ARF) in 1979 undertook a comparability study which was supposed to end the confusion.[14] But the promise never materialized. Poorly designed, the study showed what was already known—recent reading gets substantially higher audiences than through-the-book. Edgar Roll, then ARF president, summed up the chaotic situation with a befitting *non sequitur*: "The thing to remember," he said, "is that all these numbers are estimates. . . No one

TABLE 14–1 *Comparative Audiences for Select Publications*

Publication	MRI Audience as a Percentage of SMRB Audience
Better Homes & Gardens	173
Family Circle	170
Family Weekly	81
Good Housekeeping	168
Ladies' Home Journal	151
McCall's	143
National Geographic	138
Newsweek	146
Parade	93
People	127
Playboy	148
Reader's Digest	147
Sports Illustrated	124
Time	124
TV Guide	123
Woman's Day	167

Note: MRI data courtesy of Mediamark Research, Inc. Percentage calculation by the author.

service can be used for everything, and if anyone thinks he can, he's just whistling 'Dixie.' "[15]

The lesson is not to use a single service for everything. But the relevant question remains whether any service can be used for anything.

Although advertising investments in consumer magazines are substantially lower than in television, the audience measurement problem may be more severe. The reason is two-fold: reporting frequency and segmented media schedules.

Unlike television, where audience data are reported at periodic intervals throughout the year, advertising schedules in magazines are developed from static concepts. SMRB reports a single audience figure which makes up the average, until the next survey a year later. MRI reports twice a year, but as a twelve-month moving average. This, too, would produce a lag in any observable change. By reporting an average issue audience, readership is treated as though it were uniform for all issues and for all times. Readership dynamics lie buried in an inscrutable average, and advertisers cannot adjust to short-term changes.

Since advertisers use magazines to a large degree to reach selective audiences, the redeeming quality of compensating error does not hold. If the measurement is not right, messages may be going to the wrong segments. No amount of scattering advertisements among a longer list of magazines can rectify an error of messages going to wrong target audiences. For this reason, the validity question assumes prominence.

QUESTIONS OF VALIDITY

There are at least two conditions necessary for survey validity, neither of which are satisfied by the research services. These criteria are:

1. People must be willing to answer the questions asked.
2. People must be able to answer the questions asked.

These prescriptions were forcefully demonstrated by a well-known survey in which people were asked about their opinions on the Metallic Metals Act. Some 70 percent ventured an opinion, though no such legislation ever existed. Here, people were willing but unable to give acceptable answers.

Audience figures are similar in the sense that reading represents a subjective activity, intrinsically personal. Measurements are subject to all the vagaries of surveys—response bias, interview bias, and faulty questionnaires. These sources of error are pervasively present even in the most costly surveys. But print audience studies make them prominent.

For instance, broadcast measurements are done on the basis of coincidental reporting. Even diaries, in theory at least, are supposed to record behavior the instant it occurs. But the through-the-book method asks people to recall reading of ten to twelve week-old issues. The recent reading method, with weaker cues, puts equally onerous burdens on respondents' memories. Broadcast ratings not reported immediately are mistrusted. Reading done three months ago is taken literally. To assume both broadcast and print surveys as being valid, one must make the bizarre assumption that Americans suffer from mental lapses with respect to television viewing but enjoy almost infallible memories when it comes to magazine reading.

The fact is that response errors are rampant in both SMRB and MRI surveys. For example, people read and forget they did and people don't read and think they did. The first instance leads to understated readership, the second to inflated reading claims.

The aspects of forgetting are especially large with respect to the more casual, out-of-home reading. Eric Marder and Associates, in 1965, stationed investigators in barber shops and medical offices around the New York and Albany areas, and had them take careful notes as to what people read while waiting to be groomed or diagnosed. All observed readers were called upon later and interviewed by the conventional through-the-book method. Fully 75 percent of those who were seen reading smaller publications like *Harper's* and *Atlantic Monthly* denied ever having looked into the issues they were observed reading. Larger, more popular magazines, such as *Life* and *Look*, exhibited memory failure of 14 percent and 29 percent respectively. Recent experiments conducted by the Advertising Research Foundation seem to have come up with similar results.[16]

Exaggerated reading claims are more difficult to document, but evidence points to their existence. These errors are also more critical than audience deflation because larger numbers are imputed to the relative errors.

Time, Inc., in 1981, ran an experiment which virtually duplicated the MRI method. But twenty-two of the logo cards used in the interview bore fictitious titles, including those of defunct magazines such as *This Week, Look, Colliers,* and *Literary Digest.* Inflated reading claims ranged from 0.6 percent to 11.6 percent.[17] On the face of it, the wrong figures do not seem large. But when these seemingly small percentages are projected to a universe of 150 million persons, as is customary with national samples, magazines can pick up as many as 17 million invalid readers.

Incredulous reading claims are also inherent in the through-the-book method. Alfred Politz Research in 1956 carried out studies with advanced copies using the through-the-book method. This survey was conducted with two issues of *Life, Saturday Evening Post,* and *Reader's Digest,* one of the issues being a prepublication copy. Dates were masked so that respondents could not readily tell the real from the decoys. People claiming to have read issues which were, in fact, nonexistent, if projected to the U.S. population, would have amounted to three million plus readers for each magazine.

The experiments with bogus issues do not prove that inflation in the reporting of magazine reading exists. But it does offer strong presumptive evidence of audience inflation, especially since the errors are much higher for some magazines than for others.

Long and tiresome interviews reinforce response errors. Both services leave behind product data questionnaires calling for minute details about hundreds of products to which very few people could possibly supply accurate answers, even if they had the time and the inclination. When SMRB picks up the product questionnaires, a reinterview on magazine readership is attempted. In 1977, an ARF audit found 51 out of 61 magazines had lower audiences on the second interview, as compared with the first. This divergence exceeds chance expectations. Apparently, respondents sped up the second round of interviewing by giving negative answers so that they wouldn't have to go through a lot of questions.

Response errors affect particular population segments in different ways. Since magazines are used for their selective characteristics, the differential effects of response errors impair magazine audience estimates.

For example, Simmons has consistently credited leading women's magazines with more readers per copy in the South, especially the rural South, than in any other section of the country. Perhaps it is because southern women are more willing to spend time talking with interviewers about magazines. In contrast, the New York metropolitan area, where people seem more impersonal, has one of the lowest incidents of reading.

Can anything be done to get more dependable statistics? It would be foolhardy, even arrogant, for an academician to draw up a blueprint for the industry. Yet the analysis of research methodology carries with it implications for certain approaches which could lead to improvement.

The research problem can be thought of as a series of trade-offs. Though the idea may seem distasteful to many, not all information can be made known or can be measurable.

The trade-off of accuracy for desired information has been practiced in television for many years. By accepting metered ratings, which indicate set tuning, the industry has substituted inferences about viewing for measurements of viewing. For magazines, the question boils down to the exact point at which one substitutes data of questionable value for data of better quality.

SMRB and MRI estimates are most accurate when dealing with subscribers and hard-core readers. The estimates are farthest apart with respect to casual, out-of-home readers.[18]

One approach, then, is to measure subscribers and non-subscribers separately. In fact, subscription lists can be used to validate survey results, or even to draw samples of the subscriber universe. If audience relationships can be found—and there is no reason why they cannot if research is conducted properly—building a computer model would be a relatively easy matter. Samples of subscribers can be matched with census information for any territorial division, even one as small as a zip code, and statistics can be projected accurately. Population characteristics here are ascertainable, can be imputed to valid counts, and using a computer, would reduce research costs substantially. There would be less interviewing.

The "passalong" and newsstand portion of total audience presents a problem in determining a feasible memory threshold. The longer the lapse of time from when reading took place, and the vaguer the cue or memory aid given to respondents, the larger the error.

For instance, reducing the time gap between an issue's age and the interview by the through-the-book method would lighten the memory burden. Actually, not a shred of evidence exists which says that an interview which takes place ten weeks after a monthly's publication is optimum. This practice doesn't seem to have been based on any factual information and has been followed for decades. The author's experience with readership studies indicates audiences accumulate much faster then currently imagined. Likewise, the recent reading method need not confine its period to thirty days for monthlies. It can shorten it to fifteen, or for that matter, to only yesterday. If out of line reading claims are still suspected, some playback of content remains a possibility.

The main point, however, is not this or that method, or this or that question. The idea is to substitute some reasonable evidence of reading—actual or implied—for largely unsubstantiated claims. This approach would eliminate many casual readers that just "leaf through" a publication along with the survey guesswork. This type of reader has little meaning to advertisers, and to the publishers.

Structural changes in the advertising industry would probably have to accompany such changes in research. Publishers support the service which gives them the most favorable statistics, not the one that provides the most accurate information. If advertisers want research devoid of promotional overtones, they cannot expect media sellers to pick up the tab. They must be willing to pay for it. Nor can research firms be counted upon for reform. Their interests may dictate a contrary course of action. The lengthy interviews, for example, afford them a means of increasing their prospective customers by having more publications in their studies. Computer modeling may mean less revenue for research houses by reducing the number of surveys and field interviews.

In 1961, Jay Forrester of the Massachusetts Institute of Technology rattled a convention of the Advertising Research Foundation when he characterized advertising research as 98 percent promotion and two percent research. While his verdict might be a bit more charitable today, advertising remains one of the few industries in which research in a developmental sense is not done. If firms would contribute from their advertising budgets a small fraction of a percentage point, it would go a long way towards solving the media audience confusion.

COMPUTER MODELS: AN UNFULFILLED PROMISE

As electronic data processing made deeper and deeper inroads into business, it was only a matter of time until mathematical models and computers were applied to media selection. The great surge of computer models came during the 1960s. The marriage of computer modeling and media scheduling seemed natural. As enumerated by professors Little and Lodish at the New England Media Evaluators Association meeting in 1976, the advantages of model building were as follows:

- Computers are enthusiastic clerks. They can evaluate many more alternatives within reasonable time and cost limits than can people.
- Computers can handle complexity with ease.
- Computer models permit the joining of field data and expert judgment in a unifying structure. With such a structure, the alternatives can be evaluated quickly, consistently, and cheaply.
- Models provide a structure for thinking about the problem and set up requirements for data and judgments. Models clarify the elements that go into a media decision, and facilitate matters for people who do not think about advertising every day.
- In the long run, the use of models and computers seems likely to stimulate better media data.

The popular models during the mid-1970s were essentially decision models. Some took an optimizing approach. Others sought a comparatively superior solution, though nonoptimal. The major mathematical approaches were linear programing, marginal analysis, and simulation.[19]

Linear programing, first espoused by BBDO in 1962, attempted to fit media selection problems into a mathematical mold which had been employed successfully in physical distribution and business logistics. A linear program optimizes an objective function under given constraints. BBDO defined its objective function as "rated exposure units," which turned out to be an audience figure weighted by marketing and advertising factors.

The chief proponent of marginal analysis was J. Walter Thompson. Using iterative procedures, defined as successive approximations moving towards an optimum, the program attempted to build a media schedule by manipulating weighted net unduplicated audiences.

The main supporter of the simulation approach was a group of ten agencies which hired the Diebold Corporation to construct a computer model called COMPASS (Computer Optimal Media Planning and Scheduling Systems). Simulation manipulates units in an imaginary universe kept in a computer memory to evaluate alternative schedules. Its results are nonoptimal.

Despite their variety, all of these computer models consist of inputs and outputs, connected to each other by intervening variables. The in-betweens are critical, for they form the rationale of the system. They explain how the inputs influence outputs, so that the system comes under control of the decision maker. Unfortunately, the nature of the relationships among variables are not really known. They are postulated, and often from a thin, almost nonexistent theoretical base.

For example, the BBDO linear program made assumption upon assumption which had little basis in fact. It assumed no differential effect from repeat exposures, constant media costs, and validity of highly subjective data about copy and media environment. It also omitted from consideration audience duplication and timing of messages.[20] Similar limitations were inherent in other models as well. After a thorough investigation and trial of linear programing, Bass and Lonsdale concluded that the model yielded solutions that were similar to cost-per-thousand calculations which could just as easily have been done on a desk calculator.[21]

The 1970s saw the eclipse of decision models, whose sun had never really shone and whose once bright future had never come to pass. The models could demonstrate little improvement over contemporary practices, and offered no reduction in media department budgets. A recent survey of the leading advertising agencies by the author failed to turn up a single company using decision models for media selection.

The setback did not spell the end of computer models. Rather, they reverted to a more rudimentary form. Media planners scaled down their expectations, settling for less ambitious objectives and spending less in the process.

Computers are currently used to store and retrieve media data. Today's programs are primarily data generating devices, but more sophisticated than those of an earlier period. One such program is that which produces reach and frequency estimates for various combinations of media vehicles. But the focus is on data analysis for practical, everyday applications.

SUMMARY

The audience concept involves an intangible, mental activity, such as listening, viewing, reading. These activities are qualitatively different; hence, audience definitions of diverse media are not exactly comparable.

Network television is measured by the Nielsen Television Index, based on a consumer panel with television sets hooked up to audimeters. Though the method eliminates error in reporting, it suffers from unrepresentativeness.

Spot television audiences are derived from diaries kept for one-week periods. Two research firms measure spot markets: Arbitron and Nielsen Station Index. The research limitations inherent in each service may result in misallocations of advertising expenditures.

Magazine audiences are reported by SMRB and MRI. Though both services use different methods, they both aim at measuring average issue audiences. But their results are highly disparate. Both methodologies have such serious shortcomings that it is doubtful whether either produces valid audience estimates.

With advances in computer technology, a number of decision models for media selection emerged during the 1960s. But the models never fulfilled their promises, and gradually gave way to more rudimentary but practical data generation models.

Questions for Chapter 14

1. Compare the reliability and validity of personal coincidental ratings with Nielsen's metered ratings for network tv. Why do you think advertising agencies and networks have never supported the former methods despite widespread acknowledgement of their greater accuracy?

2. From what standpoint of a media buyer at an advertising agency, what are the major limitations of local tv ratings?

3. If you were the brand manager of a packaged good, would you want more detailed audience statistics for television than are currently available?

4. What are the strengths and weaknesses of Nielsen metered ratings for network tv?

5. An advertising agency uses an average of Simmons and MRI data to estimate audience size of various magazines. Do you agree with this procedure?

6. Would local tv ratings be more accurate if sample size were increased by 50 percent?

7. The ANA and AAAA have recommended more frequent ratings to eliminate tv "hypoing." Why do you think the industry has failed to adopt these recommendations?

8. Since circulation policy affects readership, why don't publications generally not base their circulation planning on audience measurements?

9. What is the rationale for a through-the-book interview asking respondents about which articles look "interesting" when the objective is to measure readership? Do you think that this is necessary?

10. Why have advertisers and advertising agencies abandoned the use of computer models for media selection?

Footnotes for Chapter 14

[1] Churchill, *Marketing Research*, pp. 71–73.

[2] Churchill, *Marketing Research*, pp. 74–75.

[3] Bob Marich, "Metered Ratings Muddle L.A. TV Market." *Advertising Age* (May 11, 1981), p. 58.

[4] For details of rating methods used, see The Arbitron Company, *Description of Methodology* (October 1980).

[5] Alan D. Fletcher and Thomas A. Bowers, *Fundamentals of Advertising Research* (Columbus, Ohio: Grid, 1979), p. 234.

[6] The Arbitron Company, *Description of Methodology*, p. 70.

[7] "May Sweeps Termed 'Atypical' Again by ARF," *Advertising Age* (July 24, 1978), p. 46; "ARF Index Discounts 'Hyped' Sweep Ratings," *Advertising Age* (July 11, 1977), p. 156.

[8] See Colby Coates, "Rating Services Updating Census Data," *Advertising Age* (April 20, 1981), p. 20.

[9] Mediamark Research, Inc., *The Procedure For Measuring Magazine Audience* (1981), p. 3.

[10] Stuart Emmerich, "Simmons Out and Surprise! Challenges Fly," *Advertising Age* (September 28, 1981), p. 1.

[11] Bob Donath, "New Storm Brews on Simmons Reader Data," *Advertising Age* (October 31, 1977), p. 3.

[12] Based on "Comparative Magazine Audience Estimates," *Advertising Age* (October 31, 1977), p. 96.

[13] Leah Rozen, "Slugging It Out: A Research Fray," *Advertising Age* (October 27, 1980), p. S-22.

[14] Advertising Research Foundation, *ARF Comparability Study* (New York: Advertising Research Foundation, 1980).

[15] Rozen, "Slugging it Out," p. S-22.

[16] Advertising Research Foundation, *ARF Compatability Study*, p. 10.

[17] Clark Shiller, "Remembered, But Never Read," *Advertising Age* (October 26, 1981), pp. S-14–S-15.

[18] Timothy Joyce, "The 'Incredible Shrinking Machine,' or When is Through-the-Book No Longer Through-the-Book?" (Mimeographed paper, 1981), p. 8.

[19] Dennis H. Gensch, "Computer Models in Advertising Media Selection," *Journal of Marketing Research* (November 1968), pp. 414–424.

[20] Philip Kotler, "Computerized Media Planning Techniques, Needs and Prospects," *Occasional Papers in Advertising* (Urbana, Ill.: American Academy of Advertising, 1965).

[21] Frank M. Bass and Ronald T. Lonsdale, "An Exploration of Linear Programming in Media Selection," *Journal of Marketing Research* (May 1966), pp. 179–188.

15 *Business-to-Business Advertising*

Many have maintained that advertising to business differs little from consumer advertising. In fact, the two types of advertising have important characteristics in common. Both are forms of national advertising and seek to achieve marketing goals by communicating product offerings through mass media. The largest difference is actually designated markets, or target audiences, and, holds the advertising-is-advertising school of thought, the difference is only a matter of degree, not of kind.

But the differences in markets makes for rather large differences in degree. Business advertising faces problems which are different from those of consumer advertising.

The differences between business and consumer advertising can be seen in this chapter's discussion of:
- **Nature of business markets and implication for advertisers**
- **Role of business advertising in a firm's marketing mix**
- **Trend toward rational copy treatment and inverted authority-information pyramids**
- **Media selection in business-to-business advertising**

THE INDUSTRIAL MARKET

Business-to-business advertising represents a huge market. But the number of buying units in business fields are relatively small. Compared to 82 million households and nearly three times as many individuals, the industrial market contains a much smaller number of buying units, close to 12 million.[1] This market, though, is highly diversified, requiring many different kinds of goods and services. The normal practice of advertisers is to subdivide this market by various methods, depending on the output of a particular company.

When a product is tailored to one or several specific industries, it is said to have a vertical market. When there is a demand for a product in many different industries, its market is regarded as horizontal. In the latest *Census of Manufactures*, all establishments in this sector of the economy came to about 360,000.[2] Certain products are highly specialized, such as precision instruments, oil drilling equipment, and large metal-working machinery. Other products are used by a wide variety of firms, such as lubricating oils, small hand tools, and office supplies.

Products or services having wider markets have a greater need for advertising. It is a way of gaining market coverage when other means

TABLE 15–1 *Number of Establishments in Manufacturing Sectors*

Major Industry Group	Number of Establishments	
	Total	With 20 or more employees
Food	26,656	11,038
Tobacco	228	123
Textile mill products	7,202	4,131
Apparel	26,505	11,932
Lumber	37,302	7,056
Furniture	10,235	3,588
Paper	6,545	3,999
Printing and publishing	49,767	9,132
Chemicals	12,173	4,602
Petroleum & coal	2,206	773
Rubber & plastics	11,943	5,294
Leather	3,075	1,486
Stone, clay, glass	17,744	5,201
Primary metal	7,375	3,980
Fabricated metal	33,712	12,739
Machinery	48,200	12,446
Electric equipment	14,973	6,338
Transportation equipment	10,176	3,653
Instruments	7,481	2,538

Source: U.S. Census Bureau, *1977 Census of Manufactures.*

might be sorely strained. Firms serving horizontal markets have more media options open to them in communicating with customers, and there is more money available for media support.

The number of business units which make up a market depend upon the degree of concentration and firm size. For example, of the 360,000 manufacturing establishments, more than half had less than ten employees and accounted for only some two percent of value added.[3] Some idea of the nature of vertical markets can be gleaned from Table 15–1, which dissects total manufacturing into selective two-digit SIC classifications. For each category, the table shows the number of all establishments and those with twenty or more employees.

When a firm's goods and services are tailored to specific industries, marketing targets shrink to dwarfish proportions. The entire tobacco industry is made up of only 228 establishments, equaling only 123 units with twenty or more employees. Firms manufacturing petroleum and coal total 2,206 establishments. The subcategory, petroleum refining, contains only 349 business units. Marketers selling specialized machinery to paper mills have a market potential of a meager 45 establishments. (See Table 15–1.)

Small buying unit figures, however, do not necessarily imply small sales. Compared to consumer markets, per unit purchasing power is immense. Paper clips bought by an individual usually comes to a paltry sum. To make an adequate profit on such transactions a firm must sell to a large number of consumers. An order for the same item by Exxon or AT&T can run into thousands of dollars. The larger an order, the more deliberation must take place in the buying process.

It might be argued that business people are no different from ordinary consumers.[4] They are human beings with the same desires, emotions and hangups. They strike up friendships with suppliers, accept their invitations to play golf at exclusive country clubs, and allow themselves to be wined and dined at the most expensive bistros. If these noneconomic activities had no influence over buying, they would quickly disappear from corporate expense accounts.

Yet, on the whole, industrial buying is a comparatively rational process. The buyer of goods and services for a company is not spending for personal consumption. The purchaser is paid to evaluate products as an expert, and is expected to approach the task rationally, not emotionally. Purchase commitments must conform to company rules and procedures, and are subject to financial control. Many goods and services require negotiations, with contracts reviewed at several levels. Though buying decisions may not always be wise, they are rational.

Narrowness of markets and deliberation in purchasing have affected business-to-business advertising in three major ways. First, they have deemphasized advertising in favor of personal selling. Advertising budgets in the industrial field are sharply lower than in the consumer field. Second, they have made copy focus on rational appeals. Third, they have dictated the choice of selective media. Business-to-business advertising actually uses a variety of media types, some of which are the same as those used in consumer advertising. But it falls back on some which are highly specialized and not pursued by consumer product manufacturers at all. Thus, there are different requirements for business-to-business advertising than for consumer advertising.

DEEMPHASIS OF ADVERTISING

The elevation of personal selling to a position of primacy has had two main effects on business-to-business advertising: budgets and objectives. Because advertising is relegated to a subordinate level in the marketing mix, it must do with small budgets. Most marketing funds go into sales. This situation requires advertising to serve as a support function for the sales force.

There are no exact statistics regarding the magnitude of business advertising. On the basis of available information, a rough approximation would place the figure at about 7.5 percent of total advertising expenditures. Total advertising expenditures in 1981 amounted to about $61.3 billion.

Many valuable insights into budgeting for business-to-business advertising can be gathered from the ADVISOR project, conducted at the Massachusetts Institute of Technology, which studied marketing expenditures of some 200 industrial products. The estimated median marketing-to-sales ratio was found to be ten times larger than the median advertising-to-sales ratio.[5] The latter came to 0.6 percent, which by all accounts is decidedly low. The major part of marketing budgets is siphoned off by the sales force.

According to ADVISOR, the median advertising-to-marketing ratio ranges from five percent to nineteen percent. This multiplier of four between top to bottom range compares with a multiplier of eighteen in advertising-to-sales ratios.[6] These relationships suggest that advertising budgets are dependent upon marketing budgets rather than actual sales.

The conventional wisdom in the industrial field sees an advertisement by itself as incapable, in most instances, of closing a sale. Since personal selling dominates marketing, advertising is conceived of as an aid to sales personnel. Of course, business-to-business advertising spans a wider range of functions. But its most important role is to act as a salesperson's assistant, to pave the way for a cordial customer reception.

Advertising which does this performs no mean accomplishment. The average industrial sales call in 1982 vaulted to $178.[7] Assuming it took 4.3 calls, on the average, to close a sale, the cost of a close can be calculated at $765 ($178 × 4.3 = $765). If advertising can make calls more productive, or decrease the number of necessary calls, potential gains can be substantial.

Advertising does sales preparatory work in three ways: it generates leads for salespeople; makes prospects aware of product offerings; and builds a favorable company image. The latter function serves as corporate advertising, and will be discussed in Chapter 16. As can be seen, these three functions of advertising are designed to assist sales personnel. The now famous McGraw-Hill advertisement, seen in Figure 15–1, dramatically illustrates the preparatory selling function of business-to-business advertising.

AWARENESS-SALES RELATIONSHIP

The three main functions of business-to-business advertising—generating leads, transmitting product offers, and building image—are often classified as "awareness" functions. Probably the most complete study undertaken to assess the effects of awareness was that of PIMS. This is a research project of the Strategic Planning Institute which has been in progress for

"I don't know who you are.

I don't know your company.

I don't know your company's product.

I don't know what your company stands for.

I don't know your company's customers.

I don't know your company's record.

I don't know your company's reputation.

Now–what was it you wanted to sell me?"

MORAL: Sales start **before** your salesman calls–with business publication advertising.

McGRAW-HILL MAGAZINES
BUSINESS • PROFESSIONAL • TECHNICAL

Fig. 15–1 *McGraw-Hill. The Man in the Chair. Courtesy of McGraw-Hill Publications Company.*

almost a decade. In cooperation with Cahners Publishing Company, a major publisher of business publications, PIMS investigated links between awareness, share of market, and profitability.[8]

Market share and profit information came from seventy-three lines of business in the PIMS data base. The awareness data was derived from reader surveys of four Cahners' business publications: *Design News, Plastics World, Professional Builder,* and *Specifying Engineer.* Respondents to the Cahners' survey were asked to indicate three of four preferred suppliers for a variety of products sold in their markets. A mention of a supplier was taken as demonstrated awareness.

This study found awareness strongly linked to market share. That is, when a regression line is drawn through the paired points, awareness corresponds with market share almost one for one. From these results, PIMS researchers postulated what was, in effect a hierarchy model, the influences of which flow in the sequence seen in Figure 15–2.

According to the model in Figure 15–2, the degree of brand awareness is determined by both past and current effort. Companies then have options of converting the intangible quality of awareness into a larger market share. Those successful in doing so benefit from reduced costs arising from the experience curve and from economies of scale. Both of these factors lower operating costs which, in turn, translate into greater profitability. Past PIMS research has demonstrated a relationship between market share and return on investment.[9]

This chain-of-influence explanation is intuitively appealing and apparently plausible. Unfortunately, it rests on rather tenuous assumptions and questionable research.

A sequential cause between awareness and brand share cannot be determined from a cross-sectional study. A longitudinal study is necessary to show that changes in awareness led to changes in share. Even worse, awareness is a cognitive factor, and is not measured by asking questions about supplier preferences. The latter is a conative measure. The results then say nothing more than this: if you ask people about the brand they prefer, they are apt to tell you the brand they buy. Under these circumstances, a close relationship between response about preference and share of market is to be expected. If preference is called awareness,

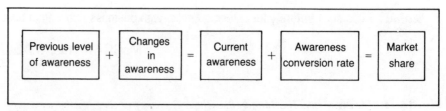

Fig. 15–2 *Visualization of PIMS Awareness-Brand Share Model.*

then the flow of influence can just as easily go from personal selling to awareness to buying.

PIMS concluded that "managing brand awareness . . . should be a major concern of management."[10] No one can really argue with that platitude. But the more meaningful question of how to manage brand awareness lingers. Cognition can be accomplished in a large number of ways: by direct response, trade shows, telephone solicitations, public relations, and sales calls themselves. All these methods are, in fact, used by industrial marketers.

USE OF THE RATIONAL APPEAL

Since business people are regarded as buyers who deliberate, sift through relevant data, and compare alternative offers, message content follows a rational line. This type of message is often referred to as "reason-why copy." Its proposition is supported by relevant data and tied logically to a warrant.

For example, Crest toothpaste runs emotionally-charged commercials on television which show parents brimming with joy when their youngsters come back from dental checkups without any cavities. Crest stresses the same cavity-protection theme when advertising in *Dental Economics*, a magazine published for the dental profession. But even the most optimistic brand manager can hardly expect dentists to recommend Crest to their patients because of an ad showing a kid smiling and shouting, "Look mom, no cavities." When Crest advertises to the profession, its copy is highly technical. One advertisement claims that "exposure of incipient carious lesions to free fluoride accelerates the remineralization process." This statement is further documented with elaborate footnotes.

Likewise, Aqua-fresh ran an ad in the same issue, also heavily footnoted, illustrating results of clinical tests. One chart graphs caries reduction in a series of controlled lab experiments. Another compares "extrinsic stain reduction" of Aqua-fresh with that of "brushing with a water control." Advertising to the profession parallels the same basic proposition made to the consumer—that of a toothpaste with protective and freshening properties. But a general consumer reading the ad in *Dental Economics* would have a great deal of difficulty in connecting the two, or in translating the message phrased in dental terminology.

The amount and type of detail depend upon the nature of markets, and consequently upon the audience for whom communication is intended. Since markets are diverse, so are copy approaches. In general, vertical markets call into being specialized audiences, and copy relates to specific applications. Advertising to horizontal markets must communicate with a more diversified audience, and if the message is to be understood at all, it cannot be composed in esoteric terms. It may still adhere to a rational format, but it must come dressed in everyday attire. For example, the aver-

Is your small copier a dog?
Or just working like a dog?

It works days. It works nights. It works harder than was ever intended, simply because you underestimated your needs.

So when it breaks down, don't be surprised.

And don't call it those awful names. After all, most small copiers weren't made for big work loads.

Of course, the compact Minolta EP 530R isn't like most small copiers. It was designed to do a bigger job. The very reason we call it the bigger small copier.

It even takes big copier options. A document feeder. A sorter. And a counter to help keep track of the copies.

The Minolta EP 530R also has a self-diagnostic system. It helps keep little problems, little problems.

And because of Minolta's exclusive micro-toning system, you get crisp, clear copies. Edge to edge.

Up to 11″ x 17″.

The EP 530R makes reduced copies. But if you don't need reduced copies, you can get the EP 530R without the R. (Now you know what the R stands for.)

The Minolta EP 530R. The copier that will become the office pet because it will never be the office dog.

For the name of your nearest authorized Minolta dealer, look under our trademark in the Yellow Pages. Or call toll-free 800-526-5256. In New Jersey, 201-797-7808.

**The EP 530R.
The bigger small
copier.**

©1982 Minolta Corporation

MINOLTA

Fig. 15–3 *Minolta. A Copier Advertisement for Horizontal Markets. Courtesy of the Minolta Corporation.*

age businessperson can readily grasp the information given in the advertisement for the copier shown in Figure 15–3. The tenor of this advertisement is not atypical of that for similar products. Compare the simplicity of this message with the one in Figure 15–4, run in *Computer Design*, a publication edited for engineers and engineering managers working with computer equipment and systems design. Addressing an audience of technicians, the message speaks directly to these experts in their own terms.

In many respects, business-to-business advertising must adapt the same principles as those which apply to internal business communication. One such doctrine refers to inverted authority-information pyramids.[11]

Both authority and information requirements of a firm have pyramidal structures (Figure 15–5). For example, a company has only one president. It may have a few executive vice-presidents, vice-presidents, and a number of managers all the way down the line. As authority increases, the number of executives wielding such power decreases, and vice versa. But as the authority pyramid narrows, information requirements become broader and more general in scope. At the lower ends of the pyramid, information becomes constricted and prescribed. Subordinates are charged with more limited tasks, and consequently need restricted but detailed information.

Industrial products are often highly complex, and advertisements cannot possibly contain all information required by buyers. What can be said in a commercial message may be too limited to have any influence over purchase decisions. These situations are common when messages must be conveyed to technically-minded audiences. One solution is for advertisements to make offers of further information, such as pamphlets, brochures, research reports, and catalogs, to assist the buyer in reaching a decision. These requests also serve as leads for salespeople.

McGraw-Hill, the leading business magazine publisher, runs a service called Qualified Lead Service (QLS). It is an inquiry followup system, which sends out questionnaires for purposes of classifying requests for information in terms of purchase likelihood. QLS sends the "live" leads directly to the appropriate sales office of the advertiser so that action can be taken as quickly as possible. The charge for this service in 1982 amounted to about $12 per followup, which was not exactly cheap. Nevertheless, it was low in relation to the cost of a personal call.[12]

MEDIA SELECTION

Since industrial markets are generally small, media for business-to-business advertising tends to be selective. Major determinants, as with consumer advertising, are the product and market characteristics. When products are used by many industries, industrial advertisers have more latitude in their choices of horizontal or vertical media.

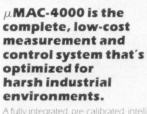

Fig. 15—4 *Analog Devices. An Advertisement Addressed to Technicians.*
Courtesy of Analog Devices, Inc.

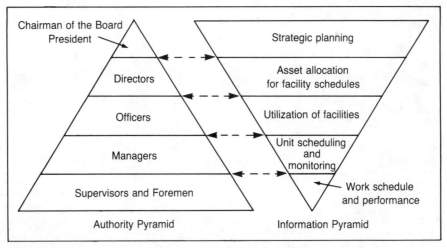

Fig. 15—5 *Inverted Authority-Information Pyramids.*

But communication takes place between people, not firms. Advertising plans must therefore modify pure market analysis in terms of number of firms and dollar volume of expenditures by considering decision-making units within firms. These are called "buying centers."

For some products, as many as fifteen to twenty people might be involved in a company purchase decision. In general, the costlier the product, the larger the buying center. A decision concerning a major installation normally draws into the decision process the ideas and opinions of many people—technicians, financial experts, department heads, directors, and top management, including the chief operating officer. On the other hand, a decision to buy a hand tool is made with little fanfare by a low-level manager at the operating end. Consequently, target markets are not determined solely by the extent of product usage among companies. The nature of buying centers and company objectives become factors which are handled in conjunction with the critical product-market use patterns.

How participants in buying centers interact with one another, and how they eventually achieve a group decision, forms a vast literature. Of the different patterns which have been observed, four basic descriptions have emerged.[13]

One popular prototype is that of autocracy. One person is responsible for the decision of the group. But there still remain questions as to how the autocrat weights all individual opinions. Another model resembles the American political system, in which the choice depends upon the largest number of votes. The winner can have a majority or a plurality. A variation of this view is one in which any choice requires a certain predesignated

WHERE'S THE FIRST PLACE TO LOOK FOR QUALITY OPTICS EQUIPMENT?

YOU'VE GOT IT!

It's the Ealing Optics Catalog and it's probably already on your bookshelf. No matter what your optics requirement, you should look to your Ealing catalog first. Because chances are the catalog lists exactly the item you need, along with comprehensive applications and engineering data. In the Ealing Optics Catalog you've got a definitive source for a broad spectrum of optics equipment and a name that's become synonymous with quality and value. It's the first place to look for the last word in products for optics research and development.

If you haven't received the latest Ealing Optics Catalog, be sure to call or write for your complimentary copy.

Ealing   THE EALING CORPORATION

Pleasant St., So. Natick, MA 01760 • (617) 655-7000/Newport Beach, CA • (714) 833-9826
International Offices in: Watford, England • Les Ulis, France • Höchst, W. Germany • Novara, Italy • Montreal, Canada

Fig. 15—6 *Ealing. An Advertisement Offering Further Information.* Courtesy of the Ealing Corporation.

number of votes. Here, voting takes place over and over until one alternative reaches the magic quota. A fourth model of buying center behavior sees the accepted choice as that which perturbs the least number of individuals. The alternative that wins is least offensive to members of the buying group.

The way one thinks buying centers arrive at decisions influences the choice of both message content and media. For example, if technical people make all recommendations for a particular product or service and these are seldom altered, a firm may decide to make sales calls to all technicians and reach purchase decision approvers with advertising only. In these latter circumstances, messages will be nontechnical and media will probably be of the vertical kind. If approvers are also technicians, copy would tilt toward the technical side. If approvers are few in number, advertising may not be used at all. When decisions are handed down from above, personal selling will concentrate on higher authority. But advertising can go in several directions. One might be to gain acceptance or approval—even if only a passive acquiesence—from product users.

When a product cuts across industries, and buying centers are large, the advertiser may opt for using horizontal media. In that event, copy will lean toward the general reader or viewer. There is an endless array of options brought about by product-market and buying center configurations. These basics are further modified by company specifics, such as manufacturing for inventory or order, product life cycle, use of direct or indirect channels of distribution.[14]

The degree of "horizontalness" or "verticalness" of media represents a trade-off between coverage and waste. As a rule, greater relative waste is associated with more "horizontalness." Waste is defined as messages transmitted to people who have little or nothing to do with purchases of the advertised product. If markets or prospective customers spill over into many different kinds of businesses, the media planner may have to overlook the unavoidable waste in order to achieve adequate market coverage.

At the extreme end of the horizontal range is the employment of undifferentiated consumer media to reach business audiences. A notable example of this kind of horizontal approach is Federal Express, helped by its spat of eye-catching and theatrical commercials, vaulted into air freight leadership. Since Federal Express specializes in light packages under 70 pounds, part of its clientele is made up of consumers. But the largest body of customers are businesses. Following Federal's example, other air freight companies plunged into electronic media. United Airlines, a new entrant, was said to have budgeted at least $13 million for its introduction in 1982. United Parcel's new service called "Gold Label Express" was expected to come into the market with an advertising budget of $20 million earmarked for television.[15] Whether shipments will yield any sort of payback from these large expenditures in undifferentiated media—a question which has produced a variety of opinions within the industry—can only be ascertained by market results.

A more common approach to horizontal advertising is the use of print media having large executive readership, such as *Fortune, Business Week,* and the *Wall Street Journal.* Several mass consumer magazines offer demographic editions with high concentrations of professional and managerial audiences, such as *Time B* and *Executive Newsweek.*

Some advertising to businesses actually verges on consumer advertising, so that it is difficult to differentiate between the two. This melding occurs when a good or a service is used personally, but for business purposes.

Airline travel and hotel accommodations fall into this business-individual union. About half of all passenger trips by air are made for business purposes. But the service is intensely personal. Advertising may thus stress individual benefits, which general consumers are interested in as well, though be directed towards the business community. In fact, such advertising may even be regarded as consumer advertising, because the service is consumed by individuals who in this instance happen to be business executives. Advertising its Ambassador Class seat for business travelers, TWA emphasizes comfort, sumptuous meals and personal convenience services on the ground (See Figure 15–7.) Whether advertising is treated as business or consumer depends on the objectives of a firm and its internal organization.

THE BUSINESS PRESS

The largest chunk of business-to-business advertising—estimated at about 40 percent in terms of dollar expenditures—is carried by the business press.[16] There are essentially three major types of business publications: trade, vertical, and professional.

Trade publications are a merchandising vehicle, reaching distributors and various people in the middle. Consumer goods companies, which are more dependent than industrial manufacturers upon indirect distribution channels, make greater use of trade publications.

Vertical magazines are published for people within an industry, regardless of position. *Iron Age,* for example, appeals to a wide range of executives within the metal fabricating industry. Advertisers wishing to cover an industry can probably reach a majority of executives in a field with one or two leading vertical publications.

Professional magazines are available for a great many occupations. The *Journal of Accountancy* gets mailed to the accounting professionals irrespective of the industry in which they work. *Laboratory Management* caters primarily to technicians and technologists working in various types

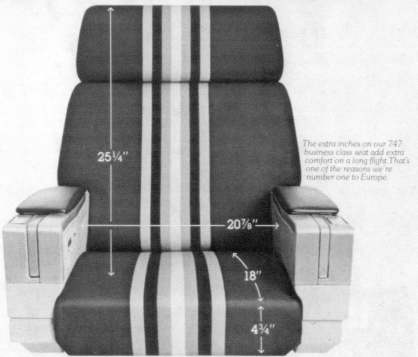

Why is TWA number one to Europe? Have a seat and find out.

25¼"

20⅞"

18"

4¾"

The extra inches on our 747 business class seat add extra comfort on a long flight. That's one of the reasons we're number one to Europe.

Our Ambassador Class℠ seat is the most comfortable business class seat to be had.

There are only six of them across the Ambassador Class cabin on all our 747's. With more recline, and more legroom, than ever before.

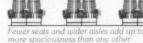

Fewer seats and wider aisles add up to more spaciousness than any other business class cabin.

But our seat is just one of a host of reasons we're the number one host across the Atlantic.

Take our Royal Ambassador℠ Service. A First Class that sets the standard. With free cocktails, assorted vintage wines and brandies, and a range of entrees presented with a style

of service that's warm and personal.

And after your sumptuous meal, you can lie back in our 747 Sleeper-Seat.℠ It stretches out when you do—the length of three full windows. Put your feet up for a good flight's sleep.

Consider our aircraft. Only 747's and L-1011's, the widebodies people prefer. We fly them nonstop to more cities in Europe than anyone.

We offer conveniences on the ground too—like Airport Express®

For First Class travel, our 747 Sleeper-Seat reclines more than ever—a full 60 degrees.

which can give you all your boarding passes in the U.S. So you'll get through the airport faster in London, Paris, and other European cities.

The only planes we fly to Europe are the widebodies people prefer most— the L-1011 and 747.

Combine all these reasons with a thirty-year tradition of service in international flight, and you've got TWA to Europe.

We're the number one choice to Europe for the seventh year in a row. We just wanted you to know why.

You're going to like us / TWA

Fig. 15—7 *TWA. An Advertisement Offering Comfort and Convenience to the Business Traveler. Reproduced by permission of TransWorld Airlines.*

Fig. 15—8 *Beau Sol. A Consumer Product Advertised to the Trade. Courtesy of Las Entreprises Beau Sol Ltee.*

of organizations, such as hospitals, medical centers, clinics, pharmaceutical firms, and independent laboratories. These magazines tend to cut across industrial classifications. In this sense, they are "horizontal" with respect to industry, but "vertical" in relation to occupational skills and interests.

While some magazines boast circulations running into six figures, the average falls somewhere in the neighborhood of 50,000. Yet a circulation of such modest proportions may provide adequate market coverage in a narrow industrial segment. Advertising revenues of the largest business magazines pale in comparison with the large consumer magazines. Costs per advertising page are similarly related. Table 15–2 shows revenue and advertising pages in 1981 for the five largest business publications. A comparison of these figures with those of leading consumer magazines would show truly substantial differences.[17]

Production costs are proportionately higher than space costs in the business press than the consumer magazines. If the same ads can be run a number of times, cost per message can be reduced. Most industrial advertisers, though, frown on this practice as being counterproductive. Because markets are relatively small, reader cumulation rates are thought to be low. Advertisements would thus be giving no new facts to interested, information-seeking audiences.

In recent years some business publications have emerged with geographically limited circulation. These are horizontal publications, and useful to marketers offering goods or services to more than one business field, such as commercial banks, real estate, construction, personnel services, and local data processing houses. Small geographic editions of news weeklies are directly competitive with these regional or local business publications. The choice of each depends upon a consideration of costs, coverage and waste. The advertisement in Figure 15–9 was made by a

TABLE 15–2 *Revenue and Number of Advertising Pages for the Five Largest Business Publications in 1981*

Magazine	Advertising Revenue ($000)	Advertising Pages (Number of Pages)	Dollars per Page
Women's Wear Daily	22,652	5,921	3,803
Computerworld	21,184	4,487	4,721
Advertising Age	17,547	3,761	4,666
Electronic News	17,218	6,538	2,634
Oil & Gas Journal	16,398	6,093	2,691

Source: Derived from Jack Hofferkamp, "The Presses Get Down to Business," *Advertising Age* (May 10, 1982), p. M-8.

Temporary problem?

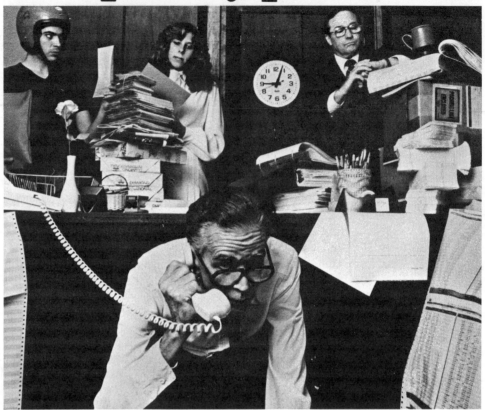

No problem.

Need a typist? A computer programmer? A stenographer? A packer? One call solves it all at the temporary service in town. Whether your temporary problem is one hour or one month, one person or fifty, your temporary problems are our full-time business. We can solve it all with one service, one invoice, one phone call. So the next time work is piling up, or a deadline is due...

Make one call and solve it all!

HIPPWATERS AMTEMP

(203) 661-1300
HIPPWATERS AMTEMP

Fig. 15—9 *Hippwaters Amtemp. Advertising to Business in a Geographically-Limited Edition. Courtesy of Hippwaters, Inc.*

local advertising agency, and the people in the illustration are employees of the client company.

ADVERTISING RATES AND CIRCULATION

Advertising rates follow the same basic patterns as those of consumer magazines. Color commands a premium over black and white. Covers represent preferred positions and go for higher prices than run-of-press (ROP). Advertisers can take advantage of volume and frequency discounts in setting their advertising schedules. Since circulation governs publishing costs, small circulation rate bases place unit page costs within the means of most business-to-business advertisers. Several hundred to several thousand dollars can buy a full-page advertisement in a leading business magazine. Such meager amounts afford low-budget brands opportunities to communicate with some degree of regularity.

Media planners select business publications on the basis of circulation, not audience. They infer market coverage and audience characteristics from circulation audit information. Audience statistics are not available, though the lack thereof has been a major criticism of media users. The reason is because small, specialized circulations do not make audience studies practical. Since these publications have a relatively small number of readers, samples would have to be inordinately large to yield reliable statistics. Such high costs can hardly be justified in light of advertising outlays.

Some business publications have paid circulation, which is audited by ABC. But the majority are controlled circulation publications. That is, they are sent free to "qualified" people who send in cards requesting the magazine. This method of distribution is apparently more economical than that of paid circulation in many lines of business, and usually obtains the desired market coverage.

Besides ABC, two other organizations audit circulation of the business press: Business Publications Audit of Circulation (BPA) and Verified Audit Circulation Corporation (VAC). By far the more important is BPA. This organization audits roughly 900 publications, which together with the 250 appraised by ABC, accounts for about 40 percent of all magazines which make up the business press. More than half are still unaudited, and can provide advertisers with no verified figures as to copy delivery. But about 70 percent of all advertising expenditures go to audited publications.[18]

An audit of a business publication describes the key aspects of its circulation. It classifies the job title of the recipient, as well as the business and SIC industry. The number of copies are also broken down by geographic areas, time intervals between last subscriber qualification, and qualified or nonqualified recipients of the magazine. Some publishers

RATE CARD 37

DENTAL ECONOMICS

1. MAILING INSTRUCTIONS
a. **Mailing Instructions**—General: Contracts, insertion orders, correspondence, proofs, copy and complete advertising materials to Advertising Production Department, Dental Economics, P.O. Box 3408, Tulsa, OK 74101. For non-postal delivery, street address is 1421 S. Sheridan Rd., Tulsa, OK 74112.
b. **Shipping Instructions**—Inserts: Ship inserts prepaid to Dental Economics, c/o PennWell Publishing Co., 1421 S. Sheridan Rd., Tulsa, OK 74112.

2. GENERAL ADVERTISING RATES
a. **Black and White Rates:** The total number of full page and fractional ads used within one year from date of first insertion determines the frequency rate earned. Each page of multi-page unit counts as one insertion towards an earned frequency. See paragraph 11 for Continuity Bonus information (13th insertion free.) Space purchased by a parent company and its subsidiaries is combined to determine earned black and white frequency rate. Four color usage may not be so combined.

	1 Page	2/3 Page	1/2 Isl Page	1/2 Std Page	1/3 Page	1/4 Page	1/6 Page
1 time	3180	2445	2320	2060	1520	1270	960
6 time	2890	2215	2110	1875	1385	1160	870
12 time	2635	2025	1925	1710	1265	1055	795
18 time	2565	1970	1875	1640	1225	1020	765
24 time	2485	1910	1810	1610	1190	995	745
30 time	2450	—	—	—	—	—	—
36 time	2360	—	—	—	—	—	—
48 time	2285	—	—	—	—	—	—
60 time	2230	—	—	—	—	—	—
72 time	2165	—	—	—	—	—	—

b. **Color Rates:** Color charge is to be added to earned black and white space rate. Four color earns frequency separately. Example: advertiser using 24 pages, 12 of which are 4-color, earns the 24 time rate for space and the 12 time rate for 4-color.

Standard colors: Red, Blue, Green, Yellow.
Second Color, Standard: $325 per page or fraction.
Second Color, Matched: $455 per page or fraction.
Second Color, Metallic Ink: $500 per page or fraction.
Three Color: $990 per page or fraction.
Four Color: See frequency discount below.

1x	6x	12x	24x	36x
990	975	935	865	820

c. **Bleed:** No charge for bleed.
d. **Cover Rates:**
2nd Cover add 25% to earned black and white rate.
3rd Cover add 20% to earned black and white rate.
4th Cover add 40% to earned black and white rate.
(Only 4-color advertising accepted on covers.)

e. **Special Position Rates:** Space cost plus 15% on all run-of-book positions and all unusual configurations. Consult publisher for availabilities.

3. GENERAL REGULATIONS
a. **Terms:** Net 30 days. Balances over 30 days are subject to carrying charges at the rate of 1½% per month.
b. **Agency Commissions:** 15% of gross billing allowed to recognized advertising agencies on space, provided account is paid within 30 days of invoice date. Commission not allowed on miscellaneous, mechanical or classified charges. Cash discount, none. Payment with order is required from all first-time advertisers and/or agencies.
c. **Short Rates and Rebates:** Advertisers will be short-rated if within a 12 month period from the date of the first insertion, they do not use the amount of space upon which their billings have been based. Advertisers will be rebated if within a 12 month period from the date of first insertion, they have used sufficient space to warrant a lower rate.
d. **Rate Protection:** When new rates are announced, advertisers will be protected at their contract rates until the effective date. Orders may be cancelled at the time the change in rates becomes effective without incurring a short rate adjustment provided the rate has been earned up to date of cancellation.
e. **Publisher's Protective Clauses:** Advertisers and advertising agencies assume liability for all content (including text, representation and illustrations) of advertisements printed, and also assume responsibility for any claim arising therefrom made against the publisher. The publisher reserves the right to insert the word 'advertisement' when in the publisher's opinion, an advertisement resembles editorial material.
PennWell Publishing Company engages in interstate commerce from its facilities in Oklahoma. All orders are subject to acceptance or rejection by the publisher at its place of business in Tulsa, Oklahoma.
Publisher cannot be held responsible for circumstances beyond his control, such as a postal strike, or an Act of God.

4. INSERTS
a. **Rates:** Furnished inserts ready for binding, black and white page rates at earned frequency apply.
Back-up charge, one-color, $1400 per spread. Supply four page inserts folded. If 4 pager must be backed-up supply flat and 2-up. Rates for gate-fold or special inserts available upon request. Mechanical charges are non commissionable.
b. **Specifications:** Single sheet inserts: 8 1/2" X 11 1/4". 3/16" trimmed off backbone and top in binding. Inserts jog to top.
c. **Maximum Paper Stock:** For single leaf: 100 lb. basis-coated stock, 80 lb. basis-uncoated stock. For inserts of more than single leaf, consult publisher. *Sample of all insert stock must be submitted for publisher approval.*
d. **Postcard Inserts:** Postcards can be used with a minimum of one page of accompanying space. Cards to be furnished by advertiser. Minimum card size acceptable is 5" deep by 7" wide. *Card jogs to top.* Consult publisher for specifications. Cost: $2365 (commissionable). If pre-tipping required: $5,000.
e. **Undersized Inserts:** Publisher cannot back-up. Any single-leaf insert which physically covers one-half page or less will be billed at $2365, and will contribute as one page toward the earned frequency. Any single-leaf insert which covers more than one-half page, but less than one full page will be billed as a full-page, single-leaf insert, and will contribute as two pages toward earned frequency.
f. **Direct Reply Cards:** $2245. Publisher-printed card adjacent to Reader Service Card available on a limited basis. Check with publisher for schedule and positioning. Printed in one color. Card counts as one page toward earned frequency rate.
g. **Regional Inserts:** Furnished by advertiser. See insert specifications above. Rates: For a **two page insert,** $155.00 per M; 50,000 or more, $130.00 per M. For a **four page insert,** $175.00 per M; 50,000 or more, $145.00 per M. Minimum quantity charged for in all cases, 10,000. Available whole states only. Only one advertising split available per issue. Insertion orders honored on a first-come first-served basis.
h. **Shipping Instructions:** Inserts should be shipped prepaid to Dental Economics, c/o PennWell Publishing Co., 1421 S. Sheridan Rd., Tulsa, OK 74112. Specify on each carton - number of cartons in shipment, number of inserts in each carton, and issue in which inserts run.

5. CLASSIFIED
a. **Rates: Display Classified,** $110.00 per column inch. 10% discount per insertion for three consecutive insertions, or more. Reader service number available at $30.00 per insertion. Ads must be vertical, and maximum depth is 4". No agency commission allowed. Payment with order, please.
Personal Classified: Restricted to dentists with practices for sale and/or help wanted. 30 words or less, $25.00. Each additional word, 65¢. Blind box number, $5.00. Payment with order, please.

6. ISSUE AND CLOSING DATES
a. **Issuance:** Monthly on the 25th of the preceding month.
b. **Closing Date:** Closing is **27th of second preceding month.**
c. **Cancellations:** No cancellations accepted after the **1st of month preceding** publication.

7. MECHANICAL DATA
a. **Publication Trim Size:** 8⅛" x 10⅞". Three columns to a page. Live matter should be kept ⅛" inside trim edge. Single page bleed is 8⅛" x 11¼". Spread bleed is 16¼" x 11¼".
b. **Binding:** Perfect binding. 3/16" milled off backbone.
c. **Method of Printing:** Web offset. Covers are sheetfed offset.
d. **Halftone Screen Requirements:** Maximum screen for two color ad is 133 line. Maximum screen for four color is 150 line. Maximum density on four color ads is 260%.
e. **Reproduction Requirements:** OFFSET FILM NEGATIVES REQUIRED. Negatives on .003' or .004' stable base material must have register marks, center marks, and trim marks clearly indicated. Each negative must be marked for color and be right reading with emulsion side down. Split film must be supplied for spread ads.
PROGRESSIVE PROOFS REQUIRED on all four color ads. Two sets of progressive proofs and two sets of engraver's proofs must be supplied. Please pull proofs on Dental Economics' stock or its equivalent. We provide stock for this purpose upon request. If progressive proofs are not supplied, color keys will be made at advertiser's expense. PMS number must be supplied on matched color ads.
f. **Printing Specifications:** Specifications for Web Offset Publications (SWOP) adopted. Publisher cannot be responsible for quality of ad reproduction if SWOP specifications not followed. Request SWOP Specification Booklet from Publisher.
g. **Ad Page Dimensions:**

1 page	7" x 10"
2/3 page (vertical)	4 1/2" x 10"
1/2 page (horizontal)	7" x 4 7/8"
1/2 page (island)	4 1/2" x 7 1/8"
1/2 page (vertical)	3 3/8" x 10"
1/3 page (horizontal)	7" x 3 1/3"
1/3 page (two column)	4 1/2" x 4 7/8"
1/3 page (vertical) •	2 3/16" x 10"
1/4 page (horizontal)	7" x 2 3/8"
1/4 page (two column)	4 1/2" x 3 1/2"
1/4 page (vertical)	3 3/8" x 4 7/8"
1/6 page (vertical)	2 3/16" x 4 7/8"

h. **Storing of Advertising Materials:** Ad materials will be stored for 12 months, then destroyed unless otherwise advised.

8. CIRCULATION DATA
a. **General Description of Audience:** Dental Economics is distributed to practicing dentists from year of graduation to age 60. In addition, it is distributed to dental school faculty, dentists in the military and Public Health Service and all retail dental dealers. Senior dental students are also included for nine months each year.
b. **Method of Distribution and Audit Organization:** Distributed on a qualified, controlled circulation basis. Audited by Business Publication Audit of Circulation, Inc.
c. **Association Affiliation:** Member of Business Publication Audit of Circulation and American Business Press.
d. **Subscription Prices:** For non-qualified recipients in U.S.A., one year - $30.00. For all other countries, $45.00. Overseas airmail subscription $60.00.

9. STATEMENT OF EDITORIAL SCOPE
Founded in 1911, Dental Economics is an independent national practice administration and money management journal for dentists. Its objective is to help the dentist administer a more efficient, satisfying and rewarding practice. Through its original feature stories, many of them dentist authored, it treats the business aspects of dentistry, including office organization and administration, patient relations and motivation, auxiliary staff recruiting, training and utilization, professional relations, money management, investments, estate planning, taxes. It also provides reports on social, economics and political issues facing dentistry.

10. OWNER & KEY PERSONNEL
a. PennWell Publishing Company, P.O. Box 1260, Tulsa, OK 74101, 918-835-3161, Telex: 49-2345, Cable: PENNPUBCO
b. Joseph T. Bessette, Publisher; Pat Muchmore, Executive Editor; Richard L. Hale, Editor; Marvin R. Ashworth, Manager, Marketing Services; Jill Tenzythoff, Production Manager; Barbara Polin, Assistant Production Manager.

11. MISCELLANEOUS
GUARANTEED ADVERTISING CONTINUITY BONUS — A bakers dozen. Run at least one paid insertion in 12 consecutive issues and receive the 13th free. Different size ad units can be used. Just total your 12 month space and color expenditure and divide by 12. The product is your dollars with which to buy bonus ad space. Purpose of bonus program is to encourage advertising continuity for each marketing group. Space from parent or other divisions cannot be combined. Ask your representative (listed overleaf) for more information.

12. REGIONALS & SPLIT RUNS
Available whole states only. One split per issue. Insertion orders honored on a first-come first-serve basis. Consult publisher for availabilities and prices.

13. COLLATERAL SERVICES
Reader Service Card in each issue. Reprints available.
Circulation list available for direct mail purposes and DENTIST'S CARD SHOPPER direct response card mailings available. Consult Marvin Ashworth.
VIEWPOINTS newsletter for dental marketers.
Harvey Advertising Communication Surveys available. Harvey Advertising Testing Service (HATS) available. Consult publisher.
Annual GOLD BOOK Directory of dental equipment, products and services published each August.

Fig. 15–10 *Business Publication Rate Card. Illustration of a Business Publication's Rate Card.* Courtesy of PennWell Publishing.

offer advertising readership surveys, which are generally of low quality and of limited value in assessing the effects of an advertisement.

READER SERVICE CARDS

A unique feature of industrial magazines is the widespread use of reader service cards, sometimes referred to as bingo cards. Readers check off requests for various information offers and mail the cards back to the publication's designated clearing house. These inquiries are for both editorial and advertising matter. The latter comes from an advertisement carrying a number which, if circled on the reader service card, generates a request for information about the product advertised.

Opinions about the effectiveness of advertising-generated inquiries are varied among practitioners. On the negative side are those who claim the inquiry is of little or no value. This group argues that if bona fide prospects must resort to filling out inquiries to learn about a company's products, the sales force is not doing a good job. Sales managers of leading brands, with sales staffs large enough to cover prospective customers, are apt to find themselves in this negative-opinion camp.

The positive thinkers view the inquiry system as a potential source of sales leads, but are of various opinions as to their quality. These range from mildly to highly enthusiastic. Most of them believe that proper follow-ups bring in sales which would not have occurred otherwise. Sometimes, a reader service card will attempt to qualify the inquiry by having one number circled for information or literature and another for a demonstration or a call by a company representative.

There have been a number of studies which seem to indicate that the percentage of qualified leads are at respectable levels.[19] However, these studies have been conducted *ad hoc*, with no attempt to relate results to marketing factors. It is not at all clear whether inquiries are substitutable for, or complementary to, regular sales calls. With escalating costs of sales calls, any elimination of nonselling duties can amount to substantial savings.

ADVERTORIALS

The business press more than any other medium blends advertising and editorial techniques into a single message. While its frequency of occurrence is rather low, these hybrid messages have appeared enough times to earn the singular designation, "advertorial." The message is actually an advertisement insofar as it is paid for by the advertiser. It was given the name advertorial because it combines advertising with simulated editorial material.[20]

There are two basic kinds of advertorials. One is the spread, two or four pages. Product advertising is placed in juxaposition to text which resembles editorial matter, often on a facing page. These messages are easily

Fig. 15—11 Offshore *Reader Service Card. Illustration of a Reader Service Card. Courtesy of PennWell Publishing.*

identified as advertisements, and seldom confused with editorial articles in the magazine.

The second kind of advertorial is where a whole section, running to some fifty or more pages, is placed in the magazine. The section is made up of text written in the editorial style of the magazine and interspersed with product messages which look quite different from the editorial. Text material usually contains technical news and subject matter of current interest. A firm may resort to this advertising-editorial format when it wants to announce a significant development.

Advertisers can reap advantages from advertorials, especially those printed as special supplements. When the text material is informative, the editorial writing style has great reader impact. It is highly believable, and carries over to the promotional portions. But advertisers may encounter problems when soliciting the help of editorial staffs to prepare advertorial messages.

SUMMARY

The number of buyers in industrial markets is small compared to consumer markets. These business markets can be vertical or horizontal. Purchase decisions in the business sector are regarded as outcomes of rational, deliberating processes.

Fig. 15—12   *TEK. Qualifying Inquiries of Reader Service Numbers. Courtesy of Tektronix, Inc.*

Business-to-business advertising has three major characteristics. First, personal selling dominates the marketing mix. Thus, advertising must enhance the objectives of the sales force. Second, advertising copy focuses on rational appeals in keeping with the nature of buying decisions. Third, media is usually limited because markets are narrow.

Principles of internal business communication are often applied to advertising in the industrial field. One such principle refers to inverted authority-informational pyramids.

The largest portion of business-to-business advertising is carried by business publications. There are three major types: vertical magazines, trade publications, and professional journals.

Advertising rates in the business press follow the same patterns as those of consumer magazines, but circulations are limited and advertising page rates are relatively low. Circulation analysis rather than audience forms the basis for media selection.

A unique feature of business publications is the widespread use of reader service cards. These are used to generate sales leads.

Though not used frequently, the advertorial can have a great impact on magazine readers. But advertisers may encounter resistance from editorial writers if they are asked to prepare copy for a magazine section.

Questions for Chapter 15

1. Why do products going to horizontal markets usually get larger advertising budgets than products for vertical markets?

2. What are the main differences between business customers and consumers?

3. Why would advertisements in a magazine such as *Laboratory Management* stress specific applications and use technical language?

4. In what ways can advertising to business make salesmen more productive?

5. Because the Pims study found a correlation between "awareness" and market share, is it correct to conclude that a company can build share by increasing advertising?

6. How does the inverted authority-information pyramid principle apply to advertising to business?

7. What is the difference between a professional journal and a trade publication?

8. Would not Xerox advertising copiers on television incur a large amount of media waste?

9. Why would a software house be reluctant to run the same advertisement many times in *Computer Decisions*?

10. What are the main values of reader service cards?

11. Why might journalists writing for the business press oppose working on advertorials?

Footnotes for Chapter 15

[1]William J. Stanton, *Fundamentals of Marketing* (New York: McGraw-Hill, 1981), p. 137.

[2]U.S. Census Bureau, *1977 Census of Manufactures.*

[3]U.S. Census Bureau, *1977 Census of Manufactures.*

[4]See Jagdish N. Sheth, "A Model of Industrial Buyer Behavior," *Journal of Marketing* (October 1973), pp. 50–56; W. M. Pride and O. C. Ferrell, *Marketing* (Boston: Houghton Mifflin, 1980), p. 648.

[5]Gary L. Lilien and John D. C. Little, "The ADVISOR Project: A Study of Industrial Marketing Budgets," *Sloan Management Review* (Spring 1976), pp. 21–22; G. L. Lilien, "ADVISOR 2: Modelling the Marketing Mix Decision for Industrial Products," *Management Science* (February 1979), p. 193.

[6]Lilien and Little, "The ADVISOR Project," p. 22.

[7]McGraw-Hill Research, *Lab Report #8013.6,* (1982).

[8]See William L. Burke and Ruth G. Newman, "Brand Awareness and Profitability," *The Pimsletter on Business Strategy, No. 24* (Strategic Planning Institute, 1980).

[9]Robert D. Buzzell et. al., "Market Share—A Key to Profitability," *Harvard Business Review* (January/February 1975), p. 96–97.

[10]Burke and Newman, "Brand Awareness," p. 1.

[11]Edward W. Smykay, *Physical Distribution Management* (New York: Macmillan, 1973), pp. 240–243.

[12]Belinda Hulin-Salkin, "Publications Go Straight to Their Market," *Advertising Age* (May 10, 1982), pp. M-12–M-17.

[13]Jean-Marie Choffray and Gary L. Lilien, *Market Planning for New Industrial Products* (New York: John Wiley & Sons, 1980), pp. 136–140.

[14]Choffray and Lilien, pp. 194–196.

[15]Robert Raissman, "Federal Fuels War in Packet Delivery," *Advertising Age* (July 12, 1982), p. 73.

[16]Charles S. Mill, "Special Need Grows for the Specialists," *Advertising Age* (May 11, 1981), p. S-1.

[17]Refer to Chapter 13, Table 1.

[18]"Circulation is BPA's Beat," *Advertising Age* (May 10, 1982), p. M-17.

[19]Frank S. Hill, "Inquiries: Bridging Advertising and Sales," *Industrial Marketing* (September 1979), pp. 70–72.

[20]See Anna Sobezynski, "Editorials vs Advertorials: It's a Separate Piece," *Advertising Age* (May 10, 1982), pp. M-24–M-27.

16 Corporate Advertising

Corporate advertising embraces both consumer and industrial marketing targets. It uses national media. It conforms to general advertising in all respects save one—it does not advertise products.

This uniqueness, superficially at least, poses somewhat of a contradiction. Corporate advertising represents an economic activity insofar as organizational funds are exchanged for creative services and media time and space. But the messages transmitted carry not even a suggestion of transactional utility in an economic sense. To assist in understanding this type of general advertising, this chapter covers:

- **Characteristics of companies and organizations which engage in corporate advertising**
- **Main purposes of corporate advertising**
- **Type of messages, as defined by their content, and the kind of media used**
- **Controversies engendered by policies relating to public issue advertising**

CHARACTERISTICS OF CORPORATE ADVERTISING

Corporate advertising is a somewhat amorphous term for describing an activity. Leading National Advertisers, Inc., which compiles expenditure statistics, puts corporate advertising under the heading "general promotion advertising." Thomas Garbett, senior vice-president of Doyle, Dane, Bernbach, characterizes corporate advertising as a "catchall term for a type of advertising run for the direct benefit of the corporation rather than for its products and services."[1]

The term "corporate" can include associations as well as other non-profit organizations, although the major part of corporate advertising expenditures comes from profit-seeking businesses in the private sector. The distinguishing feature of corporate advertising, however, is not who does it but how it is done. The products of specific organizations are not advertised directly. Rather, emphasis rests on some aspect of the organization. The advertising gives no details about product features or prices. It does not urge the reader to buy, either now or later, and does not contain directions as to where or how to buy. Hence, corporate advertising can be defined as paid communication in mass media, but with no direct presentation of products sold or no direct solicitation of productive inputs.

Nevertheless, identifying corporate advertisements presents difficulties. Many large companies in consumer fields are apt to classify corporate advertising as trade advertising. Conversely, small industrial agencies may mistakenly treat corporate advertising as though it were consumer advertising.[2] Sometimes an advertisement may have both corporate and product features, as those of department stores, which are invariably categorized as product advertisements.

Because corporate advertising refrains from any kind of product sell, it has no overnight success stories. It cannot point to measurable increases in brand share. It cannot demonstrate immediate payoffs that could be traced to its persuasive powers. The result has been an almost total neglect by marketing scholars and advertising practitioners alike. This inattention has been reenforced by the relatively small corporate budgets. Annual expenditures for corporate advertising have been variously estimated as running from one to two percent of the U.S. advertising total.[3]

Yet the practice of corporate advertising is widespread. Better than half the companies which make up the Fortune 500, the largest manufacturing firms ranked by dollar sales volume, engage in some form of corporate advertising. The comparable figure for the leading service companies, exclusive of retail establishments, runs close to two-thirds.[4] The importance of corporate advertising is underscored by the fact that almost 80 percent of companies require the objectives and expenditures for the advertising programs to be approved by the highest level of management— the president, the chairman of the board, the chief executive officer.[5] Thus, the job of corporate communication falls squarely on the shoulders of the senior management.

Another characteristic of corporate advertising, as distinct from product advertising, is the role of public relations. The ties of corporate advertising to public relations remain intimate, and indeed firmly entwined. Most managements assign to their public relations department the task of building favorable attitudes towards the corporate entity. Among the 100 leading corporate advertisers, public relations personnel serve as the principle originators of corporate advertising concepts. They also have the strongest voice in theme generation and media selection.[6]

Supplementing traditional public relations activities with paid messages in mass media offers a firm a number of advantages. Information can be presented in the form and manner desired by the sender, subject only to the general restrictions of the medium in which it appears. Communication is more organized and planned. Message content is always under the control of the information source, in this instance, the company, and is thus more forceful than a press release. Media are preselected from the standpoint of audience appropriateness. The volume and timing of messages become primarily a matter of planning, scheduling, and monitoring.

CHARACTERISTICS OF CORPORATE ADVERTISERS

There are three main sources of information about the practices of corporate advertisers—the *Public Relations Journal,* a monthly periodical, the Association of National Advertisers (ANA), and National Geographic Magazine. The *Journal* devotes a full issue each year to corporate advertising. These issues carry the latest research results, some undertaken by the *Journal* itself. The ANA and National Geographic, over a number of years have conducted a series of studies on corporate advertising practices. The ANA surveys are with member firms, primarily large advertisers. The National Geographic surveys have been with Fortune 500 companies, and with 250 leading service corporations. The latter includes the fifty largest firms in each of the following five fields: transportation, utilities, insurance, finance, and banking.

Although the ANA and National Geographic surveys probe somewhat different universes and emphasize different aspects, the main conclusions are strikingly similar. Both surveys indicate products and markets as a major determinant of corporate advertising.[7] Table 16–1 shows the relationship between corporate advertising and major product lines, as derived from the latest National Geographic survey, conducted in 1981.

Consumer goods manufacturers had the lowest incidence of corporate advertising, at 41 percent. This compares with 66 percent for industrial marketers who ran corporate advertising at any time from 1976 to 1980 inclusive. Service industries were on par with industrial goods manufacturers.

Table 16–1 does not tell the whole story. Greater insights can be derived by considering each producing segment separately.

Consumer Goods Manufacturers

According to the National Geographic Survey, done in 1981, this segment had the smallest proportion of companies placing corporate advertising,

TABLE 16–1 *Corporate Advertising by Major Product Line*

Ran corporate advertising 1976–1980	All Companies (Percent)	Consumer Goods Manufacturers (Percent)	Industrial Products Manufacturers (Percent)	Service Companies (Percent)
Yes	61	41	66	65
No	39	59	34	35
Total	100	100	100	100
Sample base	(329)	(61)	(142)	(126)

Source: Based on Sachs, *Corporate Advertising,* p. 5.

although it was not uniformly so. A closer inspection of survey returns revealed a sharp division within the consumer goods field. The bulk of corporate advertising came from firms making high-priced durables, such as automobiles, appliances, and articles of recreation. Very little was done by manufacturers of packaged goods and convenience products.

When low-priced, high-turnover items are the mainstay of revenue inflows, emphasis rests on individual products. All brands and product lines must stand alone, unless they are marketed under a family name. But even family-named brands have identities of their own, and must vie with potential substitutes for a share of the consumer's dollar. And, all brands must justify their claims on corporate resources on the basis of their own expected returns.

Low-priced, mass-marketed brands often find competitors within the parent company. This situation is a common one with multibrand marketers, many of whom refrain from any action which encourages an individual brand to become identified with the company name. Consumers know products by their brand names, such as Dial, Camay, or Lifebuoy, and not by the corporate entities producing them, such as Armour, Procter & Gamble, or Lever Brothers. Thus, it makes little sense to try enhancing the reputation of a company when its customers have no notion of what the firm sells. In fact, corporate advertising might conflict with the firm's marketing objective of having all brands promote their individual indentities, with no reference to the parent company.

In contrast, company reputation and goodwill become highly prized objectives for marketers of more expensive durables. Product quality assumes a greater importance to the consumer because risk is higher. Purchase selection is made with more deliberation, though not necessarily with logic or wisdom. Who of us has not been seduced into choosing a product because of its maker's reputation for fine quality, fair dealing, or superior service?

Industrial Products Manufacturers

Manufacturers of industrial products have relatively small advertising budgets and low advertising-to-sales ratios. They rely mainly on personal selling, not advertising, as the dominant transactional force.[8] Products are often listed by initials and numbers, with no attempt made to differentiate these nameless items by promotion. Many of them have a sales volume which is so low that they cannot support an advertising budget. Consequently, product managers do not look at corporate advertising as a competitive source of funds, as money that is taken out of their budgets. The corporate program is seen as an incremental effort which acts as an aid to salespeople. Corporate advertising in many industrial companies thus emerges as a form of promotion which individual products or product lines would not normally enjoy.

TABLE 16–2 *Corporate Advertising by Size of Firm*

Ran Corporate Advertising 1976–1980	Percent by Size of Company	
	Top 250 Manufacturing Companies	Next 250 Manufacturing Companies
Yes	67	48
No	33	52
Total	100	100
Sample base	(106)	(96)

Source: Based on Sachs, *Corporate Advertising.*

Services Organizations

Firms operating in the service sector regard reputation as paramount. The rendition of a service often cannot be disassociated from the company which renders it. If that is so, strategy dictates a positioning of the company rather than its products. It is not enough that actual differences exist. They must be perceived to exist. Hence, a favorable corporate image becomes a strong plus in a customer's choice of services.

Industrial goods and consumer durables also possess service characteristics. Many such items come bundled with services—warranties, service contracts, technical support. And their makers are as much concerned with reputation and company image as service-producing firms.

SIZE OF FIRM

A second characteristic associated with corporate advertising is the size of the firm. Table 16–2 divides the Fortune 500 Companies in half, according to their respective sales volume. The incidence of corporate advertising is then broken out for both halves. Of the top 250 manufacturing firms, 67 percent ran corporate advertising between 1976 and 1980. In the next 250 companies, 48 percent ran corporate advertising. If the percentages for the two groups of companies were adjusted for variations in major product line, the difference would be even wider than that shown in Table 16–2.

Corporate advertising can be viewed in one of two ways. First, it is a revenue producer but works indirectly and over the long term. Second, it is a cost of doing business because results cannot be measured.

Either way, large firms are more likely to run corporate advertising. Its indirectness and long-term aspects make outlays appear as discretionary or incremental, to be budgeted for after essentials are taken care of. The bigger companies have more funds available for such peripheral undertakings, the value of which is futuristic and difficult to ascertain. A company cannot worry about the future when resources are tight in the present. If

TABLE 16–3 *Ten Leading Company Advertisers*

January–December 1980—In dollar (thousands) rank order

Six-Media Totals

American Telephone & Telegraph Co.	$ 30,887.0
General Motors Corp.	29,267.6
Atlantic Richfield Co.	12,838.4
Exxon Corp.	11,130.2
Shell Oil Co.	10,222.0
Texaco Inc.	10,157.9
General Electric Co.	9,937.8
International Telephone & Telegraph Corp.	7,536.3
E.I. Du Pont De Nemours & Co., Inc.	6,884.6
McDonnell Douglas Corp.	6,876.3
Totals	$135,738.1

Source: *Public Relations Journal* (November 1981), p. 39.

corporate advertising is regarded as a cost, the larger firm is still more apt to use it since the overhead cost can be spread over a wider sales base.

The leading corporate advertisers in the private sector are lodged in the highest tier of firms. Table 16–3 shows the top ten firms in 1980 doing corporate advertising in six media (consumer magazines, Sunday magazine supplements, network television, spot television, radio, and outdoor), as reported by *Public Relations Journal*. These ten leaders collectively spend about one-third the total amount expended by all firms on corporate advertising in the six media.

Larger firms run corporate campaigns with greater continuity. Frequency estimates for the past five years are shown in Table 16–4.

Almost three-fourths of the largest manufacturing firms that placed corporate advertising from 1976 to 1980 did so every year. In the second half of the Fortune 500 list, only 54 percent advertised continuously. The remaining 46 percent handled corporate advertising as an on-again, off-again proposition. This lack of regularity reflects budget variations. The average frequency of the entire service sector was about equal to that of the median manufacturing firm.

On the whole, corporate advertising for the majority of users was an ongoing activity, done regularly year after year, without abrupt stops and starts. Most managements have come to recognize that establishing a corporate position requires time, patience, and continuity. The vast majority of executives responsible for these corporate efforts evaluate them from the same standpoint—as a long-term activity which cannot be effective if interrupted.[9]

TABLE 16–4 *Frequency of Corporate Advertising*

Number of Years Advertised in Past Five Years	All Companies	Percent of Corporate Advertisers		
		Top 250 Mfg. Companies	Next 250 Mfg. Companies	Service Companies
Five out of five	64	71	54	64
Four out of five	8	9	9	7
Three out of five	10	10	11	9
Two out of five	11	9	13	11
One out of five	7	1	13	9
Total	100	100	100	100
Sample base	(200)	(71)	(46)	(82)

Source: Based on Sachs, *Corporate Advertising.*
Note: Breakout of manufacturing companies by size derived from cross-tabulations of survey data, and not published in the National Geographic report.

PURPOSES OF CORPORATE ADVERTISING

Corporate advertising, like all business activity, might be said to be undertaken for the purpose of advancing the interests of the organization. But this says nothing. It does not differentiate corporate advertising from any other course of action.

The fact is that a business must deal with many elements—employees, financial organizations, customers, suppliers, educators, and law makers. Its advertising may have many faces, and its image may range over a broad spectrum. The perception which a public holds of a company is often referred to as the corporate image.

Management cannot control these perceptions. But it can influence them. A corporate image, the way in which a company is perceived, depends in large measure upon what a company does and how it does it. This aspect is frequently termed the corporate identity, defined as the sum of all elements that make a company what it is and, by extension, all the ways in which it chooses to communicate to its various constituencies.[10]

From the standpoint of advertising, a corporation has numerous options in the way it projects itself to the public. It may talk about its policies, its philosophies, or its operations. But the decisive factor is the advertising objective, the task that is supposed to be accomplished.

Since it is impossible to examine every advertising plan, plan objective information is gained through surveys. Both the ANA and National Geographic studies asked about the goals of corporate campaigns. Because the specifics of company programs are highly diverse, and often ambiguous, both surveys end up with all-encompassing and overlapping categories of objectives. The ANA, for example, asks executives to place their particular campaign objectives into one or more of the following six categories:[11]

1. To improve the level of awareness of the company, the nature of its business, profitability, etc.
2. To enhance or maintain the company's reputation and goodwill.
3. To provide unified marketing support for the company's present and future products, services or capabilities.
4. To inform or educate about subjects of importance to company's future (e.g., economics, resource allocations, government policies, etc.)
5. To advocate specific actions, or counter the advocacy of others, on issues of importance to the company, its industry or to business in general.
6. To communicate the company's concern and record of achievement in social and environmental issues.

The 1981 National Geographic report also lists six objectives, which were derived from multiple choice, closed-ended questions. The descriptions were phrased somewhat differently from those of the ANA questionnaire, but were about equally broad and overlapping. The act of information transfer—making the goals of an advertising plan fit into a particular questionnaire format—requires interpretation which contains obvious personal biases and ambiguities. The National Geographic survey inserted a quality control check, a rudimentary one, wherein a dozen questionnaires were returned by two executives in the same company. Both managers were apparently involved in planning corporate advertising. Yet the two answers failed to agree on what the objectives were in the majority of cases. This could mean that corporate objectives were ill-defined and indefinite, or it could mean a deficiency in the survey; managers having trouble classifying their individual goals on a survey questionnaire.

Despite the survey shortcomings, the important points fell neatly in place. First, corporate campaigns are multipurpose. They have more than one objective, though some are undoubtedly more important than others. As a result, they also have more than one target audience. The ANA survey disclosed an average of 2.7 objectives per campaign. The National Geographic study reported an average of 2.5. In part, the number of objectives yielded by a survey is a function of the number of categories carried by the checklist. But when the responses are sorted out, the basic purposes of corporate messages can be divided into three groupings. These, in order of importance, are as follows:

1. To enhance the sales-generating ability of the corporation. This objective makes advertising essentially a tool of marketing.
2. To facilitate the acquisition of productive inputs, the main ones being capital and labor. From this standpoint, advertising serves in the interests of finance and personnel.

3. To influence an exogenous factor, which may or may not be related to corporate performance. In this instance corporate advertising becomes an engine of social change, allied with what is often described as "social marketing."

Organizations which market their own outputs use corporate advertising for all three purposes. Associations usually concern themselves with the first, and sometimes with the last objective, but almost never with the second.

Sales-Generating Messages

Marketing-oriented messages are the mainstay of corporate advertising. This is why companies' major product lines were associated with the incidence of corporate advertising. The product-market factor is not merely reflected in designations of broad categories of objectives which imply sales—such as overall marketing support—but in choices of target audiences. Firms which sell goods or services to consumers invariably define their target audiences as the public at large or segments thereof. Firms which sell products to other companies lean towards the business community as their primary targets.

Because industrial goods manufacturers have the highest incidence of corporate advertising, the business community becomes the chief target for corporate messages. Table 16–5, based on survey findings, shows target audience relationships of the last corporate campaign.

TABLE 16–5 *Major Target Audiences of Last Campaign by Type of Corporate Advertiser*

Major Target Audience	Percent of Corporate Advertisers		
	All Companies*	Industrial Goods Manufacturers**	Service Companies
Business community	56	68	50
Financial community	46	56	34
Specific segments of the public	29	28	33
Public at large	24	12	31
Stockholders	18	23	9
Government officials and agents	17	20	15
Employees, plant communities	13	16	5
Other	4	5	4

Source: Sachs, *Corporate Advertising.*
*Includes consumer goods companies which are not shown separately.
**Figures for industrial firms are unpublished, and were derived by cross-tabulating survey data.
Note: Percentages add up to more than 100% because of multiple answers.

According to Table 16–5, 68 percent of industrial producers chose the business community as a major advertising target. The service sector, with products going to both individuals and businesses, directed their corporate messages to both types of customers.

A common approach of sales-oriented messages is to promote an entire product line under a corporate umbrella. Another is to emphasize corporate attributes which are closely related to products, such as technical efficiency, reliability, high quality, and excellent service, with the hope that these traits will rub off on the company's products. Both approaches are not mutually exclusive, and frequently are combined.

Illustrative of the umbrella principle are the AMF advertisements which appear both on television and in print, built around the theme, "We make weekends." Each message displays a number of products snugly fitted under the AMF leisure-time umbrella, while conveying a crisp impression of corporate leadership in recreational fields. The advertisement of an interview with Johnny Rutherford, professional race car driver, is an excellent example of good execution (Figure 16–1). Rutherford's exposition on the value of exercise adroitly brings the discussion around to bowling, swimming, skiing, and golf. The copy at the bottom, along with the logo, then lists the related products made by AMF.

Another approach to achieving a sales-generating objective with corporate advertising is to identify with some sort of expertise or technological leadership. This is expertly done in the advertisement of Bell Laboratories, which presents a summary of what the firm is doing in programming computers to talk or to synthesize voices (Figure 16–2). This advertisement, focusing on research in microelectronics, leaves the reader with an unmistaken impression of Bell Laboratories standing ready to solve communication problems for businesses operating in a world of increasing automation.

Regardless of how the task is approached, promoting the corporation as a way of building favorable attitudes towards its many products implies a "trickle down" philosophy. Its underlying assumption is that corporate images become associated in consumers' minds with company products; if a customer has a high regard for the company, he or she will think well of all items it produces. This concept is similar to that of the "halo effect" noted by psychologists, but the direction of attitude carryover is perceived as going from the top down.

This theory stands in sharp contrast to the widely-held multiattribute concept of consumer behavior. The conventional view sees customer attitudes emanating from mental processes linked with individual products. The overall attitude towards a firm's many different outputs is, therefore, the sum of attitudes toward individual items. In contrast, corporate advertising conducted for marketing ends suggests a scheme whereby attitudes filter down from the corporate entity to particular goods and services.

"You know you have to exercise. But unless it's fun, you know you won't."

Johnny Rutherford

© AMF Incorporated, 1979

(A lot of us drive to work. But for Johnny Rutherford, driving _is_ his work—at speeds over 200 miles an hour. In his 20 years of racing, he has won the Indianapolis 500 twice, was United States Auto Club National Sprint Car Champion, and has been named USAC Driver of the Year.)

Q. Then pushups really aren't your speed?

A. No way. Pushups, sit-ups, knee bends—they may build me up, but they bore me to tears. I do them to help build the stamina I need for auto racing, but I have to force myself. I'd much rather do something I can get my head into as well as my body.

Q. What exactly is your idea of exercise that's fun?

A. Any recreation that's a challenge, not a ritual. I happen to like bowling, swimming, skiing and golf because they absorb me and demand my attention. I can really get into them and enjoy them. And I particularly like sports where the idea is winning.

Q. So you're as competitive off the racetrack as on it?

A. I sure am. Although on the bowling lanes you'd have to label me a rookie. But that's one neat thing about bowling. You don't have to be a pro. You can get a group together and go have fun and hoot and holler and the one who knocks down the most pins is the winner. And you can do it anywhere, any weather, any season.

Q. Are you ever tempted to just lie back and do nothing?

A. You bet. Especially the older I get. But none of us can afford to. Before you know it, you're short of breath, overweight, and out of shape. I simply can't let down. My life depends on keeping fit. So does yours.

This is one in a series of messages brought to you by AMF. We make Voit Balls and Sporting Goods; Tyrolia Ski Bindings; Head Skis, Tennis Rackets, and Sports Wear; Roadmaster Bicycles and Mopeds; AMF Bowling Products; Slickcraft Boats; Alcort Sunfish Sailboats; Hatteras Yachts; Crestliner Boats; Ben Hogan Golf Equipment; Harley-Davidson Motorcycles and Golf Cars; Whitely Physical Fitness Products and American Athletic Equipment.

AMF
We make weekends

Fig. 16—1 _AMF. The Umbrella Principle of AMF. Courtesy of AMF._

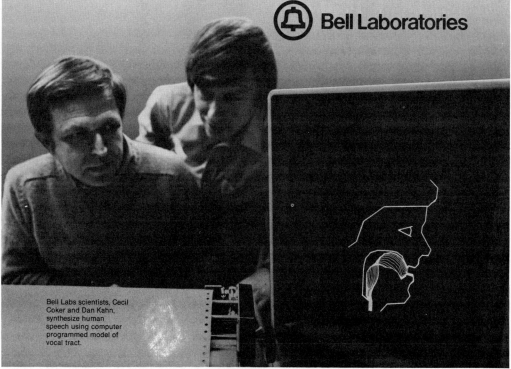

In the Information Age, computers should talk and listen.

The Information Age is here. And Bell Labs is developing the technology you need to succeed in it. Talking and listening computers are part of that technology.

It's natural for people to communicate by voice. That's why researchers at Bell Labs have been studying how machines can be taught to talk and respond to voice commands. With such a capability, the complex information-management systems of the future will be simpler to use. Now, talking and listening computers are becoming more practical — thanks to recent advances in computer programming, microelectronics technology and research in how people communicate.

The payoff? Someday, even if you have no computer training,

you'll have the convenience of phoning a computer that'll recognize your voice, call you by name, and obey your spoken command. To bring that day closer, we've been studying how people generate and recognize speech.

Our research on the human larynx and vocal tract shows us how to program computers to talk or synthesize voices. These voices can speak electronically stored information as diverse as telephone numbers, inventory data, and airline timetables.

Our understanding of human speech recognition shows us how to program computers to listen — a capability that, in laboratory demonstrations, allows people to "dial" telephone numbers simply by speaking a person's name or

phone number. The computer can also verify that the talker is who he or she claims to be — an important concern in automated systems.

And our advances in microelectronics enable us to use the latest technology. For example, we're using a new digital chip that performs more than a million functions per second to synthesize speech.

Improving communication between people and machines — one of the many ways Bell Labs applies its knowledge to help the Bell System meet the information management needs of business.

Bell Laboratories
600 Mountain Avenue
Murray Hill, New Jersey 07974

ⓑ **Bell Laboratories**

Bell Labs scientists, Cecil Coker and Dan Kahn, synthesize human speech using computer programmed model of vocal tract.

8101   Bell Laboratories advertisement appears in: BUSINESS WEEK and WALL STREET JOURNAL

Fig. 16–2 *Bell. A Technological Leadership Theme. Courtesy of Bell Laboratories.*

Hence, the AMF advertising makes the implicit assumption that a favorable image of the corporation will be transferred to its bowling balls, golf clubs, and boats. The General Motors corporate campaigns postulate that if consumers associate GM with hot dogs and apple pie, they will also do so with respect to all of its automotive models. Bell Laboratories assumes that an image as a technological innovator will help create a preference for its products related to automated systems.

These "trickle down" concepts have been incorporated into formal attitudinal models. As applied to buying behavior, a model of this sort would visualize a hierarchy where attitude change starts from the top, proceeds downward, and is capable of spreading horizontally at each of the lower levels. In a two-level hierarchy, for example, attitude change can be described mathematically as follows:[12]

$$\Delta x = \propto (M - x)$$
$$\Delta y = \propto (My - y) + \beta(x - y),$$

where

x = Attitude toward an object at the top of the hierarchy and y is that at the bottom

Mx, My = Attitude change messages concerning x and y

$\propto$ = Parameter reflecting the impact of the external message

β = Internal processing parameter

This model can easily be extended to a three-level system. On the other hand, no messages about y would necessitate dropping $\propto (My-y)$ from the equation for Δy.

The top-down hierarchy model, like the conventional ones, regards attitudes as precursors to action. But the attitude-shaping process here is different insofar as it takes place within a logical hierarchical structure which goes from the top down. Under an assumption of perfect attitude transference from higher to lower level objects, all attitudes in the long run would theoretically equal Mx. This result, in turn, would minimize advertising expenditures, for the attitude achieved by corporate advertising would also be obtained for all the company's products.[13] Although the model is intuitively appealing, it has still to prove itself capable of being operational.

Input-Acquiring Messages

The input-acquisition motive ranks second to that of sales generation as a legitimate purpose of corporate advertising. The productive inputs of greatest concern to top management are finance and people.

The financial ends of corporate advertising are various. The needs for capital are ever present—to build assets, to grow, to compete. Handling these financial resources once fell within the sole province of investment bankers. But no more. No longer do corporations place complete reliance for funding on outside specialists and remain content to play a passive role. Senior corporate executives today pursue the acquisition of financial assets with as much vigor as that of physical assets. This has become a management imperative with the rise of conglomerate organizations.[14]

A one point rise in the price of a widely-held stock can run into millions of dollars. A higher price-earnings ratio offers a company notable advantages in mergers and acquisitions, especially when the transaction involves an exchange of stock. Higher quotes on security exchanges assist capital-raising endeavors and stock option policies. Because stock and bond prices are valuations that financial markets place upon a company, communication with the financial community becomes the responsibility of top management.

How is the financial community defined? It is made up of organizational elements like brokerage houses, financial analysts, fund and portfolio managers, banks, and institutional investors. Some 46 percent of all corporate advertisers listed the financial community as a major target audience. Though not mutually exclusive, individual stockholders were listed as a major target for financial messages by 18 percent (see Table 16–5.)

Advertising with financial overtones must be done with caution so as not to run afoul of the law. Security trading is regulated by government. The Securities and Exchange Commission, the leading regulatory agency, must not construe advertisements as attempts to manipulate, tout or influence the price of a security.

Corporate advertisements directed to the financial community or individual stockholders are usually of a banal, matter-of-fact nature. There are two main types. One provides information about key aspects of a company's economic performance, such as resource allocation, markets, growth, profits, earnings per share, and dividends. Advertisements often contain offers for company literature or annual reports.

A second type of advertisement presents related or correlative information, and any conclusions about company performance is inferential on the part of readers. For example, a utility may talk about the growth in the area it supplies. Whether the company or its earnings will grow at the same rate as the region is strictly inferential.

Of course, company performance information also requires that readers make interpretations and draw inferences, but not about past or current results. These are explicit. Either type of advertisement, however—explicit or implicit—offers audiences a rational presentation. Figures 16–3 to 16–5 illustrate both types of approaches.

Advertisements for both InterNorth and Middle South Utilities can be called inferential. They both stress certain aspects of operations which should translate into higher market valuation of the company—the acqui-

Exploration revenues of $1 billion a year by the 1990's.

And in that time frame we expect to reach $4 billion in exploration and production assets—more than present total assets of all the InterNorth companies combined.

In the early 1970's InterNorth made the decision to undertake exploration and production operations on its own, to help assure the reliability of natural gas supplies for our pipeline system, natural gas liquids and petrochemical operations, and to

further diversify our mix of energy-related businesses.

In 1977 InterNorth formed a new operating company to quicken the pace of our exploration and production operations. This strategic commitment has resulted in acquisition of 1.7 million acres of leaseholds and addition of 223 billion cubic feet of proved reserves of natural gas and its equivalent.

InterNorth, a natural gas pipeline pioneer, today is an international

complex of natural resource companies in natural gas, natural gas liquids, petrochemicals, exploration and production and coal. Natural gas provides a solid foundation of income for our shareholders while our other businesses offer opportunity for capital growth.

For further information on InterNorth, call Roy A. Meierhenry, Vice President and Treasurer, 402-633-4937.

Northern Natural Gas Company • Peoples Natural Gas Company • Northern Plains Natural Gas Company • Northern Natural Resources Company • Northern Liquid Fuels Company • Northern Petrochemical Company • Nortex Gas & Oil Company • Northern Coal Company

The right mix at the right time

International Headquarters, Omaha, Nebraska 68102

Fig. 16—3 *InterNorth. Advertising Asset Acquisitions to the Financial Community. Courtesy of InterNorth.*

sition of exploration assets for InterNorth, the ability to service above-average growth areas for Middle South Utilities.

The explicit approach is demonstrated by the Tyler Corporation advertisement, which was run in the *Wall Street Journal* (Figure 16–5). This small space ad, only one column wide and a little more than four inches deep, gets its performance story across at an extremely low cost to the advertiser.

Corporate advertising to the financial community takes place most frequently among industrial goods manufacturers. About 56 percent of these firms designated the financial community as a major target, as compared with only 34 percent for service companies. Figures for stockholders as a desirable target group were 23 percent and nine percent respectively. (See Table 16–5.)

Many reasons suggest themselves for the extremes between the two major proponents of corporate advertising. Manufacturers of industrial products, unlike their counterparts in consumer fields, have low visibility. All but the largest companies are either ignored or covered lightly by financial researchers. It has been estimated that approximately 3,000 investment-worthy companies are not currently followed by security analysts.[15] The question then becomes how to gain awareness or get information disseminated except by affirmative action.

The service sector contains forces which pull in an opposite direction. Firms offering banking and investment services are part of the financial community, and have no need to make themselves known there. A portion of the service economy is regulated, and its activities, including those of advertising, are influenced by government officials. Commissions which oversee utilities, for example, may not allow corporate advertising as a proper expense in the determination of a firm's rate base. The Interstate Commerce Commission might act similarly in computations of allowable "common costs" in rate-setting cases for transportation companies. Regulation tends to discourage corporate advertising, especially for purposes which are not directly related to new or current business.

Corporate advertising can be used to acquire human resources, such as for personnel recruitment. The National Geographic study indicated that about 13 percent of all corporate advertisers, primarily manufacturing firms, claimed employees and plant communities as major target audiences. (See Table 16–5).

There are innumerable ways of assisting personnel departments with corporate advertising. The Aramco Corporation once ran a series of advertisements showing its employees in Saudi Arabia enjoying various activities, such as golf and sailing, apparently to get people to perceive the desert kingdom as a pleasant place to live and work. Some advertisements which stress company attempts to create a better environment in plant communities are actually aimed at facilitating recruitment. A company

Middle South Utilities is in the right place at the right time. The Middle South area—Arkansas, Louisiana, Mississippi and southeast Missouri— is recognized for its significant economic potential.

We're prepared for continued growth; in fact, we've helped shape it. The area's natural and developed resources, combined with our ability to produce efficient and reliable electric power, are assets which make the Middle South an area whose time has come.

Symbolic of the region's potential is the Mississippi River, our nation's greatest water resource. Uniquely, it's a two-way street, providing the Middle South with avenues of trade not only to and from vast areas of America's heartland through inland waterways, but to and from the world as well through the nation's leading port, New Orleans. The river is the bonding force of the area we serve.

With such resources, and with so much potential still to be developed in our service area, Middle South Utilities and its nearly 200,000 investor-owners are looking to the future with great anticipation.

MIDDLE SOUTH.

Floyd W. Lewis, Chairman and President, Middle South Utilities, Inc., with the area served by the Middle South System.

THE AREA WHOSE TIME HAS COME.

MⱫ MIDDLE SOUTH UTILITIES

Arkansas Power & Light Company   Louisiana Power & Light Company   Mississippi Power & Light Company   New Orleans Public Service Inc.

Fig. 16—4 *Middle South. Financial Advertising by a Utility Stressing a Growth Area. Courtesy of Middle South Utilities.*

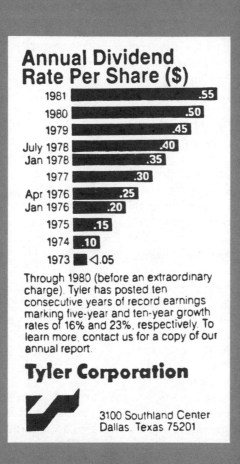

Fig. 16—5 *Tyler Corp. Small Space Performance Ad. Courtesy of the Tyler Corporation.*

perceived as being concerned with the environment in which it operates, it is reasoned, suggests one where people like to work. These suggestive advertisements normally have more than one objective, with input-acquisition often being of secondary importance.

Public Issue Messages

Advertising which involves public issues, regardless of how important they may be to corporate well-being, represents an attempt to influence social factors. These are outside the normal channels of commerce. Messages which address themselves to societal concerns embrace a form of communication which can be described as "social marketing." Its immediate objective is to effect some sort of political or social result.

Many organizations which advertise public issues are nonprofit, such as government agencies, foundations, or churches. But firms in the private sector also produce advertising campaigns on public issues. Their expenditures for these purposes make up a small fraction of total corporate advertising, which by itself is relatively minor. Business executives, on the whole, do not favor corporate funds going to public issues.[16] Nor have bursts of advertising earmarked for public issue, when they do occur, make any significant impact on society. They have engendered more debate by their very existence than by their effects.[17] However, performance to date does not say what their future potential might be.

In fact, some public issues are not debatable at all. These causes are almost universally accepted as good, and promoting them can be thought of as public service advertising. Under these conditions, the advocates of social marketing may be correct in equating the promotion of social goals with the public good, and in adoring the promise "for planning and implementing social change."[18]

Public service advertising is exemplified by campaigns which encourage such things as safe driving, eradication of litter, donations to blood banks, and prevention of forest fires. The advertisement on how to write a resume, run by International Paper, illustrates public service advertising related, though somewhat loosely, to a company's products. (See Figure 16–6). Examples with closer product ties would be messages by oil and utility companies explaining to consumers how to save energy; by MasterCard during the credit crunch of 1979–80 urging people to buy now and pay now; by forest product companies expounding on reforestation techniques.

A classic public service campaign is the "Great Idea" advertising of Container Corporation of America, begun in 1938 and still running. The company has maintained a steadfast dedication to using mass media to communicate moral, political and social philosophies. An in-house committee selects the great ideas through individual reading and outside sug-

Today, the printed word is more vital than ever. Now there is more need than ever for all of us to *read* better, *write* better, and *communicate* better.

International Paper offers this series in the hope that, even in a small way, we can help.

Since we started printing it in 1979, we have sent out—at requests from people everywhere, including students, teachers and business people—several million reprints.

If you would like reprints of this advertisement, write: "Power of the Printed Word," International Paper Co., Dept. 10, P.O. Box 954, Madison Square Station, New York, N.Y. 10010. © 1981. INTERNATIONAL PAPER COMPANY

 **INTERNATIONAL PAPER COMPANY**

We believe in the power of the printed word.

Printed in U.S. on International Paper Company's Springhill® Offset, basis 60 lb.

Fig. 16–6 *International Paper Co. Advertisement from International Paper's "Power of the Printed Word" Program. Courtesy of International Paper Co.*

gestions. The committee then contracts with an artist, who is given complete freedom to interpret the quotation graphically.[19] The rendition of a quotation from Adlai Stevenson is shown in Figure 16–7. Though undoubtedly of esthetic and social value, the campaign also contains a subtle sales-generating message. It upholds the company as innovative in design and creative in packaging graphics—most sought-after attributes in Container Corporation's line of business.

Other public issues, however, are inherently controversial, and herein lies the fallacy of social marketing. A social good acclaimed by one person may appear antisocial to another individual. When such causes are promoted with paid messages in media, the practice is called "advocacy" or "adversary" advertising.

The content of advocacy advertising is extremely diverse, and can range from government policy, such as to oppose or support certain legislation, or to individual behavior, such as to stop smoking or practice birth control. Many companies, even when forced into public controversy, express their opinions through industry associations or house organs rather than run the risk of antagonizing important seqments of the population. But some companies are more prone than others to air their views in mass media under their own signatures, presumably because the issues are company specific instead of industry specific. Oil companies and utilities, highly diverse both operationally and locationally, are not likely to achieve industry-wide agreement on public issues, and if they are drawn into controversial campaigns, they must do it alone. Another factor in a company engaging in advocacy advertising is the philosophy of its top management, particularly the chief executive.[20] How else could one explain Mobil's or Exxon's pugnacious defense of their profits during the energy crises, while the other oil companies were content to maintain a low profile? One of the Exxon advertisements, run in newspapers during December 1979, featured a picture of C. C. Garvin, Jr., Chairman, and his explanation as to why large profits were necessary.

The issues arise primarily from sources outside the corporation. Advertisers choose the argument, but not the subject. In controversy advertising, messages are almost never addressed to the general public, but to those segments already supporting the advocated position or to those who are uncommitted. Advertisements seldom go into media with contrary points of view.[21] This is in keeping with the philosophy that advertising does not change attitudes but simply reenforces those in existence.

Advocacy advertising in the United States is regarded as a traditional right of persons, including that of corporations, to free speech. The landmark case was the First National Bank of Boston *v.* Bellotti in 1978. The Supreme Court set aside as unconstitutional a Massachusetts' law which prevented the bank from advertising its views on a state referendum.

Great Ideas, one of a series

Photographer: Gene Ku

CCA

If we value the pursuit of knowledge
we must be free to follow
wherever that search may lead us.

Adlai Stevenson

Fig. 16—7 *Stevenson Quotation. A Graphic Rendition of a Quotation by Adlai Stevenson. Courtesy of Container Corporation of America.*

The right to free speech, however, is a sterile prerogative without the means to exercise it. An expression of opinion requires access to media. Print media pose no problems to corporate paid messages. But broadcasting companies, especially the networks, have thrown up formidable barriers.

Ironically, these obstacles have been erected on the foundation of the Fairness Doctrine, originally enunciated by the Federal Communications Commission (FCC) to give the public a balanced presentation of conflicting opinions. If broadcasters accept advertisements on a controversial issue, they may be obliged to give free reply time to opposing positions. But under the FCC Editorializing Broadcast Licensees decision of 1949, broadcasters have the "right to edit." They decide which issues to put on the air, and they select the contrasting points of view. Broadcasters have used this so called Editorializing Report as a justification for not accepting opinion advertising. Controversial issues, they hold, are best covered in news and public affairs programs. The rationale was upheld by the Supreme Court in 1973 when it exonerated CBS from refusing to run advertisements submitted by Business Executives Move for a Vietnam Peace.

Those opposing the use of editing rights to refuse advertising charge broadcasters with censorship of corporate communications. The only reason for network intransigence, they claim, is not a public-spirited concern with an objective presentation to the audience but a self-interested attempt to avoid having to donate free time. As former FCC Commissioner, Nicholas Johnson remarked, "Many broadcasters are fighting not for free speech, but for profitable speech."[22]

The networks have been especially loathe to accept any advertising which might obligate them to provide equal time for opposing points of view. The acceptance rates for individual television stations, however, have been quite high. A 1980 survey of Television Bureau of Advertising reported that eighty-nine percent of stations will accept advocacy advertising. But the same survey showed that only six percent have policies to accept any advocacy commercial. The remaining eighty-three percent said that acceptance is "based on considerations of individual taste."[23] No matter how widespread the acceptance by stations, however, controversy advertisements are denied in-program positions in prime time on network-affiliated stations.

More important than advertiser-broadcaster squabbles is the broader question of advocacy advertising itself, not only by private firms but by nonprofit organizations. The right to bring their views into the public arena is not a point of contention. Nor is the rightness or wrongness of any particular position. Instead, the question which intrudes itself is: Should an organization express social or political views through advertising? And does society benefit from such action?

Like any controversial issue, that of advocacy advertising is likely to be answered in different ways. The majority opinion, with certain reservations, sees "opinion" advertising as making a positive contribution to the public's understanding. The traditional view, steeped in rationalism, asserts that people have a right to know and an inherent ability to choose. As expressed by Thomas Garbett, "The truth will ultimately surface. The more powerful . . . the ad campaign, the more quickly the truth will surface."[24] This proposition assumes, perhaps naively, that blatant distortions of facts will be offset by counter-claims for the opposing party, and that through this dialectic of charges and counter-charges the public will screen out the falsehoods and arrive at pure truth.

But this philosophical position rings true only from a distance. A more realistic scenario is that of the defeated politician who outwardly accepts his adversity with grace but mutters to himself, "The people have spoken—the bastards!"

It is always possible for a challenger to counter hyperbole with even more exaggerated claims of his own. And who will stop him? As with political advertising, no government agency has the slightest desire to get involved in communications about social issues. The FTC maintains a strict, hands off policy. Kysor Industries in 1979 placed ads with prominent headlines: "Deregulation has shot down more planes than the Red Baron." Industry leaders winced. Even Kysor's supporters squirmed. The chairman of the Civil Aeronautics Board fumed and growled. But he could do nothing about it and in the end his soaring protestations, like the Baron's quarries, went down in flames.

The underlying motivation of social marketing, which includes advocacy advertising, is that ideas can be sold like soap. The typical commercial on television, for example, is only thirty seconds. But how much can be said, or shown, in this limited span of time? For this reason, advertising makes use of stereotypes to capture one essential meaning. By necessity, it departs from reality in doing so. When this departure is relatively large, it is called deception. There are safeguards against product deception, but not against misrepresentation of ideas. As so aptly stated by Mel Grayson, a former political speech writer and now a public relations executive, "in the United States today we can malign, ridicule, belittle and disparage . . . as long as there's no profit in it."[25]

One of the first successful uses of emotionally-charged messages to influence public policy was advertising to reverse a House vote on the "Rat Extermination" bill in 1967.[26] This advertisement showed a picture of a rat, with the bold caption: "Cut this out and put it in bed next to your child." Since then, more and more serious public issues have been presented with irrational appeals. Planned Parenthood in 1981 ran advertisements against the antiabortion amendment, headlined, "Should you be forced to bear your rapist's child?" Messages from Pro Life advocates have been equally distorted. To defeat an abortion bill in Michigan, advertisements showed the destruction of fetuses in their later stages. And politicians have long ago mastered the art of exploiting people's hopes and expectations to win votes.

Advocacy messages from business organizations have been in much better taste than those from nonprofit organizations. Corporate messages have been well-researched, carefully considered, and more rational. Still, abuses exist. One is the advocacy of solutions in commercials which are thinly disguised as news communications. Another concern is that over the argument of "deep pockets." Organizations with the deepest pockets, or the most money, it is contended, will speak the loudest and drown out all the others.

Media Access Project, a public interest law firm, examined three referendum campaigns in Colorado in 1976: a nuclear safety proposal, a container recycling bill, and a public utilities reform measure. Its report documents how each started with strong public support, encountered strong corporate opposition, and lost by landslide margins. The report maintains that the amount of money spent on a campaign correlated with the number of votes received. On this basis, Media Access Project recommended either improving the position of the advocate group that spent the least money or curbing one-sided expenditures in a referendum campaign.[27]

A study by professor S. Prakash Sethi of the University of California concluded that under certain circumstances, advocacy campaigns can "sharply reduce the expression of alternative viewpoints on important issues affecting society."[28] He therefore proposed the establishment of a National Council of Public Information which, among its other duties, would purchase advertising space for public expression of viewpoints having no exposure by virtue of lack of funds.[29] This recommendation assumes that a balanced presentation of all views is desirable.

But it is doubtful that this suggestion will soon be implemented even in watered-down form. The reason stems from the basic purpose of social marketing, which is not to shape a society that makes collective decisions equitably and rationally. Its goal, like that of product marketing, is to sell—in this case, a particular point of view. Whether an idea enhances public welfare is coincidental; it will be promoted if it has adherents or financial backing, and preferably both. As long as advocacy advertising is operated from this particular perspective, it must remain an instrument of contesting groups jockeying for position among conventional sources of power.

SUMMARY

Corporate advertising, though vague, involves no direct presentation of products or solicitation of productive inputs. Its objectives and budgets in most corporations are under the direction of senior management.

Products and markets are major determinants of corporate advertising. The highest incidence occurs among industrial manufacturers and service companies. Size of company is also an important factor. There is a positive relationship between the size of the firm and the probability of corporate advertising.

Corporate advertising has three main purposes. These are: to enhance sales, to facilitate the acquisition of productive inputs, to influence an exogenous factor.

Sales-generating messages are the mainstay of corporate advertising. The business community is the chief target for this type of advertising. The sales-generating objective implies a "trickle down" theory of customer attitudes.

Input-acquisition messages are meant to assist financial and personnel departments. Manufacturing firms are more apt to advertise to the financial community than the service sector.

Public service advertising has two faces. When issues are widely accepted, advertising works to enhance public welfare. But when issues are controversial, advertising serves the interests of particular groups without necessarily being conducive to the welfare of society at large.

This chapter concludes the section on general advertising in national media. The next section takes up sales-specific advertising, where sales results can be traced directly to individual messages.

Questions for Chapter 16

1. How does the administration of corporate advertising differ from that of product advertising?

2. Why would product managers in industrial companies be more prone to favor corporate advertising than managers in consumer goods companies?

3. What are the major differences between associations and their members with respect to corporate advertising?

4. Why is print media more popular than television among corporate advertisers?

5. Why is the *Wall Street Journal* a favorite medium for corporate advertisements?

6. Compare the flow of attitudes conceptualized by corporate advertising and by the Fishbein model.

7. What specific corporate functions can corporate advertising perform for an investment bank?

8. What benefits do electric utilities seek from corporate advertising?

9. Although the advertising content has almost universal approval, a program to promote good citizenship by a major corporation might still be regarded as controversial. Why?

10. Can advertising significantly change attitudes on a public policy issue?

11. Are the networks censoring free speech by refusing to run advertising on controversial issues?

12. Is the public better informed on issues as a result of "advocacy" advertising?

Footnotes for Chapter 16

[1]Thomas Garbett, "What Companies Project to Public," *Advertising Age* (July 6, 1981), p. S-1.

[2]Garbett, *Advertising Age.*

[3]Thomas A. Garbett, *Corporate Advertising* (New York: McGraw-Hill, 1981), pp. 67–69.

[4]See Joseph Chasin and William S. Sachs, *How Companies Evaluate Their Corporate Advertising* (New York: National Geographic Magazine, 1978), p. 6; and William S. Sachs, *Corporate Advertising as Perceived by Advertising Executives* (New York: National Geographic Magazine, 1981), p. 5.

[5]Association of National Advertisers, *Current Company Practices in the Use of Corporate Advertising* (New York: Association of National Advertisers, Inc., 1980), pp. 20–21.

[6]"Public Relations' Role in Corporate Advertising," *Public Relations Journal* (November 1977), pp. 34–35.

[7]See William S. Sachs, "Corporate Advertising: Ends, Means, Problems," *Public Relations Journal* (November 1981), p. 15; Peg Dardenne, "The Cost of Corporate Advertising," p. 30.

[8]See Paul W. Farris and Mark S. Albion, *Determinants of Variations in the Advertising-to-Sales Ratio: A Comparison of Industry and Firm Studies* (Cambridge, Mass.: Marketing Science Institute, 1980), Report No. 80-107.

[9]W. S. Sachs and J. Chasin, "How Companies Evaluate Their Corporate Advertising," *Public Relations Journal* (November 1977), p. 15.

[10]Walter P. Margulies, "How Banks Stress Corporate Image," *Advertising Age* (May 19, 1980), p. 85.

[11]*Current Company Practices*, Association of National Advertisers, pp. 7–10.

[12]See John E. Hunter et. al., "Attitude Change in Hierarchical Belief Systems and Its Relationships to Persuasibility, Dogmatism and Rigidity," *Human Communication Research* (Fall 1976), pp. 3–28.

[13]Jeffrey E. Danes and Gregory D. Upah, "A Hierarchical Approach to Advertising Strategy," Bellur, ed., pp. 262–264.

[14]See Oliver E. Williamson, "The Modern Corporation: Origins, Evolution, Attributes," *The Journal of Economic Literature* (December 1981), pp. 1557–1560.

[15]Garbett, *Corporate Advertising*, p. 109.

[16]See Joseph Chasin and William S. Sachs, *How Executives of America's Top 500 Corporations View Corporate Advertising* (New York: National Geographic Magazine, 1976), p. 7; William S. Sachs, "The Anatomy of Corporate Advertising," *Review of Business* (Spring 1980), pp. 11–13.

[17]See "How to Organize for Controversy Advertising," *Public Relations Journal* (November 1976), pp. 23–25; S. P. Sethi, "Dangers of Advocacy Advertising," pp. 42, 46–47.

[18]P. Kotler and S. J. Levy, "Broadening the Concept of Marketing," *Journal of Marketing* (January 1969), pp. 10–15; P. Kotler and G. Zaltman, "Social Marketing: An Approach to Planned Social Change," *Journal of Marketing* (July 1971), pp. 3–12.

[19]Janet Neiman, "CCA Breaks Latest Great Idea," *Advertising Age* (June 8, 1981), p. 14.

[20]See Paul Blustein, "Tavoulareas Puts Firm On a Separate Course From Most of Big Oil," *Wall Street Journal*, February 14, 1980, pp. 1, 18.

[21]Albert Stridsberg, *Controversy Advertising* (New York: International Advertising Association, 1977), pp. 48–51.

[22]*At Issue: Access to Television* (Oakland, Calif.: Kaiser Aluminum & Chemical Corporation, 1980), p. 20.

[23]"89% of TV Stations Will Air Corporate Advocacy Ads: Survey," *Marketing News* (October 31, 1980), p. 4.

[24]Garbett, *Corporate Advertising*, p. 61.

[25]Melvin J. Grayson, "Freedom of the Press: Our Double Standard," *Review of Business* (Spring 1980), p. 5.

[26]Stridsberg, *Controversy Advertising*, p. 108.

[27]"Corporate Spending in Vote Swamps Foes: Study," *Advertising Age* (April 28, 1980), p. 38.

[28]S. Prakash Sethi, *Advocacy Advertising and Large Corporations* (Lexington, Mass.: D. C. Heath, 1977), pp. 292–293.

[29]Sethi, *Advocacy Advertising and Large Corporations*, pp. 305–308.

SALES-SPECIFIC
ADVERTISING

17 Retail Advertising

Although retail advertising may amount to as much as one-third of all advertising in the United States, it has been underemphasized in the literature. The main reason is presumably its local, highly dispersed nature. Enterprises operating at local levels are relatively small compared with those competing on a national scale. But when individual local businesses are added together, sales volume assumes imposing proportions, and retailers' decisions, taken collectively, have important consequences for national advertisers.

The goals of this chapter are to:

- **Delineate the primary characteristics of retail advertising**
- **Examine direct advertising links between retailers and manufacturers, such as those of cooperative advertising**
- **Analyze the composition of advertising messages designed for retail goals**
- **Explore media cost structures and retailers' use of local media**

THE RETAIL TRADES

The Bureau of the Census defines the retail trades as "all establishments engaged in selling merchandise for personal or household consumption, and rendering services incidental to the sales of goods."[1] This definition pins down retailing to the exchange of goods. It eliminates all other local services, such as banking, financial services, real estate, transportation, and utilities.

Given this definition, the classification of national and local advertising suffers from certain ambiguities. Though most retail advertising is local, a good deal of local advertisements do not come from retailers. A savings and loan association may pay newspapers local rates to run its advertisements. But though the bank's messages are those of a local business, they are not those of a retailer.

Some authors have attempted to reconcile industry and government concepts by expanding the Census Bureau's definition of "retail" to encompass the service industries. But there are still difficulties. Large retail chains, such as Sears and J. C. Penney, advertise both nationally and locally. The national effort pushes the firm's own brands and engages in corporate image-building; the local effort offers direct support for individual stores. Thus, not all retail advertising is local.

According to the *1977 Census of Retail Trade*, there were slightly more than 1.85 million retail establishments in the United States. The total

TABLE 17–1 *Sales by Types of Retail Establishments*

Type of Establishment	Sales (Billions of Dollars)
Food stores	158
Automotive dealers	150
General merchandise	94
Eating and drinking	64
Gasoline service stations	56
Building material, hardware	39
Apparel, accessories	35
Furniture, home furnishings	33
Drug and proprietary	23
Miscellaneous	71
Total retail	723

Source: U.S. Bureau of the Census, *1977 Census of Retail Trade*, II, 10–11.

value of sales ran to more than $723 billion.[2] Sales for different types of retail establishments can be seen in Table 17–1.

Like manufacturing industries, retail categories have different advertising-to-sales ratios. The highest are those of general merchandisers, most sales of which are accounted for by department stores and food stores. The latter is dominated by supermarkets. A National Retail Merchants Association study found the average department store reporting an expenditure equal to 3.8 percent of sales for all phases of promotion.[3] Yet this small percentage, on the average, exceeds net after tax profit. This would also hold true for the grocery trades, where a typical supermarket has about a 1.3 percent profit-to-sales ratio. In general, retailers' advertising expenditures are exceeded only by costs of merchandise purchased for resale, payroll, and occupancy expenses.[4]

A major characteristic of retailing is its local nature. A store's customers are usually drawn from an adjoining area. But the extent of a local area is elastic, depending upon the dispersion or clustering of population and the types of goods that are being offered.

The theory of a "hierarchy of centers" was first propounded in 1933 by the German geographer, Walter Christaller, in his classic work, *Die Zentralen Orte in Süddeutschland (Central Locations in South Germany)*. Christaller developed the notion that the position any market center holds in the hierarchy is linked to the assortments it carries. For example, customers will not travel long distances for "lower order" goods, such as groceries. These would then sell in numerous small centers distributed in accordance with population. On the other hand, people are apt to travel considerable distances for goods which are unique, such as antiques, art, and other specialty items. These goods would then locate outlets in a few large centers.

In general, a more specialized supply or demand requires a larger market area to support it economically. More generalized goods tend to follow patterns of dispersion. To retranslate Christaller's descriptions of half a century ago for modern day marketing, the hierarchy can be visualized, starting from the top, as regional centers, large city centers, small city centers, large towns, small towns, villages. As populations are not uniformly distributed, marketing areas will overlap. And local media, partly because of physical constraints, and partly because of economic ones, will weave contradictory coverage patterns of overlapping markets.

CHARACTERISTICS OF RETAIL ADVERTISING

Retail advertising has two chief aims, merchandising and store image. Actually, both types of promotion have sales of goods as their ultimate goals. But because the movement of goods can often be traced directly to merchandising efforts, that aspect assumes the greater importance in advertising plans.

Most retail advertisements emphasize sales, items, or events — things that would draw customers into the store. This is product advertising, pure and simple. Retailers also attempt to create or maintain a store image. They refer to advertising as institutional when it conveys an impression about the store rather than about merchandise a store offers for sale.

The dichotomy between product advertising and institutional advertising, however, is not as sharp as might appear at first sight. Advertisements which combine the two seem to be the rule rather than the exception. The basic reason is because the selection of merchandise a store carries cannot realistically be disassociated from the store's identity.[5]

For example, a store perceived as a leader in fashions will feature new, innovative designs. Likewise, a store associated with "high quality" will carry expensive merchandise and offer a high level of service.

Retailers appealing to middle America, such as Sears, stock large assortments of widely-accepted products, good in quality and moderate in price. Discounters feature low prices, but must cut back on service, store decor, and sell merchandise that has already attained popularity in use. A certain degree of commonness is a must.

Bloomingdale's, which has been promoting itself as a trend setter, in 1980 sponsored a special event featuring Chinese merchandise. Artisans were even brought in from China to demonstrate their crafts. In 1978 and 1979 Bloomingdale's ran promotions for wares from India and Israel respectively.[6] The merchandise a store carries tells the public something about the store. And the store image implies the kind of items consumers expect to find on its shelves. Woolworth's and Tiffany's are not competitors. Although product advertising dominates retailing, it remains permeated by an institutional flavor.[7]

Product Advertising

Merchandising and product advertising are closely intertwined. Goods offered to the public are the essentials of both activities. The advertising in fact becomes an extension of the retailer's window displays and show cases.

The primary purpose of product advertising is immediate sales. The choice of items advertised becomes important, not only because they are objects of transactions but because they build store traffic. The content of advertisements thus depends heavily upon merchandising considerations. Almost all advertisements of discounters, mass merchandisers and supermarkets are framed in this type of format.

Seeking quick, tangible results, the advertising messages convey a sense of urgency to "buy now," that quantities are limited. The offer stands for a given period and won't be available later. These advertisements contain more or less rational arguments, quoting prices and terms of sale.

Expenditures for product advertising are highly correlated with sales. Periods of high sales witness high advertising outlays and vice versa. Clothing stores, toy shops, jewelry centers, music marts, and department stores reach their highest advertising peaks in December, the season to be jolly and give presents. Shoe stores promote heaviest in August to take advantage of back-to-school buying before Labor Day. The timing of these expenditures accepts the proposition that advertising will not alter established shopping habits. In the main, retailers see advertising expenditures as most productive when they follow the flow of sales, and swim, so to speak, with the direction of the current.

Some authorities have advanced a contra-seasonal theory, arguing that more advertising should be done in poor months to perk up sales and less should be done in busy months. This view assumes that advertising can change seasonal buying patterns. If people can be made to buy air conditioners in winter and snow tires in summer, a firm can even out its seasonal revenue fluctuations. Off-season promotions, however, are mainly for clearance sales to get rid of old stock. White sales abound in January and car dealers mark down their prices at the end of summer or early fall before the new models come out. Otherwise, the levels of retail advertising go up and down with the wavelike movement of sales.

Institutional Advertising

The main purpose of institutional advertising is to promote the store. Goods are often identical, regardless of the place in which they are sold. Then why should consumers prefer to purchase in one place over another?

There are many reasons for consumer location preferences, some tangible and some not. Among the former, the most obvious one is transportation. The element of distance holds a central place in location theory. But there are other, less definable qualities which influence consumer choice, such as store atmosphere or image. These institutional advertisements espouse a soft sell, as contrasted with the appeals of product advertising. But results are as soft as the sell. They cannot be measured by the hard figures of the cash register, and are, therefore, difficult to assess.

Some of the large retail chains run image-building campaigns in national media, such as magazines and network television. Sears, K-Mart Corporation, and J. C. Penney were listed among the top fifty national advertisers in 1980.[8] Most of the national advertising by retailers are product advertising, not institutional. Either can be done in this manner when a chain's stores achieve nationwide coverage. Not counting "image" carryovers into product advertising, it is estimated that retailers traditionally assign some five to ten percent of their store's budgets to institutional tasks.[9]

COOPERATIVE ADVERTISING

A substantial portion of retail advertising, perhaps half, involves cooperative ventures. Two or more parties join in an advertising program. There are basically three kinds of cooperative advertising on the retail level: horizontal, ingredient producer, and vertical.[10]

The horizontal type occurs when retailers band together and conduct a common advertising campaign. An example of this form is merchants of a shopping center jointly advertising their location. The more typical horizontal advertising is that conducted by franchised dealers of a branded durable good, such as automobiles, appliances, or hardware.

Ingredient producer cooperative advertising arises when a supplier of raw materials attempts to encourage retailers to merchandise finished goods which contain the supplier's materials. DuPont giving promotional support to stores selling carpeting made of 501 Nylon exemplifies this pattern of cooperative advertising.

The overwhelming proportion of cooperative advertising is vertical. This calls for advertising placed by retailers to be financed, wholly or partially, by manufacturers.

There are no reliable figures for the volume of cooperative advertising. Robert F. Young places the yearly total at approximately $3 billion.[11] But estimates vary widely. Some sources have put estimates of "available" funds for cooperative advertising at about $7.5 billion per annum.[12] Since roughly thirty to forty percent of all appropriated funds are not used, this estimate would put the manufacturers' contribution as high as $5 billion. Add to that the retailer's matching funds, and the cooperative peak estimate goes to some $10 billion — much too high. If the more moderate

Young estimate is adjusted for inflation, the 1981 cooperative advertising total would come to between $3.6 billion and $4.0 billion. This figure would represent at least half of all advertising placed by retailers to advertise locally.

Cooperative advertising has had a long history, tracing its origins back to the turn of the century. Its reason for being is the same now as then. Large retailers clamor for promotional assistance from their suppliers, and manufacturers harbor the belief that local advertising and store promotions will increase their sales.

But not all goods are equally benefited. Cooperative advertising achieves the best results for brands which are retail-dependent. In these instances, the national brand gets an added push at the retail level, where the manufacturer's influence is weak. The retailer acquires additional funds to promote a brand, where his influence and expertise are strong. Such goods are apt to have the following characteristics: high price, infrequent purchase, durability, low manufacturer loyalty, selective distribution, and personal selling.[13]

When manufacturers act as channel captains and are able to create demand, they are less dependent upon retailer efforts. It is the store that is impelled to stock the national brand if it wishes to maximize revenue per linear foot of space. The manufacturers will then put more emphasis on sales promotion devices such as couponing in order to draw customers to the brand.

Cooperative funds from manufacturers come in a variety of forms. Some manufacturers allow a fixed dollar amount per item or case. The dollars-per-case method is fairly typical of the food and drug industry. The other method is to set a fixed percentage of the dollar volume purchased by the store. This percentage can range from two to five percent. Either way, unit or percent of sales, the retailer must match the supplier's contribution. The most common matching plan is 50-50, splitting the cost of advertising down the middle.

In any event, retail purchases form the basis of vendor funds. Suppliers must also comply with the provisions of the Robinson-Patman Act, which prohibits discrimination among dealers and retailers. The Federal Trade Commission, the watchdog agency, has ruled that manufacturers must make available funds proportionally equal to all retailers handling their lines of merchandise.

Retailers can derive many advantages from cooperative advertising programs run by manufacturers. If a store does not substitute vendor advertising funds for its own, it increases its advertising budget with vendor money. This addition can mean more frequent advertising messages, and in print media, larger-sized advertisements than normally placed. Both strategies enhance public exposure and store traffic. By raising the volume and frequency discounts given by advertising carriers, the retailer reduces per unit media costs. Consequently, the store enjoys a net gain in the productivity of its advertising.

It might be argued that many manufacturers are able to build cooperative, or coop, programs into the prices they charge for their goods. In these instances, the cooperative dollars are not incremental at all to the retailer. But failure to make use of the coop program leaves the store with less value for the merchandise it buys. The reduction is equal to the amount of cooperative advertising shifted into the final price.

Lastly, retailers joining a cooperative advertising program can often obtain advertising materials from the manufacturer. The art and copy are put together professionally, and are usually better than the retailer could do on his own.

Yet cooperative advertising is beset by difficulties and controversies. The most serious source of conflict is differing objectives between manufacturers and retailers. The latter is indifferent to what brand is carried. The selection must be in accordance with the interests of the store. If a cooperative item sells poorly in relation to a brand leader, the store has no reason to alter its stocking or selling policies. If the cooperative item is not a fast-moving staple, retailers must think twice about expending energy to promote it. Retail advertisements emphasize price. Should a store then change its advertising copy because a manufacturer sees the "bargain basement atmosphere" as conflicting with the image by which the brand had been promoted in national advertising?

In fact, some retailers regard cooperative advertising as "promotional allowances" which are little different from other types of discounts. Major grocery chains look upon cooperative advertising funds as belonging to the price at which they buy, and upon the manufacturer as disposer of the money to buyers under the guise of cooperating in an advertising program. These budgets are actually converted into price discounts, either passed on to customers or used to widen store margins.[14]

THE USE OF NEWSPAPERS

Retailers spend most of their ad budgets — about seventy-five percent — on newspapers. Their appeal to retailers lies in their local nature. Of a total of $15.6 billion worth of advertising carried by American newspapers in 1980, some $13.3 billion or eighty-five percent was local. The $15.6 billion newspaper tab represents slightly less than twenty-nine percent of all U.S. advertising, national and local.[15]

Among the dailies in 1980, there were almost four times as many evening as morning newspapers: 1.388 vs 387.[16] The attraction of the evening paper is that it supposedly gets higher readership, being available to all family members. These papers may be favored by advertisers for items which involve joint purchase decisions, such as furniture, household furnishings, and appliances. The morning paper, which is often read

TABLE 17–2 *Daily Newspaper Circulation (In Millions)*

Year	Morning	Evening	Sunday
1950	21.3	32.6	46.6
1960	24.0	34.9	47.7
1970	25.9	36.2	49.2
1971	26.1	36.2	49.7
1972	26.1	36.4	50.0
1973	26.5	36.6	51.7
1974	26.1	35.7	51.7
1975	25.5	35.2	51.1
1976	25.9	35.1	51.6
1977	26.7	34.8	52.4
1978	27.7	34.3	54.0
1979	28.6	33.6	54.4
1980	29.4	32.9	54.7

Source: American Newspaper Publishers Association, *Facts About Newspapers* (1981), p. 3.

on the way to work, is thought to have an advantage over evening editions for advertising products bought individually, such as cosmetics, jewelry, shirts, ties, and hosiery.

The average morning paper, however, has a circulation of more than three times that of the typical evening newspaper. The number of AM newspapers increased toward the end of the 1970s, while PM papers declined slightly. In terms of circulation, morning papers have grown steadily over the last decade. Their rate of growth has paralleled that of population but lagged somewhat behind the increase in household formation. Sunday circulation exhibits much the same trend. But circulation of evening newspapers has declined absolutely, falling from 36.2 million to 32.9 million copies from 1970 to 1980 inclusive. Table 17–2 shows the trends in daily newspaper circulation for morning, evening and Sunday editions.

The circulation trends shown in Table 17–2 are in many ways reflective of population and social changes, and thus reflective of changes in retailing. The upsurge of working women abetted what some regarded as the irrepressible deterioration of the family as a unit. Alterations in reading habits have also resulted from population and social changes. The shift of population to suburbs, which had been going on for more than three decades, was accompanied by mass relocation of retail stores. The major share of consumer spending, already lodged in suburban areas by the early 1970s, leaned more heavily towards the outlying city districts as time went on.[17]

Large metropolitan dailies, offering high coverage of a wide marketing area, were well suited to retail advertising when consumer buying focused on downtown shopping centers. But today, the locus of shopping is dif-

TABLE 17–3 *Weekly U.S. Newspaper Circulation*

Year	Number of Weeklies	Total Weekly Circulation (000,000)
1970	7,610	29.4
1971	7,567	30.5
1972	7,553	32.0
1973	7,641	34.9
1974	7,612	35.8
1975	7,486	35.2
1976	7,530	37.3
1977	7,466	37.9
1978	7,673	40.2
1979	7,954	42.3
1980	7,602	41.0

Source: American Newspaper Publishers Association, *Facts About Newspapers* (1981), p. 14.

ferent, and suburban stores cannot expect much business from inner city residents. Advertisements in full-run editions of a metropolitan daily, with certain exceptions, encounter more and more "waste" circulation. City papers have responded with zoned editions and suburban sections. About eighty-seven percent of newspapers with circulations of 100,000 and more, and roughly half of the smaller-circulation newspapers, published zoned editions in 1981. Some newspapers, especially those with high proportions of home deliveries, permit advertisers to select different combinations of zip code areas in which to run their ads.

Growth of the suburbs has given impetus to a host of suburban newspapers featuring local news. They may be sold by subscription or distributed free of charge. The latter are sent to all residents of an area in order to achieve full saturation in selected localities. Many suburban newspapers, paid or free, are issued weekly to coincide with heavy shopping days. Suburban publishing efforts have also sported "shoppers," which are usually tabloids carrying no news, just advertisements. Another type of publication is the "pennysaver," the format of which imitates the shopper but relies more heavily on reader classified ads.

The number of weekly newspapers over the past decade has remained fairly constant. But the average circulation has grown by about forty percent. The circulation of weeklies has increased at about twice the rate of daily newspapers, reaching approximately 41 million copies in 1980. These trends are shown in Table 17–3.

Newspaper advertisements take up more than sixty percent of the available space in an issue, and come in two forms, classified and display. The classified sections account for roughly thirty percent of all advertising revenue in newspapers. These advertisements require no creative talent.

Regular classified advertisements are listings set in the format of the newspaper. A classified display advertisement, set apart from the rest of the classified ads by a border, makes little or no use of art work or design.

A display advertisement, which is the mainstay of a newspaper, is often designed and made up by the publisher. Typesetting services are included in local advertising rates. Newspapers actually perform creative functions for advertising agencies in many instances, and certainly production functions. The publication is able to do so because local advertisements are essentially simple, announcement messages, where layout and design are not important. Compared to magazines, printing is low quality, using thin, coarse newsprint. A newspaper advertisement has, at best, a one-day life, for yesterday's newspaper is as out of date as last year's fashions. Under these conditions, it is hardly worthwhile to spend much time and money on elaborate artwork and graphics.

Never was the futility of creative talent better illustrated than when a computer was programed to write real estate advertisements. Developed by Computer Advertising Company, the program was sold to a chain of weekly papers in northern Ohio and to more than a dozen real estate companies around the country. After the client supplies relevant information about the property, the computer takes only seconds to spit out a 50 to 60 word copy block under a catchy headline, at least for realtors. And the service charge is only three dollars per ad. According to those who have tried the computer-written ads, results were entirely satisfactory.[18]

Stores which belong to a chain frequently receive the basic advertising design from corporate headquarters. These central planning procedures give all of the chain's advertisements a common look. But local stores always make minor adjustments to suit their merchandising plans, and often at the last possible moment. Newspapers are flexible enough to accommodate these changes, even right up to press time.

An important trend in chain store use of newspaper advertising is that of rotogravure and inserts. Nationally-distributed preprints via newspapers give the large retailer better control of merchandising. Color provides a higher response, while printing in large batches offers a low per unit cost.

Institutional ads are usually single item, and similar to those of national advertising. But the more common product advertising utilizes multiple item messages. A number of different items share the cost of an advertisement, reducing the outlay per item. The joint expense also permits the use of larger space units.

From a creative standpoint, many of these so-called "omnibus ads" present a crowded appearance. If they use heavy borders and boxes, reverse blocks, and prominent illustrations, they convey an impression of bargains and inexpensive merchandise.[19]

NEWSPAPER ADVERTISING RATES

Space units for advertising are figured in one of two ways, by column inches or by agate lines. The first method specifies the basic unit as being one inch deep by one column wide. An advertisement ten inches deep stretching three columns across the page would thus be thirty column inches (10 × 3 = 30). The agate line is a printer's measure, 1/14th of a column inch as calculated from ascender to descender letters.

Besides receiving quotations of lower-than-national rates, local advertisers enjoy volume and frequency discounts. Recently, these discounts were extended to national advertisers by Newsplan, an industry-wide experiment for newspapers to compete more vigorously in the national arena. Newspaper participants in the program offer special discounts to national advertisers who agree to run some minimum advertising schedule.[20] But the differential between local and national advertising rates remains. The main reason is that newspapers pay no commissions to advertising agencies for local advertisements.

If an advertiser defaults on a contract by not running the volume specified, the advertiser is short-rated. Retailers should always keep their records current. If actual volume appears to fall short of contracted volume, a retailer can run "rate holders." These are advertisements placed solely to fulfill contracts when their cost is lower than the amount that must be returned to the medium because of default. Many of these advertisements are run off season and have an institutional flavor.[21]

Most contracts for advertising space calls for ROP, which stands for "run of press." The advertiser has no say about the position in the issue; the newspaper places the advertisement wherever it wishes. But layout people usually make every effort to place an advertisement near the appropriate editorial material. Sporting goods will find themselves among the sports pages. Movies will appear near the entertainment features. Messages to the financial community will show up in the business section. An advertiser who insists on certain preferred positions must pay a premium over ROP rates.

Retailers evaluate the potential market coverage of a newspaper primarily by its circulation. Audience studies have been conducted *ad hoc* and irregularly. The first syndicated audience study began in 1980 when Three Sigma, now a part of SMRB, surveyed 180 newspapers. It was supported by practically all major dailies, and as of November 1981, serviced forty-one ad agency subscribers. But retailers have persisted in assessing their advertising results by overt behavior, such as sales and store traffic, and have evinced no great interest in readership surveys. Unless there is a known relationship between audience and behavior — and none has been established to date — there is no reason to believe that "soft" survey data would lead to better performance.

A popular method for comparing different newspapers is the milline rate. This technique estimates the cost of placing an agate line in one million copies of circulation. The formula is: Milline rate = Line rate × 1 million/Circulation.

For example, if the line rate is $2 for 500,000 circulation, the milline rate is calculated as $2 × 1,000,000/500,000 = $4.

The lower the milline rate, the more efficient the purchase is presumed to be. But the retailer must also consider the absolute circulation size for assessment of market coverage.

USES OF RADIO

Radio, like newspapers, is mainly a local medium. Of close to $3.8 billion spent on radio advertising in 1980, some 75% was local. But this total local budget of more than $2.8 billion was only about a fifth as large as that of newspapers. The main users of local radio — not all of whom are retailers — are auto dealers, department stores, banks, clothing stores, restaurants and supermarkets. Some idea about the relative size of funds committed to local radio by various businesses can be gleaned from a 1980 Radio Advertising Bureau (RAB) survey of its membership. Since the 3,500 or so RAB members have the lion's share of radio advertising, survey percentages can be projected to U.S. expenditures. The result of this computation, done by Radio Advertising Bureau, is shown in Table 17–4. The amounts are slightly lower than the McCann-Erickson figures of $2.8 billion because totals are based on FCC estimates of station revenues. They do not include advertiser production expenses. Any projection to the larger total must assume that production expenses are proportionally distributed by business category.

Radio is ubiquitous. Virtually every home in the U.S. has one, and an estimated 457 million were in use in 1981.[22] This figure would put the average number of sets per household at about 5.7.

The greatest advantage of radio for advertisers is audience selectivity, which is determined by the station's format. Stations attract different population segments by differentiating their program offerings, such as featuring news, rock or classical music. Radio can thus complement newspapers by concentrating on select audiences, especially when promoting store events such as end-of-month clearances, January white sales, or product specials. Highly flexible in scheduling and making quick copy changes, the medium lends itself to the frantic, unsettling pace of retailing.

Advertising rates are geared to audience size, as determined by ratings. These measurements are derived from diaries placed by Arbitron with consumers in local markets. Dayparts are designated by letters, starting with AA or A and going sequentially to B, C, etc. The top letters signal the top viewing levels, with AA or A being the highest-rated time period.

TABLE 17–4 *Leading Advertiser Categories in 1980 on Local Radio*

Category	Advertising Expenditure	
	Percentage	Amount (in Millions of Dollars)
Auto dealers	10.7	278
Department stores	8.4	219
Banks	8.0	208
Clothing stores	7.7	200
Restaurants	7.0	182
Supermarkets	6.7	174
Furniture stores	6.4	166
Bottlers	5.9	153
Appliance stores	4.9	127
Savings & Loans	4.2	109
.	.	.
.	.	.
.	.	.
All Businesses	100.0	2,601

Source: Radio Advertising Bureau, *Radio Facts* (1981), p. 40. Projections made by Radio Advertising Bureau's research department.

Unlike television, prime time for radio takes place in the morning, called "drive time," when people are going to work. From then on, it's all downhill. Radio usage generally declines throughout the day and into the evening. But teenage patterns are somewhat different, peaking from 3PM to 7PM.[23] The "graveyard hours" of midnight to dawn have the lowest incidence of listening.

Volume and frequency discounts pervade the rate structure. A common practice is the weekly discount, with prices scaled downward according to the number of announcements running each week. Local rate cards begin at about six spots each week and go up to sixty plus. The week is considered a convenient span because retail activity fluctuates greatly, and many retailers build their media schedules in weekly flights.[24] Periods of broadcast inactivity can last anywhere from two to six weeks. But stations also sell at bulk rates on an annual basis, usually starting with 250 spots and lowering the price at certain points. Some stations give discounts for consecutive weekly usage, such as five percent for thirteen weeks, ten percent for twenty-six weeks, and fifteen percent for fifty-two weeks. In general, larger purchases are favored by lower costs per commercial message.

Retailers can buy radio time in a number of different ways. The most common are fixed position spots, total audience plan (TAP), run of station (ROS) or best times available (BTA).[25]

TABLE 17–5 *Leading Categories of Local TV Advertisers in 1980*

Business Category	Expenditures (In Millions of Dollars)
Restaurants & drive-ins	287.9
Food stores & supermarkets	148.7
Banks, savings & loan associations	140.9
Department stores	131.2
Furniture stores	111.4
Movies	102.4
Auto dealers	99.1
Discount department stores	73.5
Radio stations & cable tv	69.3
Amusements & entertainment	68.0

Source: Television Bureau of Advertising, *Tv Basics 24* (1981).

Fixed position spots are the most expensive. Here the advertiser contracts for commercials to be run at specified times on given days. TAP plans call for commercials to be spread among all time periods — morning, noon and night — and during all days of the week. The stations have the right to decide what gets aired where and when. ROS and BTA positions, also controlled by the stations, are billed at the lowest rates. But these plans have no guarantees as to the time the commercials will run. Because few stations have open slots in the morning, it is most unlikely that commercials would be broadcast at these preferred hours. If the retail outlet does not require drive-time announcements, however, it can usually acquire efficient buys on ROS or BTA.

Stations contract on a weekly, monthly or annual basis. The annual plans are cheapest because time is sold at bulk rates. But an advertiser has to have a need for a relatively large volume of spots to take advantage of these big discounts.

Commercials on radio can be broadcast live or prerecorded. The live commercial is tied to the style or personality of the announcer. He or she usually receives a fact sheet instead of a formal script, and emphasizes the major points in his or her own way. The voice and manner of presentation determines the success of the commercial as much as its content or data. Prerecorded commercials provide better control over the presentation. Each commercial comes over the air in the same way no matter how many times it is run. But it incurs production costs which the live commercial does not.

USES OF TELEVISION

From an operational point of view, local television advertising is identical to spot television. Stations, coverage areas, audiences, and rating measurements are the same. The only difference is that the term "spot tv" applies to national advertisers running a commercial not being telecast on a network lineup. Local tv advertising operates in the same way, except that the advertiser is engaged in a "retail" business. However, the word "retail" has been stretched from its traditional meaning, as used in government business censuses, to include service industries dealing directly with consumers on a local level. Table 17–5 shows the top ten business categories in 1980 classified as local tv advertisers. This table also demonstrates the strong ties of service industries to this media classification.

The ten leading business categories listed in Table 17–5 accounted for about forty-two percent of the total U.S. advertising on local television, which ran to almost $3.0 billion in 1980.[26] This dollar volume of tv advertising by local businesses actually exceeded that of local radio. But television still remains a mass communication device dominated by national advertisers. Local advertising on television amounted to only twenty-six percent of all tv advertising, and stood far behind newspapers as an advertising medium for local businesses.

From 1970 to 1980, advertising budgets in local television rose from $704 million to $2,967 million.[27] Although at least half the average annual increase can be traced to inflation, growth was nevertheless impressive. Still, retailers face many difficulties in using television.

One stumbling block is cost, especially for the small merchant. Stations have innovated a number of "package deals" to appeal to low-budget advertisers. Most of them, however, offer daytime and late night availabilities. Consequently, audiences are relatively small and may not reach the marketer's desired levels.

Besides media outlays, there are also production costs to consider. These can be high in relation to other types of media expenses, since production is not an in-house, do-it-yourself activity. It is possible to produce commercials cheaply with local facilities and talent. But they often turn out amateurish and tasteless.

One way of evading the dilemma of high cost or shoddy work is the so-called sandwich commercial.[28] The opening and closing parts are done by an outside agency and production house, and are served up like the two slices of bread which make up the sandwich. The middle, which can be changed inexpensively, is left to the retailer, who decides on the daily tidbits that go between the bread.

These commercial sandwiches appeal to retailers' palates and pocket books. The opening and closing parts of the commercial imbue the entire message with professionalism and quality. Individual items of merchandise can be changed frequently and expeditiously, yet every commercial will have a common family look which can be identified with the store. Although original production costs may be high, unit costs decline with each rerun. Sandwiches can be planned with proper lead time to support items and events, and even to emphasize institutional copy points.

Another difficulty encountered by retailers is that of television coverage. A typical VHF station has an effective transmission range of some sixty miles. If its ADI is roughly drawn as a circle, the diameter would stretch to 120 miles. Except for chain store operations or locations which draw customers from great distances, local stores must be prepared to accept substantial amounts of "waste circulation" in television.

A third major problem for local advertisers is direct competition with national advertisers for television time. Most stations have network affiliations, and have no empty slots in programs during prime time. Adjacencies which remain during peak hours are often sold long in advance to national advertisers and large chains. The typical retailer is thus left with the least desirable daytime and late night spots.

SUMMARY

The main characteristic of retailing is its local nature. But the size of a locale varies because of a hierarchy of centers.

Merchandising and store image are the twin objectives of retail advertising. The first is more important, since it is is more closely related to observable sales results.

Product advertising attempts to stimulate immediate sales. Institutional advertising aims at promoting the store rather than goods. In reality, these two phases are often present in the same advertisement.

A considerable part of retail advertising is cooperative, wherein two or more parties — usually a manufacturer and a retailer — join in the program. The best results are achieved for goods which are retailer dependent. Although retailers derive many advantages from a cooperative program, their interests may often conflict with those of the manufacturer.

Most retail budgets for advertising are spent in newspapers. There are many more evening than morning dailies, but the latter has a larger average circulation. Population movement out of central cities has spurred an increase in suburban newspaper circulation.

Creative design is not important in newspaper advertising. Layout, make-up and typesetting services are often furnished by the newspapers. Local advertising rates are lower than national rates because newspapers pay no commission to advertising agencies. Retailers use circulation rather than audience as the main criterion for media selection.

Other local media are radio and television, with advertising expenditures split almost evenly between the two. Radio offers audience selectivity, and can be used to complement advertising in newspapers. Prime time in radio is in the morning, and commercials can be broadcast live or pre-recorded.

Commercial production in television is relatively expensive. One way of overcoming this obstacle is the sandwich commercial, which gives the message a quality appearance and permits the retailer to make frequent changes inexpensively.

Questions for Chapter 17

1. Why would a food store have a higher advertising-to-sales ratio than a furniture store?

2. Is there a relationship between K-Mart merchandise and the image the advertising projects?

3. Why would coop advertising be more effective for a refrigerator than for a brand of toothpaste?

4. What are the advantages of newspapers for retail advertisers?

5. What difficulties does a local store encounter when advertising in a metropolitan daily? On a local tv station?

6. What are the positives and negatives of a suburban store advertising in suburban newspapers?

7. Why do many retailers refrain from using advertising agencies?

8. Why do most retailers use circulation rather than audience figures in newspaper selection?

9. Why is TAP a more preferable radio buy than ROS or BTA?

10. Why do national advertisers make relatively little use of newspapers?

Footnotes for Chapter 17

[1]U.S. Bureau of the Census, *1977 Census of Retail Trade.*

[2]U.S. Bureau of the Census, *1977 Census of Retail Trade.*

[3]"Store Ads Aim At Suburb Boom, Working Women," *Advertising Age* (November 21, 1977), p. S–1.

[4]William Haight, *Retail Advertising* (Morristown, N.J.: Silver Burdett, 1976), p. 102.

[5]Shirley F. Milton, *Advertising For Modern Retailers* (New York: Fairchild Publications, Inc., 1974), pp. 46–47.

[6]Anne Estes, "How Retailers Promote, Entertain," *Advertising Age* (April 6, 1981), p. 47.

[7]Haight, *Retail Advertising*, p. 105.

[8]*Advertising Age* (September 10, 1981), p. 1.

[9]Haight, *Retail Advertising*, p. 143.

[10]See Robert F. Young, "Cooperative Advertising: Its Uses and Effectiveness: Some Preliminary Hypotheses," Marketing Science Institute, *Working Paper*, Report No. 79–112, 1979, p. 2.

[11]Young, *"Cooperative Advertising,"* p. 3.

[12]Renee Blakkan, "Partnership Perks Up Profits," *Advertising Age* (August 17, 1981), p. S–1.

[13]Young, *"Cooperative Advertising,"* p. 7.

[14]Edward C. Crimmins, "A History of Problems and Promise," *Advertising Age* (September 1, 1980), p. S–1.

[15]Coen.

[16]American Newspaper Publishers Association, *Facts About Newspapers* (1981), p. 2.

[17]U.S. Department of Commerce, *Market Center Shifts* (Washington, D.C.: Office of Consumer Goods and Service Industries, 1978).

[18]Jacques Neher, "Computer As Ad Writer? Realtors Claim It Works," *Advertising Age* (August 11, 1980), pp. 3, 60–61.

[19]Nelson, *The Design of Advertising,* p. 209.

[20]See *Advertising Age* (September 22, 1980), p. 1.

[21]Haight, *Retail Advertising,* p. 261.

[22]Radio Advertising Bureau, *Radio Facts* (1981), p. 2.

[23]Grey Advertising, *Pocket Media Modules 1982.*

[24]Heighton and Cunningham, p. 237.

[25]Jonne Murphy, *Handbook of Radio Advertising* (Radnor, Pa: Jonne Murphy, 1980), pp. 190–191.

[26]Coen.

[27]Coen.

[28]See Howard P. Abrams, *Making TV Pay Off* (New York: Fairchild Publications, Inc., 1975), pp. 86–88.

18 Direct Marketing

Direct marketing melds elements of retailing and national advertising into unique forms of economics and communication. Like retailing, direct marketing has a strong merchandising orientation, and some of its prominent practitioners are themselves retailers. But transactions do not take place in fixed, geographic locations. Nor are they confined to local trading areas; marketing targets can be nationwide. Yet even here direct marketing deviates from national advertising patterns by resting its emphasis on unconventional media, or at least those not used widely in national advertising.

Departure from the more typical forms of general advertising are particularly evident in discussions of:

- **Scope and salient characteristics of direct marketing, particularly its use of advertising**
- **Products and markets on which direct marketing centers its attention**
- **Media usage and copy treatment by direct marketers**
- **Evaluation of advertising messages and advertising carriers in the direct marketing area**

WHAT IS DIRECT MARKETING?

Marketing circles in recent years have heard increasingly the refrains of "go direct." Only here the advice refers not to a locality but to a marketing practice.

There are many ways to go direct—direct mail, direct advertising, mail order, and direct response. All of these are subsumed under the term "direct marketing."

Direct mail is in fact a promotional medium; commercial messages are disseminated by the postal service. The messages delivered by the post office are called "junk mail" by critics. They come in various forms and sizes—letters, postcards, leaflets, catalogs, and coupons. The variations along with their sheer physical volume has been continuously increasing. Hardly a mailbox in America has escaped the bold assaults of corporate mail rooms. The average household receives one piece of third class mail each day.[1]

Direct advertising has slightly broader connotations. The term is usually taken to mean that advertising is conveyed directly to the intended recipient, either through mail, point-of-purchase counters, in pack, or handouts. The advertiser does not send a message through agencies looked upon as go-betweens, such as magazines or television.[2]

Mail order can use any medium, direct or indirect. Only customer orders come through the mail, though today the order route has been expanded to include telephone.[3] In this sense, mail order is basically a method of product distribution.

Direct response is any advertising technique which solicits an immediate response. The action can be of various sorts: an order, an inquiry, or a visit to a store or showroom.[4] The most frequent type in the consumer field is the order. In the industrial sector, direct response aims at eliciting inquiries, which serve as leads for follow-ups by sales personnel.

Direct marketing embraces all the above somewhat overlapping concepts—direct mail, direct advertising, mail order, direct response. The most widely accepted definition of direct marketing is probably that drawn up by a committee of the Direct Mail Marketing Association (DMMA), a trade association:[5]

> Direct marketing is an interactive system of marketing which uses one or more advertising media to effect a measurable response and/or transaction at any location.

The description of direct marketing as an interactive system is highly debatable, and itself more promotional than dispassionately analytical. But the DMMA definition contains the essential elements. The key concepts are the use of media and objective of direct response. These two factors set direct marketing apart from other forms of promotion employed in marketing. Direct advertising plays a major part in the marketing mix, but it differs from the usual type of general advertising. General advertising lacks the quality of directness—the ability to trace action directly to a message, whereas direct advertising is judged only by results. Direct marketing can thus be thought of as impersonal promotion—in the sense of not being face to face—which seeks to evoke direct action.

There are four important characteristics of direct marketing. These are:

1. Union of advertising and selling into a single function
2. Prominence of a service concept to affect repetitive buying
3. A strong tendency towards specificity
4. Existence of a built-in feedback mechanism

The Advertising-Selling Function

Advertising used in direct marketing performs the entire job of obtaining a response. In most instances, it does the entire selling job, at least with respect to consumer products. There are no intermediaries. A mailing piece or a mail order advertisement makes the sale without benefit of a salesperson, a checkout counter, or a store. Advertising and selling are inextricably bound together into a single function which, like the itinerant vendor of a bygone era, completes the entire transaction.

Direct marketing may share transactional duties with other members of the distribution channel. Coupon redemption, for example, necessitates the cooperation of retailers. But the store assumes a passive role; it acts as an agency that facilitates the transaction. The real selling job was done by the offer via media. The advertisement was the attention-getter, pulling the customer, coupon in hand, into the store and to the shelf displaying the bargain.

By taking on the dual functions of advertising and selling, direct marketing employs the techniques of both professions. Those of advertising include media selection and the creation of persuasive messages. Those of selling take on the sense of urgency for prompting immediate action and closing the sale. In this respect, direct marketing exhibits many characteristics of merchandising, but without sales personnel.

The elimination of the people in the middle also does away with their markups. This, in turn, increases financial leverage. Given the same price level, direct marketing enjoys a widening spread between operating revenue and cost of sales.

But the entire increment does not end up as profit. The direct marketer saves on store overhead, direct labor, and transportation. But the firm is forced to spend more on media to make up for the lack of personal selling and retail marketing effort. Direct advertising expenditures ranging from ten to twenty percent of sales are not uncommon.[6] In contrast, such ratios are considered especially high for general advertisers, and not at all typical of them.[7] Relatively few companies outside of direct marketing can maintain such lofty advertising-to-sales ratios without eroding their profit margins.

The Service Concept

Direct marketing features both one-time products and repeat lines. The former comprise isolated, single unit sales, with little or no connection between them. The latter involve repeat buying by customers, such as catalog businesses and educational, in-home services. The establishment of a long-term relationship with customers is a major objective of most direct marketers.[8] A purchaser who comes back again and again is infinitely more valuable than one who is not heard from again after the first sale. Even marketers of such products as swimming pools, seemingly one-time buys, can reap undeniable benefits from referrals by sending promotional material to past customers or by servicing the installations. Some developers of recreational communities have on-going direct mail programs which seek referrals as their main source of sales.

There are many methods of building enduring bridges to consumers. These attempts seem to be channeled in a service-oriented direction. Jim Kobs frankly declares that direct marketing "converts products into services," and cites numerous examples to support his point of view.[9] When books are offered by mail, individualistic, autonomous behavior of purchasers are turned into the more structured behavior required of a book club. Similarly, magazine subscriptions turn single copy sales into a home delivery service. When direct marketing takes this service-creating route, repetitive buying implies some form of product fulfillment.

The two types of direct marketing, single product sales and repeat lines, call for different methods of economic evaluation. In the one time sale, the value of a customer is simply the excess of revenue over cost arising from the transaction. Repeat line sales includes cost of goods sold plus order fulfillment. Advertising is profitable as long as its costs do not exceed a cash inflow calculated as the number of resulting customers multiplied by a customer's value.

When contemplating repetitive business, the value of subsequent purchases must be taken into account. Because any list of buyers will undergo attrition, net value over time is affected by a decay rate. That is, given a number of original buyers from an advertisement, each successive message will produce less and less purchasers from the initial set. Profit over time can thus be expressed as purchase probabilities of each period multiplied by the respective net value of a transaction. And the value of a customer in any period is expressed as:

$$[P]\ B \times VB$$

where

$$[P]\ B = \text{an individual's probability of buying}$$
$$VB = \text{value of a buyer.}$$

Since repetitive business is a long-term affair, profit estimates from an advertisement must be adjusted by the time value of money. This concept proposes that the future value of the advertisement investment is enhanced by cash returns accumulating at compound interest. This is figured by the standard compound interest formula,

$$FV = \frac{I}{(1 + i)^n}$$

where

$FV =$ future value of an investment (or the future value of customers produced by an advertisement)
$I =$ initial sum invested (cost of advertising)
$i =$ interest rate for each period
$n =$ number of periods in which interest is paid.

The more common way of evaluating an investment, however, is to use present value (*PV*). This conversion from future to present value is done by using the formula $PV = FV\ (I/1+i)^n$. This method discounts the expected net value from advertising to the present time at a compound rate of

TABLE 18–1 *Estimated Advertising Expenditures for Direct Marketing (in Millions)*

Medium	1980 Amount (In Millions of Dollars)	1980 Percent	1979 Amount (In Millions of Dollars)	1979 Percent
Direct mail	9,998.7	44	8,876.7	45
Telephone	9,845.0	44	8,555.6	43
Newspaper preprints	2,032.4	9	1,779.5	9
Television	253.0	1	217.0	1
Magazines (mail order merchandise only)	135.0	1	123.0	1
Coupons	84.2	1	72.0	1
Newspapers	60.6	—	54.4	—
Business magazines (industrial products only)	53.0	—	47.0	—
Radio	26.0	—	23.0	—
Total	22,487.9	100	19,748.2	100

Source: *Advertising Age* (October 26, 1981), p. 92.

interest, and then compares it with the initial investment. It is worthwhile to advertise for new customers as long as the acquisition cost of a customer does not exceed the customer's value, discounted by the time cost of capital. This comparison, known as the present value (PV) ratio, should yield a figure which is greater than 1.0 in order for advertising to be productive.[10]

This method amortizes the cost of customer acquisition over time, usually the average life span of buyers. It regards customers acquired by advertising as an asset, the undepreciated portion of which is valued at acquisition cost. The concept applies to new customers only. It encounters difficulties when direct marketing sells to people who would have bought through normal retail channels. For example, a sale to a regular department store customer purchasing from a catalog cannot be credited wholly to direct mail.

Specificity

Communication in direct marketing encompasses a wide variety of media. Some of them embellish advertisements with an editorial environment. These are the vehicles used prominently by general advertisers, and can be regarded as "conventional." Other media employed by direct marketing carry no editorial whatsoever, such as direct mail, coupons, telephone, and, for lack of a better name, they might be called "special." Table 18–1 shows how direct marketing expenditures are allocated among the major media.

Communications in conventional media, nondirectional as it were, account for about ten percent of all direct marketing expenditures. Almost 90 percent go to special media, those which possess characteristics of specificity. The messages, as phone calls and direct mail, are directed to specific homes or individuals.

The bulk of direct marketing advertisements in conventional media is carried by newspapers. There are basically three media forms made available by newspapers: run-of-press (ROP), supplements, and preprints.

The ROP advertising is carried as display, and mingles with editorial material and other advertisements. Because direct response ads carry coupons, their placement is of utmost importance. First, they must be in the newspaper section which is related to the product. For example, an ad for sporting goods should be in the sports section. An offer pertaining to office supplies should be in the business section. Second, these ads should be at the outer edge of the page, preferably the lower right-hand corner. This makes it easier for readers to cut out the coupon.

Supplements are magazines distributed by a newspaper. Sunday editions offer advertisers several supplements, such as magazines and book reviews. These magazines usually have high readership, as compared with the body of the Sunday paper, and often present advertisers with the option of advertising in color. But page placement, as with ROP, is essential for getting a good response to a coupon.

Preprints came into existence during the 1960s, and their popularity has continued to grow. They come in many forms, such as eight-page sections of advertisements, postcards or ad inserts slipped into the newspaper or sections thereof. These preprints are prepared entirely by the advertiser, and either left loose or tipped into the publication.

Regardless of where they appear—in ROP, supplements, or preprints, cents-off coupons have been the backbone of direct advertising in newspapers. According to A. C. Nielsen's Clearing House, 102.4 million cents-off coupons were distributed in 1981. Of this total, 78.5 percent appeared in newspapers: 45.0 percent in dailies, and the remaining 33.5 percent in Sunday papers or Sunday inserts. Some 11.8 percent of these coupons were carried by magazines, 6.4 percent in pack, and 3.3 percent by direct mail.[11]

Direct mail and telephone comprise the overwhelming portion of special media, and together account for 88 percent of all advertising expenditures for direct marketing. But special, like conventional media, are perceived selectively, and advertisers control only message transmission. Though the messages are directed to specific destinations, people may throw mailings into the trash can without reading them. They may hang up on telephone solicitors, not wishing to be bothered. The form and content of an advertisement undoubtedly affects its perception. But beyond that, the sender exercises no control over the reception of messages, much less over how recipients act on them.

In most instances, a response rate of from two to four percent would be considered highly satisfactory. For this reason, the same advertising can be presented to the same audience several times. If only two percent of magazine readers respond to an advertisement, the buying potential of a vehicle is hardly diminished. Some 98 percent still remain as possible customers. The same is true for a mail or telephone list. Hanover House, in 1981, sold goods by mail to almost four million people, and sent out the same catalog to customers three times at short intervals. The only change was the front and back covers, to give the catalog the appearance of newness. According to the company's president, each mailing picked up business from customers who were tempted to order before but didn't.[12] Other factors also come into play. Many recipients may not have had a chance to peruse the previous catalog. Circumstances change for some proportion of the audience, and offers given little thought in one situation become compelling in another.

Advertising copy tends to be straightforward but lengthy. Attention getting and image building are of little practical value in direct marketing, which cannot abide the luxury of waiting. It must create an atmosphere of immediate action, and close the sale. Copy must therefore ignore uninvolved or mildly-interested customers, and speak to those who have a high interest in acquiring the product.[13] They represent the best prospects for buying now.

Because copy addresses itself to highly involved consumers, it can be long without losing the interest of its potential buyers. Printed advertisements containing 1,000 or more words of text are fairly common in direct marketing. Even television commercials for direct response items generally run a full two minutes in a medium which has a standard message length of 30 seconds.[14] Since buyer interest is assumed to be present, the copy must be long enough to cover the subject adequately and perform all of its varied tasks.

Built-In Feedback

Direct marketing can claim the advantageous application of feedback principles more than any other branch of selling or advertising. The key to this quality lies in measurability. Message transmission, and to a larger extent message response, are specific. Resulting actions are thus traceable to particular sources. Consequently, firms can test, monitor, and analyze their direct marketing programs. They must, however, key their messages. The possibility of measuring input-output relationships with a relatively high degree of accuracy provides a ready method for pinpointing trouble spots and correcting them.

Testing in direct marketing equates to test marketing. Advertisements are run in actual media and results are evaluated on the basis of behavior response. How much did the advertisements pull? Consumer state-of-mind measurements like awareness, recall, predilections, attitudes are irrelevant. What a direct marketer gets from any test program is what he sees. There are no imperceptible, might-be-so intangibles.

The emphasis on hard data stems from a high degree of control which direct marketing exercises over its operations. There is virtually no dependence upon wholesalers, retailers, or other outsiders. Nevertheless, not all major variables which influence response are internal to the advertiser. If results are to be generalized or projected to a larger universe, the direct marketer must pay attention to positioning in conventional media.

There are essentially two types of direct marketing tests, a test of the offer, and a test of the medium. Research which tests offers runs a wide gamut from comparisons of different selling propositions to different ways of presenting them. The latter is essentially a copy test. Media tests deal with evaluation of different advertising carriers, such as magazines vs direct mail, or of particular vehicles within a media type, such as specific lists used for direct mailings.

Methods of researching advertising response attempt to keep all factors constant except the test variable. Copy tests, for example, vary the advertisements while keeping media effects constant. A popular method is the A/B split, wherein an ad appears in every other printing of an issue. Presumably, media effects are cancelled out by two statistically-equivalent samples. Any difference in response can then be attributed to the pulling power of the respective advertisements.

On the other hand, media tests must hold copy effects constant. Research of this nature is enjoined to use advertisements with past records, the results of which are known. But then a medium being tested reaches different market segments, or calls for different communication techniques, so new offers and new copy approaches may well prove more productive than their predecessors. In that event, the old standbys can be used as a sort of "control" against which to gauge response of the newly-created messages.

A serious limitation of direct market tests is the low level of response. The observed percentages lie on the extreme end of a statistical distribution. These numerical extremities — normal for direct response but abnormal from a statistical point of view — produce test results with sizable relative errors. Reliable data, therefore, require large samples. Some idea of the necessary sample size may be gleaned by examining sampling errors associated with what would be considered a good response rate, say two percent. The following table shows such estimates for samples of various sizes at the 95 percent level of confidence, which assumes that a manager wants decisions to be correct 19 out of 20 times.

TABLE 18–2 *Sampling Errors When a Response Rate is Two Percent*

Sample Size	Absolute Sample Error (Percent)	Relative Error of the Estimate (Percent)
1,000	.88	44
3,000	.50	25
5,000	.40	20
7,000	.34	17
10,000	.28	14

The absolute errors are based on the standard formula of a random sample,

$$S_p = \sqrt{\frac{pq}{N}}$$

where

S_p = sampling error of a proportion
p = probability of getting a response, or .02
$q = 1 - p$, or .98.

Many small lists are precluded from being tested because of comparatively large sample sizes and high costs. Similarly, testing of copy should not be done unless test materials differ substantively and are thought capable of altering response in major ways. For example, suppose that one advertisement pulled 2.0 percent and another 2.5 percent from a given list. To be reasonably sure that this differential rate could not have occurred by pure chance, the comparison must be based upon two samples of at least 7,000 mailouts each.[15]

WHAT DOES DIRECT MARKETING SELL?

Sales from direct marketing for the first time in 1980 climbed over the $100 billion mark. Some 20 percent of this total took place in the industrial area; the remaining 80 percent came from consumers. The value of sales from the consumer sector amounted to approximately $88 million, or nine percent of all U.S. sales at retail.

There are two kinds of direct marketers. One relies on direct marketing as a prime means of distribution and selling. The number of firms which make up this group is rather small, and its prominent members are specialized, mail order houses like Franklin Mint, Publishers Clearing House, and L. L. Bean. Credit card companies might also be included. For instance, American Express in 1980 alone sent out close to 50 million letters in order to attract new members in addition to 8 million monthly bills stuffed with attractive offers.[16]

The second kind of direct marketer represents a firm wherein the activity is supplementary to its existing sales channels. These firms are far more numerous than the first type. The majority of the Fortune 500 companies fall into this category. Under this group falls virtually every major department store putting out catalogs as part of its merchandising program.

Products sold through direct marketing span a wide range of classifications. The main determinants are the nature of markets and the characteristics of products.

On the market side, product unavailabilities at retail have sparked direct marketing. Spotty distribution, whatever its reasons, provide sellers with incentives to adopt direct marketing methods. This situation is the exact opposite of one which encourages firms to advertise in conventional media. Thin markets do not justify intensive distribution and media with generalized audiences. And neither of these elements are present in direct marketing.

On the product side are the qualities of dependability and safety. Unable to see, feel, or check products before buying, consumers are not prone to order products which are risky. They must have some assurance that the products will work as represented. This obstacle to ordering blind, as it were, can be removed by an unconditional guarantee.[17]

The most successful products marketed through direct means have these qualities built in. Prominent are such items as magazine subscriptions, books, film processing, records, and tapes. Direct marketing accounts for 70 percent of magazine subscriptions, 50 percent plus of all book sales, and some 20 percent of film processed.[18] Table 18–3 shows the leading products sold through direct marketing in terms of dollar volume.

In recent years a number of advertising agencies have expanded their operations and gone into the business of offering direct marketing services. This activity is, of course, related to the activities of their clients. As more firms turn to exploit direct marketing techniques, their agencies expand servicing facilities. The leader in the direct marketing field is giant Young & Rubicam, which acquired Wunderman, Ricotta & Kline, in 1974. The small shop was then billing $37 million. By 1981 the billings of this Y&R subsidiary had swelled to $167 million. While such growth is exceptional, it has enhanced the perception of direct marketing as a fast-growing specialty which advertising agencies can take on and make profits. Table 18–4 provides 1981 billings of the leading direct marketing agencies.

DIRECT MAIL

Direct mail is the oldest method used by direct marketers to make contact with customers. Though the mail route has grudgingly relinquished ground to newer media forms, it still remains the mainstay of the industry.

TABLE 18–3 *Estimated Sales For Selected Products Sold by Direct Marketing*

Product	1980 Sales (In Millions of Dollars)
Insurance	5,000
Magazine subscriptions	2,225
Books	1,485
Multi-product marketers	1,030
Ready-to-wear	1,010
Collectibles	950
Gifts	550
Sporting goods	525
Records & tapes	460
Crafts	460

Source: Craig Campbell, "The Scope of Direct Marketing," *1982 Fact Book on Direct Response Marketing,* (New York: Direct Mail Marketing Association, 1982), p. 4.

TABLE 18–4 *U.S. Gross Billings of Top Twelve Direct Marketing Agencies*

Agency	1981 Billings (In Millions of Dollars)
Young & Rubicam	166.7
Ogilvy & Mather Direct	55.6
Rapp & Collins	36.5
Smith, Hemmings, Gosden	22.7
Compton Direct Marketing	23.5
Kobs & Brady Advertising	21.5
The DR Group	20.5
TIK Direct Marketing	20.0
Soskin/Thompson	19.6
N. W. Ayer	17.7
MARCOA	13.0
Grey Direct	11.7

Source: Campbell, "The Scope of Direct Marketing," p. 7.

The prominent status of direct mail is owing to its flexibility. First, operations can be scaled to fit any budget. Mailings can vary from several hundred to several million. They can be run in sequences and be adjusted to actual response rates. Or smaller quantities can be used for testing before making commitments of larger sums.

Second, direct mail offers geographic flexibility. The marketer may direct messages to an area as small as a zip code or to one as large as the entire nation. The firm is not bound by any particular geographical boundary or minimum size imposed by a medium. Mailings can be arranged in patterns of almost infinite variety, depending upon the objectives of a company and the imagination of its decision makers.

Third, mail can go out to different kinds of recipients—building occupants, present customers, prospects, individuals stratified by demographic parameters. The varieties here, too, are virtually endless.

Fourth, the message itself is highly versatile with respect to the data it carries. Catalog selection is limitless: sportwear, jewelry, household supplies, snack foods, stationery, and bric-a-bracs. Items can be similarly bundled in mailouts other than catalogs.

The majority of dispatches go via third class mail. Rates are lower than first class, but the sender must comply with certain postal regulations in order to qualify. While many regard third class mail as junk mail, some junk may actually be looked upon with favor. The computer has made it possible to reduce hostility by personalizing letters in mass mailings. Key information in the mailing record such as name, street, and city, can be inserted at designated sections of the mailing piece to give each message an individual tone. These computerized letters enhance response rates, but are costlier than preprinted versions.

Success in direct mail depends on the quality of the mailing list. According to SRDS's directory, *Direct Mail Lists Rates and Data*, there are approximately 28,000 lists available through rentals. This estimate excludes lists of companies and nonbusiness organizations kept for private use.

Most lists can be rented through list brokers. Prices range from as low as $12.50 to as high as $500.00 per thousand, with the average price being about $50. The exact price depends upon several factors, such as demand and selectivity of the list. Making the correct list choice is important since total mailing costs run close to $300 per thousand for mass mailings.[19]

There are basically three types of lists; house lists, responder lists, and compiled lists. A house list is made up of customers and prospects assembled internally by an organization. Responder lists are composed of individuals who have acted on a mail offer. These names are sometimes characterized in the trade as "direct mail junkies," because they represent people who ostensibly like to shop by mail. Compiled lists consist of names taken from various sources, which fall into six broad market categories: consumers, businesses, volunteer organizations, professional disciplines, educational groups, and government.[20]

The strongest pull comes from house lists, proving the common sense adage that a firm's best prospects are its present customers. Because of their relatively high value, house lists should be kept current. One form of updating is in address changes, for about a fifth of all American households move each year. Productivity is further enhanced when information on responses to offers is coded into each individual record. This permits a marketer to identify specific segments and determine which might be appropriate for specific situations.

A policy of focusing on the best customers long predated the modern segmentation concept. Sears Roebuck, in the 1930s, defined catalog markets in terms of buying patterns. The firm divided its customers into three groups according to recency, frequency and size of purchase. If a customer didn't buy within a three year period, no catalog mailings would go to the nonpurchaser.

Most of the current selection methods still follow the route marked out by Sears about half a century ago.[21] These three groupings are the most popular used to segment house lists. The net result is few cells containing large numbers within, which raises questions about the extent of homogeneity within a segment.[22] In practice, however, the three-factored criterion is used to determine whether solicitations should be made or withheld, and not to match offers to particular segments.

Many marketers assign values to the three factors, with the following weightings: recency—.50; frequency—.35; purchase amount—.15.[23] This model is based on the rationale of attrition among buyers, which may easily come to 50 percent a year. The mailing pull is said to increase substantially when frequency and volume are added to recency. However, these weightings have no theoretical basis.

Recent advances in computer technology make list segmentation possible using data base models and multivariate statistical techniques. Buyers can be linked to particular product categories by "descriptive billings." Other possibilities are adjusting response patterns to special offers, seasonal promotions, quality, and price levels. These methods hold out a promise of making offers more relevant to buyers than is now the case.

Responder lists, often called mail-order lists, usually outpull compiled lists and therefore sell at a premium. These lists are subdivided into broad categories, such as gifts, books, plants, self-improvement, financial services, etc. When lists are selected on a classification basis, the choice assumes that lists within the same classification work equally well for all items in a product category. This presumption, however, is not always justified. People buying women's service magazines are not necessarily good prospects for specialized publications. Or purchasers of rock records may not be likely buyers of classical music.

Though compiled lists have generally lower response rates, they are valuable when a high level of penetration is sought in a given universe. For example, a retailer wishing to build store traffic by couponing may do a mailing to all households in a limited trading area. Or a medical journal may intend to solicit subscriptions from all doctors, and use a list from the American Medical Association.

These compiled lists, like mail-order lists, can be bought by classification. Assemblers have broken their mass listings into smaller, more homogeneous segments. For example, an entire list of doctors may be coded by particular medical specialties. Consumer household compilations are widely segmented by zip codes or census tracts. These small geographic units can be stratified by many demographic and socio-economic characteristics, such as age, income, occupation of the labor force, home value, etc. The U.S. Bureau of the Census makes summary tapes available for conducting such analyses. A number of large list houses own these tapes and offer computation facilities to clients.

TELEMARKETING

Marketing by telephone is of recent vintage, tracing back to the introduction of WATS lines in the 1960s. Despite its recency, the telephone is now the second most important mode used in direct marketing. The greatest advantage of the telephone is both speed and intimacy. Next to personal selling, it represents a one-on-one contact with the consumer.

There are two types of WATS lines—incoming and outgoing. Most of the outgoing calls involve some kind of solicitation or sales pitch. The incoming calls include those for service, inquiries, orders. The last is the most important, and their greatest incidence comes as responses to offers.

As with direct mail, house lists are more effective than those assembled on the outside for outgoing calls. The latter is referred to as "cold calls." The fixed costs of telemarketing are comparatively low. But a successful product must have a built-in margin for marketing by phone which ranges from 20 percent to 30 percent of sales.[24]

Telephone calls can be either live or prerecorded. A popular kind of prerecorded call in recent times has been the celebrity tape. An operator makes the initial contact and then offers to put on the prerecorded voice of the celebrity. Though these messages have engendered several success stories, most telemarketers are cool to the idea. One reason is the lack of intimacy. This characteristic is deemed important because many individuals regard unsolicited phone calls as an invasion of privacy.

The greatest growth of telemarketing has occurred with incoming WATS, particularly the toll-free 800 number. The volume of such calls exceeds 1.6 billion a year. The 800 number is used primarily in conjunction with other media. About a third of all catalog orders today come in on these toll-free WATS lines. Response to a combination of phone and mail will usually run 20 percent higher than that to mail alone.[25] Television commercials asking viewers to call 800 numbers require facilities capable of receiving and processing hundreds of orders in a short time.[26] However, television time is relatively expensive and few products are suited to broadcast media.

SUMMARY

Direct marketing includes different ways of dealing directly with customers—direct mail, direct advertising, mail order, and direct response. But all forms involve impersonal promotion which seeks to evoke direct action.

There are four main characteristics of direct marketing. These are: the combination of advertising and selling; service functions to encourage repeat buying; specificity; and feedback devices.

There are two kinds of direct marketers. One type relies on it as a prime means of selling. The other uses it to supplement marketing activities.

Products sold by direct marketing depend upon two factors: characteristics of products and markets. Among the former are qualities of dependability and safety. Among the latter are gaps in distribution and retail availabilities.

The oldest and most important method is direct mail. Success in this endeavor rests heavily on mailing list selection. House lists pull best, but mail-order and compiled lists can be used to advantage in many circumstances.

Telemarketing is of recent origin and owes its growth to developments in WATS line technology. WATS lines are of two types, incoming and outgoing. The incoming 800 number is usually used in combination with other direct marketing media.

Questions for Chapter 18

1. In what ways would direct response advertising differ between the consumer and industrial sector?

2. Is direct marketing complementary to or substitutable for conventional retailing?

3. Should a department store which spends 4 percent of every sales dollar on advertising spend 20 percent of sales on a catalog?

4. If you were an advertising manager, would you use your agency media department to select advertising carriers for products sold by direct marketing? Why or why not?

5. Direct marketers refrain from advertising to build awareness and product image. Why?

6. How do copy tests of direct response advertising differ from those of general advertising?

7. What product-market characteristics are most suitable for direct marketing?

8. What are the advantages of direct mail?

9. What are the primary criteria which direct marketers use to segment lists?

10. To what do you attribute the growth of telemarketing?

Footnotes for Chapter 18

[1] Ed Burnett, "A Look at Non-Household to Non-Household Mail," *Direct Marketing* (January 1980), p. 60.

[2] Wright et. al., *Advertising*, p. 189.

[3]Julian L. Simon, *How to Start and Operate a Mail-Order Business*, 2nd ed. (McGraw-Hill, 1976), p. 9.

[4]Jim Kobs, *Profitable Direct Marketing* (New York: Direct Mail/Marketing Association, Inc., 1982), p. 2.

[5]Direct Mail Marketing Association, *1982 Fact Book on Direct Response Marketing* (New York: Direct Mail/Marketing Association, 1982), p. xxiii.

[6]Kobs, *Profitable Direct Marketing*, p. 8.

[7]*Advertising Age* (September 10, 1981) and *Advertising Age* (October 19, 1981), p. 42.

[8]See Andrew J. Byrne, "The ABC's of Insurance Direct Marketing," *Direct Marketing* (August 1981), pp. 66–68, Al Migliaro, Sr. and Migliaro, Jr., "Profit Management in Direct Marketing," *Direct Marketing* (October 1979), pp. 122–130.

[9]Kobs, *Profitable Direct Marketing*, p. 8.

[10]Simon, *How to Start and Operate a Mail Order Business*, pp. 109–115; Chaman L. Jain and Al Migliaro, *An Introduction to Direct Marketing* (New York: AMACOM, 1978), pp. 11–16.

[11]*Advertising Age* (February 22, 1982), p. 80.

[12]Herb Drill, "Small-town Catalog House Makes It Big," *Advertising Age* (July 5, 1982), p. 20E.

[13]Jain and Migliaro, *Introduction to Direct Marketing*, p. 26.

[14]Grey Advertising, Inc., *Grey Matter*, vol. 53, no. 1 (1982), p. 4.

[15]The calculation is based on estimations of the critical value of $z = 1.96$, or a significance level of $a = .05$.

[16]Walter McQuade, "There's a Lot of Satisfaction (Guaranteed) in Direct Marketing," *Fortune* (April 21, 1980), pp. 110–112, 117, 121, 124.

[17]Michael Granfield and Alfred Nicols, "Economic and Marketing Aspects of the Direct Selling Industry," *Journal of Retailing* (Spring 1975), p. 33.

[18]Kobs, *Profitable Direct Marketing*, p. 3.

[19]Lauren R. Januz, "Marketing Lists Key Success in Direct Marketing Efforts," *Marketing News* (June 25, 1982), sec. 1, p. 4.

[20]Jain and Migliaro, *Introduction to Direct Marketing*, p. 43.

[21]Robert D. Kestnbaum, "List Segmentation: Profit vs Privacy," *Direct Marketing* (August 1981), p. 24; "Bloomingdale's Makes the Move to Mail Order," *Direct Marketing*, (September 1980), p. 64.

[22]See R. C. Blattberg and S. K. Sen, "Market Segmentation Using Models of Multidimensional Purchase Behavior," *Journal of Marketing* (October 1974), pp. 17–28.

[23]Bob Stone, *Successful Direct Marketing Methods*, 2nd. ed. (Chicago: Crain Communications, Inc., 1979), p. 90.

[24]"Telephone Marketing: 54 Practical Ideas," *Direct Marketing* (October 1979), p. 60.

[25]"Telephone Marketing," p. 64.

[26]Lauren R. Januz, "How to Get the Most Out of TV Spots Using 800 Numbers," *Marketing News* (April 16, 1982), p. 8.

PART SEVEN

REGULATION OF
ADVERTISING

19 *Legal Environment of Advertising*

Advertising is so widespread in our society that, like a utility, it comes clothed with the public interest. Under such conditions, numerous groups exert political pressure to affect their desired outcomes. Many of their efforts are reflected in government legislation and the establishment of regulatory agencies.

This chapter deals with the following major governmental and legal actions which affect advertising:

- **Federal laws which were enacted to regulate advertising in the public interest**
- **Rulings and procedures of the Federal Trade Commission, the most important regulatory agency**
- **Role of the courts in determining the legalities, and the regulatory limits of advertising practices**
- **Attempts at advertiser self-regulation, and activities of special interest groups**

THE ADVERTISING ENVIRONMENT

Advertising, like all business, operates in a social context or environment. These surroundings are outside the confines of the business firm. Though advertising attempts to sell products or ideas to outside groups, its scope of influence is relatively narrow. The organization can only influence behavior in relation to the specific product or service advertised, and usually accepts the judgments, values and beliefs of the outside in order to do so. Since environmental factors are settings for advertising, they are conventionally regarded as something that is given. The firm has little, if any, control over its environment. But these external forces impinge on advertising decisions, and in recent years their influence has expanded enormously.

The functions advertising performs seem as though they were being displayed in a window showcase. Of all business practices, none is more open to public scrutiny than advertising. Its messages are fully exposed to public view. They are everywhere, in the press, in broadcasts, on trains and buses, on the highways. It almost seems as though the greatest preoccupation of Americans is selling each other on the respective qualities of their products—and perhaps that impression is more than meets the eye in a highly commercialized culture.

A product manager may see advertising primarily as a sales instrument, and indeed it is. But when messages get into the public domain, as it were, they become more than simple business communications from seller to buyer. Advertisements intrude on the lives of buyers and non-buyers alike, who, while they may build mental defenses against unwanted solicitations, must suffer communication assaults against their persons. The torrent of commercial messages runs not merely into economic gullies, but into social and ethical ones as well.

Along with product data, advertising affects the way people perceive the world about them. Commercial messages do more than make gracious offers of material things. They flatter. They compromise. They sanctify. They sting.

Advertising was the main cause of resolutions introduced by women and church groups at a Procter & Gamble annual meeting. The resolutions urged the company to change its advertising which depicted women in stereotyped roles of housekeeper, mother and sex object. Advertising for custom jeans that presented a well-fitted female bottom with bawdy sayings brought a flood of complaints from outraged parents of teenagers.[1] In short, the open nature of advertising endows it with a mantle of public interest.

Advertising decisions cannot escape the long net of societal values. The messages blared over the airwaves and displayed in printed material interact with society in many ways. The resulting beliefs are expressed in acceptable styles of dress, preparation of meals, interior decor, and family relations. A large corporation in particular may have an impact on society at large by virtue of its size. In turn, advertising cannot stray too far from the prevailing values of a culture, and so acts as a mechanism which institutionalizes tastes and preferences.

But social values are also in a state of flux to which advertising, like business in general, must adjust. These adjustments do not proceed in a straight line. Rather, they get caught up in social cross-currents, the strongest of which have been consumerism, government regulation, and the rise of various interest groups. These movements are often intertwined, modifying each other.

GOVERNMENT REGULATION

Advertising is subject to laws and regulations at many government levels. Local and state governments have from the very earliest times regulated trade to protect the interests of their citizens. They issue licenses for businesses to operate, and make rules for those lines of commerce which affect public health and welfare. Eating and drinking places, for example, are inspected for compliance with laws and ordinances. City and state governments set prices in some industries, such as carting and carriage. The promotion of such goods and services obviously cannot be divorced from their production and distribution, and regulation of one means regulation of the other.

Advertising has long since outgrown its local roots, and the laws and regulations affecting the most important segments of the industry are promulgated at the national level. Several federal agencies have some voice in what is advertised. The Food and Drug Administration, by a series of enactments going back to 1906, has acquired regulatory powers over labeling and packaging of foods, drugs, medicines, and cosmetics. The Alcohol and Tobacco Tax Division of the Treasury Department has regulatory powers over misleading advertising of liquor and smoking products. The Federal Communications Commission, by its licensing of broadcast stations, affects advertising indirectly. But the major regulator of advertising is the Federal Trade Commission (FTC).

This agency was established in 1914 by the Federal Trade Commission Act. The law set up an agency headed by five commissioners, no more than three of which can come from the same political party. The agency's charter specified making more effective the operations of antitrust laws, primarily by taking action against unfair methods of competition. To do so, the Commission was given broad investigative and regulatory powers over business.

The antitrust laws were initially designed to protect the interests of producers, not consumers. Contemporary opinion at the time made the implicit assumption that competition automatically put buyers into a favorable negotiating position, and that they needed no protection from a paternalistic government. If only the government were to act as a referee, enforcing the competitive code with an even hand, the marketplace could be relied upon to allocate society's resources in the most economical way. The public servants at the FTC were public watchdogs. They would bring violations of competitive behavior to impartial judges to uphold laws enacted by partial people. The Supreme Court, in 1929, held that FTC watchdogs would roam beyond their proper bounds were they to act on behalf of the public when competitive practices were not at issue.[2]

It was not until the Wheeler Lea Amendments of 1938 that the FTC was given legal justification to involve itself with advertising. The new legislation declared unlawful "unfair and deceptive acts and practices." The change in wording of the law allowed the commission to move against anything "unfair or deceptive" in trade without having to show that the alleged infraction injured competition.

For almost half a century the FTC pursued business peccadilloes, and was derisively called "the little old lady of Pennsylvania Avenue." Policing policies stayed focused on trademark infringement and false labeling cases. Under urging from labor unions in the 1920s and 1930s, the FTC required importers of Japanese and German goods to designate with a label the respective countries of origin. Furriers enlisted FTC aid for mandatory labeling of synthetics, and subsequently these efforts resulted in passage of the Fur Products Labeling Act. Later, the Commission spent a good deal of its energy in enforcing the promotional allotment and cooperative advertising provisions of the Robinson-Patman Act. This law was put on the books in 1934 in order to prevent discriminatory practices which were thought injurious to small businesses.

By the end of the 1930s the most vital parts of legislation, regulatory procedures, and supporting legal precedents were in place. They had been built up gradually over the years, and though the regulatory machinery was not fully utilized, it stood ready to serve vigorous enforcement.

Federal Trade Commission Procedures

The FTC can on its own monitor advertising to see that the messages do not violate the forbidding doctrines of "deception and unfairness." Today, media submit routinely to the FTC thousands of advertisements which are processed and scanned for improprieties. But complaints about advertisements may also come from business firms, other government agencies, or segments of the public.

When the FTC comes across advertising which might be considered illegal, it launches an investigation. It has the right to request all material related to the specific advertisement in question. The field investigators prepare a report, and if the proper authorities within the FTC deem proceedings to be justified, it issues a complaint. The alleged offender has thirty days to reply.

If the case is contested, hearings are held before an administrative judge employed by the FTC. When a determination is made, it becomes the ruling of the commission unless either side files an appeal. In that event, the commissioners can accept, modify, or reject the decision of the trial examiner. The final verdict, however, can be brought for review before any federal court of appeal, and ultimately before the Supreme Court.

The FTC has four major powers at its command to enforce compliance with its decisions. These are cease and desist, assurance of voluntary compliance, consent decree, and publicity.

An order to cease and desist is tantamount to a legally-enforceable decree enjoining a company from undertaking certain actions. Unless the firm has petitioned for judicial review, the cease and desist order becomes final and legally binding sixty days after its issuance. Noncompliance brings assessed penalties of $5,000 for each violation.

The assurance of voluntary compliance and consent orders are out-of-court settlements arrived at through negotiation. In neither case does a firm's acquiescence to a negotiated settlement constitute an admission of guilt. In fact, companies will often favor this course of action since the evidence of wrongdoing cannot be used against them in civil suits.

Publicity accompanies all judicial proceedings. The FTC puts texts of all complaints into the public domain, and makes them available to the press. It issues press releases on its actions, decisions of its examiners, and the final ones of the commission itself. As a public servant, the FTC must put its actions and decisions within the public domain.

Throughout FTC history, most cases dealt with deceptive practices rather than monopoly. There were two reasons for this development. First, the majority of complaints arise from day-to-day operations. These by far outnumber all others that come before the commission. Second, it is cheaper and quicker to prosecute and win a case involving a deceptive practice than one dealing with monopoly.[3] The suit against the cereal companies on grounds of a "shared monopoly" dragged on for some nine years until the FTC administrative judge rendered a decision in 1981—and then it was in favor of the defendants. The IBM antimonopoly case ran for thirteen years before being dropped by the government, with astronomical costs to both the company and the public. With few exceptions, advertising cases fall into the area of practices which are deceptive or unfair to consumers.

Guidelines by which to judge deception are not exactly distinct and taut. Two basic questions are foremost:

1. What evidence can the commission use to judge deception or unfairness?
2. How much deviation from truth is tolerable?

The question about evidence is fairly straightforward. The FTC will use market research data submitted by private firms if certain professional standards are met.[4] The FTC also conducts research on its own. In 1980, the agency spent more than a million dollars to study potential damages inflicted on the marketplace and their possible remedies.[5] However, the ultimate criteria are the knowledge and experience of the commissioners and judges. A regulatory commission is presumed to have sufficient expertise to assess the effect of behavior over which it has jurisdiction. This reduces the chances of civil courts reversing FTC orders on grounds that they were not supported by adequate evidence.[6] The "expertise doctrine" in effect means that an advertisement is deceptive if the FTC says it is.

The second question pertains to the standards which the FTC will accept for commercial messages. A Benrus survey which indicated 14 percent of consumers misunderstood the advertising content was enough for the FTC to judge the message misleading. On the other hand, a Firestone-sponsored survey led to dismissal of charges that the name "Safety Champion" suggested a tire safer than others. That survey showed only 1.4 percent of people interviewed selecting that tire as one that was uniquely constructed for safety.[7]

In general, however, the criterion is the potential effect not on the average consumer, but on the most gullible. As outlined by the courts, the FTC may insist on advertising so clear that, in the words of Isaiah, "wayfaring men, though fools, shall not enter therein." Thus, the FTC has the power to proscribe any advertisement which in its judgment contains implied claims having the capacity to mislead the wayfaring fool.

The American Association of Advertising Agencies, apparently to counteract the stringent FTC standards, sponsored a study of television comprehension in 1980 conducted by Jacob Jacoby of Purdue University, in association with two doctoral students. The study involved sixty 30-second segments of news, entertainment, commercials, and public announcements. Participating in the survey were 2,700 consumers recruited in twelve shopping malls dispersed throughout the country. Each respondent watched two segments and answered six true and false questions about each. Only 3.5 percent of the sample answered all twelve questions correctly. The levels of misunderstanding ranged from 11 percent to 50 percent, and mistakes ran higher for news and entertainment than for commercials.[8] These findings, however, have been hotly contested as flawed by both industry spokespersons and FTC consultants.[9]

Federal Trade Commission Decisions and Consumerism

Until the 1960s the FTC stayed on the periphery of advertising, involving itself mainly in matters of trade disputes or flagrant violations of law. As the 1960s wore on, the FTC discarded its mild, devitalizing demeanor and, in response to the rising tide of consumerism, more and more assumed a new role as a defender of consumer rights. The 1970 reorganization plan formalized this decision by setting up within the FTC a Bureau of Consumer Protection.[10]

The first major move into the consumer area came with the ruling that cigarette companies label their packages as being dangerous to health. The cigarette cases established three principles which the FTC subsequently extended to advertising: substantive, remedial, and procedural.

The Substantive Doctrine Though cigarette promotions made no claims that were wrong, they were, nevertheless, judged to be misleading. This assessment came about because the overall impression did not square with material facts about the product. Hence, packages and advertisements were made to carry warnings about potential health hazards.

The substantive principle means that an advertisement can be misleading even though its expressed or implied representations are true. This suggests that advertising which fails to disclose material facts is tainted with falsehood. Copywriters can no longer be told to say something that should not be said but to keep it legal by carefully choosing their words. The adoption of the substantive principle transformed the FTC from a passive to an active force in encouraging affirmative disclosure of relevant facts.

Similarly, an unsubstantiated claim may be unlawful even if it cannot be proven incorrect. The FTC can request that advertisers substantiate any claim made in the advertisement, and that proof must be in hand before, not after, the claim is made.[11] Unless adequate evidence is available to support the copy, the FTC holds, the advertisement is unfair and deceptive. Whether the claim is truthful is irrelevant at this stage of the advertising process.

The advertising substantiation program was instituted by the FTC in 1971. Since then the doctrine has been expanded to include firms and individuals other than advertisers. The widening net of substantiation now includes retail stores, celebrities who endorse products, and advertising agencies which produce the messages. All parties involved have a responsibility to ascertain for themselves that what they represent possesses prior verification.

A consent order with Allied Stores in 1975 prohibited the retailer from making claims for certain cosmetics unless "written verification" is obtained before ads are run and that there is a "reasonable scientific basis" for the claim.[12] Recently, the FTC has entered into consent agreements with advertising agencies containing "escape clauses." To encourage agencies to request supporting data, the FTC permits them to escape prosecution if they received adequate substantiation and discussed all reasonable interpretation of a message with the advertiser.[13]

It has sometimes been argued that the prior substantiation doctrine reduces the amount of information in advertising. For example, an advertiser might be prone to omit all claims which are too costly to prove. A common view among experienced lawyers, however, is that advance substantiation has resulted in a sharp decline of irresponsible advertising claims. There is also a strong likelihood that even should the FTC refrain from vigorous enforcement of this principle, the courts will uphold the doctrine and grant speedy relief in private suits.[14]

The Remedial Principle The directive to cigarette companies for affixing appropriate health warnings to their packages and promotions contained the notion of remedial action. The same firms which had touted nicotine must now promote health hazards of smoking to rectify false impressions they had created previously. This concept was extended to what became known as corrective advertising.

The remedial doctrine recognizes that the mere cessation of deceptive advertising under certain circumstances would not eradicate the false impressions already created. For example, the FTC found that Warner-Lambert for fifty years had been advertising Listerine as a cure for colds and sore throats. An FTC survey indicated more than half of all consumers—product users and nonusers—believed the mouthwash prevented colds and ameliorated cold symptoms.[15] As noted by Judge Skelly Wright of the U.S. Circuit Court of Appeals:

> When viewed from this perspective, advertising which fails to rebut the prior claims as to Listerine's efficacy inevitably builds upon those claims; continued advertising continues the deception, albeit implicitly rather than explicitly.[16]

In an early case against Profile bread, which had promoted itself as a diet food, the FTC ruled for corrective advertising. Julia Mead appeared in a commercial with the following message:

> I'd like to clear up any misunderstandings you may have about Profile bread from its advertising or even from its name. Does Profile bread have fewer calories than other breads? No. Profile has about the same per ounce as other breads. To be exact, Profile has seven fewer calories per slice. That's because it's sliced thinner. But eating Profile bread will not cause you to lose weight. A reduction of seven calories is insignificant.

To dispel implications that Vivarin contained an ingredient that made for a more harmonious marriage, or even better sex relations, J. D. Williams Co. was forced to advertise that its product contained caffeine equal to two cups of coffee. In another situation, the Amstar Corporation, as part of its corrective advertising program, placed advertisements which read:[17]

> Do you recall some of our past messages saying that Domino sugar gives you strength, energy, and stamina? Actually, Domino is not a special or unique source of strength, energy or stamina. No sugar is, because what you need is a balanced diet and plenty of rest and exercise.

On the whole, FTC orders for corrective advertising are restorative in intent, not punitive. The objective is to correct a wrong impression, not to punish the offender. The emphasis upon changing people's cognitions accords with our cultural values which sanctify freedom of choice for individuals. Logically following this proposition is the concept of consumer sovereignty, with its corollary that, given adequate information, consumers have the ability to make correct choices.

Changes in cognitions, however, cannot take place by themselves. Sales of Profile bread in the year corrective advertising was run was said to have fallen about 20 percent. In another situation, the public's purchase intentions of Fresh Horizons bread were negatively affected after the FTC disclosed that the fiber content touted in the advertising was wood pulp. A similar result took place after STP was forced to publicize settlement costs to business audiences as part of its corrective advertising program. Up to now, the FTC has regarded buying behavior ensuing from its actions as only side effects. This view may rationalize the nonpunitive intent of the FTC. But when the side effects translate into drooping sales, corrective advertising assumes greater power as a deterrent to making false claims. It may also become a factor in FTC directives, if the agency begins to weigh the sales consequences of its actions in ordering corrective advertising.

The Procedural Rule This precept implies that a regulatory agency can apply the standards of one case to all other firms in the same industry, provided the issue in question is a common one. Thus, the FTC ruled that all tobacco companies must display health warnings based on its ruling against R. J. Reynolds. This action helped establish the precedent that, when dealing with a common issue, the facts of one proceeding cannot be reexamined in subsequent hearings.

The procedural rule can in effect be used to promulgate industry-wide norms of conduct without case-by-case proceedings, which are costly and time consuming. This procedure was formalized and expanded by the Magnuson-Moss FTC Improvements Act in 1975, which empowered the agency to set industry trade rules. The act envisioned advertising rules which were appropriate to particular lines of commerce. In this way, each industry would have a uniform and definite code of business practices which its members could follow.

But the actual effects of the act were not what was anticipated. Before Congress gave the FTC power to formulate trade regulation rules, government intervention in business was firm-specific. Now it became industry-specific, and a number of industries were caught up in the regulatory network. Of particular importance was that many of the FTC's proposed rules were directed against small businesses with political influence, such as optometrists, hearing aid dealers, used car dealers, funeral directors, health spa operators, finance companies, and the like.[18] That these businesses were the worst offenders did not matter. Their lobbies inundated Congress with tales of punctilious bureaucrats and overzealous regulators seeking to do them in.

Oddly enough, the issue that surfaced from this maelstrom of controversy was advertising to children. More specifically, the FTC took under consideration the restriction of television advertising to children. Though not limited to sugared cereals and so-called junk foods, the proposed rules became so identified with those products that they were generally referred to as "kid-cereal" regulations.

From a strictly legal point of view, the FTC position seemed unassailable in the courts. The law had always regarded children as vulnerable and in need of special protection because their cognitive skills are not fully developed. Children are treated differently from adults in matters of voting, holding elective office, driving vehicles, drinking alcoholic beverages, working for wages, and entering into contracts. Though the opponents of the proposed "kid-cereal" regulations raised constitutional arguments, these had little merit and probably would never have gone beyond an academic exercise.[19]

The issue, however, was not resolved in the courts. Although the FTC is an independent agency, it is the creature of Congress. The legislature gives the FTC its jurisdictional powers—indeed, its very existence—and what Congress creates, it can modify or terminate.

The shift of political winds towards less government regulation brought a chill to Pennsylvania Avenue. The FTC Amendments Act passed by Congress in 1980 suspended for three years FTC's authority to write industry rules that are "unfair." The agency subsequently dropped proposals for children's advertising rules because it lacked legal justification. Congress also reserved for itself the right of review and veto before any rule can be put into effect. This provision was ruled unconstitutional by a federal appeals court in 1982, but the final verdict awaits a Supreme Court ruling.

The advent of the more conservative Reagan administration presages less FTC powers. For one thing, the FTC will receive a smaller budget for advertising regulation. But the FTC as a regulatory agency will not be dismantled. Nor will advertising ever revert to its former free-wheeling style. Curbs on the vague notions of unfairness will undoubtedly reduce bureaucratic excesses. But the concept of deception will probably be enforced with the same degree of stringency as before. Industry itself favors ethical standards, if they are clear and understandable. Advertising to children will also receive special consideration, but on grounds of deception rather than unfairness.

THE COURTS

Besides the legislature and regulatory agencies, the courts have played a key role in how society controls the flow of commercial messages. The courts have sometimes been called the third branch of the American legislature. In the process of interpreting statutes, the law becomes what the courts say it is.

The wheels of regulatory agencies grind slowly. Cases before the FTC can go on for many years before coming to a final resolution, and by then, the issue which sparked the complaint is often no longer relevant. When a firm thinks that the FTC will drag its feet, or receive a complaint unsympathetically, it has the option of going to court and seeking speedy relief from the bench. In these instances, the courts act as instruments of regulation.

Johnson & Johnson, in 1977, bypassed the FTC and went directly to court, challenging American Home Products' advertising which stated that Anacin relieved inflammation while Tylenol did not. The court found in favor of the plaintiff and ordered the advertising discontinued.[20] Since then there has been a constant stream of private cases seeking injunctive relief against deceptive advertising.

Charges of deception in advertising can be brought into the federal courts under Section 43(a) of the Lanham Act, which prohibits false descriptions or representations involving products. The courts have interpreted the wording of that clause to include deceptive advertising.

Courts will grant injunctions under two conditions. First, if the advertisement contains statements which are untrue, the court will rule that a deception exists and grant relief. Second, an advertisement can be literally true but still retain a potential to deceive. This is more difficult to ascertain, and the court usually requires evidence of deception before it enjoins the practice. Legal evidence can include market research or expert opinion, with greater weight seemingly given to the former.[21]

The other major legal trend has been the extension of First Amendment protection to advertising. This landmark decision came in 1976 when the Supreme Court ruled that commercial speech qualifies under constitutional guarantees.

The occasion came about when a consumer group brought suit against the state of Virginia for prohibiting pharmacists for advertising or publishing prices of prescription drugs. The court declared the Virginia law unconstitutional because it violated the free speech guarantees under the First Amendment. The free flow of information, said the court, includes "communication to its source and to its recipients both." It thus follows that a right to advertise involves a "reciprocal right to receive the advertising."[22]

How does this decision affect regulation of advertising? For a while, some segments of the advertising industry hoped—and some people still do—that copywriters would have the same freedom of action as news reporters and commentators. That is, they would be able to write anything they wished, except obscenities, libel, and incitement to riot. As expressed by Richard C. Christian, Chairman of Marsteller, Inc., Chicago, "The plain truth is that advertising copywriters need liberty, license and breathing space just as do poets, politicians and headline writers."[23]

But the courts quickly dashed cold water on such notions. A U.S. circuit court of appeals in 1977 left virtually unchanged an FTC order against Warner-Lambert to do $10 million worth of corrective advertising for Listerine. The court ruled that the First Amendment did not preclude government regulation of false and deceptive advertising. The refusal of the Supreme Court to hear the appeal let stand the decision.

The application of First Amendment rights to commercial speech has effectively barred advertising prohibitions, as with pharmacists in Virginia. The New York Public Service Commission was enjoined from preventing electric utilities to advertise in order to encourage electric consumption. New York, the court said, violated the constitution, and cannot "promote energy conservation by keeping the public in ignorance." An edict limiting Consolidated Edison from promoting nuclear power with inserts in its monthly bills was similarly struck down.[24] But the right of government to regulate misleading messages was upheld, and a double standard still exists between commercial speech and noncommercial communications.

SELF-REGULATION

There are a number of self-regulation agencies formed by both trade associations and media. The most notable of the first kind is the National

Advertising Review Board (NARB), sponsored by the Council of Better Business Bureaus (CBBB). The nationwide system of Better Business Bureaus had long been concerned with the promotion of ethics in business transactions. In its sponsorship of NARB, it was supported by several advertising trade associations, such as the American Advertising Federation, Association of National Advertisers, and American Association of Advertising Agencies.

The NARB began operations in 1971. The immediate objective for its establishment was to head off government regulation which was indicated by the FTC hearings on advertising practices that year.

The NARB is composed of fifty members, thirty of which represent national advertisers. Ten are drawn from advertising agencies, and the remaining ten come from outside the advertising industry. Cases are brought before the board by the National Advertising Division (NAD) of the Council of Better Business Bureaus.

Actually, NAD is the evaluative and investigative arm of the Council of Better Business Bureaus. The NAD monitors advertising and evaluates all complaints. If the evidence indicates misleading advertising, NAD contacts the offender and tries to get a satisfactory change in the copy. Failure to resolve the issue brings the case before the NARB. In practice, most complaints are settled satisfactorily by NAD and never get to NARB.

The biggest advantage of this self-regulatory system is that many disputes are settled speedily and at a fraction of the cost had the case gone to court or to the FTC. However, neither NAD nor NARB has powers to enforce compliance with its decisions. If a company refuses to accept their rulings, the agencies can publicize their findings or refer them to the proper governmental authorities.

Individual buyers or consumer groups have been reluctant to lodge their complaints with NAD, but have relied upon government agencies for redress of grievances. Since the main motive of self-regulation is to prevent government regulation, industry codes tend to be more lax than those of government. If industry is trying to avoid severe restrictions, why should it impose upon itself more onerous burdens? Consequently, industry-sponsored organization seldom solves the problems which inaugurated self-regulation in the first place.

Of all regulation by media, probably the strictest are those in the broadcast industry. The most notable is the Television Code Review Board of the National Association of Broadcasters. But standards are lax, as compared with those of government agencies. Many stations do not subscribe to the code, and there is no way of achieving compliance if a broadcaster chooses to act in contrary fashion. In 1975, for example, Spiderman vitamins were advertised to children in spite of NAB code prohibitions. It was not until FTC intervention that the practice was stopped.[25]

Some magazines such as Good Housekeeping and Parents, supposedly test products to ascertain that performance accords with advertising claims. Good Housekeeping issues a seal of approval to advertisers in its various issues. But the magazine does not undertake product testing primarily as a means of protecting consumers. Its advertisements in the trade press and solicitations on sales calls at advertising agencies stress the seal as a sales tool for marketers. In short, Good Housekeeping uses the seal as a gimmick to sell advertising space. Other magazines do not accept certain advertisements. For example, the New Yorker will not accept advertisements for feminine hygiene products. National Geographic accepts no advertisements for liquor or cigarettes. But these policies have nothing to do with consumer protection. They are editorial policies aimed at creating a certain editorial environment for readers.

SPECIAL INTEREST GROUPS

Almost any activity of a public nature has special interest groups trying to influence its direction. Inevitably, an activity as public as advertising is bound to have a number of such organizations as part of its environment. Consumer advocates are prominent here. They have looked mainly to government regulation to ameliorate their perceived abuses in the marketplace.

In recent years, the national scene has witnessed the appearance of a group whose aims are noneconomic but whose actions affect national advertisers. This is the Coalition for Better Television, formed at the end of 1980 by Rev. Donald Wildmon. Its aim is to rid the airwaves of programs with excessive sex and violence. To further this objective, the coalition allied itself with Rev. Jerry Falwell of the Moral Majority and other evangelical groups with fundamentalist leanings, the so-called "New Religious Right." The coalition has no dispute with advertising. It has no interest in methods by which commercial transactions are carried out. But as advertising provides the financial support to programs which the coalition deems insufferable, advertisers have been swept into the controversy.

Issues of sex and violence on television are of long standing, and concerns go far beyond the Moral Majority and Protestant fundamentalism. A congressional subcommittee headed by Senator Pastore in 1969 held hearings on the matter. As a result, the U.S. Surgeon General undertook an exhaustive investigation into the effects of television violence. After three years of study, at the cost of more than $1 million, the Surgeon General issued a report to Congress that "solid scientific data" provides ample evidence that "televised violence does have an adverse effect on certain members of society." One scientist estimated that by age fifteen, an average child will have witnessed more than 13,000 homicides as part of home entertainment, and countless fist fights, robberies, rapes and beatings.[26] Studies by psychologists and sociologists are in general agreement that heavy television viewing among young audiences is associated with antisocial behavior, such as aggression and insensitivity to human suffering.

In the bright glare of unfavorable publicity, the networks made some concessions. They reduced somewhat the humor-wrapped violence on Saturday morning cartoon shows. Beginning in September 1975, they instituted the Family Hour, a neutral time zone devoid of violence and sex so that the entire family can watch the screen. But after this happy hour, critics charge, it's violence as usual.

The Justice Department subsequently cited the networks for violating antitrust laws by banding together to affect programing, even though the move was initiated by the FCC. All networks, however, have announced their adherence to the Family Hour on the basis of individual rather than collective decisions.

The purveyors of mass culture have, in the main, invoked the First Amendment to protect themselves against outside interference. Television stations and producers regard attempts by government and special interest groups to influence programing as unwarranted censorship. The mark of success is a show's ability to pull high ratings, despite the fact that its contents antagonize large segments of our population. Thus, violence and sex continue unabated.

Children's shows serve up violence with wit and good humor. Cartoons build their stories around such episodes as a red-bearded pirate plotting to decapitate Bugs Bunny, or an evil coyote hatching schemes to do in a looney-looking bird navigating on the ground instead of in the air. Newscasts more and more tend toward a tabloid format which emphasizes the sensational—crime, murder, arson. These events, such broadcasts would have their audiences believe, are basic in shaping society and the world.

Many advertisers are painfully aware of the growing dissatisfaction with programing, and its possible carry-over to advertising. A study conducted by Warwick, Welsh & Miller (WWM), found more than half the respondents (55 percent) claiming to avoid products whose commercials aired on television programing they consider in poor taste. Some 20 percent of the 5,000 Home Testing Institute panelists who made up the sample thought tv programs to be in bad taste.

But research results gave ambiguous answers. Behavior was not always consistent with opinions. The same study found "Dallas," the show which pulled the highest ratings in 1981, to be among the most distasteful. "Three's Company," another top-rated program, received the largest number of negative comments. Although soap operas attract large audiences, the WWM survey found substantial criticism and disapproval of these shows.[27] In fact, "Dallas" has a format and expounds themes not unlike the afternoon soap operas that are so popular with women at home and teenagers.

Government efforts to cleanup the airwaves produced meager results, and even less could be expected from the television industry itself. Advertisers seemed to care more about cost-per-thousands than public morals. Into this void stepped the Coalition for Better Television, with a program of direct action. In the words of Rev. Wildmon,

> The only way you can change television is through your pocketbook and through the people that pay the bills . . . and that's the only people the networks listen to. They don't listen to the public.[28]

In June, 1981, the coalition announced it would begin a boycott of advertisers who use objectionable programs to convey their selling messages. Procter and Gamble, the largest national advertiser, quickly endorsed the goals of the coalition. Other companies followed suit, taking a socially-responsible position and promising to withdraw advertising schedules from abusive programs.

The boycott was called off, but only temporarily. The coalition obtained merely a promise of reform, and its attitude was one of wait and see. A number of other groups, such as the Knights of Columbus, also stand poised to apply the economic boycott as a weapon in a crusade for decency. As of this writing, the Drama of Salvation, with advertising as a pawn, is still being played out in a modern setting, where the main concern is how Americans are to be amused on their home video sets.

SUMMARY

Since advertising is exposed to public view, its influence spreads beyond the purely economic domain. The three strongest environmental factors affecting advertising are consumerism, government, and special interest groups.

Consumerism has usually worked through government to change practices it finds objectionable. The major regulator at the national level is the Federal Trade Commission. This agency has four means of enforcing its decisions: cease and desist, assurance of voluntary compliance, consent decree, and publicity. Any decision of the commission, however, is subject to judicial review.

Most FTC cases in advertising deal with deception. The criterion used is the possible effect on the most vulnerable group of consumers.

From the 1960s onward, the FTC has assumed the role of defender of consumer rights. The first major move into this area was the proceedings against the cigarette companies. These cases established three principles which were later extended to advertising: substantive, remedial, and procedural.

In 1976, the Supreme Court extended First Amendment protection to advertising. This legal doctrine prevents governments and private associations from placing certain restrictions on advertising, but not from regulating unfair and deceptive practices.

To ward off government regulation, the advertising industry has set up self-regulatory agencies, notably the National Advertising Review Board. This agency has settled many complaints speedily and inexpensively. But self-regulation has serious shortcomings as a protective device for consumers.

Recently, we have witnessed the rise of the Coalition for Better Television. Though its aims are noneconomic, its actions affect advertising.

Questions for Chapter 19

1. Advertising is an activity clothed with the public interest. Do you agree?

2. Is advertising a conservative force or an agent of change with respect to social values?

3. Some leaders of the advertising industry have maintained that advertising should have the same rights of free speech as journalists. Comment.

4. Why might attorneys favor out-of-court settlements of an FTC complaint?

5. What are the *pros* and *cons* of the substantiation doctrine?

6. In what ways has the FTC tried to promote conditions of consumer sovereignty?

7. What is the main criticism of advertising to children on television programs designed especially for children?

8. What have been the main arguments of critics of self-regulation of advertising by industry?

9. When Procter & Gamble endorsed the goals of the Coalition for Better Television, the networks termed it a "capitulation to censorship." P&G claimed it was discharging a social responsibility. Comment.

Footnotes for Chapter 19

[1]Dan Kelly, "Jeans Advertising a Case of Shooting From the Hip," *Advertising Age* (May 11, 1981), p. 54.

[2]See *F.T.C. v. Klesner*, 280 U.S. 19 (1929); also see *F.T.C. v. Raladam*, 283 U.S. 643 (1931).

[3]Richard A. Posner, "Truth in Advertising: The Role of Government," Yale Brozen, ed., *Advertising and Society* (New York: New York University Press, 1974), p. 112.

[4]"Research presented to FTC Must Hold Up Under Cross-examination," *Marketing News* (December 26, 1980), p. 8.

[5]"FTC Now Conducts Attitude Research Before Entering Costly Legal Battles," *Marketing News* (May 16, 1980), p. 1.

[6]Posner, "Truth in Advertising," p. 115.

[7]"Research Presented to FTC," p. 8.

[8]Fred Danzig, "Keep It Simple, 4A's Study Shows," *Advertising Age* (May 19, 1980), p. 128.

[9]See "Mizerski Points Out Major Problems in 4As Pioneering Study on TV Miscomprehension," *Marketing News* (June 12, 1981), pp. 7–8.

[10]See Federal Trade Commission, *Annual Report, 1970*, pp. 7–8.

[11]J. J. Boddewyn, "The Global Spread of Advertising Regulation," *MSU Business Topics* (Spring 1981), pp. 5–6.

[12]Roger L. Jenkins, "Managers Must Develop Tactics to Handle FTC Probes of Ad Claims," *Marketing News* (May 30, 1980), p. 4.

[13]"FTC Consent Pacts Set Test, Survey Guides," *Advertising Age* (January 12, 1981), p. 10.

[14]"FTC Consent."

[15]*F.T.C. v. Warner-Lambert Co.*, Docket no. 8891 (1975).

[16]"Court Reaffirms FTC on Ordering Listerine Corrective Ads," *Advertising Age* (October 3, 1977), p. 6.

[17]Marianne M. Jennings, "FTC Will Order Corrective Ads On Case-By-Case Basis," *Marketing News* (June 13, 1980), p. 16.

[18]Stanley E. Cohen, "Will Business Help Rebuild FTC?" *Advertising Age* (November 3, 1980), p. 34.

[19]John P. Clark, "Whither FTC?" *Review of Business* (Spring 1980), pp. 1–2.

[20]"Anacin Ad Ruling May Mean Trouble: Ex-FTC Aide," *Advertising Age* (October 24, 1977), p. 10.

[21]Robert G. Sugarman, "Recent Developments in Advertising Litigation," *Marketing Review* (November/December 1980), pp. 23–29.

[22]*Virginia State Board of Pharmacy v. Virginia Citizens Consumer Council*, 425 U.S. 748.

[23]Richard C. Christian, "Ads and First Amendment Rights," *Advertising Age* (September 3, 1979), p. 35.

[24]George E. Hartman, "Supreme Court Resolves Conflicts Over Commercial Freedom of Speech," *Marketing News* (December 26, 1980), p. 12.

[25]Peggy Charren, "The Thirty-Second Prospectus," *Review of Business* (Spring 1980), p. 9.

[26]Niel Hickey, "Does TV Violence Affect Our Society? Yes," *TV Guide* (June 14, 1975), p. 9.

[27]Warwick, Welsh & Miller, *A Study of Consumer Attitudes Toward TV Programming and Advertising* (February 1981).

[28]Craig Endicott, "Television's Watchdog," *Advertising Age* (August 31, 1981), p. 30.

Subject Index

Name Index